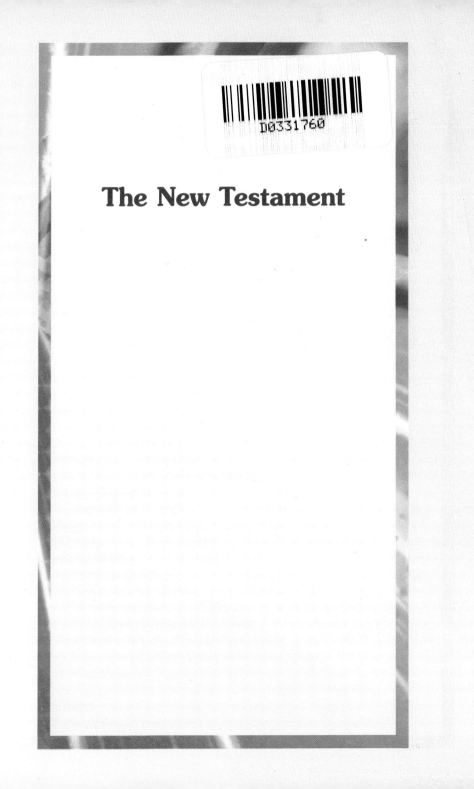

The New Testament

THE NEW TESTAMENT

St. Paul Catholic Edition

Library of Congress Cataloging-in-Publication Data

Bible. N.T. English. Wauck. 1994.
    The New Testament: St. Paul Catholic Edition/ translated by Mark A. Wauck.
        p. 656   cm. 15 x 21
        ISBN 0-8189-0657-X
        I. Wauck, Mark A. II. Title
        BS2095.W32   1996
        225.5'209 — dc20   94-25709
                                CIP

Nihil Obstat:
    Msgr. Daniel Murray, Rector St. Charles Borromeo Seminary, Overbrook, PA
    Rev. Robert Hayden, Vice Rector Immaculate Conception Seminary, Huntington, NY
Imprimi Potest:
    Most Rev. Emil A. Wcela, Vicar Eastern Vicariate
    Diocese of Rockville Centre, NY
Imprimatur:
    Most Rev. Daniel E. Pilarczyk
    President, National Conference of Catholic Bishops
    March 22, 1991
Rescript:
    In accord with canon 825, §1 of the Code of Canon Law, the National Conference
    of Catholic Bishops hereby approves for publication the Books of the New Testament,
    a translation by Mark A. Wauck, submitted by Alba House.
    Most Rev. William H. Keeler
    President, National Conference of Catholic Bishops
    Washington, DC
    May 6, 1994

Produced and designed by the
Fathers and Brothers of the Society of St. Paul,
as part of their communications apostolate.

ISBN: 0-8189-0657-X (Society of St. Paul)
ISBN: 0-8198-5139-6 (Daughters of St. Paul)

Printing Information:
    Current Printing - first digit   1   2   3   4   5   6   7   8   9   10

    Year of Current Printing - first year shown
    2000   2001   2002   2003   2004   2005   2006   2007   2008   2009

TABLE OF CONTENTS

*This is also the introduction to the Letter of Jude

TRANSLATOR'S PREFACE

This new English version of the New Testament has been translated directly from the Greek and generally follows the texts of the 3rd edition of the United Bible Society's *The Greek New Testament* and the 26th edition of Nestle-Aland's *Novum Testamentum Graece*, although, in places, variant readings have been preferred. In general, the text followed is intended to reflect the current consensus of Catholic scholarship.

The one overriding concern has, of course, been to render the sacred text as faithfully as possible and in a style which will be readily grasped. While slang has been avoided, a conscious effort has been made to model the text after the spoken language, since the Greek of the New Testament, generally speaking, reflects the spoken Koine Greek of the first century A.D.

BIBLICAL ABBREVIATIONS

OLD TESTAMENT

Gn	Genesis	Tb	Tobit	Ezk	Ezekiel
Ex	Exodus	Jdt	Judith	Dn	Daniel
Lv	Leviticus	Est	Esther	Ho	Hosea
Nb	Numbers	1 M	1 Maccabees	Jl	Joel
Dt	Deuteronomy	2 M	2 Maccabees	Am	Amos
Jos	Joshua	Jb	Job	Ob	Obadiah
Jg	Judges	Ps	Psalms	Jon	Jonah
Rt	Ruth	Pr	Proverbs	Mi	Micah
1 S	1 Samuel	Ec	Ecclesiastes	Na	Nahum
2 S	2 Samuel	Sg	Song of Songs	Hab	Habakkuk
1 K	1 Kings	Ws	Wisdom	Zp	Zephaniah
2 K	2 Kings	Si	Sirach	Hg	Haggai
1 Ch	1 Chronicles	Is	Isaiah	Ml	Malachi
2 Ch	2 Chronicles	Jr	Jeremiah	Zc	Zechariah
Ezr	Ezra	Lm	Lamentations		
Ne	Nehemiah	Ba	Baruch		

NEW TESTAMENT

Mt	Matthew	Eph	Ephesians	Heb	Hebrews
Mk	Mark	Ph	Philippians	Jm	James
Lk	Luke	Col	Colossians	1 P	1 Peter
Jn	John	1 Th	1 Thessalonians	2 P	2 Peter
Ac	Acts	2 Th	2 Thessalonians	1 Jn	1 John
Rm	Romans	1 Tm	1 Timothy	2 Jn	2 John
1 Cor	1 Corinthians	2 Tm	2 Timothy	3 Jn	3 John
2 Cor	2 Corinthians	Tt	Titus	Jude	Jude
Gal	Galatians	Phm	Philemon	Rv	Revelation

ACKNOWLEDGMENTS

It should be apparent to all that no translation of Scripture can be done unaided, by a single person, and I am no exception. I have gratefully relied upon and availed myself of the work of generations of scholars and translators. Above all I want to express my gratitude for the patience and understanding of my wife Mary Ellen and our children, Martin, Monica, Stephen, and Joseph.

THE
GOSPELS

GENERAL INTRODUCTION TO THE GOSPELS

The good news

While each of the evangelists wrote from a distinct perspective, a common purpose is evident in all four Gospels: to proclaim the "good news." What is the good news? Essentially, it is summarized by the primitive *kerygma* or preaching of the early Church: a) Jesus is the Son of God; b) he went about teaching, healing, and proclaiming the advent of the Kingdom of God; c) he was rejected by his own people, died as a sacrifice to redeem both Jews and Gentiles, and rose triumphantly; d) he passed on his authority to his successors, the apostles; e) he will come again in glory from the right hand of God where he has been exalted; f) all of this happened or will happen "in accordance with the Scriptures." This basic *kerygma* serves as the framework around which all four Gospels were written. As can be seen, at the center of the good news is a real person, Jesus of Nazareth, the Messiah, who came to transform our lives.

From this it is clear that the Gospels are not simply theological treatises or mythical constructs — they are necessarily concerned not only with ideas or theories but also with concrete facts and events. Jesus of Nazareth did, in fact, live; he did, in fact, die and later rise again; the proof of his message can be found in what he actually said and did. At the same time, it is also clear that the Gospels do not pretend to be biographies in the modern sense — those events related are not recounted for their own sake but were selected because they could help reveal the meaning of the good news. It is this concern with the concrete, factual, and historical which sets off Christianity from gnosis in every day and age, and it was this double perspective — concern for concrete events and concern for their transcendent meaning and significance — which gave rise to the Gospel as a distinct literary genre.

An important corollary to the basic fact that the purpose of the Gospels is to proclaim is that they explicitly (Jn 20:30-31) disclaim any pretension to be exhaustive, either in the biographical or theological sense. We must not expect either a complete biography or a complete account of the Christian faith. The former is not available to us, and the latter, to the extent that it's possible, is the province of the Church, for which the Gospels are no substitute.

Date and authorship

As is well known, the history of New Testament scholarship has witnessed repeated and heated debates over the date of composition for the four Gospels. What might be termed a middle ground of scholarship supports the following dates: Mark, prior to 70 A.D., probably the late 60's; Luke and Matthew, 75-85; John, the 90's. The dating of John relies in large part upon the highly developed nature of Johannine theology as well as ancient tradition concerning John which states that he lived to an advanced old age.

The traditional datings differ in that they place Matthew first, followed by Mark and Luke, all prior to 70 A.D. Tradition holds that Matthew the Evangelist is identical with Matthew the publican (Mt 9:9 ff.) and that he wrote first, in the "Hebrew" language (which may have meant Aramaic). The precise form this early version of Matthew took — whether it was similar to the hypothetical Q document or also included narrative — is not clear from our sources.

As to Mark, he is said to have drawn heavily from the teaching of St. Peter, having been his "interpreter," but the Gospel may not have reached final form until after Peter's death. Luke is familiar to all as the companion of St. Paul. Under the traditional scheme he would have completed his Gospel by the early 60's A.D.

Tradition is usually considered to state that the Fourth Gospel was written by the Apostle John around 90-100 A.D., a date which most modern scholarship also accepts. Nevertheless, there have been, over the years, several dissenting voices who have held out for an earlier date. In the first place, it is clear that the Johannine historical tradition is quite early and reliable. In addition, it is possible that tradition only states that St. John lived to an advanced age, not that he wrote as an old man. Finally, the highly developed nature of Johannine theology is no longer regarded as an indication of late composition: the basic Christological doctrines were probably largely formulated within a few years of the death of the Lord.

THE GOSPEL
ACCORDING TO

MATTHEW

Introduction to the Gospel
According to Matthew

Tradition maintains that the apostle Matthew was the first to write down "reports" about the Lord, that he wrote in "Hebrew" (which many believe meant Aramaic), and that "everyone" subsequently translated these reports to the best of their ability.

Although not a great deal is known about Matthew, one thing is certain: he was quite familiar with Palestinian Judaism at the time of Jesus' ministry. He appears to have been well informed concerning Jewish traditions and in his Gospel the Pharisees appear as the typical representatives of Judaism. For this reason many scholars believe that this Gospel was written with Jewish converts in mind, although it clearly affirms the universality of Jesus' mission and from an early date was widely used by Gentile Christians as well.

A. THE GENEALOGY OF JESUS

1 1 •[a] A record of the lineage of Jesus Christ, son of David, son of Abraham.

2 •Abraham fathered Isaac, and Isaac fathered Jacob, and Jacob fa-
3 thered Judah and his brothers, •and Judah fathered Perez and Zerah by
4 Tamar, and Perez fathered Hezron, and Hezron fathered Ram, •and Ram
fathered Amminadab, and Amminadab fathered Nahshon, and Nahshon
5 fathered Salmon, •and Salmon fathered Boaz by Rahab, and Boaz fa-
6 thered Obed by Ruth, and Obed fathered Jesse, •and Jesse fathered
David, the King.

7 And David fathered Solomon by Uriah's wife, •and Solomon fathered
Rehoboam, and Rehoboam fathered Abijah, and Abijah fathered Asa,
8 •and Asa fathered Jehoshaphat, and Jehoshaphat fathered Joram, and
9 Joram fathered Uzziah, •and Uzziah fathered Jotham, and Jotham fa-
10 thered Ahaz, and Ahaz fathered Hezekiah, •and Hezekiah fathered Man-
11 asseh, and Manasseh fathered Amos, and Amos fathered Josiah, •and
Josiah fathered Jechoniah and his brothers at the time of the Babylonian Exile.

12 •After the Babylonian Exile Jechoniah fathered Shealtiel, and Shealtiel
13 fathered Zerubbabel, •and Zerubbabel fathered Abiud, and Abiud fa-
14 thered Eliakim, and Eliakim fathered Azor, •and Azor fathered Zadok,
15 and Zadok fathered Achim, and Achim fathered Eliud, •and Eliud fathered Eleazar, and Eleazar fathered Matthan, and Matthan fathered Ja-
16 cob, •and Jacob fathered Joseph the husband of Mary, who gave birth

---

[a] *Lk 3:23-28.*

1:1 *Jesus* is the Greek form of the Hebrew *Joshua* and the Aramaic *Yeshua*, which mean "YHWH or God is salvation."
1:16 Up to this point the genealogy of Jesus has been traced through the male line. Here, however, there is an abrupt break at the final, crucial, link. Matthew clearly states that Jesus was generated from Mary, even though the whole genealogy led up to Joseph and Mary's lineage was nowhere mentioned. The inescapable conclusion is that Joseph was not Jesus' natural father, and beginning at 1:18 Matthew explains the origins of Jesus. It should be noted, however, that since Jesus' legal father, Joseph, was of the line of David, Jesus was entitled to claim the title "Son of David."

to Jesus, who is called Messiah. •So all the generations from Abraham 17 up to David were fourteen generations, and from David up to the Babylonian Exile were fourteen generations, and from the Babylonian Exile up to the Messiah were fourteen generations.

Bethlehem: crypt of the Nativity.

B. THE BIRTH OF JESUS

•[b] Now the birth of Jesus Christ came about in the following manner. 18 When his mother Mary was betrothed to Joseph, but before they came together, she was found to be with child by the Holy Spirit. •Joseph her 19 husband was a good and upright man so he was planning to put her

[b] *Lk 2:1-7.*

1:18 "Came together"; i.e., had marital relations.
1:19 The Greek word *dikaios*, usually translated "righteous," does not carry the legalistic connotations that the English word does. Rather, it conveys the notion of conformity to the will of God or the possession of a Godlike character.
1:23 Is 7:14 (Septuagint). The reference to "Emmanuel" foreshadows Jesus' promise at the conclusion of Matthew's Gospel: "I'll be with you."

20 away, but quietly because he didn't wish to disgrace her. •But while he was thinking these things over, behold, an angel of the Lord appeared to him in a dream and said, "Joseph son of David, don't be afraid to take your wife Mary into your house — the child who has been con-
21 ceived in her is from the Holy Spirit. •She'll give birth to a son and you
22 shall name him Jesus, because he'll save his people from their sins." •All this took place to fulfill what was declared by the Lord through the prophet when he said,

23 **•Behold, the virgin shall be with child**
and will give birth to a son,
And they shall give him the name Emmanuel,

24 which is translated, "God with us." •When Joseph rose from his sleep he did as the angel of the Lord had commanded him and took his wife
25 into his house, •but he hadn't known her before she gave birth to her son, and he gave him the name Jesus.

C. THE WISE MEN AND THE FLIGHT INTO EGYPT

1 2 •When Jesus was born in Bethlehem of Judea in the days of King
2 Herod, behold, Magi from the east arrived in Jerusalem •asking, "Where is the newborn King of the Jews? We saw his star rising and
3 came to worship him." •When King Herod heard this he was troubled,
4 and all Jerusalem with him, •so he gathered all the chief priests and scribes of the people and inquired of them where the Messiah was to
5 be born. •"In Bethlehem of Judea," they told him, "for thus has it been written by the prophet,

6 **•And you, Bethlehem**, land of Judah,
are by no means **least among the rulers of Judah**;
For from you will come the ruler
who will shepherd my people Israel."

1:25 "Hadn't known"; i.e., "had not had sexual intercourse with." Traditionally this verse has been translated: "he did not know her until she gave birth....," which leads many not conversant with the Greek to assume that after Jesus' birth Joseph did "know" Mary. Unlike the English, however, the Greek carries no such implication as to the future. 2:1 The term "Magi" originally referred to Persian wise men of the priestly class, but was later applied to other eastern nations. Magi were considered to be especially learned in astrological lore. 2:6 Mi 5:2, 2 S 5:2.

•Herod secretly summoned the Magi and found out from them the ⁷ time the star had appeared, •then he sent them to Bethlehem, saying, ⁸ "Go search carefully for the child and send for me as soon as you find him, so I can go worship him, too." •After listening to the king they de- ⁹ parted, and, behold, the star they had seen rising went before them un- til it came and stopped above where the child was. •When they saw the ¹⁰ star they rejoiced exceedingly, with great joy, •and when they entered ¹¹ the house they saw the child with its mother, Mary. They fell on their knees and worshipped him, and they opened their treasures and offered him gifts — gold and frankincense and myrrh. •Then, having been ¹² warned in a dream not to go back to Herod, they departed for their coun- try by another way.

•When they had departed, behold, an angel of the Lord appeared in a ¹³ dream to Joseph and said, "Get up, take the child and its mother and flee to Egypt and stay there until I tell you — Herod is going to search for the child to kill it." •So Joseph got up and took the child and its mother and ¹⁴ departed by night for Egypt, •and he stayed there until Herod's death to ¹⁵ fulfill what was stated by the Lord through the prophet when He said,

I called my son out of Egypt.

•When Herod saw that he'd been tricked by the Magi he became ab- ¹⁶ solutely furious, and he ordered the killing of all the boys in Bethlehem and all its neighborhood who were two years old or younger, based on the time he'd ascertained from the wise men. •Then what was declared ¹⁷ by Jeremiah the prophet was fulfilled, when he said,

•A voice was heard in Rama,
   wailing and great mourning;   ¹⁸
Rachel weeping for her children,
   and she would not be comforted,
   because they were no more.

•After Herod died, behold, an angel of the Lord appeared in a dream ¹⁹ to Joseph in Egypt •and said, "Get up, take the child and its mother ²⁰ and go to the land of Israel — those who sought the child's life are dead." •So Joseph got up and took the child and its mother and went into the ²¹

2:11 Is 60:1-6.
2:15 Ho 11:1. This brief reference is complex in its allusions and has several levels of meaning. Most literally, Hosea has referred to the whole people of Israel as God's son. Matthew, on the other hand, uses the text to highlight the unique Sonship of Jesus. These two sonships dovetail in the doctrine of the adoptive sonship of all believ- ers who form the Church, the Mystical Body of Je- sus, the new Israel. There is also an allusion to the new Exodus which Jesus will lead, which is re- ferred to more explicitly at Lk 9:31.
2:18 Jr 31:15.

22 land of Israel. •But when he heard that Archelaus was ruling over Judea in place of his father Herod he was afraid to go there; so, having been
23 warned in a dream, he departed for the district of Galilee, •and he went and settled in a town called Nazareth to fulfill what was said by the prophets, "he shall be called a Nazorean."

D. JESUS AND JOHN THE BAPTIST

1 3 •ᶜ In those days John the Baptist appeared, preaching in the desert
2 of Judea •and saying, "Repent, for the Kingdom of Heaven is at
3 hand!" •He was the one Isaiah the prophet was referring to when he said,

A voice crying out in the desert,
Prepare the way of the Lord,
   make straight his paths.

4 •John had clothing made from camel hair and wore a leather belt
5 around his waist, and his food was locusts and wild honey. •At that time the inhabitants of Jerusalem and all Judea used to go out to him and all
6 the people from the region around the Jordan, •and he baptized them in the river Jordan while they confessed their sins.
7 •But when he saw many of the Pharisees and Sadducees coming to be baptized by him he said to them, "You brood of vipers! Who warned
8 you to flee the coming wrath? •Produce evidence of your repentance,
9 then, •and don't think you can say to yourselves, 'Abraham is our father!', for I tell you God can raise up children to Abraham from these
10 stones. •The axe has already been laid at the root of the trees; any tree
11 not producing good fruit will be cut down and thrown into the fire. •I baptize you with water as a token of repentance, but the one coming after me is more powerful than I am — I'm not worthy to carry his san-
12 dals; he'll baptize you with the Holy Spirit and fire. •His winnowing shovel is in his hand; he'll clean out his threshing floor and gather his grain into the barn, but he'll burn up the chaff with unquenchable fire."

ᶜ Mk 1:1-8; Lk 3:1-18; Jn 1:19-28.

3:2 "Heaven" or "the Heavens" was a circumlocution for the Divine name, direct mention of which was avoided by devout Jews of that time.
3:3 Is 40:3 (Septuagint).
3:7-12 Of particular interest in the Baptist's indictment of the Jewish leaders is v. 9, in which he states that descent from Abraham merits no special consideration from God and will not save them from God's wrath. In Ch. 23 Jesus presents a more detailed but basically similar indictment of the Pharisees, concluding with a lament at their refusal to repent.
3:11 According to the Talmud, cleansing by fire is superior to cleansing by water. *Baptizo* was the common word meaning to wash or cleanse.

•[d] At that time Jesus came from Galilee to be baptized by John at the 13 Jordan. •John tried to prevent him and said, "*I need to be baptized by* 14 *you*, and *you're* coming to *me*?" •But in answer Jesus said to him, "Let 15 it be, for now — it's fitting for us to fulfill all God's will in this way." Then he let him. •After he was baptized Jesus at once came up from 16 the water, and, behold, the heavens were opened and he saw the Spirit of God descending upon him like a dove. •And, behold, a voice from 17 Heaven said, "This is My Beloved Son in whom I am well pleased!"

E. THE TEMPTATION OF JESUS

4 •[e] Then Jesus was led into the desert by the Spirit to be tempted by 1 the Devil. •After fasting for forty days and forty nights he at last be- 2 came hungry, •and the Tempter approached him and said, "If you're 3 the Son of God, tell these stones to become loaves of bread." •But in 4 answer Jesus said, "It is written,

Not by bread alone shall man live,
    but by every utterance proceeding
        from the mouth of God."

•Then the Devil took him to the Holy City. He set him on the para- 5 pet of the Temple •and said to him, "If you're the Son of God, throw 6 yourself down, for it's written,

He will give His angels orders concerning you,
    and on their hands they will carry you,
        lest you strike your foot against a stone."

•Jesus said to him, "It is further written, **You shall not tempt the** 7 **Lord your God**!" •So then the Devil took him up a very high moun- 8 tain and showed him all the kingdoms of the world and their splendor, •and he said to him, "All these things I'll give you, if you'll fall down and 9 worship me!" •But Jesus said to him, "Begone, Satan! For it is written, 10

The Lord your God shall you worship,
    and Him alone **shall you adore."**

•Then the Devil left him and, behold, angels came and served him. 11

[d] *Mk 1:9-11; Lk 3:21-22.* [e] *Mk 1:12-13; Lk 4:1-13.*
4:4 *Dt 8:3.* 4:6 *Ps 91:11-12.* 4:7 *Dt 6:16.* 4:10 *Dt 6:13.*

Jericho: Mount of the Temptations.

F. JESUS BEGINS HIS MINISTRY IN GALILEE

12 •ᶠ When Jesus heard that John had been arrested he returned to 13 Galilee. •He left Nazareth and went and settled in Capharnaum by the 14 sea, in the regions of Zebulon and Naphtali, •to fulfill what was said by Isaiah the prophet, when he said,

15 **•Land of Zebulon and land of Naphtali,**
the sea road, beyond the Jordan,
Galilee of the Gentiles,
16 **•The people living in darkness**
have seen a great light,
And for those living in the land and shadow of death
a light has dawned upon them.

17 •From that time on Jesus began to preach and to say, "Repent, for the Kingdom of Heaven is at hand!"

ᶠ *Mk 1:14-15; Lk 4:14-15.*   4:15-16   Is 9:1-2.

•[g] Now as he was walking along the sea of Galilee he saw two broth- 18
ers —Simon, who is called Peter, and his brother Andrew — casting a
throw net into the sea — they were fishermen. •And he said to them, 19
"Follow me, and I'll make you fishers of men!" •So they left their nets 20
at once and followed him. •He continued on from there and saw two 21
more brothers, James son of Zebedee and his brother John, mending
their nets in the boat with their father Zebedee, and he called them.
•They left the boat and their father at once and followed him. 22

•[h] He travelled throughout all Galilee, teaching in their synagogues, 23
proclaiming the good news of the Kingdom, and healing every disease
and illness among the people. •News of him went out through all Syr- 24
ia, and they brought him all who were sick with various diseases and
were suffering torments — the demon-possessed, epileptics, paralytics — and he healed them. •And large crowds followed him from 25
Galilee and the Decapolis and Jerusalem and Judea and from beyond
the Jordan.

G. THE SERMON ON THE MOUNT

Characteristics of members of the Kingdom

5 •When he saw the crowds he went up the mountain. After he sat 1
down his disciples came to him, •and he opened his mouth and 2
taught them, saying,

> •[i]"Blessed are the poor in spirit, 3
>   for theirs is the Kingdom of Heaven.
> •Blessed are those who mourn, 4
>   for they shall be comforted.
> •Blessed are the meek, 5
>   for they shall inherit the earth.
> •Blessed are those who hunger and thirst to do God's will, 6
>   for they shall have their fill.
> •Blessed are the merciful, 7
>   for they shall receive mercy.
> •Blessed are the pure of heart, 8
>   for they shall see God.

[g] Mk 1:16-20; Lk 5:1-11.   [h] Lk 6:17-19.   [i] Lk 6:20-23.

4:25 "The Decapolis" was a confederation of largely Hellenized cities. They were ten in number (Greek
deka = ten) and all but one were located east of the Jordan.

MATTHEW

9 •Blessed are the peacemakers,
    for they shall be called sons of God.
10 •Blessed are those who are persecuted for doing God's will,
    for theirs is the Kingdom of Heaven.

11 •Blessed are you when they insult you and persecute you and say every
12 sort of evil thing against you on account of me; •rejoice and be glad,
because your reward will be great in Heaven — they persecuted the
prophets before you in the same way."

13 •ʲ "You are the salt of the earth,
    But if the salt should lose its taste,
    What can it be salted with?
    It's good for nothing but to be thrown outside
    And be trampled underfoot."
14 •"You are the light of the world.
    A city cannot be hidden,
    if it's set atop a mountain.
15 •Nor do you light a lamp and set it beneath a bushel;
    you set it on the lampstand, instead,
    so it gives light to everyone in the house.
16 •Let your light so shine before men
    that they'll see your good works
    and glorify your Father in Heaven."

True meaning of the Torah

17 •"Don't think that I came to overturn
        the Torah or the Prophets;
    I came not to destroy, but to fulfill.

18 •For, amen, I say to you,

ʲ Mk 9:50; Lk 14:34-35.

5:17 "Torah," or "law," referred to the totality of God's revelation which could serve as a guide for one's life. Torah was, therefore, quintessentially, the Decalogue, but it also extended far beyond the confines of the Pentateuch to areas which we would never characterize as "law."
5:18 Many writers have noted that Jesus' use of "Amen" differs significantly from the standard usage of that time. Normally it was used to in-voke an authority other than oneself, but Jesus invariably uses it to invoke his own authority, un-supported by Scripture or tradition. Some writers consider this to be another example of Jesus claiming Divine authority for himself. In any event, the novelty of Jesus' attitude was not lost on his listeners: cf. 7:29. Iota is the Greek equiv-alent of the smallest letter of the Hebrew al-phabet, yod.

Until the heavens and the earth pass away,
Not one iota or one stroke of a letter will be dropped
from the Torah,
Until everything has come to pass.
•So whoever breaks one of the least of these   19
commandments, and teaches others to do so,
shall be called least in the Kingdom of Heaven;
But whoever obeys and teaches the commandments,
he shall be called great in the Kingdom of Heaven.

•For I tell you,   20

Unless your righteousness greatly exceeds
that of the scribes and Pharisees,
you'll never enter into the Kingdom of Heaven."

•"You've heard that it was said to the ancients, **You shall not mur-** 21
der, and that whoever does commit murder shall be liable to judgment.
•But *I* say to you,   22

Anyone who's angry with his brother
shall be liable to judgment,
And whoever says to his brother, 'Raqa!'
shall be liable to the Sanhedrin,
And whoever says, 'You fool!'
shall be liable to the fire of Gehenna.

•So if you're presenting your offering at the altar and remember there 23
that your brother has something against you, •leave your offering there 24
before the altar and first go be reconciled with your brother, and then
you can come and make your offering. •Come to terms quickly with your 25
opponent while you're on your way with him, or your opponent may
hand you over to the judge, and the judge to the guard, and you'll be
thrown into prison. •Amen, I say to you, you won't come out of there 26
until you pay back the last penny."
•"You've heard that it was said, **You shall not commit adultery!** 27
•but *I* say to you that anyone who looks at a woman with lust for her 28
has already committed adultery with her in his heart.

5:21 Ex 20:13.
5:22 The exact meaning of *Raqa* is unclear, but
in the context it is clearly abusive or insulting and
is probably equivalent to "fool." *Gehenna* refers
to the Hinnom Valley outside Jerusalem, where
the bodies of executed criminals were burnt. In
the Gospels it refers to Hell. The Sanhedrin was
the highest court of Judaism.
5:27 Ex 20:14.

Justice on a Greek weight, c. 23 B.C. (Mt 5:6)

29 •If your right eye causes you to sin,
   pull it out and throw it away from you!
It's better for you to lose one part of your body
   than to have your whole body thrown into Gehenna.
30 •And if your right hand causes you to sin,
   cut it off and throw it away from you!
It's better for you to lose one part of your body
   than to have your whole body go off to Gehenna."

31 •[k] "And it was said, **Whoever puts his wife away must give her**
32 **a written notice of divorce.** •But *I* say to you,

[k] *Mk 10:11-12; Lk 16:18.*

5:31 Dt 24:1.
5:32 The traditional translation of this verse is usually "except by reason of immorality," or a similar variant. That translation, however, does not adequately explain the Greek. Most literally, the Greek reads, "except by reason of fornication," fornication being a term of art in rabbinical circles indicating that, since a true marriage had not been entered into, the relationship was one of fornication. The usual reason was attempted marriage within forbidden degrees of kinship. It is clear, therefore, that Jesus is not stating an exception to the general rule forbidding divorce in valid marriages. Rather, he is distinguishing valid marriages from other relationships which do not constitute true marriages. The general rule regarding marriage naturally does not apply to such illicit or otherwise defective relationships. This has been the consistent teaching of the Church.

Anyone who puts his wife away —

except by reason of an unlawful union —

>makes her an adulteress,
>And whoever marries a divorced woman commits adultery."

• "Again, you've heard that it was said to your ancestors, **You shall** 33 **not break your oaths!** and, **You shall fulfill your oaths to the Lord!** •But *I* tell you not to swear at all, neither **by Heaven,** because 34 **it's the throne of God,** •nor by **the earth,** because **it's the foot-** 35 **stool for His feet,** nor by Jerusalem, because it's **the city of the Great King,** •nor shall you swear by your head, because you're not 36 able to make one hair white or black. •Let your 'yes,' be 'yes,' and your 37 'no,' 'no'; anything more than that is from the Evil One."

•[l] "You've heard that it was said, **an eye for an eye** and **a tooth** 38 **for a tooth.** •But *I* tell you *not* to resist the evildoer; on the contrary, 39

>If anyone strikes you on the right cheek,
>>turn the other to him as well;
>•If anyone wants to go to law with you and take your tunic, 40
>>give him your cloak as well,
>•And if anyone forces you to go one mile, 41
>>go with him for two.
>•Give to those who ask of you, 42
>>and don't reject those who wish to borrow from you."

•[m] "You've heard that it was said, **Love your neighbor!** and hate 43 your enemy. •But *I* say to you, 44

>Love your enemies,
>And pray for those who persecute you,

•so that you'll become sons of your Father in Heaven, because 45

>He causes His sun to rise on the evil and the good,
>>and rain to fall on the just and the unjust.

[l] *Lk 6:29-30.* [m] *Lk 6:27-28, 32-36.*

5:33 Nb 30:2.   5:34 Is 66:1.
5:35 Is 66:1.   5:38 Ex 21:14.
5:41 "Forces"; this word refers to a requisition of services under compulsion, probably by the Romans. It is the same word which is used to describe the requisition of Simon of Cyrene's services to carry the cross.

5:43 Lv 19:18. It was a common teaching of the rabbis that "neighbor" referred only to fellow Jews. Non-Jews were in opposition to God and were therefore "enemies." Other currents of rabbinic thought, however, did manifest a more conciliatory view toward Gentiles.

46 •For if you love those who love you,
    what reward will you have?
        Don't even the tax collectors do the same?
47 •And if you greet only your brothers,
    what great thing are you doing?
        Don't even the Gentiles do the same?
48 •So you be perfect
    as your Heavenly Father is perfect."

True practice of the Torah

1 **6** •"Take care not to perform your good deeds in front of others in order to be seen by them; if you do, you'll have no reward from your Father in Heaven."

2 •"Whenever you give alms,
    don't sound a trumpet before you,
Like the hypocrites do in the synagogues
    and in the streets,
    so people will praise them.
Amen, I say to you,
    they have their full reward!
3 •But when you give alms,
    don't let your left hand know what your
        right hand is doing,
4 •So that your alms may be in secret,
    and your Father Who sees in secret will reward you."
5 •[n] "And when you pray,
    don't be like the hypocrites —

They love to pray standing in the synagogues
    and on the corners of wide streets,
        so people will notice them.
Amen, I say to you,

---

[n] Lk 11:2-4.

5:46 Publicans or tax collectors were considered outcasts, not because of objections to the payment of taxes per se, but because they collected taxes for the Romans and were often extortionate and dishonest.

6:1-18 Jesus now turns to religious practice. Almsgiving, prayer, and fasting were considered exemplary expressions of piety and devotion.

they have their full reward!

•But when you pray, **6**
    go into your storeroom and
        shut the door;
Pray to your Father Who is hidden,
    and your Father Who sees what's hidden
        will reward you."

•"And when you're praying, **7**
    don't babble on like the Gentiles —
They think their wordiness
    will gain them a hearing.

•But don't be like them, **8**
    for your Father knows what you need
        before you ask Him.

•Pray, therefore, like this: **9**
Our Father Who art in Heaven,
    hallowed be Your name,

•Your Kingdom come, Your will be done, **10**
On earth, as it is in Heaven.

•Give us this day our daily bread, **11**

•And forgive us our debts, **12**
    as we forgive our debtors;

•And lead us not into temptation, **13**
    but deliver us from the Evil One."

•"For if you forgive others their offenses, **14**
    your Heavenly Father will forgive you, too;

•But if you don't forgive others, **15**
    neither will your Father forgive your offenses."

•"When you fast, **16**
    don't be gloomy like the hypocrites —
They make their faces unsightly
    to let others see they're fasting.
Amen, I say to you,
    they have their full reward!

•But when *you* fast, anoint your head **17**
    and wash your face,

    •so others won't see that you're fasting, **18**

6:9 Several authors have suggested that "hallowed be Your name" is best understood as a prayer that God should manifest His glory, as specified in the following verses.

6:13 "Evil One" is often translated, simply, "evil." The use of the masculine article, however, makes the former the preferred reading. Cf. 5:37.

But only your Father Who is hidden will see,
and your Father Who sees what's hidden will reward you."

Jerusalem: cloister of the Church of the Pater Noster.

Exhortations to trust in God

19 •° "Don't store up treasures for yourselves on earth,
where moth and rust destroy,
and where thieves break in and steal;

20 •Store up treasures for yourselves in Heaven,
where neither moth nor rust destroy,
and where thieves neither break in nor steal.

21 •For where your treasure is,
there will your heart be too."

22 •ᵖ "The eye is the lamp of the body.
Now if your eye is generous,
Your whole body will be full of light;

° *Lk 12:33-34. 12:22-31.* ᵖ *Lk 11:34-36.*

6:22-23 A "grudging" or "evil" eye describes the envious or acquisitive attitude toward worldly goods,
which Jesus is counselling against in this extended passage.

•But if your eye is grudging,
Your whole body will be in darkness.
So if the light in you is darkness,
How great is the darkness!" 23

•[q] "No one can serve two masters; 24
Either he'll hate the one and love the other,
Or be loyal to one and despise the other.
You cannot serve God and Mammon!"

•"Therefore, I tell you, 25
Don't worry about your life,
    what you'll eat,
Or about your body,
    what you'll wear;
Isn't life more than food,
    and the body more than clothing?

•Look at the birds of the sky — they neither sow nor reap nor gath- 26
er into barns, yet your Heavenly Father feeds them; aren't you worth
more than they are? •But which of you can add any time to your life by 27
worrying? •And why do you worry about clothing? Look how the lilies 28
of the field grow; they neither work nor spin. •But I tell you, even 29
Solomon in all his glory wasn't arrayed like one of them. •But if God 30
so clothes the grass of the fields, which is here today and thrown into
the oven tomorrow, won't He clothe you much better, O you of little
faith? •So don't go worrying, saying, 'What will we eat?' or, 'What will 31
we drink?' or, 'What will we put on?' •for the Gentiles seek all those 32
things. Your Heavenly Father knows you need them! •But first seek the 33
Kingdom and the will of God and all those things will be given to you
also. •So don't go worrying about tomorrow — tomorrow will worry for 34
itself. One day's evil is enough for a day."

Further exhortations and warnings

7 •[r] "Don't judge, 1
   so that you won't be judged,
•For with the judgment you judge, 2

---

[q] Lk 16:13. [r] Lk 6:37-38, 41-42.

6:24 *Mammon* was an Aramaic word which probably referred to worldly wealth.

you will be judged,
And with the measure you measure,
    it will be measured out to you.

3 •But why do you see the speck in your brother's eye,
    yet don't notice the log in your own eye?

4 •Or how can you say to your brother,
        'Let me take the speck from your eye,'
    when there the log is in *your* eye!

5 •You hypocrite!
First take the log out of *your* eye,
    and then you'll see clearly to take the speck
        from your brother's eye."

6 •"Don't give what's holy to the dogs,
    nor throw your pearls before the swine,
Lest they trample the pearls underfoot,
    and then turn and attack you."

7 •[s] "Ask! and it shall be given to you;
    Seek! and you shall find;
        Knock! and it shall be opened to you.

8 •For everyone who asks, will receive,
    and whoever seeks, will find,
        and to those who knock, it shall be opened.

9 •Or which of you, if his son
        asked for a loaf,
    would hand him a stone?

10 •Or if he asked for a fish,
    would hand him a snake?

11 •So if you who are evil know how
    to give good gifts to your children,
All the more will your Father in Heaven
    give good things to those who ask Him!

12 •Therefore, whatever you want others to do for you,
    do so for them as well;
For this is the Torah and the Prophets."

13 •[t] "Go in through the narrow gate,
For wide is the gate and broad the way
        leading to destruction,
    and many are those who enter through it;

[s] *Lk 11:9-13.* [t] *Lk 13:24.*

7:6 Several authors believe that "what's holy" is a mistranslation of an Aramaic word meaning "rings."

•How narrow the gate and difficult the way   14
    leading to life,
    and few are those who find it!"
•[u] "Beware of false prophets who come   15
    to you in sheep's clothing,
But within are savage wolves.
•By their fruit you will know them!   16
You don't gather grapes from thorns,
    or figs from thistles, do you?
•Likewise, every good tree produces good fruit,   17
But the worthless tree produces bad fruit;
•A good tree can't produce bad fruit,   18
Nor can a worthless tree produce good fruit.
•Every tree not producing good fruit is cut down   19
    and thrown into the fire.
•And so, from their fruit you will know them."   20

•[v] "Not everyone who says to me, 'Lord, Lord!' will enter the King- 21
dom of Heaven; no, the one who does the will of my Father in Heav-
en will. •Many will say to me on that day, 'Lord, Lord, didn't we proph- 22
esy in your name and drive out demons in your name and do mighty
works in your name?' •And then I'll declare to them, 'I never knew you; 23
get away from me, you evildoers!'"

•[w] "Therefore, everyone who hears these words of mine   24
    and acts on them
    is like a wise man who built his house on rock.
•And the rain fell and the floods came   25
    and the winds blew and beat against that house,
Yet it didn't fall,
    for its foundations had been set on rock.
•Everyone who hears these words of mine   26
    and doesn't act on them
    is like a foolish man who built his house on sand.
•And the rain fell and the floods came,   27
    and the winds blew and beat against that house,
And it fell,
    and great was its fall."

•And it happened that when Jesus had finished these words the 28

u Lk 6:43-44.   v Lk 13:25-27.   w Lk 6:47-49.

MATTHEW

Capharnaum: ruins of the synagogue and of the village. (Mt 8:5)

29 crowds were amazed at his teaching •because he was teaching them on his own authority, and not like their scribes.

H. JESUS TRAVELS, TEACHING AND HEALING

1 8 •ˣ Large crowds followed him when he came down from the moun-
2 tain •and, behold, a leper came up, knelt before him, and said, "Lord,
3 if you wish to, you can make me clean." •Jesus reached out his hand, touched him, and said, "I *do* wish it, be made clean!" and at once his
4 leprosy was made clean. •Then Jesus said to him, "See that you tell no one, but go show yourself to the priest and present the offering Moses commanded, as a witness to them."
5 •ʸ When he entered Capharnaum a centurion came up to him, ap-
6 pealing to him •and saying, "Lord, my servant is lying paralyzed at

ˣ *Mk 1:40-45; Lk 5:12-16.* ʸ *Lk 7:1-10; Jn 4:43-54.*

home, terribly tormented." •Jesus said to him, "I'll come heal him." •In 7,8
response the centurion said, "Lord, I'm not worthy to have you come
under my roof — just say a word and my servant will be healed. •For 9
I, too, am subject to authority and have soldiers under me, and if I say
to this one, 'Go!' he goes, or if I say to another, 'Come!' he comes,
and if I tell my slave, 'Do this!' he does it." •When Jesus heard this he 10
was amazed and said to those who were following, "Amen, I say to you,
nowhere have I found such faith in Israel! •I tell you, many will come 11
from east and west and will recline at table with Abraham and Isaac
and Jacob in the Kingdom of Heaven, •but the sons of the Kingdom 12
will be thrown out into the outer darkness;

> There there will be wailing
> and gnashing of teeth!"

•Then Jesus said to the centurion, "Go your way! Let it be done 13
for you as you have believed," and the servant was healed at that very
moment.

•[z] And when Jesus entered Peter's house he saw Peter's mother-in- 14
law lying in bed, sick with a fever; •he touched her hand and the fever 15
left her, and she got up and began to serve him. •When evening came 16
they brought him many people who were demon-possessed, and he
drove the spirits out with a word and cured those who were sick, •to ful- 17
fill what was said by Isaiah the prophet when he declared,

> **He took away our illnesses**
> **and removed our diseases.**

•[a] When Jesus saw a crowd around him he gave orders to go off to 18
the other side. •A scribe came up and said to him, "Teacher, I'll follow 19
you wherever you go." •Jesus said to him, 20

> "Foxes have holes
> And the birds of the sky have nests,
> But the Son of Man has nowhere to lay his head."

---

[z] Mk 1:29-34; Lk 4:38-41. [a] Lk 9:57-62.

8:8,16 "a word," i.e., a word of command or power.
8:17 Is 53:4.
8:20 The "foxes," of proverbial cunning, may refer to Herod and his hated Idumaean followers who played one side off against the other to their own advantage. The "birds of the air" were the Roman overlords. Jesus would then be warning his followers about what to expect: his Kingdom would be very different.
8:29 It was a common belief at that time that the demons had power until judgment day, hence their question of Jesus.

21 •Another of his disciples said to him, "Lord, let me first go bury my
22 father." •But Jesus said to him, "Follow me, and let the dead bury their
own dead."

23,24 •[b] When he got into the boat his disciples followed him. •And, behold, such a violent storm arose on the sea that the boat was being
25 swamped by the waves, but he went on sleeping. •They came to him
26 and got him up and said, "Lord, save us, we're going to die!" •And he
said to them, "Why are you afraid, O you of little faith?" Then he got
up and rebuked the winds and the sea, and there was a profound calm.
27 •The men were amazed and said, "What sort of man is this, that even
the winds and the sea obey him?"

28 •[c] When he came to the other side, to the region of the Gadarenes,
two demon-possessed men who had come out from the tombs met him;
29 they were so violent that no one could go by on that road. •And, behold, they cried out and said, "What do you want with us, Son of God?
30 Have you come here to torment us before the appointed time?" •Now
31 some distance away from them was a herd of many swine, feeding. •The
demons kept begging him and saying, "If you drive us out, send us in-
32 to the herd of swine." •And he said to them, "Begone!" So when they
went out they went off into the swine and, behold, the whole herd rushed
33 down the slope into the sea and died in the water. •Then the herdsmen
fled, and when they came to the town they announced everything, in-
34 cluding what had happened to the demon-possessed men. •And, behold,
the whole town went out to meet Jesus, and when they saw him they
begged him to leave their region.

1 **9** •[d] After embarking on a boat he crossed over and came to his own
2 city. •And, behold, they brought him a paralytic who was lying on
a bed. When Jesus saw their faith he said to the paralytic, "Take
3 courage, child, your sins are forgiven!" •And, behold, some of the
4 scribes said to themselves, "This fellow is blaspheming!" •Jesus, knowing their thoughts, said, "Why do you harbor evil thoughts in your
5 hearts? •What's easier, to say, 'Your sins are forgiven,' or to say, 'Get
6 up and walk'? •But so you'll know that the Son of Man has authority
on earth to forgive sins" — then he said to the paralytic, "Get up, pick
7 up your bed and go to your house!" •And he got up and went off to
8 his house. •When they saw this the crowds became frightened and glorified God, Who had given such authority to men.

[b] *Mk 4:35-41; Lk 8:22-25.* [c] *Mk 5:1-20; Lk 8:26-39.* [d] *Mk 2:1-12; Lk 5:17-26.*

•[e] As Jesus travelled on from there he saw a man named Matthew 9 seated at a tax booth, and he said to him, "Follow me!" And he got up and followed Jesus. •And it happened that he reclined at table in the 10 house, and, behold, many tax collectors and sinners had come and were at table with Jesus and his disciples. •When the Pharisees saw this they 11 said to his disciples, "Why does your teacher eat with tax collectors and sinners?" •But when Jesus heard this he said, "The healthy aren't in need 12 of a doctor — the sick are. •So go learn what *this* means, **I desire mer-** 13 **cy and not sacrifice,** for I came not to call the righteous, but sinners."

•[f] Then John's disciples came to him and said, "Why do we and 14 the Pharisees fast often, but your disciples don't fast?" •And Jesus 15 said to them,

> "Can the groomsmen mourn while the bridegroom
>   is with them?
> But the day will come when the bridegroom will
>   be taken from them, and then they'll fast.
> •No one puts a patch of new cloth   16
>   on an old cloak,
> For its fullness pulls away from the cloak
>   and the tear becomes worse.
> •Nor do you put new wine into old skins;   17
> For then the skins burst and the wine is spilled,
>   and the skins are ruined.
> Instead, you put new wine into new skins
> And then both are preserved."

•[g] While he was telling them these things, behold, a ruler came and 18 knelt before him and said, "My daughter has just died, but come lay your hand on her and she'll live." •So Jesus and his disciples got up and fol- 19 lowed him. •And, behold, a woman who had had a chronic bleeding for 20 twelve years came up and touched the tassel of his cloak from behind, •for she said to herself, "If I just touch his cloak I'll be saved." •But Je- 21.22 sus, turning and seeing her, said, "Take courage, daughter! Your faith has saved you!" And the woman was saved from that hour.

---

[e] *Mk 2:13-17; Lk 5:27-32.*   [f] *Mk 2:18-22; Lk 5:33-39.*   [g] *Mk 5:21-43; Lk 8:40-56.*

9:11 In Judaism table-fellowship established solidarity of the participants before God. Fellowship with sinners was therefore both a scandal and a source of ritual impurity.
9:13 Ho 6:6.
9:20 Devout Jews wore tassels on the four cor-
ners of their cloaks to remind them to obey the commandments (Nb 15:38-39). This woman, because of her continuous menstrual flow, was a source of ritual impurity to anyone she touched (Lv 15:25-30).

23 •When Jesus came to the ruler's house and saw the flute players and
24 the crowd in an uproar •he said, "Out with you! — the girl hasn't died,
25 she's sleeping!" And they laughed at him. •But when the crowd had been
26 driven out he went in and grasped the girl's hand, and she got up. •And
this news went out through all that land.

27 •As Jesus travelled on from there two blind men followed him, cry-
28 ing out and saying, "Have mercy on us, Son of David!" •When he had
gone into the house the blind men came to him and Jesus said to them,
29 "Do you believe that I can do this?" They said to him, "Yes, Lord!" •He
touched their eyes and said, "Let it be done to you according to your
30 faith!" •and their eyes were opened. Then he spoke sternly to them and
31 said, "See that no one hears about this!" •But they went out and spread
the news about him throughout that region.

32 •As they were leaving, behold, the people brought him a demon-pos-
33 sessed dumb man, •and when the demon had been driven out the dumb
man spoke. The crowds were amazed and said, "The like of this has
34 never been seen in Israel!" •But the Pharisees said, "He drives out
demons by the power of the prince of demons!"

A tax booth in a relief sculpture (2nd century A.D.). (Mt 9:9)

MATTHEW

I. THE MISSION OF THE DISCIPLES

•Then Jesus went around all the cities and villages, teaching in their 35 synagogues, proclaiming the good news of the Kingdom and healing every disease and illness. •When he saw the crowds he was moved with 36 pity for them because they were worried and helpless, like sheep without a shepherd. •And he said to his disciples, 37

"The harvest is plentiful,
But the laborers are few;

•so implore the Lord of the harvest to send out laborers to his harvest." 38

10•[h] Then he summoned his twelve disciples and gave them authority over unclean spirits, so they could drive them out and heal 1 every disease and illness. •These are the names of the twelve apostles; 2 first Simon who is called Peter and his brother Andrew, and James son of Zebedee and his brother John, •Philip and Bartholomew, Thomas 3 and Matthew the tax collector, James son of Alpheus and Thaddeus, •Simon the Cananean and Judas Iscariot, who handed him over. 4
•[i] Jesus sent these twelve out after instructing them and saying, 5

"Don't go off on the road to the Gentiles,
And don't enter a Samaritan city;
•Go, instead, to the lost sheep of the house of Israel. 6

•As you go, proclaim the good news, and say, 'The Kingdom of Heav- 7 en is at hand!'

•Heal the sick, 8
    raise the dead,
Cleanse lepers,
    drive out demons;
Freely you have received,
    freely give.
•Don't keep gold or silver, 9
    nor brass in your belts,
•Neither a bag for the road 10
    nor two tunics,

[h] Mk 3:13-19; Lk 6:12-16.   [i] Mk 6:7-13; Lk 9:1-6.

10:4 "Simon the Cananean." This is generally considered to be a designation for the ultranationalist (and, therefore, anti-Roman) Zealots.

Nor sandals
    nor staff,
For the worker is deserving of his living.

11 •"Whatever town or village you enter, ask who in it is worthy and stay there until you leave.

12   •When you enter the house,
        pay your respects,
13   •And if that house is worthy,
        let your peace come upon it,
    But if it isn't worthy,
        let your peace return to you.
14   •And whoever doesn't receive you
        or hear your words,
    When you leave that house or city,
        shake the dust from your feet.

15 •Amen, I say to you, it will be more tolerable for the land of Sodom and Gomorrah on the day of judgment than for that city!"

16   •ⁱ "Behold, I'm sending you off like sheep among wolves;
        Be as wise as serpents and guileless as doves.

17 •But beware of men —

    They'll hand you over to councils,
        and scourge you in their synagogues,
18   •And you'll be led before governors and kings
        for my sake,
        as a witness to them and to the Gentiles.
19   •But when they hand you over, don't worry about
        how to speak or what you should say;
        for what you should say will be given you
        in that hour,
20   •For it won't be you speaking,
        but the Spirit of my Father speaking in you.
21   •Brother will hand brother over to death,
        and father, child.
    and children will rebel against parents
        and put them to death.

ⁱ Mk 13:9-13; Lk 21:12-17.

•And you'll be hated by all because of my name,   22
  but whoever holds out till the end,
    they will be saved.

•And when they persecute you in one such city, flee to another; for, 23
amen, I say to you, you will not finish with the cities of Israel before the
Son of Man comes."

  •[k] "The disciple is not above the teacher,   24
    nor the servant above his master.
  •It's enough for the disciple to become   25
    like his teacher,
  and the servant like *his* master.
  If they've called the householder Beelzebul,
    All the more will they revile his dependents!"

•[l] "Therefore, don't be afraid of them —   26

Nothing is concealed
  that will not be revealed,
Nor hidden
  that will not be made known.
•What I tell you in darkness,   27
  speak in the light,
And what you hear whispered,
  proclaim on the roof tops.
•Don't fear those who can kill the body   28
  but can't kill the soul;
Fear, instead, the One Who can kill
  both soul and body in Gehenna.

•Aren't two sparrows sold for a few cents? Yet not one of them will fall 29
to the earth without your Father's leave. •But as for you, even the hairs 30
of your head are all numbered. •So don't be afraid; you're worth more 31
than many sparrows."

  •[m] "Therefore, whoever acknowledges me   32
    before men,
  I, too, will acknowledge him before my Father
    in Heaven;
  •But whoever denies me before men,   33

[k] *Lk 6:40.* [l] *Lk 12:2-7.* [m] *Lk 12:8-9.*

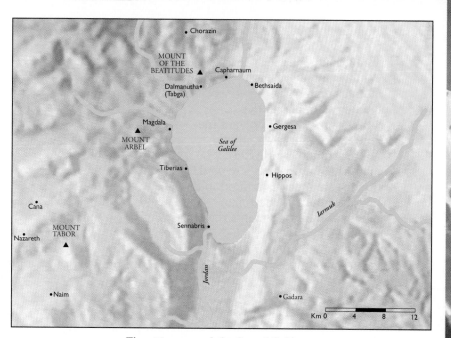

The cities around the Sea of Galilee.

I, too, will deny him before my Father
in Heaven."

34 •[n] "Don't think that I came to spread peace
on the earth;
I came not to spread peace but the sword.

35 •I came to turn a man **against his father,**
And a daughter against her mother,
And a daughter-in-law against her mother-in-law,

36 •**And a man's enemies will be the members**
of his household.

37 •Whoever loves his father or mother more than me
is not worthy of me,
And whoever loves his son or daughter more than me
is not worthy of me.

38 •And whoever doesn't take up his cross and follow
behind me isn't worthy of me.

[n] *Lk 12:51-53; 14:26-27.*   10:35-36 Mi 7:6.

•Whoever finds his life will lose it, 39
And whoever loses his life for my sake
    will find it."
•° "Whoever receives you 40
    receives me,
And whoever receives me
    receives the One Who sent me.
•Whoever receives a prophet 41
    because he's a prophet
    will receive a prophet's reward,
And whoever receives a good man
    because he's a good man
    will receive a good man's reward.

•And whoever gives even a cup of cold water to one of these little 42
ones because he's a disciple, amen, I say to you, he will not lose his
reward."

11 •And it happened that when Jesus had finished instructing his 1
twelve disciples he left there to teach and preach in their cities.

J. RESPONSE IN FAITH AND REPENTANCE

•ᵖ Now when John heard in prison about the works of the Messiah 2
he sent by means of his disciples •and said to him, "Are you he who is 3
to come, or are we to expect another?"
    •In answer Jesus said to them, "Go tell John what you hear and see: 4

•The blind can see again and the lame walk, 5
Lepers are made clean and the deaf hear,
The dead are raised and **the poor are given the good news;**
    •And blessed is whoever is not scandalized by me." 6

•After they had left, Jesus began to speak to the crowds about John. 7

"What did you go out to the desert to see?
    A reed, shaken by the wind?
•But what did you go out to see? 8
    A man wearing luxurious clothing?

° Mk 9:41. ᵖ Lk 7:18-35.   11:5 Is 35:5-6; 61:1.

Behold, those in luxurious clothing
   are in the houses of kings!
9 •But what did you go out to see?
   A prophet?
Yes, I tell you, and one greater than a prophet.
10   •He it is of whom it is written,
Behold, I'm sending my messenger before your face,
** who will prepare your way before you.**
11 •Amen, I say to you, among those born of women
   there has not risen one greater than John
    the Baptist,
But the lowliest person in the Kingdom of Heaven
   is greater than he is.
12 •From the days of John the Baptist
   until the present
The Kingdom of Heaven has been breaking in,
   and the violent have been seeking to take it by force.
13 •For all the Prophets and the Torah
   up to John prophesied,
14 •And if you can accept it, he's Elijah — he
   who is destined to come.
15 •Whoever has ears,
   let them hear!"

16   •"But to what shall I compare this generation? It's like children sitting
17 in the marketplace who call to each other •and say,

   'We piped for you and you didn't dance,
    we wailed and you didn't mourn.'
18 •For John came neither eating nor drinking,
    and they said,
   'He has a demon';
19 •The Son of Man came eating and drinking,
    and they said,

11:10 MI 3:1. This prophecy continues by stating that God Himself will come in judgment. If John the Baptist is the messenger, as Jesus says, then Jesus is equating himself with God, a point likely not missed by his listeners.
11:12 This obscure verse probably refers to attempts by those hostile to Jesus to prevent the acceptance of the Kingdom or to co-opt the Kingdom for their own purposes.
11:13 Jesus here characterizes the Torah as a prophetic witness, perhaps in opposition to the understanding of it as a code of law which will remain entirely unchanged for all time.

'Look at him, a glutton and a drunkard, a friend
of tax collectors and sinners!'
Yet wisdom is justified by her works!"

•[q] Then he began to denounce the cities in which most of his mighty 20
works had taken place, because they hadn't repented. •"Woe to you, 21
Chorazin! Woe to you, Bethsaida! Because if the mighty works that happened in you had taken place in Tyre or Sidon, they would have repented
in sackcloth and ashes long ago. •But I say to you, it will be more tol- 22
erable for Tyre and Sidon on the day of judgment than for you. •And 23
you, Capharnaum!

You'll be exalted to Heaven, will you?
You'll be brought down to Hell!

because if the mighty works that happened in you had taken place in Sodom
it would have remained to this day. •But I say to you, it will be more tol- 24
erable for the land of Sodom on the day of judgment than for you!"

•[r] At that time Jesus raised his voice and said,   25
"I praise you, Father,
    Lord of Heaven and earth,
Because You hid these things from the wise
        and intelligent,
    and revealed them to babes;
•Yes, Father,   26
    for such was Your desire.
•All things have been given to me by my Father,   27
    and no one knows the Son except the Father,
Nor does anyone know the Father except the Son,
    and whoever the Son chooses to reveal Him to.
•Come to me, all you grown weary and burdened,   28
    and I will refresh you.
•Take my yoke upon you   29
    and learn from me,

---

[q] *Lk 10:13-15.* [r] *Lk 10:21-22.*

11:19 This accusation against Jesus meant that his
accusers considered him to be deserving of stoning. Cf. Dt 21:20. Also cf. 9:11 regarding table-fellowship with sinners. The final line of v. 19 appears
to identify Jesus as the incarnate Wisdom of God,
and the words "her works" would then refer to "the
works of the Messiah" (11:2, 11:5).

11:23 Is 14:13, 15.
11:28-30 "Yoke." This was a common way of referring to the Torah, and every pious Jew was to
accept this "yoke" joyfully. The Torah was also
seen as the expression of the divine Wisdom, and
it is probable that Jesus speaks here as the personification of divine Wisdom (Si 51:23-26).

For I am gentle and humble hearted,
    and you will find rest for your souls;
30 •For my yoke is easy,
    and my burden light."

Chorazin: ruins of the synagogue (4th century A.D.). (Mt 11:21)

K. CONTROVERSY WITH THE PHARISEES

The Lord of the Sabbath

1 **12**•ˢ At that time Jesus was going through the grain fields on the Sabbath; now, his disciples became hungry and began to pluck
2 the heads of grain and eat them. •When the Pharisees saw this they said to him, "Look, your disciples are doing what it's unlawful to do

ˢ *Mk 2:23-28; Lk 6:1-5.*

on the Sabbath!" •But he said to them, "Haven't you read what David 3 did when he was hungry, as well as those with him? •How he went 4 into the house of God and ate the loaves of offering, which it wasn't lawful for him to eat nor for those with him but was for the priests alone? •Or haven't you read in the Torah that on the Sabbath the 5 priests serving in the Temple violate the Sabbath yet are not considered guilty? •But I say to you, something greater than the Temple is 6 here. •If you had known what this means, **I desire mercy and not** 7 **sacrifice,** you wouldn't have condemned the innocent. •For the Son 8 of Man is Lord of the Sabbath."

•[t] He left there and went to their synagogue, •and, behold, a man 9,10 with a withered hand was there. And they asked him, "Is it lawful to heal on the Sabbath?" in an effort to find an accusation they could bring against him. •But he said to them, "Which of you, if you had 11 one sheep and it fell into a ditch on the Sabbath, wouldn't take hold of it and pull it out? •Yet a man is certainly worth far more than a 12 sheep! And so it's lawful to do good on the Sabbath." •Then he said 13 to the man, "Hold out your hand." He held it out and it was restored, as sound as the other. •But the Pharisees went out and plotted to do 14 away with Jesus.

•Now Jesus realized this and departed from there. Many people fol- 15 lowed him and he healed them all •and commanded them not to make 16 him known, •so he would fulfill what was said by Isaiah the prophet, 17 when he proclaimed,

> •**Behold my Servant whom I have chosen,** 18
> **my Beloved in whom my soul is well pleased;**
> **I will put my Spirit upon him,**
> **and he will proclaim justice to the Gentiles.**
> •**He will not quarrel or shout out angrily,** 19
> **nor will anyone hear his voice in the streets.**
> •**He will not snap off a broken reed,** 20
> **and he will not snuff out a smoldering wick,**
> **Until he leads justice to victory,**
> •**and the Gentiles will hope in his name.** 21

[t] *Mk 3:1-6; Lk 6:6-11.*

12:5-6 Performance of their priestly duties on the Sabbath involved the priests in technical breaches of the Sabbath rest, which Jesus says is justified because in this case the Temple service takes precedence over the Sabbath laws. 12:7 Ho 6:6. 12:18-21 Is 42:1-4 (Septuagint).

Jesus and Beelzebul

22 •[u] Then they brought him a demon-possessed blind and dumb man,
23 and he healed him so that the dumb man could speak and see. •All the
24 crowds went wild and said, "Could this be the Son of David?" •But when
the Pharisees heard this they said, "If it weren't for the power of Beelzebul, prince of demons, this fellow wouldn't be able to drive out demons!"
25 •Now he knew their inmost thoughts and so he said to them,

> "Every kingdom divided against itself
>   is laid waste,
> And no city or house divided against itself
>   will stand.
26 > •And if Satan drives out Satan,
>   he's divided against himself;
> How, then, will his kingdom stand?
27 > •And if I drive out demons by Beelzebul,
> By whom do *your* followers drive them out?
> Therefore, *they'll* be your judges!
28 > •But if I drive out demons by the Spirit of God,
> Then the Kingdom of God has come upon you!

29 •How can someone enter a strong man's house and carry off his possessions if he doesn't first tie the strong man up? *Then* he can plunder
the house.

30 > •Whoever isn't with me is against me,
> And whoever doesn't gather with me scatters.
31 > •Therefore I say to you,
> Every sin and blasphemy will be forgiven you,
> But blasphemy against the Spirit
>   will not be forgiven.
32 > •And whoever says a word against the Son of Man,
>   will be forgiven,
> But whoever speaks against the Holy Spirit
>   will not be forgiven, neither in this age
>   nor in the age to come.

[u] *Mk 3:20-30; Lk 11:14-23; 12:10.*

12:29 Here Jesus compares Satan to a "strong man" and the present age to Satan's house. It is Jesus who has entered Satan's house, bound him, and freed those in Satan's power. Jesus' power over demons is a sign of this mastery and of the coming of the Messianic age.

•ᵛ Either make the tree good and its fruit good,   33
Or make the tree bad and its fruit bad,
For from the fruit the tree is known.
•You brood of vipers!   34
How can you speak good things
    when *you're* evil?
For the mouth speaks from the abundance
    of the heart.
•The good bring out good things   35
    from their store of good,
And the evil bring out evil things
    from their store of evil.
•But I tell you that for *every* slighting   36
    utterance you make,
You'll give an accounting on the day
    of judgment,
•For by your words you'll be acquitted,   37
And by your words you'll be condemned."

The sign of Jonah

•ʷ Then some of the scribes and Pharisees spoke up and said to him, 38
"Teacher, we want to see a sign from you." •But in response he said 39
to them,

"A wicked and adulterous generation seeks a sign,
Yet no sign will be given it but the sign of Jonah the prophet.
•For just as **Jonah was in the belly of the whale**   40
    for three days and three nights,
So will the Son of Man be in the heart of the earth
    for three days and three nights.
•The men of Nineveh will stand in judgment   41
    against this generation and will condemn it,
Because they repented as a result of Jonah's preaching,

ᵛ *Lk 6:43-45.*   ʷ *Mk 8:11-12; Lk 11:29-32.*

12:36 Often translated "every idle word." The context makes it abundantly clear, however, that Jesus is addressing those attempting to simply dismiss him, cf. 11:32 above.

12:39 "The sign of Jonah" probably referred primarily to the extension of God's mercy to the Gentiles and their preference over those Jews who rejected Jesus.
12:40 Jon 1:17.

The Sea of Galilee. Region of the ministry of Jesus.

And, behold, one greater than Jonah is here.
42 •The queen of the South will rise up at the judgment
    against this generation and condemn it,
Because she came from the ends of the earth
    to hear the wisdom of Solomon,
And, behold, one greater than Solomon is here."

43 •ˣ "When an unclean spirit comes out of a man it goes about through
44 waterless places seeking relief, and finds none. •Then it says, 'I'll return
to the house I left,' and when it comes it finds the house empty, swept
45 out, and decorated. •Then it goes and brings with it seven other spirits
worse than itself, and it goes in and settles there, and the last state of
that man becomes worse than the first. That's how it will be with this
evil generation, too."

ˣ Lk 11:24-26.

•[y] While he was still speaking to the crowds, behold, his mother and 46
brothers came and stood outside, seeking to speak with him. [•Some- 47
one said to him, "Look, your mother and your brothers are standing outside — they want to speak with you!"] •But in response he said to the 48
one who had spoken to him, "Who is my mother, and who are my brothers?" •And stretching out his hand to his disciples he said, "Here are 49
my mother and my brothers, •for whoever does the will of my Father 50
in Heaven, he's my brother and sister and mother."

L. PARABLES OF THE KINGDOM
AND REJECTION AT NAZARETH

13 •[z] That day when Jesus left the house he sat down by the sea, 1
•and such large crowds gathered around him that he got into a 2
boat and seated himself, while the whole crowd stood on the shore.
•Then he spoke to them at length in parables, saying, 3

"Behold, the sower went out to sow!
•And as he sowed, some seed fell along the path, 4
and the birds came and ate it up.
•Other seed fell on rocky ground, where it 5
didn't have much soil
and it sprouted at once, since the soil
had no depth.
•But when the sun rose it got scorched, 6
and since it had no roots it withered away.
•Other seed fell among the thorns, 7
and the thorns came up and choked it.
•Still other seed fell on the good earth 8
and gave fruit,
the one a hundredfold, the other sixtyfold,
yet another thirtyfold.
•Whoever has ears, 9
let them hear!"

•[a] The disciples came and said to him, "Why are you speaking to them 10

---

[y] Mk 3:31-35; Lk 8:19-21.   [z] Mk 4:1-9; Lk 8:4-8.

12:46 In Semitic usage, close relatives such as
cousins could be referred to as brothers or sisters. That these "brothers" were not additional
sons of Mary, the mother of Jesus, can be seen
from other passages such as Mt 27:60. Cf. below
at 13:55 for a further discussion.

11 in parables?" •In answer he said, "To you it's given to know the secrets of the Kingdom of Heaven, but to them it isn't given.

12 •For whoever has, to him it will be given
and it will be more than enough,
But whoever does not have, even what he has
will be taken from him.

13 •Therefore, I speak to them in parables, because

Although they look,
they don't see,
And though they listen,
they neither hear nor understand,

14 •and in them is being fulfilled the prophecy of Isaiah, who said,

**For all you listen,
you will hear yet not understand,
And though you look,
you will see yet not perceive.**
15 **•For the heart of this people has been hardened,
and it has been difficult for them to hear
with their ears,
And they closed their eyes lest they see with their eyes
and hear with their ears
And understand with their heart and return,
and I will heal them.**

16 •But blessed are your eyes because they see,
and your ears because they hear.

17 •Amen, I say to you,
Many of the prophets and the righteous longed
to see what you're seeing,
yet didn't see,
And to hear what you're hearing,
yet didn't hear."

18,19 •[b] "Listen, then, to the parable of the sower. •When anyone hears the word of the Kingdom yet doesn't understand, the Evil One comes and snatches away what was sown in his heart; this is the one who was
20 sown along the footpath. •The one sown on the rocky ground, this is

[a] Mk 4:10-12; Lk 8:9-10.   [b] Mk 4:13-20; Lk 8:11-15.

13:14-15 Is 6:9-10 (Septuagint).

the one who hears the word and at once receives it joyfully, •but he's 21 not well rooted but is only for the moment and when trouble or persecution arises because of the word he at once falls away. •Now the one 22 sown among the thorns, this is the one who hears the word, yet worldly cares and the deception of wealth choke the word and it's unfruitful. •But the one sown on good earth, this is the one who hears the word 23 and understands, who, indeed, bears fruit, and produces a hundredfold, or sixtyfold, or thirtyfold."

•He presented another parable to them and said, "The Kingdom of 24 Heaven has been compared to a man who sowed good seed in his field. •While everyone was sleeping his enemy came and sowed weeds among 25 the wheat and went off, •so when the shoots sprouted and bore fruit 26 the weeds appeared then, too. •The householder's servants came to him 27 and said, 'Master, didn't you sow good seed in your field? Then where did the weeds come from?' •He said to them, 'An enemy did this.' So 28 the slaves said to him, 'Do you want us to go gather the weeds up, then?' •'No,' he said, 'you might uproot the wheat at the same time you're gath- 29 ering the weeds. •Let them both grow together until the harvest, and at 30 the harvest time I'll tell the harvesters, "First gather the weeds and tie them in bundles to be burned, but gather the wheat into my barn."'"

•[c] He presented another parable to them and said, "The Kingdom of 31 Heaven is like a grain of mustard seed, which a man took and sowed in his field. •Although it's the smallest of seeds, when it's fully grown it's 32 the biggest of garden plants and becomes a tree, so that the birds of the air come and nest in its branches."

•He told them another parable. "The Kingdom of Heaven is like yeast 33 that a woman took and mixed into a bushel of wheat flour until all of it was leavened."

•[d] Jesus spoke all these things to the crowds in parables and he said 34 nothing to them except in a parable, •so that what was said by the 35 prophet would be fulfilled, when he said,

I will open my mouth in parables,
I will proclaim what has been hidden since
the beginning of the world.

•Then after dismissing the crowds he went into the house. His disci- 36 ples came to him and said, "Explain the parable of the weeds in the field to us." •In response he said, "The one who sowed good seed is the Son 37

[c] *Mk 4:30-32; Lk 13:18-21.* [d] *Mk 4:33-34.* 13:35 *Ps 78:2.*

38 of Man, •while the field is the age; now the good seed, these are the children of the Kingdom, while the weeds are those who belong to the
39 Evil One, •and the enemy who sowed them is the Devil; now the har-
40 vest is the end of the age, and the harvesters are the angels. •Just as the weeds are gathered and burned with fire, so also will it be at the end
41 of the age; •the Son of Man will send his angels, and they'll gather all who cause others to sin from his Kingdom and all who do evil,
42 •and they'll thrust them into the furnace of fire;

> There there will be wailing
> and gnashing of teeth!

43 •Then the righteous will shine like the sun in the Kingdom of their Father.

> Whoever has ears,
> let them hear!"

*Winnowing of the wheat. The parables of Jesus reflect
an agricultural society of fishermen and shepherds.*

•"The Kingdom of Heaven is like a treasure hidden in a field which ⁴⁴ a man found and hid, and in his joy he went off and sold all he had and bought that field."

•"Again, the Kingdom of Heaven is like a merchant seeking fine ⁴⁵ pearls; •when he found one very precious pearl he went and sold off all ⁴⁶ he had and bought it."

•"Again, the Kingdom of Heaven is like a dragnet cast into the sea ⁴⁷ which gathered every sort of fish; •when it was filled they dragged it ⁴⁸ ashore, sat down, and gathered the good ones into containers, but they threw the bad ones out. •It will be like that at the end of the age; the ⁴⁹ angels will go out and sort the evil out from among the righteous •and ⁵⁰ throw them into the furnace of fire;

There there will be wailing
    and gnashing of teeth."

•"Have you understood all these things?" "Yes," they said to him. ⁵¹ •Then he said to them, ⁵²

"Every scribe who is a disciple
    of the Kingdom of Heaven
Is like a man who is master of a house,
Who brings from his storeroom
    both new things and old."

•ᵉ And it happened that when Jesus finished these parables he left ⁵³ there. •When he came to his home town he taught them in their syna- ⁵⁴ gogue, with the result that they were amazed and said, "Where does this fellow get this wisdom and these mighty works? •Isn't this the carpen- ⁵⁵ ter's son? Isn't his mother called Mary, and his brothers James and Joseph and Simon and Judas? •And his sisters — aren't they all here ⁵⁶ among us? Where did he get all this?" •And they rejected him. But Je- ⁵⁷ sus said to them, "A prophet is without honor only in his hometown and in his own house." •And because of their unbelief he didn't do many ⁵⁸ mighty works there.

ᵉ Mk 6:1-6; Lk 4:16-30.

13:55 Church tradition has consistently main- tained that the "brothers" of Jesus referred to here were merely close relatives, not sons of the same mother. It is instructive to compare this passage to 27:56 (and parallel passages in the other Gospels, esp. Mk 15:40 - 16:1 and Lk 23:49 - 24:10) where these brothers are again referred to as sons of "Mary," but this time it is unambigu- ously clear that *this* Mary was not Mary the moth- er of Jesus. Such usage was typically Semitic.

M. THE DEATH OF THE BAPTIST AND TWO SIGNS

1,2 **14** •[f] At that time Herod the Tetrarch heard reports about Jesus, •and he said to his servants, "This is John the Baptist; he's been raised 3 from the dead and that's why these powers are at work in him." •For Herod had seized John, bound him, and thrown him into prison because 4 of Herodias, the wife of his brother Philip, •because John had been 5 telling Herod, "It isn't lawful for you to have her." •Although Herod wanted to kill him, he feared the reaction of the people, because they re-6 garded John as a prophet. •Now when Herod's birthday celebration was held Herodias' daughter danced before the guests, and she pleased 7 Herod so much •that he promised with an oath to give her whatever 8 she asked for. •So, prompted by her mother, she said, "Give me, right 9 here on a platter, the head of John the Baptist." •The king was grieved but, because of his oath and those reclining at table with him, he or-10 dered that it be given to her. •He sent and had John beheaded in prison 11 •and his head was brought on a platter and given to the girl, and she 12 brought it to her mother. •His disciples came and took the corpse and buried it. Then they went and informed Jesus.

13 •[g] Now when Jesus heard about it he left there privately by boat for a desert place, and when the crowds heard where he'd gone they fol-14 lowed him on foot from the cities. •When he got out of the boat he saw a large crowd, and he was moved with pity for them and healed their 15 sick. •When evening had come his disciples came to him and said, "This is a desert place and the day has already come to a close; send the crowds away so they can go off to the villages and buy themselves some food." 16 •But Jesus said to them, "There's no need for them to go away; you 17 give them something to eat." •They said to him, "We have nothing here 18,19 except five loaves and two fish." •"Bring them here to me," he said. •After ordering the crowds to recline on the grass he took the five loaves and the two fish and, looking up to Heaven, he gave a blessing, and after breaking them he gave the loaves to his disciples and his disciples 20 gave them to the crowds. •They all ate and were filled, and they picked 21 up what was left of the bread — twelve baskets full. •Now there were about five thousand men who ate, not counting women and children.

22 •[h] At once he made his disciples get into the boat and go on ahead 23 of him to the other side while he sent the crowds away, • and after sending the crowds away he went up the mountain to pray in private. 24 When evening came on he was there alone, •while the boat, already

---

[f] *Mk 6:14-29; Lk 9:7-9.* [g] *Mk 6:30-44; Lk 9:10-17; Jn 6:1-14.* [h] *Mk 6:45-52; Jn 6:15-21.*

several miles away from land, was being tossed about by the waves, for the wind was against it. •Shortly before dawn he came toward 25 them, walking on the sea. •When the disciples saw him walking on 26 the sea they were terrified and said, "It's a ghost!" and they cried out in fear. •But he spoke to them at once and said, "Take courage! It's 27 me! Don't be afraid!" •In answer to him Peter said, "Lord, if it's you, 28 command me to come to you on the water." • "Come!" he said. Pe- 29 ter got out of the boat and began to walk on the water and came toward Jesus, •but when he saw the wind he became frightened and, as 30 he began to sink, he cried out and said, "Save me, Lord!" •At once 31 Jesus reached out his hand and caught him and said to him, "O you of little faith, why did you doubt?" •And when they got into the boat 32 the wind ceased. •Those in the boat worshipped him and said, "Tru- 33 ly you're the Son of God!"

•ⁱ After crossing over they came to land at Gennesaret. •The men of 34,35 that place recognized him and sent to all that neighborhood, and they brought all who were sick to him •and begged him to just let them touch 36 the tassel of his cloak, and all who touched it were cured.

N. TRUE PURIFICATION

15 •ʲ Then Pharisees and scribes from Jerusalem came to Jesus and 1 said, • "Why do your disciples disobey the tradition of the elders? 2 They don't wash their hands when they eat bread!" •In reply he said to 3 them, "And why do *you* disobey the commandment of God for the sake of your tradition? •God said, **Honor your father and your mother,** 4 and, **Let whoever curses his father or mother be put to death,** •but you say, 'Whoever says to his father or mother, "Whatever benefit 5 you might have had from me is an offering to God," •need not honor 6 his father,' and you've set aside the word of God for the sake of your tradition. •You hypocrites! Surely Isaiah prophesied about you when he said, 7

> •**This people honors me with their lips,** 8
> **but their heart is far distant from me;**
> •**In vain do they worship me,** 9
> **teaching as doctrines the commandments of men.**"

ⁱ *Mk 6:53-56.* ʲ *Mk 7:1-23.*
15:4 Ex 20:12, Dt 5:16.   15:8-9 Is 29:13 (Septuagint).

10 •Then he called the crowd to himself and said to them, "Hear and understand!

11 •What goes into the mouth
    is not what makes a man unclean;
On the contrary, what comes out of his mouth,
    that makes a man unclean."

*Place of worship on the plain of Gennesaret,
on the shore of the Sea of Galilee.*

12 •The disciples came and said to him, "Do you know that the Phar-
13 isees took offense when they heard what you said?" •But in answer he
said, "Every plant not planted by my Heavenly Father will be pulled out
14 by the roots. •Let them be. They're blind guides.

    If a blind man leads a blind man,
    Both will fall into a ditch."

15,16 •In response Peter said to him, "Explain the parable to us." •Jesus
17 said, "Can you still be that dense? •Don't you see that everything that

15:16 "You." The Greek word is plural, so that Jesus is not singling Peter out.

enters the mouth goes into the stomach and is expelled into the latrine? •But the things that come *from* the mouth come from the heart, and 18 *those* are the things that make a man unclean. •For from the heart come 19 wicked thoughts, murder, adultery, fornication, theft, false witness, and blasphemy. •These things are what make a man unclean, but eating with 20 unwashed hands doesn't make a man unclean."

O. HEALINGS AND SIGNS

•[k] When he left there Jesus withdrew to the district of Tyre and 21 Sidon. •And, behold, a Canaanite woman from that region came and 22 cried out, "Have mercy on me, Lord, Son of David! My daughter is severely tormented by a demon!" •But not a word did he answer her. 23 His disciples came and begged him, saying, "Send it away — she keeps crying out behind us!" •But in reply he said, "I was sent only to the 24 lost sheep of the house of Israel." •So the woman came and knelt before him and said, "Lord, help me!" •In reply he said, "It isn't right to 26 take the children's bread and throw it to the pups." •But she said, "O 27 yes, Lord — even the pups eat the crumbs that fall from their master's table!" •In answer, then, Jesus said to her, "O woman, great is 28 your faith! Let it be done for you as you wish!" And her daughter was healed from that very hour.

•After leaving there Jesus went along the sea of Galilee, and he ascended the mountain and sat down there. •Large crowds came to him 30 who had with them lame, blind, crippled, dumb people, and many others, and they put them down at his feet and he cured them, •so that 31 the crowd marvelled when they saw the dumb speaking, cripples sound, the lame walking, and the blind seeing, and they glorified the God of Israel.

•[l] Then Jesus called his disciples together and said, "I'm overcome 32

---

[k] *Mk 7:24-30.* [l] *Mk 8:1-10.*

15:23 "Send it away." Literally, "send *her* away." The substitution of "it" presupposes an Aramaic original. Since Aramaic has no neuter gender, it was possible to mistakenly translate an Aramaic feminine pronoun literally rather than changing it to the neuter, if that would be required in Greek. The context appears to support this interpretation. If it is read "her," then Jesus' reply to the disciples is a nonsequitur, since he would be granting nei-ther the woman's request that her daughter be healed, nor the disciples', that she be sent away. On the other hand, if "it" is substituted, it makes excellent sense: the disciples beg Jesus to grant the woman's request and send *it* (the demon) away just to quiet the woman, but he at first declines to grant the woman this favor because she is a non-Israelite. This is clearly seen in the parallel passage at Mk 7:24 ff.

with pity for the crowd — they've stayed with me for three days now and don't have anything to eat, yet I don't want to send them away
33 hungry — they might faint on the way." •And the disciples said to him, "Where can we get enough loaves in the desert to feed such a large
34 crowd?" •Jesus said to them, "How many loaves do you have?" "Sev-
35 en, and a few fish," they replied. •After ordering the crowd to sit down
36 on the ground •he took the loaves and the fish and gave thanks, and he broke them and began giving them to his disciples, and the disci-
37 ples gave them to the crowds. •They all ate and were filled, and they
38 picked up the leftover pieces of bread — seven large baskets full. •Now there were four thousand men who ate, not counting the women and
39 children. •Then after sending the crowds away he got into the boat and came to the regions of Magadan.

1 **16** •[m] The Pharisees and Sadducees came to test him, and they asked
2 him to show them a sign from Heaven. •But in answer he said
3 to them, ["In the evening you say, 'Fair weather — the sky is red,' •and in the morning, 'Today will be stormy — the sky is red and darkened.' You know how to read the face of the sky, yet you can't tell the signs of the times!]

4   •[n] A wicked and adulterous generation seeks a sign,
        Yet no sign will be given it but the sign of Jonah."

Then he left them and went away.
5   •And when the disciples went to the other side they forgot to bring
6 bread. •Now Jesus said to them, "Take care, and guard against the leav-
7 en of the Pharisees and Sadducees!" •But they began arguing among themselves, saying, "Is he [saying that] because we didn't bring bread?"
8 •So Jesus, realizing this, said, "O you of little faith, why are you argu-
9 ing among yourselves because you don't have bread? •Do you still not understand? Don't you remember the five loaves for the five thousand
10 and how many baskets you picked up? •Or the seven loaves for the four
11 thousand and how many large baskets you picked up? •How can you not understand that I wasn't talking to you about bread? Be on guard,
12 then, against the leaven of the Pharisees and Sadducees." •Then they realized that he wasn't saying to be on guard against the *leavening* but against the *teaching* of the Pharisees and Sadducees.

[m] *Mk 8:11-13; Lk 12:54-56.*   [n] *Mk 8:14-21.*

P. JESUS, PETER, TRANSFIGURATION

•° When Jesus came to the district of Caesarea Philippi he began to 13 question his disciples, "Who do men say the Son of Man is?" •"Some 14 say John the Baptist," they said, "others, Elijah, still others, Jeremiah or one of the prophets." •Then he asked them, "But who do *you* say I 15 am?" •Simon Peter replied, "You're the Messiah, the Son of the Living 16 God!" •In response Jesus said to him, 17

"Blessed are you, Simon bar Jonah,
For it wasn't flesh and blood that
    revealed this to you,
But my Father in Heaven.
•And now *I* tell *you*, that you are Peter, 18
And on this rock I will build my church,
And the gates of Hell will not prevail
    against it.
•I will give you the keys to the Kingdom of Heaven, 19
And whatever you bind on earth
    will have been bound in Heaven,
And whatever you loose on earth
    will have been loosed in Heaven."

•Then he ordered the disciples not to tell anyone that he was the Messiah. 20
•ᵖ From then on Jesus began to explain to his disciples that he had 21 to go on to Jerusalem and suffer terrible things at the hands of the elders and chief priests and scribes and be put to death and rise on the third day. •Peter took him aside and began to remonstrate with him, saying, 22 "God be merciful to you, Lord! This will never happen to you!" •But Je- 23 sus turned to Peter and said, "Get behind me, Satan! You're an occasion of sin for me — you're not thinking the thoughts of God but of men." •Then Jesus said to his disciples, 24

° *Mk 8:27-30; Lk 9:18-21.*   ᵖ *Mk 8:31 - 9:1; Lk 9:22-27.*

16:17 "Simon bar Jonah"; "bar" is Aramaic for "son of."

16:18 "Peter...rock"; a play on words is involved here. In Greek, "Peter" = *Petros* and "rock" = *petra*. This play on words undoubtedly was derived from the original Aramaic; Peter was known in the early Church as "Kephas," derived from *kepha*, the Aramaic word for "rock." Verse 19 with its symbolism of the keys and reference to binding and loosing makes it clear that Peter will receive both Divine authority and Divine guidance in matters relating to the Kingdom, which the Church has taught as pertaining to faith and morals.

"Church"; in the OT this term designated the assembly of God's people Israel, as, e.g., at Mt. Sinai where God manifested Himself to Israel through Moses.

"Whoever would be my disciple must deny himself,
He must take up his cross and follow me.
25 •For whoever would save his life will lose it,
While whoever loses his life for my sake will find it.
26 •For what good would it do a man to gain the whole world,
but forfeit his life?
Or what could a man give in exchange for his life?
27 •For the Son of Man will come in the glory
of his Father with his angels,
And then he'll pay each according to their work.

28 •Amen, I say to you, some of those standing here will not taste death
until they see the Son of Man coming in his Kingdom."

Church of the Transfiguration on Mount Tabor. (Mt 16:13)

17 •[q] Six days later Jesus took Peter and James and his brother John 1
along and led them up a high mountain by themselves. •And he 2
was transformed in front of them and his face shone like the sun, while
his clothing became as white as light. •And, behold, Moses appeared to 3
them as well as Elijah, speaking with him. •In response Peter said to Je- 4
sus, "Lord, it's good for us to be here; if you wish, I'll put up three
dwellings here, one for you, one for Moses, and one for Elijah." •While 5
he was still speaking, behold, a bright cloud overshadowed them and,
behold, a voice from the cloud said, "This is My Beloved Son, in whom
I am well pleased; hear him!" •When the disciples heard the voice they 6
fell on their faces and were overwhelmed with fear, •but Jesus came and 7
touched them and said, "Get up; don't be afraid any more!" •And when 8
they raised their eyes they saw no one but Jesus alone.

•As they were coming down from the mountain Jesus commanded 9
them, "Tell no one about the vision until the Son of Man has risen from
the dead." •The disciples questioned him, saying, "Why, then, do the 10
scribes say that Elijah must come first?" •In answer he said, "Elijah *is* 11
coming and he'll restore all things; •but I say to you that Elijah has *al-* 12
ready come, yet they didn't acknowledge him; instead, they did to him
whatever they wanted. So, too, the Son of Man will suffer at their
hands." •Then the disciples realized that he was talking to them about 13
John the Baptist.

•[r] And when they came to the crowd a man approached Jesus, knelt 14
before him, •and said, "Lord, have mercy on my son. He's epileptic and 15
suffers terribly — he often falls into the fire and also into the water. •I 16
brought him to your disciples, but they couldn't heal him." •In response 17
Jesus said,

"O unbelieving and perverse generation!
How long will I be with you?
How long will I put up with you?

Bring him here to me!" •And Jesus rebuked it and the demon left him, 18
and the boy was healed from that very hour. •Then the disciples came 19
to Jesus privately and said, "Why couldn't *we* drive it out?" •"Because of 20
your weak faith," he said, "for, amen, I say to you, if you have faith like

[q] *Mk 9:2-13; Lk 9:28-36.* [r] *Mk 9:14-29; Lk 9:37-43.*

17:2-3 Jesus is glorified, flanked by the representatives of the Torah and the Prophets, which he brings to fulfillment.
17:4 "Dwellings." This Greek word also means "tents," but was applied to the booths which the Jews constructed during the Feast of Tabernacles; they were meant to recall the way the Israelites lived during the Exodus.

a grain of mustard seed you'll say to this mountain, 'Move from here to
21 there!' and it *will* move, and nothing will be impossible for you." [•]
22 •ˢ While they were together in Galilee Jesus told them, "The Son
23 of Man is going to be handed over into the hands of men •and they'll
put him to death, but on the third day he'll rise." And they were terribly distressed.
24 •When they came to Capharnaum those who were collecting the Temple tax came up to Peter and said, "Doesn't your Teacher pay the Tem-
25 ple tax?" • "Certainly he does!" he said. And when he entered the house
Jesus anticipated him by saying, "What do you think, Simon? The kings
of the earth — from whom do they collect tax or toll? From their fol-
26 lowers or from others?" •When Peter said, "From others," Jesus said to
27 him, "So then their followers are exempt! •But so we don't offend them,
go to the sea, cast a hook in, and take the first fish that comes up, and
when you open its mouth you'll find a silver coin, worth twice the Temple tax; take it and give it to them for me and you."

Q. TRUE AUTHORITY AND FORGIVENESS

1 18 •ᵗ At that time the disciples came to Jesus and said, "Who's the
2 greatest in the Kingdom of Heaven?" •He called a child forward,
3 stood it before them, •and said, "Amen, I say to you,

Unless you turn about and become like children,
you won't ever *enter* the Kingdom of Heaven!
4 •Therefore, whoever humbles himself like this child,
he's the greatest in the Kingdom of Heaven.
5 •And whoever receives one such child in my name,
receives me."

6 •ᵘ "But whoever causes one of these little ones who believe in me to
sin, it would be better for him to have a donkey's millstone hung around
7 his neck and be sunk in the depths of the sea. •Woe to the world because of occasions of sin! It's inevitable that occasions of sin should come,
yet woe to the man through whom the occasion of sin comes!

ˢ *Mk 9:30-32; Lk 9:43-45.* ᵗ *Mk 9:33-37; Lk 9:46-48.* ᵘ *Mk 9:33-37; Lk 9:46-48.*

17:21 The best manuscript tradition omits this verse: "But this type doesn't come out except through prayer and fasting."
17:24 This was the annual Temple tax which every Jew was required to pay.

18:6 For everyday household use in Palestine a stone hand mill or quern was used. The millstone referred to here was a much larger and heavier one, requiring the use of a donkey for its operation.

•If your hand or your foot causes you to sin, 8
    cut it off and throw it away from you!
It's better for you to enter that life crippled or lame,
than to have two hands or two feet and be thrown
     into eternal fire.
•And if your eye causes you to sin, 9
    pluck it out and throw it away from you!
It's better for you to enter that life one-eyed,
    than to have two eyes and be thrown
     into the fire of Gehenna."

•[v] "See that you don't look down on one of these little ones, for I tell 10 you, their angels in Heaven continually look upon the face of my Father in Heaven. [•] •What do you think? If a man has a hundred sheep 11,12 and one of them strays away, won't he leave the ninety-nine on the mountainside and go look for the one that went astray? •And if he happens to find it, amen, I say to you, he rejoices over it more than over the ninety-nine that *didn't* go astray. •Likewise, it isn't the will of your 14 Father in Heaven that one of these little ones should be lost."

•[w] "If your brother should sin [against you], go show him his error 15 between you and him alone. If he listens to you, you've won your brother back; •but if he doesn't listen, take one or two others with you, so 16 that **every statement may stand upon the testimony of two or three witnesses.** •If he refuses to listen to *them,* tell the church, but 17 if he refuses to listen *even* to the church, regard him as you would a Gentile or a tax collector."•"Amen, I say to you, 18

Whatever you bind on earth
    will have been bound in Heaven,
And whatever you loose on earth
    will have been loosed in Heaven.

•Again I say to you, if two of you agree on earth about any matter they 19 ask for, it will come to be for them through my Father in Heaven. •For 20 where two or three are gathered in my name, I am there among them."

---

[v] *Lk 15:3-7.*   [w] *Lk 17:3.*

18:8-9 "That life"; i.e., the life of the Kingdom.
18:11 The best manuscript tradition omits this verse: "For the Son of Man came to save the lost."
18:16 Dt 19:15.

18:20 According to the rabbis, God was present when at least two studied the Torah. It is probable that Matthew presents Jesus here as "God with us" (1:23, 28:20).

MATTHEW

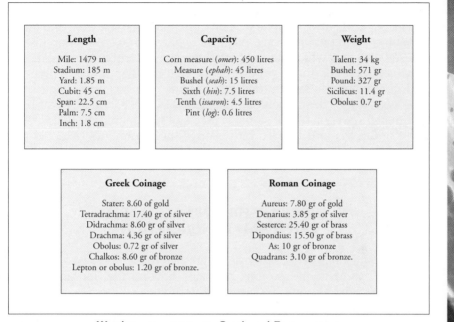

Length	Capacity	Weight
Mile: 1479 m	Corn measure (*omer*): 450 litres	Talent: 34 kg
Stadium: 185 m	Measure (*ephah*): 45 litres	Bushel: 571 gr
Yard: 1.85 m	Bushel (*seah*): 15 litres	Pound: 327 gr
Cubit: 45 cm	Sixth (*hin*): 7.5 litres	Sicilicus: 11.4 gr
Span: 22.5 cm	Tenth (*issaron*): 4.5 litres	Obolus: 0.7 gr
Palm: 7.5 cm	Pint (*log*): 0.6 litres	
Inch: 1.8 cm		

Greek Coinage	Roman Coinage
Stater: 8.60 of gold	Aureus: 7.80 gr of gold
Tetradrachma: 17.40 gr of silver	Denarius: 3.85 gr of silver
Didrachma: 8.60 gr of silver	Sesterce: 25.40 gr of brass
Drachma: 4.36 gr of silver	Dipondius: 15.50 gr of brass
Obolus: 0.72 gr of silver	As: 10 gr of bronze
Chalkos: 8.60 gr of bronze	Quadrans: 3.10 gr of bronze.
Lepton or obolus: 1.20 gr of bronze.	

Weights, measurements, Greek and Roman coins.

21 •Then Peter came and said to him, "Lord, how many times can my brother sin against me and I'll have to forgive him? Up to seven times?"
22 •Jesus said to him, "I don't say to you up to seven times, but instead up
23 to seventy-seven times. •Therefore, the Kingdom of Heaven can be com-
24 pared to a king who wanted to settle accounts with his servants. •When he began settling the accounts a debtor was brought to him who owed
25 ten thousand talents. •Since the man was unable to repay the debt the lord ordered him to be sold, along with his wife and children and every-
26 thing he had, and payment made. •The servant fell down, therefore, knelt before the king, and said, 'Be patient with me and I'll pay you back
27 everything!' •Deeply moved, the lord of that servant released him and
28 forgave him the debt. •But when that servant went out he found one of his fellow servants who owed him a hundred denarii, and he grabbed
29 him and began choking him saying, 'Pay back what you owe!' •The fel-

18:24 An astronomically large sum, impossible to repay, since each talent was worth 5,000 - 6,000 denarii.

low servant fell down and pleaded with him, saying, 'Be patient with me and I'll pay you back!' •But he wouldn't listen; instead, he went and threw 30 him into prison until he could pay back what was owed. •When his fel- 31 low servants saw what had happened they were terribly distressed, and they went and told their lord everything that had happened. •Then the 32 lord summoned the servant and said to him, 'You wicked servant! I forgave you all that debt when you pleaded with me; •shouldn't you have 33 had mercy on your fellow servant, too, as I had mercy on you?' •And 34 in his anger the lord handed him over to the jailors until he could pay back all that was owed. •That's what my Heavenly Father will do to you, 35 too, unless each of you forgives your brother from your heart."

R. DISCIPLESHIP AND AUTHORITY, FAITH AND RENUNCIATION

19•[x] And it happened when Jesus finished these words he left Galilee and went to the regions of Judea beyond the Jordan. •Large 1 crowds followed him and he healed them there. 2

•And Pharisees came up to him and tested him by asking, "Is it lawful for a husband to put his wife away for any reason he wants?" •In re- 3 sponse he said, "Haven't you read that from the beginning the Creator 4 **made them male and female**? •And He said, **For this reason a man shall leave father and mother and be united with his wife,** 5 **and the two shall become one flesh.** •So, then, they're no longer two but instead are one flesh. Therefore, 6

> What God has joined together
> let man not separate."

•"Then why," they asked, "did Moses command us **to give a notice of divorce and put her away**?" •He said to them, "Moses allowed 7 you to put your wives away because of the hardness of your hearts, but 8 it wasn't that way from the beginning. •But *I* tell you, whoever puts his wife away — not in the case of an unlawful union — and marries an- 9

---

[x] *Mk 10:1-12.*

19:4 Gn 1:27.   19:5 Gn 2:24.   19:7 Dt 24:1.
19:9 The words "the case of" are not in the original. For a more detailed discussion of Jesus' teaching on divorce cf. above at 5:32. Jesus is not stating an exception to the general rule forbidding divorce in valid marriages. Rather, he is distin-guishing valid marriages from other relationships which do not constitute true marriages. The general rule regarding marriage naturally does not apply to such illicit or otherwise defective relationships. This has been the consistent teaching of the Church.

10 other commits adultery." •His disciples said to him, "If *that's* the rela-
11 tionship between a man and his wife, it's better not to marry!" •"Not everyone can accept this teaching," he said, "only those to whom it's
12 been given. •For there are some who are eunuchs from their birth, and some who are eunuchs were made eunuchs by men, and some who are eunuchs make themselves eunuchs for the sake of the Kingdom of Heaven. Let whoever is able accept this!"
13 •[y] Then children were brought to him so he could lay his hands on
14 them and pray, but the disciples rebuked them. •Jesus said,

> "Let the children be,
> And don't stop them from coming to me,
> For of such as these
> Is the Kingdom of Heaven!"

15 •And after laying his hands on them he went away from there.
16 •[z] And, behold, a certain man came up to Jesus and said, "Teacher,
17 what good must I do in order to gain eternal life?" •"Why do you ask *me* about what is good?" Jesus said. "One there is Who is good. If you
18 want to enter into life, keep the commandments." •"Which ones?" he asked. Jesus said, "These — **you shall not murder, you shall not commit adultery, you shall not steal, you shall not bear false**
19 **witness, •honor your father and mother, and love your neigh-**
20 **bor as yourself."** •The young man said to him, "I've obeyed all of
21 these; what else do I need to do?" •Jesus said to him, "If you want to be perfect, go sell your possessions and give to the poor and you'll have
22 treasure in Heaven, and come follow me." •When the young man heard this he went away sadly, because he had many properties.
23 •Then Jesus said to his disciples, "Amen, I say to you, with difficulty
24 will a rich man enter the Kingdom of Heaven! •Yet again I say to you, it's easier for a camel to go through a needle's eye than for a rich man
25 to enter the Kingdom of God." •When the disciples heard this they were
26 very much amazed and said, "Then who can be saved?" •Jesus gazed at them and said,

> "For men this is impossible,
> But for God all things are possible."

27 •Then in response Peter said to him, "You see we've left everything
28 and followed you; what will there be for us, then?" •Jesus said to them,

[y] Mk 10:13-16; Lk 18:15-17.   [z] Mk 10:17-31; Lk 18:18-30.
19:18-19 Ex 20:12-16.   19:28 Dn 7:9, 22.

"Amen, I say to you, you who have followed me — in the new age, when the Son of Man takes his seat on his throne of glory — you, too, will sit on twelve thrones judging the twelve tribes of Israel. •And everyone 29 who has left houses or brothers or sisters or father or mother or children or fields for the sake of my name will receive a hundredfold and will gain eternal life.

•But many who are first will be last, 30
and the last, first."

20•"For the Kingdom of Heaven is like a landowner who went out 1 early in the morning to hire workers for his vineyard •and, after 2 agreeing with the workers on a denarius for the day, he sent them into his vineyard. •And when he went out at about nine o'clock he saw oth- 3 ers standing idle in the market place, •and he said to them, 'You go in- 4 to the vineyard, too, and I'll give you whatever's just.' •So they went off. 5 When he went out again at about noon and three o'clock he did the same. •Now at about five o'clock when he went out he found others standing 6 there, and he asked them, 'Why have you stood here idle the whole day?' •They said to him, 'Because nobody hired us.' He said to them, You go 7 into the vineyard, too.' •When evening came the lord of the vineyard said 8 to his foreman, 'Call the workers and pay them their wages, beginning from the last up to the first.' •When those who started at five o'clock came 9 they each got a denarius. •And when the first ones came they thought 10 they'd receive more, yet they, too, each received a denarius. •When they 11 received it they began to grumble against the landowner, •saying, 'These 12 came last and worked only one hour, yet you've made them equal to us, who endured the whole day and the scorching heat!' •In response to one 13 of them the landowner said, 'My friend, I do you no injustice; didn't you agree on a denarius with me? •Take what's yours and go! I wish to give 14 this last one the same as I gave to you. •Can't I do what I want with what's 15 mine? Or are you jealous because I'm generous?' •Thus, 16

The last shall be first,
and the first, last."

•ᵃ As Jesus was going up to Jerusalem he took the Twelve aside pri- 17 vately, and as they walked he said to them, •"Behold, we're going up 18 to Jerusalem, and the Son of Man will be handed over to the chief priests and the scribes; they'll condemn him to death •and will hand him over 19

ᵃ Mk 10:32-34; Lk 18:31-34.

Greek statue of a child (2nd century B.C.). (Mt 19:13)

to the Gentiles to be mocked and scourged and crucified, and on the third day he'll rise."

20 •[b] Then the mother of the sons of Zebedee came up to him with her
21 sons and knelt down to make a request of him. •So Jesus said to her, "What do you want?" She said to him, "Say that these two sons of mine can sit, one at your right hand and one at your left hand, in your King-
22 dom." •In response Jesus said, "You don't know what you're asking for! Can you drink the cup *I'm* going to drink?" They said to him, "We can."
23 •He said to them, "You will, indeed, drink my cup, but as for sitting at my right hand or left, that isn't mine to give — it's for those for whom
24 it's been prepared by my Father." •When the other ten heard this they
25 became indignant at the two brothers. •So Jesus called them together and said, "You know that

> The rulers of the Gentiles lord it over them,
> And their leaders exercise authority over them,

26 •but it won't be like that among you; instead,

[b] Mk 10:35-45.

Whoever would be great among you,
    he shall be your servant,
•And whoever would be first among you,   27
    he shall be your slave;
•Just as the Son of Man came, not to be served, but to serve,   28
    and to give his life as a ransom for many."

•[c] When they were leaving Jericho a large crowd followed him. •And, 29,30
behold, there were two blind men sitting by the road, and when they
heard that Jesus was passing by they began to cry out, "Have mercy on
us, Son of David!" •The crowd ordered them to be quiet, but they cried 31
out all the more, "Lord, have mercy on us, Son of David!" •Jesus 32
stopped, called them over, and said, "What do you want me to do for
you?" •They said to him, "Lord, let our eyes be opened!" •So Jesus, 33,34
deeply moved, touched their eyes, and at once they recovered their sight
and followed him.

S. JESUS' MINISTRY IN JERUSALEM

21 •[d] When they drew near to Jerusalem and had come to Beth- 1
phage, on the Mount of Olives, then Jesus sent two disciples,
•telling them, "Go into the village opposite you, and at once you'll find 2
a donkey tied up and a colt with it; untie them and lead them to me.
•And if anyone says anything to you, say, 'The Lord needs them,' and 3
he'll send them at once." •This took place to fulfill what was said by the 4
prophet when he said,

•Tell the daughter of Zion,   5
'Behold your king is coming to you,
    humble, and mounted on a donkey,
  and on a colt, the offspring of an ass.'

•When the disciples had gone and done as Jesus had instructed them 6
•they led the donkey and the colt to him and put their cloaks on them, 7

---

[c] Mk 10:46-52; Lk 18:35-43.   [d] Mk 11:1-11; Lk 19:28-38; Jn 12:12-19.

21:1ff Beginning with Jesus' entry into Jerusalem the fulfillment of Jesus' mission moves inexorably to its climax. As seen through the eyes of faith, all these events are "in accordance with the Scriptures," and the account is punctuated with frequent references to Scripture in order to under-line this. All Jesus' words and actions are now seen in their full eschatological significance: the Kingdom has come and, following the Lord's atoning death, it will be proclaimed to all nations. 21:5 Is 62:11.

8 and he sat upon them. •The large crowd spread their cloaks on the road, while others began cutting branches from the trees and spreading them
9 on the road. •The crowds that were going ahead, as well as those following him, kept shouting and saying,

> "**Hosanna** to the Son of David!
> **Blessed is he who comes in the name of the Lord!**
> **Hosanna** in the highest!"

10 •When he entered Jerusalem the whole city was caught up in the ex-
11 citement and asked, "Who is this?" •The crowds said, "This is the prophet Jesus, from Nazareth in Galilee!"
12   •ᵉ Then Jesus went into the Temple and drove out all who were selling and buying in the Temple, and he overturned the tables of the mon-
13 eychangers and the seats of those who sold the doves, •and he said to them, "It is written,

> **My house shall be called a house of prayer,**
>   but you're making it **a robbers' den**!"

14   •And the blind and the lame came up to him in the Temple, and he
15 healed them. •When the chief priests and scribes saw the wonders he was performing and the children who were shouting in the Temple and
16 saying, "Hosanna to the Son of David!" they became indignant •and said to him, "Do you hear what they're saying?" But Jesus replied, "Certainly. Haven't you ever read that

> **Out of the mouths of babes and nursing infants**
> **You have brought forth perfect praise.**"

17 •Then he left them and went out of the city to Bethany and spent the night there.
18   •ᶠ Early in the morning, as he was returning to the city, he was hun-
19 gry. •He noticed a fig tree by the road and so he went over to it, but he found nothing on it but leaves, and he said to it, "May no fruit ever come from you again, forever!" And the fig tree shrivelled up immediately.
20 •When the disciples saw this they were amazed and said, "How did the
21 fig tree shrivel up immediately?" •In answer Jesus said to them, "Amen, I say to you, if you have faith and never doubt, you'll not only do what was done to the fig tree but also, if you say to this mountain, 'Be lifted

---

ᵉ *Mk 11:15-19.*   ᶠ *Mk 11:12-14, 20-24.*

21:9 Ps 118:26. *Hosanna* probably signified "royal power."

21:13 Is 56:7
21:16 Ps 8:2 (Ps 8:3 in the Septuagint).

up and thrown into the sea,' it will happen. •Whatever you ask for in 22
prayer and believe, you'll receive."

•ᵍ And when he entered the Temple the chief priests and elders of 23
the people came up to him as he was teaching and said, "By what authority do you do these things? Who gave you this authority?" •In re- 24
sponse Jesus said to them, "I'll ask you one question, too; if you answer
it for me I'll tell you by what authority I do these things. •Where was 25
John's baptism from? From Heaven or from men?" They began to argue among themselves, saying, "If we say, 'From Heaven,' he'll say,
'Then why didn't you believe him?' •But if we say, 'From men,' we're 26
afraid of the people — they all consider John a prophet." •So in an- 27
swer to Jesus they said, "We don't know." And he said to them, "Nor
will I tell you by what authority I do these things."

•"What do you think, now? A man had two boys. He came up to the 28
first one and said, 'My boy, go work in the vineyard today.' •In reply 29
the boy said, 'I don't want to!' but later he changed his mind and went.
•When the man came to the other boy he said the same thing. The sec- 30
ond boy answered, 'I'll go, lord!' but he didn't go. •Which of the two 31
did the will of the father?" "The first," they said. Jesus said to them,
"Amen, I say to you, tax collectors and prostitutes are entering the Kingdom of God ahead of you. •For John came to you preaching the way 32
of fulfillment of God's will and you didn't believe him, whereas the tax
collectors and prostitutes *did* believe him, but though you saw it you did-
n't change your minds and believe him."

•ʰ "Listen to another parable! There was a man, a landowner, who 33
**planted a vineyard and put a hedge around it and dug a wine-
press in it and built a tower.** Then he leased it to farmers and left
on a journey. •When harvest time drew near he sent his servants to 34
the farmers to get his share. •But the farmers took his servants and 35
beat one, killed another, and stoned yet another. •Once more he sent 36
other servants, more than the first group, and they did the same to
them. •So, finally, he sent his son to them, saying, 'They'll feel shame 37
before my son.' •But when the farmers saw the son they said to them- 38
selves, 'This is the heir; come on, let's kill him and have his inheritance!' •And they took hold of him, threw him out of the vineyard, 39
and killed him. •So, then, when the lord of the vineyard comes, what 40

ᵍ *Mk 11:27-33; Lk 20:1-8.*   ʰ *Mk 12:1-12; Lk 20:9-19.*

21:32 Literally, "in the way of righteousness."   preaching of such obedience.
This phrase appears to emphasize John's active   21:33 Is 5:1-2.
obedience to God's will as well as (implicitly) his

The Temple of Jerusalem (reconstruction).

⁴¹ will he do to those farmers?" •They said to him, "He'll put those evil men to a miserable death and lease the vineyard to other farmers who ⁴² will turn over to him his share of the harvest." •Jesus said to them, "Haven't you ever read in the Scriptures,

**The stone rejected by the builders
has become the cornerstone;
By the Lord has this been done,
and it is wonderful in our eyes.**

⁴³ •Therefore, I say to you, the Kingdom of God will be taken from you ⁴⁴ and given to a people who will produce its fruits." [•]
⁴⁵ •When the chief priests and Pharisees heard his parables they knew ⁴⁶ that he was speaking about them, •and although they considered seizing him they feared the crowds, for they regarded him as a prophet.

21:42 Ps 118:22-23.
21:44 The best manuscript tradition omits this verse: "And whoever falls on this stone will be broken to pieces, while it will crush whoever it falls upon."

22 •[i] And in response Jesus spoke to them again in parables, say- 1 ing, • "The Kingdom of Heaven may be compared to a man, a 2 king, who held a wedding feast for his son. •And he sent his servants 3 to summon those who had been invited to the feast, but they refused to come. •Once more he sent other servants, saying, 'Tell those who were 4 invited, "Behold, I've prepared my dinner; my steers and fatted calves have been slaughtered and everything's ready; come to the feast!"' •Some of those who had been invited ignored the invitation and went 5 off, one to his farm and another to his business, •and the rest seized his 6 servants, treated them shamefully, and killed them. •The king became 7 furious, then, and he sent his soldiers to kill those murderers and burn their city. •Then he said to his servants, 'The wedding feast is ready, but 8 those invited weren't worthy. •So go to the highways and invite who- 9 ever you find to the wedding feast.' •The servants went out on the roads 10 and gathered everyone they found, evil as well as good, and the feast was full of guests. •But when the king went in to see the guests he saw 11 there a man who wasn't dressed in a wedding garment, •and he asked 12 him, 'My friend, how did you come in here without a wedding garment?' But the man remained silent. •Then the king said to his servants, 'Tie 13 his hands and feet and throw him out into the outer darkness;

> There there will be wailing
>> and gnashing of teeth,'
> •For many are called, 14
>> but few are chosen."

•[j] Then the Pharisees went off and came up with a plan to entrap 15 him in his speech. •They sent their disciples to him with the Herodians 16 to say, "Teacher, we know you're truthful and truly teach the way of God and are influenced by no one, for you don't consider the person. •So 17 tell us what you think; is it lawful to pay the tax to Caesar or not?" •But 18 Jesus, aware of their evil intent, said, "You hypocrites! Why are you test- ing me? •Show me the coin for the tax!" So they brought him a denar- 19 ius. •And he said to them, "Whose image is this, and whose inscription?" 20 •They said to him, "Caesar's." Then he said to them, 21

> "Render, therefore, to Caesar
>> the things that are Caesar's,
> And to God
>> the things that are God's."

[i] Lk 14:15-24. [j] Mk 12:13-17; Lk 20:20-26.

22 •When they heard this they were amazed, and they left him and went away.

23 •[k] That same day the Sadducees came to him claiming that there's
24 no resurrection, and they put this question to him: •"Teacher, Moses said, **If anyone should die without children, his brother shall**
25 **marry his wife and raise up offspring for his brother.** •Now there used to be seven brothers among us, and the first married and died,
26 and since he had no offspring he left his wife to his brother. •Likewise
27 also the second and the third, up to the seventh. •Last of all the woman
28 died. •At the resurrection, then, whose wife will she be of the seven, since they all had her?"

29 •In reply Jesus said to them, "You go astray because you neither un-
30 derstand Scripture nor realize the power of God — •at the resurrection they'll neither marry nor be given in marriage but will be like angels in
31 Heaven. •But as for the resurrection of the dead, haven't you read what
32 was said to you by God when He declared, •**I am the God of Abra-ham and the God of Isaac and the God of Jacob.** He's not God
33 of the dead but of the living." •And when the crowds heard this they were astounded at his teaching.

34 •[l] When the Pharisees heard that he'd silenced the Sadducees they
35 came in a group, •and one of them, an expert in the Torah, asked him
36 as a test, •"Teacher, which is the greatest commandment in the Torah?"
37 •Jesus said to him, **"You shall love the Lord with all your heart**
38 **and with all your soul and with all your understanding;** •this is
39 the first and greatest commandment. •And the second is like it, **You**
40 **shall love your neighbor as yourself.** •All the Torah and the Prophets rests on these two commandments."

41 •[m] While the Pharisees were gathered there Jesus questioned them,
42 •saying, "What do you think about the Messiah? Whose son is he?"
43 "David's," they replied. •"Then how," he asked, "can David, in the Spir-it, call him 'Lord' when he says,

44   •**The Lord said to my Lord,**
       'Sit at My right hand
         till I put your enemies under your feet.'

k Mk 12:18-27; Lk 20:27-40. l Mk 12:28-34; Lk 10:25-28. m Mk 12:35-37; Lk 20:41-44.

22:24 Dt 25:5; Gn 38:8.
22:32 Ex 3:6.
22:37 Dt 6:5.
22:39 Lv 19:18.
22:44 Ps 110:1

•If David calls him 'Lord,' how can he be David's son?" •And no one [45,46] could answer him a word, nor from that time on did anyone dare question him further.

T. DENUNCIATION OF THE PHARISEES

23 •[n] Then Jesus spoke to the crowds and to his disciples, •saying, [1,2]

"The scribes and the Pharisees sit
   on the chair of Moses
      •so do and observe whatever they tell you, [3]
But don't imitate their actions,
   for they don't do what they say.
•Instead, they tie up heavy burdens and put them [4]
      on men's shoulders,
   but they won't lift a finger to move them.
•Everything they do [5]
   they do to be seen by others;
They broaden their phylacteries
   and enlarge their tassels,
•They love the first place at banquets [6]
   and the first seats in the synagogues,
•And greetings in the markets [7]
   and being called 'Rabbi,'
•But don't *you* be called 'Rabbi,' [8]
   for One is your teacher, and all of you are brothers.
•And call no one on earth your father, [9]
   for you have one father — your Father in Heaven.
•Nor shall you be called teachers, [10]
   for you have one teacher, the Messiah.
•Instead, the greatest among you [11]
   shall be your servant.

[n] Mk 12:38-40; Lk 11:37-52, 20:45-57.

23:1ff. Cf. the note on 3:7-12. At the time of Jesus the rabbis were adopting ever more restrictive and burdensome interpretations of the Torah. A primary purpose for this was to maintain the purity of Israel against the immorality that was rampant in the surrounding Gentile cultures. However, the tendency to put ritual obligations on the same level as moral obligations was recognized to be a danger in rigoristic interpretations of the Torah – hypocrisy and formalism were known even then as "the plague of the Pharisees."
23:8-10 Jesus here warns against excessive respect for merely human authority, using the hyperbolic style favored in these types of orations.

MATTHEW

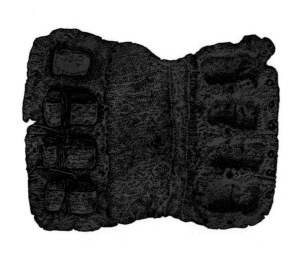

Phylacteries made of black leather (from Qumran, 1st century A.D.). (Mt 23:5)

12 •For whoever exalts himself will be humbled,
    And whoever humbles himself will be exalted."
13 • "But woe to you, scribes and Pharisees,
        you hypocrites!
    You shut the door to the Kingdom of Heaven
        in men's faces —
    you aren't going in, but you won't allow
14   those who *are* trying to enter to go in." [•]
15 • "Woe to you, scribes and Pharisees,
        you hypocrites!
    You travel over land and sea to win one proselyte,

23:13 In the "seven woes" Jesus condemns, not outward expressions of piety *per se*, but their self-serving use to enhance personal prestige.
23:14 The best manuscript tradition omits this verse: "Woe to you, scribes and Pharisees, you hypocrites! because you eat up widows' homes and as a pretense say long prayers; therefore, you will receive the greater condemnation."

23:15 This verse reflects the extensive missionary efforts of the Pharisees prior to the destruction of the Temple. A proselyte was a Gentile who accepted all the requirements of the Torah, including circumcision. For obvious reasons, Gentile sympathizers, known as Godfearers, were more numerous than actual proselytes.

and when he becomes one you make him twice
    the son of Gehenna that *you* are."
•"Woe to you,   16
    blind guides! who say,
'Whoever swears by the sanctuary,
    that's nothing,
    but whoever swears by the gold
    of the sanctuary is bound.'
•You're foolish and blind!   17
For what's greater, the gold
    or the sanctuary that sanctifies the gold?
•And, 'Whoever swears by the altar,   18
    that's nothing,
    but whoever swears by the offering
    upon it is bound.'
•You're blind! For what's greater, the offering   19
    or the altar that sanctifies the offering?
•Therefore, whoever swears by the altar   20
    swears by the altar
    and also by everything on it,
•And whoever swears by the sanctuary   21
    swears by the sanctuary
and also by the One Who dwells within,
•And whoever swears by Heaven swears   22
    by the throne of God
    and also by the One seated upon it."
•"Woe to you, scribes and Pharisees,   23
    you hypocrites!
You tithe mint and dill and cumin,
    yet you've neglected the weightier things
    of the Torah, justice and mercy and faith.
You should have acted upon these things
    without neglecting the others!
•Blind guides!   24
You strain out the gnat
    and swallow the camel."
•"Woe to you, scribes and Pharisees,   25
    you hypocrites!
You purify the outside of the cup and the plate,
    but inside they're full of greed
    and self indulgence.

26 •Blind Pharisees!
First purify the inside of the cup
   so the outside will also be pure."
27 •"Woe to you, scribes and Pharisees,
   you hypocrites!
You're like whitewashed tombs, which outside
   appear beautiful,
      but inside are full of dead men's bones
      and every sort of impurity.
28 •You too appear to be righteous on the outside,
   but inside you're filled with hypocrisy and lawlessness."
29 •"Woe to you, scribes and Pharisees,
   you hypocrites!
You restore the tombs of the prophets
   and adorn the monuments of the righteous,

30 •and you say, 'If we had been there in the days of our fathers, we
31 wouldn't have taken part in shedding the blood of the prophets!' •Thus
you bear witness against yourselves, because you're the sons of the
32 prophets' murderers. •Go ahead, then; complete the work of your fa-
33 thers! •You snakes! You brood of vipers! How will you escape being
34 condemned to Gehenna? •Therefore, behold, I'm sending you
prophets and wise men and scribes, some of whom you'll kill and crucify, and some of whom you'll scourge in your synagogues and pur-
35 sue from city to city, •so that all the guilt will come upon you for every
righteous man who died on earth, from Abel the Righteous to Zechariah the Righteous, son of Barachiah, whom you murdered between the
36 sanctuary and the altar. •Amen, I say to you, all these things will befall this generation!"

37 •° "Jerusalem, Jerusalem!
You kill the prophets
   and stone those sent to you!
How often I wished
   to gather your children,
The way a hen gathers her brood
   under her wings,
But you would not!

° Lk 13:34-35.

•Behold, **there remains to you** 38
   your desolate house.
•For I say to you, you shall not see me until you say, 39
   Blessed is he who comes in the name of the Lord!"

U. PROPHECIES AND PARABLES OF THE END TIME

24 •[p] When Jesus came out of the Temple he left, and his disciples 1
came up to him to show him the Temple buildings, •but in reply 2
he said to them, "Do you see all these things? Amen, I say to you, not
a stone here will be left upon a stone which will not be torn down."

•[q] While he was sitting on the Mount of Olives his disciples came up 3
to him privately and said, "Tell us when these things will happen, and
what will be the sign of your coming and of the end of the age." •In re- 4
ply Jesus said to them, "See that no one leads you astray, •for many 5
will come in my name, saying, 'I'm the Messiah,' and they'll lead many
astray. •You're going to hear of wars and rumors of wars; take care not 6
to be alarmed, for all this must happen, but it won't be the end yet.

•For nation will rise against nation, 7
   and kingdom against kingdom,

and there will be famines and earthquakes in various places; •all this will 8
be the beginning of the birth pains. •Then they'll hand you over to suf- 9
fering and will kill you, and you'll be hated by all nations because of my
name. •Many will lose their faith then and they'll hand each other over 10
and they'll hate each other, •and many false prophets will rise up and 11
will lead many people astray, •and because of the increase of lawless- 12
ness the love of many will grow cold. •But whoever holds out till the 13
end, he will be saved. •And this good news of the Kingdom will be pro- 14
claimed in all the inhabited world as a witness to all the nations, and then
the end will come."

•[r] "So when you see **the Abomination of Desolation** spoken of 15
by Daniel the prophet set **in the holy place** — let the reader understand — •then those in Judea must flee to the mountains, •the man on 16,17

[p] Mk 13:1-2; Lk 21:5-6.   [q] Mk 13:3-13; Lk 21:7-19.   [r] Mk 13:14-23; Lk 21:7-19.

23:38 Jr 22:5.
23:39 Ps 118:26.
24:8 "The birth pains" referred, in Jewish writings,
to the coming of the Messiah.
24:15 Dn 9:27, 11:31, 12:11. "The Abomination

of Desolation" refers to the desecration of the
Temple by the Seleucids in 167 B.C. The Feast
of Hanukkah celebrates the rededication of the
Temple in 164 B.C.

The Western Wall and the Esplanade of the Temple. (Mt 24:1-2)

18 his housetop must not descend to take things from his house, •and the
19 man in his field must not turn back to get his cloak. •But woe to women
20 who are with child and women who are nursing in those days! •Pray
21 that your flight will not take place in winter or on the Sabbath, •for then
there will be great **suffering such as has not been from the be-**
22 **ginning of the world until now,** nor will be. •And if those days were
not cut short no creature of flesh would be saved, but for the sake of
23 those who were chosen those days will be cut short. •Then, if anyone
says to you, 'Look, here's the Messiah!' or, 'Over here!' don't believe
24 it, •for false messiahs and false prophets will rise up and they'll produce
great signs and wonders so as to deceive, if it were possible, even those
25,26 chosen [by God]; •behold, I've told you ahead of time! •So, if they say
to you, 'There, he's in the desert!' don't go out; 'Here, in the inner
27 room!' don't believe it. •For as lightning comes from the east and can
be seen clear to the west, so it will be with the coming of the Son of
28 Man. •Where the corpse is, there will the vultures gather!

24:21 Dn 12:1; Jl 2:2.

•"But immediately after the suffering of those days,   29

The sun will be darkened,
   and the moon will not give its light,
And the stars will fall from the heavens,
   and the powers of the heavens will be shaken.

•Then the sign of the Son of Man will appear in the heavens, and then 30
all the tribes of the earth will mourn and they'll see **the Son of Man coming on the clouds of Heaven** with power and great glory. •He'll send his angels forth with a great trumpet blast, and they'll 31 gather his chosen ones from the four winds, from one end of the heavens to their other end."

•[t] "Learn the parable from the fig tree. As soon as its branch becomes 32 tender and is putting out leaves, you know that summer is near. •So also you, when you see all these things, you'll know that he's near, at the 33 very gates. •Amen, I say to you, this generation will not pass away until all these things come to pass. 34

•The heavens and the earth will pass away,   35
But my words will not pass away."
•[u] "But as for that day and hour,   36
   no one knows —
Not the angels in Heaven, nor the Son,
   but only the Father.
•But just as the days of Noah were,   37
   so will the coming of the Son of Man be.
•For just as they kept on eating and drinking,   38

marrying and giving in marriage in the days before the flood right up to the day Noah entered the ark, •and didn't find out until the flood came 39 and swept them all away,

      that's how the coming of the Son of Man will be.
•Then if two men are in the field —   40
   one will be taken and one will be left;
•If two women are grinding at the mill —   41
   one will be taken and one will be left.

[s] *Mk 13:24-27; Lk 21:25-28.*   [t] *Mk 13:28-31; Lk 21:29-33.*   [u] *Mk 13:32-37; Lk 17:26-30, 34-36.*

24:29 Is 13:10.
24:30 Dn 7:13-14.

24:36 Several important manuscripts omit the words "nor the Son."

MATTHEW

42 •So stay awake! because you don't know what day your Lord is com-
43 ing. •But remember this, if the householder had known at what hour
the thief was coming he would have stayed awake and wouldn't have
44 let his house be broken into. •Therefore, you be ready too! because the
Son of Man will come at an hour when you don't expect him."

45   •ᵛ "Who, then, is the wise and faithful servant
       whom the Lord set over his household servants
    To give them their share of food
       at the proper time?
46   •Blessed that servant who, when his lord comes,
       is found performing his duties!
47   •Amen, I say to you,
       his lord will set him over all his possessions.
48   •But if that wicked servant says in his heart,
       'My master is delayed,'
49   •And begins to beat his fellow servants
       and to eat and drink with drunkards,
50   •The master of that servant will come on a day
        he doesn't expect,
       and at an hour he doesn't know.
51   •He'll cut him in pieces
       and assign him the lot of the hypocrites.
    There there will be wailing
       and gnashing of teeth."

1 **25** •"At that time the Kingdom of Heaven will be compared to ten
virgins who took their lamps and went out to meet the bride-
2,3 groom. •Five of them were foolish and the other five were wise, •for
when the foolish ones took their lamps they didn't take oil with them,
4,5 •while the wise ones *did* take oil in vessels along with their lamps. •Now
when the bridegroom was delayed they all grew drowsy and fell asleep.
6 •At midnight the cry arose, 'Here he is, the bridegroom! Come out to
7,8 meet him!' •Then all those virgins got up and trimmed their lamps. •The
foolish ones said to the wise ones, 'Give us some of your oil — our lamps
9 are going out!' •But the wise ones answered by saying, 'If we do there
may not be enough for us as well as for you! You'd better go to the deal-
10 ers and buy some for yourselves.' •But when they went off to buy some
the bridegroom came, and the virgins who were ready went in with him

ᵛ *Lk 12:41-48.*

to the wedding feast and the door was locked. •Then, finally, the other 11
virgins came, too, and said, 'Lord, lord, open up for us!' •But in reply 12
he said, 'Amen, I say to you, I don't know you!' •Stay awake, therefore, 13
because you don't know the day or the hour."

•ᵂ "For it's like when a man who was going on a journey called his 14
servants and turned over his possessions to them, •and to one he gave 15
five talents, and to one, two talents, and to one, one talent; to each according to their ability. Then he left. At once •the servant who got the 16
five talents went and invested them and earned another five. •Likewise, 17
the servant with the two talents earned another two. •But the servant 18
who got the one talent went off and dug a hole in the ground and hid
his lord's money. •After a long time the lord of those servants came and 19
settled accounts with them. •And when the servant who got the five tal- 20
ents came forward he brought the other five talents and said, 'Lord, you
turned five talents over to me; look! I've earned another five talents.'
•His lord said to him, 21

'Well done, good and faithful servant!
You were faithful over a few things,
So now I'll set you over many.
Come into your master's joy!'

•When the servant who got the two talents came forward he said, Lord, 22
you turned two talents over to me; look! I've earned another two talents.' •His master said to him, 23

'Well done, good and faithful servant!
You were faithful over a few things,
So now I'll set you over many.
Come into your master's joy!'

•But when the servant who got the one talent came forward he said, 24
'Lord, I knew that you're a hard man, who reap where you didn't sow
and gather where you didn't scatter, •and since I was afraid I went off 25
and hid your talent in the ground; look! you have what's yours.' •In 26
response his lord said to him, 'You evil and lazy servant! You knew
that I reap where I didn't sow and gather where I didn't scatter, did
you? •You would have done better to give my money to the bankers, 27
and when I came I would have received what was mine with interest.
•Therefore, take the talent from him and give it to the one with ten 28
talents,

ᵂ *Lk 19:11-27.*

29 •For all who have will receive,
      and will have more than enough,
   But as for the one who doesn't have,
      even what he has will be taken from him.

30 •And throw the worthless servant out into the outer darkness;

      There there will be weeping
         and gnashing of teeth.'"
31   •"But when the Son of Man comes in his glory,
         and all his angels with him,
      He'll sit on the throne of his glory,
32   •and all the nations will be gathered before him,
      And he'll separate them from each other,
         the way a shepherd separates the sheep from the goats,
33   •And he'll set the sheep at his right hand
         and the goats at his left hand.

Aerial view of the coastal strip of Palestine.

•"Then the King will say to those at his right hand,   34
   'Come, you blessed of my Father,
Receive the Kingdom prepared for you
   from the foundation of the world,
•For I was hungry and you gave me to eat,   35
   I was thirsty and you gave me to drink,
I was a stranger and you took me in,
   •naked and you clothed me,   36
   I was sick and you cared for me,
I was in prison and you came to me.'
•"Then the righteous will answer him by saying,   37
'Lord, when did we see you hungry and feed you,
   or thirsty and give you to drink?
•When did we see you a stranger and take you in,   38
   or naked and clothe you?
•When did we see you sick,   39
   or in prison and come to you?'
•"And in answer the King will say to them,   40
   'Amen, I say to you,
Insofar as you did it for one of these least of my brothers,
   you did it for me.'"
•"Then he'll say to those at his left hand,   41
'Get away from me, you cursed,
   into the eternal fire prepared for the Devil and his angels,
•For I was hungry and you *didn't* give me to eat,   42
   I was thirsty and you *didn't* give me to drink,
•I was a stranger and you *didn't* take me in,   43
   naked and you *didn't* clothe me,
Sick and in prison
   and you *didn't* come to me.'

•Then they'll answer by saying, 'Lord, when did we see you hungry   44
or thirsty or a stranger or naked or sick or in prison and not care for you?'

•Then he'll answer them by saying,   45
   'Amen, I say to you,
Insofar as you didn't do it for one
   of the least of these brothers,
   you didn't do it for me, either.'
•And these will go off to eternal punishment,   46
   but the righteous to eternal life."

MATTHEW

V. LAST SUPPER AND PASSION OF JESUS

1 **26** •ˣ And it happened when Jesus had finished all these words he
2 said to his disciples, •"You know that the Passover will be in two
3 days, and the Son of Man will be handed over to be crucified." •Then
the chief priests and elders of the people gathered in the palace of the
4 high priest, who was named Caiaphas, •and they plotted to seize Jesus
5 on a pretext and kill him, •but they said, "Not at the festival, or there
might be an outcry among the people."

6,7 •ʸ Now while Jesus was at Bethany in Simon the leper's house •a
woman came up to him with an alabaster jar of a precious oil and poured
8 it over his head as he reclined at table. •When the disciples saw this they
9 were indignant and said, "To what purpose was this waste? •It could have
10 been sold for a great deal of money and given to the poor!" •When Jesus became aware of this he said to them, "Why are you bothering the
woman? She's done a beautiful thing for me.

11 •For the poor you always have with you,
But me you will not always have.

12 •When she poured this oil on my body she did it to prepare me for bur-
13 ial. •Amen, I say to you, wherever this good news is proclaimed in the
whole world, what she did will also be told in memory of her."

14 •ᶻ Then one of the Twelve, the one called Judas Iscariot, went to the
15 chief priests •and said, "What are you willing to give me if I hand him
16 over to you?" **So they counted out thirty silver coins** for him, •and
from then on he sought the right time to hand him over.

17 •ᵃ On the first day of the Unleavened Bread the disciples came to Jesus and asked, "Where do you want us to prepare for you to eat the
18 Passover?" •"Go into the city," he said, "to a certain man and say to
him, 'The Teacher says, "My time is at hand; I'll celebrate the Passover
19 at your house with my disciples."'" •The disciples did as Jesus had instructed them, and they prepared the Passover.

20,21 •When evening came he reclined at table with the Twelve, •and while
they were eating he said, "Amen, I say to you, one of you will hand
22 me over." •They were greatly distressed and one after the other they

ˣ Mk 14:1-2; Lk 22:1-2; Jn 11:45-53.   ʸ Mk 14:3-9; Jn 12:1-8.
ᶻ Mk 14:10-11; Lk 22:3-6.   ᵃ Mk 14:12-21; Lk 22:7-14, 21-23; Jn 13:21-30.

26:15 Zc 11:12.
26:17 The eight day period during which unleavened bread was eaten was closely linked to the

Passover, but had its origins in a festival marking
the beginning of the barley harvest.

said to him, "Surely not me, Lord?" •But in answer he said, "One who 23 dipped his hand into the bowl with me will be the one to hand me over. •The Son of Man is going as it's written about him, but woe to that 24 man by whom the Son of Man is handed over; it would be better for that man if he had never been born!" •In response Judas, the one who 25 handed him over, said, "Surely it isn't me, Rabbi?" Jesus said to him, "You said it."

•[b] While they were eating Jesus took bread, blessed it, broke it, gave 26 it to his disciples and said, "Take and eat it; this is my body." •Then he 27 took the cup and after blessing it he gave it to them and said, "Drink from it, all of you, •for this is my blood of the covenant which will be 28 poured out for many for the forgiveness of sins. •I say to you, I will not 29 drink again of the fruit of the vine until that day when I drink it new with you in my Father's Kingdom." •And after singing a hymn they went out 30 to the Mount of Olives.

•[c] Then Jesus said to them, "This night you'll all lose your faith in 31 me, for it is written,

I will strike the shepherd,
and the sheep of the flock will be scattered,

•but after I rise I'll go ahead of you into Galilee." •In response Peter said 32,33 to him, "Even if all the others lose faith in you, I will never lose faith!" •Jesus said to him, "Amen, I say to you, this night, before the cock crows, 34 you'll deny me three times." •Peter said to him, "Even if it comes to dy- 35 ing with you, I won't deny you!" And all the other disciples said so, too.

•[d] Then Jesus came with them to a place called Gethsemane, and he 36 said to the disciples, "Sit here while I go over there and pray." •He took 37 Peter and the two sons of Zebedee along and he began to be upset and troubled. •Then he said to them, "My soul is greatly distressed, to the 38 point of death; stay here and stay awake with me." •And he went ahead 39 a little and fell face down in prayer, and he said, "My Father, if it's pos- sible, let this cup pass away from me, yet not as I wish but as You do." •When he came to the disciples he found them sleeping, and he said to 40 Peter, "So, you couldn't stay awake with me for one hour? •Stay awake 41 and pray that you won't come to the test,

For the spirit is willing,
But the flesh is weak."

[b] Mk 14:22-26; Lk 22:15-20.   [c] Mk 14:27-31; Lk 22:31-34; Jn 13:36-38.
[d] Mk 14:32-42; Lk 22:39-46.

26:31 Zc 13:7.

⁴² •He went off a second time and prayed again, saying, "My Father, if it isn't possible for this cup to pass by without me drinking it, let Your ⁴³ will be done." •And when he came he again found them sleeping, for ⁴⁴ their eyes were heavy. •And he left them and went off again and prayed ⁴⁵ for the third time, saying the same thing once more. •Then he came to the disciples and said to them, "Are you still sleeping and resting? Behold, the hour has arrived and the Son of Man will be handed over in-⁴⁶ to the hands of sinners. •Get up! Let's be going! Behold, the one who will hand me over has come!"

The grotto of arrest in Jerusalem. (Mt 26:48ff)

⁴⁷ •^e While he was still speaking, behold, Judas, one of the Twelve, came, and with him a large crowd with swords and clubs from the chief priests ⁴⁸ and elders of the people. •Now the one handing him over had arranged ⁴⁹ to give them a sign, saying, "Whoever I kiss is the one; seize him!" •And he came up to Jesus at once and said, "Hail, Rabbi!" and kissed him. ⁵⁰ •But Jesus said to him, "What are you here for, my friend?" Then they ⁵¹ came forward, laid hands on Jesus, and seized him. •And, behold, one

^e *Mk 14:43-50; Lk 22:47-53; Jn 18:3-12.*

of those with Jesus reached out his hand, drew his sword, and struck the high priest's slave and cut off his ear. •But Jesus said to him, "Put 52 your sword back in its place — all who take up the sword will die by the sword! •Or do you think that I couldn't call on my Father and have him 53 at once send me more than twelve legions of angels? •But then how 54 could the Scriptures be fulfilled, that this is the way it must be?" •Then 55 Jesus said to the crowds, "You came out with swords and clubs to seize me, as if you were after a robber? Every day I sat in the Temple teaching, yet you didn't seize me! •But all this has happened so that the writ- 56 ings of the prophets would be fulfilled." Then all the disciples forsook him and fled.

•[f] Those who had seized Jesus led him off to Caiaphas, the high priest, 57 where the scribes and elders had gathered. •Peter followed him at a dis- 58 tance up to the courtyard of the high priest, then went inside and sat down with the Temple attendants to see the outcome. •The chief priests 59 and the whole Sanhedrin were seeking false testimony against Jesus so they could put him to death, •but they found none, although many false 60 witnesses came forward. Finally two men came forward •and said, "This 61 fellow said, 'I can tear down the sanctuary of God and in three days build it up.'" •The high priest stood up and said to him, "Do you make no 62 answer? Why are these men testifying against you?" •But Jesus remained 63 silent. Then the high priest said to him, "I put you under oath by the Living God to tell us if you're the Messiah, the Son of God." •Jesus said 64 to him, "*You* said it. Moreover, I say to you, from now on you will see **the Son of Man, seated at the right hand of Power, and coming on the clouds of Heaven**!" •Then the high priest tore his robes 65 and said, "He has blasphemed! What further need do we have for witnesses? Look! Now *you* heard him blaspheme! •What's your opinion?" 66 In answer they said, "He deserves to die!" •Then they spit in his face 67 and struck him, while some hit him, •saying, "Prophesy to us, O Mes- 68 siah! Who was it that struck you?"

•[g] As Peter was sitting outside in the courtyard a certain maidservant 69 came up to him and said, "You were with Jesus of Galilee, too!" •But 70 he denied it in front of everyone and said, "I don't know what you're talking about." •As he was going out to the gate another maidservant 71 saw him and said to those who were there, "This fellow was with Jesus of Nazareth!" •And he denied it again with an oath: "I don't know the 72

[f] *Mk 14:53-65; Lk 22:54-55, 63-71; Jn 18:13-14, 19-24.*
[g] *Mk 14:66-72; Lk 22:56-62; Jn 18:15-18, 25-27.*

26:64 Ps 110:1; Dn 7:13.

73 man!" •But a little later those who were standing there came up to Peter and said, "Surely *you* were one of them, too — even your speech
74 gives you away!" •Then he put himself under a curse and swore, "I don't
75 know the man!" At once a cock crowed, •and Peter remembered what
Jesus told him when he said, "Before the cock crows you'll deny me three
times," and he went outside and wept bitterly.

1 **27** •ʰ When morning had come all the chief priests and elders of the
people came up with a plan against Jesus in order to put him to
2 death, •and after binding him they led him off and handed him over to
Pilate, the governor.
3   •Then when Judas, the one who handed him over, saw that Jesus had
been condemned, out of remorse he returned the thirty silver coins to
4 the chief priests and elders •and said, "I sinned when I handed over in-
5 nocent blood." "What's that to us?" they said. "*You* take care of it!" •And
after flinging the silver coins into the sanctuary he left, and he went off
6 and hung himself. •Now when the chief priests had picked up the silver
coins they said, "It isn't lawful to put these into the Temple treasury, since
7 it was the price of blood." •So after conferring they used them to buy
8 the Potter's Field for the burial of strangers. •Therefore, to this day that
9 field has been called the Field of Blood. •Then what was said by Jeremiah the prophet was fulfilled, when he stated, **and they took the thirty pieces of silver, the price of a man with a price set on him,**
10 **the price set on him by some of the Sons of Israel, •and they
gave them for the potter's field, as the Lord instructed me.**
11   •ⁱ Now Jesus stood before the governor, and the governor questioned
him and said, "Are *you* the King of the Jews?" Jesus said, "*You* say so."
12 •And he made no answer while the chief priests and elders were mak-
13 ing accusations against him. •Then Pilate asked him, "Don't you hear
14 how many things they're alleging against you?" •But not one word did
he answer him to anything, to the great amazement of the governor.
15   •ʲ Now at the festival it was the governor's custom to release to the
16 crowd any one prisoner they wanted. •At that time they had a notori-
17 ous prisoner named Barabbas, •so when they had gathered, Pilate said
to them, "Who do you want me to release to you, Barabbas or Jesus,
18 who's called the Messiah?" — •he knew they'd handed him over out of

ʰ *Mk 15:1; Lk 23:1-2; Jn 18:28-32.* ⁱ *Mk 15:2-5; Lk 23:3-5; Jn 18:33-38.*
ʲ *Mk 15:6-15; Lk 23:13-25; Jn 18:39 - 19:16.*

26:73 Apparently Peter had a Galilean accent; 27:9 Zc 11:12-13; Jr 32:6-9.
cf. Mk 14:70.

envy. •And while he was sitting on the judgment seat his wife sent to 19
him and said, "Have nothing to do with that innocent man — I suffered
greatly in a dream today because of him!" •Now the chief priests and 20
elders persuaded the crowds to ask for Barabbas but to have Jesus killed.
•So in response the governor said to them, "Which of the two do you 21
want me to release to you?" "Barabbas!" they said. •Pilate said to them, 22
"Then what should I do with Jesus, who's called the Messiah?" They all
said, "Let him be crucified!" •"But what wrong has he done?" he asked. 23
But they shouted all the more and said, "Let him be crucified!" •When 24
Pilate saw that he was doing no good, but instead a riot was beginning,
he took water and washed his hands in full view of the crowd, saying,
"I'm innocent of this man's blood! See to it yourselves!" •In reply the 25
whole people said, "His blood be upon us, and upon our children!"
•Then he released Barabbas to them, but he had Jesus scourged and 26
then handed him over to be crucified.

•[k] Then the governor's soldiers took Jesus along to the praetorium 27
and gathered the whole cohort around him. •They stripped him and put 28
a scarlet robe on him, •and after weaving a crown of thorns they put it 29
on his head and placed a reed in his right hand, then they'd kneel before him and mock him, saying, "Hail, King of the Jews!" •and after 30
spitting on him they'd take the reed and beat him over the head. •And 31
when they were done mocking him they stripped the robe off him and
dressed him in his own clothes and led him off to be crucified.

•[l] As they were going out they found a man named Simon of Cyrene; 32
they forced this man to carry his cross. •And when they came to the 33
place called Golgotha, which is to say "the Place of the Skull," •they 34
gave him wine mixed with gall to drink, but when he tasted it he refused
to drink it. •After crucifying him they divided his clothes among them 35
by casting lots, •then they sat down and kept watch over him there. •And 36,37
over his head they placed the written charge against him, "This is Jesus the King of the Jews." •Then two robbers were crucified with him, 38
one on his right hand and one on his left hand. •The passersby kept 39
blaspheming him, **shaking their heads** •and saying, "You who were 40
going to tear down the sanctuary and build it up in three days, save yourself! If you *are* the Son of God, come down from the cross!" •The chief 41

---

[k] Mk 15:16-20; Jn 19:2-3.   [l] Mk 15:21-32; Lk 23:26-43; Jn 19:28-30.

27:35 The best manuscript tradition omits: "to **They divided my garments among them,**
fulfill what was spoken through the prophets **and for my clothing they cast lots.**" (Ps 22:19)
when they said,   27:39 Ps 22:7.

Jerusalem. Basilica of the Holy Sepulchre. (Mt 27:66)

42 priests along with the scribes and elders also mocked him, saying, •"He saved others but can't save himself! If he's the King of Israel, let him
43 come down now from the cross and we'll believe in him. •**He trusted in God, let God deliver him** now **if He wants him,** since he said,
44 'I'm the Son of God.'" •Even the robbers who were crucified with him derided him in the same way.
45   •ᵐ Now from about noon darkness came upon the land until about
46 three o'clock. •Then at about three Jesus cried out with a loud voice and said, *"Eli, Eli, lema sabachthani?"* that is, **"My God, my God,**
47 **why have You forsaken me?"** •When some of those who were stand-
48 ing there heard this they said, "The fellow's calling Elijah!" •At once one of them ran and took a sponge and filled it with wine, and he placed it
49 on a reed and tried to give him a drink. •But the rest said, "Hold on,
50 let's see if Elijah will come to save him!" •But Jesus cried out again in

ᵐ *Mk 15:33-41; Lk 23:44-49; Jn 19:28-30.*

27:43 Ps 22:8; Ws 2:18.   27:46 Ps 22:2.

a loud voice and gave up the spirit. •And, behold, the curtain of the sanc- 51
tuary was torn in two from top to bottom, and the earth was shaken
and the rocks were torn apart, •and the tombs were opened and many 52
bodies of the saints who had fallen asleep arose, •and they came out of 53
the tombs after his resurrection and went into the holy city and appeared
to many people. •When the centurion and those watching Jesus with 54
him saw the earthquake and what had happened they were terrified and
said, "Truly this man *was* the Son of God!" •There were many women 55
there, watching from a distance, who had followed Jesus from Galilee
to serve him; •among them were Mary Magdalen and Mary the moth- 56
er of James and Joseph and the mother of the sons of Zebedee.

•ⁿ When evening had come a rich man from Arimathea named Joseph, 57
who had also been a disciple of Jesus, came; •he went to Pilate and re- 58
quested the body of Jesus. Then Pilate ordered it to be given to him.
•Joseph took the body and wrapped it in a clean linen shroud •and placed 59,60
it in his new tomb, which he had hewn in the rock, and after rolling a
large stone up to the door of the tomb he went away. •Now Mary Mag- 61
dalen and the other Mary were there, sitting across from the sepulchre.

•The next day, that is, the day after the Day of Preparation, the chief 62
priests and Pharisees gathered before Pilate •and said, "Lord, we re- 63
member that that imposter said, while still alive, 'After three days I'll rise.'
•Therefore, order the sepulchre to be made secure until the third day, 64
lest his disciples come steal him and say to the people, 'He's risen from
the dead!' and the last imposture will be worse than the first." •Pilate 65
said to them, "You have a guard; go secure it as well as you know how."
•So they went and set a watch on the tomb and sealed the stone with 66
the guard.

W. RESURRECTION AND APPEARANCES OF JESUS

28 •° Now after the Sabbath, as it began to dawn on the first day of 1
the week, Mary Magdalen and the other Mary came to see the
sepulchre. •And, behold, there was a powerful earthquake; an angel of 2
the Lord came down from Heaven, came up to the stone, rolled it away
and sat upon it. •His appearance was like lightning and his clothing was 3
as white as snow, •and for fear of him those who were on guard trem- 4
bled and became like dead men. •But in response the angel said to the 5
women, "Don't be afraid — I know you're looking for Jesus, who was

ⁿ Mk 15:42-47; Lk 23:50-56; Jn 19:38-42.   ° Mk 16:1-8; Lk 24:1-12; Jn 20:1-10.

6 crucified. •He isn't here — he's risen, just like he said; come see the
7 place where he lay. •And go quickly to tell his disciples, 'He's risen from
the dead and, behold, he's going ahead of you into Galilee; you'll see
8 him there.' Behold, I've told you!" •They quickly left the tomb with fear
9 and great joy and ran to tell the disciples. •And, behold, Jesus met up
with the women and said, "Hail!" They came forward, took hold of his
10 feet, and worshipped him. •Then Jesus said to them, "Don't be afraid!
Go tell my brothers to go to Galilee, and they'll see me there."

11 •While they were on their way, behold, some of the guard came in-
12 to the city and told the chief priests all that had happened. •And after
getting together with the elders and coming up with a plan they gave
13 the soldiers a considerable amount of money •and said, "Say, 'His dis-
14 ciples came at night and stole him away while we were sleeping.' •And
if word of this gets to the governor, we'll satisfy him and keep you out
15 of trouble." •So they took the money and did as they'd been instructed. And this story has been spread among Jews to this day.

16 •ᵖ But the eleven disciples went into Galilee to the mountain Jesus
17 had directed them to. •And when they saw him they worshipped him,
18 but some were doubtful. •Jesus came to them and spoke to them, say-
19 ing, "All authority in Heaven and on earth has been given to me. •Go,
therefore, and make disciples of all nations, baptizing them in the name
20 of the Father and of the Son and of the Holy Spirit, •and teach them
to observe all that I've commanded you and, behold, I'll be with you all
the days until the end of the age."

ᵖ Mk 16:14-18; Lk 24:36-49; Jn 20:19-23.

THE GOSPEL
ACCORDING TO

MARK

Introduction to the Gospel According to Mark

Both tradition and modern scholarship are in general agreement that the author of the second Gospel was John Mark, well known to Christians from the Acts of the Apostles and also mentioned in several epistles. He apparently cooperated in the ministries of both Peter and Paul, and there is strong testimony in tradition to the effect that Mark's Gospel reflects Peter's teaching, that Mark, in fact, committed some of Peter's preaching to writing and incorporated it in his Gospel. Some scholars find support for this in the vivid eyewitness tone of those passages in which Peter is involved. At the same time, it is also clear that Mark used more than one source, and such a well travelled Christian, acquainted with important leaders of the Church, would have had access to many eyewitnesses to the ministry of Jesus. It is usually supposed that Mark's Gospel was written primarily for Gentile Christians since he shows none of Matthew's interest in specifically Jewish concerns and seems to assume his readers will need an explanation when such matters are mentioned. This accords well with the persistent tradition that Mark wrote this Gospel at the request of the church at Rome, a mixed community.

MARK

A. THE BEGINNINGS OF JESUS' MINISTRY

1 •ᵃ The beginning of the good news of Jesus Christ, the Son of God.
2 •As it is written in the prophet Isaiah —

Behold, I'm sending my messenger before your face,
who will prepare your way,
3 **•The voice of one crying out in the desert,**
'Prepare the way of the Lord,
make straight his paths' —

4 •so it was that John the Baptist appeared in the desert, proclaiming a
5 baptism of repentance for the forgiveness of sins. •People from all the
Judean countryside went out to him as well as everyone who lived in
Jerusalem, and they were baptized by him in the river Jordan while they
6 confessed their sins. •John was clothed in camel hair with a leather belt
7 around his waist, and he ate locusts and wild honey. •And he would
preach, saying, "One more powerful than I am is coming after me, the
8 strap of whose sandals I'm not worthy to stoop down and untie. •I've
baptized you with water, but he'll baptize you with the Holy Spirit."
9 •ᵇ And it happened in those days that Jesus came from Nazareth in
10 Galilee and was baptized in the Jordan by John. •As he was coming out
of the water he saw the heavens torn apart and the Spirit descending
11 upon him like a dove, •and a voice came from Heaven, "You are My
Beloved Son; in you I am well pleased!"
12,13 •ᶜ And at once the Spirit led him out into the desert. •He stayed in
the desert for forty days being tempted by Satan. He was with the wild
animals, and angels served him.

ᵃ *Mt 3:1-12; Lk 3:1-9, 15-17; Jn 1:19-28.* ᵇ *Mt 3:13-17; Lk 3:21-22.*
ᶜ *Mt 4:1-11; Lk 4:1-13.*

1:2-4 Mark opens his Gospel by likening John   1:2 Ml 3:1.
the Baptist to the herald announcing the coming   1:3 Is 40:3 (Septuagint).
of God to His people Israel, thus clearly equating
Jesus with God.

B. AUTHORITY OF JESUS AND CONFLICT
WITH THE PHARISEES

•[d] After John was arrested, Jesus came into Galilee proclaiming the 14
good news of God •and saying, "The appointed time has come and the 15
Kingdom of God is at hand; repent and believe in the good news!"

•[e] As he was walking along the Sea of Galilee he saw Simon and Si- 16
mon's brother Andrew casting throw nets into the sea — they were fishermen. •Jesus said to them, "Follow me, and I'll make you fishers of 17
men!" •And they left their nets at once and followed him. •He contin- 18,19
ued on a little way and saw James son of Zebedee and his brother, John
— they were in the boat mending the nets. •He called them at once, 20
and they left their father Zebedee in the boat with the hired men and
followed him.

•[f] They entered Capharnaum, and he went into the synagogue on the 21
Sabbath and began to teach. •The people were amazed at the way he 22
taught, for he was teaching them on his own authority, unlike the scribes.
•And there was a man with an unclean spirit in the synagogue who cried 23
out, •"What do you want with us, Jesus of Nazareth? Have you come 24
to destroy us? I know who you are — the Holy One of God!" •Jesus re- 25
buked him and said, "Be silenced and come out of him!" •And after 26
throwing him into convulsions and crying out with a loud voice, the unclean spirit came out of him. •Those gathered there were so astounded 27
that they began to argue with one another and say, "What's going on?
A new teaching given on his own authority; he even gives orders to the
unclean spirits, and they obey him!" •And word of him went out every- 28
where in the whole district of Galilee.

•[g] After leaving the synagogue he went to Simon and Andrew's house 29
with James and John. •Peter's mother-in-law was burning with fever, 30
and at once they told Jesus about her. •He went over to her, grasped 31
her hand and raised her up, and the fever left her and she began to serve
them. •When it was evening, when the sun had set, they brought him 32
all the people who were sick and were demon-possessed, •and the whole 33
city was gathered at the door. •He cured many who were sick with all 34
kinds of diseases and drove out many demons, and he didn't allow the
demons to speak, because they knew him.

[d] Mt 4:12-17; Lk 4:14-15.   [e] Mt 4:18-22; Lk 5:1-11.   [f] Lk 4:31-37.   [g] Mt 8:14-17; Lk 4:38-41.

1:22 "On his own authority," lit., "as one having authority." The scribes always invoked the authority
of the Torah.

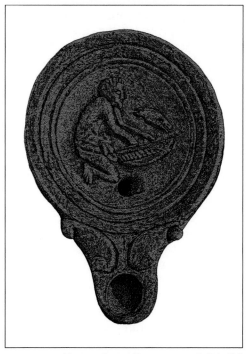

A fisherman on a Roman lamp (1st century A.D.). (Mk 1:16)

35 •ʰ Early in the morning, long before daylight, he got up, went out,
36 and went off to a desert place, and there he prayed. •Simon and those
37 with him tracked him down, •and when they found him they said to him,
38 "Everyone's looking for you!" •He said to them, "Let's go elsewhere,
to the neighboring country towns, so I can preach there as well — this
39 is what I came for!" •And he went through all Galilee, preaching in their
synagogues and driving out demons.
40   •ⁱ A leper came up to him, begging him and kneeling down and say-
41 ing to him, "If you wish to, you can make me clean!" •Greatly moved, he

ʰ *Lk 4:42-44.*   ⁱ *Mt 8:1-4; Lk 5:12-16.*

1:40-44 By touching the leper Jesus risked ritual impurity (Lv 13-14) to help the man. The
Greek indicates that Jesus was moved by a
strong emotion, but his brusqueness toward the
leper throughout the passage seems to indicate
his indignation, perhaps at the implicit assumption in the leper's words (v. 40) that Jesus might
be reluctant to help him. This shows a lack of
faith. For a similar response by Jesus to a plea
for a cure, cf. 9:17-27.

reached out his hand, touched him, and said to him, "I do wish it; be made clean!" •and at once the leprosy left him and he was made clean. •After **42,43** admonishing him Jesus at once sent him away, •saying to him, "See that **44** you tell no one, but go show yourself to the priest and offer for your cleansing what Moses commanded, as a witness to them." •But the man went **45** out and began to spread the word and proclaim it so energetically that Jesus wasn't even able to enter a city openly; instead, he stayed out in desert places, and people would come to him from all directions.

2 •[j] He came into Capharnaum again a few days later, and it became **1** known that he was at home. •So many people gathered around that **2** there was no longer room even in front of the door, and he spoke the word to them. •Then some people came to him carrying a paralytic, **3** borne by four men. •And since they couldn't bring him in because of **4** the crowd, they removed the roof where Jesus was, and after opening it up they lowered the mat on which the paralytic was laid. •When Je- **5** sus saw their faith he said to the paralytic, "My child, your sins are forgiven!" •Some of the scribes were seated there and they questioned in **6** their hearts, •"How can the fellow talk like that? He's blaspheming! **7** Who but God alone is able to forgive sins?" •Jesus realized at once in **8** his spirit that they were questioning within themselves in this way, and so he said to them, "Why are you questioning these things in your hearts? •What's easier, to say to the paralytic, 'Your sins are forgiven,' **9** or to say, 'Get up, pick up your mat, and walk'? •But so you'll know **10** that the Son of Man has authority to forgive sins on earth" — he said to the paralytic, •"I say to you, get up, pick up your mat, and go to **11** your house!" •And he got up, picked up his mat at once and went out **12** in full sight of everyone, causing everyone to be amazed and to glorify God, saying, "We've never seen anything like this!"

•[k] Once again he went out along the sea, and the whole crowd came **13** to him and he taught them. •As he walked along he saw Levi son of **14** Alpheus seated at his tax booth, and he said to him, "Follow me!" And he got up and followed him. •He reclined at table in his house, and many **15** tax collectors and sinners were at table with Jesus and his disciples; many, indeed, were there. Also following him •were scribes of the Pharisees, **16** and when they saw that he was eating with sinners and tax collectors they

[j] Mt 9:1-8; Lk 5:17-26.   [k] Mt 9:9-13; Lk 5:27-32.

2:2 "The word," i.e., the good news. This usage quickly became a technical term among the early Christians.

2:5-11 By his words and actions Jesus placed himself in a position outside and superior to the accepted Judaic cultic structures for forgiveness.

said to his disciples, "Why is he eating with tax collectors and sinners?"

17 •When he heard this Jesus said to them, "The healthy aren't in need of a doctor — the sick are! I came to call sinners, not the righteous."

18 •ˡ John's disciples and the Pharisees were fasting, and people came and said to Jesus, "Why are John's disciples and the disciples of the Phar-

19 isees fasting, but your disciples aren't fasting?" •Jesus said to them,

"Can the groomsmen fast
while the bridegroom is with them?
As long as the bridegroom is with them
they cannot fast,

20 •But the days will come when the bridegroom
will be taken from them,
and then, on that day, they'll fast.

21 •No one sews a patch of unshrunken cloth
onto an old cloak,
Otherwise, the patch tears away from it,
the new from the old,
and the tear becomes worse.

22 •And no one puts new wine
into old skins,
Otherwise, the wine will burst the skins,
and both wine and skins are ruined;

on the contrary,

new wine in new skins.'"

23 •ᵐ It happened that as he was going through the grain fields on the Sabbath his disciples began plucking the heads of the grain as they made

24 their way through. •And the Pharisees said to him, "Look! Why are they

25 doing what's unlawful on the Sabbath?" •He said to them, "Haven't you ever read what David did when *he* was in need and was hungry, as well

26 as those with him? •How he went into the house of God when Abiathar was high priest and ate the loaves of offering" — which it's only lawful for the priests to eat — "and he gave some to those with him as well?"

27 •And he said to them,

"The Sabbath was made for Man,
not Man for the Sabbath;

28 •thus the Son of Man is Lord even of the Sabbath."

ˡ *Mt 9:14-17; Lk 5:33-39.*   ᵐ *Mt 12:1-8; Lk 6:1-5.*

3 •[n] Once again he entered the synagogue. Now a man was there who had a withered hand •and they were watching closely to see whether Jesus would heal him on the Sabbath, so they could make an accusation against him. •So he said to the man with the withered hand, "Stand out in the middle." •Then he said to them,

> "Which is lawful on the Sabbath, to do good
>   or to do evil,
>   to save a life or to kill?"

But they remained silent. •And after looking around at them in anger, deeply grieved at the hardness of their hearts, he said to the man, "Hold out your hand." The man held his hand out and it was restored. •Then the Pharisees left and at once began to plot with the Herodians to do away with Jesus.

•Jesus departed with his disciples for the sea. A large crowd from Galilee followed •and, having heard all he was doing, a large crowd as well from Judea and from Jerusalem and from Idumea and beyond the Jordan and around Tyre and Sidon came to him. •He told his disciples to ready a small boat for him because of the crowd, so they wouldn't crush him — •he was curing so many that those who had diseases pressed close upon him so they could touch him. •As soon as the unclean spirits saw him they'd fall down before him and cry out, "You're the Son of God!" •And he'd sternly command them not to make him known.

•[o] Then he went up the mountain and called those he wanted, and they came to him. •He chose twelve, whom he also called apostles, to stay with him and to send them out to preach •and have power to drive out demons. •He chose the Twelve and he gave the name Peter to Simon, and James son of Zebedee •and James' brother John, and he gave them the name Boanerges, that is, Sons of Thunder, •and Andrew and Philip and Bartholomew and Matthew and Thomas and James son of Alpheus and Thaddeus and Simon the Cananean •and Judas Iscariot, who handed him over.

•[p] He went into a house, and once again such a crowd gathered that they weren't even able to eat.•When his relatives heard this they came to seize him, because people were saying, "He's out of his mind!" •And

[n] *Mt 12:9-14; Lk 6:6-11.*   [o] *Mt 10:1-4; Lk 6:12-16.*   [p] *Mt 12:22-32; Lk 11:14-23, 12:10.*

3:4 Jesus contrasts his own good intentions with his opponents' deadly intentions: he wishes to do good, while they seek to kill him.

3:18 "Simon the Cananean." Cf. the note at Mt 10:4.

MARK

Capharnaum. Aerial view.

the scribes who had come down from Jerusalem were saying, "He's possessed by Beelzebul! By the prince of demons he drives out demons!"
23 •So he called them to himself and said to them in parables, "How can Satan drive out Satan?

24 •If a kingdom is divided against itself,
that kingdom is unable to stand,

25 •If a house is divided,
that house will be unable to stand.

26 •And if Satan rebels against himself
and is divided,
he cannot last, but comes to an end.

27 •On the contrary, no one can enter the strong man's house to plunder his possessions unless he first ties the strong man up; then he can plun-
28 der his house. •Amen, I say to you,

3:27 Here Jesus compares Satan to a "strong man" and the present age to Satan's house. It is Jesus who has entered Satan's house, bound him, and freed those in Satan's power. Jesus' power over demons is a sign of this mastery and the coming of the Messianic age.

Everything will be forgiven the sons of men,
their sins and the blasphemies they
may blaspheme,
•But whoever blasphemes the Holy Spirit 29
never has forgiveness, but is liable for an eternal sin —"

•because they were saying, "He has an unclean spirit!" 30
•[q] His mother came as well as his brothers; they stood outside and 31
sent someone in for him, to call him. •A crowd was seated around him, 32
and they said to him, "Look, your mother and brothers are outside asking for you." •In answer he said to them, "Who are my mother and my 33
brothers?" •Then he looked around at those seated in a circle around 34
him and said, "Here are my mother and my brothers. •For whoever does 35
the will of God, he's my brother and sister and mother."

C. PARABLES OF THE KINGDOM

4 •[r] Once again he began to teach by the sea. And such a large crowd 1
gathered around him that he got into a boat on the sea and sat down,
while the whole crowd gathered along the sea on the land. •Then he 2
taught them many things in parables and in his teaching he said to them,
•"Listen now! 3

Behold, the sower went out to sow!
•And it happened as he sowed that some fell 4
along the footpath,
and the birds came and ate it up.
•And some fell on the rocky ground where it 5
didn't have much soil,
and it sprouted at once, since the soil
had no depth,
•And when the sun rose it got scorched, 6
and since it had no roots it withered away.

[q] *Mt 12:46-50; Lk 8:19-21.* [r] *Mt 13:1-9; Lk 8:4-8.*

3:29 The blasphemy against the Spirit consists in imputing to Satan what is in fact the lifegiving activity of the Spirit.
3:31 Church tradition has consistently maintained that the "brothers" of Jesus referred to here were merely close relatives, not sons of the same mother. It is instructive to compare this passage to 15:40-16:1 and parallel passages in the other Gospels (especially Mt 27:60 and Lk 23:49-24:10) where these brothers are again referred to as sons of "Mary," but this time it is unambiguously clear that this Mary was not Mary the mother of Jesus. Such usage was typically Semitic.

7 •And some fell among the thorns and the thorns
    grew up,
  and they choked it and it gave no fruit.
8 •And some fell on the good earth, and it grew up
    and increased and gave fruit,
  and one bore thirtyfold, and one sixtyfold,
    and one a hundredfold."

9 •Then he said,

  "Whoever has ears to hear,
  let them hear!"

10 •ˢ When he happened to be alone, those who were with him and the
11 Twelve asked him about the parables. •And he said to them, "To you is
given the secret of the Kingdom of God, but to those outside everything
12 is given in parables, •so that

Although they look,
  they may see yet not perceive,
And though they listen,
  they may hear yet not understand,
Lest they turn back
  and receive forgiveness."

13 •ᵗ Then he said to them, "You don't understand this parable? Then how
14,15 will you understand *any* of the parables? •The sower sows the word. •These
are the ones where the word is sown on the footpath — when they hear,
16 Satan comes at once and snatches away the word sown among them. •And
these are the ones sown on the rocky ground — when they hear the word
17 they at once receive it joyfully, •but they aren't well rooted and last only
for the moment, and then when trouble or persecution arises because of
18 the word they give up their faith at once. •Others are those sown among
19 the thorns, who are the ones who hear the word, •but worldly cares and
the deception of wealth and desires for all the other things come in and
20 choke the word, and it's unfruitful. •Then there are those sown on the good
earth, who are the ones who hear the word and welcome it and bear fruit,
one thirtyfold, one sixtyfold, and one a hundredfold."
21 •ᵘ And he said to them, "Is the lamp brought in to be put under the
grain basket or under the bed? Isn't it so it can be placed on the lampstand?

ˢ *Mt 13:1-17; Lk 8:9-10.*   ᵗ *Mt 13:18-23; Lk 8:11-15.*   ᵘ *Lk 8:16-18.*   4:12 Is 6:9-10 (Septuagint).

•For nothing is hidden unless it is   22
    to be revealed,
Nothing is covered up unless to be brought
    into the open.
•If anyone has ears to hear,   23
    let them hear!"

•And he said to them,   24

"Consider what you hear.
With the measure you measure, it will be measured
        out to you,
    and more will be added as well.
•For whoever has,   25
    to him it shall be given,
And whoever does *not* have,
    even what he has will be taken from him."

•And he said,   26

"This is how the Kingdom of God is,
    like a man who throws seed upon the earth
•And sleeps and rises by night and day,   27
    and the seed sprouts and grows
        while he's unaware.

The reaping: an engraved stone (3rd century B.C.). (Mk 4:28-29)

MARK

28 •The earth bears fruit on its own,
first the shoot, then the head of grain,
then the full grain in the head.
29 •When it puts forth fruit he at once sends
for the sickle,
because the harvest has come."

30 •ᵛ And he said,

"How may we compare the Kingdom of God,
or in what parable can we present it?
31 •It's like a grain of mustard seed
which, when it's sown upon the earth, is the
smallest of all the seeds on the earth,
32 •Yet when it's sown it grows and becomes
the biggest of all the garden plants
and puts out big branches, so that the birds
of the sky are able to nest
in its shade."

33 •ʷ He spoke the word to the people in many such parables, to the
34 extent that they were able to understand, •but he spoke to the people
only in parables and explained everything to his own disciples in private.
35 •ˣ That day when evening had come he said to them, "Let's cross over
36 to the other side." •After dismissing the crowd they took him as he was,
37 in the boat, and other boats were with it. •A violent wind squall came
up and the waves were breaking over the boat so that the boat was fill-
38 ing up, •yet he was in the stern, sleeping on the cushion. So they woke
him and said to him, "Teacher, doesn't it matter to you that we're go-
39 ing to die?" •Then he woke up and rebuked the wind and said to the
sea, "Silence! Be calm!" The wind ceased and there was a profound
40 calm, •and he said to them, "Why are you afraid? Don't you have faith
41 yet?" •They were seized with fear and said to each other, "Who is he,
then? Even the wind and sea obey him!"

ᵛ Mt 13:31-32; Lk 13:18-19.   ʷ Mt 13:34-35.   ˣ Mt 8:23-27; Lk 8:22-25.   4:29 Jl 3:13.

D. JESUS MANIFESTS HIS AUTHORITY
BUT IS REJECTED

5 •[y] He went to the other side of the sea to the region of the Gerasenes, 1 •and when he got out of the boat he was confronted by a man with 2 an unclean spirit who came up to him from among the tombs. •This man 3 lived among the tombs and no one could restrain him any more, even with a chain — •he'd been put in chains and restrained many times, yet 4 he'd broken the chains and restraints to bits and scattered them, and no one was able to control him. •By day and by night, among the tombs 5 and on the mountains, he was continually shouting and cutting himself with stones. •When he caught sight of Jesus from a distance he rushed 6 up and fell on his knees before him, •crying out in a loud voice, "What 7 do you want with me, Jesus, Son of the Most High God? I beg you in the name of God not to torment me!" •because Jesus had been saying 8 to him, "Come out of the man, unclean spirit!" •Jesus asked him, "What's 9 your name?" and he said to him, "My name is Legion, because there are many of us." •And he kept begging Jesus not to send them out of the 10 region. •Now there was a large herd of swine on the hillside there, feed- 11 ing, •and they begged him, "Send us into the swine; let us enter into 12 them!" •So he gave them permission and when the unclean spirits had 13 gone out they went into the swine, and the herd, numbering about two thousand, rushed headlong down the slope into the sea and was drowned. •The men who had been feeding them fled and spread the news in the 14 town and the fields, and the people came to see what had happened. •When they came up to Jesus and saw the demon-possessed man sitting 15 there, clothed and in his right mind — the one who had been possessed by Legion — they became frightened. •Then those who had seen it all 16 told them how this had come about for the demon-possessed man, and also about the swine. •And the people began to beg him to leave their 17 district. •When he had gotten into the boat the man who had been de- 18 mon-possessed begged him to let him go with him, •but he wouldn't al- 19 low him to; instead he told him, "Go off to your home, to your own peo-ple, and proclaim to them everything the Lord has done for you and how He had mercy on you." •So he went off and began to proclaim in the 20 Decapolis what Jesus had done for him, and they were all astounded.

[y] Mt 8:28-34; Lk 8:26-39.

5:1 The setting of this narrative is replete with ritual impurity – unclean spirits, tombs, demoni-acs, pigs; even the location, outside Israel and inhabited by Gentiles, lends an air of unclean-ness, a sense of lessened holiness for the de-vout Jew.

21 •[z] When Jesus had again crossed over to the other side a large crowd
22 gathered around him, as he stood by the sea. •One of the rulers of the
synagogue, Jairus by name, came and, when he saw him, fell at his feet
23 •and begged him, saying, "My little daughter is dying; please come lay
24 your hands on her and save her life!" •So he went off with him. A large
25 crowd was following him and kept crowding in on him. •Now a woman
26 was there who had had a heavy flow of blood for twelve years •and had
suffered greatly at the hands of many doctors. She'd spent all she had
but had nothing to show for it; on the contrary, her condition was get-
27 ting worse. •Having heard about Jesus, she came with the crowd and
28 touched his cloak from behind, •because she said, "If I can just touch part
29 of his clothing I'll be saved." •At once her flow of blood dried up, and
30 she knew in her body that she was cured from the illness. •Jesus himself, realizing at once that power had gone out from him, turned around
31 in the crowd and said, "Who touched my clothing?" •His disciples said
to him, "You see the crowd pressing in on you! How can you say, 'Who
32,33 touched me?'" •But he kept looking around to see who had done it. •So
the woman, trembling and afraid because she knew what had happened
34 to her, came and fell down before him and told him the whole truth. •Then
he said to her, "Daughter, your faith has saved you; go in peace and be
35 cured of your illness." •While he was still speaking some people came
from the ruler of the synagogue's household and said, "Your daughter
36 has died; why trouble the teacher further?" •But Jesus paid no attention
to what was being said and told the ruler of the synagogue, "Don't be
37 afraid; just believe!" •And he didn't allow anyone to accompany him ex-
38 cept Peter and James and James' brother John. •When they came to
the leader of the synagogue's house Jesus saw the confusion and the peo-
39 ple weeping and wailing loudly, •and when he entered he said to them,
"Why are you upset and weeping? The child hasn't died, she's sleeping!"
40 •And they just laughed at him. But after driving them all out he took the
father of the child and the mother and those who were with him, and he
41 went in to where the child was; •and taking hold of the child's hand he
said to her, "*Talitha koum*," which, translated, is, "Little girl, I say to you,
42 arise!" •At once the little girl got up and began to walk around — she

---

[z] *Mt 9:18-26; Lk 8:40-56.*

5:20 "The Decapolis" was a confederation of largely Hellenized cities. They were ten in number (Greek *deka* = ten) and all but one were located east of the Jordan. To have encountered the herd of swine in a more Jewish environment would have been unthinkable.

5:25 Because of her continual menstrual flow, almost any contact with this woman would risk ritual impurity (Lv 15:19-30). But Jesus is unfazed by her touch.

was twelve years old. And at once they were completely overcome with amazement. •Then he gave strict orders that no one should know of this 43 and said to give her something to eat.

6 •ᵃ Jesus left there and went to his hometown, and his disciples fol- 1 lowed him. •When the Sabbath came he began to teach in the syna- 2 gogue, and most of those who were listening were amazed and said, "Where did this fellow get all this? What sort of wisdom has been given to him that such mighty works should come about at his hands? •Isn't this 3 the carpenter, the son of Mary and the brother of James and Joses and Judas and Simon? Aren't his sisters right here among us?" And they re- jected him. •Jesus said to them, "A prophet is without honor only in his 4 hometown and among his kinsmen and in his own house." •He was un- 5 able to do any mighty works there, except that he cured a few sick peo- ple by laying his hands on them, •and he was astounded at their unbelief. 6

E. MISSION OF THE DISCIPLES
AND DEATH OF THE BAPTIST

ᵇThen he went around the surrounding villages teaching. •He sum- 7 moned the Twelve and began to send them out two by two, and he gave them authority over the unclean spirits •and ordered them to take noth- 8 ing on the road except a staff — not bread, not a bag, nor money in their belts — •but instead to put sandals on their feet and not to wear 9 two tunics. •And he said to them, "Wherever you enter a house, stay 10 there until you leave the place. •But if any place doesn't receive you or 11 give you a hearing, when you're leaving there shake the dust from the soles of your feet in witness against them." •So they went out and pro- 12 claimed that the people should repent, •and they drove out many 13 demons and anointed many sick people with oil and cured them.

•ᶜ King Herod heard about Jesus, for his name had become known, 14 and people were saying, "John the Baptizer has been raised from the dead, and that's why these powers are at work in him." •But others said, 15 "He's Elijah," while others said, "He's a prophet like one of the Prophets of old." •But when Herod heard he said, "It's John whom I beheaded — 16 he's been raised!" •For Herod himself had sent and had John seized and 17

ᵃ Mt 13:53-58; Lk 4:16-18.   ᵇ Mt 10:1, 5-15; Lk 9:1-6.   ᶜ Mt 14:1-12; Lk 9:7-9.

6:3 Cf. 3:31 above for more detailed discussion. In Semitic usage any close male relative could be referred to as a brother.

*The goddess Tyche (Fortune). Sculpture from Philadelphia,
a town of the Decapolis. (Mk 5:20)*

kept him in prison because of Herodias, the wife of his brother Philip,
18 because he'd married her. •For John had been telling Herod, "It isn't law-
19 ful for you to have your brother's wife." •Now Herodias held this against
20 John and wanted to have him killed, but she was unable to •because
Herod feared John, knowing him to be an upright and holy man. He kept
an eye on him and when he listened to him he was greatly disturbed, and
21 yet he liked to listen to him. •But a day of opportunity came for Herodias when Herod held a feast for his top men and the tribunes and the
22 most important men from Galilee, •and when Herodias' own daughter
came in and danced she pleased Herod and the guests. The king said to
23 the girl, "Ask me whatever you want and I'll give you it," •and he swore
to her, "Whatever you ask me for I'll give you, up to half my kingdom."
24 •She went out and said to her mother, "What should I ask for?" And her
25 mother said, "The head of John the Baptizer." •So she hurried in at once
to the king and made her request — "I want you to give me, right now,
26 the head of John the Baptist on a platter." •The king was greatly dis-

6:21 The words "for Herodias" have been added to the text.

tressed; because of the oaths and the guests he didn't want to refuse her, •so the king sent at once and ordered an executioner to bring John's head. 27 The executioner went off and beheaded John in the prison, •and he 28 brought the head on a platter and gave it to the girl, and she gave it to her mother. •And when his disciples heard they came and carried the 29 corpse away and laid it in a tomb.

F. TWO SIGNS AND LACK OF FAITH

•[d] Then the apostles gathered around Jesus and told him all they had 30 done and had taught. •And he said to them, "Come away privately, just 31 yourselves, to a desert place and rest for a bit." For there were so many people coming and going that they didn't even have time to eat. •So 32 they went off alone in the boat to a desert place, •but people saw them 33 leaving and many of them found out where he was going, and they ran ahead on foot from all the towns and got there before them. •When he 34 got out of the boat he saw a large crowd, and he was moved with pity for them because they were like sheep without a shepherd, and he began to teach them many things. •Now when it was already late in the 35 day his disciples came to him and said, "This is a desert place and it's already late; •send them away so they can go off to the farms and vil- 36 lages and buy themselves something to eat." •But in response he said 37 to them, "*You* give them something to eat." And they said to him, "Should we go buy two hundred denarii worth of bread and give it to them to eat?" •But he said, "How many loaves do you have? Go see." 38 And when they found out they said, "Five, and two fish." •Then he or- 39 dered them all to recline in groups on the green grass, •and they sat 40 down in groups of a hundred and of fifty. •Taking the five loaves and 41 the two fish, he looked up to Heaven, blessed and broke the loaves, and kept giving them to the disciples to distribute to the people, and he divided the two fish among them all. •They all ate and were filled, •and 42,43 they filled twelve baskets with what was left of the bread as well as some of the fish. •There were five thousand men who ate the bread. 44

•[e] Then he made his disciples get into the boat and go on ahead to 45 the other side to Bethsaida, while he sent the crowd away. •And after 46

[d] *Mt 14:13-21; Lk 9:10-17.*   [e] *Mt 14:22-33.*

6:39 "Green grass"; John (6:10) also mentions that "there was a lot of grass" at this spot. These details indicate that it was probably early spring, quite possibly Passover time. John specifically states (6:4) that "the Passover ... was near."

47 he took leave of them he went up the mountain to pray. •When evening came on, the boat was in the middle of the sea, while he was alone on
48 land. •He saw them straining at the oars —the wind was against them — and shortly before dawn he came toward them, walking on the sea,
49 and he was going to go past them. •Now when they saw him walking
50 on the sea they thought he was a ghost, and they cried out •because they all saw him and were terrified. But he at once spoke with them
51 and told them, "Take courage! It's me! Don't be afraid!" •Then he got into the boat with them and the wind ceased. And they were utterly
52 amazed, •for they hadn't understood about the loaves; instead, their hearts were hardened.

53   •[f] After crossing over they came to land at Gennesaret and moored
54 the boat. •And when they got out of the boat the people recognized
55 him at once — •they ran around the whole district there and began to
56 carry the sick on mats to where they heard he was. •Wherever he entered the villages or cities or farms they put the sick in the market places and begged him to let them just touch the tassel of his cloak, and all who touched it were saved.

G. ISRAEL'S HARDNESS OF HEART

1 7•[g] The Pharisees and some of the scribes from Jerusalem were gath-
2 ered around him, •and they saw that some of his disciples ate bread
3 with unclean, that is, unwashed, hands — •for the Pharisees and all the Jews don't eat unless they wash their hands, holding fast to the tradi-
4 tion of the elders, •and they don't eat after coming from the market-place unless they bathe, and there are many other things that their tradition requires, the washing of cups and pitchers and bronze vessels —
5 •the Pharisees and scribes asked him, "Why don't your disciples walk according to the tradition of the elders, but instead eat bread with un-
6 clean hands?" •He said to them, "Surely Isaiah prophesied about you hypocrites, as it is written,

> **This people honors me with their lips,**
> **but their heart is far from me;**

[f] Mt 14:34-36.   [g] Mt 15:1-20.

6:56 Devout Jews wore tassels on the four corners of their cloaks to remind them to obey the commandments (Nb 15:38-39).
7:3 These various purificatory washings were re-quired to cleanse a person of ritual impurities that might render him unfit to attend the Temple rites.
7:6-7 Is 29:13 (Septuagint).

·In vain do they worship me,   7
   teaching as doctrines the commandments of men.
   ·You forsake the commandment of God,   8
      yet hold fast to the tradition of men."

·And he said to them, "Surely you *do* set aside the commandment of   9
God so you can set up your *own* tradition. ·For Moses said, **Honor your**   10
father and your mother, and, **Let whoever curses his father or**
mother be put to death; ·but you say, 'If a man should say to his fa-   11
ther or mother, "Whatever help you might have from me is *Qorban*"'—
that is, an offering to God — ·"you no longer allow him to do anything   12
for his father or mother; ·thus you set aside the word of God for the   13
tradition you've handed down among yourselves, and you do many other similar things." ·Then he called the crowd to himself again and said   14
to them, "Listen to me, all of you, and understand!

   ·Nothing that enters a man from outside   15
      can make him unclean;
   It's what comes out of a man
      that makes the man unclean."

[·] ·When he entered the house from the crowd his disciples ques-   16,17
tioned him about the parable. ·And he said to them, "Are you that dense,   18
too? Don't you see that nothing that enters a man from outside can make
him unclean, ·because it enters his stomach, not his heart, and goes out   19
into the latrine?" — thus he declared all foods to be clean. ·Then he   20
said, "What comes *out* of a man, that's what makes him unclean, ·for   21
from within, from the hearts of men, come evil thoughts, fornication,
theft, murder, ·adultery, greed, evil intentions, deceit, indecency, jeal-   22
ousy, blasphemy, arrogance, and foolishness. ·All such evils come from   23
within and make a man unclean."

·[h] After departing from there he went off to the regions of Tyre. He   24
entered a house and didn't want anyone to find out, but he couldn't
hide; ·instead, a woman whose daughter had an unclean spirit heard   25
about him at once and came and fell at his feet. ·The woman was a   26
Greek, a Syrophoenician by birth, and she kept begging him to drive
the demon out of her daughter. ·And he said to her, "Let the children   27

---

[h] *Mt 15:21-28.*

7:10 Ex 20:12; Ex 21:17.
7:11 *"Qorban."* This "gift to God" allowed the
giver to continue using what was "given," leav-

ing open the possibility for serious abuses.
7:16 The best manuscript tradition omits this
verse: "If anyone has ears to hear, let him hear!"

MARK

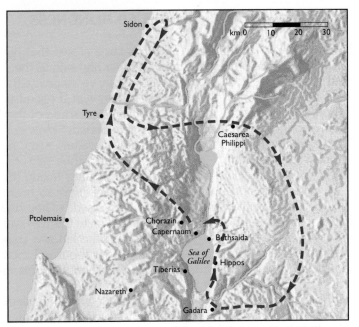

Jesus goes to the regions of Tyre and Sidon. (Mk 7:24ff)

be fed first — it isn't right to take the children's bread and throw it to
28 the pups." •But she answered and said to him, "Lord, even the pups
29 beneath the table eat the children's crumbs." •Then he said to her, "Because of what you've said, go your way; the demon has come out of
30 your daughter." •And when she went off to her house she found the
child lying on the bed, and the demon gone.
31   •When he left the region of Tyre again he went through Sidon to the
32 Sea of Galilee, through the region of the Decapolis. •The people there
brought him a deaf and tongue-tied man and begged him to lay his hands
33 on him. •He took him off alone away from the crowd and put his fin-
34 gers into his ears, and after spitting he touched his tongue. •Then he
looked up to Heaven, sighed, and said to him, "Ephphatha," that is, "Be
35 opened!" •At once his ears were opened and the knot in his tongue was
36 loosed and he began to speak properly. •Jesus ordered them to tell no
one, but the more he ordered them all the more did they proclaim it.
37 •The people were utterly astonished and said, "Surely he's done everything! He makes the deaf hear and the dumb speak!"

7:37 "He's done everything," i.e., everything the Messiah was supposed to do.

H. A SIGN AND CONTINUED BLINDNESS

8•ⁱ In those days there was once again a large crowd that had noth- 1
ing to eat. So he called his disciples together and said to them, •"I'm 2
overcome with pity for the crowd because they've stayed with me for
three days now and don't have anything to eat, •yet if I send them off 3
to their homes hungry they'll faint on the way, and some of them have
come from a long way off." •His disciples responded, "How could any- 4
one give them their fill of bread here in a desert place?" •And he asked 5
them, "How many loaves do you have?" "Seven," they said. •Then he 6
ordered the crowd to recline on the ground and, after taking the seven
loaves, he gave thanks and broke them and gave them to his disciples
to distribute, and they distributed them to the crowd. •They had a few 7
small fish, and after blessing them he said to distribute them as well. •The 8
people ate and were filled, and they picked up the leftover fragments,
seven large baskets. •Now there were about four thousand men there. 9
And he sent them away. •Then he got into the boat with his disciples 10
and went to the district of Dalmanutha.

•ʲ The Pharisees came out and began to argue with him, demanding 11
of him a sign from Heaven and putting him to the test. •And after groan- 12
ing deeply in his spirit he said,

"Why does this generation seek a sign?
Amen I say to you, *no* sign will be given
    to this generation."

•Then he left them, embarked once again, and went off to the oth- 13
er side.

•ᵏ Now they had forgotten to bring bread, and except for one loaf 14
they had none with them in the boat. •He was instructing them and say- 15
ing, "Take care! Watch out for the leaven of the Pharisees and the leav-
en of Herod!" •but they kept arguing among themselves because they 16
didn't have bread. •Realizing this, he said to them, "Why are you argu- 17
ing because you don't have bread?

Do you still neither see nor understand?
    Do *you* have hardened hearts?
•**Can't you see with your eyes?**
    Can't you hear with your ears?   18

ⁱ *Mt 15:32-39.*   ʲ *Mt 16:1-4.*   ᵏ *Mt 16:5-12.*   8:18 Jr 5:21.

19 Don't you remember •when I broke the five loaves for the five thou-
20 sand, how many baskets full of leftovers you picked up?" "Twelve," they
said. •"And the seven for the four thousand, how many large baskets
21 full of leftovers did you pick up?" "Seven," they said. •Then he said to
22 them, "Don't you understand yet?" •They came to Bethsaida. The people there brought a blind man to him and begged him to touch him.
23 •So he took the blind man by the hand and led him out of the village.
After spitting on his eyes and laying his hands on him Jesus asked him,
24 "Do you see anything?" •And when the man looked up he said, "I see
25 men, as if I'm looking at trees walking around." •Once again he laid
his hands on the man's eyes; then his vision was restored and he was
26 able to see everything clearly. •Then Jesus sent him to his house, saying, "Don't even go into the village."

I. TRANSFIGURATION AND LACK OF FAITH

27 •ˡ Then Jesus and his disciples left for the villages of Caesarea Philip-
28 pi, and on the way he asked his disciples, "Who do people say I am?" •So
they told him, "Some say, 'John the Baptist,' and others, 'Elijah,' while
29 others say, 'One of the prophets.'" •"But you," he asked them, "who do
30 you say I am?" In answer Peter said to him, "You're the Messiah!" •Then
Jesus commanded them not to tell anyone about him.
31 •ᵐ Then he began to teach them that the Son of Man would have
to suffer greatly and be rejected by the elders and the chief priests and
32 the scribes and be put to death and rise after three days, •and he said
this openly. Peter took him aside and began to remonstrate with him,
33 •but Jesus turned and, looking at his disciples, rebuked Peter and said,
"Get behind me, Satan — you're not thinking the thoughts of God but
34 of men!" •Then he called the crowd to him, along with his disciples,
and said to them,

> "If anyone would be my disciple, he must deny himself
> And take up his cross and follow me.
35 •For whoever would save his life will lose it,
> And whoever loses his life for my sake and the sake
> of the good news will save it.
36 •For what good does it do to gain the whole world
> yet forfeit your life?

ˡ *Mt 16:13-20; Lk 9:18-21.*   ᵐ *Mt 16:13-20; Lk 9:22-27.*

8:27 This area was north of Galilee, near the foothills of Mount Hermon.

•For what would you give in exchange for your life? 37

•Anyone in this adulterous and sinful generation 38
who is ashamed of me and my words,
Of him will the Son of Man also be ashamed
when he comes in the glory of his Father
with the holy angels."

9 •And he said to them, "Amen, I say to you, there are some who are 1
standing here who will not taste death until they see the Kingdom of
God has come with power."

•[n] Six days later Jesus took Peter and James and John along and led 2
them up a high mountain all alone. He was transformed in front of them
•and his clothes became an utterly glistening white, so white that no one 3
on earth could bleach them that way. •Elijah appeared to them along 4
with Moses, and they were talking together with Jesus. •So in response 5
Peter said to Jesus, "Rabbi, it's good for us to be here; let's put up three
dwellings, one for you, one for Moses, and one for Elijah." •For he did- 6
n't know what to say — they were terrified. •Then a cloud arose over- 7
shadowing them, and a voice from the cloud said, "This is My Beloved
Son, hear him!" •And suddenly as they looked around they no longer 8
saw anyone but Jesus alone with them.

•As they were coming down the mountain he commanded them not 9
to tell anyone what they'd seen until the Son of Man had risen from the
dead. •So they kept what he'd said to themselves, arguing about what 10
it meant to rise from the dead. •But they questioned him and said, "Why 11
do the scribes say that Elijah must come first?" •He said to them, "Eli- 12
jah *will* come first and restore all things, yet how can it be written of
the Son of Man that he'll suffer greatly and be scorned and rejected?
•On the contrary, I say to you that Elijah *has* come, and they did what- 13
ever they wanted with him, just as it's written of him."

•[o] As they were coming toward the disciples they saw a large crowd 14
around them and scribes arguing with them. •When they saw him the 15
whole crowd was greatly surprised and at once ran up and greeted him.

---

[n] *Mt 17:1-13; Lk 9:28-36.*   [o] *Mt 17:14-20; Lk 9:37-43.*

9:4 Moses and Elijah represent, respectively, the Torah and the Prophets, with Jesus as their fulfillment.

9:5 "Dwellings." This Greek word also means "tents," but was applied to the booths which the Jews constructed during the Feast of Tabernacles; they were meant to recall the way the Is-raelites lived during the Exodus.

9:11-13 Ml 3:23-24 (Ml 4:5-6). Jesus' words are a condemnation of Israel, for instead of repenting before the day of the Lord, John's call was not heeded, and now the day of the Lord is upon them in Jesus' ministry. Having failed to listen to John, Israel will, tragically, kill its Messiah.

MARK

16,17 •And he asked them, "What are you arguing about with them?" •One
of the crowd answered, "Teacher, I brought my son to you because he
18 has a dumb spirit; •whenever it seizes him it throws him to the ground
and he foams at the mouth and grinds his teeth and becomes stiff, and
19 I told your disciples to drive it out but they couldn't." •In answer to
them he said,

> "O unbelieving generation!
> How long will I be with you?
> How long will I put up with you?

20 Bring him to me!" •So they brought him to Jesus, and when the spirit saw him it at once threw the boy into convulsions, and he fell down
21 and kept rolling around, foaming at the mouth. •Jesus asked his father,
"How long has it been like this for him?" "From childhood," he said,
22 •"and it's often thrown him both into fire and into water in order to
23 kill him, but if you can do anything, help us and take pity on us." •Je-
sus said to him, "'*If* you can?' — all things are possible for the believ-
24 er!" •The father of the child cried out at once and said, "I believe; help

The "Gate of the Wind" which gives access to the fortress
which surrounds Mount Zion.

my unbelief!" •When Jesus saw that a crowd was quickly rushing over 25 he rebuked the unclean spirit and said to it, "Deaf and dumb spirit, I command you, come out of him and may you go into him no more!" •And after crying out and convulsing violently it came out, and the boy 26 lay as if he were dead, leading most of the people to say that he had died. •But Jesus took hold of his hand and raised him and he got up. 27 •When he entered the house his disciples asked him privately, "Why 28 couldn't we drive it out?" •And he said to them, "This kind can't be 29 driven out by anything but prayer."

J. TRUE AUTHORITY

•[p] After leaving there they went through Galilee, and he didn't want 30 anyone to know •because he was teaching his disciples and telling 31 them, "The Son of Man will be given over into the hands of men. They'll put him to death, and when he's been killed, after three days he'll rise." •But they couldn't understand what he meant and were 32 afraid to ask him.

•[q] Then they came to Capharnaum. When he was inside the house 33 he asked them, "What were you arguing about on the way?" •But they 34 were silent, because on the way they'd been arguing among themselves about who was the most important. •He sat down and called the Twelve 35 and said to them, "If anyone wishes to be first, he must be the last of all and the servant of all." •Then he took a child and stood it before them, 36 and he put his arms around it and said to them,

•"Whoever receives one such child in my name 37
    receives me;
And whoever receives me,
    receives not me but the One Who sent me."

•[r] John said to him, "Teacher, we saw someone driving out demons 38 in your name and we tried to stop him, because he wasn't following us." •But Jesus said, "Don't stop him — no one who does a mighty work in 39 my name will be able to speak ill of me soon afterwards, •for whoever's 40 not against us is for us. •Whoever gives you a cup of water in my name 41 because you're followers of the Messiah, amen, I say to you, he will not lose his reward."

[p] Mt 17:22-23; Lk Lk 9:43-45.   [q] Mt 18:1-5; Lk 9:46-48.   [r] Lk 9:49-50.

42 •ˢ "But whoever causes one of these little ones who believe in me to sin, it'd be better for him if a donkey's millstone were tied around his neck and he were thrown into the sea.

43 •If your hand causes you to sin, cut it off!
It's better for you to enter that life a cripple,
Than to go off with two hands to Gehenna,
44   to the unquenchable fire. [•]
45 •If your foot causes you to sin, cut it off!
It's better for you to enter that life lame,
46 Than to be thrown with two feet into Gehenna. [•]
47 •If your eye causes you to sin, pull it out!
It's better for you to enter the Kingdom of God one-eyed,
Than to have two eyes and be thrown into Gehenna,
48 •Where **their worm does not die,
and the fire is not extinguished,**
49 •For each will be salted with fire.
50 •Salt is good, but if the salt becomes unsalty,
   how will you season it?
Have salt within yourselves
   and be at peace with one another!"

K. OBSTACLES TO FAITH

1 **10**•ᵗ When he went up from there he went to the region of Judea [and] beyond the Jordan. Once again crowds gathered around 2 him, and again, as was his custom, he taught them. •Then the Pharisees came forward and asked him if it's lawful for a husband to put 3 his wife away, testing him. •In answer he said to them, "What did 4 Moses command you?" •They said, "Moses permitted a husband **to** 5 **write a bill of divorce and put his wife away.**" •Jesus said to them, "He wrote that commandment for you because of the hardness 6 of your heart. •But from the beginning of creation **He made them**

ˢ Mt 18:6-9; Lk 7:1-2.   ᵗ Mt 19:1-12.

9:43-45 "That life," i.e., the life of the Kingdom, as is made explicit in v. 47.
9:44 The best manuscript tradition omits this verse: "Where their worm doesn't die and the fire is not extinguished."
9:46 The best manuscript tradition omits this verse: "Where their worm doesn't die and the fire is not extinguished."
9:48 Is 66:24.
10:6 Gn 1:27.
10:4 Dt 24:1, 3.
10:7-8 Gn 2:24.

male and female; •for this reason a man shall leave his father 7
and mother and be united with his wife •and the two shall be- 8
come one flesh. So, then, they're no longer two but one flesh.
•Therefore, 9

> What God has joined together,
> Let man not separate."

•In the house the disciples asked him about this again. •And he said to 10,11
them, "Whoever puts his wife away and marries another woman commits adultery against his wife, •and if a wife puts her husband away and 12
marries another man, she commits adultery."

A Roman couple in a fresco of the 1st century A.D. (Mk 10:9)

•ᵘ People were bringing children to him for him to touch, but the 13
disciples rebuked them. •When Jesus saw this he became indignant 14
and said to them, "Let the children come to me! Don't stop them! For

ᵘ *Mt 19:13-15; Lk 18:15-17.*

15 of such as these is the Kingdom of God! •Amen, I say to you, whoever doesn't accept the Kingdom of God like a child shall not enter
16 it!" •Then he put his arms around the children and blessed them, laying his hands upon them.

17 •ᵛ As he was setting out on the road a man ran up and knelt before him. "Good Teacher," he asked, "what should I do to gain eternal life?"
18 •Jesus said to him, "Why do you call me good? No one is good but God
19 alone! •You know the commandments, **You shall not murder, you shall not commit adultery, you shall not steal, do not bear false witness, do not defraud, honor your father and mother.**"
20,21 •"Teacher," he said, "I've obeyed all these from my youth." •As Jesus gazed upon him he was moved with love for him and said, "One thing is left for you; go sell what you have and give to the poor and you'll have
22 treasure in Heaven, and come follow me." •But he was shocked by what Jesus had said and went off saddened, because he had many properties.

23 •Then Jesus looked around and said to his disciples, "How hard it will
24 be for those with wealth to enter the Kingdom of God!" •His disciples were astonished at his words. But Jesus, in response, again said to them,
25 "My children, how hard it is to enter the Kingdom of God; •it's easier for a camel to go through a needle's eye than for a rich man to enter the
26 Kingdom of God." •They were even more amazed and said to each oth-
27 er, "Then who can be saved?" •Jesus gazed at them and said,

> "For men it's impossible,
> But not for God;
> All things are possible for God."

28 •Peter spoke up and said, "You see we've left everything and followed
29 you." •Jesus said to him, "Amen, I say to you, there's no one who has left his house or brothers or sisters or mother or father or children or
30 fields for my sake and for the sake of the good news •who will not receive now, in this time, a hundredfold in houses and brothers and sisters and mothers and fields along with persecution, and in the coming age, life eternal.

31 •But many who are first will be last,
    and the last, first."

ᵛ Mt 19:16-30; Lk 18:18-30.   10:19 Ex 20:12-16.

L. TRUE AUTHORITY AND SPIRITUAL BLINDNESS

•^w Now they were on the road going up to Jerusalem and Jesus was 32 leading them, and they were amazed, but those following were afraid. Once again he took the Twelve and began to tell them the things that were going to happen to him. •"Behold, we're going up to Jerusalem, 33 and the Son of Man will be handed over to the chief priests and the scribes. They'll condemn him to death and hand him over to the Gentiles; •they'll mock him and spit on him and scourge him and kill him, 34 and after three days he'll rise."

•^x Then James and John, the sons of Zebedee, approached him and 35 said to him, "Teacher, we want you to do for us whatever we ask of you." •"What do you want me to do for you?" he asked. •"Grant," they said, 36,37 "that we may sit, one at your right hand and one at your left hand, in your glory." •But Jesus said to them, "You don't know what you're asking for! 38

Can you drink the cup I am drinking,
Or be baptized with the baptism with which
I am being baptized?"

•"We can," they said. But Jesus said to them, 39

"The cup I am drinking,
you will drink,
And with the baptism with which
I am being baptized,
you will be baptized,
•But sitting at my right hand or left is not 40
mine to give —
it's for those for whom it's been prepared."

•When the other ten heard about this they became indignant at James 41 and John. •So Jesus called them all together and said, "You know that 42

Those considered rulers among the Gentiles
lord it over them,
And their leaders exercise authority over them.

•But it must not be like that among you; instead, 43

Whoever would be great among you,
must be your servant,

---

^w *Mt 20:17-19; Lk 18:31-34.*   ^x *Mt 20:20-28.*

44 •And whoever would be first among you,
        must be the slave of all;
45 •For even the Son of Man came, not to be served,
        but to serve,
        and to give his life as a ransom for many."

46 •[y] Then they came to Jericho. When he was leaving Jericho, with both his disciples and a considerable crowd, blind Bartimaeus — the son of
47 Timaeus — was sitting by the road, begging. •And when he heard that it was Jesus of Nazareth he began to cry out, "Jesus, Son of David, have
48 mercy on me!" •Many of the people were telling him to be quiet, but he
49 cried out all the more, "Son of David, have mercy on me!" •Jesus stopped and said, "Call him!" They called the blind man and said to him, "Take
50 courage! Get up! He's calling you!" •So he threw off his cloak, jumped
51 up, and came to Jesus. •And in answer to him Jesus said, "What do you want me to do for you?" The blind man said to him, "Rabbi, please let
52 me see again!" •Jesus said to him, "Go your way, your faith has saved you!" At once he regained his sight and followed him along the road.

M. JESUS' MINISTRY IN JERUSALEM

1 **11** •[z] When they drew near to Jerusalem, to Bethphage and Bethany
2 at the Mount of Olives, he sent two of his disciples •and told them, "Go into the village opposite you, and immediately upon entering it you'll find a colt tied up, which no one has ever sat on before; untie it and
3 bring it. •And if anyone says to you, 'Why are you doing that?' say, 'The
4 Lord has need of it and will send it back here again at once!'" •They went off and found the colt tied by the door out on the street, and they
5 untied it. •Some of those standing there said to them, "What are you
6 doing, untying the colt?" •They told them just what Jesus had said, and
7 they let them go. •So they took the colt to Jesus and threw their cloaks
8 over it and he sat on it. •Many people spread their cloaks on the road,

[y] Mt 20:29-34; Lk 18:35-43.   [z] Mt 21:1-11; Lk 19:28-40; Jn 12:12-19.

11:1 Beginning with Jesus' entry into Jerusalem the fulfillment of Jesus' mission moves inexorably to its climax. As seen through the eyes of faith, all these events are "in accordance with the Scriptures," and the account is punctuated with frequent references to Scripture in order to underline this. All Jesus' words and actions are now seen in their full eschatological significance: the Kingdom has come and, following the Lord's atoning death, it will be proclaimed to all nations. 11:7 Significantly, the colt is the mount of the Prince of Peace for all nations at Zc 9:9. Jesus graphically indicates in his triumphal entry to the Holy City of the Jews that his mission is to all nations.

while others spread leafy branches which they had cut from the fields. •Both those going ahead and those following kept shouting,   9

> "Hosanna!
> Blessed is he who comes in the name of the Lord!
> •Blessed is the coming Kingdom of our father David!   10
> Hosanna in the highest!"

•When he entered Jerusalem he went to the Temple and, after looking   11 around at everything, since it was by now the evening hour he went out to Bethany with the Twelve.

•[a] The next day as they were leaving Bethany Jesus was hungry. •And   12,13 seeing from a distance a fig tree which had leaves on it, he went to see if he could find anything to eat, but when he came up to it he found it had nothing but leaves, because it wasn't the season for figs. •And in   14 response he said to it, "May no one ever eat fruit from you ever again!" And his disciples heard it.

•[b] When they came to Jerusalem he went into the Temple and began   15 to drive out those who were selling and buying in the Temple. He over-turned the tables of the moneychangers and the seats of those who sold the doves, •and he didn't let anyone carry anything through the Tem-   16 ple. •And he taught and said to them, "Is it not written,   17

> **My house shall be called a house of prayer**
> **for all the nations,**
> But you have made it a **robbers' den**!"

•When the chief priests and scribes heard this they began to consid-   18 er how they could do away with him, for they were afraid of him be-cause all the people were astonished at his teaching. •And in the evening   19 Jesus and his disciples left and went outside the city.

•[c] As they were passing by early in the morning they saw the fig   20 tree shrivelled up from its roots. •Peter remembered and said to him,   21 "Rabbi! Look! The fig tree you cursed has shrivelled up!" •In response   22 Jesus said to them, "If you have faith in God, •amen, I say to you,   23 whoever says to this mountain, 'Be taken away and thrown into the sea!' and doesn't doubt in his heart but believes that what he says will

[a] Mt 21:18-19.   [b] Mt 21:12-17; Lk 19:45-48; Jn 2:13-22.   [c] Mt 21:20-22.

11:15-17 In quoting Scripture Jesus combines Is 56:7 and Jr 7:11.

24 happen, it will come to be for him. •Therefore I say to you, whatever you pray for and ask for, believe that you've received it and it will
25 be yours. •And whenever you stand in prayer, forgive whatever you have against anyone so that your Father in Heaven will also forgive
26 you your offenses." [•]

Money-changer on a Roman engraved stone (2nd century A.D.). (Mk 11:15)

N. CONFLICT WITH THE LEADERS OF ISRAEL

27 •[d] They came to Jerusalem again, and as he was walking about in the Temple the chief priests and scribes and the elders came up to him
28 •and said, "By what authority do you do these things? Who gave you
29 the authority to do these things?" •But Jesus said to them, "I'll ask you one question; answer me and I'll tell you by what authority I do these
30 things — •John's baptism, was it from Heaven or from men? Answer
31 me!" •They began to argue among themselves, saying, "If we say, 'From
32 Heaven,' he'll say, 'Then why didn't you believe him?' •but can we say, 'From men'?" — they were afraid of the people because they all held

[d] Mt 21:23-27; Lk 20:1-8.

11:26 Some manuscript traditions include v. 26 here: "But if you don't forgive, neither will your Father in Heaven forgive you your trespasses."

that John had, indeed, been a prophet. •So in answer to Jesus they 33
said, "We don't know." And Jesus said to them, "Nor will I tell you by
what authority I do these things."

12 •ᵉ Then he began to speak to them in parables. "A man **plant-** 1
ed a vineyard, and he placed a hedge around it, dug a
trough for the wine press, and built a tower. Then he leased it to
farmers and went off on a journey. •When the proper time came he sent 2
a servant to the farmers so he could take some of the fruits of the vineyard, •but they took him and beat him and sent him away empty-hand- 3
ed. •Again he sent another servant to them, and they beat that one about 4
the head and treated him shamefully. •He sent another, and they killed 5
that one. And he sent many others, some of whom were beaten while
others were killed. •He still had one, a beloved son; he sent him to them 6
last, saying, 'They'll feel shame before my son.' •But these farmers said 7
to each other, 'This is the heir; come on, let's kill him and the inheritance
will be ours!' •So they took and killed him and threw him outside the vine- 8
yard. •What, then, will the lord of the vineyard do? He'll come and do 9
away with the farmers and give the vineyard to others. •Haven't you read 10
this passage?

The stone which the builders rejected
    has become the cornerstone;
•Through the Lord has this been done 11
    and it is wonderful in our eyes."

•They wanted to seize him but they were afraid of the people, because they 12
knew he'd spoken the parable against them. So they left him and went off.

O. TRUE TORAH AND TRUE AUTHORITY

•ᶠ Next they sent some of the Pharisees and Herodians to him to trap 13
him in speech. •They came and said to him, "Teacher, we know that 14
you're truthful and are influenced by no one, for you don't consider the
person but truly teach the way of God; is it lawful to pay the tax to Caesar or not? Should we pay or should we not pay?" •But he realized their 15
hypocrisy and said to them, "Why are you testing me? Bring me a denarius so I can look at it." •So they brought one. Then he said to them, 16

ᵉ Mt 21:33-46; Lk 20:9-19.   ᶠ Mt 22:15-22; Lk 20:20-26.

12:1 Cf. Is 5:1-2.   12:10-11 Ps 118:22-23.

"Whose image is this, and whose inscription?" "Caesar's," they said.
17 •Then Jesus said,

> "Render to Caesar the things that are Caesar's,
> and to God the things that are God's."

And they were amazed at him.

18 •[g] Then the Sadducees came to him — those who say there's no res-
19 urrection — and they questioned him, saying, •"Teacher, Moses wrote for us that if a man's brother should die and leave a wife behind but not leave a child, the brother should take his wife and raise up offspring for
20 his brother. •There were seven brothers, and the first took a wife and
21 he died without offspring; •and the second took her and died without
22 leaving offspring, and the third likewise; •and the seven left no offspring.
23 Last of all the woman died, too. •When they rise at the resurrection
24 whose wife will she be? — all seven brothers had her as wife." •Jesus said to them, "Isn't this the reason you go astray, that you understand
25 neither the Scriptures nor the power of God? •For when you rise from the dead you neither marry nor are given in marriage, but are like the
26 angels in Heaven. •But as for the dead rising, haven't you read in the scroll of Moses, at the passage about the thorn bush, how God spoke to him, and said, **I am the God of Abraham and the God of Isaac**
27 **and the God of Jacob**? •He's not God of the dead but of the living; you've gone seriously astray."

28 •[h] One of the scribes who had been listening to them arguing came forward when he saw that Jesus had answered them well and asked him,
29 "What commandment is the first of all?" •Jesus answered, "The first is,
30 **Hear, O Israel, the Lord your God is One, •and you shall love the Lord your God with your whole heart and with your whole soul** and with all your understanding, **and with your whole strength.**
31 •This is the second, **You shall love your neighbor as yourself.** There
32 is no other commandment greater than these." •And the scribe said to him, "Indeed, Teacher, you spoke truly when you said that **There is One**
33 **and there is no other beside Him,** •and, **Love Him with your whole heart and your whole mind and your whole strength,** and, **Love your neighbor as yourself**, are greater than all the burnt of-
34 ferings and sacrifices." •Jesus, seeing that he had answered wisely, said to him, "You're not far from the Kingdom of God." And no one dared to question him any more.

[g] Mt 22:23-33; Lk 20:27-40.   [h] Mt 22:34-40; Lk 1:25-28.

12:26 Ex 3:6, 15, 16.	12:31 Lv 19:18.	12:33 Dt 6:5; Lv 19:18.
12:29-30 Dt 6:4-5.	12:32 Dt 4:35.	

•[i] And in response, while teaching in the Temple, Jesus said, "How 35 can the scribes say that the Messiah is the son of David? •David himself 36 said in the Holy Spirit,

> **The Lord said to my lord,**
> **'Sit at My right hand**
> **till I put your enemies under your feet.'**

•David himself calls him 'lord,' so how can he be David's son?" And a 37 large crowd listened to him eagerly.

•[j] And in his teaching he said, 38

> "Beware of the scribes,
> Who like walking about in long robes
>   and greetings in the marketplaces,
> •And seats of honor in the synagogues 39
>   and places of honor at the banquets;
> •They eat up the houses of widows 40
>   and say long prayers as a pretense —
> These will receive the greater condemnation!"

•[k] Then he took a seat opposite the offering box and watched the 41 crowd toss money into the offering box. Many rich people tossed in a great deal, •but when one poor widow came she tossed in two small 42 coppers, that is, about a penny. •He called his disciples together and 43 said to them, "Amen, I say to you, this poor widow tossed in more than all the others who tossed money into the offering box — •they all tossed 44 in from their abundance, but she from her want tossed in all that she had, her whole livelihood."

P. PROPHECIES OF THE END TIME

13 •[l] As he was leaving the Temple one of his disciples said to him, 1 "Teacher, look at how wonderful the stones and the buildings are!" •Jesus said to him, "Do you see these great buildings? Not a stone 2 will be left here upon a stone that won't be torn down."

---

[i] Mt 22:41-46; Lk 20:41-44.   [j] Mt 23:1-36; Lk 20:45-47.   [k] Lk 21:1-4.   [l] Mt 24:1-2; Lk 21:5-6.

12:36 Ps 110:1.
12:38-40 The tendency for Pharisaism to de- recognized in ancient times, cf. 7:5-13 and the
generate into formalism and hypocrisy was well note at Mt 23:1ff.

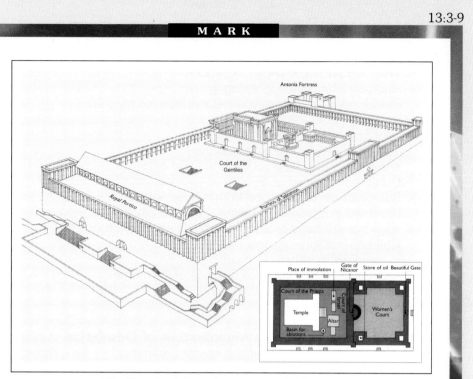

The Temple of Jerusalem at the time of Jesus.

3 •ᵐ While he was sitting on the Mount of Olives, opposite the Temple, Peter and James and John and Andrew questioned him privately.
4 •"Tell us when these things will happen, and what the sign will be that
5 all these things are about to be fulfilled." •So Jesus spoke out and told
6 them, "See that no one leads you astray; •many will come in my name
7 saying, '*I'm* the one,' and they'll lead many astray. •But when you hear of wars and rumors of wars, don't be alarmed; this must happen, but it's not yet the end.

8 •For nation shall rise against nation,
    and kingdom against kingdom,
There will be earthquakes in various places,
    there will be famines;

9 these things are the beginning of the birth pains. •But look out for yourselves;

ᵐ Mt 24:3-14; Lk 21:7-19.

They will hand you over to councils,
And you'll be beaten in synagogues.
Before rulers and kings you'll stand firm for my sake,
As a witness to them.
•But first to all the nations   10
The good news must be proclaimed.
•And when they lead you to hand you over,   11
Don't worry ahead of time what you will say;
But whatever is given you in that hour, say it;
For it will not be you speaking, but the Holy Spirit.
•Brother will hand brother over to death, and father, child.   12
Children will rebel against parents,
        and will put them to death;
•And you'll be hated by all because of my name.   13
But whoever holds out to the end,
        he shall be saved."

•[n] "But when you see **the Abomination of Desolation** standing 14
where he should not be — let the reader understand — then those in
Judea must flee to the mountains, •the man on his housetop must not 15
descend nor go in to take anything from his house, •and the man in his 16
field must not turn back to get his cloak. •But woe to women who are 17
with child and to those who are nursing in those days! •Pray that it won't 18
happen in winter, •for in those days there will be **suffering such as** 19
has not been since the beginning of the creation God created **up till**
now, and will not be. •And if the Lord had not shortened those days 20
no fleshly creature would be saved, but for the sake of those whom He
has chosen He did shorten those days. •And then, if anyone says, 'Look, 21
here's the Messiah!' or 'Look there!' don't believe it. •For false messi- 22
ahs and false prophets will rise up and will produce signs and wonders
to deceive, if possible, the chosen ones. •But look out for yourselves; 23
I've told you everything ahead of time."

•[o] "But in those days,   24
        after that suffering,
The sun will be darkened
        and the moon will not give its light,

[n] Mt 24:15-28; Lk 21:20-24.   [o] Mt 24:29-31; Lk 21:25-28.

13:14 Dn 9:27. "Abomination of Desolation."   crating it.
This phrase from Daniel envisions a Gentile, here   13:19 Dn 12:1.
a Roman, presence in the Temple, thus dese-   13:24-25 Is 13:10, 34:4; Ezk 32:7-8.

25   •**And the stars will be falling** from the heavens,
        and the powers in the heavens will be shaken.
26   •Then they'll see **the Son of Man**
        coming on clouds with great power and glory.
27   •And then he'll send the angels
        and will gather the chosen from the four winds,
      From the ends of the earth to the ends of the heavens."

28   •[p] "So learn the parable from the fig tree. As soon as its branch be-
      comes tender and is putting out leaves, you know that summer is near.
29   •So, too, when you see these things happening, you'll know that he's
30   near, at the very gates. •Amen, I say to you, this generation will not pass
      away until all these things take place.

31   •The heavens and the earth will pass away,
      But my words will not pass away."

32   •[q] "But as for that day or hour, no one knows — not the angels in
33   Heaven nor the Son, but only the Father. •See that you're watchful, for
34   you don't know when the appointed time is. •It's like a man leaving on
      a journey. When he left his household he gave authority to his servants
      — each received a task — and he ordered the doorkeeper to stay awake.
35   •So stay awake, for you don't know when the lord of the household is
      coming, whether in the evening or in the middle of the night or at cock
36   crow or in the morning. •You don't want him to come suddenly and find
37   you sleeping! •But what I say to you I say to all — stay awake!"

Q. THE PASSION

1   **14** •[r] Now the Passover and feast of Unleavened Bread was in two
              days and the chief priests and scribes were considering how they
2   could seize Jesus on a pretext and kill him, •for they said, "If we wait
    till the festival there might be an outcry among the people."
3   •[s] While he was at Bethany, reclining at table in Simon the leper's
    house, a woman came with an alabaster jar of pure oil of nard, of great

[p] Mt 24:32-35; Lk 21:29-33.   [q] Mt 24:36-44.
[r] Mt 26:1-5; Lk 22:1-2; Jn 11:45-53.   [s] Mt 26:6-13; Jn 12:1-8.

13:26 Dn 7:13-14.
14:1 The eight day period during which unleavened bread was eaten was closely linked to the

Passover, but had its origins in a festival marking
the beginning of the barley harvest.
14:2 Literally, "Not during the festival."

value; after breaking the alabaster jar she poured the oil over his head. •But there were some there who were indignant and said to themselves, 4 "To what purpose was this waste of oil? •It could have been sold for more 5 than three hundred denarii and given to the poor," and they criticized her harshly. •But Jesus said, "Let her be! Why are you bothering her? 6 She's done a beautiful thing for me.

•For the poor you always have with you — 7

and whenever you want you can do good to them,

but me you will not always have.

•She's done what she could; she's anointed my body in advance in prepa- 8 ration for burial. •Amen, I say to you, wherever the good news is proclaimed 9 in all the world, what she did will also be told in memory of her."

•[t] Then Judas Iscariot, one of the Twelve, went off to the chief priests 10 in order to hand him over to them. •When they heard this they were 11 overjoyed and promised to pay him with silver money, and he began to consider when the best time to hand Jesus over would be.

•[u] On the first day of the Unleavened Bread, when they sacrificed the 12 Passover lamb, his disciples said to him, "Where do you want us to go to prepare for you to eat the Passover?" •He sent two of his disciples 13 and told them, "Go into the city, and a man carrying a clay jar of wa- ter will meet you; follow him, •and wherever he goes in, say to the house- 14 holder, 'Teacher says, "Where is my room where I'll eat the Passover with my disciples?"' • And he'll show you a large, furnished, upstairs 15 room which has been prepared; make ready for us there." •So the dis- 16 ciples left and went to the city and found it just as he told them, and they prepared the Passover.

•When it was evening he came with the Twelve. •And while they were 17,18 reclining and were eating, Jesus said, "Amen, I say to you, one of you will hand me over, **one who is eating with me.**" •They became dis- 19 tressed and asked him, one by one, "Surely not me?" •but he said to 20 them, "One of the Twelve, one who is dipping [bread] into the bowl with me. •Because the Son of Man is going as it is written about him, but 21 woe to that man by whom the Son of Man is handed over; it would be better for him if that man had not been born."

---

[t] Mt 26:14-16; Lk 22:3-6.   [u] Mt 26:17-25; Lk 22:7-14, 21-33; Jn 13:21-30.
[v] Mt 26:26-30; Lk 22:15-20.

14:5 Since a denarius was equal to a laborer's daily wage, 300 denarii was a truly large amount of money.
14:18 Ps 41:9.

The "Little Cenacle" near Mount Zion and Jerusalem.

22 •ᵛ And while they were eating he took bread, blessed it, broke it, gave
23 it to them and said, "Take it; this is my body." •And taking the cup, he
24 blessed it and gave it to them and they all drank from it. •Then he said
to them, "This is my blood of the covenant, which will be poured out
25 for many. •Amen, I say to you, I will not drink again of the fruit of the
26 vine until that day when I drink it new in the Kingdom of God." • And
after singing a hymn they went out to the Mount of Olives.
27 •ʷ Then Jesus said to them, "All of you will lose your faith, because
it is written,

**I will strike the shepherd
and the sheep will be scattered,**

28,29 •but after I rise I'll go ahead of you into Galilee." •But Peter said to him,
30 "Even if they all lose their faith, *I* won't!" •Jesus said to him, "Amen, I
say to you, today, this very night, before the rooster crows twice, you'll

ʷ *Mt 26:31-35; Lk 22:31-34; Jn 13:36-38.*

14:26 "Hymn." This term refers to Ps 114-118, which were sung as part of the Passover supper liturgy.
14:27 Zc 13:7.

deny me three times." •But Peter kept saying, "Even if it comes to dy- 31
ing with you, I won't deny you." And they all said the same, too.

•[x] When they came to a place named Gethsemane he said to his dis- 32
ciples, "Sit here while I pray." •He took Peter and James and John along 33
with him and he became very distressed and troubled, •and he said to 34
them, "My soul is greatly distressed, to the point of death; stay here and
keep watch." •Then he went ahead a little, fell on the ground, and prayed 35
that, if it were possible, this moment might pass away from him, •and 36
he said, "Abba, Father, all things are possible for You; take this cup from
me, but not what I wish, but what You do." •When he came back he 37
found them sleeping, and he said to Peter, "Simon, are you sleeping?
Couldn't you stay awake for one hour? •Stay awake and pray that you 38
won't come to the test,

> For the spirit is willing,
> But the flesh is weak."

•Then he went off and prayed again, saying the same words. •When he 39,40
came again he found them sleeping, for their eyes were very heavy, and
they didn't know what to answer him. •He came the third time and said 41
to them, "Are you going to keep sleeping and resting? It's settled; the
hour has come; behold, the Son of Man will be handed over into the
hands of sinners. •Get up! Let's be going! Behold, the one who will hand 42
me over has come."

•[y] And right then, while he was still speaking, Judas, one of the 43
Twelve, arrived, and with him a crowd with swords and clubs from the
chief priests and the scribes and the elders. •Now, the one handing him 44
over had arranged to give them a signal, saying, "Whoever I kiss is the
one; seize him and lead him away under guard." •Judas came right up 45
to him and said, "Rabbi!" and kissed him. •So they laid hands on him 46
and seized him. •Then one of those present drew his sword, struck the 47
high priest's slave, and cut off his ear. •In answer Jesus said to them, 48
"You came out with swords and clubs to seize me, as if you were after
a robber? •I was among you daily, teaching in the Temple, yet you did- 49
n't seize me; but let the Scriptures be fulfilled." •Then they all aban- 50
doned him and fled.

•A certain young man was following, wearing a linen cloth on his 51
bare body, and they seized him, •but he left the linen behind and fled 52
naked.

[x] Mt 26:36-46; Lk 22:39-46.   [y] Mt 26:47-56; Lk 22:47-53; Jn 18:3-12.
[z] Mt 26:57-68; Lk 22:54-55, 63-71; Jn 18:13-14, 19-24.

53 •ᶻ So they led Jesus off to the high priest, and all the chief priests and
54 elders and scribes came together. •Peter had followed him at a distance
right inside into the courtyard of the high priest and was sitting with the
55 Temple attendants, warming himself at the fire. •Now the chief priests
and the whole Sanhedrin were seeking testimony against Jesus in order
56 to put him to death, yet they found none; •although many gave false
57 testimony against Jesus, their testimony didn't agree. •Some had stood
58 up and given false testimony against Jesus and said, •"We heard him
say, 'I'll tear down this sanctuary made by hands and in three days I'll
59 build another not made by hands.'" •Yet their testimony didn't agree in
60 this, either. •Then the high priest stood up and questioned Jesus, saying, "You make no answer? Why are these men testifying against you?"
61 •But he remained silent and made no answer. Again the high priest questioned him and said to him, "Are you the Messiah, the Son of the Blessed
62 One?" •Jesus said, "I am, and

**You will see the Son of Man
seated at the right hand of Power
and coming with the clouds of Heaven."**

63 •At this the high priest tore his clothing and said, "What further need do
64 we have for witnesses? •You heard the blasphemy! What's your opinion?"
65 And they all judged him to be deserving of death. •Then some began to
spit on him and cover his face and strike him, and to say, "Prophesy!"
and the Temple attendants took him away, beating him as they went.

66 •ᵃ While Peter was down in the courtyard one of the high priest's maid-
67 servants came, •and when she saw Peter warming himself she took a
closer look at him and said, "You were with Jesus the Nazarene, too!"
68 •But he denied it and said, "I neither know nor understand what you're
saying!" And he went outside into the gateway [and a rooster crowed].
69 •When the maidservant saw him she again began to tell the bystanders,
70 "This fellow's one of them!" •but he denied it again. After a little while
the bystanders again said to Peter, "Surely you're one of them — you're
71 a Galilean, too!" •And he put himself under a curse and swore an oath,
72 "I don't know the man you're talking about!" •At that moment a cock
crowed a second time. Then Peter remembered what had been said, how
Jesus had told him, "Before a cock crows twice you'll deny me three
times," and he stormed out weeping.

ᵃ Mt 26:69-75; Lk 22:56-62; Jn 18:15-18, 25-27.

14:62 Dn 7:13.

15 •[b] As soon as it was morning the chief priests held a council with 1 the elders and scribes and the whole Sanhedrin. They bound Jesus, sent him off, and handed him over to Pilate. •And Pilate asked him, 2 "Are you the King of the Jews?" But in answer he said to him, "You say so." •And the chief priests kept making accusations against him. •But 3,4 Pilate questioned him again and said, "Do you have no answer? Look how many accusations they're bringing against you!" •But Jesus made 5 no further reply, to Pilate's amazement.

•[c] At the festival Pilate used to release to them any one prisoner 6 they asked for. •Now there was a man called Barabbas who was im- 7 prisoned with the rebels who had committed murder in the revolt, •and 8 when the crowd came it began to request him to do what he usually did for them. •Pilate responded, "Do you want me to release to you 9 the King of the Jews?" •for he was aware that the chief priests had 10 handed Jesus over out of envy. •But the chief priests stirred up the 11 crowd to get him to release Barabbas to them instead. •So in answer 12 Pilate again said to them, "Then what shall I do with the King of the Jews?" •Again they cried out, "Crucify him!" •So Pilate said to them, 13,14 "But what wrong has he done?" but they cried out all the more, "Crucify him!" •So Pilate, because he wanted to satisfy the crowd, released 15 Barabbas to them, and after having Jesus scourged he handed him over to be crucified.

•[d] So the soldiers led him away inside the courtyard, that is, the prae- 16 torium, and called the whole cohort together. •They dressed him in a 17 purple robe and put on him a crown they had woven from thorns, •and 18 they began to greet him, "Hail, King of the Jews!" •Then they'd hit his 19 head with a reed, and spit on him and kneel and worship him. •And 20 when they had mocked him they stripped the purple robe off him, dressed him in his own clothes, and led him out to be crucified.

•[e] They forced a passerby, one Simon of Cyrene, father of Alexan- 21 der and Rufus, who was coming from the country, to take up his cross, •and they brought him to the place called Golgotha, which, translated, 22 is, "the Place of the Skull." •They tried to give him wine mixed with 23 myrrh, but he didn't take it. •Then they crucified him, 24

and they **divided** his **clothes among them,**
casting lots for them to see who would take what.

[b] Mt 27:1-2, 11-14; Lk 23:1-5; Jn 18:28-38.   [c] Mt 27:15-26; Lk 23:13-25; Jn 18:39 - 19:16.
[d] Mt 27:27-31; Jn 19:2-3.   [e] Mt 27:32-44; Lk 23:26-43; Jn 19:17-27.

15:24 Ps 22:18.

25,26 •Now it was mid morning when they crucified him. •The inscription of
27 the charge against him was written, "The King of the Jews," •and they
28 crucified two robbers with him, one on his right and one on his left. [•]
29 •The passersby blasphemed him, **shaking their heads** and saying,
"Ha! You who would tear down the sanctuary and build it up in three
30,31 days, •save yourself by coming down from the cross!" •The chief priests,
likewise, made fun of him to each other and to the scribes and said, "He
32 saved others but can't save himself! •Let the Messiah, the King of Israel, come down now from the cross so we can see and believe!" Those
crucified with him also derided him.

*Archaeological inscription found at Caesarea which mentions
"Pontius Pilate, prefect of Judea".*

33 •ᶠ Now at about noon darkness came over the whole land until three.
34 •And at three o'clock Jesus cried out with a loud voice, *"Eloi, Eloi, lema
sabachthani?"* which, translated, is, **"My God, my God, why have
35 You forsaken me?"** •Some of the bystanders heard it and said, "See?

ᶠ *Mt 27:45-46; Lk 23:44-49; Jn 19:28-30.*

15:28 The best manuscript tradition omits this
verse: "And the scripture was fulfilled which says,   **He was numbered among criminals."** Is 53:12.
15:29 Ps 22:7.   15:34 Ps 22:1.

M A R K

He's calling Elijah!" •Someone ran and, filling a sponge with sour wine, 36 put it on a reed and gave it to him to drink, saying, "Let's see if Elijah comes to take him down." •But Jesus let out a loud cry and died, •and 37,38 the curtain of the sanctuary was torn in two from top to bottom. •When 39 the centurion standing facing him saw that he'd died in this way he said, "Truly this man *was* the Son of God!" •There were also women there 40 watching from a distance, among them Mary Magdalen and Mary mother of James the younger and Joses, Salome — •they had followed him 41 when he was in Galilee and served him — and many other women who had come up with him to Jerusalem.

•[g] Evening had now come. Since it was the Day of Preparation, that 42 is, the day before the Sabbath, •Joseph of Arimathea, a respected Coun- 43 cil member who himself was also awaiting the Kingdom of God, dared to go in to Pilate and ask for the body of Jesus. •But Pilate was amazed 44 that he was already dead, and he called in the centurion and asked whether Jesus had been dead for very long, •and after learning it from 45 the centurion he bestowed the corpse on Joseph. •So Joseph bought a 46 linen shroud and took Jesus down, wrapped him in the linen shroud, and placed him in a tomb that had been hewn out of rock. Then he rolled a stone up against the door of the tomb. •But Mary Magdalen and Mary 47 mother of Joses watched where he was laid.

R. THE RESURRECTION
AND APPEARANCES OF JESUS

16 •[h] When the Sabbath was over Mary Magdalen and Mary the 1 mother of James and Salome bought spices so they could go anoint him. •And very early in the morning of the first day of the week 2 they came to the tomb when the sun had risen. •They were saying to 3 each other, "Who will roll the stone away from the door of the tomb for us?" •but when they looked up they saw that the stone had been 4 rolled away, for it was very large. •When they went into the tomb they 5 saw a young man seated on the right hand side, dressed in a white robe, and they were astonished. •"Don't be alarmed," he said, "you're look- 6

---

[g] *Mt 27:57-61; Lk 23:50-56; Jn 19:38-42.*   [h] *Mt 28:1-8; Lk 24:1-12; Jn 20:1-10.*

15:43 The bodies of executed criminals were not usually turned over for decent burial but were ig- nominiously disposed of in the Hinnom valley. Joseph may have been performing a pious act in accordance with Dt 21:22-23.

ing for Jesus the Nazarene who was crucified; he's risen, he's not here;
7 look at the place where they laid him! •But go tell his disciples and Peter, 'He's going ahead of you into Galilee; you'll see him there just as
8 he told you.'" •Then the women went out and fled the tomb, for trembling and amazement had seized them, and they said nothing to anyone because they were afraid.

9 •[i] Now when he rose in the early morning of the first day after the Sabbath he appeared first to Mary Magdalen, from whom he had driv-
10 en out seven demons. •She went to announce it to those who had been
11 with him, who were mourning and weeping; •and when they heard that he was alive and had been seen by her they refused to believe.

12 •[j] After this he appeared in a different form to two of them as they
13 were walking into the countryside, •and when they went and told the rest they didn't believe them either.

14 •[k] But later he appeared to the Eleven themselves as they reclined at table and reproached them for their unbelief and hardness of heart, be-
15 cause they hadn't believed those who had seen him risen. •And he said to them, "Go into the whole world and proclaim the good news to all cre-
16 ation. •Whoever believes and is baptized will be saved, but whoever does-
17 n't believe will be condemned. •But these signs will follow with those who believe — they'll drive out demons in my name, they'll speak in new
18 tongues, •they'll pick up snakes in their hands, and if they drink poison it won't harm them; they'll lay their hands on the sick and they'll be well."

19 •[l] So then the Lord, after speaking to them, was raised up to Heav-
20 en and took his seat at the right hand of God. •But they went out to proclaim the good news everywhere, the Lord working with them and confirming the word through the signs following upon it.

[i] Mt 28:9-10; Jn 20:11-18.   [j] Lk 24:13-35.
[k] Mt 28:16-20; Lk 24:36-49; Jn 20:19-23.   [l] Lk 24:50-53.

16:9-20 Some of the oldest manuscripts end the Gospel at 16:8, while other manuscripts continue with 16:9-20. There is also a shorter ending attested to, which adds immediately after 16:8: "And all these commands they told briefly to those around Peter. But after these things Jesus himself sent out through them, from the east unto the west, the holy and undying message of eternal salvation. Amen."

THE GOSPEL
ACCORDING TO

LUKE

Introduction to the Gospel
According to Luke

There is general agreement that Luke the physician, Paul's companion in Acts, was the author of the third Gospel.

Luke shares many of the same concerns that we have already seen in Matthew and Mark but, in addition, there is an emphasis that is unique in degree to Luke alone. This is his emphasis on God's loving forgiveness and the need for self-renunciation on the part of disciples. In addition, in this Gospel we see Jesus, time after time, reaching out to and championing the weak, the outcast, and the underdog, challenging shallow prejudices and presuppositions. Luke clearly had a flair for storytelling and many of the best loved Gospel stories (the Prodigal Son, the Good Samaritan, the Sinful Woman, etc.) are found in his Gospel, precisely in the context of God's, and Jesus', mercy and loving forgiveness and radical openness to all sinners. As in Mark, however, the unifying theme is Jesus' mission to all nations and his rejection by his own people, whose truest hopes he had fulfilled.

A. PROLOGUE

1 •Inasmuch as many others have undertaken to draw up an account
2 of the events which have been accomplished among us — •just as
those who were eyewitnesses and servants of the word from the be-
3 ginning have handed them down to us — •it seemed proper that I,
too, after carefully examining everything anew, should write you an
4 orderly account, most excellent Theophilus, •so that you may recognize the certainty of the words concerning which you have been instructed.

B. ORIGINS OF THE BAPTIST AND JESUS

5 •In the days of Herod, King of Judea, there was a priest named
Zechariah from the division of Abijah, and he had a wife from among
6 the daughters of Aaron whose name was Elizabeth. •They were both
righteous before God, blamelessly following all the commandments and
7 regulations of the Lord, •yet they had no child because Elizabeth was
8 barren, and they were both on in years. •Now it happened that when
he was doing his priestly service before God when his division was on
9 duty, •according to the custom of the priestly office, he was chosen by
10 lot to enter the sanctuary of the Lord to offer incense. •All the multitude of the people were outside praying at the hour of the incense of-
11 fering •when an angel of the Lord appeared to him, standing to the right

1:2 "Servants of the word." Elsewhere, the word translated "servant" is translated "attendant." The word has two principal uses in the Gospels, in the context of contemporary Judaism: (1) It refers to members of the Temple police force, and (2) it also refers to the synagogue official who had custody of the Scriptures, cf. Lk 4:20.

1:2 The expression "handed down" most probably refers to oral tradition, although it is entirely possible that by the time Luke began to compose

his Gospel some of the early traditions had been committed to a written form.

1:5 So that all priests could participate in the Temple services in an orderly fashion, the Judaic priesthood was divided into twenty-four "divisions." Each division served in the Temple twice a year, for a week at a time.

1:8-10 The action of the Gospel opens with the assembly of Israel gathered in the Temple under the Old Covenant.

of the incense altar. •Zechariah was terrified when he saw the angel and 12
was overcome with fear, •but the angel said to him, 13

"Fear not, Zechariah —
your petition has been heard.
Your wife Elizabeth will bear you a son,
and you shall name him John.
•Joy and gladness will be yours, 14
and many will rejoice at his birth.
•For he will be great before the Lord 15
and shall drink neither wine nor strong drink.
He will be filled with the Holy Spirit
right from his mother's womb,
•And he will bring back many of the sons of Israel 16
to the Lord their God.
•He will go before Him 17
in the spirit and power of Elijah,
To bring back the hearts of fathers to the children
and the rebellious to the wisdom of the upright,
To make ready for the Lord
a people made perfect."

•Zechariah said to the angel, "How can I be sure of this? — I'm elder- 18
ly and my wife is advanced in years." •And in answer the angel said to 19
him,

"I am Gabriel
who stands before God,
I was sent to speak to you
and bring you these good tidings,
•Now, behold, you shall be silent 20
and unable to speak until the day these things happen,
Because you did not believe my words,
which will be fulfilled at their proper time."

•Meanwhile the people were waiting for Zechariah and were won- 21
dering at how long he was staying in the sanctuary. •When he came out 22
he was unable to speak to them and they realized that he'd seen a vision in the sanctuary, because he kept making signs to them but remained mute. •And it happened that when the days of his liturgical serv- 23
ice were fulfilled he went off to his home. •After these days his wife Eliz- 24

1:17 MI 3:23-24 (MI 4:5-6).

LUKE

abeth became pregnant, and she secluded herself for five months, say-
25 ing, •"Thus has the Lord dealt with me in the days He deigned to take
away my disgrace before men."

26 •In the sixth month the angel Gabriel was sent from God to a city of
27 Galilee named Nazareth, •to a virgin who was betrothed to a man of
the house of David named Joseph, and the virgin's name was Mary.
28 •And when he came into her presence he said, "Hail, full of grace, the
29 Lord is with you!" •She was perplexed by these words and wondered
30 what sort of greeting this could be. •Then the angel said to her,

> "Fear not, Mary —
> you have found grace before the Lord.
31 •And, behold, you will conceive in your womb
> and will bear a son,
> and you shall name him Jesus.
32 •He will be great and will be called
> Son of the Most High,

Nazareth. Basilica of the Annunciation.

and the Lord God will give him the throne
   of his father, David.
•He will reign over the house of Jacob forever,   33
   and his Kingdom will have no end."

•Mary said to the angel, "How will this come about, since I do not know 34
man?" •And in answer the angel said to her,   35

"The Holy Spirit will come upon you,
And the power of the Most High
   will overshadow you;
Therefore, the holy child to be born
   will be called Son of God.
•And, behold, your kinswoman Elizabeth, even she   36
   conceived a son in her old age,
And this is the sixth month for her who was called barren.
•For **nothing will be impossible for God.**"   37

•Mary said,   38

"Behold, the handmaid of the Lord;
   let it be done to me according to your word."

Then the angel left her.
  •In those days Mary set out and went with solicitude into the hill coun- 39
try to a city of Judah, •and when she entered the house of Zechariah 40
she greeted Elizabeth. •And it happened when Elizabeth heard Mary's 41
greeting the baby leapt in her womb, Elizabeth was filled with the Holy
Spirit, •and she exclaimed with a loud cry, "Blessed are you among 42
women, and blessed is the fruit of your womb! •But how is it that the 43
mother of my Lord should come to *me*? •For, behold, when the sound 44
of your greeting came to my ears, the baby in my womb leapt with a
great joy. •Blessed is she who believed that there would be a fulfillment 45
of what was spoken to her by the Lord."
  •And Mary said,   46

"My soul gives praise to the Lord,
  •and my spirit rejoices in God my Savior;   47
•Because He had regard for the lowliness of His handmaid,   48

1:37 Gn 18:14.
1:42 The hymns which follow are replete with al- Magnificat, in particular shows a number of
lusions to the Old Testament. Mary's hymn, the marked similarities to the hymn at 1 S 2:1-10.

behold, henceforth all generations shall call me blessed,

49 •For the Mighty One has done great things for me,
and holy is His name,

50 •And His mercy is from generation to generation
toward those who fear Him.

51 •He has shown might with His arm,
scattered the arrogant in the conceit of their heart,

52 •He has pulled down the mighty from their thrones,
and exalted the lowly,

53 •The hungry He has filled with good things,
and the rich He has sent away empty.

54 •He has come to the aid of His servant, Israel,
mindful of His mercy,

55 •Just as He promised our fathers,
Abraham and his descendants forever."

56 •Mary remained with her for three months and then returned to her home.

57,58 •The time came for Elizabeth to give birth, and she bore a son. •And when the neighbors and her relatives heard that the Lord had manifested 59 His mercy to her they rejoiced with her. •And it happened that on the eighth day they went to circumcise the child, and they were going to 60 call him by his father's name, Zechariah. •But his mother answered, "No! 61 He shall be called John, instead!" •And they said to her, "None of your 62 relatives is called by that name!" •So they asked the father by signs what 63 *he* wanted the child to be called. •And after asking for a writing tablet 64 he wrote, "His name is John." And they were all amazed. •Then his mouth was immediately opened as well as his tongue, and he spoke, 65 blessing God. •Fear came upon all their neighbors and throughout the 66 Judean hill country they discussed all these events, •and all who heard kept it in their hearts and said, "What, then, will this child be?" For the hand of the Lord was with him as well.

67 •Then his father Zechariah was filled with the Holy Spirit and prophesied, saying,

68 •"Blessed be the Lord God of Israel —
He has visited and set His people free,

69 •And He has raised up a horn of salvation for us
in the house of His servant David,

70 •Just as He promised through the mouths of His
holy prophets from of old:

•to save us from our enemies and from the hand   71
    of all who hate us;
•To show mercy to our fathers and to be mindful   72
    of His holy covenant,
    •of the oath He swore to our father Abraham,   73
To grant us, •saved from the hand of enemies,   74
    that we might worship Him without fear,
    •in holiness and righteousness, in His presence all our days.   75
•And you, child, will be called a prophet of the Most High,   76
    for you will go before the Lord to prepare His ways,
•To give knowledge of salvation to His people   77
    through forgiveness of their sins,
•Through the tender mercy of our God,   78
    whereby the Shining Light from on high will visit us,
•To give light to those in darkness and   79
    in the shadow of death,
    to guide our feet into the way of peace."

•The child grew and became strong in spirit, and he was in the deserts   80
until the day of his manifestation before Israel.

C. BIRTH AND EARLY YEARS OF JESUS

2 •[a] Now it happened that in those days a decree went out from Cae-   1
sar Augustus that all the world should be registered. •This first cen-   2
sus took place when Quirinius was governor of Syria. •So everyone went   3
to be registered, each to his own city. •Since Joseph was of the house   4
and family of David he went up from Nazareth in Galilee to Bethlehem
of Judea, the city of David, •to be registered with Mary, who was be-   5
trothed to him and who was pregnant. •It happened that while they were   6
there the day came for her to give birth. •She gave birth to her firstborn   7
son, wrapped him in swaddling clothes, and laid him in a manger, because there was no room for them in the inn.

•There were shepherds in the same region, living out of doors and   8
keeping guard at night over their flock. •An angel of the Lord appeared   9

[a] Mt 1:18-25.

1:78 Ml 4:2; Is 60:1-2. The Shining Light was understood to be the Messiah.
2:8 As always, Luke emphasizes Jesus' openness to the outcasts of society. Shepherding
was considered an unclean occupation by the
Pharisees.

Caesar Augustus (sculpture, 1st century B.C.).

to them and the glory of the Lord shone around them, and they were
10 greatly afraid. •And the angel said to them, "Fear not! for, behold, I bring
11 you good news which will give joy to the whole nation, •because this
day a savior has been born for you in the city of David who is the Mes-
12 siah, the Lord, •and this will be the sign for you — you will find a ba-
13 by, swaddled and lying in a manger." •And, suddenly, with the angel was
an assembly of the heavenly host, praising God and saying,

14 •"Glory to God in high Heaven,
   and, on earth, peace to those in whom
      He is pleased."

15 •And it happened that when the angels had left them to return to
Heaven the shepherds said to one another, "Let's go over to Bethlehem and see this thing that has happened, which the Lord has made
16 known to us." •They hurried off and found Mary and Joseph and the
17 baby, which was lying in the manger. •Now when they saw the child

2:13 "Host." The Greek word means "army."

they let them know what they had been told about him, •and when they 18
all heard it they were amazed at what the shepherds told them. •Mary 19
remembered all this and pondered it in her heart, •and the shepherds 20
returned, glorifying and praising God for all they had heard and seen,
just as they had been told.

•And when eight days had passed for his circumcision they gave him 21
the name Jesus, the name given him by the angel before he was conceived in the womb.

•When the day came for their purification according to the Torah 22
of Moses they took the child up to Jerusalem to present him to the
Lord — •as it is written in the Torah of the Lord, every **firstborn male** 23
shall be called holy to the Lord, — •and to offer a sacrifice ac- 24
cording to what is said in the Torah of the Lord, **a pair of turtle
doves or two young pigeons.**

•And, behold, there was a man in Jerusalem named Simeon. He was 25
an upright and devout man who awaited the liberation of Israel, and the
Holy Spirit was upon him; •moreover it had been revealed to him by 26
the Holy Spirit that he would not see death before he saw the Messiah
of the Lord. •He was led by the Spirit to come to the Temple, and when 27
the parents brought the child Jesus in to do for him what was in accordance with the custom of the Torah •he, too, took him in his arms and 28
blessed God, saying,

> •"Now You send Your servant away in peace, O Master, 29
> according to Your word,
> •Because my eyes have seen Your salvation 30
> •prepared in the presence of all the peoples, 31
> •A light of revelation to the Gentiles 32
> and glory to Your people Israel."

•His father and mother were amazed at what was said about Jesus. •And 33,34
Simeon blessed them and said to his mother, Mary,

> "Behold, he's destined to bring about the fall
> and rise of many in Israel,

2:22 "Torah," or "law," referred to the totality of God's revelation which could serve as a guide for one's life. Torah was, therefore, quintessentially, the Decalogue, but it also extended far beyond the confines of the Pentateuch to areas which we would never characterize as "law," as can be seen in several New Testament passages.
2:23 Ex 13:2, 12, 15.

2:24 Lv 12:8.
2:25-38 The nationalist hopes of Simeon and Anna are raised once again by the two disciples on the road to Emmaus (24:21), but Jesus explains the true meaning of the liberation which has come to Israel.
2:32 Here at his birth Jesus is proclaimed to be "a light of revelation to the Gentiles," and at the

and to be a sign that will be opposed
35 •(And a sword will pierce your own soul,)
so that the thoughts of many hearts may be revealed."

36 •The prophetess Anna was there, too, the daughter of Phanuel from the tribe of Asher; she was greatly advanced in years, having lived sev-
37 en years with her husband from her virginity •and alone as a widow up to eighty-four years, never leaving the Temple and worshipping night
38 and day with fasts and prayers. •And she came up at that very hour and began to give thanks to God, and spoke about him to all who were awaiting the liberation of Israel.

39 •When they had carried out everything in accordance with the Torah
40 of the Lord they returned to Galilee to their own city, Nazareth. •The child grew and became strong and was filled with wisdom, and the grace of God was on him.

41 •His parents used to go to Jerusalem every year for the festival of
42 the Passover. •And when he was twelve years old they went up to
43 Jerusalem in accordance with the custom of the feast, •and after they had fulfilled the days, while they were returning, the child Jesus re-
44 mained in Jerusalem, but his parents didn't know. •Since they thought he was in their group of travellers they went a day's journey and then
45 looked for him among their relatives and acquaintances, •and when
46 they didn't find him they returned to Jerusalem in search of him. •And it happened that after three days they found him in the Temple, seated in the midst of the teachers, both listening to them and asking them
47 questions, •and all those listening to him were amazed at his intelli-
48 gence and his answers. •When his parents saw him they were amazed, and his mother said to him, "Son, why did you do this to us? You see
49 your father and I have been looking for you, worried to death!" •And he said to them, "Why were you looking for me? Didn't you know that
50 I have to concern myself with my Father's affairs?" •And they didn't
51 understand what he was telling them. •Then he went down with them and went to Nazareth, and he was subject to them. His mother kept
52 all these things in her heart, •and Jesus **progressed** in wisdom and age **and grace before God and men.**

end of the Gospel (24:47), when Jesus appears to the disciples in Jerusalem, he sends them forth to bring the light to "all nations."
2:42 Twelve was the age when Jewish boys be-gan scriptural studies, so Jesus would have just been beginning those studies.
2:52 1 S 2:26.

D. THE MINISTRY OF THE BAPTIST

3 •[b] In the fifteenth year of the reign of Tiberius Caesar, when Pon- 1
tius Pilate was governing Judea and Herod was Tetrarch of Galilee,
while his brother Philip was Tetrarch of the region of Iturea and Tra-
chonitis and Lysanias was Tetrarch of Abilene, •during the high priest- 2
hood of Annas and Caiaphas, the word of God came to John son of
Zechariah in the desert. •And he came to the whole region around the 3
Jordan, proclaiming a baptism of repentance for the forgiveness of sins,
•as it is written in the book of the words of the prophet Isaiah, 4

The voice of one crying out in the desert,
'Prepare the way of the Lord,
   make straight his paths.'
•Every valley shall be filled in 5
   and every mountain and hill brought low,
The crooked ways shall be made straight,
   and the rough ways made into smooth ways,
•And all flesh shall see the salvation of God. 6

•And to the crowds that were coming out to be baptized by him he 7
said, "You brood of vipers! Who warned you to flee from the coming
wrath? •Produce evidence of your repentance, then, and don't go say- 8
ing to yourselves, 'Abraham is our father!' for I say to you that God
can raise up children to Abraham from these stones. •Already now the 9
axe is laid at the root of the trees; any tree, then, not producing good
fruit will be cut down and thrown into the fire." •So the people ques- 10
tioned him and asked, "Then what should we do?" • In response he 11
told them, "Whoever has two tunics should share with the one who
has none, and whoever has food should do likewise." •Tax collectors 12
came to be baptized as well, and they asked him, "Teacher, what should
we do?" •"Collect nothing more than what has been designated for 13
you," he told them. •Soldiers questioned him as well, saying, "What 14
about us, what should we do?" "Don't rob or cheat anyone," he told
them, "and be satisfied with your wages."

[b] Mt 13:1-12; Mk 1:1-8; Jn 1:19-28.

3:4-6 Is 40:3-5 (Septuagint).
3:7-9 Of particular interest in the Baptist's indictment of the Jewish leaders is v. 8, in which he
states that descent from Abraham merits no spe-
cial consideration from God and will not save them from God's wrath. In chapter 13 Jesus takes
this theme up (v. 28) and concludes that the Gen-
tiles will be admitted to the Kingdom before the
descendants of Abraham.

15 •The people were in suspense and were all wondering in their hearts
16 whether John might be the Messiah. •John responded by telling everyone, "I baptize you with water, but one more powerful than I am is coming, the strap of whose sandal I'm not worthy to untie; he'll baptize you
17 with the Holy Spirit and fire — •his winnowing shovel is in his hand to
clean out his threshing floor and gather his grain into the barn, but he'll
18 burn up the chaff with unquenchable fire." •And so he proclaimed the
19 good news to the people with many other words of encouragement; •but
Herod the Tetrarch, who had been rebuked by John on account of Herodias, his brother's wife, and on account of all the evil things Herod had
20 done, •added this to them all — he shut John up in prison.

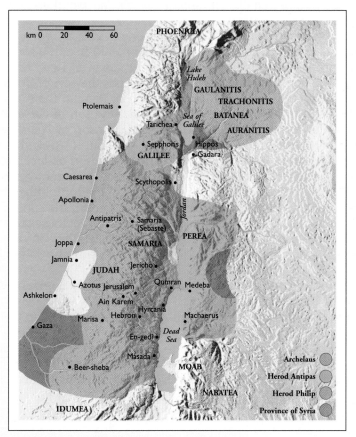

The division of Herod's Kingdom.

L U K E

E. THE BEGINNINGS OF JESUS' MINISTRY

•[c] Now it happened that when all the people had been baptized, and 21 when Jesus had been baptized and was in prayer, the sky was opened •and the Holy Spirit descended upon Jesus in bodily form like a dove, 22 and a voice came from Heaven, "You are My Beloved Son; in you I am well pleased!"

•[d] And Jesus himself, when he started out, was about thirty years old, 23 being the son, as was supposed, of Joseph the son of Heli, •the son of 24 Matthat, the son of Levi, the son of Melchi, the son of Jannai, the son of Joseph, •the son of Mattathias, the son of Amos, the son of Nahum, 25 the son of Esli, the son of Naggai, •the son of Maath, the son of Mat- 26 tathias, the son of Semein, the son of Josech, the son of Joda, •the son 27 of Joanan, the son of Rhesa, the son of Zerubbabel, the son of Shealtiel, the son of Neri, •the son of Melchi, the son of Addi, the son of Cosam, 28 the son of Elmadam, the son of Er, •the son of Joshua, the son of Eliez- 29 er, the son of Jorim, the son of Matthat, the son of Levi, •the son of 30 Simeon, the son of Judah, the son of Joseph, the son of Jonam, the son of Eliakim, •the son of Melea, the son of Menna, the son of Mat- 31 tatha, the son of Nathan, the son of David, •the son of Jesse, the son 32 of Obed, the son of Boaz, the son of Sala, the son of Nahshon, •the 33 son of Amminadab, the son of Admin, the son of Arni, the son of Hezron, the son of Perez, the son of Judah, •the son of Jacob, the son 34 of Isaac, the son of Abraham, the son of Terah, the son of Nahor, •the 35 son of Serug, the son of Reu, the son of Peleg, the son of Eber, the son of Shelah, •the son of Cainan, the son of Arphaxad, the son of Shem, 36 the son of Noah, the son of Lamech, •the son of Methuselah, the son 37 of Enoch, the son of Jared, the son of Mahalaleel, the son of Cainan, •the son of Enos, the son of Seth, the son of Adam, the son of God. 38

4 •[e] Jesus returned from the Jordan full of the Holy Spirit and was led 1 by the Spirit through the desert •for forty days, while being tempt- 2 ed by the Devil. He ate nothing during those days, and when they were completed he was hungry. •Then the Devil said to him, "If you're the 3 Son of God, tell this stone to become a loaf of bread." •Jesus answered 4 him, "It is written, **Not by bread alone shall man live.**" •Then he 5 led Jesus up and showed him all the kingdoms of the world in an instant

[c] Mt 3:13-17; Mk 1:9-11.   [d] Mt 1:1-17.   [e] Mt 4:1-11; Mk 1:12-13.

4:4 Dt 8:3.

6 of time, •and the Devil said to him, "I can give you all this power and glory, because it's been given to me and whoever I want to give it to.
7,8 •So, if you'll worship before me, it'll all be yours." •And in answer Jesus said to him, "It is written,

The Lord your God shall you worship,
and Him alone shall you adore."

9 •Then he led Jesus to Jerusalem and set him on the parapet of the Temple and said to him, "If you're the Son of God, throw yourself down from
10 here, •for it's written,

He will give His angels orders concerning you,
to protect you.

11 •and,

On their hands they will carry you
lest you strike your foot against a stone."

12 •In answer Jesus said to him, "It is said, **You shall not tempt the Lord**
13 **your God.**" •And when the Devil had finished all his tempting he left him until an opportune time.

F. THE GALILEAN MINISTRY

14 •ᶠ Jesus returned to Galilee in the power of the Spirit, and word of
15 him went out through all the surrounding region. •And he taught in their synagogues, praised by all.
16 •ᵍ He went to Nazareth, where he'd been brought up, and as was his custom he went into the synagogue on the Sabbath day, and he stood
17 up to read. •They handed him the scroll of the prophet Isaiah, and when he unrolled the scroll he found the place where it was written,

18 •**The Spirit of the Lord is upon me,**
because He has anointed me
to bring the good news to the poor,
He has sent me to proclaim release to captives

ᶠ Mt 4:12-17; Mk 1:14-15.   ᵍ Mt 13:53-58; Mk 6:1-6.

4:8 Dt 6:13-14.
4:10 Ps 91:11.   4:12 Dt 6:16.
4:11 Ps 91:12.   4:18 Is 61:1-2 (Septuagint).

and recovery of sight to the blind,
to set at liberty the oppressed,
•**To proclaim the acceptable year of the Lord.**   19

•When he had rolled up the scroll and handed it back to the attendant 20
he sat down, and the eyes of everyone in the synagogue were fixed on
him. •Then he began to tell them, "Today this Scripture has been ful- 21
filled in your hearing." •All the people bore witness against him and were 22
amazed at the words of mercy that came from his mouth, and they said,
"Isn't this fellow Joseph's son?" •So he said to them, "No doubt you'll 23
quote me this parable, 'Physician, heal thyself!' 'Do here, too, in your
hometown, what we heard was done in Capharnaum.'" •Then he said, 24
"Amen, I say to you, no prophet is acceptable in his hometown. •But I 25
tell you in truth,

There were many widows in Israel in the days of Elijah,

when the sky was shut up for three years and six months while there
was a severe famine over all the land,

•Yet Elijah was sent to none of them except to   26
Zarephath of Sidon, to a woman, a widow.
•And there were many lepers in Israel in the time   27
of Elisha the prophet,
Yet none of them was cleansed except Naaman
the Syrian."

•All the people in the synagogue who heard these things were enraged. 28
•They rose up and threw him out of the city and took him to the brow 29
of the hill on which their city was built in order to throw him over the
edge, •but he passed through the middle of them and went away.   30
•[h] Then he went down to Capharnaum, a city of Galilee. He taught 31
them on the Sabbath, •and they were amazed at the way he taught be- 32
cause he spoke with authority. •Now in the synagogue was a man who 33
had the spirit of an unclean demon, and he cried out with a loud voice,
•"Ah! What do you want with us, Jesus of Nazareth? Have you come 34
to destroy us? I know who you are — the Holy One of God!" •Jesus re- 35
buked him and said, "Be silenced and come out of him!" Then the de-

[h] Mk 1:21-28.

4:22 Jesus may have outraged his listeners by
breaking off the quote in mid-sentence, omitting
all reference to divine vengeance against the
Gentiles.

4:32 Or perhaps, "on his own authority." The
scribes always invoked the authority of the
Torah.

*El-Muraga. The chapel which commemorates Elijah
on the top of Mount Carmel. (Lk 4:25)*

mon threw the man down in their midst and came out of him without
36 harming him. •All the people were overcome with wonder and kept saying to one another, "What sort of word is this? — he gives orders to the
37 unclean spirits with authority and power, and they leave!" •And news
of him went out to every place in the surrounding region.

38 •ⁱ When he left the synagogue he went into Simon's house. Now Simon's mother-in-law was suffering from a high fever, and they appealed
39 to him on her account. •And when he stood over her he rebuked the
fever and it left her; she got up immediately and began to serve them.
40 •Now when the sun was setting everyone who had people sick with various diseases brought them to him, and he laid his hands on each one
41 of them and healed them. •Demons also came out of many people,
shouting and saying, "You are the Son of God!" And he rebuked them
and wouldn't let them speak, because they knew he was the Messiah.

ⁱ *Mt 8:14-17; Mk 1:29-34.*

•[j] At daybreak he slipped out and went to a desert place. The peo- 42 ple began to search for him and when they came to where he was they tried to keep him from leaving them. •But he said to them, "I must 43 proclaim the good news of the Kingdom of God to the other cities, too, because I was sent for this purpose." •And he preached in the 44 synagogues of Judea.

5 •[k] It happened that the people were pressing in on him as they lis- 1 tened to the word of God. He was standing by the Lake of Gennesaret •and he saw two boats pulled up on the shore — the fishermen had got- 2 ten out and were washing the nets. •So he got into one of the boats — 3 it was Peter's — and asked him to put out from land a little, and when he had seated himself he taught the crowds from the boat. •When he 4 finished speaking he said to Simon, "Put out to the deep and lower your nets for a catch." •In response Simon said, "We've been at it all night, 5 working hard, and have caught nothing, but at your word I'll lower the nets." •And when they did this they took in a tremendous number of 6 fish, but their nets began to rip. •So they signalled to their companions 7 in the other boat to come help them, and they filled both boats to the point that they began to sink. •When Simon Peter saw this he fell down 8 at the knees of Jesus and said, "Leave me, Lord, for I'm a sinful man!" •For wonder at the catch of fish they had taken in seized him and all 9 those with him, •and likewise James and John the sons of Zebedee, who 10 were partners with Simon. Jesus said to Simon, "Don't be afraid; from now on you'll be catching men." •And when they brought their boats 11 to land they left everything and followed him.

•[l] It happened that he was in one of the cities and a man was there 12 who was full of leprosy, and when the man saw Jesus he fell on his face and begged him, saying, "Lord, if you wish to, you can make me clean!" •He reached out his hand, touched him, and said, "I *do* wish it, be made 13 clean!" And at once the leprosy left him. •Then he ordered the man to 14 tell no one, but instead "go show yourself to the priest and make an of- fering for your cleansing as Moses commanded, as a witness to them." •But word of him spread all the more and large crowds kept gathering 15 to listen and to be healed of their illnesses, •but he used to withdraw in- 16 to the deserts to pray.

•[m] It happened that one day he was teaching, and Pharisees were 17 seated there as well as teachers of the Torah who had come from every village of Galilee and Judea and Jerusalem, and the power of the Lord

[j] Mk 1:35-39.   [k] Mt 4:18-22; Mk 1:16-20.   [l] Mt 8:1-4; Mk 1:40-45.   [m] Mt 9:1-8; Mk 2:1-12.

18 was in his healing. •There were some men carrying a paralyzed man on a bed and they were trying to bring him in and set him in front of him.
19 •And since they couldn't find a way to carry him in because of the crowd, they took him onto the roof and lowered him through the tiles of the
20 roof with the bed into the middle, in front of Jesus. •When he saw their
21 faith he said, "Man, your sins are forgiven you!" •Then the scribes and Pharisees began to object and say, "Who is this fellow who speaks blas-
22 phemies? Who can forgive sins but God alone?" •Now Jesus was aware of the objections they were raising and he said to them in response, "Why
23 are you raising objections in your hearts? •What's easier, to say, 'Your
24 sins are forgiven you,' or to say, 'Get up and walk'? •But so you'll know that the Son of Man has authority on earth to forgive sins —" he said to the paralytic, "I say to you, get up, pick up your bed and go to your
25 house!" •Immediately he got up in front of them, picked up what he was
26 lying on, and went off to his house, glorifying God. •Amazement seized them all and they glorified God, and they were filled with fear and said, "We've seen incredible things today!"
27 •[n] After this he went out and he noticed a tax collector named Levi
28 seated at his tax booth, and he said to him, "Follow me!" •He left every-
29 thing, got up, and followed him. •Later Levi held a big banquet for him in his house, and there was a large crowd of tax collectors and others
30 who were reclining with them. •The Pharisees and their scribes com- plained to his disciples and said, "Why do you eat and drink with tax
31 collectors and sinners?" •In response Jesus said to them, "Those in good
32 health are not in need of a doctor — the sick are; •I've come to call, not the righteous, but sinners to repentance!"
33 •[o] Then they said to him, "John's disciples often fast and offer prayers,
34 and so do the disciples of the Pharisees, but yours eat and drink." •So Jesus said to them,

> "How can the groomsmen fast
> while the bridegroom is with them?
35 > •But days will come, and when the groom
> is taken from them,
> then they'll fast in those days."

36 •He also told them a parable.

> "No one tears a patch from a new cloak
> and puts it on an old cloak —

[n] Mt 9:9-13; Mk 2:13-17.   [o] Mt 9:14-17; Mk 2:18-22
5:27 Regarding tax collectors, cf. the note at Mt 5:46.

If you do, the new cloak will be torn
    and the patch from the new cloak won't match the old cloak.
•And no one puts new wine into old skins —   37
If you do, the new wine bursts the skins;
    the wine itself will be spilt and the skins will be ruined;

•On the contrary,   38

    'new wine should go in new skins.'

•No one who has drunk old wine wants new wine, for he says, 'The old   39
wine is better.'"

6 •[p] Now it happened on a Sabbath as he was going through some   1
grainfields that his disciples began plucking and eating the ears of
grain, rubbing them in their hands to remove the husks. •Some of the   2
Pharisees said, "Why are you doing what's unlawful on the Sabbath?"
•And in answer he said to them, "Haven't you read what David did when   3
he was hungry, as well as those with him? •He went into the house of   4
God and took and ate the Loaves of Offering and gave them to those
with him, which it wasn't lawful for them to eat but only for the priests."
•And he said to them, "The Son of Man is Lord of the Sabbath."   5
    •[q] It happened on another Sabbath that he went into the synagogue   6
and taught, and there was a man there whose right hand was withered.
•Now the scribes and Pharisees were watching him closely to see   7
whether he healed on the Sabbath, so they could find something to accuse him of. •Jesus knew their thoughts, so he said to the man with the   8
withered hand, "Get up and stand in the middle." So he got up and stood
there. •Then Jesus said to them, "I ask you,   9

    Is it lawful on the Sabbath to do good or do evil,
        to save a life or to kill?"

•And after looking around at them all he said to the man, "Hold out   10
your hand." The man did, and his hand was healed. •They were filled   11
with rage and began to discuss among themselves what they could do
about Jesus.
    •[r] It happened in those days that he went out to the mountain to pray,   12
and he spent the night in prayer to God. •When day came he called his   13

---

[p] Mt 12:1-8; Mk 2:23-28.   [q] Mt 12:9-14; Mk 3:1-6.   [r] Mt 10:1-4; Mk 3:13-19.

6:1 The words "to remove the husks" have been added.
6:2 The disciples were technically "reaping" on the Sabbath.

Sanctuary of the Beatitudes. (Lk 6:20ff)

disciples to him and he chose twelve of them, whom he also called apos-
14 tles — •Simon, whom he also named Peter, and Andrew his brother, and
15 James and John and Philip and Bartholomew •and Matthew and Thomas
16 and James son of Alpheus and Simon, who was called the Zealot, •and
Judas son of James and Judas Iscariot, who became a traitor.
17   •ˢ When he came down with them he stood on a level place, and a
large crowd of his disciples as well as a great number of the people from
18 all Judea and Jerusalem and the coastal district of Tyre and Sidon •came
to hear him and be healed of their diseases, and those troubled by un-
19 clean spirits were cured. •All the people kept trying to touch him, because power kept coming out from him and healing them all.
20   •ᵗ Then he raised his eyes to his disciples and said,

> "Blessed are you poor,
>   for yours is the Kingdom of God.
21 •Blessed are you who hunger now,
>   for you shall have your fill.

ˢ *Mt 4:23-25.*   ᵗ *Mt 5:1-12.*

6:15 "Simon the Zealot." This is generally considered to be a designation for the ultranationalist (and, therefore, anti-Roman) Zealots.

Blessed are you who weep now,
> for you shall laugh.
•Blessed are you when men hate you 22

and exclude you and insult you and reject your name as evil on account of the Son of Man; •rejoice on that day and leap for joy — behold, your 23 reward will be great in Heaven,

> because their fathers did the same to the prophets.
•But woe to you rich, 24
> for you *have* your delights!
•Woe to you who are full now, 25
> for you shall be hungry!
Woe, you who laugh now,
> for you shall mourn and wail!
•Woe, when all men speak well of you, 26
> for their fathers did the same
> > to the false prophets!"
•ᵘ "But to you who are listening, I say, 27
Love your enemies,
> do good to those who hate you,
•Bless those who curse you, 28
> pray for those who insult you.
•To the one who strikes you on one cheek, 29
> offer your other cheek as well,
And from the one who takes your cloak,
> don't hold back your tunic.
•Give to all who ask of you, 30
> and don't demand what's yours
> > from the one who took it.
•As you wish others to do for you, 31
> do likewise for them.
•And if you love those who love you, 32
> what kindness is that in you?
Even sinners love those who love them!
•And if you do good to those who do good to you, 33
> what kindness is that in you?

ᵘ *Mt 5:38-48, 7:12.*

6:27 It was a common teaching of the rabbis that "neighbor" referred only to fellow Jews. Non-Jews were in opposition to God and therefore "ene-mies." Other currents of rabbinic thought, however, did manifest a more conciliatory view toward Gentiles.

Even sinners do the same!

34 •And if you lend to those from whom you
expect to receive,
what kindness is there in you?
Even sinners lend to sinners,
to get back equal amounts.

35 •But love those who hate you,
do good, and lend when you have no hope of return,
And your reward will be great,
and you'll be sons of the Most High,
Because He's kind to the ungrateful
and to those who are evil.

36 •Be merciful, as your Father is merciful.

37 •ᵛ Don't judge, and you won't be judged;
Don't condemn, and you won't be condemned.
Forgive, and you will be forgiven,

38 •Give, and it will be given to you.
Good measure, pressed down, shaken together,
Overflowing, they shall give into your bosom,
For with the measure you measure
it will be measured out to you in return."

39 •He also told them a parable.

"Can a blind man lead a blind man?
Won't they both fall into a ditch?

40 •A disciple is not above his teacher but, when fully trained, each disciple will be like his teacher.

41 •But why do you see the speck in your brother's eye,
yet don't notice the log in your own eye?

42 •Or how can you say to your brother, 'Brother, let me
take the speck from your eye!'
while you don't see the log in your own eye?
You hypocrite!
First take the log out of your own eye,
and then you'll see clearly to take the speck
from your brother's eye."

43 •ʷ "For a good tree doesn't bear rotten fruit,
Nor, again, does a rotten tree bear good fruit;

ᵛ Mt 7:1-5.   ʷ Mt 7:17-20, 12:34-35.

•For each tree is known by its own fruit. 44
For you don't gather figs from thorn bushes,
Nor pick grapes from brambles.
•The good bring forth good from the store of good 45
    in their hearts,
And the evil bring forth evil from their store of evil,
For the mouth speaks from the abundance of the heart."

•ˣ "But why do you call me, 'Lord, Lord,' yet don't do the things I 46
say? •Everyone who comes to me, hears my words, and acts upon them, 47
I'll show you what he's like. •He's like a man building a house, who dug 48
and went deep and laid the foundation on rock; when a flood came the
river burst upon that house, yet it wasn't able to shake it because it had
been well built. •But the one who heard but didn't act is like a man who 49
built a house on the ground without a foundation, and when the river
burst upon it, it collapsed at once, and great was the ruin of that house."

7 •ʸ After he finished everything he had to say in the hearing of the 1
people he went into Capharnaum. •Now a certain centurion had a 2
servant whom he valued, and the servant was sick and at the point of
death. •When the centurion heard about Jesus he sent Jewish elders to 3
him to ask him to come save his servant. •The elders appeared before 4
Jesus and began to beg him earnestly, saying, "He's worthy that you
should do this for him — •he loves our nation and built our synagogue 5
for us." •So Jesus set out with them. When he was no longer far from 6
the house the centurion sent friends to say to him, "Lord, don't put yourself to the trouble — I'm not worthy to have you come under my roof.
•Nor, therefore, did I consider myself worthy to come before you; just 7
say a word, and my servant will be healed! •For I, too, am subject to au- 8
thority, with soldiers under me, and when I tell this one, 'Go!' he goes,
and if I tell another, 'Come!' he comes, and if I say to my servant, 'Do
this!' he does it." •When Jesus heard these things he was amazed at him, 9
and turning to the crowd that was following him he said, "I tell you, not
even in Israel have I found such faith!" •And when those who had been 10
sent got back home they found the servant in good health.

•It happened that soon afterwards he went to a city called Nain, and 11
his disciples and a large crowd went with him. •Now as he approached 12

ˣ Mt 7:24-27.   ʸ Mt 8:5-13; Jn 4:43-54.

7:6-7 The centurion may have doubted whether Jesus would be willing to enter the house of a Gentile. The strictest sects of Judaism considered such contact to be a cause of ritual impurity.

Nain. Church which commemorates the resuscitation of the the widow's son.

the city gate, behold, a dead man was being carried out for burial. He was the only son of his mother, who was a widow, and a considerable
13 crowd from the city was with her. •The Lord was moved with pity when
14 he saw her and said, "Don't weep!" •Then he went forward and touched the bier and the bearers stood still, and he said, "Young man, I say to
15 you, arise!" •Then the dead man sat up and began to speak, and Jesus
16 gave him to his mother. •Fear seized them all and they glorified God, saying, "A great prophet has risen among us! God has visited His peo-
17 ple!" •And this account of him went out through all Judea and the whole surrounding region.

18 •ᶻ John's disciples informed him of all these things. So John sum-
19 moned two of his disciples and •sent them to the Lord to ask, "Are you
20 he who is to come or are we to expect another?" •When they came to him the men said, "John the Baptist sent us to you to ask, 'Are you he

ᶻ *Mt 11:2-19.*

7:14 Contact with a corpse was commonly held to cause ritual impurity.

171

who is to come or are we to expect another?'" •At that very hour he 21
cured many people from diseases and illnesses and evil spirits, and he
bestowed sight on many who were blind. •Then in answer he said to 22
them, "Go tell John what you saw and heard,

> **The blind can see again,** the lame walk,
>   lepers are made clean and the deaf hear,
> The dead are raised, **the poor are given
>   the good news,**
>   •and blessed is whoever is not scandalized by me." 23

•When John's messengers had gone he began to speak to the crowds 24
about John.

> "What did you go out to the desert to see?
>   A reed, shaken by the wind?
> •But what did you go out to see? 25
>   A man in luxurious robes?
> Behold, those in expensive and luxurious clothing
>   live in palaces.
> •But what did you go out to see? 26
>   A prophet?
> Yes, I tell you, and one greater than a prophet.
>   •He it is of whom it is written, 27
> **Behold, I'm sending My messenger before your face,
>   who will prepare your way before you.**
> •I say to you, among those born of women 28
>   none is greater than John,
> But the lowliest in the Kingdom of God
>   is greater than he is."

•When they heard this all the people as well as the tax collectors praised 29
the righteousness of God's plan because they had been baptized with
John's baptism, •but the Pharisees and lawyers had rejected God's plan 30
for them, since they hadn't been baptized by him.

> •"To what shall I compare the men of this generation, 31
>   and to what are they similar?

•They're like the children who sit in the marketplace and call to each 32
other,

7:23 Jesus again omits all reference to Divine   7:22 Is 35:5, 61:1.
vengeance against the Gentiles.   7:27 Ml 3:1.

'We piped for you and you didn't dance,
   we wailed and you didn't weep.'
33 •For John the Baptist came neither eating bread
   nor drinking wine, and you said,
   'He has a demon';
34 •The Son of Man came eating and drinking, and you said,
   'Look at him, a glutton and a drunkard, a friend
   of tax collectors and sinners!'
35 •Yet wisdom is justified by all her children."

36 •Now one of the Pharisees asked Jesus to eat with him, so he went
37 into the Pharisee's house and reclined at table. •There was a woman who
was a sinner in the city, and when she learned that "he's reclining at table
38 in the Pharisee's house!" she bought an alabaster jar of perfumed oil •and
stood behind by his feet, weeping, and she began to wet his feet with her
tears and to wipe them with the hair of her head, and she kissed his feet
39 repeatedly and anointed them with the oil. •When the Pharisee who had
invited him saw this he said to himself, "If this fellow were a prophet he'd
realize who and what kind of woman it is who's touching him — she's a
40 sinner!" •In response Jesus said to him, "Simon, I have something to say
41 to you." "Speak, Teacher," he said. •"Two men were debtors of a certain moneylender; the one owed five hundred denarii, the other, fifty.
42 •When they were unable to repay, he forgave them both. Which of them,
43 then, will love him more?" •In reply Simon said, "I suppose the one he
44 forgave the most." "You've judged correctly," he said. •Then turning to
the woman he said to Simon, "You see this woman?"

I came into your house —
   you gave me no water for my feet,
But she wet my feet with her tears
   and dried them with her hair.
45 •You gave me no kisses,
   but she, from the moment she came in,
   has not stopped kissing my feet.
46 •You didn't anoint my head with olive oil,
   but she anointed my feet with perfumed oil.
47 •Therefore I tell you: her sins, many as they are,
   have been forgiven,

7:47 "Have been forgiven"; this is an example of the so-called Divine Passive, occasioned by the Jewish desire to avoid using the name of God. The meaning is: "her sins... have been forgiven by God."

and so she has shown great love;
But whoever is forgiven little, loves little."

•Then he said to her, "Your sins are forgiven." •And those reclining at ₄₈,₄₉ table began to say to themselves, "Who is this fellow who even forgives sins?" •Then he said to the woman, "Your faith has saved you, go in ₅₀ peace!"

8 •It happened next that he went travelling through city and village, ₁ preaching and proclaiming the good news of the Kingdom of God, and the Twelve were with him •as well as some women who had been ₂ healed from evil spirits and illnesses — Mary, who was called the Magdalen, from whom seven demons had gone out, •and Joanna, the wife ₃ of Chuza, Herod's steward, and Susanna, and many others who provided for them out of their possessions.

•ᵃ Now when a large crowd had gathered, including people who had ₄ come to him from every city, he said in a parable, •"The sower went ₅ out to sow his seed. And as he sowed some fell along the footpath, and it was trampled underfoot and the birds of the sky ate it up. •And oth- ₆ er seed fell on rock, and when it grew up it was scorched because it had no moisture. •And other seed fell among the thorns, and when the ₇ thorns grew up with it they choked it. •And other seed fell on the good ₈ earth, and when it grew up it gave fruit a hundredfold." After he had said these things he cried out,

"Whoever has ears to hear,
let them hear!"

•ᵇ His disciples asked him what this parable could mean. •"To you it's ₉,₁₀ given to know the mysteries of the Kingdom of God," he said, "but to the rest of them it's given in parables, so that

**Seeing they may not see,
And hearing they may not understand.**

•ᶜ "This is the parable. The seed is the word of God. •Those on the ₁₁,₁₂ footpath are those who hear, and then the Devil comes and snatches the word from their heart, so they won't believe and be saved. •Those ₁₃ on the rock are those who, when they hear, accept the word joyfully,

---

ᵃ *Mt 13:1-9; Mk 4:1-9.* ᵇ *Mt 13:10-17; Mk 4:10-12.* ᶜ *Mt 13:18-23; Mk 4:13-20.*

8:10 Is 6:9-10 (Septuagint).

yet these have no root; they believe for a time but forsake the word in
14 time of trial. •Now the seed that fell among the thorns, these are those
who hear but are choked by the worries and wealth and pleasures of life
15 as they proceed, and they don't mature. •But the seed on the good earth,
these are those who listen to the word with an honest and good heart,
hold fast to it, and bear fruit with perseverance."

16 •[d] "No one, after lighting a lamp, covers it with something or puts it
under a bed; on the contrary, he puts it on a lampstand so those who
enter will see the light.

17 •For nothing is hidden that will not be revealed,
Nor secret that will not be made known
and brought into the open.

18 •Therefore, watch how you listen;

For whoever has, it will be given to him,
And whoever does not have, even what he thinks he has
will be taken from him."

19 •[e] His mother and brothers showed up where he was, but they could-
20 n't get near him because of the crowd. •So he was informed, "Your
mother and your brothers are standing outside and wish to see you."
21 •But in response he said to them, "My mother and my brothers are those
who hear the word of God and do it."

22 •[f] Now it happened that on one of those days both he and his disciples got into a boat, and he said to them, "Let's go over to the other
23 side of the lake," and so they set sail. •While they were sailing he fell
asleep and a wind squall descended on the lake, and they were being
24 swamped and were in danger. •So they came and woke him, saying,
"Master, master, we're going to die!" He woke up and rebuked the wind
25 and the waves of water, and they stopped and there was a calm. •Then
he said to them, "Where's your faith?" But they were amazed and fearful and said to each other, "Who *is* he, then? When he rebukes the winds
and the water *even they* obey him!"

---

[d] Mk 4:21-25.   [e] Mt 12:46-50; Mk 3:31-35.   [f] Mt 8:23-27; Mk 4:35-41.

8:19 Church tradition has consistently maintained that the "brothers" of Jesus referred to
here were merely close relatives, not sons of the
same mother. It is instructive to compare this
passage to 23:49-24:10 (and parallel passages
in the other Gospels, esp. Mk 15:40-16:1 and Mt

27:60) where these brothers are again referred
to as sons of "Mary," but this time it is unambiguously clear that this Mary was not Mary the
mother of Jesus. Such usage was typically Semitic.

Pagan altar from the region of the Gerasenes (1st century A.D.). (Lk 8:26)

•[g] Then they sailed to the region of the Gerasenes, which is opposite 26 Galilee. •When Jesus came ashore a certain man from the city who had 27 a demon confronted him. This man hadn't worn a cloak for a long time; he didn't live in a house but instead lived among the tombs. •When he 28 saw Jesus he cried out and fell down before him and said in a loud voice, "What do you want with me, Jesus, Son of the Most High God? I beg you, don't torment me!" •because he had commanded the unclean spir- 29 it to come out of the man. Many times it had seized him, and he was kept under guard and bound with chains and leg irons, and when he'd break the chains he was driven into the deserts by the demon. •So Je- 30 sus asked him, "What's your name?" "Legion," he said, because many demons had gone into him. • And they kept begging him not to order 31 them to go off to the abyss.

[g] *Mt 8:28-34; Mk 5:1-20.*

8:26-39 This episode is replete with sources of impurity – it takes place in Gentile territory, the demoniac lives among the tombs, and a herd of pigs is present.

32 •Now a fair sized herd of swine was feeding on the hillside there, and they begged him to let them go into the swine, and he gave them per-
33 mission. •So when the demons came out of the man they went into the swine, and the herd rushed headlong down the slope into the lake and
34 drowned. •When the herdsmen saw what had happened they fled and told
35 those who were in the city and the fields. •When the people went out to see what had happened and came to Jesus they found the man from whom the demons had gone out — clothed and in his right mind — seated at
36 Jesus' feet, and they became frightened. •Then those who had seen what
37 happened told them how the demon-possessed man had been saved. •And the whole crowd from the district of the Gerasenes asked him to leave them, because they were seized with a great fear. So he got into a boat
38 and returned. •The man from whom the demons had gone out begged
39 to stay with Jesus, but he sent him off, saying, •"Return to your house and announce what God has done for you." And he went off through the whole city, proclaiming what Jesus had done for him.

40 •[h] When Jesus returned the crowd welcomed him, because they'd all
41 been looking for him. •And, behold, a man named Jairus came — he was a ruler of the synagogue — and he fell at Jesus' feet and begged
42 him to come to his house, •because he had an only daughter about twelve years old who was at the point of death.

Now as Jesus slowly made his way the crowd kept pressing in on him.
43 •A woman was there who had had a heavy flow of blood for twelve years. She [had spent her whole livelihood on doctors but] couldn't be cured
44 by anyone. •She came up and touched the tassel of his cloak from be-
45 hind, and immediately the flow of blood stopped. •And Jesus said, "Who was it that touched me?" When everyone denied it Peter said, "Master,
46 the crowd is pressing in on you and crowding around!" •But Jesus said,
47 "Someone touched me — I could feel power going out from me." •When the woman saw that she couldn't hide she came, trembling, and fell down before him and, in the presence of all the people, she told why she'd
48 touched him and how she'd been immediately cured. •"Daughter," he said to her, "your faith has saved you; go in peace!"

49 •While Jesus was still speaking someone came from the ruler of the synagogue's and said, "Your daughter has died; don't trouble the Teacher
50 further." •When Jesus heard this he told the man, "Don't be afraid! Just

[h] Mt 9:18-26; Mk 5:21-43.

8:44 Devout Jews wore tassels on the four cor- ners of their cloaks as a reminder to obey the commandments (Nb 15:38-39). Because of her continual menstrual flow almost any contact with this woman would risk ritual impurity (Lv 14:19- 30). But Jesus is unfazed by her touch.

believe and she'll be saved!" •When he came to the house he didn't al- 51
low anyone to go in with him except Peter, John, and James, and the
mother and father of the child. •Everyone was weeping and mourning 52
for her, but Jesus said, "Don't weep — she hasn't died, she's sleeping!"
•And they laughed at him because they knew she *had* died. •Then he 53,54
grasped her hand and called out, "Child, arise!" •Her spirit returned and 55
she immediately sat up, and he gave instructions that she be given something to eat. •Her parents were beside themselves, but he ordered them 56
to tell no one what had happened.

9 •[i] Then he called the Twelve together and gave them power and au- 1
thority over all the demons and to cure diseases, •and he sent them 2
off to proclaim the Kingdom of God and to heal, •and he said to them, 3

"Take nothing for your journey,
     neither staff nor bag,
Nor bread nor silver,
     nor two tunics.
•And whatever house you enter,   4
     stay there and go on from there.
•And whoever doesn't receive you,   5
     when you leave that city
Shake its dust from your feet
     as a witness against them."

•So they went out and travelled through the villages, proclaiming the 6
good news and healing everywhere.
    •[j] Now Herod the Tetrarch heard everything that was going on, and 7
he was perplexed because some were saying, "John has risen from the
dead!" •while others said, "Elijah has appeared!" and others, "One of 8
the prophets of old has risen!" •But Herod said, "John, I beheaded! Who 9
is this, then, I hear so much about?" And he kept trying to see him.
    •[k] When the apostles returned they told him what they'd done. Then 10
he took them along and withdrew privately to a city called Bethsaida,
•but when the crowds found out they followed him. After greeting them 11
he spoke to them about the Kingdom of God and cured those who were
in need of healing. •Now as day was coming to an end the Twelve came 12
up to him and said, "Send the crowd away so they can go to the surrounding villages and farms and find food and lodging, because we're
in a desert place here." •"*You* give them something to eat." he said. 13

[i] Mt 10:5-15; Mk 6:7-13.   [j] Mt 14:1-12; Mk 6:14-29.   [k] Mt 14:13-21; Mk 6:30-44; Jn 6:1-14.

"We have no more than five loaves and two fish," they said, "unless we

14 go buy food for all these people!" •There were about five thousand men. Then he said to his disciples, "Have them recline in groups of fifty."

15,16 •They did so and they had them all recline. •Then he took the five loaves and the two fish and, after looking up to Heaven, he blessed them and broke them into pieces and kept giving them to the disciples to distrib-

17 ute to the crowd. •And they all ate and were filled, and they picked up what was left over — twelve baskets of fragments.

Tabgha. Mosaic from the Church of the Multiplication of the Loaves.

18 •ˡ And it happened that while he was praying alone the disciples were

19 with him, and he asked them, "Who do the crowds say I am?" •In response they said, "Some say, 'John the Baptist,' while others say, 'Elijah,' and others say, 'One of the prophets of old has risen.'" •Then he

20 said to them, "But *you*, who do *you* say I am?" And in answer Peter said, "The Messiah of God!"

21 •ᵐ Jesus gave them strict orders and commanded them to tell no one

22 about this •and said, "The Son of Man must suffer greatly and be re-

ˡ *Mt 16:13-19; Mk 8:27-29.* ᵐ *Mt 16:20-28; Mk 8:30-9:1.*

jected by the elders and chief priests and scribes and be put to death
and rise on the third day." •Then he said to everyone,   23

"If anyone would be my disciple,
   he must deny himself,
And take up his cross daily
   and follow me.
•For whoever would save his life   24
   will lose it,
While whoever loses his life for my sake,
   he will save it.
•For what good is it if you gain   25
   the whole world,
   but lose or forfeit your life?
•For whoever is ashamed of me and my words,   26
   of him will the Son of Man be ashamed
When he comes in his glory and in the glory
   of his Father,
   and of the holy angels.

•But I tell you truly, there are some who are standing here who will not   27
taste death until they see the Kingdom of God."

•[n] It happened that about eight days after he spoke these words he   28
took Peter, John, and James and went up the mountain to pray. •And   29
it happened that while he was praying the appearance of his face was
altered, and his clothing became a dazzling white. •And, behold, two men 30
were speaking with him, Moses and Elijah, •who were seen in glory   31
speaking about his Exodus, which he would bring to completion in
Jerusalem. •Peter as well as those with him had been overcome by sleep,   32
but when they were fully awake they saw his glory and the two men
standing with him. •And it happened that as Moses and Elijah were leav-   33
ing him Peter said to Jesus, "Master, it's good for us to be here; let's
put up three dwellings, one for you, one for Moses, and one for Elijah"
— he didn't really know what he was saying. •As he was saying this a   34

[n] *Mt 17:1-8; Mk 9:2-8.*

9:31 "Exodus"; this expression is difficult to render adequately in English. The word has as its basic meaning a departure or going out but is also used to signify a departure from this life, i.e. decease. It clearly has this last meaning in this passage, but just as clearly retains all the connotations associated with the word Exodus as referring to the Israelites' departure from their slavery in Egypt. Jesus, through his death, leads the New Israel out of slavery and into the Promised Kingdom.
9:33 Cf. the note to Mt 17:4. Luke specifically states (v. 31) that Jesus was discussing "his Exodus."

cloud arose and overshadowed them; then they were afraid when they
35 went into the cloud. •And a voice came from the cloud, saying, "This
36 is My Son, My Chosen; hear him!" •After the voice had spoken Jesus
was found alone, and they kept silent and told no one in those days anything they'd seen.
37 •[o] It happened that on the next day when they were coming down
38 from the mountain a large crowd met him. •And, behold, a man from
the crowd called out and said, "Teacher, please look at my son — he's
39 my only child •and, behold, a spirit takes hold of him and cries out suddenly, then it throws him into convulsions with foam at the mouth and
40 will hardly stop battering him. •I asked your disciples to drive it out, but
41 they couldn't." •In answer Jesus said, "O unbelieving and perverse generation, how long will I be with you and put up with you? Bring your
42 son here." •But while he was coming the demon threw the boy to the
ground and convulsed him, so Jesus rebuked the unclean spirit and
43 healed the child and gave him back to his father. •And they were all
amazed at God's greatness.
[p] But while they were marvelling at all the things he was doing he
44 said to his disciples, •"Listen closely to what I'm going to tell you:
the Son of Man is going to be handed over into the hands of men."
45 •But they didn't understand this saying and it was hidden from them
so they wouldn't ask about it, and they were afraid to ask him about
this saying.
46 •[q] Now a disagreement arose among them as to which of them was
47 the most important. •Jesus, aware of the disagreement in their hearts,
48 took a child and stood it next to himself, •and he said to them,

"Whoever receives this child in my name
receives me,
And whoever receives me
receives the One Who sent me,
For the least of all of you —
that's who's the greatest."

49 •[r] In response John said, "Master, we saw someone driving out
demons in your name, and we tried to stop him because he doesn't fol-
50 low with us." •But Jesus said to him, "Don't stop him, for

Whoever isn't against you
is with you."

[o] *Mt 17:14-18; Mk 9:14-27.* [p] *Mt 17:22-23; Mk 9:30-32.* [q] *Mt 18:1-5; Mk 9:33-37.* [r] *Mk 9:38-40.*

G. HEALING AND TEACHING
ON THE ROAD TO JERUSALEM

•It happened that as the days were drawing near for Jesus to be tak- 51
en up he set his face to go to Jerusalem, •and he sent messengers on 52
ahead of him. They went and entered a Samaritan village to prepare for
him, •but the people didn't welcome him because his face was set on 53
going to Jerusalem. •When his disciples James and John saw this they 54
said, "Lord, do you want us to call down **fire from Heaven to consume** them?" •But he turned and rebuked them, •and they went to an- 55,56
other village. •ˢ As they were going along the road someone said to him, 57
"I'll follow you wherever you go." •And Jesus said to him, 58

"Foxes have holes,
And the birds of the sky have nests,
But the Son of Man has nowhere to lay his head."

•To another he said, "Follow me!" "Let me first go bury my father," said 59
the man. •Jesus said to him, 60

"Let the dead bury their own dead,
But you, go proclaim the Kingdom of God!"

•Then another said, "I'll follow you, Lord, but first let me take leave of 61
those at home." •But Jesus said, 62

"No one who puts his hand to the plow
And looks behind
Is fit for the Kingdom of God."

10 •After this the Lord appointed seventy-two others and sent them 1
in twos ahead of him to every town and place he was going to
go to. •Then he said to them, 2

"The harvest is great,
But the laborers are few,

ˢ Mt 8:19-22.

9:58 Some have suggested that the "foxes," of
proverbial cunning, are Herod and his hated Idumaean followers who played one side off against
the other to their own advantage. The "birds of the
air" were the Roman overlords. Jesus would then
be warning his followers about what to expect: his
Kingdom would be very different.

10:1 Gn 10:1-32. Seventy-two is the number of
the nations of the world. The symbolism indicates
that Jesus' mission is to all nations. When taken
in conjunction with Jesus' instruction to eat what
was placed before them, contrary to Jewish dietary laws, some authors have suggested that this
particular mission was to an area where large
numbers of Gentiles lived, perhaps Transjordan.

so implore the Lord of the harvest to send out laborers to his harvest.
3,4 •Go now! Behold, I'm sending you out like sheep among wolves. •Don't
5 carry a wallet or a bag or sandals, and greet no one along the way. •And
6 to whatever house you enter, first say, 'Peace be to this house.' •If there's
a son of peace there your peace will rest upon him, but, if not, your
7 peace will return to you. •Stay, then, in that house and eat and drink
what they have, for the laborer is worthy of his reward. Don't move from
8 house to house. •And in whatever town you enter and they receive you,
9 eat what's set before you, •heal the sick in it, and say to them, 'The
10 Kingdom of God has come upon you!' •But whatever town you enter
11 and they don't receive you, go out into its streets and say, •'Even the
dust of your town that stuck to our feet we wipe off against you, but
12 know this, the Kingdom of God is at hand!' •I say to you,

> It will be more tolerable for Sodom on that day
> Than it will be for that town."

*Caravanserai of the Good Samaritan
on the road which connects Jerusalem to Jericho. (Lk 10:35)*

•[t] "Woe to you, Chorazin! Woe to you, Bethsaida! because if the 13
mighty works that took place in you had taken place in Tyre and Sidon,
they would have repented long ago and sat in sackcloth and ashes. •But 14
it will be more tolerable for Tyre and Sidon at the judgment than for
you. •And you, Capharnaum, 15

> **You'll be exalted to Heaven, will you?**
> **You'll be brought down to Hell!**

•Whoever hears you, 16
    hears me,
And whoever rejects you,
    rejects me.
And whoever rejects me,
    rejects the One Who sent me."

•The seventy-two returned joyfully, saying, "Lord, even the demons 17
are subject to us in your name!" •And he said to them, "I watched Sa- 18
tan falling like lightning from Heaven. •Behold, I've given you the pow- 19
er to step on snakes and scorpions and to trample on all the power of
the Enemy, and nothing can harm you. •But don't rejoice in the fact 20
that the spirits are subject to you — rejoice because your names are
recorded in Heaven."

•[u] At that very hour he rejoiced in the Holy Spirit and said, 21

"I praise you, Father,
    Lord of Heaven and earth,
Because You hid these things from the wise
    and intelligent
    and revealed them to babes;
Yes, Father,
    for such was Your desire.
•All things have been given to me by my Father, 22
    and no one knows who the Son is
        except the Father,
Nor who the Father is except the Son,
    and whoever the Son chooses to reveal Him to."

•And when he turned to the disciples in private he said, 23

"Blessed are the eyes that see
    what you're seeing,

---

[t] *Mt 11:20-24.*   [u] *Mt 11:25-27.*   10:15 Is 14:13-15.

24 •For I tell you,

Many prophets and kings wished to see what you're seeing,
    yet didn't see,
And to hear what you're hearing,
    yet didn't hear."

25   •And, behold, a certain lawyer stood up to put Jesus to the test and
26 said, "Teacher, what must I do to gain eternal life?" •Jesus said to him,
27 "What's written in the Torah? How do you read it?" •In reply he said,
**"You shall love the Lord your God with your whole heart and
with your whole soul and with your whole strength** and with your
whole understanding, and **you shall love your neighbor as yourself.**"
28 •Then Jesus said to him, "You've answered correctly; do this and you'll
29 live." •But the lawyer wished to find favor with God and so he said to Je-
30 sus, "And who is my neighbor?" •After considering, Jesus said, "A certain man was going down from Jerusalem to Jericho and ran into robbers who, after stripping and beating him, went off leaving him half dead.
31 •Now a priest happened to be going down by that road, but when he
32 saw the man he passed by on the other side of the road. •Likewise a
Levite was also going past the spot, and when he saw the man he passed
33 by on the other side of the road. •But a certain Samaritan who was on
34 a journey came upon the man, and when he saw him he took pity. •He
went up to him and bandaged his wounds, poured oil and wine on them,
set him on his own mount, brought him to an inn, and took care of him.
35 •The next day he took out two denarii, gave them to the innkeeper, and
said, 'Look after him, and any additional amount you spend I'll repay you
36 on my way back.' •Which of these three, do you think, was a neighbor
37 to the man who ran into the robbers?" •The lawyer said, "The one who
had mercy on him." Then Jesus said to him, "Go, and you do likewise."
38   •In the course of their journey he entered a certain village where a
39 woman named Martha received him. •She had a sister named Mary who
40 seated herself at the Lord's feet and listened to his teaching. •But Martha
was distracted with all the serving, so she came up and said, "Lord, does-
n't it matter to you that my sister has left me to serve alone? Tell her to
41 give me a hand!" •In response the Lord said to her, "Martha, Martha!
42 You're anxious and upset over many things, •but one thing is necessary.
Mary has chosen the better part, which will not be taken from her."

10:31-32 The priest and Levite presuming the
man to be dead or near death place the risk of
ritual impurity from contact with a corpse ahead
of aid to a fellow man.

10:35 "Two denarii." Silver coins, each worth a
laborer's daily wage.
10:27 Dt 6:5.

11 •ᵛ It happened that Jesus was praying at a certain spot, and when 1
he was done one of his disciples said to him, "Lord, teach us to
pray, like John taught his disciples." •So he said to them, "When you 2
pray, say,

> Father, Your name be blessed;
>> may Your Kingdom come;
> •Give us each day our daily bread 3
> •And forgive us our sins, 4
>> for we also forgive all who are indebted to us,
> And lead us not into temptation."

•Then he said to them, "If any of you had a friend and you went to 5
him at midnight and said to him, 'Friend, lend me three loaves — •my 6
friend has arrived on a journey to me and I haven't a thing to set before him,' •would he answer from inside, 'Don't bother me! The door's 7
already locked and my children are with me in the bed; I can't get up
and give you anything.' •I tell you, even if he doesn't get up and give 8
you something because he's your friend, he'll get up and give you whatever you need out of a sense of shame. •And to you I say, 9

> Ask! and it shall be given to you;
>> Seek! and you shall find;
>>> Knock! and it shall be opened to you.
> •For everyone who asks, receives; 10
>> And whoever seeks will find;
>>> And to those who knock it shall be opened.
> •But is there a father among you who, 11
>> if his son asks for a fish,
>> instead of a fish will hand him a snake?
> •Or if he asks for an egg, 12
>> will hand him a scorpion?
> •So if you who are evil know how 13
>> to give good gifts to your children,
> All the more will the Father from Heaven
>> give the Holy Spirit to those who ask Him!"

•ʷ And he was driving out a dumb demon; now it happened that 14
when the demon had gone out the dumb man spoke. The crowds were
amazed, •but some of them said, "He drives out demons by Beelzebul, 15
the prince of demons," •while others demanded that he show them a 16

ᵛ Mt 6:9-15. ʷ Mt 12:22-30; Mk 3:20-27.

LUKE

Church of the "Pater Noster" on the Mount of Olives at Jerusalem.

17 sign from Heaven, as a test. •But he knew their thoughts and so he said to them,

> "Every kingdom divided against itself is laid waste,
> and a house divided against itself falls.

18 •Now if Satan, too, is divided against himself — because you say I drive
19 out demons by Beelzebul — how will his kingdom stand? •But if I do drive out demons by Beelzebul, by whom do *your* followers drive them
20 out? Therefore, they'll be your judges. •But if I drive out demons by the
21 finger of God, then the Kingdom of God has come upon you. •When the strong man guards his own palace fully armed his possessions are
22 safe; •but when someone stronger than he is comes and conquers him, he takes away the armor on which the strong man had relied, and distributes his spoils.

11:21-22   Here Jesus compares Satan to a "strong man" and the present age to Satan's house. It is Jesus who has entered Satan's house, bound him, and freed those in Satan's power. Jesus' power over demons is a sign of this mastery and of the coming of the Messianic age.

•Whoever isn't with me is against me, 23
And whoever doesn't gather with me scatters."

•ˣ "When the unclean spirit comes out of the man it goes about 24
through waterless places seeking relief, and when it finds none it says,
'I'll return to the house I came from,' •and when it comes it finds the 25
house swept and decorated. •Then it goes and brings along seven oth- 26
er spirits worse than itself, and it goes in and settles there, and the last
state of that man becomes worse than the first."

•Now it happened that while he was saying these things a woman in 27
the crowd raised her voice and said to him,

"Blessed is the womb that bore you,
and the breasts that you nursed at!"

•But he said, "Rather, 28

Blessed are those who hear the word of God
and keep it!"

•ʸ As the crowds pressed around he said, 29

"This generation is a wicked generation;
it seeks a sign,
Yet no sign will be given it but the sign of Jonah.
•For just as Jonah became a sign for the Ninevites, 30
So also will the Son of Man be for this generation.
•The Queen of the South will rise up at the judgment 31
against this generation and will condemn it,
Because she came from the ends of the earth
to hear the wisdom of Solomon,
And, behold, something greater than Solomon is here.
•The Ninevites will stand up at the judgment 32
against this generation and will condemn it,
Because they repented at the preaching of Jonah,
And, behold, something greater than Jonah is here!"

•ᶻ "No one, after lighting a lamp, puts it in the cellar — he puts it on 33
the lampstand so those who enter will see the light.

•Your eye is the lamp of the body. 34
When your eye is generous,

ˣ Mt 12:43-45.   ʸ Mt 12:38-42; Mk 8:12.   ᶻ Mt 5:15, 6:22-23.   11:29 Cf. the note at Mt 12:39.

Your whole body is full of light, too,
But when it's grudging,
Your body, too, is full of darkness.

35 •Take care, then — perhaps the light within you
   is darkness!

36 •So if your whole body is full of light, having no part darkened, it will be full of light, like when the lamp flashes its light on you."

37 •[a] After he was done speaking a Pharisee asked him to eat with him,
38 so he went and sat down. •Now when the Pharisee saw, he was amazed
39 that Jesus didn't first wash before the meal. •But the Lord said to him,
"Now you Pharisees, you cleanse the outside of the cup and the dish,
40 but your inside is full of greed and wickedness. •You fools! Didn't He
41 Who made the outside make the inside as well? •But give what's within as alms and then everything will be clean for you.

42 •But woe to you Pharisees!
   You tithe mint and rue and every herb,
      and neglect judgment and the love of God;
   These are the things you should have done,
   and what you should not have neglected.

43 •Woe to you Pharisees!
   You love the first seat in the synagogues,
      and greetings in the marketplaces.

44 •Woe to you!
   You're like unmarked tombs,
      and those who walk over them don't know it."

45 •In response one of the lawyers said to him, "Teacher, you insult us, too,
46 by saying these things!" •But he said,

   "And woe to you lawyers!
   You load men down with heavy burdens,
      yet you don't touch the burdens
         with one of your fingers.

[a] *Mt 23:1-36; Mk 12:38-40.*

11:37-52 The tendency for Pharisaism to degenerate into formalism and hypocrisy was well recognized in ancient times, cf. Mt 23:1ff.
11:41 Several authors have suggested that "give what's within as alms" is a mistranslation of an Aramaic original and that Mt 23:26 renders this passage correctly.

11:44 Contact with a dead body or a tomb was a serious matter for the Pharisees, since it made them ritually unclean. Here, Jesus compares the Pharisees themselves to the cause of uncleanness. As the lawyer's response shows, this was a grave insult, indeed.

•Woe to you! 47
You build the monuments of the prophets,
     but your fathers killed them.
•So you're witnesses, 48
     and you approve of your fathers' works —
They killed them,
     while you build their tombs.

•Therefore the Wisdom of God also said, 'I will send them prophets and 49
apostles and they will kill and persecute some of them,' •so that this gen- 50
eration might be responsible for the blood of all the prophets that was
shed from the creation of the world, •from the blood of Abel to the blood 51
of Zechariah, who was killed between the altar and the sanctuary; yes,
I tell you, this generation will be responsible.

•Woe to you lawyers! 52
     because you've taken the key of knowledge;
You wouldn't go in,
     and you hindered those who *were* going in."

•When he left there the scribes and Pharisees began to bitterly op- 53
pose him and to press him with questions about many things, •lying in 54
wait for him to pounce on something he said.

12 •When the countless thousands of the crowd had gathered, so that 1
they were trampling on one another, he said to his disciples first, "Be
on your guard against the leaven of the Pharisees, which is hypocrisy.

•Nothing is concealed 2´
     that will not be revealed,
Nor hidden
     that will not be made known.
•Therefore, what you have said in the darkness 3
     will be heard in the light,
And what you whispered in inner rooms
     will be proclaimed from the roof tops."

•b "But I say to you, my friends, 4

Fear not those who kill the body,
     and after that can do no more.

---

b *Mt 10:28-31.*   11:49 "The Wisdom of God." At Mt 23:34 it is Jesus himself who speaks, perhaps
identified by Matthew as the personification of the divine Wisdom.

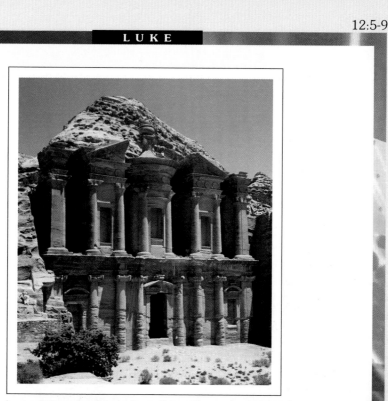

Facade of one of the splendid tombs at Petra. The work of the Nabateans, these are more elaborate than the Jewish tombs mentioned in Lk 11:48.

5   •But I'll let you know whom to fear!

Fear the One Who, after killing,
   has power to thrust into Gehenna.

6 Yes, I tell you, fear *Him*! •Aren't five sparrows sold for a few cents? Yet
7 not one of these is overlooked in the presence of God! •On the contrary, even the hairs of your head are all numbered. Fear not! You're
worth far more than sparrows."

8   •ᶜ "But I tell you,

Everyone who acknowledges me before men,
   the Son of Man will acknowledge him, too,
      before God's angels;
9   •But whoever denies me before men
      will be denied before God's angels.

ᶜ *Mt 10:32-33; 12:32; 10:19-20.*

•And everyone who utters a word against the Son of Man,   10
  he'll be forgiven,
But whoever blasphemes the Holy Spirit
  will not be forgiven.

•But when they bring you before the synagogues and rulers and officials,   11
don't worry how to speak your case or what to say — •the Holy Spirit   12
will teach you what to say at that very hour."

•Then someone from the crowd said to him, "Teacher, tell my broth-   13
er to share the inheritance with me!" •But he said to him, "Man, who   14
made me judge or arbitrator over you?" •Then he said to them, "Watch   15
out for and guard against all greed, because your life doesn't consist in
the abundance of your possessions." •Then he told them a parable and   16
said, "The land of a certain rich man produced good crops. •So he con-   17
sidered to himself, 'What shall I do — I have nowhere to gather my
grain!' •'This is what I'll do!' he said, 'I'll pull down my barns and build   18
bigger ones, and I'll gather all my grain and my goods there, •and I'll   19
tell my soul, "Soul, you have many goods laid up for many years. Re-
lax; eat, drink, be merry!"' •But God said to him, 'You fool! This night   20
they'll demand your soul of you. But the things you prepared, whose
will *they* be?' •That's how it will be for whoever accumulates treasure   21
for himself, yet is not generous toward God."

•[d] Then he said to his disciples, "Therefore I say to you,   22

Don't worry about your life, what you will eat,
  or about your body, what you will wear.
•For life is more than food,   23
  and the body more than clothing.
•Consider the ravens —   24
  they neither sow nor reap,
Nor have either storeroom or barn,
  yet God feeds them;
Of far greater value are *you* than *birds*!
•But which of you can add   25
  any time to your life by worrying?
•So if you can't even do such a little thing,   26
  why do you worry about the rest?
•Consider how the lilies grow —   27
  they neither work nor spin,
But I tell you, not even Solomon in all his glory

[d] Mt 6:25-34, 19-20.

was arrayed like one of them!

28 •If God so clothes the grass in the field,
which is here today and thrown
into the oven tomorrow,
All the more will He clothe *you*,
O you of little faith!

29 •And *you* — don't ask what you'll eat
and what you'll drink,
and don't get upset.

30 •All the nations of the world seek these things,
but your Father knows that you need them.

31 •Instead, seek His Kingdom
and these things will also be given to you.

32 •Fear not, little flock,
for it pleased your Father
to give you the Kingdom.

33 •Sell your possessions and give alms;
make yourselves purses that don't grow old,
An inexhaustible treasure in the heavens,
where no thief approaches nor moth destroys;

34 •For where your treasure is,
there will your heart be, too!"

35 •[e] "Let your loins be girt
and your lamps burning,

36 •And you like men awaiting their lord,
when he at last returns from the wedding feast,
So that when he comes and knocks
they can open up for him at once.

37 •Blessed those servants who, when he comes,
the lord will find still awake!
Amen I say to you, he'll get himself dressed
and have them recline at table,
and he'll come wait on them.

38 •And if he comes in the middle of the night
and finds them thus,
they are blessed!

39 •But know this — if the householder had known
at what hour the thief was coming
he wouldn't have let his house be broken into.

[e] Mt 24:45-51.

•You be ready, too,   40
    because you don't know the hour
      when the Son of Man is coming!"

Christ on the throne. Church of the Fountain (Nazareth).

•Then Peter said, "Lord, are you telling this parable for us or for every- 41
one?" •And the Lord said,   42

"Who, then, is the faithful steward,
    the wise one,
Whom the lord will set over his staff
    to give them their ration at the proper time?

43 •Blessed that servant who, when his lord comes,
he finds doing so!
44 •Surely, I tell you,
he'll set him over all his possessions.
45 •But if that servant says in his heart,
'My lord is long in coming,'
And begins to beat the servants and maids,
eating and drinking and getting drunk,
46 •The lord of that servant will come
on a day he doesn't expect,
and at an hour he doesn't know,
And he'll cut him in pieces
and assign him the lot of the unbelievers.
47 •The servant who knew his lord's will,
yet didn't prepare or act according to his will,
will be severely beaten,
48 •Whereas, the one who didn't know,
but did what deserved a beating,
will receive fewer blows.
But to whomever much has been given,
much will be required of him,
And to whomever much was entrusted,
they will ask still more of him."
49 •[f] "I came to spread fire on the earth,
and would that it were already kindled!
50 •But I have a baptism to be baptized with,
and how apprehensive I am until it is
accomplished!
51 •Do you think I came to bring peace to the earth?
no, I tell you, but division instead!
52 •For from now on five in one house will be divided,
three against two and two against three,
53 •Father against son will be divided
and son against father,
Mother against daughter
and daughter against mother,
Mother-in-law against daughter-in-law
and daughter-in-law against mother-in-law."

[f] Mt 10:34-36.

•Then he said to the crowds, "When you see a cloud rising in the 54 west you say at once, 'A rainstorm is coming!' and so it is, •and when 55 a south wind blows you say, 'There will be scorching heat!' and it hap- pens. •You hypocrites! You know how to interpret the face of the earth 56 and the sky, so how is it you don't know how to interpret these times?"

•[g] "Why, then, don't you judge for yourselves what's right? •While 57,58 you're going with your opponent to the official, make an effort to set- tle with him on the way, lest he drag you before the judge, and the judge will hand you over to the officer, and the officer will throw you into prison. •I tell you, you won't come out of there until you pay back 59 the very last penny."

13 •Now some people came at that very time and told him about 1 the Galileans whose blood Pilate had mixed with their sacrifices. •And in response he said to them, 2

"Do you think these Galileans were worse sinners
　　than all the other Galileans were
　　　　because they've suffered these things?
•No, I tell you, 3
　　but unless you repent
　　　　you'll all die the same way.
•Or those eighteen on whom the tower fell in Siloam 4
　　and killed them —
　　do you think they were guiltier
　　　　than everyone else living in Jerusalem?
•No, I tell you, 5
　　but unless you repent
　　　　you'll all die the very same way."

•Then he told them this parable. "A man had a fig tree planted in his 6 vineyard, and he came looking for fruit on it and found none. •So he 7 said to the vinedresser, 'For three years now I've come looking for fruit on this fig tree and I haven't found any. Cut it down — why should it use up the land, after all?' •But in answer the vinedresser said, 'Lord, let it 8 be for this year, too, until I dig around it and put down manure, •and 9 maybe it'll produce fruit for next year — but, if it doesn't, have it cut down.'"

•Now he was teaching in one of the synagogues on the Sabbath. 10 •And, behold, a woman was there who for eighteen years had had a 11

[g] Mt 5:25-26.

crippling spirit, and she was bent over double and unable to straighten
12 herself up fully. •When Jesus saw her he called out to her and said,
13 "Woman, you've been set free from your illness!" •Then he laid his hands
on her and she straightened up immediately and began glorifying God.
14 •The ruler of the synagogue was indignant that Jesus had healed on the
Sabbath, so in response he said to the crowd, "There are six days on
which it's proper to perform work, so come be healed on those days
15 and not on the Sabbath!" •But the Lord answered him and said, "You
hypocrites! Don't each of you untie your ox or donkey from the manger
16 and lead it off to water on the Sabbath? •Wasn't it proper for this daughter of Abraham, whom Satan had bound for all these eighteen years, to
17 be released from this bond on the Sabbath day?" •And when he said
these things all his opponents were put to shame, and the whole crowd
rejoiced at all the glorious things that were done by him.
18   •[h] So he said,

>   "What is the Kingdom of God like,
>   and to what shall I compare it?

19 •It's like a grain of mustard seed which a man took and threw into his
garden, and it grew and became a tree, and the birds of the sky nested
in its branches."
20   •And again he said, "To what shall I compare the Kingdom of God?
21 •It's like yeast that a woman took and mixed into a bushel of wheat flour
until all of it was leavened."
22   •[i] And he travelled around the cities and villages, teaching and jour-
23 neying toward Jerusalem. •Now someone said to him, "Lord, will only
a few be saved?" So he said to them,

24   •"Strive to come in
              through the narrow gate,
>   Because many, I tell you, will try to come in,
>   but won't be able to.
25 •Once the householder has risen
              and locked the door,
>   You'll stand outside
>   and knock on the door,
>   Saying, 'Lord, open up for us!'
>   and in answer he'll say to you,
>   'I don't know you,
>   where you're from!'

[h] Mt 13:31-33; Mk 4:30-32. [i] Mt 7:13-14, 21-23.

•Then you'll try to say, 26
'We ate and drank in your presence
      and you taught in our streets!'
•And he'll say to you, 27
'I don't know you,
      where you're from!
Get away from me,
      all you evildoers!'
•There there will be wailing 28
      and gnashing of teeth,
When you see Abraham and Isaac and Jacob
      and all the prophets in the Kingdom of God,
      while you're thrown outside.
•People will come from east and west 29
      and from north and south
      and will recline at table in the Kingdom of God.
•And, behold, some who are last will be first, 30
      and some who are first will be last."

•ʲ At that very time some Pharisees came and said to him, "Leave 31
and go away from here — Herod wants to kill you!" •And he said to 32
them, "Go tell that fox, 'Behold, I'll drive out demons and do cures today and tomorrow, and on the third day I'll be done with my work.' •But 33
I must keep travelling today and tomorrow and the next day, because
it's unacceptable for a prophet to be killed outside Jerusalem.

•Jerusalem, Jerusalem, 34
You kill the prophets
      and stone those sent to you!
How often I wished
      to gather your children,
Like a hen gathers her brood
      under her wings,
But you would not!
•Behold, your house is left to you. 35

ʲ Mt 23:37-39.

13:29 Probably a reference to the Gentiles being saved and welcomed into the Kingdom.
13:32 "That fox"; cf. 9:58, note. Jesus may be
referring to Herod's fox-like cunning in playing off
various competing powers against each other.
13:35 Ps 118:26. Jesus no longer calls the Temple "my Father's house" but "your house."

I tell you, you will not see me
     until you say,
     **'Blessed is he who comes
     in the name of the Lord!'"**

View of Jerusalem.

1 **14** •It happened that when he went to the house of one of the rulers of the Pharisees on the Sabbath to eat bread they were watching 2 him closely. •And, behold, a man with dropsy was there in front of him. 3 •In response Jesus spoke to the lawyers and Pharisees, saying, "Is it law- 4 ful to heal on the Sabbath or not?" •But they remained silent. So he 5 took hold of him, cured him, and sent him away. •Then he said to them, "Can any of you imagine having a son or ox fall into a well, and not at 6 once pulling him out on the Sabbath day?" •And they were unable to respond to these things.

7   •Then he told a parable to those who had been invited, having not- ed how they had selected the places of honor for themselves, and he 8 said to them, •"When you're invited by someone to a wedding feast,

don't recline at the place of honor, because if someone more eminent than you was invited by him, •the man who invited you and him will 9 come say to you, 'Give the place to this man!' and then you'll shame-facedly proceed to take the last place. •Instead, when you're invited and 10 arrive, sit at the last place, so that when the one who invited you comes he'll say to you, 'Friend, move up higher!' Then you'll receive honor in the presence of all those reclining with you.

•Because everyone who exalts himself will be humbled,   11
And whoever humbles himself will be exalted."

•He also said to the one who invited him, "When you give a meal or a 12 feast, call neither your friends, nor your brothers, nor your kinsmen, nor rich neighbors, lest they also invite you in turn and repay you. •Instead, 13 when you give a banquet, invite the poor, crippled, lame, and blind, •and 14 you'll be blessed because they won't have anything to repay you with — you'll be repaid at the resurrection of the righteous!"

•ᵏ One of those reclining with him heard these things and said to him, 15 "Happy is he who will eat bread in the Kingdom of God!" •But he said 16 to him, "A man was giving a big banquet and invited many people, •and 17 he sent his servant at the time of the banquet to tell those who had been invited, 'Come — everything's ready now!' •But they one and all began 18 to make excuses. The first said, 'I bought a field and I have to go see it; I beg you, consider me excused.' •Another said, 'I bought five yoke of 19 oxen and I'm setting out to examine them; I beg you, consider me ex-cused.' •And another said, 'I've just married a wife and therefore can't 20 come.' •And when the servant returned he told these things to his lord. 21 The householder was furious and said to his servant, 'Go quickly to the streets and alleys of the city and bring the poor and crippled and blind and lame here.' •The servant said, 'Lord, your commands have been car- 22 ried out, but there's still room.' •Then the lord said to the servant, 'Go 23 out along the roads and hedges and force them to come in, so my house may be filled — •I tell you, not one of those men I invited will taste my 24 banquet!'"

•ˡ Now large crowds were travelling with him, and he turned and said 25 to them, •"If anyone comes to me and doesn't hate his own father and 26 mother and his wife and children and his brothers and sisters, even his own life, he cannot be my disciple. •Whoever doesn't pick up his cross 27

ᵏ Mt 22:1-10.   ˡ Mt 10:37-38.

14:13 The meal of this parable and the next is clearly the Messianic banquet of the Kingdom. The Essenes, who celebrated a type of Messianic ban- quet, excluded those with physical deformities from their table-fellowship, perhaps because no man with a deformity could be a priest under the Torah.

28 and follow me cannot be my disciple. •After all, wouldn't any of you who wanted to build a tower first sit down and figure out the expense
29 to see if you had enough to complete it? •Otherwise, if you lay the foundation but are unable to finish it, all the onlookers will begin to make
30 fun of you •and say, 'This man began building but he couldn't finish.'
31 •Or wouldn't a king setting out to meet another king in war first sit down and consider if he's able to oppose with ten thousand the one who's
32 coming against him with twenty thousand? •If he can't he sends an en-
33 voy to request peace terms while his enemy is still a long way off. •So in the same way, no one who doesn't part with all his possessions can be my disciple."
34 •[m] "Therefore, salt is good, but if the salt, too, has lost its taste, what
35 can it be seasoned with? •It's good neither for the land nor for manure — they throw it out.

> Whoever has ears to hear,
> let them hear!"

1 15•[n] Now the tax collectors and sinners were all drawing near to lis-
2 ten to him, •and the Pharisees and scribes were muttering among
3 themselves, "This fellow welcomes sinners and eats with them!" •So he
4 told them this parable, •"What man among you who had a hundred sheep and lost one of them wouldn't leave the ninety-nine in the desert
5 and set out after the lost one until he found it? •And when he finds it
6 he puts it on his shoulders, rejoicing, •and when he comes home he calls his friends and neighbors together and says to them, 'Rejoice with me
7 — I've found my lost sheep!' •I say to you that this is the type of joy there will be in Heaven at the repentance of one sinner, rather than at ninety-nine of the righteous who had no need of repentance."
8 •"Or a woman who has ten drachmas — if she loses one drachma, won't she light a lamp and sweep her home and search carefully until
9 she finds it? •And when she finds it she calls her friends and neighbors
10 and says, 'Rejoice with me, because I've found the drachma I lost!' •This, I tell you, is how God's angels will rejoice over one sinner who repents."
11,12 •Then he said, "A man had two sons, •and the younger of them said to his father, 'Father, give me the share of the property that falls to me.'

[m] Mt 5:13; Mk 9:50.   [n] Mt 18:12-14.

15:1 Table-fellowship was a serious matter in Judaism because it was viewed as establishing a fellowship before God. To eat with sinners was to be in solidarity with them, in the Pharisees' eyes.

15:8 A drachma was a Greek silver coin worth about the same as a denarius, i.e., the daily wage of a laborer.

So the man divided his belongings between them. •Not many days lat- 13 er the younger son sold everything and left home for a far off country, and there he squandered his wealth, leading a profligate life. •After he 14 had spent everything a severe famine came to that country and he found himself in need, •so he went and attached himself to one of the citizens 15 of that country, who sent him into his fields to feed pigs. •And he longed 16 to fill himself with the carob pods the pigs were eating, but no one gave him anything. •Then he came to himself and said, 'How many of my 17 father's hired men have more than enough bread, while I'm here dying of hunger. •I'll get up and go to my father and I'll say to him, "Father, 18 I've sinned against Heaven and before you; •I'm no longer worthy to be 19 called your son; treat me like one of your hired men."' •So he got up 20 and went to his father. While he was still far away his father saw him and took pity, and he ran and fell upon his neck and kissed him re- peatedly. •His son said to him, 'Father, I've sinned against Heaven and 21 before you; I'm no longer worthy to be called your son.' •But his father 22 said to his servants, 'Quick, bring out the best robe and clothe him in it, and put a ring on his hand and sandals on his feet, •and bring the 23 fatted calf — slaughter it and let's eat and celebrate —

The Merciful Father, by Giulio Carpioni (1611-1674).

24 •This son of mine was dead,
    and has come back to life,
He was lost,
    and has been found.'

And they began to celebrate.
25 •"Now his older son was in the field, and when he was coming and
26 had approached the house he heard music and dancing, •and he called
27 one of the servants over and asked what these things meant. •'Your brother has come and your father has slaughtered the fatted calf,' the servant
28 told him, 'because he's gotten him back in good health.' •Then he became furious and refused to go in. His father came out and appealed to
29 him. •But in answer he said to his father, 'I've slaved all these years for
you now and never went against your command, and you never gave me
30 a kid goat so I could celebrate with my friends, •but when this son of yours
who devoured your living with whores came, you slaughtered the fatted
31 calf for him!' •'My child,' he said, 'you're always with me and everything
32 of mine is yours, •but we *had* to celebrate and rejoice —

This brother of yours was dead,
    and has come back to life,
He was lost,
    and has been found!'"

1 **16** •He also said to his disciples, "There was a rich man who had
a steward, and a report came to him that this steward had been
2 squandering his possessions. •So he summoned him and said to him,
'What's this I hear about you? Turn in the accounts of your steward-
3 ship — you can no longer be steward!' •The steward said to himself,
'What can I do? — my lord is taking the stewardship away from me!
4 I can't dig; I'm ashamed to beg. •I know what I can do so that when
I'm removed from the stewardship people will welcome me into their
5 homes!' •So he called his lord's debtors in one by one and said to
6 the first, 'How much do you owe my lord?' •'Eight hundred gallons
of oil,' said the debtor. 'Take your bills,' he told him, 'sit down, and
7 quickly write four hundred.' •Next he said to another debtor, 'You
now, how much do *you* owe?' 'A thousand bushels of wheat,' said
8 the debtor. 'Take your bills,' he said, 'and write eight hundred.' •And
the lord commended the dishonest steward because he'd acted wise-

^b *Mk 10:35-45.*

ly, for the sons of this age are wiser than the sons of light are in their own generation. •And to you I say, make friends for yourselves with 9 unrighteous mammon so that when it runs out they'll receive you into the eternal dwellings.

> •Whoever is faithful in very little 10
> is also faithful in much,
> And whoever is dishonest in very little
> is also dishonest in much.
> •So if you haven't been faithful with 11
> unrighteous mammon,
> Who will entrust you with the true riches?
> •And if you haven't been faithful 12
> with what's another's,
> Who will give you what is yours?
> •No steward can serve two lords, 13
> For either he'll hate the one and love the other,
> Or be loyal to one and despise the other.
> You cannot serve God and Mammon!"

•° The Pharisees, who loved money, were listening to all these things 14 and began making fun of him. •And he said to them, "You're the ones 15 who hold yourselves out as righteous before others, but God knows your hearts, because

> What is exalted among men
> Is an abomination before God.

•The Torah and the Prophets lasted until John; from then on 16

> The Kingdom of God is proclaimed in the good news,
> And everyone seeks to force his way into it.
> •But it's easier for the heavens and the earth to pass away 17
> Than for one stroke of a letter to fall from the Torah.
> •Anyone who puts his wife away and marries another 18
> commits adultery,
> And whoever marries a woman put away by her
> husband commits adultery."

•"There was a certain rich man who used to dress in purple and fine 19 linen and who feasted splendidly every day. •A certain poor man named 20 Lazarus used to lay at his gate, covered with sores, •and he longed to fill 21

° Mt 11:12-13.

himself with what fell from the rich man's table; why, even the dogs used
22 to come and lick his sores! •It happened that the poor man died and was
carried away by the angels to the bosom of Abraham. The rich man al-
23 so died and was buried, •and in Hades when he lifted his eyes — he was
in torments — he saw Abraham from a great distance, and Lazarus in
24 his bosom. •He called out and said, 'Father Abraham! Have mercy on
me and send Lazarus to dip the tip of his finger in water and cool my
25 tongue, for I'm in great pain in these flames!' •But Abraham said, 'My
child, remember that you got your good things during your lifetime, and
Lazarus, likewise, his bad things, but now he's being comforted here while
26 you're in pain. •Besides, a yawning chasm has been placed between you
and us, so that those who wish to cross over from here to you are un-
27 able to, nor can anyone cross over from there to us.' •Then the rich man
28 said, 'Then I beg you, father, to send him to my father's house — •for I
have five brothers — to solemnly warn them so they won't come to this
29 place of torment, too.' •But Abraham said, 'They have Moses and the
30 prophets; let them listen to *them*!' •'Oh no, Father Abraham!' he said,
31 'but if someone came to them from the dead, they'd repent.' •But Abraham said to him, 'If they won't listen to Moses and the prophets, they
won't be convinced even if someone rises from the dead.'"

1 **17** •p Then he said to his disciples, "For scandal not to come is im-
2 possible, but woe to the one through whom it comes! •It would
be better for him to have a millstone placed around his neck and be
thrown into the sea, rather than to scandalize one of these little ones.
3 •Keep an eye on one another.

> If your brother sins,
>   rebuke him,
> And if he repents,
>   forgive him,

4   •and if he sins against you seven times in a day and turns to you sev-
en times, saying, 'I repent,' you must forgive him."
5,6   •And the apostles said to the Lord, "Increase our faith!" •So the Lord
said, "If you have faith like a grain of mustard seed you could say to
this mulberry tree, 'Be uprooted and be planted in the sea,' and it would
obey you."
7   •"But would any of you who had a slave who was plowing or tend-
ing sheep say to him when he came in from the field, 'Go sit down at

p *Mt 18:6-7, 21-22; Mk 9:42.*

the table at once.' •On the contrary, wouldn't you say to him, 'Fix me 8 something to eat and dress yourself and serve me while I eat and drink. After that, you can go eat and drink.' •The servant isn't owed any thanks 9 because he did what he was commanded, is he? •Likewise, you, too, 10 when you do everything you were commanded, should say, 'We're servants of no special merit; we only did what we should have done.'"

•It happened during his journey to Jerusalem that he was crossing 11 the border of Samaria and Galilee. •As he was entering a village he 12 was met by ten lepers who stood at a distance, •and they raised their 13 voices and cried out, "Jesus, master, have mercy on us!" •When he 14 saw them he said, "Go show yourselves to the priests!" And it happened that they were made clean while they were on their way. •One 15 of them, when he saw he'd been cured, returned, glorifying God in a loud voice, •and he fell face down at Jesus' feet and thanked him. He 16 was a Samaritan. •In response Jesus said, "Weren't ten made clean? 17 Where, then, are the other nine? •Did no one return to give glory to 18 God except this foreigner?" •Then he said to him, "Arise and go; your 19 faith has saved you."

•q Now when he was asked by the Pharisees, "When is the Kingdom 20 of God coming?" he answered them and said, "The Kingdom of God is not coming in a way that can be observed, •nor will they say, 'Look, 21 here it is!' or, 'There it is!' — behold, the Kingdom of God is in your midst!" •Then he said to his disciples, "The days will come when you'll 22 long to see one of the days of the Son of Man, but you *won't* see it. •And they'll say to you, 'Look, it's there!' 'Look, it's here!' Don't go 23 off and don't follow them, •because just as the lightning, when it flash- 24 es, lights up from one side of the sky to the other side of the sky, so will the Son of Man be. •But first he must suffer many things and be 25 rejected by this generation. •Just as it happened in the days of Noah, 26 so, too, will it be in the days of the Son of Man. •They ate, they drank, 27 they married, they gave in marriage, until the day Noah went into the ark and the deluge came and destroyed them all. •Likewise, it happened 28 like that in the days of Lot; they ate, they drank, they bought, they sold, they planted, they built; •but on the day Lot came out of Sodom, fire 29 and brimstone rained down from Heaven and destroyed them all. •It 30 will be the same on the day the Son of Man is revealed. •On that day 31 whoever is on his roof and has his things in the house must not go down

q Mt 24:23-28, 37-41.

17:21 Jesus appears to be telling the Pharisees that the Kingdom has already arrived and is right there among them, if they have eyes to see it.

Salty formations in the vicinity of Sodom on the Dead Sea.

to get them, and, likewise, whoever is in his field must not return for
32 what was left behind. •Remember Lot's wife!

33   •Whoever tries to save his life will lose it,
       While whoever loses it will save his life.
34   •I tell you,
       On that night there will be two men in one bed —
           one will be taken and the other will be left.
35   •There will be two women grinding together —
36   one will be taken while the other will be left." [•]

37   •In response they asked him, "Where, Lord?" But he said to them,

       "Where the body is,
       There, too, will the vultures be gathered."

17:36 The best manuscript tradition omits v. 36: "Two in the field — one will be taken and the
other will be left."

18 •Then he told them a parable about the need for them to pray al- 1
ways and not become discouraged, •saying, "There was a judge 2
in a certain city who neither feared God nor felt shame before men.
•Now there was a widow in that city and she kept coming to him and 3
saying, 'Do me justice against my adversary!' •For a while he didn't want 4
to, but later he said to himself, 'Even though I neither fear God nor feel
shame before men, •still, because of the way this widow keeps bother- 5
ing me, I'll do her justice so she won't keep coming and finally wear me
out.'" •Then the Lord said, "Listen to what the unjust judge says! •Won't 6,7
God, then, vindicate His chosen ones when they cry out to Him day and
night and be patient with them? •I tell you, He'll do them justice with 8
all speed. But, nevertheless, when the Son of Man comes, will he find
faith on earth?"

•He also told this parable to some of those who self-confidently be- 9
lieved in their own righteousness and looked down on others. •"Two 10
men went up into the Temple to pray, one a Pharisee and the other a
tax collector. •The Pharisee stood [by himself] and made these prayers. 11
'O God, I give You thanks because I'm not like other men, greedy, unjust, adulterers — or even like this tax collector. •I fast twice a week, I 12
tithe everything I earn.' •But the tax collector stood at a distance and 13
didn't want to even lift his eyes up to Heaven; instead, he kept beating his breast, saying, 'O God, forgive me, a sinner!' •I tell you, *he* went 14
down to his house pardoned and reconciled with God rather than the
other one, because

> Everyone who exalts himself will be humbled,
> While whoever humbles himself will be exalted."

•ʳ Now people were even bringing babies to him to have him touch 15
them, but when his disciples saw this they rebuked the people. •But Je- 16
sus called the children over and said,

> "Let the children come to me,
> And don't stop them,
> For of such as these is the Kingdom of God.

•Amen, I say to you, whoever doesn't accept the Kingdom of God 17
like a child will not enter it."

•ˢ Then a ruler asked him, "Good Teacher, what should I do to gain 18

ʳ Mt 19:13-15; Mk 10:13-16.   ˢ Mt 19:16-30; Mk 10:17-31.

18:7 "be patient"; i.e., God will bear with the human failings of "His chosen ones," who are also
not perfect.

19 eternal life?" •"Why do you call me good?" Jesus asked. "No one is good
20 but God alone! •You know the commandments — **you shall not commit adultery, you shall not murder, you shall not steal, you shall
21 not bear false witness, honor your father and mother.**" •"I've
22 obeyed all these from my youth," said the ruler. •When Jesus heard that
he said to him, "You still lack one thing. Sell everything you have and
give to the poor and you'll have treasure in Heaven, and come follow
23 me." •When the ruler heard this he became very sad, for he was extremely
rich.

24 •When Jesus saw him so saddened he said,

> "How hard it is
> for those who are wealthy
> to enter the Kingdom of God!
25 •It's easier for a camel to go through
> a needle's eye
> than for a rich man
> to enter the Kingdom of God!"

26,27 •Those who were listening said, "Then who can be saved?" •But Jesus said,

> "What is impossible for men
> is possible for God."

28 •Then Peter said, "You see we've left our homes and followed you."
29 •Jesus said, "Amen, I say to you, there's no one who has left his house
or wife or brothers or parents or children for the sake of the Kingdom
30 of God •who will not receive many times more in this time, and in the
coming age, life eternal."

H. THE MINISTRY IN JERUSALEM

31 •[t] Then he took the Twelve and said to them, "Behold, we're going
up to Jerusalem where all the things written by the prophets about the
32 Son of Man will be brought to completion, •for he'll be handed over to
33 the Gentiles and he'll be mocked and insulted and spit upon. •Then
they'll scourge him and put him to death, and on the third day he'll rise."
34 •But they understood none of this; the meaning of the words was kept
hidden from them, and they didn't realize what had been said.

[t] Mt 20:17-19; Mk 10:32-34.   18:20 Ex 20:13-16.

LUKE

•[u] Now it happened that when he was approaching Jericho a blind man 35 was seated beside the road, begging. •When the man heard the crowds 36 going by he asked what was going on, •and they informed him that "Je- 37 sus of Nazareth is passing by." •So the man cried out and said, "Jesus, 38 Son of David, have mercy on me!" •Those who were going ahead or- 39 dered him to be silent, but he kept crying out all the more, "Son of David, have mercy on me!" •Jesus stopped and ordered the man to be brought 40 to him, and when he approached he asked him, •"What do you want me 41 to do for you?" "Lord," he said, "please let me see again!" •Jesus said 42 to him, "Regain your sight! Your faith has saved you!" •Immediately he 43 regained his sight and followed Jesus, glorifying God. And all the people, when they saw this, gave praise to God.

19 •Then he entered Jericho and passed through the town. •And, 1,2 behold, a man named Zacchaeus was there; he was chief tax collector and he was rich. •He was trying to see who Jesus was, but he 3 was short of stature and wasn't able to see because of the crowd. •So 4 he ran on ahead to the front and climbed up into a sycamore tree in order to see him, because he was going to be passing by that way. •When 5 Jesus came to that place he looked up and said to him, "Zacchaeus! Hurry on down — today I must stay at your house!" •So he hurried down 6 and welcomed him joyfully. •When everyone saw this they complained 7 and said, "He went in as the guest of a sinful man!" •But Zacchaeus stood 8 up and said to the Lord, "Look, Lord, I'm giving half of my possessions to the poor, and if I've cheated anyone of anything I'm paying back four-fold." •Then Jesus said to him, "Today salvation has come to this house, 9 because he's a son of Abraham, too. •For the Son of Man came to seek 10 out and save what was lost."

•[v] While they were listening to these things he continued and told them 11 a parable, because he was near Jerusalem and they thought the Kingdom of God was going to appear immediately. •So he said, "A noble born man 12 departed for a distant country to receive the kingship for himself and then return. •So he summoned ten of his servants and gave them ten gold coins 13 and said to them, 'Do business till I come.' •But his citizens hated him and 14 sent a representative after him to say, 'We don't want this man to reign over us.' •And it happened that when he returned after receiving the king- 15 ship he ordered the servants to whom he'd given the money to be summoned so he could find out what profit they'd made. •The first one ap- 16

[u] Mt 20:29-34; Mk 10:46-52.   [v] Mt 25:14-30.

19:13 The gold coin, or mina, was a Greek coin worth 100 denarii or 1/60 talent.

View of Jericho, the city of Zacchaeus.

17 peared and said, 'Lord, your one coin made ten more.' •And he said to
him, 'Well done, good servant! Because you've been trustworthy in a small
18 affair, you shall have authority over ten cities!' •The second servant came
19 and said, 'Your one coin made five.' •So to this one he said, 'And *you*
20 shall be over *five* cities.' •Then the other came and said, 'Lord, behold
21 your coin, which I had tucked away in a handkerchief — •I feared you,
because you're a stern man — you take what you didn't set down and
22 reap what you didn't sow.' •He said to him, 'I'll judge you from your own
mouth, wicked servant! You knew that I'm a stern man, taking what I did-
23 n't set down and reaping what I didn't sow, did you? •Why then didn't
you give my money to a bank? Then when I came I would have collected
24 it with interest!' •And he said to those who were standing by, 'Take the
25,26 coin from him and give it to the one who has the ten. [•] •I say to you,

> To the one who has, it will be given,
> But from the one who doesn't have,
>   even what he has will be taken.

19:25 The best manuscript tradition omits v. 25: "And they said to him, 'Lord, he *has* ten coins!'"

•But bring those enemies of mine here who didn't want me ruling over 27 them, and slaughter them in front of me.'"

•[w] And after saying these things he went on ahead, going up to 28 Jerusalem. •It happened that when he drew near to Bethphage and 29 Bethany at the mount called Olivet he sent two of his disciples •and said, 30 "Go into the village opposite you. When you enter it you'll find a colt tethered on which no man has ever sat; untie it and bring it. •And if 31 anyone asks you, 'Why are you untying the colt?' this is what you'll say, 'The Lord has need of it.'" •When they went off, those who were sent 32 found it just as he'd told them. •Now when they were untying the colt 33 its owners said to them, "Why are you untying the colt?" •So they said, 34 "The Lord has need of it." •They led it to Jesus and, after spreading 35 their cloaks on the colt, they had Jesus mount it. •Then as he proceeded 36 they spread their cloaks out on the road.

•By this time he was approaching the descent from the Mount of 37 Olives and the whole crowd of the disciples began to praise God in a loud voice, rejoicing at all the mighty works they had seen and •saying, 38

> "Blessed is the king
>   who comes in the name of the Lord;
> Peace in Heaven
>   and glory in the highest!"

•Some of the Pharisees from the crowd said to him, "Teacher, rebuke 39 your disciples!" •He answered and said, "I tell you, if *they* were silent 40 the *stones* would cry out!"

•When Jesus drew near and caught sight of the city he began to weep 41 over it •and said, "If only you had realized on this day what leads to 42 peace — but now it's been hidden from your eyes. •Because days will 43 come upon you,

> And your enemies will set up a siege wall
>   around you,
> They'll surround you and close you in
>   on all sides,

---

[w] Mt 21:1-11; Mk 11:1-11; Jn 12:12-19.

19:28f Beginning with Jesus' entry into Jerusalem the fulfillment of Jesus' mission moves inexorably to its climax. As seen through the eyes of faith, all these events are "in accordance with the Scriptures," and the account is punctuated with frequent references to Scripture in order to underline this. All Jesus' words and actions are now seen in their full eschatological significance: the Kingdom has come and, following the Lord's atoning death, it will be proclaimed to all nations.
19:38 Ps 118:26.

44 •And utterly destroy you, and your children
within you,
And they will not leave a stone upon a stone
within you,

because you didn't recognize the appointed time of your visitation."
45 •ˣ And when he went into the Temple he began to drive out those
46 who were selling •and he said to them, "It has been written,

And my house shall be a house of prayer,
but you have made it a **robbers' den**!"

47 •And he taught daily in the Temple. Now the chief priests and the
scribes as well as the leaders of the people sought to do away with him,
48 •yet they couldn't find anything to do, because all the people hung upon his words.

1 **20** •ʸ It happened that on one of the days when he was teaching
the people in the Temple and proclaiming the good news the
2 chief priests and scribes along with the elders came up •and said to him,
"Tell us by what authority you do these things, or who it is who gave
3 you this authority." •In answer he said to them, "I'll ask a question, too,
4 and *you* tell *me*! •John's baptism — was it from Heaven or from men?"
5 •They conferred with each other, saying, "If we say, 'From Heaven,'
6 he'll say, 'Then why didn't you believe him?' •But if we say, 'From men,'
all the people will stone us because they're convinced John was a
7 prophet." • So they answered that they didn't know where John's bap-
8 tism was from. •And Jesus said to them, "Nor will I tell you by what
authority I do these things."

9 •ᶻ Then he went and told the people this parable. "A man planted a
vineyard and leased it to farmers and left home on a journey for a con-
10 siderable time. •And at the proper time he sent a servant to the farmers to have them give him some of the fruit of the vineyard, but the farm-
11 ers sent him away empty handed after beating him. •Again he sent another servant, but after beating that one and treating him shamefully they
12 sent him away empty handed. •And again he sent yet a third, but after
13 injuring this one, too, they threw him out. •Then the owner of the vineyard said, 'What can I do? I'll send my beloved son; maybe they'll feel

ˣ *Mt 21:12-17; Mk 11:15-19; Jn 2:13-22.* ʸ *Mt 21:23-27; Mk 11:27-33.* ᶻ *Mt 21:33-46; Mk 12:1-12.*

19:46 Is 56:7; Jr 7:11.
20:9 Is 5:1. The vineyard was a well-known symbol for Israel.

shame before him.' •But when the farmers saw him they conferred with 14
one another and said, 'This is the heir — let's kill him so the inheritance
will be ours!' •Then they threw him out of the vineyard and killed him. 15
What will the owner of the vineyard do to them? •He'll come and de- 16
stroy those farmers and give the vineyard to others." Those who were
listening said, "God forbid!" •But he gazed at them and said, "What, 17
then, is this that is written,

> The stone which the builders rejected
>   has become the cornerstone.
> •Everyone who falls on that stone 18
>   will be broken to pieces,
>   while whoever it falls upon it will crush."

•The scribes and chief priests wanted to get their hands on him at that 19
very hour, yet they feared the people because they knew he'd spoken
this parable against them.

•[a] Then they kept him under observation and sent spies who pre- 20
tended to be upright men so they could seize on what he said in order
to hand him over to the authority and power of the governor. •And they 21
put this question to him, "Teacher, we know you speak and teach plainly and without regard for the person; instead, you truly teach the way
of God. •Is it lawful for us to pay the tax to Caesar or not?" •Realizing 22,2
their deceit, he said to them, •"Show me a denarius; whose image and 24
inscription does it have?" "Caesar's," they said. •Then he said to them, 25

> "Then render to Caesar the things that are Caesar's
>   and to God the things that are God's."

•And they weren't able to catch him in what he said before the peo- 26
ple, and they remained silent, amazed at this answer.

•[b] Then some of the Sadducees came forward — those who say 27
there's no resurrection — and they put this question to him, •"Teacher, 28
Moses wrote for us, if a brother with a wife should die, and he should
be childless, then his brother should take the wife and raise up offspring
for his brother. •So then, there were seven brothers, and the first, after 29
taking a wife, died childless; •the second •and the third also took her 30,3
and, likewise, the seven, too, left no children and died. •Finally the 32

[a] Mt 22:15-22; Mk 12:13-17.   [b] Mt 22:23-33; Mk 12:18-27.

20:17 Ps 118:2.
20:24 A denarius was a Roman silver coin equal to the daily wage of a laborer.

LUKE

Monastery of Saint Catherine at Mount Sinai.

33 woman died, too. •So at the resurrection, whose wife will the woman
34 be? — all seven had her as wife." •Jesus said to them, "The children of
35 this age marry and are given in marriage, •but those counted worthy of
that age and resurrection from the dead neither marry nor are given in
36 marriage, •because they are no longer able to die — they're angel-like
37 and are children of God, since they've attained the resurrection. •But
that the dead rise Moses, too, made known at the passage about the
thorn bush, when he calls the Lord **God of Abraham and God of**
38 **Isaac and God of Jacob.** •Now He's not God of the dead but of the
39 living — for Him they're all alive." •In answer some of the scribes said,
40 "Teacher, you spoke well," •and no one dared to question him any
longer.
41   •c Then he said to them, "How can they say the Messiah is the son
42 of David? — •David himself says in the Book of Psalms,

The Lord said to my lord,
'Sit at My right hand

c *Mt 22:41-46; Mk 12:35-37.*   20:37 Ex 3:6   20:42-43 Ps 110:1.

215

**·till I make your enemies a footstool
for your feet.'** 43

·If David calls him 'lord,' how can he be David's son?" 44
    ·[d] Then with the whole people listening he said to the disciples, 45

    ·"Beware of the scribes, 46
Who like to walk about in long robes,
    and love greetings in the markets,
And seats of honor in the synagogues,
    and places of honor at the banquets;
    ·They eat up the houses of widows, 47
    and as a pretense make long prayers —
These will receive the greater condemnation!"

21 ·[e] Then he looked up and saw the rich dropping their offerings 1
into the offering box. ·Now he saw a poor widow drop two small 2
coins there ·and he said, "Truly, I say to you, this poor widow put in 3
more than all of them. ·All the others gave offerings from their abun- 4
dance, while she from her want gave all the livelihood she had."

·[f] And when some of them were talking about the Temple, that it had 5
been decorated with beautiful stones and votive offerings, he said,
·"These things you see — the days will come in which not a stone will 6
be left upon a stone which will not be torn down."

·[g] "Teacher," they asked him, "when will these things be, and what 7
will be the sign when they're about to happen?" ·"See that you're not 8
led astray," he said, "for many will come in my name, saying, 'I am he!'
and, 'The time has come!' Don't follow them. ·But when you hear of 9
wars and insurrections, don't be terrified — these things must happen
first, but the end will not come at once." ·Then he said to them, 10

"Nation will rise against nation,
    and kingdom against kingdom,
·There will be powerful earthquakes 11
    and famines and plagues in various places,
There will be dreadful sights
    and great signs from Heaven.
·But before all this they'll lay hands on you 12
    and they'll persecute you —

[d] Mt 23:1-36; Mk 12:38-40. [e] Mt 12:41-44. [f] Mt 24:1-2; Mk 13:1-2. [g] Mt 24:3-14; Mk 13:3-13.

Handing you over to the synagogues and prisons,
   having you brought before kings and governors
     for the sake of my name;

13,14 •this will lead to you giving witness. •So resolve in your hearts not to
15 prepare ahead of time how to defend yourselves — •I'll give you eloquence and wisdom which all those opposing you will not be able to re-
16 sist or refute. •But you'll be handed over by parents and brothers and
17 kinsmen and friends. They'll kill some of you •and you'll be hated by all
18 because of my name, •yet not a hair on your head will be destroyed.
19 •You'll gain your lives by your endurance."

20   •ʰ "But when you see Jerusalem surrounded by an army,
     know, then, that its desolation has come.
21   •Then those in Judea must flee to the mountains, and
      those inside it must leave,
    and those in the countryside must not enter it.
22   •Because these are days of retribution,
    of the fulfillment of everything
     that has been written.
23   •Woe to women who are with child,
    and to those who are nursing in those days,
  For there will be great distress over the land,
    and wrath to this people,
24   •And they will fall by the edge of the sword,
    and be made captive in all nations,
  And Jerusalem will be trampled by the Gentiles
    until the times of the Gentiles are fulfilled."
25   •ⁱ "And there will be signs in the sun
    and moon and stars,
    and distress of nations on the earth in despair
     at the roaring of the sea and waves,
26   •Men fainting from fear and foreboding of what
    is coming upon the world,
    for **the powers of the heavens** will be shaken.
27   •And then they'll see **the Son of Man**
    coming on a cloud with power and great glory.

ʰ Mt 24:15-21; Mk 13:14-19. ⁱ Mt 24:29-31; Mk 13:24-27.

21:26 Hg 2:6,11.   21:27 Dn 7:13.

•Now when these things begin to happen, stand up 28
    and raise your heads,
        because your deliverance is at hand."

•[j] And he told them a parable. "Look at the fig tree and all the trees. 29
•When they put out leaves you see for yourselves and know that spring 30
is near. •So, too, you, when you see these things happening, you'll know 31
that the Kingdom of God is near. •Amen, I say to you, this generation 32
will not pass away until all these things come to pass.

•The heavens and the earth will pass away, 33
But my words will *not* pass away."

•"But take care for yourselves lest your hearts be weighed down with 34
dissipation and drunkenness and everyday cares, and that day come upon you unexpectedly, •like a trap, for it will come upon all those living 35
on the face of the whole earth. •But be alert at all times, and pray that 36
you'll have the strength to escape all these things that are going to happen, and to stand before the Son of Man."

•Now during the days he taught in the Temple, while at night he'd 37
go out and spend the night on the mount called Olivet, •and all the peo- 38
ple came early in the morning to listen to him in the Temple.

I. LAST SUPPER AND PASSION

22 •[k] Now the feast of Unleavened Bread was approaching, which 1
is called the Passover, •and the chief priests and scribes kept con- 2
sidering how they could do away with him, because they feared the people. •Then Satan entered into Judas — the one called Iscariot — who 3
was numbered among the Twelve, •and he went off and spoke with the 4
chief priests and officers as to how he should hand him over to them.
•They were overjoyed and agreed to pay him with silver money, •and 5,6
he agreed and began to seek the right time to hand Jesus over to them
away from the crowd.

•[l] Now the day of Unleavened Bread came, on which the Passover 7
lamb was supposed to be sacrificed. •Jesus sent Peter and John and said, 8

[j] Mt 24:32-35; Mk 13:28-31.   [k] Mt 26:1-5; Mk 14:1-2; Jn 11:45-53.
[l] Mt 26:17-25; Mk 14:12-21; Jn 13:21-30.

22:1 The eight day period during which unleavened bread was eaten was closely linked to the
Passover, but had its origins in a festival marking
the beginning of the barley harvest.

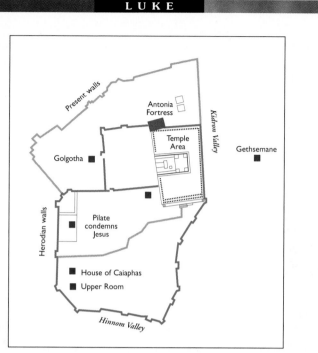

Jerusalem. The places of the Passion. (Lk 22-23)

9 "Go prepare the Passover for us to eat." •So they said to him, "Where
10 do you want us to prepare it?" •"Behold," Jesus told them, "when you
go into the city a man carrying a clay jar of water will meet you; follow
11 him to the house he enters. •Tell the master of the house, 'The Teacher
says to you, "Where's the room where I'll eat the Passover with my dis-
12 ciples?"' •He'll show you a large, furnished, upstairs room; make ready
13 there." •When they went off they found it just as he'd told them, and
they prepared the Passover.

14,15 •ᵐ When the hour came he sat down at table with the apostles. •And
he said to them, "With what longing have I longed to eat this Passover
16 with you before I suffer, •for I tell you that I will not eat it until it's ful-
17 filled in the Kingdom of God." •Then he took a cup, blessed it, and
18 said, "Take this and divide it among yourselves, •for I tell you I will not
drink the fruit of the vine from this moment until the Kingdom of God
19 comes." •Then he took bread, blessed it, broke it, and gave it to them,
saying, "This is my body which is given up for you — do this in my re-

ᵐ Mt 26:26-30; Mk 14:22-26.

membrance." •Likewise he took the cup after they had eaten and said, 20 "This cup is the new covenant in my blood which is poured out for you. •But, behold, the hand of the one who will hand me over is on the table 21 with me, •because the Son of Man is going as it has been decided, but 22 woe to the man through whom he's handed over!" •And they began 23 to argue among themselves as to which of them it could be who intended to do this.

•Now a dispute also arose among them as to which of them should 24 be considered the greatest. •But he said to them, 25

"The kings of the Gentiles lord it over them,
And those who exercise authority over them
    are called 'benefactors.'

•But not so with you! Instead, 26

The greatest among you shall be like the youngest,
    and the ruler like the one who serves.

•For who is greater, the one reclining at table or the one serving? Is-27 n't it the one reclining at table? But I'm among you as the one who serves. •You're the ones who stayed with me in my trials •and I grant 28,29 to you dominion, just as my Father granted it to me, •so you can eat 30 and drink at my table in my Kingdom, and you can sit on thrones judging the Twelve Tribes of Israel."

•[n] "Simon, Simon! Behold, Satan has been demanding you Twelve, 31 to sift you like wheat, •but I've prayed for you, Peter, so that your faith 32 may not fail, and you, when you return, strengthen your brothers." •Peter said to him, "Lord, I'm ready to go with you even to prison 33 and to death." •But Jesus said, "I tell you, Peter, the cock will not crow 34 today until you deny you know me three times."

•And he said to them, "When I sent you without a purse and bags 35 and sandals you didn't lack for anything, did you?" "Nothing," they said. •Then he said to them, 36

"But now, let whoever has a purse take it,
    and likewise a bag,
And let whoever is without one
    sell his cloak and buy a sword.

[n] Mt 26:31-35; Mk 14:27-31; Jn 13:36-38.

22:31-32 In v. 31 "you" is plural and refers to all the disciples, but in v. 32 it is singular and refers to Peter, clearly giving primacy to Peter. The words "Twelve" and "Peter" are added for clarity.

37 •For I tell you that this Scripture must
come to completion in me,
And he was counted among the outlaws,
for that, too, which was written about me,
has its completion."

38 •Then they said, "Lord, look, we have two swords here." But Jesus
said to them, "That's enough."
39 •[o] And he went out and left for the Mount of Olives, as was his cus-
40 tom, and the disciples followed him, too. •When he came to the place
41 he said to them, "Pray that you won't be put to the test." •Then he withdrew about a stone's throw away from them, knelt down, and began to
42 pray, •saying, "Father, if it's Your will, take this cup away from me, but
,44,45 not my will but Yours be done." [•] [•] •When he rose from his prayer
46 and came to the disciples he found them sleeping, out of grief, •and he
said to them, "Why are you sleeping? Get up and pray that you won't
come to the test."
47 •[p] While he was still speaking a crowd came with the one called Judas, one of the Twelve, at the head of them, and he approached Jesus
48 to kiss him. •But Jesus said to him, "Judas, would you hand over the Son
49 of Man with a kiss?" •Now when those around him saw what was com-
50 ing they said, "Lord, shall we strike with the sword?" •And one of them
51 struck the high priest's servant and cut off his right ear. •But in response
Jesus said, "Enough of this!" and he picked up the ear and cured him.
52 •Then Jesus said to those who had come out after him, chief priests and
Temple officers and elders, "You came out with swords and clubs as if
53 after a robber? •When I was with you daily in the Temple you didn't lay
hands on me, but this is your hour and the power of darkness."
54 •[q] After they seized him they led him away and brought him into the
55 high priest's house, while Peter followed at a distance. •Now when they'd
lit a fire in the middle of the courtyard and had sat down together Pe-
56 ter sat down with them. •A maidservant who saw him as he sat in the
57 light stared at him and said, "This fellow was with him, too!" •But he
58 denied it and said, "I don't know him, woman!" •A little later someone
else saw him and said, "You're one of them, too!" But Peter said, "Man,

[o] *Mt 26:36-46; Mk 14:32-42.* [p] *Mt 26:47-56; Mk 14:43-50; Jn 18:3-11.*
[q] *Mt 26:57-58, 69-75; Mk 14:53-54, 66-72; Jn 18:12-18, 25-27.*

22:37 Is 53:12.
22:43-44 The best manuscript tradition omits vv. 43-44: "Then there appeared to him an angel from Heaven to strengthen him, and in his anguish he prayed more earnestly, and his sweat became like drops of blood falling to the ground."

I'm not!" •And when an hour or so had passed, still another insisted, 59 saying, "Of course this fellow was with him — he's a Galilean, too!" •But 60 Peter said, "Man, I don't know what you're talking about!" Immediately, while he was still speaking, a cock crowed. •And the Lord turned and 61 looked right at Peter, and Peter remembered what the Lord said when he told him, "Before a cock crows today you'll deny me three times." •And he went outside and wept bitterly. 62

•ʳ Then the men guarding him began to make fun of him and beat him. 63 •After blindfolding him they'd ask him, "Prophesy! Who was it that struck 64 you?" •And they spoke many other blasphemies against him. 65

•ˢ When day came the Body of Elders of the people was gathered, 66 both chief priests and scribes, and they led him away to their Sanhedrin •and said, "If you *are* the Messiah, tell us!" But he said to them, 67

"If I tell you, you won't believe me,
•And if I ask you questions, you won't answer me. 68

•But from this moment **the Son of Man will be seated at the right** 69 **hand of the power of God.**" •Then they all said, "Then you *are* the 70 Son of God?" But he said to them, "*You* say that I am." •Then they said, 71 "What further need do we have for testimony? — we've heard it from his own mouth!"

23 •ᵗ Then their whole assembly rose and led him to Pilate. •They 1,2 began to accuse him and said, "We found this fellow misleading our nation — forbidding payment of taxes to Caesar and calling himself Messiah, a king." •Then Pilate questioned him, saying, "Are you the King 3 of the Jews?" But in answer Jesus said, "You say so." •Pilate said to the 4 chief priests and the crowds, "I find no case against this man." •But they 5 insisted and said, "He's inciting the people, teaching throughout all of Judea, starting from Galilee as far as here."

•When Pilate heard this he asked if the man was a Galilean, •and when 6,7 he found out that Jesus was from Herod's jurisdiction he sent him to Herod, who was himself also in Jerusalem at that time. •Herod was ex- 8 tremely pleased to see Jesus — he'd been wanting to see him for a considerable time because he'd heard about him and was hoping to see some sign performed by him. •He questioned Jesus at some length, but Jesus 9

ʳ *Mt 26:67-68; Mk 14:65.*   ˢ *Mt 26:59-66; Mk 14:55-64; Jn 18:19-24.*
ᵗ *Mt 27:1-2, 11-14; Mk 15:1-5; Jn 18:28-38.*

22:69 Ps 110:1.
22:70 "You say that I am." This seemingly non-committal reply is a tacit acceptance of the truth of what was said, but not necessarily as it was understood by Jesus' interrogators.

*The "Holy Steps" which led from the Kidron Valley
to the house of Caiaphas.*

10 gave him no answer. •Meanwhile the chief priests and scribes were stand-
11 ing by, accusing him vehemently. •But after Herod and his soldiers had
treated him with contempt and mocked him Herod had him dressed in
12 fine apparel and sent him back to Pilate. •On that very day Herod and
Pilate became friends — previously they'd been hostile to each other.
13   •[u] Now when Pilate had called together the chief priests and the rulers
14 and the people •he said to them, "You brought me this man as one who
was misleading the people and, behold, after interrogating him in your
presence, I've found no case against this man concerning what you al-
15 leged against him; •moreover, neither has Herod — *he* sent him back
16 to *us*. And, behold, he's done nothing deserving of death. •So, I'll re-
17,18 lease him after teaching him a lesson." [•] •But they all cried out together

---

u *Mt 27:15-26; Mk 15:6-15; Jn 18:39 - 19:16.*

23:16 Perhaps, "after having him scourged." Cf. also v. 22.

23:17 The best manuscript tradition omits this verse: "By custom he released one prisoner to them during the festival."

and said, "Take this fellow away and release Barabbas to us!" — •who 19 had been thrown into prison during a riot in the city and for murder. •So Pilate addressed them again, wanting to release Jesus, •but they kept 20,21 shouting and saying, "Crucify him, crucify him!" •Then for a third time 22 he said to them, "But what wrong has the fellow done? I've found no charge against him deserving death, so I'll teach him a lesson and release him." •But they were insistent, demanding with loud cries that he 23 be crucified, and their outcries prevailed. •Pilate decided that their de- 24 mand should be carried out. •So he released the one they were asking 25 for, who had been thrown in prison for rioting and murder, while Jesus he handed over to their will.

•ᵛ As they were leading him away they seized Simon, a Cyrenean, 26 who was coming from the country, and laid the cross on him to carry behind Jesus. •Now a large crowd of the people was following him, as 27 well as women who were lamenting and wailing for him. •But Jesus 28 turned to them and said, "Daughters of Jerusalem, don't weep for me; weep, instead, for yourselves and for your children, •because, behold, 29 the days are coming in which people will say,

'Blessed are those who are barren,
    and the wombs that did not give birth,
    and the breasts that did not nurse!'
•Then **they will say to the mountains, 'Fall on us!'** 30
    and to the hills, 'Cover us!'

•Because if they do these things when the wood is green, what will hap- 31 pen when it's dry?"

•They also led away two other criminals with him to be killed, •and 32,33 when they came to the place called "the Skull" they crucified him there as well as the criminals, one on his right and one on his left. •Then Je- 34 sus said, "Father, forgive them, for they don't know what they're doing." Then **they divided his clothes and cast lots for them.** •And 35 the people stood there watching while the rulers made fun of him, saying, "He saved others, let him save himself, if this fellow is God's Mes-

---

ᵛ Mt 27:32-44; Mk 15:21-32; Jn 19:17-27.

23:26 Cyrene was a North African city which had a large Jewish community.
23:30 Ho 10:8.
23:31 This seemingly enigmatic statement is believed to have the following meaning: if "they" (the Romans) react so violently against Jesus, who opposed the extreme nationalists (and thus was "green," not ready for the fire), what will be the result when those who were pushing for confrontation with the Romans get their way? The result will be the tragic conflagration prophesied in the preceding verse.
23:34 Ps 22:18.

36 siah, the Chosen One!" •The soldiers who had come also mocked him,
37 offering him sour wine •and saying, "If you're the King of the Jews,
38 save yourself!" •There was also an inscription above him which read,
"This is the King of the Jews."

39 •One of the criminals who was hanging blasphemed him and said,
40 "Aren't you the Messiah? Save yourself and us!" •But in response the
other rebuked him and said, "Don't you fear God? — you're under the
41 same sentence! •And we justly, for we're being paid back fittingly for what
42 we did, while this fellow has done nothing wrong." •Then he said, "Je-
43 sus, remember me when you come into your Kingdom!" •Jesus said to
him, "Amen, I say to you, this day you'll be with me in Paradise."

44 •[w] It was already about noon and darkness came over the whole land
45 until about three o'clock, •the sun having failed, while the sanctuary cur-
46 tain was torn down the middle. •Then Jesus called out with a loud voice
and said, "Father, **into Your hands I entrust my spirit!**" And after
47 saying this, he breathed his last. •When the centurion saw what had hap-
48 pened he glorified God and said, "This man really was innocent!" •And
all the crowds who had assembled for this spectacle, when they saw what
49 had happened, returned, beating their breasts. •But all those who had
known him stood there at a distance, and the women who had followed
with him from Galilee watched these things.

J. RESURRECTION,
APPEARANCES, AND ASCENSION OF JESUS

50 •[x] There was a man named Joseph who was a Council member, a
51 good and upright man from the Judean city of Arimathea — •he had
not agreed with their plan and deed — who looked forward to the King-
52,53 dom of God; •he came to Pilate and asked for Jesus' body, •and after
taking it down he wrapped it in a linen shroud and placed it in a tomb
54 hewn out of rock in which no one had yet been laid. •And it was the
55 Day of Preparation and the Sabbath was about to begin. •Now the
women had followed along, those who had come with him from Galilee,
56 and they saw the tomb and how his body was laid, •and they returned
and prepared aromatic spices and perfumed oils. Then they rested on
the Sabbath, in accordance with the commandment,

w Mt 27:45-46; Mk 15:33-41; Jn 19:28-30.   x Mt 27:57-61; Mk 15:42-47; Jn 19:38-42.

23:46 Ps 31:5.

225

24 •ʸ but on the first day of the week, at early dawn, the women came 1 to the tomb bringing the aromatic spices they had prepared. •They found the stone rolled away from the tomb •and when they went 2,3 in they didn't find the Lord Jesus' body, •and it happened that when 4 they were at a loss over this, behold, two men in dazzling clothes stood near them. •The women were terrified and bowed their faces to the 5 ground, and the men said to them, "Why are you looking for He Who Lives among the dead? •He isn't here — he's risen. Remember — he 6 spoke to you when he was still in Galilee, •and said that the Son of Man 7 would have to be handed over into the hands of sinners and be crucified and rise on the third day." •Then they remembered what he had 8 said, •and when they returned from the tomb they told all these things 9 to the Eleven and to all the rest. •Now it was Mary Magdalen and Joan- 10 na and Mary mother of James and the rest with them who told these things to the apostles. •And it all seemed like nonsense to them, and 11 they didn't believe the women. •But Peter got up and ran to the tomb, 12 and when he stooped down he saw only the linen cloths, and he went away wondering to himself at what had happened.

•ᶻ And, behold, two of them were travelling the same day to a village 13 seven miles away from Jerusalem named Emmaus, •talking to each oth- 14 er about all these events. •And it happened while they were talking and 15 discussing these things that Jesus himself approached and began to walk with them, •but their eyes were kept from recognizing him. •So he said 16,17 to them, "What are these words you're exchanging with each other as you walk?" They stopped, gloomily, •and in answer one named Cleopas 18 said to him, "Are you the only person staying in Jerusalem who's unaware of the things that have happened there in these days?" •"What 19 things?" he said. So they told him, "Those concerning Jesus of Nazareth, who was a prophet mighty in word and deed before God and all the people, •how the chief priests and our rulers handed him over to a sentence 20 of death and had him crucified. •We were hoping that he was the one 21 who was coming to liberate Israel, but with all these things it's now the third day since this happened. •Moreover, some women from among 22 us have amazed us. They were at the tomb early in the morning •and 23 didn't find his body, and they came and said they'd even seen a vision of angels, who said he was alive. •Some of those with us went off to 24 the tomb, and they, too, found it just as the women said, but they didn't see him." •He said to them, "How dense you are, and how slow of 25

ʸ Mt 28:1-10; Mk 16:1-8; Jn 20:1-10.   ᶻ Mk 16:12-13.

24:21 Cf. note at 2:25, 38.

²⁶ heart to believe all the prophets said! •Didn't the Messiah have to suf-
²⁷ fer all these things and enter into his glory?" •And starting from Moses
and all the prophets he interpreted for them what was in all the Scriptures about himself.

²⁸ •They were approaching the village to which they were travelling, and
²⁹ when he made as if to travel further •they urged him and said, "Stay
with us, because it's near evening and the day has already come to a
³⁰ close." So he went in to stay with them. •And it happened that when
he reclined at table with them he took the bread and blessed it, broke
³¹ it, and gave it to them. •Then their eyes were opened and they recog-
³² nized him, and he disappeared from them. •And they said to each oth-
er, "Weren't our hearts burning within us while he spoke to us on the
³³ road, as he opened up the Scriptures to us?" •They got up and returned
to Jerusalem that very hour, and they found the Eleven and those with
³⁴ them gathered together, •who said, "The Lord has really risen and has

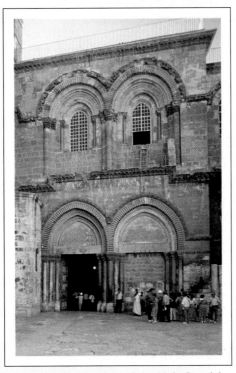

Entrance to the Basilica of the Holy Sepulchre.

been seen by Simon!" •And they related what had happened on the ³⁵ road, and how they recognized him in the breaking of the bread.

•ª As they were speaking of these things Jesus stood among them ³⁶ and said to them, "Peace be with you!" •They were startled and terri- ³⁷ fied, thinking they were seeing a spirit. •And he said to them, "Why are ³⁸ you frightened, and why are doubts arising in your hearts? •Look at my ³⁹ hands and my feet — it's me! Touch me and see, because a spirit does- n't have flesh and bones, as you see I do!" •And as he said this he ⁴⁰ showed them his hands and feet. •But since they were still incredulous ⁴¹ and wondering for joy, he said to them, "Do you have anything to eat here?" •So they gave him a piece of broiled fish •and he took it and ate ⁴²,⁴³ it in front of them.•Then he said to them, "These are my words which ⁴⁴ I spoke to you while I was still with you, that everything written about me in the Torah of Moses and in the Prophets and in the Psalms had to be fulfilled." •Then he opened their minds so they could understand ⁴⁵ the Scriptures. •And he said to them, "So it is written, that the Messi- ⁴⁶ ah would suffer and rise from the dead on the third day, •and repen- ⁴⁷ tance and forgiveness of sins for all nations would be proclaimed in his name — starting from Jerusalem."

•"You are witnesses of these things. •And, behold, I'm sending the ⁴⁸,⁴⁹ promise of my Father upon you, so stay in the city until you're clothed with power from on high."

•ᵇ Then he led them out to Bethany, and he lifted up his hands and ⁵⁰ blessed them. •And it happened that as he was blessing them he passed ⁵¹ away from them and was carried up to Heaven. •After they worshipped ⁵² him they returned to Jerusalem with great joy, •and they were constantly ⁵³ in the Temple, blessing God.

ª Mt 28:16-20; Mk 16:14-18; Jn 20:19-23.   ᵇ Mk 16:19-20.

24:50-53 As the Gospel opens with the assem- bly of Israel, so it ends. The New Israel, the Church, assembles under the New Covenant as Jesus raises his hands in blessing, the high priestly gesture now used by the Messianic high priest.

THE GOSPEL
ACCORDING TO

JOHN

Introduction to the Gospel According to John

The last several decades have seen a drastic reevaluation of the Gospel of John. Whereas previously it was held by many to have been written late, c. 130-150 A.D., it is now generally believed that John's Gospel was completed by 100 A.D. at the latest. Once regarded as the product of a Hellenistic mind and environment, it is now recognized that this Gospel's roots are deep within Palestine and the Judaism of our Lord's time. Once considered to be primarily a theoretical theological creation only tenuously linked to the Jesus of history, modern scholarship has established that, in fact, the sources behind the Gospel of John embody some of the oldest and most reliable of all Gospel traditions. Finally, it is now realized that the Johannine portrait of Jesus is in fundamental harmony with that of the Synoptic Gospels.

The basic conceptual framework for John's meditative narration can be briefly summarized. The Word of God became man in Jesus. This is fundamental for John. For him, the truth is not theory, it is a living Person, and this explains the wealth of detail in his narratives. The Word came accredited. God Himself bore witness to him, as did John the Baptist, the Scriptures, the disciples, as well as Jesus through his signs and life-giving words. Nevertheless, Jesus was rejected by the World (specifically, by his own, the Jewish authorities) and died as a sacrifice of love in accordance with the Divine plan to bring light, sight, belief, and life into the darkness and blindness of the World. Yet to those who believe, Jesus still offers life, and his resurrection is a witness to his victory and his life-giving power, not as a symbol but as a fact that has been seen and touched. And when we believe the witness that is given we begin to live the life that Jesus has shown us; we begin to know that God is Love.

A. PROLOGUE

1 **1** •In the beginning was the Word,
And the Word was with God,
And the Word was God.
2 •He was in the beginning with God.
3 •All things came to be through him,
And without him nothing came to be.
4 What came to be •through him was life,
And the life was the light of men,
5 •And the light shines in the darkness,
And the darkness did not overcome it.

6,7 •There was a man sent by God named John. •He came as a witness to bear witness concerning the light, so that all might believe through **8** him. •He was not the light, but came to bear witness concerning the **9** light. •It was the true light that enlightens every man that was coming into the world.

10 •He was in the world, and the world
came to be through him,
Yet the world did not know him.
11 •He came to his own home,
Yet his own people did not receive him.

12 •But all who did receive him, to them he gave the power to become **13** sons of God, to those who believe in his name, •those who were born, not of blood nor of the will of flesh nor of the will of a man, but of God.

14 •And the Word became flesh
And dwelt among us,
And we saw his glory,
Glory as of the only begotten of the Father,
Full of grace and truth.

•John bore witness concerning him and cried out, saying, "This was 15
the one of whom I said, 'The one who's coming after me is above me,
because he was before me.'"

•For we have all received of his fullness, 16
and grace upon grace,
•For the Torah was given through Moses, 17
Grace and truth came through Jesus Christ.
•No one has ever seen God; 18
The only begotten Son of God,
who is in the bosom of the Father, he has revealed Him.

B. THE BAPTIST AND THE FIRST DISCIPLES

•[a] And this was John's witness when the Jews of Jerusalem sent priests 19
and Levites to ask him, "Who are you?" •He stated plainly and didn't 20
deny it, and he stated plainly, "I'm not the Messiah." •"Then what are 21
you?" they asked him, "Are you Elijah?" "I'm not," he said. "Are you
the Prophet?" "No," he answered. •So they said to him, "Who are you? 22
Give us an answer for those who sent us! What do you say about yourself?" •He said, 23

**"I am the voice of one crying out in the desert,
'Make straight the way of the Lord,'"**

as Isaiah the prophet said. •There were also some who had been sent 24
from the Pharisees, •and they asked him, "Then why do you baptize if 25
you're neither the Messiah nor Elijah nor the Prophet?" •John answered 26
them by saying, "I baptize with water; among you stands one you don't
know, •the one who comes after me, the strap of whose sandal I'm not 27
worthy to untie." •These things took place at Bethany beyond the Jor- 28
dan, where John was baptizing.

[a] Mt 3:1-12; Mk 1:2-8; Lk 3:15-17.

1:14 The verb translated "dwelt" literally means, "set his tent," and referred in the Old Testament to God's presence in the tabernacle. "Glory" refers to God's power as manifested, then in the tabernacle, and now in the person of Jesus.
1:17 "Torah," or "law," referred to the totality of God's revelation which could serve as a guide for one's life. Torah was, therefore, quintessentially, the Decalogue, but it also extended far beyond the confines of the Pentateuch to areas which we would never characterize as "law," as can be seen in several New Testament passages.
1:21-25 "The Prophet" is the figure referred to in Dt 18:15-19. Cf. Jn 6:14; 7:40.
1:23 Is 40:3 (Septuagint).

River Jordan to the south of the Sea of Galilee:
place where pilgrims repeat their baptismal promises.

29 •The next day he saw Jesus coming toward him and said, "Here is the
30 Lamb of God who takes away the sin of the world! •This is the one of
whom I said, 'After me comes a man who is above me, because he was
31 before me.' •I didn't know him; instead, I came baptizing with water for
32 this reason — so he might be revealed to Israel." •Then John bore witness and said, "I saw the Spirit descending like a dove from Heaven, and
33 it remained upon him. •I didn't know him, but He Who sent me to baptize with water, He said to me, 'Whoever you see the Spirit descending
upon and remaining upon, he's the one who baptizes with the Holy Spir-
34 it.' •And I've seen and have borne witness that this is the Son of God."

35 •The next day John was again standing there, as well as two of his
36 disciples, •and, as Jesus walked by, John looked right at him and said,
37 "Here is the Lamb of God." •His two disciples heard him speaking and
38 they followed Jesus. •When Jesus turned and saw them following him
he said to them, "What are you looking for?" So they said to him, "Rabbi" — which, translated, means "Teacher" — "where are you staying?"

1:29 At 19:36 we will see Jesus explicitly compared to the Paschal lamb that saved Israel from death.

•"Come and you'll see," he said to them. So they came and saw where 39
he was staying, and they stayed with him that day; it was about four in
the afternoon. •Now Andrew, the brother of Simon Peter, was one of 40
the two who were listening to John and had followed him. •He first found 41
his own brother, Simon, and said to him, "We've found the Messiah!"
— which, translated, is "Christ." •He brought him to Jesus. Jesus gazed 42
at him and said, "You are Simon son of John; you shall be called
'Kephas'" — which is translated, "Peter."

•The next day he decided to go to Galilee, and he found Philip. And 43
Jesus said to him, "Follow me!" •Now Philip was from Bethsaida, from 44
Andrew's and Peter's city. •Philip found Nathanael and said to him, 45
"We've found the one Moses wrote about in the Torah, as well as the
Prophets — Jesus son of Joseph from Nazareth!" •And Nathanael said 46
to him, "Can anything good come from Nazareth?" Philip said to him,
"Come and see!" •Jesus saw Nathanael coming toward him and said 47
about him, "Here's a true Israelite, in whom there's no guile!" •Nathanael 48
said to him, "Where do you know me from?" Jesus answered and said
to him, "Before Philip called you, while you were under the fig tree, I
saw you." •Nathanael answered him, "Rabbi, you're the Son of God, 49
you're the king of Israel!" •Jesus answered and said to him, "Do you 50
believe because I told you I saw you beneath the fig tree? You'll see
greater things than this!" •And he said to him, "Amen, amen, I say to 51
you, you'll see **Heaven opened up and the angels of God ascending and descending** upon the Son of Man!"

C. A SIGN AT CANA

2 •On the third day there was a wedding in Cana of Galilee, and Jesus' mother was there. •Now Jesus and his disciples had also been 2
invited to the wedding, •and when the wine ran out Jesus' mother said 3
to him, "They have no wine." •Jesus replied, "What do you want from 4
me, woman? My hour hasn't come yet." •His mother said to the ser- 5
vants, "Do whatever he tells you." •Now six stone water jars were stand- 6
ing there, in accordance with the Jewish purification rites, each holding
twenty to thirty gallons. •Jesus said to them, "Fill the water jars with wa- 7
ter." And they filled them to the brim. •Then he said to them, "Now 8

1:51 Gn 28:12.
2:4 "What do you want from me, woman?" This
difficult idiom literally means: "What to you and to
me?" The context seems to indicate that the
meaning cannot be the brusque dismissal many
interpreters have made it sound like, since Jesus,
quite to the contrary, is fully cooperative.
"Woman" was a respectful form of address.

9 draw some out and take it to the head steward." So they took it. •When the head steward tasted the water which had become wine — and he didn't know where it came from, while the servants who had drawn the
10 water did know — the head steward called the bridegroom •and said to him, "Every man first puts out the good wine, then when they're drunk
11 he puts out the lesser wine; *you've* kept the good wine till *now!*" •Jesus did this, the first of his signs, at Cana in Galilee and revealed his glory, and his disciples believed in him.
12 •After this he, as well as his mother and brothers and his disciples, went down to Capharnaum and stayed there for a few days.

D. THE CLEANSING OF THE TEMPLE

13 •[b] When the Jewish Passover was near Jesus went up to Jerusalem.
14 •He found in the Temple those who sold oxen and sheep and doves,
15 and the moneychangers were also sitting there, •and making a whip out of rope, he drove them all out of the Temple, along with the sheep and the oxen. He poured out the moneychangers' coins and overturned their
16 tables, •and he told those who were selling the doves, "Get them out of
17 here! Don't make my Father's house a market house!" •His disciples remembered that it is written, **Zeal for Your house will consume me.**
18 •So in response the Jews said to him, "What sign can you show us to
19 justify your doing these things?" •Jesus answered and said to them, "De-
20 stroy this sanctuary, and in three days I'll raise it up." •So the Jews said, "This sanctuary has been forty-six years in the building, and you claim
21 you can raise it up in three days?" •But he was speaking about the sanc-
22 tuary of his body. •So, when he rose from the dead, his disciples remembered that he'd said this, and they believed the Scripture and the word Jesus had spoken.
23 •Now while he was in Jerusalem for the Passover, at the festival, many
24 believed in his name when they saw the signs he was doing, •but Jesus
25 didn't trust himself to them because he understood everyone •and because he had no need for anyone to tell him about human nature — he was well aware what was in men.

[b] *Mt 21:12-13; Mk 11:15-17; Lk 19:45-46.*

2:12 In Semitic usage, close relatives such as cousins could be referred to as brothers or sisters. That these "brothers" were not additional sons of Mary, the mother of Jesus, can be seen from other passages such as Mt 27:60. Cf. Mt 13:55 for a further discussion.

2:17 Ps 69:10.

E. JESUS AND NICODEMUS

3 •There was a man of the Pharisees named Nicodemus, a ruler of the ¹ Jews. •He came to Jesus at night and said to him, "Rabbi, we know ² that you're a teacher come from God, because no one can do the signs you're doing unless God is with him." •Jesus answered and said to him, ³ "Amen, amen, I say to you, unless you're born from above, you cannot see the Kingdom of God." •Nicodemus said to him, "How can a man be ⁴ born when he's old? Surely he can't go into his mother's womb and be born a second time?" •Jesus answered, "Amen, amen, I say to you, if ⁵ you're not born of water and the Spirit you cannot enter the Kingdom of God. •What's born of the flesh is flesh and what's born of the Spirit ⁶ is spirit. •Don't wonder that I told you, 'you must be born from above.' ⁷ •The wind blows where it pleases and you hear its voice, but you don't ⁸ know where it comes from or where it goes. So it is with everyone who's born of the Spirit." •Nicodemus answered and said to him, "How can ⁹ these things be?" •Jesus answered and said to him, "You're a teacher of ¹⁰ Israel and don't know these things? •Amen, amen, I say to you, ¹¹

We speak of what we know, and we bear witness
    to what we've seen,
Yet you don't accept our witness.
•If I told you about earthly things and you   ¹²
    didn't believe,
How will you believe if I tell you about
    heavenly things?
•Yet no one has gone up to Heaven   ¹³
Except the one who came down from Heaven,
    the Son of Man.
•And just as Moses lifted up the serpent   ¹⁴
    in the desert, so must the Son of Man
      be lifted up
•So that everyone who believes in him may have   ¹⁵
    eternal life."
•For God so loved the world that He gave   ¹⁶
    His only begotten Son,
So that everyone who believes in him will not die
    but will have eternal life.

3:3 "From above." This Greek adverb also means "again," which is how Nicodemus (v. 4) misunderstands it.
3:8 The Greek word *pneuma* means both "wind" and "spirit," and is used in both senses in this verse. Such word play is very typical of Semitic style.
3:11 "You don't accept"; at this point Jesus switches to the second person plural.

17 •For God didn't send His Son into the world
    to judge the world,
But to save the world through him.
18 •Whoever believes in him is not condemned;
Whoever doesn't believe in him is already condemned,
Because he hasn't believed in the name
    of the only begotten Son of God.

19 •And this is the condemnation —

The light came into the world,
Yet men loved the darkness rather than the light,
    for their works were evil.
20 •For everyone who does evil hates the light,
And doesn't come into the light lest his works
    be made known,
21 •But whoever does the truth comes to the light
So his works may be revealed as wrought in God.

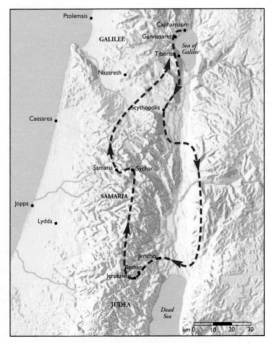

The journeys of Jesus to Jerusalem according to John's Gospel.

F. THE WITNESS OF THE BAPTIST

•After this Jesus and his disciples went to the Judean countryside 22 and he stayed there with them and baptized. •John was also baptiz- 23 ing at Aenon near Salim because water was plentiful there, and people would come and be baptized — •John had not yet been thrown 24 into prison. •So a dispute arose between some of John's disciples and 25 a Jew regarding purification. •And they came to John and said to him, 26 "Rabbi, the one who was with you beyond the Jordan, to whom you bore witness, here he is, baptizing, and everyone is going to him!" •John answered and said, "A man can receive nothing unless it's giv- 27 en to him from Heaven. •You yourselves can bear witness to me that 28 I said, 'I'm not the Messiah,' but instead said, 'I'm the one sent before him.' •The one who has the bride is the bridegroom. The friend of 29 the bridegroom, who stands and listens to him, rejoices with joy at the bridegroom's voice. So this my joy has been fulfilled. •He must increase 30 while I must decrease."

•Whoever comes from above is above everything, 31
Whoever is from the earth is of the earth
   and speaks of the earth.
Whoever comes from Heaven is above everything,
•What he has seen and heard, 32
   this he bears witness to,
Yet no one receives his witness.
•Whoever receives his witness 33
   attests that God is true.
•For the one God sent speaks the words of God, 34
For He gives the Spirit without measure.
•The Father loves the Son 35
And has given all things into his hand.
•Whoever believes in the Son has eternal life; 36
Whoever doesn't obey the Son shall not see life,
   instead God's wrath remains upon him.

4 •So when Jesus learned that the Pharisees had heard that Jesus was 1 making and baptizing more disciples than John — •although Jesus 2 himself wasn't baptizing; his disciples baptized instead — •he left Judea 3 and went off to Galilee again.

G. THE SAMARITAN WOMAN

4,5 •He had to pass through Samaria, •and he came to a Samaritan city
6 named Sychar, near the field Jacob gave to his son Joseph. •Now Jacob's well was there. So Jesus, tired out from the journey, simply sat down at the well. It was about noon.

7 •A Samaritan woman came to draw water. Jesus said to her, "Give
8,9 me a drink" — •his disciples had gone off to the city to buy food. •So the Samaritan woman said, "How is it that you, a Jew, ask me, a Samar-
10 itan woman, for a drink?" — Jews don't associate with Samaritans. •Jesus answered and said to her, "If you knew the gift of God and who it is who's saying to you, 'Give me a drink,' you would have asked him
11 and he would have given you living water." •The woman said to him, "Lord, you have no bucket and the well is deep, so where do you get
12 the living water from? •Surely you're not greater than our father Jacob who gave us the well and drank from it himself, as well as his sons and
13 his herds?" •Jesus answered and said to her, "Everyone who drinks this
14 water will thirst again. •But whoever drinks the water I'll give him will never thirst; instead, the water I'll give him will become a spring of wa-
15 ter welling up in him to eternal life." •The woman said to him, "Lord, give me this water so I won't become thirsty and won't have to come over here to draw water."

16,17 •He said to her, "Go call your husband and come here." •The woman answered and said to him, "I don't have a husband." Jesus said to her,
18 "You were right when you said, 'I don't have a husband' — •you've had five men and the one you have now isn't your husband. You've spoken
19 the truth." •The woman said to him, "Lord, I see that you're a prophet.
20 •Our fathers worshipped on this mountain but you say that in Jerusalem
21 is the Place where we should worship." •Jesus said to her, "Believe me, woman, the hour is coming when you'll worship the Father neither on
22 this mountain nor in Jerusalem. •You worship what you don't know; we
23 worship what we know, because salvation is from the Jews. •But the hour is coming, and is now, when the true worshippers will worship the Father in spirit and truth, for indeed the Father seeks such people to wor-
24 ship Him. •God is spirit, and those who worship Him must worship in
25 spirit and truth." •The woman said to him, "I know that the Messiah is

---

4:16-18 In Greek the word translated "man" and "husband" is the same, as in many other languages.
4:20 "This mountain." I.e., Mt. Gerezim near Sychar, where the ancestors of the Samaritans had set up an altar in opposition to the Temple in Jerusalem. "Place," a common euphemism for the Temple; cf. 11:48.

coming, who is called the Anointed; when he comes he'll tell us everything." •Jesus said to her, "I who am speaking to you am he."   26

•At this point his disciples came, and they were amazed that he was   27
speaking to a woman. Nevertheless, no one said, "What do you want?"
or, "Why are you speaking with her?" •So the woman left her water jar   28
and went off to the city and said to the men, •"Come see a man who   29
told me everything I've done! Could this be the Messiah?" •They went   30
out of the city and came to him.

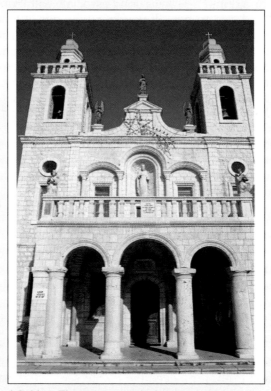

*Cana of Galilee. The sanctuary which commemorates the miracle
of water changed into wine. (Jn 2:1-11)*

•In the meantime the disciples were urging him, "Rabbi, eat!" •But he   31,32
said to them, "I have food to eat that you don't know about." •So the dis-   33
ciples said to each other, "No one brought him anything to eat, did they?"

34 •Jesus said to them, "My food is to do the will of the One Who sent me,
35 and to bring His work to completion. •Don't you say, 'There are still four months, and then comes the harvest'? Behold, I tell you, lift up your eyes
36 and look at the fields, because they're white for the harvest. Already •the reaper receives his pay and gathers fruit for eternal life, so that the sow-
37 er and reaper rejoice together. •For in this the saying is true, 'One is the
38 sower and another the reaper.' •I sent you to reap what you didn't labor for. Others have labored and you've come into their labor."

39 •Many of the Samaritans from that city believed in him, based upon the word of the woman who bore witness that "He told me everything
40 I've done!" •So when the Samaritans came to him they asked him to
41 stay with them, and he stayed there for two days. •And far more be-
42 lieved based upon his word, •and they said to the woman, "No longer do we believe because of what you said — we've heard for ourselves and we know that this man is truly the savior of the world."

43,44 •[c] After the two days he set out from there for Galilee, •because Jesus himself bore witness that a prophet gets no honor in his own coun-
45 try. •So when he came to Galilee the Galileans received him because they'd heard all the things he did in Jerusalem during the festival, since they, too, had gone to the festival.

H. A SECOND SIGN IN GALILEE

46 •So he came to Cana of Galilee again, where he made the water in-to wine. There was a royal official there whose son was ill in Caphar-
47 naum, •and when he heard that Jesus had come from Judea into Galilee he went off to him and urged him to come down and cure his son, be-
48 cause he was about to die. •So Jesus said to him, "Unless you see signs
49 and wonders you don't believe." •The royal official said to him, "Lord,
50 come down before my child dies!" •Jesus said to him, "Go your way, your son will live." The man believed what Jesus told him and went his way.
51 •While he was going down his servants met him and said that his son
52 would live. •So he asked them the hour at which he got better, and they said to him, "Yesterday at about one in the afternoon the fever left him."
53 •The father realized that it was at that hour that Jesus had said to him, "Your son will live," and he believed, along with his whole household.
54 •Jesus did this second sign as he was coming from Judea into Galilee.

[c] Mt 8:5-13; Lk 7:1-10.

I. CONTROVERSY IN JERUSALEM

5 •After these things there was a festival of the Jews, and Jesus went ₁
up to Jerusalem. •Now in Jerusalem by the Sheep Gate is a pool — ₂
called Bethzatha in Hebrew — which has five porticoes. •In these would ₃
lie a crowd of sick people — blind, lame, paralyzed. [•] •A man was there ₄,₅
who'd been sick for thirty-eight years. •When Jesus saw him lying there ₆
and learned that he'd been sick for a long time, he said to him, "Do you
want to be healthy?" •The sick man answered him, "Lord, I have no- ₇
body to put me into the pool when the water's been troubled, so while
I'm going, someone else gets there before me." •Jesus said to him, "Get ₈
up, pick up your cot and walk!" •And at once the man became healthy ₉
and picked up his cot and began to walk.

Now that day was the Sabbath. •So the Jews said to the man who ₁₀
had been cured, "It's the Sabbath, and it's not lawful for you to carry
your cot." •But he answered them, "The one who made me healthy, he ₁₁
told me, 'Pick up your cot and walk!'" •They asked him, "Who's the ₁₂
man who said to you, 'Pick it up and walk'?" •Now the man who had ₁₃
been cured didn't know who it was — Jesus had left without being noticed, since there was a crowd at the place. •After these things Jesus ₁₄
found him in the Temple and said to him, "Here you are, made healthy!
Sin no more, lest something worse happen to you!" •The man went off ₁₅
and told the Jews, "Jesus is the one who made me healthy." •And this ₁₆
is why the Jews persecuted Jesus, because he did these things on the
Sabbath. •But Jesus answered them, "My Father is still working, so I'm ₁₇
working, too." •So this is why the Jews sought all the harder to kill him ₁₈
— not only did he break the Sabbath, but he even said God was his own
Father, making himself equal to God.

•So in response Jesus said to them, "Amen, amen, I say to you, ₁₉

The Son can do nothing on his own except what
he sees the Father doing —
What He does, likewise the Son, too, does.
•For the Father loves the Son and shows him ₂₀
everything He does,
And He'll show him greater works than these,
so that you'll be amazed.

5:4 The best manuscript tradition omits this
verse: "They were waiting for the troubling of the
water, for from time to time an angel of the Lord
went down into the pool and troubled the water,
and whoever first entered the pool afterwards
was healed of whatever disease he had."
5:17 Jesus is saying that since his Father, God,
is active ("working") on the Sabbath, he too may
perform work on the Sabbath, since he shares
the Father's authority.

21 •For just as the Father raises the dead
and gives them life,
So too the Son gives life to those he wants to.
22 •For the Father judges no one;
Instead, He's given all judgment to the Son,
23 •So all may honor the Son,
just as they honor the Father.
Whoever doesn't honor the Son,
doesn't honor the One Who sent him.

24 •Amen, amen, I say to you,

Whoever listens to my word
and believes in the One Who sent me
Has eternal life and doesn't come to judgment,
but, instead, crosses over from death to life.

25 •Amen, amen, I say to you,

The hour is coming, and is now, when the dead
will hear the voice of the Son of God,
and those who listen to it will live.
26 •For just as the Father has life in Himself,
so too has He given the Son life to have in himself,
27 •And has given him authority to pass judgment,
because he's Son of Man.

28 •Don't be amazed at this,

Because the hour is coming in which all those
in the tombs will hear his voice,
29 •and they'll come out,
Those who did good deeds to the resurrection of life,
but those who wrought evil to the resurrection of judgment."
30 •"I can do nothing on my own;
Just as I hear, so do I judge,
And my judgment is just because I seek,
not my own will, but the will of the One Who sent me.
31 •If I bear witness to myself, my witness isn't true.
32 •There's another Who bears witness to me,
And I know that the witness He bears to me is true.

5:27 This is the only instance in the Gospels where "Son of Man" is not preceded by an article.
5:28-29 Dn 12:2.

•You sent to John and he bore witness to the truth, 33
•But I don't receive witness from a man; 34
Instead, I say these things so you may be saved.
•He was a lamp burning and shining, 35
So you wanted to rejoice in his light for a time.
•But I have witness greater than John's, 36
For the works the Father has given me
to bring to completion,
The very works I do,
Bear witness to me that the Father sent me,
•And the Father Who sent me, He has borne witness to me. 37
You've never heard His voice, nor seen His image,
    •And you don't have His word abiding in you, 38
Because you don't believe the one He sent.
•You search the Scriptures because you think you have 39
    eternal life in them,
Yet *they* bear witness to *me*,
•And you don't want to come to me to have life." 40

Tabgha. Church of the Multiplication of the Loaves
built on the remains of the Byzantine building.

41 •"I don't receive glory from men,
42 •But I know you, that you don't have the love
of God within you.
43 •I've come in my Father's name,
yet you don't receive me;
If another should come in his own name,
him you'll receive.
44 •How *can* you believe, who receive glory
from each other,
Yet don't seek glory from God alone?
45 •Don't think that *I'll* accuse you before the Father;
Your accuser is *Moses*, in whom you hoped!
46 •For if you believed Moses, you'd believe me,
because he wrote about me!
47 •So if you don't believe *his* writings, how can
you believe what I say?"

J. SIGNS, CONTROVERSY, AND UNBELIEF

1 6 •d After this Jesus went off to the other side of the Sea of Galilee of
2 Tiberias. •A large crowd was following him because they saw the signs
3 he was performing on the sick. •So Jesus went up the mountain and sat
4 down there with his disciples. •Now the Passover, the festival of the Jews,
5 was near. •When Jesus raised his eyes and saw that a large crowd was
coming toward him he said to Philip, "Where can we buy loaves for them
6 to eat?" •He said this to test him — he knew what he was going to do.
7 •Philip answered him, "Two hundred denarii worth of bread wouldn't be
8 enough to allow each of them to have a little!" •One of his disciples, An-
9 drew, Simon Peter's brother, said to him, • "There's a boy here who has
10 five barley loaves and two fish, but what are they for so many?" •Jesus
said, "Have the people sit down" — now there was a lot of grass at that
11 spot. So the men, numbering about five thousand, sat down. •Jesus took
the loaves and after blessing them he distributed them to those who were
12 reclining, and likewise with the fish, as much as they wanted. •When they
were full he said to his disciples, "Gather the left-over fragments so noth-

---

d *Mt 14:13-21; Mk 6:30-44; Jn 9:10-17.*

6:4 The reference to Passover is not incidental. Passover celebrated the whole Exodus experience, and by linking this sign directly to Passover John also links the Eucharist to both the Passover meal and to the Exodus from death to life.

ing will be lost." •So they gathered them and filled twelve baskets with 13 fragments of the five barley loaves which were left by those who had eaten. •When the people saw the sign he'd done they said, "Truly this is the 14 Prophet who is to come into the world!" •But when Jesus realized that 15 they intended to come and take him by force to make him king he withdrew alone to the mountain again.

•[e] Now when evening came his disciples went down to the sea, •and 16,17 they got into a boat and began to go across the sea to Capharnaum. Darkness had already come and Jesus had not yet come to them, •and 18 the sea became rough, with a strong wind blowing. •After they'd rowed 19 about three or four miles they saw Jesus walking on the sea and coming near the boat, and they were frightened. •But Jesus said to them, 20 "It's me, don't be afraid!" •So they wanted to take him into the boat, 21 and at once the boat came to land where they were going.

•The next day the crowd which had stayed on the other side saw 22 that there had been no other boat there except the one, and that Jesus had not gotten into the boat with his disciples, but instead only his disciples had set out; •in addition boats came from Tiberias to near the 23 place where they'd eaten the bread after the Lord had blessed it. •So 24 when the crowd saw that neither Jesus nor his disciples were there they got into the boats and went to Capharnaum in search of Jesus. •And 25 when they found him on the other side of the sea they said, "Rabbi, when did you come here?" •Jesus answered them and said, "Amen, 26 amen, I say to you,

You seek me not because you saw signs,
    but because you ate of the loaves
        and were satisfied.
•Labor not for food that perishes,   27
    but for food that remains for life eternal,
Which the Son of Man will give you,
    for God the Father has set His seal on him."

•So they said to him, "What should we do to do the works of God?" 28 •Jesus answered and said to them, 29

"This is the work of God,
    to believe in the one He sent."

---

[e] Mt 14:22-27; Mk 6:45-52.

6:20 "It's me." Lit., "I am." This may be intended to mirror God's words to Moses in Exodus, "I am Who am." Cf. also Jn 8:24, 26; 18:5-8.

30 •So they said to him, "Then what sign do you do, so we can see and
31 believe in you? What work do you perform? •Our fathers ate manna in
the desert, as it is written, **He gave them bread from Heaven to**
32 **eat.**" •Jesus said to them, "Amen, amen, I say to you,

It wasn't Moses who gave you bread from Heaven;
On the contrary, my Father gives you
the true bread from Heaven,
33 •For God's bread is the bread that comes down
from Heaven and gives life to the world."

34,35 •So they said to him, "Lord, give us this bread always." •Jesus said
to them,

"I am the bread of life;
Whoever comes to me will not hunger,
And whoever believes in me will never thirst.
36 •But I said to you that you've seen me,
yet you don't believe.
37 •Everything the Father gives to me
will come to me,
And whoever comes to me I will not send away,
38 •Because I've come down from Heaven
not to do *my* will,
But to do the will of Him Who sent me.
39 •Now this is the will of Him Who sent me,
that I should lose nothing of what He gave me,
but should raise it up on the last day.
40 •For this is the will of my Father,
that *everyone* who sees the Son and believes
in him should have eternal life,
and I'll raise him up on the last day."

41 •So the Jews complained about him because he said, "I am the bread
42 come down from Heaven," •and they said, "Isn't this fellow Jesus son
of Joseph? Don't we know his father and mother? How can he now say,
43 'I've come down from Heaven'?" •Jesus answered and said to them,
"Don't complain among yourselves.

44 •No one can come to me unless the Father
Who sent me draws him,
and I'll raise him up on the last day.

6:31 Ps 78:24.

•It is written in the Prophets, 45
And they will all be taught by God.
Everyone who listens to the Father and learns,
   comes to me.
•Not that anyone has seen the Father except 46
   the one who is from the Father;
   he has seen the Father.

•Amen, amen, I say to you, 47

Whoever believes has eternal life.
   •I am the bread of life. 48
•Your fathers ate manna in the desert 49
   yet they died.
•This is the bread that came down from Heaven, 50
   so that you can eat of it and *not* die.
•I am the living bread that came down from Heaven. 51
   Anyone who eats this bread will live forever,
But the bread that *I'll* give for the life of the world
   is my flesh."

•So the Jews began quarrelling among themselves, saying, "How can 52
this fellow give us his flesh to eat?" •But Jesus said to them, "Amen, 53
amen, I say to you,

Unless you eat the flesh of the Son of Man
   and drink his blood,
You do not have life within you.
•Whoever feeds on my flesh and drinks my blood 54
   has eternal life,
And I'll raise him up on the last day,
•For my flesh is true food, 55
And my blood is true drink.
•Whoever feeds on my flesh and drinks my blood 56
Remains in me, and I in him.
•Just as the living Father sent me, and I live 57
   because of the Father,
So too, whoever feeds on me will live because of me.
•*This* is the bread come down from Heaven, not like 58
   your fathers ate and they died.
Whoever feeds on this bread will live forever."

6:45 Is 54:13.

*Inside of the synagogue of Capharnaum
where the great discourse of John 6 is situated.*

59 •He said these things while teaching in a synagogue in Capharnaum.
60 •Many of his disciples who were listening said, "This teaching is hard;
61 who can accept it?" •Jesus knew in himself that his disciples were com-
62 plaining about this and he said to them, "Does this offend you? •What
if you see the Son of Man ascending to where he was before?

63 •The Spirit is the life-giver,
The flesh is profitless;
The words I speak to you are Spirit and are life.
64 •But there are some of you who don't believe."

For Jesus knew from the beginning who they were who didn't be-
65 lieve, and who it was who would hand him over. •And he said, "This
is why I told you that no one can come to me unless it's given to him
by the Father."

•Because of this many of his disciples turned back and no longer 66 walked with him. •So Jesus said to the Twelve, "Do you, too, wish to 67 turn back?" •Simon Peter answered him, "Lord, who would we go to? 68 You have the words of eternal life, •and we've believed and come to 69 know that you're the Holy One of God." •Jesus answered them, "Did- 70 n't I choose you Twelve? Yet one of you is a devil." •He was speaking 71 about Judas son of Simon Iscariot, because this fellow, one of the Twelve, intended to hand him over.

K. JESUS AT THE FEAST OF TABERNACLES

7 •After these things Jesus moved about in Galilee — he didn't want 1 to go about in Judea because the Jews were trying to kill him. •Now 2 it was near the Jewish Festival of Tabernacles. •So his brothers said to 3 him, "Leave here and go to Judea so your disciples, too, can see the works you do. •After all, no one does something in private if he wants 4 to be before the public. If you do these things, make yourself known to the world." •For his brothers didn't believe in him either. •So Jesus said 5,6 to them, "My time hasn't come yet, but your time is always at hand. •The world can't hate you, but it hates me because I bear witness against 7 it that its works are evil. •You go up to the festival; I'm not going up to 8 this festival because my time hasn't been brought to completion yet." •After he said these things he stayed in Galilee. 9

•But when his brothers had gone up to the festival he went up, too 10 — not openly, but in secret. •So the Jews were looking for him at the 11 festival and saying, "Where is he?" •and there was a great deal of ar- 12 guing about him among the common people. Some said, "He's a good man!" while others said, "No! On the contrary, he's leading the peo- ple astray!" •No one spoke openly about him, however, for fear of the 13 Jews.

•When the festival was already half over Jesus went up to the Tem- 14 ple and began to teach. •The Jews were amazed and said, "Where did 15 the fellow get this learning, since he hasn't studied?" •So Jesus an- 16 swered them and said, "My teaching isn't mine but is from the One Who sent me. •If anyone wishes to do His will, he'll know whether 17 the teaching is from God or whether I'm speaking on my own. •Who- 18 ever speaks on his own is seeking his own glory, while whoever seeks the glory of the one who sent him, he's truthful and there's no false-

7:15 "Since he hasn't studied," i.e., Jesus had not had a formal rabbinical education.

19 hood in him. •Didn't Moses give you the Torah? Yet none of you keeps
20 the Torah. Why are you trying to kill me?" •The crowd answered, "You
21 have a demon! Who's trying to kill you?" •Jesus answered and said to
22 them, "I did one work and all of you were amazed by it. •Moses gave
you circumcision — not that it's from Moses; it's actually from the fa-
23 thers — yet you'll circumcise a man on the Sabbath. •If a man can receive circumcision on the Sabbath so as not to break the Torah of
Moses, why be angry with me because I made a whole man healthy
24 on the Sabbath? •Don't judge by outward appearances; render *just*
judgment, instead."

25 •So some of the Jerusalemites were saying, "Isn't this fellow the one
26 they're trying to kill? •Yet here he is, speaking openly, and they say nothing to him. Could it be that the rulers really know that he's the Messi-
27 ah? •But we know where he's from, whereas when the Messiah comes
28 no one will know where he's from." •So as Jesus was teaching in the
Temple he cried out and said, "You both know me and know where I'm
from, yet I haven't come on my own; but the One Who sent me, Whom
29 you don't know, is true. •*I* know Him because I'm from Him and He
30 sent me." •So they wanted to arrest him, yet no one laid a hand on him
31 because his hour had not yet come. •But many of the common people
believed in him and said, "When the Messiah comes will he do more
signs than this man has done?"

32 •The Pharisees heard when the people were whispering these things
about him, and the chief priests and the Pharisees sent Temple atten-
33 dants to arrest him. •So Jesus said,

"A little while yet I'll be with you,
And then I'm going to the One
    Who sent me.
34 •You'll seek me, yet you won't find me,
And where *I* am, you cannot come."

35 •So the Jews said to themselves, "Where is he going to go that we won't
find him? He's not going to travel to the Diaspora among the Greeks
36 and teach the Greeks, is he? •What does it mean when he said,

'You'll seek me, yet you won't find me,
And where *I* am, you cannot come'?"

7:32 "Attendants." The Jewish authorities had a Temple police force, armed with staves, to keep order.

7:35 "Greeks." Cf. 12:20. While it is possible that this term refers to Gentiles, it is more likely that it refers to Jews of the Diaspora who spoke Greek.

•Now on the last day of the festival, the most important day, Jesus 37 stood up and cried out,

"If anyone thirsts,
let him come to me and drink!

•Whoever believes in me, as Scripture said, **From within him shall** 38 **flow rivers of living water!**" •Now he said this about the Spirit which 39 those who believed in him were going to receive — the Spirit hadn't come yet, because Jesus had not yet been glorified.

•Some of the people who heard these words said, "Surely he's the 40 Prophet!" •Others said, "He's the Messiah!" But some said, "The Mes- 41 siah certainly doesn't come from Galilee, does he? •Hasn't Scripture 42 said that the Messiah comes from **the seed of David** and **from Beth- lehem,** the village David was from?" •So there was a split among the 43 people over him. •Some of them wanted to arrest him, but no one laid 44 hands on him.

•So the attendants came back to the chief priests and Pharisees, who 45 said to them, "Why haven't you brought him?" •The attendants an- 46 swered, "Never did a man speak like that!" •So the Pharisees answered 47 them, "You haven't been led astray too, have you? •None of the rulers 48 or Pharisees have believed in him, have they? •But this rabble that does- 49 n't know the Torah is under God's curse." •Nicodemus said to them — 50 the one who had come to Jesus previously, he was one of them — •"Our Torah doesn't judge a man unless it first hears from him and 51 learns what he's doing, does it?" •They answered and said to him, 52 "You're not from Galilee, too, are you? Look it up and you'll see that no prophet comes from Galilee!"

•And each departed for his own house, 53

8 •but Jesus departed for the Mount of Olives. •Early in the morning 1,2 he again came to the Temple and all the people came to him, and after taking a seat he began to teach them. •Then the scribes and the 3

7:37-38 Part of the ritual of the Feast of Taber- nacles involved the priests pouring water over the altar. Jesus may have used this rite as the occa- sion for proclaiming himself the "living water."
7:38 Pr 18:4, Is 58:11, Ex 17:6, Ezk 47:1.
7:42 2 S 7:12; Ps 89:3-4.
7:49 "Rabble"; this Greek word, which literally means "crowd," also refers to the common peo- ple, here pejoratively, as used by the authorities.
7:53-8:11 While this passage is accepted by the Church as authentic and canonical, its exact po- sition is a matter of some question. The earliest texts omit it entirely from the Gospel of John, while other texts place it elsewhere in John or, sometimes, in the Gospel of Luke, with which it appears to have stylistic affinities. In this latter manuscript tradition, it appears after Lk 21:38. The Jewish authorities thought they were putting Jesus on the horns of a dilemma: either call for the woman's execution, in which case he would

The Mount of Olives with the Russian Church dedicated to Mary Magdalen.

Pharisees brought a woman who had been caught in adultery, and af-
4 ter standing her out in the middle •they said to him, "Teacher, this
5 woman was caught in the act of adultery. •Now in the Torah Moses
6 commanded us to stone such women. So what do *you* say?" •They said
this to test him, so they would have something to accuse him of. But
Jesus bent down and began to write on the ground with his finger.
7 •When they kept asking him, he straightened up and said to them, "Let
whoever is without sin among you be the first to throw a stone at her."
8 •And once again he bent down and began to write on the ground.
9 •Then those who had been listening began to go away, one by one,
beginning with the elders, and he was left alone, with the woman still

run afoul of the Romans who reserved the power of punishment in capital cases, or recommend
leniency and caution, in which case Jesus would
reveal himself as less than zealous for the Torah
and willing to acquiesce in Roman interference
in Jewish affairs.

8:12 The Feast of Hanukkah featured a torchlight
procession and, as at 7:37, this may have been

the occasion for Jesus' proclamation. Unfortunately, there are no other clear indications in the
text which would allow us to say definitely that
that was when this scene occurred. From a narrative standpoint, this passage belongs to the
section on Jesus at the Feast of Tabernacles.

8:13 The Torah required two witnesses for testimony to be admissible; cf. Dt 19:15.

in the middle. •Jesus straightened up and said to her, "Woman, where 10 are they? Has no one condemned you?" •"No one, Lord," she said. 11 Then Jesus said, "Neither do I condemn you. Go your way, and from now on sin no more."

•Jesus spoke to them again and said, 12

"I am the light of the world;
Whoever follows me will not walk in darkness,
But will have the light of life."

•So the Pharisees said to him, "You're bearing witness to yourself! 13 Your witness isn't true!" •Jesus answered and said to them, "Even if 14 I bear witness to myself my witness is true, because I know where I came from and where I'm going, but you don't know where I came from or where I'm going. •You judge according to the flesh. I judge 15 no one. •But even if I do judge, my judgment is true because I'm not 16 alone; rather, I and the Father Who sent me bear witness, •and in 17 your Torah it is written that the witness of two men is true. •I bear 18 witness to myself, and the Father Who sent me also bears witness to me." •So they said to him, "Where *is* your father?" Jesus answered, 19 "You know neither me nor my Father. If you knew me you'd know my Father, too." •He spoke these words while teaching near the Tem- 20 ple treasury in the Temple, and no one arrested him because his hour had not yet come.

•So he said to them again, "I'm going away and you'll seek me, yet 21 you'll die in your sin; where I'm going you cannot come." •So the Jews 22 said, "He won't kill himself, will he?" since he said, "Where I'm going you cannot come." •And he said to them, 23

"You're from below,
I'm from above;
You're *of* this world,
I'm *not* of this world.

•That's why I told you that you'll die in your sins — if you don't be- 24 lieve that I am, you'll die in your sins." •So they said to him, "Who are 25 you?" Jesus said to them, "Why do I talk to you in the first place? •I have many things to say about you and to condemn, but the One Who 26 sent me is true, and what I heard from Him, these things I speak to the world." •They didn't realize that he was speaking to them about the Fa- 27 ther. •So Jesus said, "When you've lifted up the Son of Man, then you'll 28 realize that I am, and I do nothing on my own; I proclaim these things just as the Father taught me to. •And the One Who sent me is with me. 29

He hasn't left me alone because I always do what's pleasing to Him."

30 •Many believed in him when he said these things.

31 •So Jesus said to those Jews who had believed in him,

"If you abide in my word,
You're truly disciples of mine,
32 •And you'll know the truth,
And the truth will set you free."

33 •They answered him, "We're Abraham's offspring and have never been
34 enslaved! How can you say, 'You'll be freed'?" •Jesus answered them,
"Amen, amen, I say to you,

Everyone who commits sin
is a slave of sin.
35 •Now the slave doesn't stay in the house forever;
the *son* stays forever.
36 •So if the son frees you,
you will, indeed, be free.

37 •I know that you're Abraham's offspring, but you're trying to kill me be-
38 cause my word finds no place in you. •I speak of what I've seen with
my Father, just as you, too, do what you've heard from your father."
39 •They answered and said to him, "Our father is Abraham!" Jesus said
40 to them, "If you're Abraham's children, do the *works* of Abraham! • But
now you're trying to kill me, a man who's told you the truth he heard from
41 God — that's not what Abraham did! •You're doing the works of your father!" They said to him, "We weren't born from fornication! We have one
42 father, God!" •Jesus said to them, "If God were your father you'd love me,
because I came forth from God and have come from God; I haven't come
43 on my own, — *He* sent me. •Why don't you understand what I say? Be-
44 cause you're unable to hear my word. •You're from your father the Devil, and you long to do your father's desires. He was a murderer from the
beginning, and doesn't stand with the truth because there's no truth in him.
When he lies, he's speaking according to his nature, because he's a liar
45 and the father of lies. •But because I speak the truth, you don't believe
46 me. •Which of you can convict me of sin? If I speak the truth, why don't
47 you believe me? •Whoever is from God hears the words of God, which is
why you don't hear, because you're not from God."

48 •The Jews answered and said to him, "Aren't we right to say that
49 you're a Samaritan and have a demon?" •Jesus answered, "I don't have
50 a demon, but I honor my Father, and you dishonor me. •I'm not seeking my own glory. One there is Who seeks it, and He's also the One

Who judges! •Amen, amen, I say to you, if anyone keeps my word, 51
he'll never see death." •The Jews said to him, "Now we *know* you 52
have a demon. Abraham died, as well as the prophets, yet *you* say,
'If anyone keeps my word he'll never taste death'! •Are you greater 53
than our father Abraham, who died? The prophets died, too! Who are
you making yourself out to be?" •Jesus answered, "If I glorify myself, 54
my glory is nothing. It's my *Father* Who glorifies me, Who you say is
your God. •Yet you haven't recognized Him, while I know Him. And 55
if I were to say that I don't know Him, I'd be like you, a liar. But I
know Him and I keep His word. •Your father Abraham rejoiced to see 56
my day; he saw it and was glad." •So the Jews said to him, "You're 57
not fifty years old yet, and you've seen Abraham?" •Jesus said to them, 58
"Amen, amen, I say to you, before Abraham came to be, I am." •They 59
picked up stones to throw at him, but Jesus hid himself and went out
of the Temple.

L. THE MAN BORN BLIND

9 •As he was passing along he saw a man who was blind from birth. 1
•The disciples asked him, "Rabbi, who sinned, this fellow or his par- 2
ents, that he should be born blind?" •Jesus answered, "Neither he nor 3
his parents sinned — he was born blind so that the works of God might
be revealed through him! •We must do the works of the One Who sent 4
me while it's day; night is coming, when no one is able to work. •As 5
long as I'm in the world, I'm the light of the world." •Having said these 6
things he spit on the ground and made clay out of the spittle, and he
smeared the clay on the man's eyes •and said to him, "Go wash your- 7
self in the pool of Siloam," which is translated, "Sent." So he went off
and washed himself and came back seeing. •His neighbors and those 8
who used to see him as a beggar said, "Isn't this the man who used to
sit and beg?" •Some said, "It *is* him!" others said, "No, it's not! He on- 9
ly looks like him." The man said, "I'm the one!" •So they said to him, 10
"How were your eyes opened?" •He answered, "The man called Jesus 11
made clay and smeared it on my eyes and said to me, 'Go to Siloam
and wash yourself'! When I went off and washed myself I could see."
•And they said to him, "Where is he?" He said, "I don't know." 12

•They brought him to the Pharisees — the man who was formerly 13
blind. •Now it was the Sabbath on the day Jesus made the clay and 14
opened his eyes. •Once again the Pharisees too asked him how it was 15
that he could see. "He put clay on my eyes," he said, "and I washed

16 myself and now I can see." •So some of the Pharisees said, "This man isn't from God because he doesn't keep the Sabbath!" Others said, "How can a sinful man do such signs?" And there was a split among them.
17 •So they said to the blind man again, "What do you say about him, since it was your eyes he opened?" Then *he* said, "He's a prophet."
18 •The Jews didn't believe that the man had been blind and had regained his sight until they called the parents of the man who was now able to
19 see •and asked them, "Is this your son, the one you say was born blind?
20 How can he now see?" •His parents answered, "We know that this is
21 our son and that he was born blind, •but how he can now see we don't know, nor do we know who opened his eyes. Ask *him*; he's of age! He
22 can speak for himself!" •His parents said these things because they were afraid of the Jews, for the Jews had already agreed that anyone who declared Jesus to be the Messiah would be banished from the synagogue.
23 •This is why his parents said, "He's of age, ask him!"
24 •So for a second time they summoned the man who had been blind and said to him, "Give glory to God! We know this man's a sinner."

Jerusalem. Ruins of Siloe.

•"Whether he's a sinner, I don't know," he answered. "One thing I do ₂₅ know — I was blind, but now I can see." •So they said to him, "What ₂₆ did he do to you? How did he open your eyes?" •"I've already told you ₂₇ but you didn't listen," he answered. "Why do you want to hear it again? Surely you don't want to become his disciples, too, do you?" •Then they ₂₈ began to insult him and said, "You're his disciple, but we're Moses' disciples! •We know that God spoke to Moses, but we don't know where ₂₉ this fellow's from!" •The man answered, "The wonder is certainly in this, ₃₀ that you don't know where he's from, yet he opened my eyes. •We know ₃₁ God doesn't listen to sinners, but if anyone is God-fearing and does His will He listens to him. •It's completely unheard of for someone to open ₃₂ the eyes of a man who was blind from birth. •If he weren't from God, ₃₃ he wouldn't be able to do anything." •They answered, "You were completely born in sin, and *you're* teaching *us*?" And they threw him out. ₃₄

•Jesus heard that they'd thrown him out, and when he found him he ₃₅ said, "Do you believe in the Son of Man?" •The man answered, "And ₃₆ who is he, Lord, so I can believe in him?" •Jesus said to him, "You have ₃₇ seen him, and the one who is speaking with you is he." •Then the man ₃₈ said, "I believe, Lord," and worshipped him. •And Jesus said, "For judg- ₃₉ ment I came into this world, so that

> Those who do not see may see,
> And those who see may become blind."

•Those of the Pharisees who were with him heard, and they said to ₄₀ him, "We're not blind, too, are we?" •Jesus said to them, "If you were ₄₁ blind you'd have no sin, but since you say, 'We see!' your sin remains."

M. THE GOOD SHEPHERD

10•"Amen, amen, I say to you, ₁

> Whoever doesn't go in by the gate
> into the sheepfold
> but enters by another way,

9:24 "Give glory to God!" This formula was used to adjure witnesses to tell the truth.
9:34 "Threw him out." This probably means he was banished from the synagogue, although he may also have been physically ejected.
10:1 The following poem is based upon Burney's retroversion of a rhyming Aramaic original and the format must be considered somewhat speculative. The translation, however, does not rely in any way on the retroversion. The image of God as a shepherd is common in the Old Testament.

he's a thief and robber.

2 •But whoever comes in by the gate,
he's the shepherd of the sheep.

3 •The gate keeper opens to him,
and the sheep hear his voice,
and he calls his own sheep by name, and leads them out.

4 •When he drives out all his own sheep
he goes before them,
and the sheep follow him
because they know his voice.

5 •But they don't follow a stranger,
instead, they flee from him,
because they don't know
the voice of strangers."

6 •Jesus told them this parable, but they didn't understand what the things
he was telling them meant.

7 •So once again Jesus said, "Amen, amen, I say to you,

I am the gate for the sheep!

8 •All those who came before me
are thieves and robbers,
But the sheep didn't listen to them.

9 •I am the gate!
Whoever comes in through me will be saved
And will enter and leave and find pasture.

10 •The thief comes only to steal and slaughter
and slay;
I've come that you might have life
and have it abundantly.

11 •I am the *good* shepherd;
The good shepherd lays down his life
for his sheep.

12 •But since the hired man is not a shepherd —
the sheep are not his own —
When he sees the wolf coming he leaves the sheep
and flees,
And the wolf carries them off and scatters them,

13 •Because he's a hired man and doesn't care
about the sheep.

14 •I am the *good* shepherd,

And I know mine and mine know me,
•Just as the Father knows me and I know the Father,   15
And I lay down my life for my sheep.
•I have other sheep who are not of this fold,   16
    and I must lead them,
And they'll listen to my voice, and become
    one flock, one shepherd.
•This is why the Father loves me,   17
Because I lay down my life in order to take
    it up again.
•No one takes it from me;   18
On the contrary, I lay it down on my own.
I have power to lay it down and I have power
    to take it up again.
This is the command I've received from my Father."

•Once again a split arose among the Jews because of these words. 19
•Many of them said, "He has a demon and is out of his mind! Why lis- 20
ten to him?" •Others said, "These are not the words of a demon-pos- 21
sessed man! Can a demon open the eyes of the blind?"

N. JESUS AT HANUKKAH

•At that time Hanukkah was taking place in Jerusalem. It was winter 22
•and Jesus was walking in the Temple in the Portico of Solomon. •So 23,24
the Jews surrounded him and said, "How long will you keep us in suspense? If you're the Messiah, tell us openly!" •Jesus answered them, 25

"I told you and you don't believe.
The works I do in the name of my Father —
    these bear witness to me,
•But you don't believe because you're not   26
    from among my sheep.
•My sheep listen to my voice, and I know them,   27
    and they follow me,
•And I give them eternal life and they'll   28
    never die,

10:22 Hanukkah, or the Feast of Dedication, cel-   Maccabees in 164 B.C., after it had been profaned
ebrates the rededication of the Temple by the   by Antiochus IV Epiphanes, the Seleucid ruler.

And no one will snatch them from my hand.
29 •My Father, Who has given them to me,
   is greater than all,
And no one can snatch them
   from the hand of the Father.
30 •The Father and I are one."

31,32 •Once again the Jews picked up stones in order to stone him. •Jesus answered them, "I've shown you many good works from the Father.
33 For which of those works are you going to stone me?" •The Jews answered him, "We're not stoning you for a good work but for blasphemy, and because you, a man, are making yourself God!" •Jesus answered
34 them, "Isn't it written in your Torah, **I said, you shall be gods**? •If
35 he called them gods, to whom the word of God came, and Scripture
36 cannot be set aside, •are you saying to the one the Father consecrated and sent into the world, 'You're blaspheming!' because I said, 'I'm the

10:34 Ps 82:6.

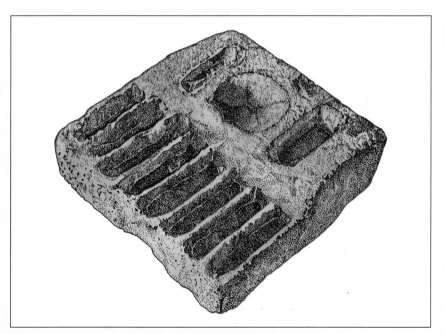

A stone lamp with 8 candles used for Hanukkah (2nd century A.D.).

Son of God'? •If I'm not doing my Father's works, don't believe me! 37
•But if I am, and you don't believe *me*, believe the *works*, so you may 38
know and understand that the Father is in me and I am in the Father."
•Once again they tried to arrest him, yet he came out from their hands. 39

O. THE RAISING OF LAZARUS

•He went off again to the other side of the Jordan to the place where 40
John first baptized, and he stayed there. •Many people came to him be- 41
cause they said, "John didn't perform any sign, but all the things John
said about this man were true." •And many believed in him there. 42

11 •Now a certain man was sick, Lazarus of Bethany, from the vil- 1
lage of Mary and her sister Martha. •Mary was the one who had 2
anointed the Lord with oil and wiped his feet dry with her hair — it was
her brother Lazarus who was sick. •So the sisters sent to tell him, "Lord, 3
behold, the one you love is sick." •When Jesus heard this he said, "This 4
sickness will not bring death — it's for the glory of God so the Son of
Man may be glorified through it." •Now Jesus loved Martha and her sis- 5
ter and Lazarus, •but after he heard that Lazarus was sick he stayed 6
where he was for two more days. •Then after this he said to the disci- 7
ples, "Let's go into Judea again." •The disciples said to him, "Rabbi, 8
the Jews were just now trying to stone you, and you're going back there
again?" •Jesus answered, "Aren't there twelve hours in a day? 9

If someone walks in the day he doesn't stumble,
because he sees the light of this world,
•But if someone walks in the night he stumbles, 10
because the light isn't with him."

•He said these things, and then he said to them, "Our friend Lazarus 11
has fallen asleep, but I'm going now to wake him up." •So the disciples 12
said to him, "Lord, if he's fallen asleep he'll recover." •But Jesus had 13
spoken about his death, while they thought he was speaking about natural sleep. •So then Jesus said to them openly, "Lazarus has died, •and 14,15
I rejoice for your sake that I wasn't there, so you may believe. But let's
go to him." •So Thomas, who was called the Twin, said to his fellow 16
disciples, "Let's go, too, to die with him!"

•When Jesus came he found that Lazarus had already been in the 17
tomb for four days. •Now Bethany was near Jerusalem, about two miles 18

19 away, •and many of the Jews had come to Martha and Mary to console
20 them over their brother. •So Martha, when she heard that Jesus was
21 coming, met him, but Mary stayed in the house. •Martha said to Jesus,
22 "Lord, if you'd been here my brother wouldn't have died! •but even now
23 I know that whatever you ask God for, God will give you." •Jesus said
24 to her, "Your brother will rise!" •Martha said to him, "I know that he'll
25 rise at the resurrection on the last day." •Jesus said to her,

> "*I* am the resurrection and the life!
> Whoever believes in me, even if he should die,
>   will live,
26 •And everyone who lives and believes in me
>   shall never die!

27 Do you believe this?" •She said to him, "Yes, Lord, I've come to
believe that you're the Messiah, the Son of God who has come into
the world!"

28 •After she said these things she went off and called her sister Mary,
29 saying quietly, "The Teacher is here and he's asking for you." •When
30 she heard that, she got up quickly and went to him. •Now Jesus had
not yet come to the village, but was still at the place where Martha had
31 met him. •So the Jews who were with her in the house, consoling her,
when they saw that Mary had quickly gotten up and gone out they fol-
32 lowed her, thinking, "She's going to the tomb to weep there." •When
Mary came to where Jesus was and saw him she fell at his feet and said
33 to him, "Lord, if you'd been here my brother wouldn't have died!" •So
when Jesus saw her weeping, and the Jews who had come with her
34 weeping, he groaned in spirit and was troubled •and he said, "Where
35 have you laid him?" They said to him, "Lord, come and see!" •Jesus
36,37 began to weep. •So the Jews said, "See how he loved him!" •But some
of them said, "Couldn't the one who opened the eyes of the blind man
have caused this man not to die?"

38 •So Jesus, again groaning within himself, came to the tomb. Now it
39 was a cave, and a stone lay on it. •Jesus said, "Take the stone away!"
Martha, the sister of the dead man, said to him, "Lord, by now he'll
40 smell — it's been four days!" •Jesus said to her, "Didn't I tell you that
41 if you believe you'll see the glory of God?" •So they took the stone
away. Then Jesus lifted up his eyes and said, "Father, I give You thanks,
42 because You heard me. •Now I knew that You always hear me, but I
said this for the sake of the crowd standing around me, so they may
43 believe that You sent me." •And after saying this he called out with a

loud voice, "Lazarus, come out!" •The dead man came out with his 44
hands and feet bound with thongs and his face wrapped with a cloth.
Jesus said to them, "Untie him and let him go!"

•ᶠ Many of the Jews who had come to Mary, and had seen what he 45
did, believed in him, •but some of them went off to the Pharisees and 46
told them what Jesus had done. •So the chief priests and Pharisees gath- 47
ered the Sanhedrin and said, "What should we do? — this man is doing many signs! •If we leave him like this everyone will believe in him, 48
and the Romans will come and destroy both our Place and our nation!"
•One of them, Caiaphas, who was the high priest that year, said to them, 49
"You don't know anything! •Don't you realize that it's better for one man 50
to die than to have the whole nation be destroyed?" •Now he didn't say 51
this on his own, but since he was high priest that year he prophesied
that Jesus would die for the nation, •and not only for the nation but al- 52
so so that the scattered children of God might gather into one. •So from 53
that day they resolved to put him to death.

•So Jesus no longer went about openly among the Jews, but instead 54
he went away from there to the country near the desert, to a city called
Ephraim, and there he remained with the disciples.

P. JESUS' GLORIFICATION IN JERUSALEM

•The Passover of the Jews was near, and many of them went up to 55
Jerusalem from the country before the Passover to purify themselves. •So 56
they were looking for Jesus and would say to each other as they stood
in the Temple, "What do you think? He won't come to the festival, will
he?" •Now the chief priests and Pharisees had given an order that any- 57
one who knew where Jesus was should report it, so they could arrest him.

12 •ᵍ Six days before the Passover Jesus came to Bethany, where 1
Lazarus was, whom Jesus had raised from the dead. •They had 2
a banquet for him there and Martha served, while Lazarus was one of
those who were reclining at table with him. •So Mary took a pound of 3
very expensive pure oil of nard and anointed Jesus' feet and wiped his
feet dry with her hair, and the house was filled with the fragrance of the
oil. •Judas Iscariot, one of his disciples, the one who was going to hand 4

ᶠ *Mt 26:1-5; Mk 14:1-2; Lk 22:1-2.*   ᵍ *Mt 26:6-13; Mk 14:3-9.*

11:48 "Place," i.e., the Temple.
11:51 The high priest was believed to have the gift of prophecy.

Bethany. Entrance to the Tomb of Lazarus.

5 him over, said, •"Why wasn't this oil sold for three hundred denarii and
6 given to the poor?" •He said this not because he was concerned about
the poor but because he was a thief, and since he kept the money bag
7 he used to take what was put in it. •So Jesus said, "Let her be; let her
keep it for the day of my burial, for

8 •The poor you always have with you,
But me you do not always have."

9 •So a large crowd of the Jews found out that he was there and they
came, not just because of Jesus, but also to see Lazarus, whom he'd
10 raised from the dead. •Now the chief priests were plotting to kill Lazarus,
11 too, •because many of the Jews were leaving on account of him and
were coming to believe in Jesus.

12:5 A denarius was a silver coin worth about a day's wage.

•[h] The next day, when the large crowd that had come to the festival 12 heard that Jesus was coming to Jerusalem, •they took the branches of 13 palm trees and went out to meet him, and they kept shouting,

> **"Hosanna!**
> **Blessed is he who comes in the name of the Lord,**
> and the king of Israel!"

•But Jesus found a young donkey and sat on it, as it is written, 14

> **•Fear not, daughter Zion!** 15
> **Behold, your king is coming,**
> **sitting on a donkey's colt.**

•His disciples didn't understand these things at first, but when Jesus was 16 glorified, then they remembered that these things had been written about him and had been done for him. •So the crowd that had been with him 17 when he called Lazarus out of the tomb and raised him from the dead was bearing witness. •This is why the crowd met him —because they'd 18 heard that he'd done this sign. •So the Pharisees said to one another, 19 "You see there's no use! Look, the whole world has gone off after him!"

•There were some Greeks among those who had come up to wor- 20 ship at the festival, •so they came up to Philip, who was from Bethsai- 21 da in Galilee, and asked him, "Sir, we want to see Jesus." •Philip came 22 and spoke to Andrew; Andrew and Philip came and spoke to Jesus. •Je- 23 sus answered them by saying, "The hour has come for the Son of Man to be glorified! •Amen, amen, I say to you, 24

> If the grain of wheat that falls to the ground
>   does not die, it remains alone,
> But if it dies, it bears much fruit.
> •Whoever loves his life, loses it, 25
> And whoever hates his life in this world
>   will save it for eternal life.
> •If anyone would serve me, let him follow me, 26
> And where I am, there will my servant be.
> If anyone would serve me,
> The Father will honor him."

[h] *Mt 21:1-11; Mk 11:1-11; Lk 19:28-40.*

12:13 Ps 118:26.
12:15 Jesus took the mount of the King of Peace for all nations (Zc 9:9), as a sign that he was not a nationalistic Messiah come to wreak vengeance on the Gentiles.
12:20 "Greeks" probably refers to Jews of the Diaspora whose first language was Greek.

27 •"Now my soul is troubled! And what shall I say? 'Father, save me from
28 this hour'? But it was for *this* that I came to this hour. •Father, glorify
Your name!" A voice came from Heaven, "I have glorified it and I will
29 glorify it again!" •So when the crowd standing there also heard it they
30 said that it had thundered. Others said, "An angel spoke to him!" •Jesus
answered and said, "This voice came, not for my sake, but for your sake.

31   •Now is the judgment of this world,
      Now the ruler of this world will be driven out!
32   •And when I'm lifted up from the earth
      I'll draw all men to myself."

33,34 •He said this to indicate the kind of death he was going to die. •So
the crowd answered him, "We've heard from the Torah that the Messiah is to stay forever, so how can *you* say that the Son of Man must be
35 lifted up? Who is this Son of Man?" •So Jesus said to them, "The light
will be with you for a little while, yet. Walk while you have the light, so
the darkness doesn't overtake you, and whoever walks in the dark does-
36 n't know where he's going. •While you have the light, believe in the light,
so you may become sons of light."
37 Jesus said these things and then went off and hid from them. •Although
he'd performed so many signs in their presence, they didn't believe in
38 him •so that the word Isaiah the prophet spoke might be fulfilled,

Lord, who has believed our report?
And to whom has the arm of the Lord been revealed?

39 •This is why they were unable to believe, because Isaiah said once again,

40   **•He has made their eyes blind**
      and made their hearts stubborn,
      Lest they see with their eyes
      and understand with their hearts
      And return,
      and I will heal them.

41 •Isaiah said these things because he saw his glory and spoke about him.
42 •Nevertheless, even many of the rulers believed in him, but because of the
Pharisees they didn't admit it, so they wouldn't be banished from the syn-
43 agogue, •for they loved the glory of men more than the glory of God.
44   •Then Jesus cried out, "Whoever believes in me doesn't believe in me
45 but in the One Who sent me, •and whoever sees me sees the One Who

12:38 Is 53:1 (Septuagint).   12:40 Is 6:10 (Septuagint).

JOHN

sent me. •I've come as a light for the world so that no one who believes 46
in me will remain in darkness. •And if anyone hears my words and does- 47
n't keep them, *I* don't judge him — I didn't come to *judge* the world,
but to *save* the world. •Whoever rejects me and doesn't accept my words 48
has something to judge him; the word I spoke — *that* will judge him on
the last day, •because I haven't spoken on my own; it's the Father Who 49
sent me Who has Himself commanded me what to say and what to
speak. •And I know that His command is eternal life. So the things I 50
say — as the Father has spoken to me, so do I speak."

Q. THE LAST SUPPER

13 •Before the festival of the Passover Jesus, knowing that his hour 1
had come to leave this world for the Father, having loved his own
in the world, he loved them to the end. •During the banquet, when the 2
Devil had already put it into the heart of Judas son of Simon Iscariot to
hand Jesus over, •knowing that the Father had given all things into his 3
hands and that he had come from God and was now returning to God,
•he got up from the banquet and laid aside his cloak, and he took a tow- 4
el and wrapped it around himself. •Then he poured water into the wash- 5
basin and began to wash the disciples' feet and wipe them dry with the
towel he'd wrapped around himself. •When he came to Simon Peter, 6
Peter said to him, "Lord, are *you* going to wash *my* feet?" •Jesus an- 7
swered and said to him, "What I'm doing you don't understand just now,
but later you'll understand." •Peter said to him, "You'll *never* wash my 8
feet!" Jesus answered him, "Unless I wash you, you'll have no share in
me." •Simon Peter said to him, "Lord, wash not only my feet, but my 9
hands and head as well!" •Jesus said to him, "Whoever has bathed has 10
no need to wash except for his feet; on the contrary, he's completely
purified; and you *are* pure, but not all of you." •For he knew who was 11
to hand him over; that's why he said, "Not all of you are pure." •After 12
he'd washed their feet and had put his cloak back on he sat down again
and said to them, "Do you understand what I've done for you? •You call 13
me 'The Teacher' and 'The Lord,' and rightly so, because I am. •So if 14
I, the Lord and Teacher, have washed your feet, you, too, ought to wash
each others' feet, •because I've given you an example so that, just as 15
I've done for you, you, too, should do. •Amen, amen, I say to you, 16

A servant isn't greater than his lord,
Nor is a messenger greater than the one who sent him.

Jerusalem: Cenacle.

17 •If you *know* these things,
Blessed are you if you *do* them.

18 •I'm not speaking about all of you. I know whom I've chosen, but let
the Scripture be fulfilled, **The one who ate my bread has raised**
19 his heel up against me. •I tell you this now before it happens so you
20 may believe, when it does happen, that I am. •Amen, amen, I say to
you,

Whoever receives anyone I send receives me,
While whoever receives me receives the One
Who sent me."

21 •[i] After saying these things Jesus became troubled in spirit, and he bore
witness and said, "Amen, amen, I say to you, one of you will hand me
22 over!" •The disciples looked at one another, uncertain whom he was speak-

[i] *Mt 26:21-25; Mk 14:17-21; Lk 22:21-23.*
13:18 Ps 41:10.

ing about. •One of the disciples, the one Jesus loved, was reclining at Je- 23
sus' bosom, •so Simon Peter nodded to the disciple to ask whom he could 24
be speaking about. •So, simply leaning onto Jesus' chest, the disciple said 25
to him, "Lord, who is it?" •Jesus answered, "It's the one I'll dip the piece 26
of bread for, and give to him." So he dipped the piece of bread and gave
it to Judas son of Simon Iscariot. •And then, after the piece of bread, Sa- 27
tan went into Judas. So Jesus said to him, "Do what you're doing quickly." •Now none of those reclining at table knew why he said this to him 28
— •since Judas kept the money bag, some thought that Jesus was telling 29
him, "Buy what we need for the festival," or to give something to the poor.
•So after taking the piece of bread Judas left at once; now it was night. 30

R. JESUS' FAREWELL TO HIS DISCIPLES
THE WAY, THE TRUTH, AND THE LIFE

•After Judas left Jesus said, 31

"Now is the Son of Man glorified, and God
    is glorified in him!
•If God is glorified in him, God will also glorify him 32
    in Himself and will glorify him at once.
•Little children, I'll be with you yet a little while; 33
You'll seek me, and just as I told the Jews,
'Where I'm going you cannot come,'
I now tell you also.
•I give you a new commandment — love one another; 34
As I have loved you, you too should love one another.
•All will know by this that you're my disciples, 35
If you have love for one another."

•ʲ Simon Peter said to him, "Lord, where are you going?" Jesus an- 36
swered, "Where I'm going you cannot follow me now, but you'll follow
later." •Peter said to him, "Lord, why can't I follow you now? I'll lay 37
down my life for you!" •Jesus answered, "You'll lay down your life for 38
me? Amen, amen, I say to you, the cock will not crow before you deny me three times!"

ʲ Mt 26:31-35; Mk 14:27-31; Lk 22:31-34.

13:23-25 The disciple Jesus loved is normally
understood as being the disciple John.
13:34 As at the Sermon on the Mount, Jesus here
proclaims himself capable of establishing laws or
commandments — considered by the Jews to be
a divine prerogative — and thus, implicitly, proclaims his equality with the Father.

1 **14** • "Let not your hearts be troubled!
Believe in God and believe in me.
2 •In my Father's house are many rooms;
Were it not so, would I have told you that I'm
    going to prepare a place for you?
3 •And if I go and prepare a place for you,
I'll come again and take you to myself,
So that where I am, you too may be.
4 •Yet where I'm going, you know the way."

5 •Thomas said to him, "Lord, we don't know where you're going!
6 How can we know the way?" •Jesus said to him,

"I am the way and the truth and the life;
No one comes to the Father except through me.
7 •If you know me you'll know the Father, too,
And from now on you'll know Him and will see Him."

8 •Philip said to him, "Lord, show us the Father and we'll be satisfied."
9 •Jesus said to him,

"Have I been with you so long and yet you
    don't recognize me, Philip?
Whoever has seen me has seen the Father!
How can you say, 'Show us the Father'?
10 •Don't you believe that I am in the Father
    and the Father is in me?
The words I speak to you I don't speak on my own,
But the Father Who abides in me does His works.
11 •Believe *me* when I say that I am in the Father
and the Father is in me,
But if you don't, believe because of the works themselves.

12 •Amen, amen, I say to you,

Whoever believes in me,
    the works I do he, too, will do,
And he'll do greater works than these,
    because I'm going to the Father!
13 •And whatever you ask for in my name, I'll do it,
    so the Father may be glorified in the Son;
14 •If you ask me for anything in my name,
    I'll do it."

•"If you love me, you'll keep my commandments,   15
•And I'll ask the Father and He'll give you   16
 another Intercessor to be with you forever,
•The Spirit of truth, whom the world cannot accept   17
 because it doesn't see or know Him.
You'll know Him, because He'll remain with you
 and be in you.
•I won't leave you orphaned — I'll come to you.   18
•In a little while the world will no longer   19
 see me, but *you'll* see me;
Because *I* will live, you, too, will live.
•On that day you'll realize that I am in my Father,   20
 and you in me and I in you.
 •Whoever keeps my commandments and obeys them —   21
he it is who loves me,
While whoever loves me is loved by my Father,
 and I'll love him and reveal myself to him."

•Judas, not the Iscariot, said to him, "Lord, why is it that you're going   22
to reveal yourself to us but not to the world?" •Jesus answered,   23

"If anyone loves me he'll keep my word,
 and my Father will love him,
And We'll come to him and make our abode
 with him.
•Whoever doesn't love me doesn't keep my words,   24
And the word you hear is not mine,
 but the Father's Who sent me."

•"I've told you these things while I'm still with you, •but the Intercessor,   25,26
the Holy Spirit the Father will send in my name, He'll teach you everything and will remind you of all the things I told you.

•Peace I leave with you,   27
 my peace I give to you;
Not as the world gives
 do I give to you.
Let not your hearts be troubled
 nor afraid.

14:26 "Intercessor." The Spirit intercedes for us, or serves as our Advocate, with God in Heaven.

28 •You've heard that I told you,
'I'm going away and I'm coming to you.'
If you loved me you'd rejoice
that I'm going to the Father,
because the Father is greater than I.

29 •And now I've told you this before it happens,
so that when it happens you'll believe.

30 •I'll speak of many things with you no longer, for the ruler of the world
31 is coming. He has no claim over me, •but the world must know that I
love the Father, and just as the Father has commanded me, that's what
I'll do. Get up, let's be going!"

The Washing of the Feet, by Duccio di Buoninsegna.

The True Vine

15 •"I am the true vine,   1
And my Father is the vinedresser.
•Every branch in me that doesn't bear fruit He'll remove,   2
And every branch that does bear fruit He'll prune
    so it will bear more fruit.
•You're already pure because of the word   3
    I've spoken to you;
•Abide in me, and I'll abide in you.   4
Just as the branch cannot bear fruit on its own
    unless it remains on the vine,
Likewise *you* cannot unless you abide in me.
•I am the vine, you are the branches.   5
Whoever abides in me, and I in him,
He it is who bears much fruit,
For apart from me you can do nothing.
•Unless someone abides in me he's thrown out   6
    like a [pruned] branch and withers,
And they gather them and throw them into the fire
    and they're burned.
•If you abide in me, and my words abide in you,   7
Ask whatever you wish and it will happen for you.
•In this is my Father glorified,   8
That you bear much fruit and become my disciples.
•As the Father loved me, I, too, have   9
    loved you;
Abide in my love.
•If you keep my commandments   10
    you'll abide in my love,
Just as I've kept my Father's commandments
    and I abide in Him."
•"I've told you these things so that my joy   11
    may be in you
and your joy may be complete.
•This is my commandment: 12
    love one another as I have loved you.
•Greater love than this no man has —   13
    to lay down his life for his friends.
•You are my friends   14
    if you do what I command you.

15   •I no longer call you servants,
     because the servant doesn't know
       what his lord does.
  I've called you friends
     because everything I've heard from the Father
       I've made known to you.

16   •You didn't choose me;
     on the contrary, I chose you,
  And I designated you to go and bear fruit
     and that your fruit should abide,
  So that whatever you ask the Father for in my name
     He'll give to you.

17   •This I command you:
     love one another."

18   •"If the world hates you,
     remember that it hated me before you.

19   •If you had been of the world
     the world would have loved its own,
  But because you're not of the world, but instead
      I chose you from the world,
     therefore, the world hates you.

20   •Remember the word I spoke to you,
     'A servant isn't greater than his lord.'
  If they persecuted me,
     they'll also persecute you,
  If they kept my word,
     they'll keep yours as well.

21   •But they'll do all these things to you
      because of my name,
     because they don't know the One
      Who sent me.

22   •If I hadn't come and spoken to them they'd
      have no sin,
     but now they have no excuse for their sin.

23   •Whoever hates me
     also hates my Father.

24   •If I hadn't done among them works that no one
      else has done,
     they'd have no sin,
  But now they've seen and hated
     both me and my Father.

•But let the word written in their Torah   25
   be fulfilled,
   They hated me without cause."
•"When the Intercessor comes, whom I'll send to you   26
   from the Father
   — the Spirit of truth that comes forth
   from the Father —
   He'll bear witness to me,
•But you, too, will bear witness,   27
   because you've been with me from the beginning."

Church of the "Dominus flevit" (the Lord's lamentation over Jerusalem)
on the Mount of Olives.

16 •"I've told you these things so you won't lose faith. •They'll have 1,2
you banished from the synagogue, but the hour is coming when
everyone who kills you will think he's performing a service to God. •And 3

15:25 Ps 69:5.

they'll do these things because they knew neither my Father nor me.
4 •But I've told you these things so that when their hour comes you'll remember that I told you."

"I didn't tell you these things from the beginning
because I was with you.
5 •But now I'm returning to the One Who sent me,
yet none of you asks me, 'Where are you going?'
6 •But because I've told you these things,
grief has filled your hearts.
7 •Still I'm telling you the truth — it's for your good
that I should go away,
Because if I don't go the Intercessor
won't come to you,
But if I depart, I'll send Him to you.
8 •And when He comes He'll expose sin
and righteousness and judgment to the world
for what it is;
9 •Sin, because they don't believe in me,
10 •Then righteousness, because I'm returning
to the Father and you'll no longer see me,
11 •Then judgment, because the ruler of this world
has been judged."
12 •"I still have many things to tell you,
But for now you cannot bear it,
13 •But when He comes — the Spirit of truth —
He'll lead you to the whole truth,
For He won't speak on His own,
But instead He'll say what He hears,
And He'll proclaim to you the things to come.
14 •He'll glorify me because He'll receive what's mine
and proclaim it to you.
15 •Everything the Father has is mine;
That's why I said that He receives what's mine
and proclaims it to you."

The victory is mine

•"A little while and you'll no longer see me,   16
    yet again a little while and you *will* see me."

•So some of his disciples said to one another, "What is this he's telling   17
us, 'A little while and you won't see me, yet again a little while you *will*
see me' and, 'Because I'm returning to the Father'?" •So they said, "What 18
is this 'little while'? We don't get what he's saying." •Jesus knew what   19
they wanted to ask him, and so he said to them, "Are you asking each
other about this because I said, 'A little while and you won't see me, yet
again a little while and you *will* see me'? •Amen, amen, I say to you,   20

You'll wail and mourn,
    but the world will rejoice;
You'll grieve,
    but your grief will turn to joy.
•When a woman is giving birth   21
    she grieves
        because her hour has come,
But when she bears a child
    she no longer remembers her suffering
        out of joy that a man has come into the world.
•So you, too, are in grief now,   22
    but I'll see you again
And your hearts will rejoice,
    and no one will take your joy from you.

•And on that day you'll ask nothing of me. Amen, amen, I say to you,   23
whatever you ask the Father for in my name He'll give you. •Up till now   24
you've asked for nothing in my name; ask and you'll receive, so your
joy may be complete."

•"I've told you these things in figures of speech; the hour is coming   25
when I'll no longer speak to you in figures of speech but will openly tell
you about the Father. •On that day you'll ask in my name and I won't   26
tell you that I'll ask the Father for you, •for the Father Himself loves you 27
because you've loved me and have believed that I've come from God.
•I came from the Father and came into the world, and now I'm leaving   28
the world and going to the Father." •His disciples said, "Look, now   29
you're speaking openly and aren't speaking in a figure of speech! •Now   30
we know that you know everything and have no need for someone to
question you! Because of this we believe that you came forth from God."

31,32 •Jesus answered them, "Do you believe for now? •Behold, the hour is coming, and has come, when each will be scattered to his home and you'll leave me alone; yet I'm not alone, because the Father is with me. 33 •I've told you these things so you'll have peace in me; you'll have suffering in the world, but take courage! I've conquered the world!"

Jesus' prayer to the Father

1 **17** •Jesus said these things, and then he lifted his eyes up to Heaven and said,

"Father, the hour has come!
Glorify Your Son so Your Son may glorify You,
2 •Just as You gave him authority over all flesh
So You may give eternal life to all those
You've given to him.
3 •Now this is eternal life, to know You —
the One, True, God —
And the one You sent, Jesus Christ.
4 •I glorified You on earth by completing the work
You gave me to do,
5 •And now You glorify me in Your presence, Father,
with the glory I had with You before the world was."
6 •"I've made Your name known to those men
You gave me from the world.
They were Yours and You gave them to me,
and they've kept Your word.
7 •Now they know that everything You've given me
is from You,
8 •Because I've given them the words You gave me,
And they received them and they truly know
that I came from You, and they believe
that You sent me.
9 •I'm praying for *them*; I'm praying, not for the world,
but for those You've given me,
10 Because they're Yours •and everything of mine
is Yours and Yours is mine, and I am
glorified in them.
11 •Yet I'm no longer in the world and they *are*
in the world,

And I'm coming to You.
Holy Father, keep them in Your name
    which You've given me,
That they may be one as We are one.
•When I was with them I kept them in Your name   12
    which You gave me and guarded them,
And none of them was lost except the son of perdition,
    so that Scripture may be fulfilled.
•But now I'm coming to You, and I'm speaking these   13
    things in the world
That they may have my joy fulfilled in them.
•I've given them Your word and the world   14
    has hated them
Because they're not of the world, just as I'm not
    of the world.
•I don't pray for You to take them out of the world,   15
But for You to preserve them from the Evil One.
•They're not of the world, just as I'm not   16
    of the world.
•Make them holy in the truth; Your *word* is truth.   17
•Just as You sent me into the world,   18
    I, too, have sent them into the world.
•And I consecrate myself for their sake   19
    that they may be made holy in truth."
•"But I'm praying not only for them   20
But also for those who believe in me
    through their word,
•So that all may be one, just as You, Father,   21
    are in me and I in You,
So they, too, may be in Us, so the world
    may believe that You sent me.
•And I've given them the glory You gave me,   22
    so they may be one as We are one,
•I in them and You in me, so they may be   23
    perfectly one,
So the world may know that You sent me
And You loved them just as You loved me.
•Father, I desire that they, too, may be with me   24
    where I am — those You gave me —
So they may see my glory that You gave me,
    because You loved me before the beginning of the world.

25   •Righteous Father, the world also doesn't know You,
       But I know You and these know that You sent me,
26   •And I made Your name known to them
           and I'll make it known,
       That the love with which You have loved me
           may be in them, and I in them."

S. THE PASSION

1 **18** •ᵏ After Jesus said these things he went out with his disciples to the other side of the Kedron Valley where there was a garden, 2 which he and his disciples entered. •Now Judas, who handed him over, also knew the spot because Jesus had often met there with his disciples.

ᵏ *Mt 26:47-56; Mk 14:43-50; Lk 22:47-53.*

Garden of Gethsemane with the centuries-old olive trees.

•So Judas took the cohort, as well as Temple attendants from the Phar- ₃ isees and the chief priests, and came there with torches and lanterns and weapons. •Jesus, knowing all that was to befall him, came out and said ₄ to them, "Who are you looking for?" •They answered him, "Jesus of ₅ Nazareth!" He said to them, "I am he!" Now Judas, who handed him over, was also standing with them. •When Jesus said to them, "I am he!" ₆ they drew back and fell to the ground. •So he asked them again, "Who ₇ are you looking for?" "Jesus of Nazareth!" they said. •Jesus answered, ₈ "I told you that I am he, so if you're looking for *me*, let these others go," •so what he said might be fulfilled: "I lost none of those You gave ₉ to me." •Simon Peter, who had a sword, drew it and struck the servant ₁₀ of the high priest and cut off his right ear. The servant's name was Malchus. •Jesus said to Peter, "Put the sword in its scabbard. Am I not ₁₁ to drink the cup my Father has given me?"

•ˡ So the cohort and their tribune and the attendants of the Jews seized ₁₂ Jesus and bound him •and led him first to Annas — he was the father- ₁₃ in-law of Caiaphas, who was high priest that year — •for it was Caiaphas ₁₄ who had advised the Jews that it was better for one man to die for the people.

•ᵐ Simon Peter and another disciple followed Jesus. That disciple was ₁₅ known to the high priest and he went in with Jesus to the high priest's courtyard •while Peter stood outside near the gate. So the other disci- ₁₆ ple, who was known to the high priest, went out and spoke to the maidservant at the gate and led Peter in. •So the gatekeeper, the maidser- ₁₇ vant, said to Peter, "Aren't you one of this man's disciples, too?" He said, "I'm not." •Now the servants and the Temple attendants had made ₁₈ a charcoal fire and were standing warming themselves, because it was cold; Peter was with them, too, standing and warming himself.

•ⁿ So the high priest questioned Jesus about his disciples and about ₁₉ his teaching. •Jesus answered him, "I've spoken openly to the world; ₂₀ I've always taught in a synagogue or in the Temple" — where all the Jews gather — "and I've said nothing in secret. •Why are you questioning ₂₁ me? Ask those who heard what I said to them. After all, they know what I said." •When he said these things one of the attendants who was stand- ₂₂ ing by gave Jesus a slap and said, "Is that how you answer the high

ˡ *Mt 26:57-58; Mk 14:53-54; Lk 22:54.*   ᵐ *Mt 26:69-70; Mk 14:66-68; Lk 22:55-57.*
ⁿ *Mt 26:59-66; Mk 14:55-64; Lk 22:66-71.*

18:3 A "cohort" was, technically, the tenth part of a Roman legion, or about 600 men. It may here mean simply a group of soldiers. The "trib- une" (v. 12) was their commanding officer. 18:15 The disciple known to the high priest is normally identified with the disciple John.

23 priest?" •Jesus answered him, "If I've spoken wrongly, bear witness
24 against the wrong, but if I've spoken rightly, why do you hit me?" •So
Annas sent him bound to Caiaphas, the high priest.
25 •[o] Now Simon Peter was standing there warming himself. So they said
to him, "Aren't you one of his disciples, too?" He denied it and said,
26 "I'm not." •One of the servants of the high priest, a kinsman of the one
whose ear Peter had cut off, said, "Didn't I see you with him in the gar-
27 den?" •Again Peter denied it, and at once a cock crowed.
28 •[p] So they led Jesus from Caiaphas to the praetorium. Now it was
early morning, and they didn't go into the praetorium so they would-
29 n't be defiled and would be able to eat the Passover. •So Pilate came
out to them and said, "What charge are you bringing against this man?"
30 •They answered, "If the fellow weren't a wrongdoer we wouldn't have
31 handed him over to you." •So Pilate said to them, "*You* take him and
judge him according to your law." The Jews said to him, "It's not law-
32 ful for us to put anyone to death," •so that Jesus' word might be fulfilled, which he said to indicate the kind of death he was going to die.
33 •So Pilate went into the praetorium again and called for Jesus and said
34 to him, "Are you the King of the Jews?" •Jesus answered, "Are you
35 saying this on your own or have others told you about me?" •Pilate answered, "Am I a Jew? It was your nation and the chief priests who hand-
36 ed you over to me; what have you done?" •Jesus answered, "My Kingdom is not of this world; if my Kingdom *were* of this world my attendants would fight so that I wouldn't be handed over to the Jews, but as
37 it is my Kingdom is not from here." •So Pilate said to him, "So you
are a king?" Jesus answered, "*You* say that I'm a king. For this I was
born and for this I came into the world — to bear witness to the truth.
38 Everyone who is of the truth hears my voice." •[q] Pilate said to him,
"What is truth?"

After saying this he went out again to the Jews and said to them, "I
39 find no case against him. •But it's your custom to have me release one
prisoner to you on the Passover. So do you want me to release the King
40 of the Jews to you?" •But they cried out again, "Not this one, but Barabbas, instead!" Now Barabbas was a robber.

[o] *Mt 26:71-75; Mk 14:69-72; Lk 22:58-62.* [p] *Mt 27:1-2, 11-14; Mk 15:1-5; Lk 23:1-5.*
[q] *Mt 27:15-31; Mk 15:6-20; Lk 23:13-25.*

18:30 The Romans normally allowed subject populations to rule themselves according to their own law. It is understood here that the offense is a breach of Roman law, i.e., rebellion, rather than solely of Jewish law, otherwise Jesus would not have been brought to Pilate.

19 •So then Pilate took Jesus and had him scourged. •And the sol- 1,2 diers wove a crown of thorns and placed it on his head, and they put a purple robe on him, •and they'd come up to him and say, "Hail, 3 King of the Jews!" and slap him. •Pilate came outside again and said to 4 them, "Look, I'm bringing him out to you so you'll know that I find no case against him." •So Jesus came outside, wearing the crown of thorns 5 and the purple robe. And Pilate said to them, "Look at the man!" •When 6 they saw him the chief priests and their attendants cried out and said, "Crucify him, crucify him!" Pilate said to them, "*You* take him and cru- cify him — I find no case against him!" •The Jews answered him, "We 7 have the Torah, and according to the Torah he deserves to die, because he made himself the Son of God!"

•Now when Pilate heard *this* being said he became more afraid than 8 ever, •and he went into the praetorium and said to Jesus, "Where are 9 you from?" But Jesus gave him no answer. •So Pilate said to him, "You 10 won't speak to me? Don't you know that I have power to release you and I have power to crucify you?" •Jesus answered him, "You'd have 11 no power over me unless it had been given to you from above; that's why the one who handed me over to you has the greater sin." •From 12 then on Pilate kept trying to release him, but the Jews kept shouting, saying, "If you release this man you're no 'Friend of Caesar'; everyone who makes himself a king is rebelling against Caesar!"

•So when Pilate heard these words he led Jesus outside and sat on 13 the judgment seat at a place called "the Pavement," but in Hebrew, Gab- batha. •Now it was the Day of Preparation for the Passover; it was about 14 noon. And he said to the Jews, "Here is your king!" •They shouted, 15 "Away with him, away with him! Crucify him!" Pilate said to them, "Shall I crucify your king?" The chief priests answered, "We have no king but Caesar!" •[r] Then he handed him over to them to be crucified. 16

So they took Jesus in charge. •And carrying the cross himself he went 17 out to what was called "the Place of the Skull," in Hebrew, Golgotha, •where they crucified him and with him two others, on either side, while 18 Jesus was in the middle. •Now Pilate wrote a notice and had it placed 19 on the cross, but it was written, "Jesus of Nazareth, the King of the Jews." •Many of the Jews read this notice, because the place where Je- 20

[r] *Mt 27:32-44; Mk 15:21-32; Lk 23:26-43.*

18:40 "Robber." This term was often applied to rebels against Roman rule.
19:12 "Friend of Caesar" was a title given high-ranking Roman officials. As used by the Jews here it takes on a threatening tone: if Pilate re- fuses to condemn Jesus he may be accused of declining to defend the supremacy of the Roman Emperor against pretenders to the royal dignity.
19:14 "About noon." This was the hour at which the Passover lambs were slaughtered.

JOHN

sus was crucified was near the city, and it was written in Hebrew, Latin,
21 and Greek. •So the chief priests of the Jews said to Pilate, "Don't write,
'The King of the Jews' but instead, 'He said, I am the King of the Jews.'"
22 •Pilate answered, "What I have written I have written!"
23   •When the soldiers had crucified Jesus they took his cloak and made
four parts, one for each soldier, plus the tunic. Now the tunic was seam-
24 less, woven from the top in one piece. •So they said to each other, "Let's
not tear it; let's draw lots for it instead," so the Scripture would be fulfilled which said,

**They divided my garments among them,
and for my clothing they cast lots.**

25   So the soldiers did these things. •Now standing by Jesus' cross were
his mother and his mother's sister, Mary the wife of Clopas, and Mary

19:24 Ps 22:19.

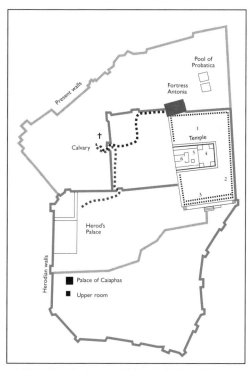

Jerusalem. Northern route: the traditional Via Crucis.
Southern route: the historical Via Crucis

Magdalen. •When Jesus saw his mother and the disciple he loved stand- 26
ing by he said to his mother, "Woman, here is your son." •Then he said 27
to the disciple, "Here is your mother." And from that hour the disciple
took her into his home.

•ˢ After this Jesus, knowing that everything had already been ac- 28
complished, in order to fulfill the Scripture, said, "I'm thirsty." •There 29
was a container there full of sour wine; so after putting a sponge full of
sour wine on some hyssop they held it up to his mouth. •When he had 30
taken the sour wine Jesus said, "All has been fulfilled!" and bowing his
head he gave up the spirit.

•The Jews, since it was the Day of Preparation and so the bodies 31
wouldn't remain on the crosses — for that Sabbath was a great day
—asked Pilate to let them break their legs and take them away. •So 32
the soldiers came and they broke the legs of the first one and then of
the other who had been crucified with him, •but when they came to 33
Jesus and saw that he'd already died they didn't break his legs, •but, 34
instead, one of the soldiers stabbed him in the side with a spear, and
at once blood and water came out. •And the one who saw it has borne 35
witness and his witness is true, and he knows that he's speaking the
truth so you, too, may believe. •For these things happened so the 36
Scripture might be fulfilled, **Not a bone of his shall be broken.**
•And again another Scripture says, **They shall look on him whom** 37
they have pierced.

•ᵗ After these things, Joseph of Arimathea — who was a disciple of 38
Jesus, but a secret one for fear of the Jews — asked Pilate to allow
him to take Jesus' body, and Pilate let him. So he came and took his
body. •Then Nicodemus came, too — the one who had first come to 39
him at night — bringing a mixture of myrrh and aloes, about a hundred pounds. •So they took Jesus' body and bound it in linen cloths 40
with the spices, as is the custom among the Jews in preparing for burial. •Now at the place where he had been crucified there was a gar- 41
den, and in the garden a new tomb in which no one had been laid yet,
•so because of the Jewish Day of Preparation, because the tomb was 42
near, they laid Jesus there.

ˢ *Mt 27:45-46; Mk 15:33-41; Lk 23:44-49.* ᵗ *Mt 27:57-61; Mk 15:42-47; Lk 23:50-56.*

19:36 Ex 12:46, Nb 9:12, Ps 34:21. The passages
in Exodus and Numbers refer to the Paschal lamb;   19:28 Ps 69:21.
Jesus is thus the new Paschal lamb.   19:37 Zc 12:10.

T. RESURRECTION AND APPEARANCES OF JESUS

1 **20** •ᵘ On the first day of the week Mary Magdalen came to the tomb in the early morning while it was still dark, and she saw the stone,
2 which had been taken away from the tomb. •So she ran and came to Simon Peter and to the other disciple whom Jesus loved, and she said to them, "They've taken the Lord out of the tomb and we don't know
3 where they've put him!" •So Peter and the other disciple went out and
4 they went to the tomb. •The two of them were running together, but
5 the other disciple ran faster than Peter and came to the tomb first, •and when he bent down he saw the linen cloths lying there, but he didn't go
6 in. •Simon Peter came, too, following him, and he went into the tomb
7 and saw the linen cloths lying there, •and the face covering, which had been on his head, wasn't lying with the linen cloths but was wrapped
8 up separately in its own place. •So then the other disciple, who had come
9 to the tomb first, went in, too, and he saw and believed, •for they did-
10 n't yet understand the Scripture that he had to rise from the dead. •So the disciples went off home again.

11 •ᵛ Now Mary was standing near the tomb, weeping outside. As she
12 wept she looked into the tomb •and saw two angels in white sitting where
13 Jesus' body had been, one at the head and one at the feet. •And they said to her, "Woman, why are you weeping?" She said to them, "They've
14 taken my Lord and I don't know where they've put him!" •After she said this she turned around and saw Jesus standing there, yet she didn't re-
15 alize that it was Jesus. •Jesus said to her, "Woman, why are you weeping? Who are you looking for?" Thinking that it was the gardener she said to him, "Sir, if you removed him tell me where you put him, and
16 I'll take him away." •Jesus said to her, "Mary!" She turned and said to
17 him, in Hebrew, "Rabboni!" which means, "Teacher!" •Jesus said to her, "Don't hold on to me — I haven't yet ascended to the Father. But go to my brothers and tell them,

'I am ascending to my Father and your Father,
And to my God and your God.'"

18 •Mary Magdalen went and told the disciples, "I've seen the Lord!" and she related the things he had told her.
19 •ʷ When it was evening on that first day of the week, and the doors had been locked where the disciples were for fear of the Jews, Jesus came and stood in their midst and said to them, "Peace be with you!"

ᵘ Mt 28:1-10; Mk 16:1-8; Lk 24:1-12.   ᵛ Mk 16:9-11.   ʷ Mt 28:16-20; Mk 16:14-18; Lk 24:36-49.

•And after saying this he showed them his hands and side. The disci- 20
ples rejoiced when they saw the Lord. •He said to them again, "Peace 21
be with you! As the Father has sent me, I, too, send you." •And after 22
saying this he breathed on them and said, "Receive the Holy Spirit!

•Whoever's sins you forgive, 23
    they've already been forgiven;
Whoever's you retain,
    they've already been retained."

•Now Thomas, one of the Twelve, called the Twin, wasn't with them 24
when Jesus came. •So the other disciples told him, "We've seen the 25
Lord!" But he told them, "Unless I see the mark of the nails in his hands
and put my finger into the mark of the nails and put my hand into his
side, I won't believe!" •And a week later his disciples were once again 26
inside, and Thomas was with them. Although the doors had been locked,
Jesus came and stood in their midst and said, "Peace be with you!"
•Then he said to Thomas, 27

"Bring your finger here
    and look at my hands,
And bring your hand
    and put it in my side,
And be not unbelieving,
    but believing!"

•Thomas answered and said to him, "My Lord and my God!" •Jesus said 28,29
to him,

"You've believed because you've seen me;
Blessed are they who haven't seen
    yet have believed!"

•Jesus also did many other signs in the presence of the disciples which 30
are not written in this book, •but these things have been written so you 31
may believe that Jesus is the Messiah, the Son of God, and so that by
believing you may have life in his name.

20:23 I.e., the disciples will be guided by the Holy Spirit to perform what God has already decided
from all eternity.

*Tabgha. Church which commemorates the apparition
of the Risen Lord narrated in John 21.*

U. JESUS AND PETER IN GALILEE

1 **21** •After these things Jesus showed himself to the disciples again at
2 the Sea of Tiberias; now he appeared in this way. •Simon Peter
and Thomas, who was called the Twin, and Nathanael, who was from
Cana in Galilee, and the sons of Zebedee and two other of his disciples
3 were together. •Simon Peter said to them, "I'm going out to fish." They
said to him, "We'll go with you, too." They went out and got in the boat
4 and that night they caught nothing. •Now as day was breaking Jesus stood
5 there on the shore, but the disciples didn't know that it was Jesus. •So
Jesus said to them, "Children, do you have any fish?" They answered
6 him, "No." •Then he said to them, "Cast the net to the right side of the
boat and you'll find some." So they cast it, and now they were unable to
7 draw it in because of the number of fish. •So the disciple Jesus loved said
to Peter, "It's the Lord!" Simon Peter, when he heard that it was the Lord,
put on his outer garment — he was stripped — and threw himself into
8 the sea. •Then the other disciples came with the boat — they weren't

far from land, about a hundred yards away — dragging the net of fish.
•So as they were coming up onto land they saw a charcoal fire started 9
and a fish laid on it and bread. •Jesus said to them, "Bring some of the 10
fish you caught just now." •So Simon Peter went aboard and dragged 11
the net to land, full of large fish — a hundred and fifty-three — yet, even
though there were so many, the net wasn't split. •Jesus said to them, 12
"Come eat breakfast." None of the disciples dared to ask him, "Who are
you?" because they knew it was the Lord. •Jesus came and took the bread 13
and gave it to them, and likewise the fish. •This was the third time now 14
that Jesus had appeared to the disciples after rising from the dead.

•After they'd eaten breakfast Jesus said to Simon Peter, "Simon son 15
of John, do you love me more than they do?" He said to him, "Yes,
Lord, you know that I love you!" He said to him, "Feed my lambs!"
•Again he said to him a second time, "Simon son of John, do you love 16
me?" He said to him, "Yes, Lord, you know that I love you!" He said to
him, "Tend my sheep!" •He said to him a third time, "Simon son of 17
John, do you love me?" Peter was distressed because he said to him a
third time, "Do you love me?" and he said to him, "Lord, you know
everything; you know that I love you!" He said to him, "Feed my sheep!
•Amen, amen, I say to you, when you were young you fastened your 18
belt and went where you wanted, but when you're old you'll stretch out
your hands and another will fasten you and bring you where you don't
wish to go." •He said this to indicate by what type of death he'd glori- 19
fy God. And after saying this he said to him, "Follow me!"

•When Peter turned he saw the disciple Jesus loved following — the 20
one who had leaned at his bosom onto his chest and said, "Lord, who
is it who will hand you over?" — •so when Peter saw him he said to 21
Jesus, "Lord, what about him?" •Jesus said to him, "If I want him to 22
stay till I come, what's it to you? Follow me!" •So this report went out 23
to the brothers, that that disciple wouldn't die. But Jesus didn't say to
him that he wouldn't die, but, instead, "If I want him to stay till I come,
what's it to you?"

•This is the disciple who bears witness to these things and has writ- 24
ten them, and we know that his witness is true.

•Now there are also many other things that Jesus did; if every one of 25
them were written down, I don't suppose the world itself would have
room for the books that would be written.

21:15-19 This passage strongly stresses the primacy of Peter. Just as Jesus is the Good Shepherd
who has a unique relationship to the Father, he now
designates Peter to be that good shepherd in his
stead, to tend and lead the flock Jesus loves and
for which he has suffered and died.

THE ACTS OF THE

APOSTLES

Introduction
to the Acts of the Apostles

Although Acts is often treated as a separate work, it is actually a continuation of the Gospel according to St. Luke, the two books forming a whole with a common purpose, often referred to by scholars as "Luke-Acts." Early and reliable tradition ascribes both books to Luke, the companion of St. Paul. Luke is usually associated with the Syrian city of Antioch and is believed to have been a Gentile.

Luke's stated purpose for his work, set out in the prologue to his Gospel, is to write an accurate, ordered account of all that had taken place and in so doing to confirm the early Christians in their faith. Many scholars maintain that Luke also had an apologetic purpose in mind, which was to convince the Gentile world, specifically the Roman authorities, that Christianity was no threat to the established order and that it deserved to be treated with tolerance.

A further, intriguing theory which scholars such as Johnson have advanced in recent years to explain Luke's purpose in writing "Luke-Acts" is that the whole work is essentially an "apologia for God," a vindication in narrative form of the justice of God's saving plan. According to this view Luke wished to show that the history of Jesus' ministry and the early Church demonstrate that, even though the Jews had by and large rejected the good news, which had been embraced, then, largely by Gentiles, God's plan of salvation had not been derailed but was continuing to achieve its glorious purpose. Luke's task would thus be to show that the call to the Gentiles had been part of God's plan from the beginning and that Israel had been given ample opportunity to accept the good news. There can be no doubt that Luke was attempting to write a history of salvation, and this theory does full justice to that intent. It also, quite interestingly, reveals Luke to have been very much a disciple of Paul in this respect, for what Luke sought to do in narrative form was precisely the purpose behind Paul's magnum opus, the Letter to the Romans.

A. THE ASCENSION;
THE SELECTION OF MATTHIAS

1 1 •I wrote my first book, O Theophilus, about everything Jesus did and
2 taught •up to the day when, after giving instructions through the
3 Holy Spirit to the apostles he had chosen, he was taken up. •He also
provided them with many proofs that he was still alive after his
sufferings; for a period of forty days he appeared to them and spoke
4 to them about the Kingdom of God. [a]• And while he was with them he
commanded them not to leave Jerusalem: "Wait for my Father's
5 promise, which you heard from me — •John baptized with water, but
you will be baptized with the Holy Spirit in just a few days."

6 •So when they were gathered together they asked him, "Lord, is this
7 when you'll restore the Kingdom to Israel?" •But he told them, "It's not
for you to know the dates and times my Father has decided upon from
8 His own authority. •When the Holy Spirit comes upon you you'll receive
power and you'll be my witnesses in Jerusalem and in all Judea and
9 Samaria, all the way to the end of the earth." •After he said these things
he was taken up while they watched, and a cloud took him out of their
10 sight. •While they were gazing up at the sky as he departed, behold, two
11 men in white garments stood beside them •and said, "Men of Galilee,
why are you standing here looking up at the sky? This Jesus who has
been taken from you up to Heaven will return in the same way you saw
him going up to Heaven."

12 •Then they returned to Jerusalem from the mountain called Olivet,
13 which is near Jerusalem, a Sabbath day's journey distant, [b]•and when
they entered the city they went to the upper room where they were
staying — Peter and John and James and Andrew, Philip and Thomas,

---

[a] *Lk 24:29* [b] *Mt 10:2-4; Mk 3:16-19; Lk 6:14-16.*

1:1 The work which Jesus "began" in the course
of his earthly life and ministry (as recorded by
Luke in his Gospel), he continues through the
Church (as demonstrated by Luke in Acts). See,
e.g., 2:47: "And day by day the Lord increased
the number of those who were being saved."

Bartholomew and Matthew, James son of Alphaeus and Simon the Zealot and Judas son of James. •They all devoted themselves single- 14 mindedly to prayer, along with some women and Mary the mother of Jesus and his brothers.

•And in those days Peter stood up before the brethren (there was a 15 crowd of about one hundred and twenty people gathered there) and said, •"My brothers, the passage of Scripture in which the Holy Spirit 16 prophesied through David's mouth concerning Judas, who served as a guide for those who arrested Jesus, was bound to be fulfilled, •for he 17 was numbered among us and received a share of this ministry. ᶜ(•He 18 purchased a field with the reward for his wrongdoing, but he fell head-long and burst open his midsection and all his insides spilled out. •This 19 became known to everyone who lived in Jerusalem and they named that field "Akeldama" in their language, that is, the Field of Blood.) •For 20 it is written in the Book of Psalms,

Let his homestead be desolate,
and let there be no one dwelling in it,

and,

Let another take his place.

•"Therefore, one of those men who accompanied us the whole time 21 the Lord Jesus came and went among us — •beginning with the bap- 22 tism of John, right up to the day he was taken from us — must become with us a witness to his resurrection." •They had two men stand up, 23 Joseph who was called Barsabbas and was surnamed Justus, and Matthias. •Then they prayed and said, "You, Lord, who know the hearts 24 of all, show which one of these two you have chosen •to take the place 25 in this ministry and apostolic mission from which Judas turned aside to go to his own place." •Then they drew lots and the lot fell to Matthias, 26 and he was counted among the eleven apostles.

ᶜ *Mt 27:3-8*

1:20 Ps 69:25; 109:8.
2:1 The Jewish feast of Pentecost (*Shavu'ot* or "Weeks" in English) was originally an agricultur-al feast but had become a commemoration of the gift of the Torah. Here we will see the contrast of written law and the law of the Spirit, written on the heart as the Torah was to be written on the hearts of devout Jews.

B. THE COMING OF THE SPIRIT AT PENTECOST

1 2 •Now when the day of Pentecost arrived they were all together in
2 one place. •Suddenly a sound like a violent rushing wind came from
3 the sky and filled the whole house where they were staying. •Tongues
as if of fire appeared to them, parting and coming to rest on each of
4 them, •and they were all filled with the Holy Spirit and began to speak
in different tongues according to how the Spirit inspired them to speak.
5   •Now in Jerusalem there lived devout Jews from every nation under
6 Heaven. •At this sound they gathered in a crowd and they were bewil-
7 dered, because each one heard them speaking in his own language. •And
as they marvelled and wondered they said, "Behold, aren't all those who
8 are speaking Galileans? •How is it, then, that we each hear them in our
9 own native language? •Parthians, Medes, and Elamites, those who live
10 in Mesopotamia, Judea, Pontus, and Asia, •in Phrygia and Pamphylia,
Egypt and those parts of Libya around Cyrene as well as Roman visitors,
11 •Jews and proselytes alike, Cretans and Arabs, we hear them speaking

Small chapel of the Ascension on the Mount of Olives.

of God's mighty acts in our own tongues!" •They were all amazed and 12
perplexed and kept saying to one another, "What does this mean?" •But 13
others mocked them and said, "They're full of new wine!"

•So Peter stood up with the Eleven, raised his voice, and spoke to 14
them, "Fellow Jews, and all you who live in Jerusalem, know this, and
give heed to what I'm saying! •These men aren't drunk, as you sup- 15
pose — it's only nine in the morning! •No, this is what the prophet 16
Joel spoke of:

•So it shall be in the last days, says God, 17
I will pour out My Spirit on all flesh,
and your sons and your daughters will prophesy,
Your young men will see visions,
and your old men will dream dreams;
•Yes, upon My servants and handmaids will I 18
pour out My Spirit in those days,
and they will prophesy.
•I will work wonders in the sky above, 19
and signs **on the earth** below,
Blood and fire
and a haze of smoke;
•The sun will be turned to darkness and the moon 20
to blood,
before the coming of the great and glorious
day of the Lord.
•And so it shall be that whoever calls on the 21
name of the Lord,
they shall be saved.

•"My fellow Israelites, listen to these words: Jesus of Nazareth was a 22
man who was vouched for by God by means of mighty works, wonders,
and signs, that God performed among you through him, as you yourselves know. •You killed this man, who had been delivered to you in ac- 23
cordance with the set purpose and foreknowledge of God, by having him
crucified at the hands of the Gentiles, •yet God raised him and released 24
him from the throes of death, because it was impossible for death to
hold him in its power. •For David says of him: 25

I kept my gaze ever on the Lord before me,
because He is at my right hand lest
I be shaken,

2:17-21 Jl 2:28-32 (3:1-5 Septuagint).   2:25-28 Ps 16:8-11 (Septuagint).

26 •**Therefore my heart has rejoiced and my tongue
has exulted,
and my flesh, too, shall dwell in hope;**
27 •**For You will not abandon my soul to the nether world
nor allow Your holy one to suffer death's decay.**
28 •**You have shown me the way of life,
You will fill me with joy in Your presence.**

29 •"My brothers, we can speak frankly about the Patriarch David —
he died and was buried and his tomb is here among us to this very day.
30 •So since he was a prophet, and remembered that God had **sworn him**
an oath that **He would set a descendant of his on his throne**,
31 •he spoke with foreknowledge about the Messiah's resurrection — that
he was neither abandoned **to the nether world nor** did his flesh **suf-**
32 **fer death's decay.** •God raised this Jesus — of this we are all wit-
33 nesses — •and when he was exalted by the right hand of God and had
received from the Father the promise of the Holy Spirit he poured it
34 forth, as you can see and hear. •For it wasn't David who ascended to
Heaven; he himself said:

**The Lord said to my lord,
'Sit at My right hand**
35 •**till I make your enemies a footstool for your feet.'**

36 •So let the whole house of Israel know beyond any doubt — this Jesus
whom you crucified, God made both Lord and Messiah."
37 •When they heard this it pierced them to the heart, and they said
to Peter and the rest of the apostles, "What should we do, brothers?"
38 •So Peter told them, "Each of you must repent and be baptized in the
name of Jesus Christ for the forgiveness of your sins, and you'll re-
39 ceive the gift of the Holy Spirit, •for the promise is to you and your
children and to all who are far away — anyone the Lord our God calls."
40 •And so with many other words he bore witness and exhorted them,
41 saying, "Save yourselves from this perverse generation." •Then those
who accepted his word were baptized, and that day about three thou-
42 sand were won over. •And so they devoted themselves to the teaching of the apostles and to the fellowship, to the breaking of the bread
and to the prayers.

2:30 Ps 132:11; 2 S 7:12-13.   2:31 Ps 16:10.   2:34-35 Ps 110:1.
2:39 Here we find the universal mission of the Church as expressed in some of the very early tradition.

•Awe was in every soul, and many wonders and signs came about ⁴³ through the apostles. •All the believers were together and had every- ⁴⁴ thing in common, •and they used to sell their property and posses- ⁴⁵ sions and distribute it to them all, according to the need of each individual. •By common consent they continued to meet daily in the Tem- ⁴⁶ ple and at home they broke bread, sharing their food with joy and simplicity of heart, •praising God and enjoying the good will of all the peo- ⁴⁷ ple. And day by day the Lord increased the number of those who were being saved.

C. PETER AND JOHN HEAL A LAME MAN
AND BEAR WITNESS BEFORE THE SANHEDRIN

3 •Now Peter and John were going up to the Temple one afternoon ¹ for the three o'clock hour of prayer. •A certain man who was lame ² from his mother's womb was being carried there. Every day they would place him near the gate of the Temple called the Beautiful Gate so he could ask for alms from the people who were going into the Temple, •so when he saw Peter and John about to enter the Temple he asked ³ them for alms. •But Peter gazed at him along with John and said, ⁴ "Look at us!" •Now the man was all attention, since he expected to ⁵ receive something from them, •but Peter said, "I have neither silver ⁶ nor gold, but what I do have I'll give to you — in the name of Jesus Christ of Nazareth, walk!" •Then Peter grasped the man's right hand ⁷ and raised him up, and his feet and ankles were immediately made strong. •The man leaped to his feet and began to walk about and en- ⁸ tered the Temple with them, walking and leaping, praising God. •All ⁹ the people saw him walking about and praising God •and they rec- ¹⁰ ognized him as the man who used to sit near the Beautiful Gate of the Temple asking for alms, and they were filled with wonder and astonishment at what had happened to him.

•Now as he clung to Peter and John all the people came running to- ¹¹ ward them in the porch called Solomon's Portico, utterly amazed at what had happened. •When Peter saw them he addressed the people: ¹² "Fellow Israelites, why are you so amazed? Why are you staring at us as if we made him walk with our own power or holiness? •**The God** ¹³ **of Abraham, Isaac, and Jacob, the God of our fathers,** has glorified His servant Jesus, whom you handed over and denounced before

3:13 Ex 3:6, 15.

People present in Jerusalem on the Day of Pentecost. (Ac 2:9-11)

14 Pilate, who had decided to release him. •You denounced a holy and
15 righteous man and asked that a murderer be released to you, •but you
killed the author of life, whom God then raised from the dead — of
16 that we are witnesses. •And through faith in the name of Jesus this man
whom you see and know has been strengthened, and faith in that name
17 has given him his health in full view of all of you. •And now, brothers,
18 I know that you acted out of ignorance, as did your rulers, •but in this
way God brought to fulfillment what He foretold through the mouths
19 of His prophets — that His Messiah would suffer. •So repent and turn
20 back, so that your sins may be wiped away •and a time of rest may
come to you from the Lord, and He will send you His chosen Messi-
21 ah, Jesus, •whom Heaven must receive until the time of universal
restoration that God spoke of through the mouths of His holy prophets
22 from of old. •For Moses said,

**A prophet like me will the Lord your God
raise up for you,**

3:15 "The author of life." This title was ordinari-
ly understood to apply to God. In this context the
phrase also refers to Jesus' saving activity.
3:18 The New Testament writers clearly saw the
Christian teaching of a suffering Messiah as a po-
tential stumbling block to belief for Jews and were
concerned to demonstrate that it had been foretold in the Old Testament.
3:22 Dt 18:15-16.

ACTS

from among your brothers;
You shall listen to everything he says to you,
•And anyone who fails to listen to that prophet   23
will be cut off from the people.

•And so from Samuel and his successors, all the prophets who spoke 24
also proclaimed these days. •You are sons of the prophets and of the 25
covenant God made with your fathers when He said to Abraham, **In
your offspring all the nations of the earth shall be blessed.** •God 26
raised His servant for you first and sent him to bless you by turning each
of you from your evil ways."

4 •While they were speaking to the people, the priests, the captain 1
of the Temple guard, and the Sadducees came up to them, •very 2
annoyed that they were teaching the people and proclaiming in Jesus
the resurrection of the dead, •and they laid hands on them and took 3
them into custody till the next day, since it was already evening. •But 4
many of those who had heard the word believed, and their number grew
to about five thousand men.

•The next day their leaders, elders, and scribes were gathered in 5
Jerusalem — •the high priest Annas, Caiaphas, John, and Alexander 6
were there, along with all who were of the high-priestly family — •and 7
they brought Peter and John into their presence and began to question them, "By what power or by what name did you do this?" •Then 8
Peter was filled with the Holy Spirit and said to them, "Leaders of the
people and elders, •if we're being questioned today about a good deed 9
done to a sick man — by what means he was saved — •then let it be 10
known to all of you and all the people of Israel that it was done in the
name of Jesus Christ of Nazareth, whom you crucified and whom God
raised from the dead; it is by his name that this man stands before you
healed. •He is   11

The stone rejected by you, **the builders,
which has become the cornerstone.**

•Salvation comes from no one else, for no other name under Heav- 12
en has been given to us by which we may be saved." •Now when they 13

3:23 Dt 18:19; Lv 23:29.
3:25 Gn 22:18, 26:4.
4:6 Annas was not the actual high priest at this
time, but as former high priest and father-in-law
to Caiaphas he retained enormous prestige. Caiaphas was deposed in 36 A.D., so this occur-
rence probably took place before that date.
4:11 Ps 118:22.

saw Peter's and John's boldness and realized that they were untrained laymen they were amazed, and they recognized them as having been
14 with Jesus. •And when they saw the man who had been healed stand-
15 ing there with them they had nothing to say in reply. •So they ordered
16 them to leave the Sanhedrin and then conferred among themselves, •saying, "What should we do with these men? Everyone living in Jerusalem knows that a remarkable sign was done by them, and we can't deny it.
17 •But so it doesn't spread further among the people, let's forbid them to
18 speak to anyone in this name ever again." •Then they called them in and warned them against any preaching or teaching whatsoever in the
19 name of Jesus. •But in response Peter and John told them, "Whether
20 it's right for us to obey you rather than God, you be the judges, •because it's impossible for us not to speak about what we've seen and
21 heard." •So after threatening Peter and John further the leaders released them, since they couldn't find any way to punish them, with all the peo-
22 ple glorifying God for what had happened. •For the man on whom this healing sign had been done was over forty years old.
23 •After they were released they went back to their companions and
24 told them what the chief priests and elders had said, •and when they heard about it they raised their voices to God with one accord and said, "O Lord, **Maker of heaven and earth and the sea and all that**
25 **are in them,** •by the Holy Spirit, through the mouth of our father, Your servant, David, You said,

> **Why did the Gentiles rage,**
> **and the nations foolishly conspire?**
26 > **•The kings of the earth took their stand**
> **and the rulers gathered together**
> **against the Lord and against His Anointed.**

27 •For in fact they gathered in this city against Your holy servant Jesus, whom You anointed — Herod and Pontius Pilate with the Gentiles and
28 the people of Israel — •in order to do what Your hand and will had pre-
29 destined. •And now, Lord, look at these things, at their threats, and grant
30 that Your servants may speak Your word boldly •as You stretch out Your hand to heal and perform signs and wonders through the name of Your
31 holy servant Jesus." •And after they had prayed the place where they were gathered shook, and they were all filled with the Holy Spirit and continued to boldly speak the word of God.

4:24 Ex 20:11; Ps 146:6.   4:25-26 Ps 2:1-2 (Septuagint).

ACTS

D. THE STATE OF THE EARLY
COMMUNITY; ANANIAS AND SAPPHIRA

•The community of the faithful were of one heart and mind, and none 32 of them said that their possessions were their own; instead, they held everything in common. •The apostles bore witness to the resurrection 33 of the Lord Jesus with great power, and great grace was on them all. •No one among them was in need, for whoever owned land or houses 34 would sell them and bring the proceeds of the sale •to lay at the feet of 35 the apostles, and it was distributed to each according to their need. •For 36 example, Joseph, who was called Barnabas by the apostles (which is translated "son of encouragement") and was a Levite, a Cypriot by birth, •when he sold a field that belonged to him he brought the money and 37 laid it at the feet of the apostles.

4:36 "Son of encouragement." This Semitic idiom indicates that Barnabas was a particularly effective speaker.

Cyprus. Basilica of the 4th century.

1 5 •But there was a man named Ananias who, with his wife Sapphira,
2 sold a piece of land •and held back part of the proceeds with the
knowledge of his wife, and he brought part of it and laid it at the feet
3 of the apostles. •So Peter said, "Ananias, why did Satan put it in your
heart to lie to the Holy Spirit and hold back part of the price of the land?
4 •While you still had it didn't it remain at your disposal, and when you
sold it didn't you retain control over it? Why did you scheme in your heart
5 to do this thing? You lied to God, not just to men." •When Ananias heard
these words he fell down and breathed his last, and all who heard of it
6 were filled with awe. •So the young men got up, wrapped him up, carried him out, and buried him.

7 •About three hours later his wife also came in, unaware of what had
8 happened. •Peter said to her, "Tell me, was this how much you were
9 paid for the land?" •She said, "that's how much." •Then Peter said to
her, "Why did you agree to test the Spirit of the Lord? Behold, the feet
of those who buried your husband are at the door and they'll carry you
10 out!" •She immediately fell at his feet and breathed her last, and when
the young men came in and found her dead they carried her out and
11 buried her with her husband. •And great awe came over the whole
church and all who heard these things.

E. THE SANHEDRIN SEEKS
TO HALT THE APOSTOLIC PREACHING

12 •Many signs and wonders were performed among the people through
the hands of the apostles, and they all used to gather in Solomon's Por-
13 tico. •Although none of the others dared to join them, the people nev-
14 ertheless held them in high regard, •and an ever greater number of be-
15 lievers — both men and women — were added to the Lord •with the
result that they even used to carry the sick out into the streets on cots
and pallets so that when Peter came by at least his shadow would fall
16 on some of them. •People from the towns around Jerusalem also came
and brought the sick and those who were tormented by unclean spirits,
and they were all healed.

17 •Then the high priest arose as well as all those with him — that is,
18 the party of the Sadducees. They were filled with jealousy •and laid hands
19 on the apostles and threw them into the public jail. •But during the night
an angel of the Lord opened the doors of the prison, led them out, and
20 told them, •"Go stand in the Temple and tell the people everything about
21 this Life." •When they heard this they went into the Temple at dawn

and began to teach. Now when the high priest came, as well as those with him, they summoned the Sanhedrin and the whole council of Israel and sent to the prison to have the apostles brought in. •But when 22 the attendants came they couldn't find them in the prison, so they returned and gave their report, •saying, "We found the jail securely locked 23 and the guards standing at the doors, but when we opened them up we found no one inside." •When the captain of the Temple guard and the 24 chief priests heard these words they were at a complete loss as to what had become of them. •Then someone came and informed them, "Be- 25 hold, the men you put in prison are standing in the Temple, teaching the people." •Then the captain came with his attendants and led them 26 away, but without violence because they were afraid that the people might stone them.

•Now when they brought them they had them stand before the San- 27 hedrin, and the high priest questioned them, •saying, "We gave you strict 28 orders not to teach in that name and, behold, you've filled Jerusalem with your teaching, and you want to hold us guilty for this man's death." •In response Peter and the apostles said, "We have to obey God rather 29 than men. •The God of our fathers raised Jesus, whom you had killed 30 by hanging him on a cross. •God exalted him by His right hand as leader 31 and savior to grant Israel repentance and forgiveness of sins. •We are 32 witnesses of these things, and so is the Holy Spirit, whom God has given to those who obey Him."

•When they heard this they were furious and wanted to kill them, 33 •but a certain Pharisee in the Sanhedrin named Gamaliel, a teacher of 34 the Torah who was respected by all the people, got up and ordered that the men be put outside for a short time. •Then he said to them, "Fel- 35 low Israelites, consider carefully what you're about to do to these men. •Some time ago Theudas arose, claiming to be someone, and he at- 36 tracted four hundred men to himself. But he was killed and all those he had persuaded were dispersed and nothing came of it. •After him Ju- 37 das of Galilee arose at the time of the census; he incited the people to revolt with him, but he was killed, too, and those he had persuaded were dispersed. •And now I tell you, stay clear of these men and let them 38 go, for if their movement or endeavor is of human origin it will be put down, •but if it's from God you won't be able to stop them — you may 39 even find yourselves fighting with God!" They were persuaded by him

5:34 Gamaliel was one of the most influential Pharisees of this period. He was active during the decades which included Jesus' ministry and most of the early development of the Church de-scribed in Acts. At 22:3 Paul boasts of having studied under Gamaliel, obviously in the conviction that this would carry considerable weight with the Pharisees.

40 •and, after summoning the apostles and having them beaten, they or-
41 dered them not to speak in the name of Jesus and released them. •So
the apostles left the Sanhedrin, rejoicing that they had been considered
42 worthy to be dishonored for the sake of the Name. •And all day long,
both in the Temple and at home, they never ceased to teach and spread
the good news of the Messiah, Jesus.

F. STEPHEN'S WITNESS AND MARTYRDOM

1 6 •Now in those days, as the number of disciples kept increasing, a
complaint arose among the "Hellenists" against the "Hebrews" to
the effect that their widows were being overlooked in the daily distri-
2 bution. •So the Twelve summoned the community of the disciples and
said, "It isn't right for us to neglect the word of God to wait on tables,
3 •so pick out seven men from among you who are well regarded, full of
4 wisdom and the Spirit, whom we can appoint to this task, •while we
5 devote ourselves to prayer and the ministry of the word." •This idea
pleased the whole community, and they chose Stephen, a man full of
faith and the Holy Spirit, Philip, Prochorus, Nicanor, Timon, Parmenes,
6 and Nicholas, a proselyte from Antioch. •They had them stand before
the apostles, who prayed and then laid their hands on them.
7 •The word of God kept spreading and the number of disciples in
Jerusalem increased tremendously, and a large number of priests also
adhered to the faith.
8 •Stephen was full of grace and power and he performed wonders and
9 great signs among the people. •So some of those from the so-called Synagogue of the Freedmen — Cyrenians, Alexandrians, and those from Cili-
10 cia and Asia — arose and began to argue with Stephen, •but they could-
11 n't withstand the wisdom and spirit with which he spoke. •Then they got
some men to say, "We heard him speak blasphemies against Moses and
12 God," •and they stirred up the people and the elders and scribes. Then
they rushed upon Stephen, seized him, and led him to the Sanhedrin,
13 •and they presented false witnesses who said, "This man never stops say-
14 ing things against the Holy Place and the Torah — •we've heard him say
that this Jesus of Nazareth will tear down this Place and change the cus-

---

6:1 Historical and archaeological research has
confirmed that many Jews in Palestine were primarily Greek-speaking.
6:14 While Stephen's opponents may have un-
fairly distorted his proclamation, this passage
shows that Stephen may well have been teaching the type of things that later got Paul in trouble — that Jesus' death and resurrection had
drastically revised what it meant to belong to Israel.

toms Moses handed down to us." •And as all those seated in the San- 15
hedrin gazed at him, his face seemed like the face of an angel.

7 •"Is this so?" the high priest asked. •Then Stephen said, "My broth- 1,2
ers and fathers, listen! The God of glory appeared to our father Abraham while he was in Mesopotamia, before he settled in Harran, **and** 3
**said to him, 'Leave your land and your relatives here and go
to a land I'll show you.'** •So he left the land of the Chaldeans and 4
settled in Harran. And from there, after the death of his father, He had
him resettle in this land where you live now, •yet He gave him no part 5
of it, not even a square foot, but promised **to give possession of the
land to him and his descendants after him,** even though Abraham
had no children. •Then God spoke as follows — **'His descendants will** 6
**be aliens in a foreign land, and they'll be enslaved and mis-
treated there for four hundred years, •and then I will pass** 7
judgment on the people who enslave them,' God said. **'And after these things they will leave and worship me in this** place.'
•Then He gave him the covenant of circumcision, and so Abraham fa- 8
thered Isaac and circumcised him on the eighth day, and Isaac did the
same with Jacob, and Jacob with the twelve patriarchs."
   •"And when the patriarchs grew jealous of Joseph they sold him off 9
to Egypt, yet God was with him •and rescued him from all his afflic- 10
tions and **gave him grace** and wisdom **in the sight of Pharaoh,
king of Egypt, so that Pharaoh made Joseph the ruler of Egypt
and put him in charge of his whole household. •Now a famine** 11
came over all Egypt and **Canaan** and great suffering, and our fathers were unable to find fodder. •So when Jacob heard there were pro- 12
visions in Egypt he sent our fathers there first, •and on their second 13
trip there Joseph made himself known to his brothers and Joseph's family became known to Pharaoh. •Then Joseph sent and summoned his 14
father Jacob and all his relations, seventy-five people in all, •and Ja- 15
cob went down to Egypt. Jacob died as well as our fathers, •and they 16
were taken back to Shechem and placed in the tomb Abraham had

---

6:15 "The face of an angel." Unlike modern representations of angels as childlike cherubs, in
Scripture they are portrayed as God's messengers and soldiers in the Divine Army ("host") who
inspire fear and awe. Stephen's face reflects his
zeal for God's message, which here takes the
form of an indictment of Israel's disobedience.
7:2-53 Stephen's speech presents the history
of Judaism as essentially the account of the

Jewish people's resistance to God's plan of salvation and their continual refusal to understand
God's message.
7:3 Gn 12:1.
7:5 Gn 12:7, 13:5, 15:8, 17:8.
7:6-7 Gn 15:13-14.
7:7 Ex 3:12.
7:10 Gn 41:37-39,41:40-44; Ps 105:21.
7:11 Gn 41:54, 42:5.

bought and paid for with silver money from the sons of Hemor in Shechem."

17 •"Now as the time grew near for the promise God had made to Abra-
18 ham to be fulfilled the people increased and multiplied in Egypt, •until a time came when another king arose in Egypt who didn't know Joseph.
19 •He took advantage of and deceived our people and oppressed our fathers by making them expose their infants, so they wouldn't survive.
20 •Moses was born at this time, and he was pleasing to God. He was raised
21 in his father's house for three months, •but when he was exposed
22 Pharaoh's daughter adopted him and raised him as her own son. •Moses was instructed in all the wisdom of the Egyptians, and he was mighty in both word and deed."

23 •"When Moses turned forty he decided to go see his brothers, the
24 Israelites, •and when he saw one of them being wronged he came to his aid and avenged the one who was being mistreated by striking down
25 the Egyptian. •He thought his brothers understood that God was grant-
26 ing them salvation by his hand, but they didn't understand. •The next day he saw some of them fighting and tried to make peace between them by saying, 'Men, you're brothers! Why are you harming one an-

Christian ossuary from the Basilica of Saint Stephen. (Ac 7:58)

other?' •But the one who was wronging his neighbor pushed him away 27
and said, **'Who made you the ruler and judge over us? •Are you** 28
going to kill me, like you killed the Egyptian yesterday?' •When 29
he heard this Moses fled Egypt and lived as an alien in the land of Midian, where he fathered two sons."

•"And after forty years had passed **an angel appeared to him** 30
in the flame of a burning bush in the desert of Mount Sinai. 31
•When Moses saw the apparition he marvelled at it, but when he approached to examine it the voice of the Lord came, •**'I am the God** 32
of your fathers, the God of Abraham, Isaac, and Jacob.'
Moses began to tremble and didn't dare look. •**Then the Lord said** 33
to him, 'Remove your sandals from your feet, for the spot
you're standing on is holy ground. •I have seen and know of 34
the oppression of My people in Egypt and have heard their
groaning, and I have come down to rescue them. And now
come, I'm sending you to Egypt!' •This Moses, whom they re- 35
jected, saying, **'Who made you ruler and judge?'** this is who God
sent as ruler and deliverer through the angel who appeared to him in
the bush. •He led them out after performing signs and wonders in 36
the land of Egypt, at the Red Sea, and for forty years in the desert.
•It was this Moses who told the Israelites, **'God will raise up for** 37
you a prophet like me from among your kinsmen.' •He it was 38
who, during the assembly in the desert, was with the angel who spoke
to him on Mount Sinai and with our fathers; he received living words
to give to us. •Our fathers didn't wish to be obedient to him; instead, 39
they rejected him and, in their hearts, they turned back to Egypt •and 40
said to Aaron, **'Make us gods who will lead us, because we**
don't know what's become of this Moses who led us out of
Egypt.' •And in those days they made a calf and offered sacrifice to 41
the idol, and they rejoiced in the work of their hands. •So God turned 42
from them and handed them over to the worship of the host of heaven, as it is written in the book of the prophet,

> **Did you offer Me victims and sacrifices**
> **those forty years in the desert, O house of Israel?**
> •**No, you took up the tent of Moloch** 43
> **and the star of your god, Rephan,**

7:27-28 Ex 2:14.
7:30 Ex 3:2-3.
7:32 Ex 3:6.
7:33-34 Ex 3:5, 7-10.

7:35 Ex 2:14.
7:37 Dt 18:15.
7:40 Ex 32:1, 23.
7:42-43 Am 5:25-27 (Septuagint).

whose images you made for your worship;
I will send you into exile beyond Babylon.

44 •"Our fathers had the Tent of Testimony in the desert, just as the One Who spoke with Moses ordered it to be made, in accordance with
45 the pattern he had seen. •It was brought in with Joshua when our fathers dispossessed the nations whom God drove out before them, and
46 so matters stood up to the days of David, •who found favor before God and asked to be allowed to find a dwelling place for the God of
47,48 Jacob. •It was Solomon, however, who built a house for Him. •But the Most High doesn't dwell in houses made by human hands, as the prophet says,

49 •**'The sky is My throne,**
     and the earth is My footstool;
   What kind of house can you make for Me,'
       says the Lord,
     'or what place for Me to rest in?
50 •**Wasn't it My hand that made all these things?'**

51 •"You're stiff necked, and uncircumcised in both heart and ears! You always resist the Holy Spirit — just as your fathers did, so you do, too.
52 •Which of the prophets didn't your fathers persecute? They killed those who foretold the coming of the Righteous One, whose betrayers and
53 murderers you have now become! •You accepted the Torah as decreed by angels, yet you haven't observed it!"
54 •When they heard these things they became enraged and gnashed
55 their teeth at him. •But Stephen was full of the Holy Spirit, and as he gazed up to Heaven he saw the glory of God, and Jesus standing at God's
56 right hand, •and he said, "Behold, I see the heavens opened up and the
57 Son of Man standing at God's right hand!" •At this they shouted out
58 loud and covered their ears, and they all rushed at him, •threw him out of the city, and stoned him. The witnesses took their cloaks off and laid
59 them at the feet of a young man named Saul. •As he was being stoned
60 Stephen cried out and said, "Lord Jesus, receive my spirit!" •And as he fell to his knees he cried out with a loud voice, "Lord, don't hold this sin against them!" And having said this, he fell asleep [in death].

1 **8**•Now Saul approved of his murder.

7:49-50 Is 66:1-2.

G. VIOLENT PERSECUTION;
PHILIP CONVERTS AN ETHIOPIAN

On that day a violent persecution began against the church in Jerusalem, and they were all scattered throughout the country districts of Judea and Samaria, except for the apostles. •Some devout men buried 2 Stephen and raised a great lamentation over him. •But Saul kept ha- 3 rassing the church, entering house after house, dragging out the men and women and sending them to prison.

•Now those who had been scattered went about proclaiming the good 4 news. •Philip went down to the city of Samaria and proclaimed the Mes- 5 siah to them. •With one mind the crowds paid close attention to the 6 things Philip was saying, as they listened and saw the signs he was per- forming; •many of those who were possessed had their unclean spirits 7 cry out in a loud voice and come out, and many paralytics and cripples were healed, •and there was tremendous joy in that city.   8

•There was a man named Simon already in the city whose practice of 9 magic used to amaze the Samaritans, and he claimed to be someone great. •All the Samaritans, both high and low, paid close attention to him 10 and said, "This man is the 'Power of God' that's called 'Great.'" •The 11 reason they paid attention to him was that for quite some time he had amazed them with his magic. •But when they came to believe Philip's 12 proclamation of the good news about the Kingdom of God and the name of Jesus Christ, both men and women were baptized. •Even Simon him- 13 self believed and was baptized and became a follower of Philip; and when he saw the signs and mighty works that were taking place he was amazed.

•Now when the apostles in Jerusalem heard that Samaria had accepted 14 the word of God they sent Peter and John to them. •When they went 15 down they prayed over them that they might receive the Holy Spirit, •for 16 it had not yet come upon any of them — they'd only been baptized in the name of the Lord Jesus. •Then they laid their hands on them, and 17 they received the Holy Spirit. •When Simon saw that the Spirit was giv- 18 en by the apostles' laying on their hands he brought them money •and 19 said, "Give me that power too, so that anyone I lay my hands on will re- ceive the Holy Spirit!" •But Peter said to him, "May your money perish 20 with you, because you thought that money could get you God's gift! •You 21 have no part or share in this teaching, because your heart is not upright

---

8:1 Up to this point the action of Acts has cen- tered on Jerusalem. The next several chapters portray a movement away from Jerusalem, both spatially and in spirit, as the young Church em- braces those who were excluded by official Ju- daism: Samaritans, a eunuch, and Gentiles.

A C T S

Samaritans celebrating Passover according to the ancient rite.

22 before God. •So turn away from this wickedness of yours and beg the
23 Lord to forgive the thoughts of your heart, •for I can see you're destined
24 for bitter gall and the bonds of iniquity." •Simon answered, "Plead for
me with the Lord so that nothing you said will come upon me!"

25 •After they had borne witness and spoken the word of the Lord they
returned to Jerusalem, proclaiming the good news to many Samaritan
villages.

26 •Then the angel of the Lord spoke to Philip and said, "Get up and
head south on the road that goes down from Jerusalem to Gaza" — this
27 is a desert road. •He got up and set out, and behold there came an
Ethiopian eunuch — an official of the Kandake, the Queen of Ethiopia
— who was in charge of the Queen's whole treasury and had come to
28 worship in Jerusalem. •He was returning and was seated in his chariot,
29 reading the prophet Isaiah. •So the Spirit told Philip, "Go, catch up with
30 the chariot." •Now when Philip ran up he heard him reading the prophet

8:27 Although the eunuch is said to have come to worship in Jerusalem, eunuchs were specifically barred from inclusion in God's people (Dt 23:2).

Isaiah, and he said, "Do you *understand* what you're reading?" •But 31 the eunuch said, "How *can* I, unless someone will guide me?" and he urged Philip to get up and sit with him. •Now this was the passage of 32 Scripture he was reading:

> **He was led like a sheep to the slaughter,**
> **and as a lamb is silent before its shearers,**
> **he opened not his mouth.**
> •**He was humiliated and justice was denied him;** 33
> **who will tell of his posterity,**
> **for his life is cut off from the earth.**

•In response the eunuch said to Philip, "Please tell me, who is the 34 prophet referring to, himself or someone else?" •So Philip opened his 35 mouth and told him the good news about Jesus, starting with that very passage of Scripture. •As they travelled down the road they came to 36 some water, and the eunuch said, "Look, here's some water! What's to keep me from being baptized?" [•] •He ordered the chariot to halt and 37,38 they both went down to the water — Philip as well as the eunuch — and Philip baptized him. •But when they came up from the water the 39 Spirit of the Lord snatched Philip away, and the eunuch saw no more of him but went on his way rejoicing. •But Philip went to Azotus, and 40 as he travelled along he proclaimed the good news in all the towns until he came to Caesarea.

H. THE CONVERSION OF SAUL

9 •But Saul was still breathing threats and murder against the disciples 1 of the Lord. He approached the high priest •and asked him for let- 2 ters to the synagogues in Damascus, so that if he found anyone who belonged to the Way — both men and women — he could bring them to Jerusalem in chains. •Now while he was on his way, as he was ap- 3 proaching Damascus, suddenly a light from Heaven shone around him. •As he fell to the ground he heard a voice saying to him, "Saul, Saul, 4 why are you persecuting me?" •"Who are you, Lord?" he asked. "I am 5 Jesus, whom you are persecuting!" the voice replied. •"Get up and go 6 into the city and you'll be told what to do." •The men travelling with him 7

8:32-33 Is 53:7-8 (Septuagint).
8:37 The best textual witnesses omit this verse: "Philip said, 'If you believe with your whole heart, you may.' And he answered and said, 'I believe that Jesus Christ is the Son of God!'"

stood there speechless, for though they heard the voice they saw no one.
8 •Saul rose from the ground but when he opened his eyes he could see
9 nothing, so they took him by the hand and led him into Damascus. •For
three days he was unable to see, and he neither ate nor drank.

10 •Now there was a disciple in Damascus named Ananias, and the Lord
11 said to him in a dream, "Ananias!" "Here I am, Lord!" he said. •The
Lord said to him, "Get up and go to the street called 'Straight' and ask
at Judas' house for a man from Tarsus named Saul, for he is in prayer
12 •and has had a vision of a man named Ananias who came and laid his
13 hands on him so he could regain his sight." •"Lord," Ananias responded, "I've heard from many others about this man, how many evil things
14 he's done to your saints in Jerusalem, •and he has authority here from
15 the chief priests to arrest all who call on your name." •But the Lord said
to him, "Go, for this man is my chosen vessel to bring my name before
16 the Gentiles and their kings and before the sons of Israel, •for I'll show
17 him how much he'll have to suffer for my name." •So Ananias went off
and came to the house, and when he laid his hands on him he said,
"Saul, my brother, the Lord has sent me — Jesus, who appeared to you
on your way here — so you could regain your sight and be filled with
18 the Holy Spirit." •And at once things like scales fell from his eyes and
19 he regained his sight, and when he got up he was baptized •and he took
food and regained his strength.

20 He stayed some days with the disciples in Damascus, •and at once
he began to proclaim Jesus in the synagogues — that he's the Son of
21 God. •All who heard him were amazed and said, "Isn't this the fellow
who was trying to destroy those in Jerusalem who called upon this name,
and didn't he come here in order to lead them back to the chief priests
22 in chains?" •But Saul grew all the stronger and confounded the Jews
who lived in Damascus by proving that Jesus is the Messiah.

23 •[d] After a considerable number of days had passed the Jews devised
24 a plot to kill him, •but Saul learned of their plot. They were watching the
25 gates both night and day in order to kill him, •so his disciples took him
by night and let him down through the wall, lowering him in a basket.

26 •When Saul arrived in Jerusalem he tried to associate with the disciples, but they were all afraid of him because they didn't believe he was
27 a disciple. •But Barnabas took him and brought him to the apostles, and
he related to the apostles how Saul had seen the Lord on the road, that
the Lord had spoken to him, and how Saul had spoken out boldly in

[d] 2 Cor 11:32-33.

9:23-25 This episode took place sometime before 40 A.D., when King Aretas died.

Damascus in the name of Jesus. •Then he came and went with them in 28
Jerusalem and spoke out boldly in the name of the Lord, •and he also 29
spoke and debated with the Hellenists, but they began planning to kill
him. •When the brothers became aware of this they took him down to 30
Caesarea and sent him off to Tarsus.

•So the church was at peace throughout all Judea and Galilee and 31
Samaria; it was being built up and proceeded in the fear of the Lord and
it grew in numbers with the encouragement of the Holy Spirit.

I. PETER BRINGS THE WORD TO GENTILES

•Now it happened that when Peter travelled throughout all these re- 32
gions he also went down to the saints who lived in Lydda. •There he 33
found a man named Aeneas who for eight years had been lying on a
cot — he was paralyzed. •Peter said to him, "Aeneas, Jesus Christ 34
heals you; get up and make your bed for yourself!" And at once he
got up. •Everyone living in Lydda and Sharon saw him, and they 35
turned to the Lord.

•At Joppa there was a woman disciple named Tabitha — or 36
Dorcas, as it's translated. This woman devoted herself to good
works and almsgiving. •And it happened in those days that she 37
took ill and died, so they washed her and placed her in an upper room. •Lydda was near Joppa and so when the disciples 38
heard that Peter was there they sent two men to him to urge
him, "Come to us without delay!" •So Peter got up and ac- 39
companied them. When he arrived they led him to the upper
room, and all the widows stood around him, weeping and point-
ing out the tunics and cloaks Dorcas had made while she was
still with them. •After Peter had sent them all out he got down 40
on his knees and began to pray, and turning to the body he
said, "Tabitha, arise!" At this she opened her eyes, and when
she saw Peter she sat up. •Then he gave her his hand and 41
raised her up, and he called the saints and the widows and presented her to them, alive. •This became known throughout all 42
Joppa and many people believed in the Lord. •And it happened 43
that he remained in Joppa for quite a few days with a certain
Simon, a tanner.

9:43 Tanning was considered an unclean occupation. Here Luke shows Peter following in Jesus'
footsteps in his openness to all levels of society,
a recurrent theme in "Luke-Acts."

Caesarea. Roman aqueduct.

10 ¹ •Now there was a man in Caesarea named Cornelius, a centurion ² from the cohort named the Italica, •who with all his household was a devout and God-fearing man. He gave large amounts of alms ³ to the Jewish people and prayed continuously to God. •At about three in the afternoon he clearly saw in a vision the angel of the Lord com- ⁴ ing in to him and saying to him, "Cornelius!" •He stared at him and, overcome with fear, said, "What is it, Lord?" He said to him, "Your prayers and almsgiving have ascended like a memorial offering before ⁵ God. •And now, send some men to Joppa and summon a man named ⁶ Simon, who is called Peter — •he's staying as a guest with Simon the ⁷ tanner, whose house is by the sea." •So when the angel who had been speaking with him went off, he called two of his household servants ⁸ and a devout soldier who was part of his staff •and after explaining everything to them he sent them to Joppa.

⁹ •The next day while they were on their way and were approaching the city, Peter went up to the roof of the house to pray at about noon.

10:2 Within Judaism prayer and alms-giving were considered fundamental expressions of righteousness under the covenant. Thus Cornelius is seen to lack only one thing for full participation in the Old Covenant: circumcision.

•He became hungry and wanted to eat, but while they were preparing 10 the meal he fell into a trance, •and he saw the heavens open up and a 11 thing like a huge sheet coming down, being lowered to earth by its four corners. •In it were all the four-footed animals and reptiles of the earth 12 and the birds of the sky. •And a voice came to him, "Get up, Peter, kill 13 and eat!" •But Peter said, "Certainly not, Lord! I've never eaten any- 14 thing unclean or impure!" •And the voice came to him a second time, 15 "What God has made clean, don't you call impure!" •This happened 16 three times and then the thing was taken back up to the heavens.

•While Peter was wondering to himself what the vision he had seen 17 could mean, behold the men who had been sent by Cornelius were ask- ing the way to Simon's house and had arrived at the entrance •and were 18 calling out, inquiring whether the Simon who was called Peter was stay- ing there. •And while Peter was trying to understand the vision the Spir- 19 it said to him, "Behold, some men are looking for you, •so get up and 20 go down and don't hesitate to go with them, because *I* sent them." •Pe- 21 ter went down to the men and said, "Behold, I'm the one you're look- ing for; what brings you here?" •They said, "The centurion Cornelius, 22 an upright, God-fearing man who is acknowledged as such by the whole Jewish nation, was instructed by an angel to summon you to his house to hear what you have to say." •So he invited them in and extended 23 hospitality to them.

The next day he got up and left with them, and some of the broth- ers from Joppa accompanied him. •The next day he came to Caesarea. 24 Cornelius was expecting them and had summoned his relatives and close friends. •Now it happened that when Peter entered he was greeted by 25 Cornelius, who fell at his feet and worshipped him. •But Peter raised 26 him up and said, "Get up, I'm just a man, too!" •And as he spoke with 27 him he entered and found many people gathered there, •and he said to 28 them, "You know that it's forbidden for a Jew to associate or visit with a Gentile, but God has shown me that no one is to be called impure or unclean. •That's why I didn't hesitate to come when I was summoned. 29 So, may I ask why you sent for me?" •Then Cornelius said, "Four days 30 ago at this hour, three in the afternoon, I was praying in my house, and behold a man in bright clothing stood before me •and said, 'Cornelius, 31 your prayer has been heard and your almsgiving has been remembered before God. •So send to Joppa and invite Simon who is called Peter — 32 he's staying at the house of Simon the tanner, by the sea.' •So I im- 33 mediately sent for you, and you were kind enough to come. And now we've all come together here in God's presence to hear all that you've been commanded by the Lord."

34 •Then Peter opened his mouth and said, "Now I truly see that God
35 doesn't play favorites; •instead, those of every nation who fear Him and
36 do what's right are acceptable to Him. •He sent His word to the sons
of Israel and proclaimed the good news of peace through Jesus Christ,
37 who is Lord of all. •You know what took place throughout all Judea,
38 starting in Galilee after the baptism which John preached. •Jesus of
Nazareth, when he had been anointed by God with the Holy Spirit and
power, travelled everywhere, doing good works and healing all who
39 were in the power of the Devil, because God was with him. •We are
witnesses of everything he did, both in the Judean countryside and in
40 Jerusalem, and then they killed him by hanging him on a tree. •God
41 raised him on the third day and granted that he should be visible, •not
to the people as a whole, but to the witnesses who had been chosen
beforehand by God — to us, who ate and drank with him after he rose
42 from the dead, •and he commanded us to proclaim to the people and
solemnly declare that he is the one God has appointed to be judge of
43 the living and the dead. •All the prophets bore witness to this, that
everyone who believes in him will receive forgiveness of sins through
his name."

44 •While Peter was still saying these things the Holy Spirit came upon
45 all who were listening to the word. •The believers who were of the circumcision who had accompanied Peter were astounded, because the gift
46 of the Holy Spirit had also been poured out upon the Gentiles — •they
could hear them speaking in tongues and glorifying God. Then Peter re-
47 sponded, •"Can anyone withhold the water of baptism from these peo-
48 ple, who have received the Holy Spirit the same as we have?" •So he
ordered that they should be baptized in the name of Jesus Christ. Then
they asked him to stay for a few days.

1 **11** •Now the apostles and the brothers who were in Judea heard that
2 the Gentiles had also received the word of God. •So when Peter
3 went up to Jerusalem those of the circumcision took issue with him •and
said, "You went into a house with uncircumcised men and ate with
4,5 them!" •Then Peter spoke and explained it to them point by point. •"I
was in the city of Joppa and was at prayer, and while in a trance I had
a vision — a thing like a huge sheet was coming down, lowered from
6 the heavens by its four corners, and it came to me. •I looked into it and
gazed at what was there and I saw the four-footed creatures of the earth
7 and wild animals and reptiles and the birds of the sky. •And then I heard

11:3 For a devout Jew, sharing table-fellowship with a Gentile made him like the Gentile: unclean.

a voice saying to me, 'Get up, Peter! Kill and eat!' •But I said, 'By no 8
means, Lord — nothing impure or unclean has ever entered my mouth!'
•But the voice answered me from heaven a second time, 'What God has 9
made clean, don't you call impure!' •This happened three times, and 10
then all these things were drawn up again to the heavens. •And behold 11
three men immediately came to the house where we were — they had
been sent to me from Caesarea. •The Spirit told me not to hesitate but 12
to accompany them. They and some of the brothers went with me and
we went into that man's house. •Then he told us how he had seen an 13
angel standing in his house, saying, 'Send to Joppa and summon Simon, who is called Peter; •he'll tell you things which will lead to the sal- 14
vation of you and your household.' •But as I began to speak the Holy 15
Spirit came upon them just as it came upon us in the beginning. •Then 16
I remembered the words of the Lord when he said, 'John baptized with
water, but you will baptize with the Holy Spirit.' •So if God gave them 17
a gift equal to what He gave us when we came to believe in the Lord
Jesus Christ, who was I to stand in God's way?" •When they heard this 18
they stopped objecting and glorified God, saying, "Then God has given
the Gentiles life-giving repentance, too!"

J. THE CHURCH SPREADS OUTSIDE PALESTINE
AND WELCOMES THE GENTILES IN ANTIOCH

•Now those who had been scattered by the persecution which arose 19
over Stephen travelled about — as far as Phoenicia, Cyprus, and Antioch
— speaking the word to no one but Jews. •Among them were some Cypri- 20
ots and Cyrenians who came to Antioch and spoke to the Greeks as well,
proclaiming the good news about the Lord Jesus. •The hand of the Lord 21
was with them and a great number of people believed and turned to the
Lord. •Word of their activities reached the ears of the church in Jerusalem, 22
and they sent Barnabas to Antioch. •When he arrived there and saw the 23
grace of God he rejoiced and urged them all to remain steadfast in heart
toward the Lord, •because he was a good man, full of the Holy Spirit and 24
faith. And a considerable number of people were added to the Lord. •Then 25
Barnabas went to Tarsus to look for Saul, •and when he found him he 26
brought him to Antioch. And it happened that for a whole year they met
with the church and taught quite a large number of people, and it was in
Antioch that the disciples were first referred to as "Christians."

11:20 Cyprus and Cyrenaica had for centuries had large Hellenized Jewish populations.

²⁷ •In those days some prophets came down from Jerusalem to Anti-
²⁸ och, •and one of them — who was named Agabus — got up and fore-
told through the Spirit a terrible famine that was about to come over
²⁹ the whole world, which came to pass under Claudius. •So the disciples
decided that, to the extent that each had the means, they should send
³⁰ help to the brothers who lived in Judea. •They did this and sent it to the
elders through Barnabas and Saul.

K. PERSECUTION BY HEROD

¹ 12 •At about that time King Herod laid hands on some members of
² the church intending to harm them, •and he put John's broth-
³ er James to the sword. •Then, when he saw that this pleased the Jews,
he proceeded to arrest Peter, too — this was during the feast of the
⁴ Unleavened Bread — •and after seizing him he put him in prison un-
der the guard of four squads, each containing four soldiers, intending
⁵ to bring him before the people after the Passover. •So while Peter was

Peter's arrest, relief on a Roman sarcophagus (4th century A.D.). (Ac 12:3)

being kept under guard in prison, the Church was offering fervent prayers to God on his behalf.

•Now when Herod was about to bring him out, that night Peter was 6 sleeping — bound with two chains — between two soldiers, and guards were keeping watch at the doors of the prison. •And, behold, an angel 7 of the Lord appeared and a light shone in the cell. He touched Peter's side, woke him, and said, "Get up at once!" And the chains fell from his hands. •Then the angel said to him, "Fasten your belt and put on 8 your sandals!" So he did it. Then he said to him, "Put on your cloak and follow me!" •Peter went out and followed him, unsure whether what the 9 angel had done was for real — he thought he was having a vision. •Af- 10 ter going past the first and second guard they came to the iron gate that led to the city, which opened for them by itself. They came out and went down a narrow street, and at once the angel left him. •When Peter came 11 to himself he said, "Now I truly know that the Lord sent His angel and delivered me out of Herod's hands and from all that the Jewish people were expecting." •And when he realized this he went to the house of 12 Mary, the mother of John who is called Mark, where a considerable number of people were gathered in prayer. •When he knocked at the en- 13 trance door a young maid named Rhoda answered it, •and when she 14 recognized Peter's voice, out of joy she didn't open the entrance but ran in and announced that Peter was standing at the entrance. •"You're 15 crazy!" they told her, but she insisted that it was so. Then they said, "It's his angel!" •But Peter kept knocking, and when they opened the door 16 and saw him they were astounded. •He motioned to them with his hand 17 to be silent and then told them how the Lord had led him out of the prison and said, "Tell this to James and the brothers!" Then he went out and left for another place.

•When day came there was more than a little consternation among the 18 soldiers over what had become of Peter. •Herod searched for him and 19 when he didn't find him he questioned the guards and ordered them put to death, and then he went down from Judea and stayed in Caesarea.

•Now for some time he had been very angry with the people of Tyre 20 and Sidon, but by common consent they presented themselves to him. And after winning over Blastus, the king's chamberlain, they sued for peace because the royal territory was the source of their land's food sup-

12:17 This is James "the brother of the Lord," who even at this time was a recognized "pillar" of the Christians in Jerusalem. His martyrdom in about 62 A.D. is reported in Josephus' *Jewish An-* *tiquities.* In Jewish usage of the time, the word "brother" often referred to cousins. That James was a cousin rather than a brother of the Lord can be seen at Mk 15:40 and Lk 24:10.

21 ply. •So on the appointed day Herod took his place on the judgment
22 seat, dressed in his royal robes, and delivered an address to them, •and
23 the crowd cried out, "It's the voice of a god, not of a man!" •And immediately the angel of the Lord struck him because he failed to give the
glory to God, and he was eaten by worms and died.

L. THE CHURCH IN ANTIOCH SENDS
PAUL AND BARNABAS AS MISSIONARIES

24 •Now the word of God continued to spread and to reach more and more
25 people. •And after completing their relief mission Saul and Barnabas returned from Jerusalem, bringing John, who is called Mark, with them.

1 **13** •There were in the church at Antioch prophets and teachers —
Barnabas and Symeon who was called Niger and Lucius the Cyrenean and Manaen, the close friend of Herod the Tetrarch, and Saul.
2 •Now as they were worshipping God and fasting the Holy Spirit said,
"Set Barnabas and Saul apart for Me for the work to which I have called
3 them." •Then, after fasting and praying and laying their hands on them,
they sent them off.
4 •So, sent forth by the Holy Spirit, they went down to Seleucia and
5 from there they sailed to Cyprus, •and when they got to Salamis they
proclaimed the word of God in the synagogues of the Jews, and they
6 also had John as an attendant. •After travelling throughout the island
as far as Paphos they met a man who was a magician, a Jewish pseu-
7 do-prophet named Bar Jesus — •he was with the proconsul Sergius
Paulus, who was an intelligent man. He summoned Barnabas and Saul
8 and wished to hear the word of God •but the magician Elymas — that's
how his name is translated — opposed them and sought to turn the pro-
9 consul away from the faith. •But Saul, also known as Paul, filled with
10 the Holy Spirit, gazed at him •and said, "You're full of every sort of deceit and villainy, you son of the Devil, you enemy of all that's right! Stop
11 twisting the straight ways of the Lord! •And now, behold, the hand of
the Lord is upon you, and you'll be blind and unable to see the sun for
a time!" Immediately mistiness and darkness came over him and he
12 walked around looking for someone to lead him by the hand. •When
the proconsul saw what had happened he believed, for he was astounded
at the teaching of the Lord.

12:23 Herod Agrippa died in 44 A.D.

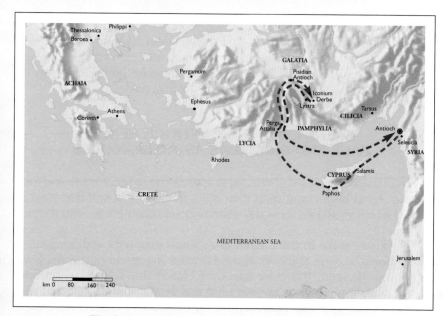

The first missionary journey of Paul. (Ac 13:1-14:28)

•Those with Paul set sail from Paphos and came to Perga in Pam- 13
phylia, but John left them and returned to Jerusalem. •They travelled 14
on from Perga and came to Pisidian Antioch, and they entered the synagogue on the Sabbath and sat down. •After the reading of the Torah 15
and the Prophets the leaders of the synagogue sent to them and said,
"Brothers, if you have any word of encouragement for the people,
speak!" •So Paul got up, motioned with his hand, and said, 16
"Israelites and you who fear God, listen! •The God of the people of 17
Israel chose our ancestors and raised them up to be a nation during the
sojourn in Egypt. With arm outstretched He led them out of there, •and 18
then for forty years He put up with their behavior in the desert. •After 19
destroying seven nations in the land of Canaan He gave them that land
as an inheritance •for some four hundred and fifty years. After that He 20
appointed judges up till the time of the prophet Samuel. •At that point 21
they asked for a king, and God gave them Saul son of Kish, a man of
the tribe of Benjamin, for a period of forty years. •Then He removed 22
Saul and raised up David to be their king, concerning whom He bore
this witness: **I have found David** son of Jesse **to be a man after My
own heart, one who will do all My will.** •Just as He promised, God 23
has brought forth a savior for Israel from among David's descendants

24 — Jesus, •whose coming John announced by proclaiming a baptism of
25 repentance for the whole people of Israel. •But when John was approaching the end of his course he said, 'I'm not who you think I am.
Behold, there is one coming after me, and I'm not worthy to untie his
sandals.'

26 •"Brothers, sons of Abraham's line and you who fear God, it is to us
27 that word of this salvation has been sent. •For the inhabitants of Jerusalem
and their rulers failed to recognize Jesus, and by condemning him they
28 fulfilled the words of the prophets which are read every Sabbath. •Even
though they couldn't find a single reason to put him to death they asked
29 Pilate to have Jesus killed, •and after fulfilling everything that had been
written about him they took him down from the cross and laid him in a
30,31 tomb. •But God raised him from the dead •and he appeared over many
days to those who had gone up with him from Galilee to Jerusalem, and
32 who are now witnesses for him before the people. •We are proclaiming
to you the good news that the promise that was made to our ancestors
33 •has been fulfilled by God for us their children through the resurrection
of Jesus, as indeed it is written in the second psalm,

You are My son,
this day I have begotten you.

34 •That He raised him from the dead, no longer to undergo decay, He
says in these words:

I will give you the blessings which were
promised to David.

35 •And therefore He said in another psalm:

You will not let Your holy one undergo decay.

36 •David, when he had served God's will in his generation, died and was
37 gathered to his ancestors and underwent decay, •whereas the one God
38 raised did *not* undergo corruption. •So know this, my brothers, that it
is through him that forgiveness of sins is being proclaimed to you —
everything for which you were unable to be pardoned under the Law of
39,40 Moses •the believer is pardoned through Jesus. •Therefore beware lest
what was spoken by the prophets should happen:

13:16-26 "You who fear God" clearly refers to   13:22 Ps 89:20; 1 S 13:14.
Gentiles, but whether they were merely sympa-   13:33 Ps 2:7.
thetic to Judaism or were full-fledged converts,   13:34 Is 55:3 (Septuagint).
as the reference to "proselytes" at 13:43 indi-   13:35 Ps 16:10 (Septuagint).
cates, is not clear.

•Watch, you scoffers, 41
  wonder and vanish,
For I will do something in your days,
  a deed which you'll never believe
    even if someone tells you."

•When Paul and Barnabas were leaving, the people urged them to 42
speak about these things again on the next Sabbath, •and after leav- 43
ing the synagogue many of the Jewish and proselyte worshippers followed Paul and Barnabas, who spoke with them and urged them to continue in the grace of God.

•On the next Sabbath nearly the whole city gathered to hear the word 44
of the Lord. •When the Jews saw the crowds they were filled with jeal- 45
ousy and began to dispute what Paul was saying and to insult him. •Both 46
Paul and Barnabas spoke out boldly and said, "It was necessary to speak
the word of God to you first, but since you reject it and condemn yourselves as unworthy of eternal life, behold, we'll turn to the Gentiles. •For 47
thus did the Lord command us:

**I have made you a light to the Gentiles,
a means of salvation to the ends of the earth."**

•The Gentiles rejoiced when they heard this and glorified the word 48
of the Lord, and all who were destined for eternal life believed, •and 49
the word of the Lord spread throughout that region. •But the Jews in- 50
cited some prominent Gentile women worshippers and leaders of the
city to stir up a persecution against Paul and Barnabas and drive them
from their region. •So they shook the dust from their feet against them 51
and went to Iconium, •and the disciples were filled with joy and the 52
Holy Spirit.

14 •In Iconium they entered the synagogue of the Jews together and 1
spoke to such effect that a considerable number of Jews as well as
Greeks believed, •but the Jews who hadn't believed stirred up the Gen- 2
tiles and poisoned their minds against the brethren. •They stayed there 3
for quite some time speaking boldly for the Lord, who confirmed the word
of his grace by causing signs and wonders to happen at their hands. •The 4
people of the city were divided — some sided with the Jews, some with
the apostles, •but when a move was made by the Gentiles and Jews along 5
with the local authorities to mistreat and stone them •they got wind of it 6

13:41 Hab 1:5 (Septuagint).   13:47 Is 49:6.

and fled to the Lycaonian cities of Lystra and Derbe and the surround-
7 ing region, •where they continued to proclaim the good news.

8 •At Lystra was a man who lacked the use of his feet — he had been
9 born crippled and had never walked. •This man listened while Paul spoke,
and when Paul looked at him and saw that the man had faith sufficient
10 to be healed •he said in a loud voice, "Get up and stand straight on your
11 feet!" And the man jumped up and began to walk around. •When the
crowd saw what Paul had done they began to shout in their Lycaonian
language, "The gods have taken human form and come down to us!"
12 •They called Barnabas Zeus and Paul Hermes, since he took the lead in
13 speaking, •and the local priest of Zeus whose temple was just outside the
city brought bulls and garlands to the city gates, intending to offer sacri-
14 fice along with the crowd. •When the apostles Paul and Barnabas heard
this they tore their garments and rushed out into the crowd, shouting,
15 •"Why are you doing this? We're men like you in every way! We're bringing you the good news that you can turn from these worthless things to
the Living God **Who made heaven and earth, the sea and all that's**
16 **in them.** •In ages past He allowed all the nations to follow their own
17 ways, •and yet His good works provided you with a witness to Himself;
He gives you rain from the heavens and fruitful seasons, He fills you with
18 food and your hearts with gladness." •By saying these things they were
with difficulty able to dissuade the crowd from sacrificing to them.

19 •But Jews showed up from Antioch and Iconium, and after winning
over the crowds they stoned Paul and dragged him outside the city,
20 thinking he was dead. •But when the disciples gathered around him
he got up and went back into the city, then the next day he left for
Derbe with Barnabas.

21 •They proclaimed the good news in that city and gained a considerable number of disciples, then they returned to Lystra, Iconium, and An-
22 tioch, •strengthening the souls of the disciples, encouraging them to persevere in the faith, and reminding them that "We must pass through
23 many tribulations in order to enter the Kingdom of God." •They appointed elders for them in each church and entrusted them to the Lord
24 in whom they had believed, with prayers and fasting. •Then they went
25 through Pisidia and came to Pamphylia, •and after speaking the word
26 in Perga they went down to Attalia. •From there they sailed to Antioch,

14:12 Zeus was the father of the other Olympian gods. Barnabas apparently had an impressive physical presence and so was thought to be Zeus, whereas Paul, who "took the lead in speak-ing," was identified as Hermes, the messenger of the gods.
14:15 Ex 20:11; Ps 146:6.

the place where they had been commended to the grace of God for the task which they had now completed. •When they arrived and had gath- 27 ered the church they reported all that God had done through them and that He had opened the door of faith to the Gentiles. •Then they stayed 28 with the disciples there for a fairly long time.

M. THE COUNCIL OF JERUSALEM
DECIDES ABOUT GENTILE CONVERTS

15 •Then some people who had come down from Judea began to 1 teach the brethren, "If you're not circumcised according to the custom of Moses you can't be saved." •After Paul and Barnabas had 2 entered into quite a disagreement and dispute with them, the people at Antioch selected Paul and Barnabas as well as certain others to go up to the apostles and elders at Jerusalem to discuss this matter. •So 3 they were sent on their way by the church and as they passed through Phoenicia and Samaria they described in detail the conversion of the Gentiles, which caused great joy among the brethren. •When they ar- 4 rived in Jerusalem they were received by the church, the apostles, and the elders and reported everything God had done through them. •Then 5 some of the believers who belonged to the party of the Pharisees stood up and said, "The Gentiles should be circumcised and required to fol-low the Torah of Moses."

•So the apostles and elders gathered to consider this matter. •After 6,7 a lengthy debate Peter got up and said to them, "My brothers, you know that long ago God decided among you that through my mouth the Gen-tiles would hear the good news and believe. •God, Who knows what's 8 in the heart, manifested His approval of the Gentiles by giving them the Holy Spirit just as He had given it to us — •He made no distinction be- 9 tween them and us, He cleansed their hearts because of their faith. •So 10 why are you putting God to the test now, putting a yoke on the necks of disciples which neither our ancestors nor we were able to bear? •On 11 the contrary, we believe that we are saved by the grace of the Lord Je-sus, just as they are, too."

•Then the whole assembly remained silent and listened as Barnabas 12 and Paul described all the signs and wonders God had performed among the Gentiles through them. •After they finished speaking James re- 13

15:13-35 The regulations embody traditional Jewish thought on the "Noachian" command-ments, a type of natural morality considered bind-ing on both Jews and Gentiles. They were also considered a basic minimum of decent behavior. 15:16-17 Am 9:11-12.

A bull with garlands has been brought to the sacrifice. (Ac 14:13)

14 sponded, "Listen to me, my brothers. •Symeon has described how God
15 first visited the Gentiles to choose a people in His name. •The words of
the prophets are also in accord with this, as it is written,

16 **•After this I will return and rebuild
the ruined dwelling of David;
I will rebuild its ruins and restore it**
17 **•So that the rest of mankind may seek out the Lord,
All the nations who are called in My name,**
18 **Says the Lord Who made these things** •known
from of old.

19 •Therefore my opinion is that we shouldn't lay extra burdens on the
20 Gentile converts; •instead, we should send them a letter instructing
them to avoid meat which was sacrificed to idols, unlawful marriages,
21 meat from strangled animals, and blood. •For from of old there have
been those who proclaim Moses in every city, and he is read in the
synagogues every Sabbath."

22 •Then the apostles and elders along with the whole church decided to
select representatives and send them to Antioch with Paul and Barnabas

— Judas, who was known as Barsabbas, and Silas, leading men among the brethren — • with a letter which read as follows: "The apostles and 23 elders to their Gentile brethren in Antioch, Syria, and Cilicia: greetings! •We have heard that certain persons from among us have disturbed you 24 and upset your peace of mind with words that we didn't authorize, •and 25 so we have unanimously decided to choose men and send them to you with our beloved Barnabas and Paul, •who have risked their lives for the 26 name of our Lord Jesus Christ. •Therefore, we are sending Judas and 27 Silas to announce the same things by word of mouth. •For the Holy Spir- 28 it and we have decided to lay no burdens on you beyond these necessary things: •to abstain from meat which was sacrificed to idols, from blood, 29 and from the meat of strangled animals, and to refrain from unlawful mar- riages. If you avoid these things you'll be doing well. Farewell!"

•And so they were sent on their way and went down to Antioch, 30 where they gathered the congregation and delivered the letter. •When 31 the people read it they rejoiced at the encouragement. •Both Judas and 32 Silas, who were prophets, encouraged and strengthened the brethren with all they had to say. •They stayed there for awhile and then the 33 brethren sent them on their way in peace, back to those who had sent them. [•] •But Paul and Barnabas remained in Antioch, teaching and 34,35 proclaiming the word of the Lord with many others as well.

N. PAUL AND BARNABAS SPLIT;
PAUL'S SECOND MISSIONARY JOURNEY

Philippi

•After some time Paul said to Barnabas, "Let's return and visit the 36 brethren in each city where we proclaimed the word of the Lord, and see how they are." •But Barnabas wanted to take John, who was called Mark, 37 with them too, •whereas Paul thought it was best not to take someone 38 who had left them in Pamphylia and had not gone with them to the work. •Such a sharp disagreement arose, that they separated from each other. 39 Barnabas took Mark and sailed for Cyprus •while Paul chose Silas and 40 left, after being commended by the brethren to the grace of God, •and 41 he went through Syria and Cilicia, strengthening the churches.

15:34 The best textual witnesses omit this verse, which is attested in several differing versions. Each version begins, "Silas decided to stay there," but while some add, "and Judas left alone," others add, "and Judas went to Jerusalem alone."

16 •Now he arrived at Derbe and Lystra, and behold there was a certain disciple there by the name of Timothy, the son of a Jewish woman who was a believer and a Greek father. •This Timothy was well spoken of by the brethren in Lystra and Iconium. •Paul wanted Timothy to go with him, so he took him and circumcised him because the Jews in those places all knew that his father was a Greek. •As they travelled through the cities they passed on to the people the rules the apostles and elders in Jerusalem had decided should be observed. •So the churches were strengthened in the faith and grew in number every day.

•They passed through the regions of Phrygia and Galatia because the Holy Spirit had forbidden them to preach the word in the province of Asia. •Jesus wouldn't allow them to, •so they went on through Mysia and went down to Troas. •That night Paul had a vision: a man from Macedonia was standing there imploring him, "Come over to Macedonia and help us!" •When he saw the vision we immediately sought to go to Macedonia, having concluded that God had called us to proclaim the good news to them.

•We set sail from Troas and made a straight run to Samothrace, reached Neapolis the next day, •and from there went to Philippi, which is a Roman colony and the leading city in that district of Macedonia. We stayed several days in that city. •On the Sabbath we went outside the gates to the river, where we thought there'd be a place of prayer, and sat down to talk with the women who had gathered there. •There was a woman named Lydia listening there — a dealer in purple cloth from the city of Thyatira and a worshipper of God — and the Lord opened her heart to heed the words Paul was speaking. •After she and her household were baptized she offered this invitation, "If you consider that I'm a believer in the Lord, come and stay in my house." And she prevailed upon us.

•Now as we were going to the place of prayer one day, we happened to meet a slave girl who had a spirit of divination and whose fortunetelling was a source of considerable profit for her masters. •She began following Paul and us and kept crying out, "These men are servants of the Most High God and are proclaiming the way of salvation to you!" •She continued doing this for many days. Now Paul was irritated by this so he turned and said to the spirit, "I command you in the name of Jesus Christ to leave her!" and it came out of her then and there. •When her

16:10-17 This is the first of the "we" sections, so-called because the narrative shifts to the first person plural. While some have suggested that this shift is simply a literary convention, it is more probable that the "we" sections truly reflect an eyewitness account (cf. also 20:5-15, 21:1-18, and 27:1-28:16).

masters saw that their hope of profit was gone they seized Paul and Silas and dragged them to the authorities in the marketplace, •and when they 20 had led them before the magistrates they said, "These men are Jews and are stirring up trouble in our city! •They're advocating practices that 21 are unlawful for us Romans to accept or perform!" •The crowd joined 22 in the attack on them and the magistrates tore the robes off Paul and Silas and ordered that they be beaten with rods. •After administering a 23 severe beating to them they threw them into prison and ordered the jailer to keep them under close guard. •Upon receiving this order he threw 24 them into the inner cell and fastened their feet in stocks.

•At about midnight Paul and Silas were praying and singing hymns 25 to God while the prisoners listened to them. •Suddenly there was such 26 a strong earthquake that it shook the foundations of the prison, causing all the doors to immediately open and all the chains to come unfastened. •When the jailer woke up and saw the prison's doors open he 27 drew his sword and was about to kill himself, because he thought the prisoners had escaped. •But Paul called out in a loud voice, "Don't harm 28 yourself — we're all here!" •So the jailer asked for a light and rushed 29 in, trembling all over, and fell down before Paul and Silas. •Then he led 30 them out and said, "Sirs, what must I do to be saved?" •"Believe in the 31 Lord Jesus and both you and your family will be saved," they said. •Then 32 they proclaimed the word of the Lord to him and to all his household. •So he took Paul and Silas at that very hour of the night and washed 33 their wounds, after which both he and his household were baptized at once. •Then the jailer led Paul and Silas to his house and fed them, while 34 he rejoiced with his whole household at having come to believe in God.

•When it was day the magistrates sent lictors to say, "Release those 35 men." •The jailer reported these instructions to Paul: "The magistrates 36 have sent to have you both released, so come out now and go in peace!" •But Paul said to them, "They beat us publicly without a trial — we who 37 are Roman citizens — then threw us into prison, and now they want to send us away secretly? Absolutely not! Let them come here themselves and release us!" •The lictors reported all this to the magistrates, and when 38 they heard that Paul and Silas were Romans they became frightened. •So 39 they went and apologized to them, released them, and asked them to leave the city. •When they left the prison they went to Lydia's house, where 40 they visited the brethren and exhorted them and then departed.

16:14 Purple cloth was a luxury item in the ancient world, so it may be assumed that Lydia was a person of some substance and social standing.

16:35 "Lictors." These officials exercised what are now considered to be police functions.

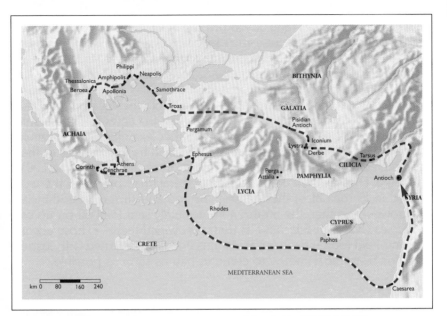

The second missionary journey of Paul. (Ac 15:36-18:22)

Thessalonica

17 1 •They travelled on through Amphipolis and Apollonia and came 2 to Thessalonica, where there was a Jewish synagogue. •As was his custom Paul joined their meetings and for three Sabbaths he argued 3 with them from the Scriptures, •explaining and demonstrating that it was necessary for the Messiah to suffer and rise from the dead, saying, "This 4 Jesus, whom I proclaim to you, is the Messiah." •Some of them were won over and joined with Paul and Silas, as did a large number of Greek 5 believers and quite a few of the leading women. •But the Jews became jealous; they gathered some worthless fellows from the marketplace, formed a mob and threw the city into an uproar, and attacked Jason's house in an attempt to find Paul and Silas and drag them in front of the 6 town assembly. •When they failed to find them, they dragged Jason and some of the brethren before the municipal authorities and shouted, "These men who have caused disturbances everywhere they've been

17:1 In Roman times Thessalonica was one of the most important trading centers in Greece. It was blessed with a fine natural harbor.

have come here now, •and Jason has taken them in! They're all violat- 7
ing Caesar's decrees because they say there's another king — Jesus!"
•These words got the mob and the municipal authorities stirred up, •and 8,9
after making Jason and the rest post a bond they let them go.

•The brethren immediately sent Paul and Silas away to Beroea by 10
night, and when they arrived there they went into the Jewish synagogue.
•These people were more open-minded than the Jews in Thessalonica 11
and received the word eagerly. Every day they examined the Scriptures
to see if these things they were being told could be true. •Many of them 12
believed, along with quite a few prominent Greek men and women. •But 13
when the Thessalonian Jews learned that Paul had preached the word
of God in Beroea also, they came there too and stirred up and incited
the crowds. •So then the brethren immediately sent Paul off on his way 14
to the sea, but both Silas and Timothy remained there. •Those accom- 15
panying Paul took him as far as Athens and then returned with instructions for Silas and Timothy to come to him as soon as possible.

Athens and Paul's discussion on the Areopagus

•While Paul was waiting for them in Athens he became irritated be- 16
cause he saw how full the city was of idols. •So he entered into dis- 17
cussions with the Jews and the Gentile worshippers in the synagogue
and every day with whoever happened to be in the marketplace. •Even 18
some of the Stoic and Epicurean philosophers had discussions with
him; some of them said, "What in the world is he trying to say, with
his bits and pieces of knowledge?" while others said, "He seems to be
a preacher of foreign gods," because Paul was proclaiming Jesus and
the resurrection. •So they took him and led him to the Areopagus and 19
said, "May we know what this new teaching is that you're preaching?
•Some of these things you're saying are strange to our ears, so we'd 20
like to know what they mean" — •all the Athenians and foreign resi- 21
dents did nothing with their free time but talk about and listen to the
latest new ideas.

•So Paul stood up in the middle of the Areopagus and said, "I can 22
see that you Athenians are extremely religious, •for as I walked about 23
and observed your places of worship I even found an altar on which was
written, 'To the unknown god.' What you worship without knowing is

17:19 The Areopagus was the Hill of Ares (Mars) in Athens where the Athenian court met. It was
also a gathering place for open air discussions.

24 what I proclaim to you. •For God Who made the world and everything in it — the Lord of the heavens and the earth — does not dwell in sanc- 25 tuaries made by human hands, •nor does He need anything we can do 26 for Him since He gives everyone life and breath and everything. •From one man He made every nation that dwells on the whole face of the earth, determining the exact periods and boundaries for their dwelling 27 places, •so that by groping about after Him they might search for and find God, for He isn't far from any of us.

28   •'In Him we live and move and exist,'

as some of your poets have said,

'For we too are His offspring.'

29 •So since we are God's offspring we shouldn't suppose that God re- sembles images of silver and gold and stone — which bear the stamp 30 of human skill and imagination. •God has chosen to overlook our peri- 31 ods of ignorance and now commands all men everywhere to repent, •be- cause He has fixed the day on which He will judge the whole world with justice through the man He has appointed. He has given proof of this to all of us by raising that man from the dead."

32   •When they heard about resurrection of the dead some of them be- gan to scoff, while others said, "We'll hear more about this from you lat- 33,34 er." •So Paul left their gathering. •Now some of the men believed and joined him, among them Dionysius, a member of the court of the Are- opagus, and a woman named Damaris as well as others with them.

Fruitful labor in Corinth and the return to Antioch

1,2 **18** •After this Paul left Athens and went to Corinth. •There he found a Jew named Aquila — a native of Pontus — who had recently come from Italy with his wife Priscilla because Claudius had ordered all 3 the Jews to leave Rome. He went to them •and since they practiced the same trade he stayed and worked with them — they were tentmakers

17:28 This appears to be a composite quote, the first part coming from Epimenides and the sec- ond from Aratus.
18:1 Corinth was perhaps the preeminent trad- ing center in Greece, due to its favorable location. Paul probably arrived in Fall of 50 A.D.
18:2 It is not clear from this account whether Aquila and Priscilla were already Christians when they met Paul. It is entirely possible that they were, because the expulsion of Jews from Rome under Claudius in about 49 A.D. is be- lieved to have been a result of civic disturbances between Jews who accepted Jesus as Messiah and those who did not.

by trade. •But every Sabbath he carried on discussions in the synagogue, ₄ trying to win over both Jews and Greeks.

•When Silas and Timothy arrived from Macedonia Paul devoted him- ₅ self to the word, solemnly assuring the Jews that the Messiah was Jesus. •But when they opposed him and insulted him he shook out his ₆ clothing and told them, "Your blood is on your heads; I'm innocent! From now on I'm going to the Gentiles." •Then he left there and went to the ₇ house of a man named Titius Justus, a Gentile worshipper of God, whose house was next door to the synagogue. •Crispus, the leader of the syn- ₈ agogue, believed in the Lord along with his whole household, and many of the Corinthians who heard the word believed and were baptized. •Then the Lord said to Paul in a vision one night, "Don't be afraid! Speak ₉ and don't be silent, •because I'll be with you and no one will try to harm ₁₀ you, because my people are numerous in this city." •So he stayed with ₁₁ them for a year and a half, preaching the word of God.

•But when Gallio became proconsul of Achaia the Jews made a con- ₁₂ certed attack against Paul and brought him into court, •saying, "This fel- ₁₃ low is inducing people to worship God contrary to the law." •Paul was ₁₄ about to open his mouth when Gallio said to the Jews, "If this were some vicious crime or misdeed I'd bear with you patiently, O Jews, •but since ₁₅ it's a dispute over words and names and your own law, see to it your-selves! I have no wish to be a judge in these matters." •With that he ₁₆ drove them from the court. •Then they all seized Sosthenes, the leader ₁₇ of the synagogue, and beat him in front of the tribunal, but Gallio paid no heed to any of this.

•So Paul stayed on for many more days and then said farewell to ₁₈ the brethren and set sail for Syria, along with Priscilla and Aquila. In Cenchreae he had his hair cut because he was under a vow. •They ar- ₁₉ rived in Ephesus and there he parted with them. While there he entered the synagogue and held discussions with the Jews. •They begged ₂₀ him to stay longer but he wouldn't agree; •instead, he bade them ₂₁ farewell and said, "God willing, I'll return to you." Then he set sail from Ephesus. •After landing at Caesarea he went up and greeted the church ₂₂ and then went down to Antioch. •He spent some time there and then ₂₃ left, travelling from place to place throughout Galatia and Phrygia, strengthening all the disciples.

18:12 Gallio was proconsul in 51-52 A.D.
18:22 The phrase "to go up" was commonly used of going to Jerusalem, so that it is proba-ble that Paul landed at Caesarea, went up to Jerusalem, and then proceeded to his base of operation, Antioch.

Ephesus: ruins of the temple of Artemis. (Ac 19:29)

Apollos

24 •Now an Alexandrian Jew named Apollos came to Ephesus — a
25 learned man, well versed in the Scriptures. •He had been instructed in
the way of the Lord and being of an ardent spirit spoke and taught ac-
26 curately concerning Jesus, but he knew only the baptism of John. •He
began to speak out boldly in the synagogue, but when Priscilla and Aquila
heard him they took him aside and explained the way of God more ac-
27 curately. •When he decided to go over to Achaia the brethren encouraged him and wrote to the disciples to receive him. When he arrived he
was of considerable assistance to those who through grace had become
28 believers, •for he vigorously refuted the Jews and publicly demonstrated through the Scriptures that Jesus was the Messiah.

18:24 Alexandria was a major center of Jewish
learning. It was in Alexandria that the Septuagint, the translation into Greek of the Old Testament, was produced by Jewish scholars about
250 years before the Christian era.

O. PAUL'S THIRD MISSIONARY JOURNEY

Ephesus

19 •Now it happened that while Apollos was in Corinth Paul trav- 1 elled through the inland districts and came to Ephesus, where he found some disciples. •He asked them, "Did you receive the Holy Spir- 2 it when you became believers?" "We've never even heard that there *is* a Holy Spirit," they said. •So Paul said, "What were you baptized into, 3 then?" "Into John's baptism," they said. •Then Paul said, "John bap- 4 tized with a baptism of repentance and told the people that they should believe in the one coming after him, that is, in Jesus." •When they heard 5 this they were baptized in the name of the Lord Jesus, •and when Paul 6 had laid his hands on them the Holy Spirit came upon them and they spoke in tongues and prophesied. •There were about twelve men in all. 7

•Paul then entered the synagogue and for three months he preached 8 boldly, arguing persuasively about the Kingdom of God. •But when some 9 of them proved stubborn and refused to believe, speaking evil against the Way in front of the congregation, Paul withdrew from them and took the disciples with him, and every day he held discussions in Tyrannus' lecture hall. •This went on for two years so that all who resided in the 10 province of Asia heard the word of God, both Jews and Greeks.

•God also performed extraordinary miracles at Paul's hands, •so that 11,12 people even took handkerchiefs and aprons from his body and carried them to the sick, and the diseases left them and the evil spirits came out of them. •Some travelling Jewish exorcists also tried to use the name of 13 the Lord Jesus on those who were possessed by evil spirits, by saying, "I adjure you by the Jesus Paul proclaims." •Seven sons of a Jewish high 14 priest named Sceva were doing this. •But in answer the evil spirit said to 15 them, "Jesus I know, and Paul I know about, but who are you?" •Then 16 the man with the evil spirit leapt upon them, overpowered them all, and so manhandled them that they had to flee that house, naked and wound- ed. •This became known to both the Jews and the Greeks who were liv- 17 ing in Ephesus — fear came over them all and they glorified the name of the Lord Jesus. •Many of those who had become believers also came 18 forward, acknowledging their past misdeeds and publicly disclosing them. •A large number of those who had practiced magic gathered their books 19

19:1 Ephesus was a major governmental, com- mercial, and cultural center on the west coast of Asia Minor. As with other trading centers in the area, numerous ethnic and religious groups were represented in its population, and there was a particularly flourishing Jewish community.

together and burned them in front of everyone. They added up the cost
20 of the books and found that it came to fifty thousand silver coins. •And
so the word of the Lord spread and grew strong.

21 •After these things happened Paul decided in the Spirit to travel
through Macedonia and Achaia and then proceed to Jerusalem, saying,
22 "After I go there I also have to see Rome." •So after sending two of
those who were assisting him to Macedonia — Timothy and Erastus —
he stayed awhile in the province of Asia.

23 •About that time there was a considerable commotion regarding the
24 Way. •A certain silversmith named Demetrius made silver shrines of
25 Artemis, which brought a considerable profit to the craftsmen. •He gathered them together, along with other workers who produced similar
things, and said, "Men, you know that our prosperity depends on this
26 business, •and you can see and hear that not only in Ephesus but in practically the whole province of Asia this Paul has persuaded and misled a
considerable number of people, by saying that gods made by human
27 hands are no gods at all. •Not only is there a danger that our business
will be brought into disrepute but also that the temple of the great goddess Artemis may count for nothing and that her splendor may even be
brought low, she whom all Asia and the whole world worships."

28 •When they heard this they became enraged and began to shout,
29 "Great is Artemis of the Ephesians!" •The city was filled with the uproar and the mob all rushed into the theater, dragging Gaius and
Aristarchus with them — they were two Macedonians who were travel-
30 ling with Paul. •Paul wanted to go before the people but the disciples
31 wouldn't allow him to, •and some high-ranking provincial officials who
were his friends also sent an appeal to him not to venture into the the-
32 ater. •Meanwhile, some people were shouting one thing while others
shouted something else — the assembly was in confusion and most of
33 them didn't even know why they had gathered. •Some of the crowd selected Alexander as a spokesman (the Jews had pushed him forward),
so Alexander waved his hand for silence and tried to address the as-
34 sembly. •But when they realized that he was a Jew they all cried out
with one voice and for nearly two hours they shouted, "Great is Artemis
35 of the Ephesians!" •The town clerk finally calmed the crowd down and
then said, "Fellow Ephesians, is there anyone who doesn't know that
the city of the Ephesians is the temple-keeper for the great Artemis and
36 the stone that fell from the sky? •Since all this is undeniable, what you

19:35 "The stone that fell from the sky." Perhaps a meteorite, associated in some way with the worship of Artemis.

should do is stay calm and not do anything rash. •You've brought these 37
two men here who have neither robbed a temple nor blasphemed our
goddess. •If Demetrius and his craftsmen have a complaint against any- 38
one the courts are open and the proconsuls are there — they can all
sue one another. •But if there's anything else you wish to address, it will 39
have to be handled at the regular assembly. •For we're in danger of be- 40
ing accused of rioting as a result of today's events, since we're unable
to give a reason for this disorderly gathering." •And with that he dis- 41
missed the assembly.

FURTHER TRAVEL IN MACEDONIA AND GREECE; PAUL'S DECISION TO GO TO JERUSALEM

20 •After the uproar had died down Paul summoned the disciples, 1
gave them encouragement, said farewell, and set out for Macedonia. •After travelling through those parts and giving them a great deal 2
of encouragement he went to Greece. •He spent three months there 3
and was planning to set sail for Syria, but because of a plot against him
by the Jews he decided to return by way of Macedonia. •Sopater son 4
of Pyrrhus from Beroea accompanied him, along with the Thessalonians Aristarchus and Secundus and Gaius from Derbe and Timothy as
well as the Asians Tychicus and Trophimus. •They went ahead and wait- 5
ed for us at Troas; •meanwhile, we set sail from Philippi after the days 6
of Unleavened Bread and in five days came to them at Troas, where we
stayed for seven days.

•On the first day of the week we gathered to break bread and Paul 7
spoke to us, since he was planning to depart the next day, and his talk
lasted until midnight. •There were quite a few lamps in the upstairs room 8
where we were gathered •and a certain young man named Eutychus, 9
who was sitting in the window, fell into a deep sleep as Paul talked on.
Since he was overcome with sleep he fell from the third floor and was
dead when they picked him up. •But Paul went down, threw himself on 10
him, and as he embraced him said, "Don't be distressed — there's life
in him!" •So Paul went back up, broke bread and ate, and talked for a 11
long time, until dawn, and in this manner he left. •Then they took the 12
boy away, alive, and were greatly comforted.

•We went ahead to the ship and set sail for Assos, intending to take 13
Paul on board there — he had arranged it this way because he intend-

20:7 "The first day of the week," i.e., Sunday, the first day after the Sabbath.

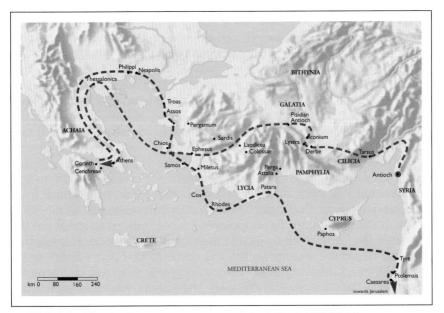

The third missionary journey of Paul. (Ac 18:23-20:14)

14 ed to go by land. •When he met up with us at Assos we took him on
15 board and went on to Mitylene. •We sailed from there and arrived the
next day opposite Chios and the next day came to Samos. The day af-
16 ter that we came to Miletus, •for Paul had decided to sail past Ephesus
so he wouldn't lose time in Asia, because he was hurrying to be in
Jerusalem, if at all possible, for Pentecost.

The farewell at Miletus

17   •From Miletus Paul sent to Ephesus and summoned the elders of the
18 church. •When they arrived he said to them, "You know how I was the
19 whole time I was with you, from the first day I set foot in Asia — •I served
the Lord in all humility, with tears and trials from the plotting I met with

20:17,28 "Elders... bishops." At this stage in the Church's development these terms appear to be essentially synonymous. The Greek for "elder" is "presbyter"; the Greek word *episkopos* or "bishop" means an "overseer." They are distinguished from deacons, rather than from priests as we know them. 20:18-35 This is the only speech in Acts in which Paul addresses people who are already believing Christians. It contains many echoes of Paul's style as we know it from his letters.

from the Jews; •I didn't keep silent about anything that could help you 20
but preached to you and taught you both in public and in your homes;
•to both Jews and Greeks I bore witness to repentance before God and 21
faith in our Lord Jesus. •And now, behold, the Spirit is compelling me 22
to go to Jerusalem, not knowing what will befall me there •except that 23
the Holy Spirit testifies to me in every city that chains and suffering await
me. •But I set no great value on my life as long as I'm able to finish the 24
course and the ministry I received from the Lord Jesus — to bear witness to the good news of God's grace."

•"I went about among you proclaiming the Kingdom, and now, be- 25
hold, I know you'll never see my face again. •Therefore I testify to you 26
this day that I'm innocent of your blood, •for I didn't hold back from 27
preaching to you all God's plan. •Watch over yourselves and all the flock, 28
in which the Holy Spirit has appointed you as bishops to shepherd the
church of the Lord which he gained through his own blood. •I know that 29
after my departure savage wolves will come to you and will not spare
the flock, •and men will arise from among you who will say perverse 30
things in order to draw the disciples after them. •So stay awake; re- 31
member that for three years, both night and day, I didn't cease exhorting each one of you with tears. •And now I commend you to God and 32
to His word of grace, which can build you up and give you an inheritance among all His holy ones. •I've never desired anyone's silver or gold 33
or clothing — •you yourselves know that these hands of mine provided 34
for my needs as well as for the needs of those who were with me. •In 35
every way possible I've shown you that we must help the weak by working hard like this, mindful of the words spoken by the Lord Jesus himself, 'It's more blessed to give than to receive.'"

•After saying these things he got on his knees and prayed with them 36
all. •They all wept a great deal and embraced Paul and kissed him, •be- 37,38
cause they were especially pained by what he said about them never seeing his face again. Then they accompanied him to the ship.

The trip to Jerusalem

21 •When we had parted from them we set sail. We set a straight 1
course and came to Cos, made Rhodes the next day, and from
there went to Patara, •and when we found a ship that was making the 2
crossing to Phoenicia we went on board and set sail. •We caught sight 3
of Cyprus and passed it on our left, sailed to Syria, and landed at Tyre,
where the ship was to unload its cargo. •We sought out the disciples 4

and stayed there for seven days with them, and they kept telling Paul
5 through the Spirit not to go on to Jerusalem, •but when our days there
were over we left and set out on our way. All of them, including the
women and children, accompanied us until we were outside the city and
6 after kneeling on the beach in prayer •we said farewell to one another.
Then we got on board the ship and they went back to their homes.

7 •We continued the voyage from Tyre and arrived at Ptolemais, where
8 we greeted the brethren and stayed with them for a day. •The next day
we left and went to Caesarea, where we went to the house of Philip the
9 Evangelist — one of the Seven — and stayed with him. •He had four un-
10 married daughters who were prophetesses. •We had been staying there
for several days when a prophet named Agabus came down from Judea.
11 •He came to us, took Paul's belt, bound himself hand and foot, and said,
"Thus says the Holy Spirit, 'Thus will the Jews in Jerusalem bind the man
12 whose belt this is, and they'll hand him over to the Gentiles.'" •When we
heard this both we and the local people begged Paul not to go up to
13 Jerusalem. •But Paul replied, "What are you doing, weeping and breaking my heart? I'm prepared not only to be bound but to die at Jerusalem
14 for the name of the Lord Jesus." •So since we were unable to convince
him we stopped trying and said, "The Lord's will be done."

15 •After these days we prepared ourselves and went up to Jerusalem.
16 •Some of the disciples from Caesarea also went with us and took us to
the house of Mnason of Cyprus — one of the early disciples — with
whom we were to stay.

P. CONFLICT AND CAPTIVITY FOR PAUL

Paul's reception in Jerusalem

17,18 •When we got to Jerusalem the brethren greeted us warmly •and the
next day we went with Paul to see James; all the elders were also pres-
19 ent. •After greeting them Paul related one by one all the things God had
20 done among the Gentiles through his ministry. •When they heard it they
glorified God and said, "Brother, you can see how many thousands of
believers there are among the Jews, and all of them are zealous follow-
21 ers of the Torah. •Now we have received reports about you to the effect
that you're teaching apostasy from Moses to those Jews who live among
the Gentiles — telling them not to circumcise their children or follow the

21:8 "Philip the Evangelist." One of the original seven deacons, cf. 6:5.

customs. •What should be done? They'll surely hear that you've come. 22 •Do what we tell you, then. We have four men who have placed them- 23 selves under a vow. •Take them and be purified with them and pay for 24 them to have their heads shaved. Then everyone will know that there's nothing to what was reported about you, but on the contrary that you live in observance of the Torah. •As for the Gentile believers, we've sent 25 them a letter instructing them that we consider that they should abstain from food that has been offered to idols, from the meat of animals that have been strangled, from blood, and from incestuous marriages." •The 26 following day Paul took the men and, after being purified with them, en- tered the Temple to give notice of when the days of purification would be completed and when the offering would be presented for each of them.

The riot in the Temple

•When the seven days were almost completed the Jews from Asia saw 27 Paul in the Temple. They stirred up the whole crowd and laid hands on him, •shouting, "Fellow Israelites, help us! This is the man who teaches 28 everywhere against the people, the Torah, and this Place! And now he's even brought Gentiles into the Temple and has desecrated this holy Place!" •For they had previously seen Trophimus the Ephesian in the city 29 with Paul and thought that Paul had brought him into the Temple. •The 30 whole city was aroused and the people formed a mob, got hold of Paul and dragged him out of the Temple, and immediately shut the gates. •As 31 they were trying to kill him word reached the tribune of the cohort that all Jerusalem was in a state of confusion. •At once he took some soldiers 32 and centurions and ran down to them, and when they saw the tribune and his soldiers they stopped beating Paul. •Then the tribune came up, 33 arrested Paul, and ordered that he be bound with two chains, and he asked who he was and what he had done. •Some in the crowd shouted one 34 thing while others shouted something else, and since he couldn't be sure of the facts because of the confusion he ordered the soldiers to bring Paul into the barracks. •Now when he got to the steps the soldiers ended up 35 having to carry Paul because of the violence of the crowd, •because a 36 mob of people was following and shouting, "Away with him!"

21:24 To pay the expenses of Nazirites under a vow was considered an exemplary act of piety in Judaism.
21:28 The presence of Gentiles in the Temple proper was forbidden under pain of death. Gen- tiles were regarded as unclean and their pres- ence would have desecrated the Temple. Warn- ing notices were posted which restricted Gentiles to the large surrounding "Court of the Gentiles."

ACTS

Jerusalem. Esplanade of the Temple.
The Fortress Antonia, where Paul was taken after the arrest (Ac 21:37),
stood on the site of the photographed edifices.

37 •They were about to take him into the barracks when Paul said to the tribune, "May I say something to you?" And the tribune said, "You know
38 Greek? •Aren't you the Egyptian who some time ago started a revolt
39 and led the four thousand Assassins into the desert?" •Paul said, "I'm a Jew from Tarsus in Cilicia, a citizen of no mean city! Please allow me
40 to speak to the people." •He gave his consent, so Paul stood on the steps and motioned with his hand, and when there was silence he addressed them in the Hebrew language.

1 **22** •"My brothers and fathers, listen to the defense I'll now set be-
2 fore you!" — •and when they heard him addressing them in the
3 Hebrew language they grew still more quiet — •"I am a Jew, born in Tarsus of Cilicia but brought up in this city at the feet of Gamaliel. I was educated strictly, according to the Torah we received from our an-

21:38 This incident is referred to by Josephus in his history of the Jewish revolt against Rome in 66-73 A.D. The assassins killed Gentile officials and Jews whom they considered collaborators by means of daggers which they concealed in their robes. Their activity reached its height in the years preceding the Jewish revolt.

cestors, and was zealous for God just as all of you are today. •As such 4 I persecuted this Way even to the death, tying up and imprisoning both men and women, •as the high priest and the Council of Elders can tes- 5 tify. I also received letters from them to the brethren in Damascus, and I went to Damascus in order to bring the people there who followed the Way back in chains to Jerusalem for punishment."

•"But as I was on my way and was drawing near to Damascus at about 6 noon a bright light from heaven suddenly shone around me. •I fell to 7 the ground and heard a voice saying to me, 'Saul! Saul! Why are you persecuting me?' •'Who are you, Lord?' I answered. The voice said to 8 me, 'I am Jesus of Nazareth, whom you are persecuting!' •Those who 9 were with me could see the light but couldn't hear the voice that was speaking to me. •So I said, 'What should I do, Lord?' And the Lord said 10 to me, 'Get up and go to Damascus, and there you'll be told everything you're to do.' •And since I was unable to see because of the brightness 11 of the light, those with me led me by the hand into Damascus."

•"Now Ananias, a devout man who revered the Torah and was well 12 spoken of by all the Jews who lived there, •came to me, stood beside 13 me, and said to me, 'Brother Saul, regain your sight!' And at that mo- ment I regained my sight and saw him. •Then he said, 'The God of our 14 fathers has chosen you to know His will, to see the Righteous One, and to hear the word of his mouth, •because you shall bear witness to all 15 men concerning what you have seen and heard. •And now, what are 16 you waiting for? Get up and be baptized — wash away your sins by call- ing on his name!'"

•"When I returned to Jerusalem and was at prayer in the Temple I 17 fell into a trance •and saw the Lord saying to me, 'Hurry! Leave 18 Jerusalem at once because they won't accept your testimony about me.' •'Lord,' I said, 'They themselves know that in every synagogue I jailed 19 and beat those who believed in you, •and when your witness Stephen's 20 blood was shed I was there, too, standing by in approval and watching the cloaks of those who killed him.' •Then he said to me, 'Go, because 21 I will send you far away to the Gentiles!'"

•Up to that point the crowd had listened to him, but then they raised 22 their voices and said, "Away from the earth with such a man! He's not fit to live!" •And as they shouted and waved their cloaks and threw dust 23 into the air •the tribune ordered Paul to be led into the barracks and 24 said that he should be interrogated under the whip to find out the rea- son they were shouting at him like that. •But when they had tied him 25 up with thongs Paul said to the centurion who was standing by, "Are you allowed to whip a Roman citizen without a trial?" •When the cen- 26

turion heard this he went to the tribune and said, "What are you doing?
27 This man's a Roman!" •So the tribune came and said to him, "Tell me,
28 are you a Roman?" "Yes," he said. •The tribune answered, "I paid a lot
of money for my citizenship." And Paul said, "But I'm a citizen by birth."
29 •At once, the men who had been about to interrogate him stepped back,
and the tribune was frightened when he realized that Paul was a Roman
and he had had him bound.

Q. PAUL SPEAKS BEFORE THE SANHEDRIN
AND IS TRANSFERRED TO CAESAREA

30 •The tribune wished to determine exactly what the Jews were accusing Paul of, so the next day he unbound him and ordered the chief priests
and the whole Sanhedrin to assemble. Then he brought Paul down and
stood him before them.

1 **23** •Paul gazed at the Sanhedrin and said, "My brothers, all my life,
to this very day, I have lived with a clear conscience before God."
2 •At this the high priest Ananias ordered those who were standing near
3 Paul to hit him across the mouth. •Then Paul said to him, "God will strike
you, you whitewashed wall! You sit there judging me according to the
4 Torah, and in violation of the Torah order me to be struck?" •Those who
5 were standing by said, "Would you slander God's high priest?" •"My
brothers," said Paul, "I didn't know he was the high priest, for it is written, **You shall not speak evil of a ruler of the people.**"
6 •Now Paul realized that one part of the assembly was made up of Sadducees while the other part was made up of Pharisees, so he cried out,
"My brothers, I'm a Pharisee, the son of Pharisees! I'm on trial for hop-
7 ing in the resurrection of the dead!" •When he said this a dispute arose
between the Pharisees and Sadducees, and the assembly was divided.
8 •For the Sadducees say that there's no resurrection, no angels, and no
9 spirits, while the Pharisees believe in all of them. •So there was a tremendous clamor, and some of the Pharisees' scribes stood up and strongly
maintained, "We can find nothing wrong in this man; maybe an angel
10 or spirit did speak to him!" •The disagreement became so heated that
the tribune, fearing that they'd tear Paul apart, ordered the soldiers to
go down and snatch him out from among them and bring him to the

23:2-3 Ananias was high priest from 47-59 A.D. and was assassinated at the beginning of the Jewish Revolt. He was notorious for his arrogant conduct. 23:5 Ex 22:28.

barracks. •The following night the Lord stood by Paul and said, "Take 11 courage! for just as you've given witness on my behalf in Jerusalem, so too must you bear witness in Rome."

•When day came the Jews entered into a conspiracy and bound them- 12 selves with an oath not to eat or drink until they had killed Paul. •There 13 were more than forty men who formed this conspiracy, •and they went 14 to the chief priests and elders and said, "We've bound ourselves under a solemn vow to taste nothing until we've killed Paul. •So you and the 15 Sanhedrin inform the tribune that he should bring Paul down to you as if you intended to consider his case more carefully, and we're prepared to kill him before he comes near." •Now the son of Paul's sister heard 16 about the ambush and he went and entered the barracks and told Paul. •So Paul summoned one of the centurions and said, "Take this young 17 man to the tribune because he has something to tell him." •The centu- 18 rion took him, led him to the tribune, and said, "The prisoner Paul sum-moned me and asked me to bring this young man to you, because he has something to tell you." •The tribune took him by the hand, led him 19 off alone, and asked, "What is it you have to tell me?" •And he said, 20 "The Jews have decided to ask you to bring Paul to the Sanhedrin to-morrow as if they were going to inquire into his case more carefully. •Don't let them persuade you — more than forty of them are going to 21 ambush him. They've put themselves under an oath not to eat or drink until they kill him and now they're ready, waiting for your decision." •So 22 the tribune sent the young man away after instructing him, "Don't tell anybody that you've informed me of these things."

•Then he summoned two centurions and said, "Have two hundred 23 soldiers ready to go to Caesarea by nine tonight, along with seventy horsemen and two hundred auxiliaries; •provide mounts for Paul to ride 24 and escort him to Felix, the governor." •Then he wrote a letter to this 25 effect: •"Claudius Lysias to his Excellency the governor Felix, greetings! 26, •This man had been seized by the Jews and was about to be killed by 27 them when I came upon the scene with the soldiers and rescued him, having learned that he was a Roman citizen. •Since I wanted to know 28 what they were accusing him of, I brought him down to their Sanhedrin. •I found that the charges against him were based on their law, but that 29 none of the charges warranted death or imprisonment. •So when it was 30 brought to my attention that there was a plot against him on the part of the Jews I sent him to you and instructed his accusers to state their case against him before you."

23:24 Felix was governor from 52-60 A.D.

A C T S

At Caesarea Paul remained prisoner for more than two years.

31 •So the soldiers took Paul to Antipatris by night, as they had been
32 ordered to do, •and the next day they let the horsemen accompany him
33 further while they returned to their barracks. •When they came to Caesarea they delivered the letter to the governor and also brought Paul
34 before him. •After reading the letter the governor asked what province
Paul was from, and when he learned that he was from Cilicia he said,
35 •"I'll hear your case when your accusers arrive," and ordered him to
be held in Herod's praetorium.

Paul defends himself before the Governor

1 **24** •Five days later the high priest Ananias came down with some elders and a professional spokesman, Tertullus, and they presented
2 their case against Paul to the governor. •When Paul was called in Tertullus began to make accusations and said, "Through you we enjoy peace to
a considerable degree, and by your foresight reforms have been introduced
3 for the benefit of our nation. •Therefore everywhere and in every way we
4 accept all this most gratefully, O excellent Felix. •But to detain you no fur-

ther, I beg you to briefly listen to us in your graciousness. •For we have ₅ found this man to be a trouble maker, a cause of strife among Jews all over the world and a ringleader for the sect of the Nazarenes — •he even ₆ tried to desecrate our Temple, but we seized him. [•] •You can learn about ₇,₈ everything we're accusing him of by questioning him yourself." •The Jews ₉ joined in the accusations and maintained that these things were true.

•When the governor nodded to him to speak Paul responded, "With ₁₀ the realization that you have been a judge for this nation for many years I confidently make my defense. •As you can ascertain for yourself, it was ₁₁ no more than twelve days ago that I went up to Jerusalem to worship. •They didn't find me arguing with anyone or stirring up the people in ₁₂ the Temple, nor did I do so either in the synagogues or the city, •and ₁₃ they can't prove the charges they're bringing against me now. •But this ₁₄ I do confess to you, that in accordance with the Way — which they call a sect — I worship the God of our fathers and believe everything that's written in the Torah and the Prophets, •hoping in the God these men ₁₅ themselves also accept that there will be a resurrection of both the good and the bad. •For this reason I strive to have a clear conscience before ₁₆ both God and men at all times. •After being away for many years I came ₁₇ to bring alms to my nation and to present offerings. •I was engaged in ₁₈ this when they found me in the Temple, purified and without any crowd or disturbance. •But it was some Jews from Asia — who should be here ₁₉ before you to accuse me if they have anything against me — •or these ₂₀ men themselves should say what wrongdoing they found when I was standing before the Sanhedrin, •except for the one thing I cried out as ₂₁ I stood before them, 'I'm on trial before you today because of my belief in the resurrection of the dead.'"

•Then Felix, who was well informed about the Way, adjourned the ₂₂ hearing and said, "When Lysias the tribune comes down I'll decide your case." •He instructed the centurion to keep Paul in custody but to give ₂₃ him some freedom and allow his friends to look after his needs.

•Several days later Felix came with his wife Drusilla, who was Jew- ₂₄ ish. He sent for Paul and listened to him speak about faith in Christ Je- sus. •As Paul was discussing righteousness and self-control and the judg- ₂₅ ment to come, Felix became alarmed and responded, "Go, for the time being. I'll call you again when I have the opportunity." •At the same time ₂₆

24:7 The best textual witnesses omit the follow- ing passage: "We were going to judge him in ac- cordance with our own law, 7 but the tribune Lysias forcibly removed him from our custody 8 and sent him to you."

24:25 Some authors believe Paul may have alarmed Felix by pointedly referring to Felix' adul- terous marriage to Drusilla, daughter of Herod Agrippa, much as John the Baptist had rebuked Herod for marrying his brother Philip's wife.

he was hoping that Paul would give him money, and so he frequently called him and talked with him.

27 •Two years later Porcius Festus succeeded Felix. Since Felix wished to gain the favor of the Jews he left Paul in prison.

Paul speaks before King Agrippa

1 **25** •Three days after Festus arrived in the Province he went up to
2 Jerusalem from Caesarea. •The chief priests and leaders of the Jews informed him of the charges against Paul and they appealed to
3 him •as a favor to have Paul sent to Jerusalem, because they were plan-
4 ning to ambush and kill him on the way. •Festus replied that Paul was being held at Caesarea and that he himself would be going there short-
5 ly. •"So," he said, "your leaders can come down with me if there's any wrongdoing they wish to charge this man with."

6 •After staying with them no more than eight or ten days he went down to Caesarea and the next day he took his seat in court and ordered Paul
7 to be brought. •When he came in the Jews who had come down from Jerusalem stood around him and began to make many serious accusa-
8 tions against him which they were unable to prove. •In defense Paul said, "In no way have I sinned against the Jewish Law, the Temple, or Cae-
9 sar." •Now Festus wanted to grant the Jews a favor and so in response he said, "Are you willing to go up to Jerusalem and be tried on these
10 charges before me there?" •So Paul said, "I stand now before the tri-bunal of Caesar, which is where I should be judged. I have done no wrong
11 to the Jews, as you know quite well. •If I'm in the wrong and have done anything deserving death, I don't refuse to face death. But if there's noth-ing in their charges against me, no one can turn me over to them. I ap-
12 peal to Caesar!" •Then Festus conferred with his council and respond-ed, "You have appealed to Caesar, to Caesar you shall go!"

13 •After several days had passed King Agrippa and Bernice arrived in
14 Caesarea to pay their respects to Festus. •Since they were spending quite a few days there, Festus explained the case against Paul to the king. "Fe-
15 lix left me a certain prisoner, •concerning whom the Jewish high priests and elders spoke to me when I was in Jerusalem and asked me to pass
16 sentence against him. •I responded that it is not the custom for us Ro-

24:27 Festus was governor from 60-62 A.D. Galilee and Perea (located in modern Jordan).
25:13 The royal title was largely honorary in re- Bernice was his sister.
ferring to Agrippa II, who ruled only portions of

mans to hand over a man before the accused has a chance to confront his accusers and offer a defense to the charges against him. •So when 17 we came here I lost no time — the next day I took my seat on the tribunal and ordered the man to be brought in. •But when his accusers 18 stood up they didn't bring any of the charges of wrongdoing I expected they would — •the issues they raised with him concerned their own 19 religion and a certain Jesus who had died, but who Paul claimed is alive. •Being at a loss in a controversy of this sort I asked if he wanted to go 20 to Jerusalem and be judged there concerning these matters. •But when 21 Paul appealed to be held for the decision of the Emperor I ordered that he be held until I could send him to Caesar." •Then Agrippa said to Fes- 22 tus, "I'd like to hear the man myself." "Tomorrow," said Festus, "you shall hear him."

•The next day Agrippa and Bernice came with great pomp and en- 23 tered the audience hall with the military commanders and the prominent men of the city, then at Festus' command Paul was brought in. •Festus 24 said, "King Agrippa and all those gathered here with us, you now see the man concerning whom the whole Jewish people petitioned me in Jerusalem, shouting that he should no longer live. •I could find nothing 25 deserving death in what he had done, but since he himself appealed to the Emperor I decided to send him. •I have nothing definite I can write 26 about him to my lord, and so I've brought him before all of you — and especially you, King Agrippa — so that after conducting a preliminary hearing I may have something to write. •For it seems unreasonable to 27 me to send a prisoner without indicating the charges against him."

26 •Agrippa said to Paul, "You have permission to speak on your 1 own behalf." Then Paul extended his hand and began his defense, •"King Agrippa, I count myself fortunate to defend myself before you 2 today against everything I've been accused of by the Jews, •especially 3 because you're familiar with all the customs and controversies of the Jews; therefore, please listen to me patiently. •All the Jews know the 4 type of life I led from my youth, which from the beginning was spent among my nation and in Jerusalem. •They've known for a long time, if 5 they're willing to testify, that I have lived as a Pharisee according to the strictest party of our religion. •And now I stand on trial for my hope in 6 the promise God made to our fathers, •which is what our twelve tribes 7 hope to attain as they earnestly offer worship both night and day. It is because of this hope that I am being accused by the Jews, your Majesty! •Why do your people consider it incredible that God should raise the 8 dead? •I myself thought that I had an obligation to strenuously oppose 9

10 the name of Jesus of Nazareth, •which is what I did in Jerusalem. I shut many of the saints up in prisons based on the authority I received from the chief priests, and when they were put to death I cast my vote against 11 them. •I also punished them many times in the synagogues and tried to force them to blaspheme against their faith. In my all-consuming rage against them I even persecuted them in foreign cities."

12 •"It was for this reason that I travelled to Damascus with the permis-
13 sion and authority of the chief priests. •I was on the road at about mid-day, your Majesty, when I saw a light more brilliant than the sun shin-
14 ing around me and those who were travelling with me. •We all fell to the ground and I heard a voice saying to me in the Hebrew language, 'Saul, Saul, why are you persecuting me? It's hard for you to kick against
15 the goad!' •'Who are you, Lord?' I said. And the Lord said, 'I am Je-
16 sus, whom you are persecuting. •Get up and stand on your feet! This is why I have appeared to you — to make you my servant and a witness
17 for what you've seen [of me] and what I'll show you. •I'll deliver you from
18 this people and from the Gentiles to whom I'll send you, •to open their

The Roman Imperial Way at Genila in Algeria.

eyes and turn them from darkness to the light — from the power of Satan to God — so that they may receive forgiveness for their sins and a place among those consecrated by faith in me.'"

•"And so, King Agrippa, rather than disobey this vision from Heaven •I began to call upon the people in Damascus, first, and then those in Jerusalem and the whole region of Judea, as well as the Gentiles, to repent and turn to God, and to do works befitting their repentance. •This is why the Jews seized me in the Temple and tried to kill me. •To this day I have received the help of God and so I stand here, bearing witness to great and small alike and saying nothing except what Moses and the prophets said would come to pass: •that the Messiah would have to suffer and that by being the first to rise from the dead he would proclaim light to the Jews and to the Gentiles."

•As Paul said these things in his defense Festus said in a loud voice, "You're mad, Paul! Your great learning is driving you to madness!" •"I'm not mad, most excellent Festus," said Paul. "What I declare is both true and reasonable. •The king knows about these things and to him I speak freely, for I'm convinced that he is aware of all these things, because they weren't done off in a corner. •Do you believe the prophets, King Agrippa? I know that you do!" •Agrippa said to Paul, "In no time at all you'll make a Christian of me!" •And Paul said, "I pray to God that whether in a short or a long time not only you but *all* those listening to me today may become what I am — except for these chains!"

•Then the king got up, along with the governor, Bernice, and those who were sitting with them, •and when they had withdrawn they said to each other, "This man is doing nothing deserving of either death or imprisonment." •And Agrippa said to Festus, "If he hadn't appealed to Caesar this man could have been set free."

R. SHIPWRECK ON THE VOYAGE TO ROME

27 •When it had been decided that we were to sail to Italy they turned Paul and some other prisoners over to a centurion of the Augustan Cohort named Julius. •We then embarked on a ship from Adramyttium that was about to sail for the ports along the coast of Asia and put out to sea. Aristarchus, a Macedonian from Thessalonica, was with us. •The next day we arrived at Sidon, where Julius kindly allowed Paul to go see his friends and be cared for by them. •From there we put out to sea and sailed under the lee of Cyprus because the winds were against us, •and after crossing the open sea near Cilicia and Pamphylia we arrived at Myra

6 in Lycia. •There the centurion found an Alexandrian ship that was sail-
7 ing to Italy and he put us on board. •For quite a few days we sailed slowly and made Cnidus only with difficulty, and since the wind would not
allow us to go any further on that course we sailed under the lee of Crete
8 past Salmone. •By hugging the coast we were able with difficulty to come
to a port called Fair Havens, near the city of Lasea.

9 •So much time had gone by that navigation was now dangerous, since
10 the Fast was now behind us. Paul advised •them, "Men, I can see that
this voyage will bring damage and severe loss not only to our cargo and
11 the ship but also to our lives." •But the centurion listened to the captain
12 and the owner of the ship rather than to Paul. •Since the harbor was un-
suitable for wintering over, the majority of them were in favor of setting
out from there in the hope of somehow reaching Phoenix, a harbor in
Crete which faces southwest and northwest, and wintering over there.

13 •When a south wind began to blow gently they decided that their ob-
jective was within their grasp, so they raised anchor and sailed along as
14 close as possible to the coast of Crete. •But soon a powerful wind called
15 the Northeaster swept down from the land. •The ship was caught up by
the wind and since it was impossible to keep it facing into the wind we
16 gave up and were driven before the wind. •As we were running under
the lee of a small island called Cauda we managed with difficulty to get
17 control of the ship's boat •and hoist it up, and then we braced the ship
by wrapping cables around it. Since they were afraid of running aground
off Libya at the Syrtis shoals they lowered the sea anchor and in this
18 manner were driven along. •We were being tossed about violently and
19 so on the next day they began to jettison the cargo •and on the third
20 day they threw the ship's gear overboard with their own hands. •For
many days neither the sun nor the stars were visible as the violent winter storm raged on, and finally we gave up all hope of being saved.

21 •When they had been without food for a long time Paul stood among
them and said, "Men, you should have heeded me and not put to sea
22 from Crete and you would have avoided all this damage and loss. •But
now I urge you to be of good cheer because there will be no loss of life
23 among you, only of the ship, •for last night an angel of the God to Whom
24 I belong and Whom I serve stood by me •and said, 'Fear not, Paul! You
must stand before Caesar, and behold, God has spared those sailing with
25 you.' •So be of good cheer, men, for I believe in God that it will turn out
26 just as I was told. •But we'll have to run aground on some island."

27:9 "The Fast." This took place on the Day of
Atonement, the holiest day of the Jewish year.
Since this fell in early to mid autumn, it was a convenient date to mark the shift in weather which
made navigation dangerous.

•On the fourteenth night we were being driven across the Adriatic, 27
and about the middle of the night the sailors began to suspect that we
were being driven toward land. •They took soundings and found twen- 28
ty fathoms, and when we had gone a little further they again took soundings and found fifteen fathoms. •They were afraid we might run aground 29
on some rocks and so they threw four anchors over the stern and prayed
for day. •Then the sailors tried to escape from the ship by letting the 30
ship's boat into the sea under the pretense of putting out anchors from
the bow. •Paul told the centurion and the soldiers, "If these men don't 31
stay on the ship you can't be saved!" •Then the soldiers cut the ropes 32
to the ship's boat and let it go.

•As day was coming Paul urged them all to take some food and said, 33
"This is the fourteenth day that you've been continually waiting without
food and have taken nothing, •so I urge you to take some food — it will 34
be of aid in saving you, for not a hair of your heads will be lost." •After 35
saying this he took some bread, gave thanks to God in front of them all,
broke it, and began to eat. •They were all cheered and took some food. 36
•There were two hundred and seventy-six souls in the ship. •After they 37,38
were filled they lightened the ship by throwing the wheat into the sea.

•When day came they were unable to recognize the land, but they 39
could see a bay with a beach onto which they planned to run the ship
if possible. •So they cut away the anchors and left them in the sea, and 40
at the same time they unfastened the ropes from the rudders, raised the
foresail to the wind, and headed for the beach. •But they struck a sand 41
bar and ran the ship aground. The prow was jammed fast and remained
immovable, but the stern was being broken up by the force of the waves.
•The soldiers' plan was to kill the prisoners so they couldn't swim away 42
and escape, •but the centurion wanted to save Paul and so he put a stop 43
to their plan. Then he ordered those who were able to swim to throw
themselves overboard first and make for land •while the rest were to go 44
on planks or pieces from the ship, and in this way they all made it safely to land.

28 •After we had all been saved we learned that the island was called 1
Malta. •The natives showed us extraordinary kindness — they 2
made us all welcome and lit a fire for us, because it had become cold
and rainy. •Now Paul had gathered up a bundle of brushwood and was 3
putting it on the fire when a viper came out because of the heat and
fastened itself onto his hand. •When the natives saw the snake hanging 4
from his hand they said to each other, "This man must be a murderer
— even though he was saved from the sea justice will not allow him to

5 live!" •But Paul shook the snake off into the fire and suffered no harm.
6 •The natives expected him to swell up or suddenly fall down dead, but after they had waited for a long time and saw that nothing out of the ordinary was happening to him they changed their minds and began to
7 say that he was a god. •Near that place were some lands that belonged to the most prominent person on the island, a man named Publius, who
8 took us in and for three days treated us as his guests. •Now Publius' father was lying down, sick with dysentery and a fever; Paul went to him,
9 prayed and laid his hands on him and healed him. •After this happened all the other people on the island who had ailments came and were
10 healed. •They also gave us many gifts, and when we set sail they put everything we needed on board.

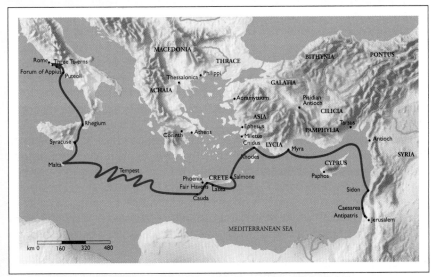

The journey of Paul towards Rome. (Ac 27:1-28:16)

S. PAUL IN ROME

11 •After three months we set sail in an Alexandrian ship that bore the
12 figurehead of the Heavenly Twins and had wintered at the island. •When
13 we arrived at Syracuse we stayed there for three days, •and from there

28:11 "The Heavenly Twins," i.e., Castor and Pollux, the pagan patron gods of sailors.

we went around the coast and arrived at Rhegium. After one day there a south wind came up and on the second day we came to Puteoli, •where 14 we found brethren who invited us to stay with them for seven days, and so we came to Rome. •When the brethren there heard about us they 15 came as far as the Forum of Appius and Three Taverns to meet us, and when Paul saw them he gave thanks to God and took courage. •And 16 when we came to Rome Paul was allowed to stay by himself, with the soldier who guarded him.

•After three days he called together the most prominent Jews there, 17 and when they had come he said to them, "My brothers, although I had done nothing against the people or the customs of our fathers I was handed over from Jerusalem into the hands of the Romans. •After they 18 had questioned me they wanted to release me because there was nothing I had done that merited the death penalty. •But when the Jews ob- 19 jected to this I was forced to appeal to Caesar, even though I had no accusation to bring against my nation. •This is why I've asked to see you 20 and speak to you, because it's for the sake of the hope of Israel that I'm wearing these chains." •They said to him, "We've received no letters 21 from Judea about you and none of the brethren who have come here have reported or spoken any evil concerning you. •But we'd like to hear 22 from you about your views, since we're aware that everywhere people are speaking against this sect."

•When they had set a day for him they came to him at his lodgings 23 in large numbers. From morning till night he explained everything to them, bearing witness to the Kingdom of God and trying to convince them about Jesus from the Law of Moses and the prophets. •Some were 24 convinced by what he said but others refused to believe, •and since they 25 disagreed with each other they departed, after Paul said one thing, "How well the Holy Spirit spoke to your fathers through Isaiah the prophet, •when he said, 26

Go to this people and say,
'Although you will listen and hear
    you will not understand,
And although you will look and see
    you will not perceive.'
•For the heart of this people has grown dull, 27
And with difficulty do they hear with their ears.
Their eyes they have closed lest they
    perceive with their eyes
Or hear with their ears

**And understand with their hearts
and turn to Me,
And I would heal them.**

28 •So let this be known to you — the salvation of God has been sent to
29 the Gentiles; they will listen!" [•]
30 •Paul stayed for two whole years in his own lodgings and received all
31 who came to him, •proclaiming the Kingdom of God and teaching about
the Lord Jesus Christ, openly and unhindered.

28:29 The best textual witnesses omit this verse: 28:26-27 Is 6:9-10 (Septuagint).
"After he said these things the Jews left, arguing 28:30 "Two whole years." Probably 60-62 A.D.
heatedly among themselves."

THE
PAULINE
LETTERS

General Introduction to the Pauline Letters

In his own day St. Paul was an influential and often controversial figure. In the course of the nearly two millennia which have passed his influence has increased so that today, as he has been for centuries, he is recognized as one of the seminal figures in the Church and Western civilization. Not only do we have in the Acts of the Apostles a narrative account of some of the events of St. Paul's ministry, we also have many of the letters which he wrote to the fledgling churches. These letters are of course of enduring theological significance and value. They also have a fascination all their own because of the personality they reveal, for Paul held little back in these letters — his passionate, questing personality is there for all to see, and the goal of his quest, Christ Jesus, is also everywhere to be felt in his letters.

THE LETTER TO THE

ROMANS

Introduction to the Letter to the Romans

By the late 50s A.D., probably about the year 57, Paul had come to believe that the time was coming for him to seek out new fields of missionary activity. He had been proclaiming the good news and establishing churches in the areas surrounding the Aegean sea as well as some inland parts of Asia Minor for the better part of ten years, and had had considerable success. He was now completing work on a very special project, the collection among the new Gentile churches which he planned to offer to the mother church in Jerusalem as a symbol of that new unity of Jew and Gentile, that universal salvation, which the good news of Jesus had brought. But even as he prepared for what he knew could be, and indeed turned out to be, a very dangerous trip to Jerusalem, he was already looking ahead.

The new field Paul had selected for his ministry was Spain. To undertake to proclaim the good news in so distant a land would take planning and preparation, and so as he wintered over in Corinth before his final trip to Jerusalem he spent part of his time composing a letter of introduction to the church in Rome. His hope was that the large Roman church would be able to assist him in his plans, and so he wished to acquaint them with his vision of the good news in so far as it concerned its proclamation to the Gentiles.

The instrument he chose with which to introduce himself has come down to us as the Letter to the Romans, generally considered to be Paul's masterwork.

Romans is certainly Paul's greatest effort at a sustained exposition of the gospel he had devoted his life to. It is not, however, a complete exposition of his gospel. The letter is concerned with the place of Israel and the Gentiles in God's plan of salvation, a subject which was still controversial. It would therefore be mistaken to seek a systematic 'theology of St. Paul' in Romans. On the other hand, because it was written — more or less — at leisure, rather than in the heat of some crisis in the life of a particular church, it presents the most systematic and considered view of Paul's ideas on almost any topic, with the possible exception of Ephesians.

A. GREETING

1 •Paul, a servant of Christ Jesus, called to be an apostle set apart for
2 the proclamation of God's good news •which He promised before-
3 hand through His prophets in the Holy Scriptures — •the good news
about His Son Jesus Christ our Lord, who was born from the line of
4 David according to the flesh •and was designated Son of God in power according to the Spirit of holiness by his resurrection from the dead.
5 •Through him we have received the grace of apostleship to bring about
6 the obedience of faith among all nations for the sake of his name. •And
7 you too are among those called to belong to Jesus Christ. •To all those
in Rome who are beloved of God and are called to be saints, grace and
peace be with you from God our Father and the Lord Jesus Christ.

B. THANKSGIVING AND THEME OF THE LETTER

8 •First of all, I give thanks to my God through Jesus Christ for all of
9 you, because your faith is being proclaimed throughout the world. •God
is my witness — Whom I serve with my spirit by proclaiming the good
10 news of His Son — that I continually mention you •in my prayers and
11 ask that somehow by God's will I'll finally manage to come to you, •for
I long to see you and to share with you some spiritual gift in order to
12 strengthen you, •that is, so we may be mutually encouraged by one an-
13 other's faith, both yours and mine. •[a] I want you to know, brothers, that
I've often planned to come to you (although I've been prevented from
doing so thus far) in order to receive some fruit among you as I've done
14 among the rest of the Gentiles. •For I'm obligated to both Greeks and
15 barbarians, to the wise and foolish alike, •and so I'm eager to proclaim
the good news to you who live in Rome as well.

---

[a] Ac 19:21.

1:5 "The obedience of faith." Obedience to a written code, the Torah, is replaced with obedience of the spirit, brought about through faith.

1:7 The Greek root for such words as "saints," "holy," and "sanctify" translated the Hebrew concept of being "set apart" or "consecrated," especially as an offering to God.

•For I'm not ashamed of the good news — it's God's saving power 16
for everyone who believes, first the Jew and then the Greek as well. •In 17
this good news God reveals His saving righteousness, from faith to faith,
as it is written, **Whoever is righteous by faith shall live.**

C. THE PROBLEM: BOTH JEW AND
GENTILE ARE IN NEED OF GOD'S GRACE

The Gentiles have incurred God's just wrath

•God's wrath is revealed from Heaven against all the wickedness and 18
evil of those who suppress the truth by their evil, •because what can be 19
known about God is evident to them, since God has revealed it to them.
•From the creation of the world God's invisible attributes — His eternal 20
power and divine nature — have been accessible to human knowledge
through what can be perceived, and so they have no excuse. •[b] They 21
knew God and yet they didn't honor Him as God or give Him thanks;
instead, their reasoning became foolish and their senseless hearts were
darkened. •They claimed they were wise but they became foolish, •ex- 22,23
changing the glory of the immortal God for an image in the likeness of
mortal man, birds, four-footed animals, or reptiles.

•And so God handed them over to the impure desires in their hearts, 24
which led them to degrade their bodies with one another. •They ex- 25
changed the truth of God for falsehood, they worshipped and did service to creatures instead of to the Creator, Who is blessed forever, amen.
•This is why God handed them over to dishonorable passions; indeed, 26
even their women exchanged natural relations for those which are
against nature, •and similarly their men also forsook natural relations with 27
women and burned with desire for one another — men committed
shameful deeds with other men, and received a fitting punishment for
their perversion in their own persons. •And since they refused to ac- 28
knowledge God, God handed them over to corrupted reasoning to do
things they shouldn't do. •They're filled with all sorts of wrongdoing, evil, 29
greed, and malice; full of envy, murder, strife, deceit, and mean spirit-

[b] *Eph 4:17-18.*

1:17 Hab 2:4.
1:20 The doctrine that God can be known from   "Through what can be perceived." Lit., "through
His works was common in rabbinic theology.   created things."

A Canaanite altar at Megiddo. The Canaanites constituted the great temptation of paganism for Israel. (Rm 2)

30 edness; they gossip, •slander, hate God, are insolent, arrogant, and
31 boastful; they invent evil, are disobedient to their parents, •are foolish,
32 disloyal, inhuman, and merciless. •Although they know that God's law says those who do such things deserve death, not only do *they* do them, they approve of *others* who do them.

The Jews too fall short in God's sight and have no special status

1 **2** •[c] But this is why all you who pass judgment on others have no excuse! For to the extent that you pass judgment on others you con-
2 demn yourself, since you who judge do the very same things. •Now we know that God's judgment against those who do such things is in accor-
3 dance with the truth. •Do you think, then, that you — who pass judg-
ment on those who do such things yet do the same things yourself — do
4 you think you can escape God's judgment? •Or do you despise the richness of His kindness, forbearance, and patience, not understanding that

[c] *Mt 7:1; Lk 6:37.*

the purpose of God's kindness is to lead you to repentance? •By your 5
hardness and your impenitent heart you're storing up wrath for yourself
on the day of wrath, when God's righteous judgment will be revealed.
•He'll reward each according to their works — •those who through per- 6,7
severance in good works seek glory, honor, and immortality will receive
everlasting life, •whereas those who act out of selfish ambition and dis- 8
obedience to the truth and who obey evil will receive wrath and anger.
•There will be tribulation and anguish upon every person who does evil, 9
Jews first and then Greeks, •but glory, honor, and peace for everyone 10
who does what's good, Jews first and then Greeks. •God doesn't play 11
favorites — •those who sin outside the Torah will also perish outside the 12
Torah, and those who sin under the Torah will be judged by the Torah.
•For those who *hear* the Torah aren't the ones who are righteous before 13
God — those who *observe* the Torah will be vindicated. •When Gentiles 14
who don't have the Torah do by nature what the Torah commands, even
though they don't have the Torah they're a law for themselves. •They 15
show that what the Torah requires is written on their hearts. Their consciences *also* bear witness, their conflicting thoughts accusing or even defending them •on the day when, according to my gospel, God judges 16
men's secrets through Christ Jesus.

•But if you call yourself a Jew and rely upon the Torah and boast about 17
God, •if you know God's will and can discern what's right as a result of 18
your instruction in the Torah, •if you're confident that you're a guide for 19
the blind, a light for those in darkness, •an instructor for the ignorant, a 20
teacher for children, if you really believe that in the Torah you have the
embodiment of knowledge and truth — •how can you teach others, yet 21
fail to teach yourself? You preach against theft, but do *you* steal? •You 22
say people shouldn't commit adultery, but do *you* commit adultery? You
abhor idols, but do *you* rob temples? •You boast about the Torah, but do 23
you dishonor God by violating the Torah? •For as it is written, **God's** 24
name is blasphemed among the Gentiles because of you. •Cir- 25
cumcision will only benefit you if you observe the Torah, but if you violate the Torah your circumcision becomes *un*circumcision. •So then, if a 26
Gentile keeps the precepts of the Torah, won't his uncircumcision be re-

2:9-15 Paul uses an allusion to Jr 31:31-33 to
show that the Gentiles are also God's people. In
this passage, God tells Israel that He will make
a new covenant with them, since they have broken the covenant which He made with them at
Sinai (as Paul has been saying). By this new
covenant the Torah will be written on their hearts,
and not just on stone tablets. Paul observes, in
this connection, that experience with conscience
shows that a "natural" version of the Torah is written on the hearts of the Gentiles as well. Thus,
from a moral standpoint Jews and Gentiles are
on the same level and are both in need of redemption.
2:24 Is 52:5.

27 garded as circumcision? •Then the man who is uncircumcised in the physical sense but keeps the Torah will pass judgment on you who, in spite
28 of the written law and circumcision, violate the Torah. •For external observance isn't what makes you a Jew, nor is circumcision an external mat-
29 ter of the flesh. •Rather, the true Jew is a Jew in an internal sense, and
circumcision is a matter of the heart, spiritual rather than literal; the true
Jew receives his praise from God rather than from men.

The dilemma of God's faithfulness and Israel's unfaithfulness

1 3 •What advantage does the Jew have, then? Is there any value in cir-
2 cumcision? •The advantage is great in every respect! First of all, the
3 Jews were entrusted with God's messages. •What does it matter if some
of them were unfaithful? Can their faithlessness cancel out God's faith-
4 fulness? •By no means! God must be faithful, even if every man were a
liar, as it is written,

**That You may be vindicated in Your words,
and be victorious when You're judged.**

5 •But if our wickedness highlights God's righteousness, what shall we say?
6 Is God unjust for inflicting His wrath? (I speak in a human manner.) •By
7 no means! Otherwise, how could God judge the world? •But if through
my falsity God's truth abounds to His glory, why am I still being con-
8 demned as a sinner? •And why not say, as some slanderously claim that
we do say, "Let's do evil that good may come of it!" Those who say
such things are justly condemned!

9 •What then? Are we Jews better off? Not at all! for I've already ar-
10 gued that everyone is under the power of sin, Jew and Greek alike. •As
it is written,

No one is righteous, not even one,
11   **•no one understands, no one seeks God.**
12 **•All have turned away, together they've
    become worthless,
    no one does what's right, not even one.**
13 **•Their throats are open graves.
    with their tongues they deceive,**

3:4 Ps 51:4.
3:9ff Paul has already stated that God will be
faithful even though Israel has been unfaithful, but
the dilemma remains: since Israel is in need of
reconciliation, what form will God's faithfulness,
His saving righteousness, take?
3:10-12 Ps 14:1-3; 53:1-3.

The venom of asps is under their lips,
  •their mouths are full of curses and bitterness.   14
•Their feet rush quickly to shed blood,   15
  •in their wake is ruin and misery,   16
•The way of peace they know not,   17
  •there is no fear of God before their eyes.   18

•Now we know that whatever the Torah says is directed to those under 19 the Torah, so that every excuse may be cut off and the whole world may be subject to God's judgment. •[d] **For no one is held to be righteous** 20 **in God's sight** based upon observance of the Torah, for the Torah gives only the consciousness of sin.

D. GOD'S SOLUTION: RESTORATION TO FELLOWSHIP WITH GOD THROUGH FAITH IN CHRIST

•But now God's saving righteousness has been revealed apart from 21 the Torah, although the Torah and the Prophets bear witness to •[e] God's 22 plan for restoring us to His fellowship through faith in Jesus Christ for *all* who believe. There can be no distinction; •all have sinned and there- 23 fore are deprived of God's glory. •They are restored to fellowship with 24 God by His freely given grace through the redemption that comes in Christ Jesus. •God put him forward to serve as an expiation for sins with 25 his blood, and that expiation is ours through faith. In this way God

[d] *Gal 2:16.*   [e] *Gal 2:16.*

3:13 Ps 5:9; 140:3.
3:14 Ps 10:7.
3:15-17 Is 59:7-8.
3:18 Ps 36:1.
3:20 Ps 143:2.
3:21-31 Paul has shown that both Jews and Gentiles are on the same level. Now he outlines the solution to the dilemma of God's faithfulness and man's unfaithfulness: God has revealed in Jesus His intent to offer reconciliation, through faith in Jesus. Since redemption is contingent only upon faith and not upon observance of the Torah, redemption is now available to all who put their faith in Jesus.
3:22 The Greek verb behind the phrase "restoration to fellowship" was often used in a secular context to mean "to acquit" or "to declare innocent." However, Paul's use of the word (usually translated "justification") takes on a very specific

and original sense when he uses it, as he does here, in the context of our redemption. Even God cannot declare the guilty to be innocent when they are not so in fact. What He does is even more wonderful: in spite of our guilt, a guilt we could never expiate on our own, God unilaterally offers us pardon, reconciliation, and restoration to His fellowship through the redemptive death of Jesus His Son. When we place our faith in Jesus the merits of his expiatory death are "credited to us as righteousness," and so through faith we are restored to fellowship with God.
3:25 According to Judaic sacrificial theology "the life of the flesh is in the blood... it is the blood that makes an atonement for the soul" (Lv 17:11). Thus the reference to blood is properly understood within a sacrificial context, whereby the shedding of blood brings life. Cf. also 5:8-9.

Roman aqueduct in Seleucia (Turkey).

26 demonstrated His saving righteousness, by overlooking past sins •in His divine forbearance — as a demonstration of His saving righteousness at the present time, showing that He Himself is righteous and will restore to His fellowship whoever puts his faith in Jesus.

27 •What basis can there be for boasting, then? All boasting is excluded. Is it excluded on the basis of works? No, boasting is excluded on the

28 basis of faith. •For we consider that a person is restored to fellowship

29 with God by faith, and not by observing the Torah. •After all, is God only the God of the Jews? Isn't He also the God of the Gentiles? Yes,

30 of the Gentiles as well, •^f since God is one, and He'll restore both cir-

31 cumcised and uncircumcised to His fellowship based on their faith. •Well then, does that mean that our faith nullifies the Torah? By no means! On the contrary, the principle of faith upholds the Torah.

---

^f *Gal 3:20.*

3:31 As Paul will go on to show, the Christian upholds the Torah in a new and deeper sense: we observe the Torah "in the new way of the spirit," rather than the old way of observing a written code (7:6). This places the Torah within the true context of God's plan for our redemption.

The example of Abraham's faith

4 •What, then, shall we say? Has Abraham been found to be our fore- 1 father according to the flesh? •If Abraham was restored to fellow- 2 ship with God by his own efforts he has something to boast about, but he has no such boast, not before God! •[g] For what does Scripture say? 3 **Abraham believed God, and it was credited to him as right- eousness.** •Now a worker's wages are credited to him not as a gift but 4 as something that's owed to him, •whereas in the case of someone who 5 doesn't work but puts his faith in the God Who pardons sinners, God accepts his faith for the purpose of restoring him to fellowship. •And so 6 David speaks of how blessed the person is whom God receives into fel- lowship without regard to his works,

> •**Blessed are they whose iniquities are forgiven,** 7
> **whose sins are covered;**
> •**Blessed the man whose sin God does not count** 8
> **against him.**

•Is this blessedness only for the circumcised, or also for the uncircumcised? 9 We say, **Abraham's faith was credited to him as righteousness,** •but when was it credited to him? Before he was circumcised or after he 10 was circumcised? It was before he was circumcised, not after. •He received 11 circumcision as a sign or seal indicating that through faith he had been re- stored to fellowship with God while still uncircumcised. This was so he would be the father of all the uncircumcised who believe and are credited with righteousness, •as well as being the father of the circumcised who 12 are not only circumcised but also follow the steps of faith that our father Abraham followed when he was still uncircumcised.

•[h] For the promise to Abraham and his descendants that they would 13 inherit the world was based not on Abraham's observance of the Torah but on the fact that he had been restored to fellowship with God through faith. •[i] If the heirs are those who observe the Torah, then faith is point- 14 less and the promise is null and void. •For the Torah paves the way for 15 God's wrath, whereas where there's no law there can be no violation of the law. •[j] The reason the promise was based on faith was so that it would 16 be a free gift and would be secured for all his descendants, not just for those who observe the Torah but also for those who follow Abraham's example of faith. (Abraham is the father of all of us, •as it is written, **I** 17

---

[g] *Gal 3:6.*   [h] *Gal 3:29.*   [i] *Gal 3:18.*   [j] *Gal 3:7.*

4:3 Gn 15:6.   4:7-8 Ps 32:1-2.   4:9 Gn 15:6.

have made you the father of many nations.) He is our father in the sight of God, God Who gives life to the dead and calls into existence what
18 doesn't exist. •Abraham believed, hoping against hope, that he would become **the father of many nations** as he had been told, **So shall your**
19 **descendants be.** •Nor did his faith weaken when he considered his own body, which was already as good as dead since he was about a hundred
20 years old, or when he considered Sarah's barrenness. •His faith in God's promise never wavered; instead, his faith grew stronger and he gave glo-
21 ry to God, •since he was fully convinced that God was able to do what
22 He had promised. •That's why Abraham's faith **was credited to him**
23 **as righteousness.** •But the words "it was credited to him" weren't writ-
24 ten for his sake alone — •they were also written for our sake, and righteousness will be credited to us who have faith in the One Who raised our
25 Lord Jesus from the dead. •He was handed over for our offenses and was raised to restore us to fellowship with God.

The extraordinary nature
and consequences of God's redemption

1 5 •Now that we've been restored to His fellowship by faith we're at
2 peace with God through our Lord Jesus Christ. •Through him we've obtained access [by faith] to God's grace in which we now stand,
3 and we rejoice in our hope of sharing in God's glory. •Not only that, we even rejoice in our afflictions, since we know that affliction pro-
4 duces steadfastness, •steadfastness produces proven character, and
5 proven character produces hope. •And this hope is no illusion, because God's love has been poured out in our hearts through the Holy Spir-
6 it which has been given to us. •For while we were still helpless Christ
7 died for the wicked at the appointed time. •It's hardly likely that someone would die even for a righteous man, although someone might have
8 the courage to die for a good man, •but the proof of God's love for
9 us is that Christ died for us while we were still sinners. •Now that we've been restored to fellowship with God by Jesus' blood we can be far
10 more certain that he'll also save us from God's wrath. •For if we were reconciled to God through the death of His Son while we were still God's enemies, now that we've been reconciled we have a much

4:17 Gn 17:5.   4:18 Gn 15:5.   4:19 Gn 17:7.   4:22 Gn 15:6.
5:9 The "far more" shows that in spite of the emphasis Paul put on restoration to fellowship the real center of his thought was the life in Christ after restoration.

greater assurance that we'll be saved by His Son's life. •Not only that, 11 we even boast of God through our Lord Jesus Christ, through whom we've now received reconciliation.

•Therefore, just as through one man sin entered the world, and through 12 sin, death, and in this way death spread to all men because they all sinned — •sin was indeed in the world before the Torah was received, although 13 sin isn't charged against anyone in the absence of a law. •But death reigned 14 from Adam until Moses even over those who hadn't sinned in the same way as Adam, who was a figure of the one who was to come.

•But God's free gift is not at all like the offense. For while it's true 15 that many died because of one man's offense, nevertheless God's grace and the free gift through the grace of the one man Jesus Christ have overflowed to far greater effect for the many. •Nor is God's free gift pro- 16 portionate to the effect of that one man's sin, for the judgment that followed the single offense brought condemnation, whereas the gift that followed many offenses brought pardon. •It may be true that as a result 17 of one man's offense death began its reign through that one man, yet how much greater is the gift! For those who receive God's abundant grace and the free gift of righteousness shall reign in life through the one man Jesus Christ. •So then, just as one man's offense resulted in 18 condemnation for all, so too one man's obedience results in pardon and life for all. •For just as many were made sinners as a result of one man's 19 disobedience, so too through one man's obedience many will be made righteous. •The Torah came in so as to increase the offense, but where 20 sin increased grace increased even more, •so that just as sin reigned in 21 death so too would grace reign in reconciliation leading to eternal life through our Lord Jesus Christ.

E. OBJECTIONS TO PAUL'S GOSPEL ANSWERED

Are we now free to sin?

6 •What shall we say, then? Should we remain in sin so grace will in- 1 crease? •By no means! How can we who died to sin still live in it? 2 •Don't you know that those of us who were baptized into Christ Jesus 3

5:19 The centrality of obedience for Paul's understanding of Christ's redemptive death flowed naturally from the Judaic concept of complete loyalty to the Torah as well as the Suffering Servant figure in Deutero-Isaiah, but it was also firm-ly founded in Jesus' own experience.
6:3ff Paul reminds the Romans that through baptism they are called to a new life, one which is dead to sin.

Baptism shown on a Roman bas-relief (4th century A.D.). (Rm 6:4)

4 were baptized into his death? •[k] Therefore, we were buried with him through our baptism into his death so that just as Christ was raised from the dead by the Father's glory we too might be able to lead a new life. 5 •For if in baptism we've become sharers in a death like his, we'll also 6 share in a resurrection like his. •We know that our old self was crucified with him in order to do away with the sinful self, so we'd no longer 7,8 be slaves to sin, •for a person who has died is set free from sin. •But if we've died with Christ we believe that we'll also come to life with him, 9 •for we know that Christ rose from the dead and will never die again 10 — death no longer has any power over him. •For the death he died he 11 died to sin once and for all, and the life he lives he lives for God. •Thus, you too should consider yourselves dead to sin and living for God in Christ Jesus.

[k] *Col 2:12.*

6:12 "Mortal bodies." It is important to remember that for Paul "body" could refer to more than just the physical aspects of human beings — it referred to the human person as a totality. There-fore the sins of the body included non-sensual sins such as greed and pride, although in our disordered state (the effect of sin) sins of the flesh (in the modern sense) naturally bulk large.

•Therefore, don't let sin reign in your mortal bodies so that you obey 12 bodily desires. •Don't yield your members to sin as weapons of evil; in- 13 stead, offer yourselves to God as raised from the dead and now living, and offer your members to God as weapons of righteousness. •For sin 14 has no power over you, since you're under grace, not under law.

•What shall we do then? Since we're under grace instead of under 15 law shall we sin? By no means! •Don't you know that if you offer your- 16 selves to someone as obedient slaves, you're slaves of the one you obey, be it sin which leads to death or obedience which leads to right- eousness? •But thanks be to God, for you who were once slaves to 17 sin have become obedient from the heart to the pattern of teaching which was handed down to you — •you've been set free from sin and 18 have become slaves of righteousness. •(I'm speaking in terms suitable 19 to the weakness of your human nature.) For just as you once allowed your bodily members to become slaves of impurity and ever greater wickedness, so now you offer your bodily members as slaves to right- eousness so that they may be sanctified. •When you were slaves of sin 20 you were free of righteousness — •so what benefit did you derive from 21 those things you're now ashamed of? Those things lead only to death. •But now that you've been freed from sin and have become slaves of 22 God the benefit you derive is sanctification, which leads to eternal life. •The wages of sin is death, whereas God's free gift is eternal life in 23 Christ Jesus our Lord.

7 •Don't you know, my brothers — for I'm speaking to people who 1 understand legal matters — that law has power over you only as long as you're alive? •For example, a woman is by law bound to her 2 husband while he's alive, but if he dies she's released from the law with respect to her husband. •So then, she'll be branded an adulteress if she 3 marries another man while her husband is alive, but if her husband dies she's free as far as the law is concerned and she won't be an adulter- ess if she marries another man. •And so it is, my brothers — you've 4 been put to death with respect to the Torah through Christ's body. You may now belong to another, to him who was raised from the dead, so that we may produce fruit for God. •For when we were in the flesh the 5 sinful desires stirred up by the Torah were at work in our bodily mem- bers so as to bear fruit for death. •Now, however, we've been freed from 6 the Torah; we've died to what had held us fast so that we'll be able to serve in the new way of the Spirit, rather than in the old way of ob- serving a written code.

The role of the Torah in God's saving plan

7 •What shall we say, then? Is the Torah sin? By no means! But I never would have known what sin is if it hadn't been for the Torah. I never would have known what it is to covet if the Torah hadn't said, **You shall**
8 **not covet!** •Sin took advantage of the opportunity provided by the commandment to produce all sorts of covetousness in me, for apart from law,
9 sin is dead. •I once was alive apart from law, but when the command-
10 ment came sin came to life •and I died — it turned out that, for me, the
11 commandment that was supposed to bring life brought death, •for sin took advantage of the opportunity provided by the commandment to de-
12 ceive me and kill me by means of the commandment. •So the Torah itself is holy, and the commandment is holy, just, and good.
13 •Well then, did something good cause death? By no means! It was sin that brought about my death by *using* what was good, so that the reality of sin might be revealed and so sin would, through the commandment,
14 reach the extreme of sinfulness. •We know that the Torah is spiritual, but
15 I am of the flesh, sold and subjected to sin. •[1] I don't even choose my own
16 actions, because instead of doing what I want to do I do what I hate. •Now if I don't want to do the very thing that I actually do, then I agree that the
17 Torah is, in fact, good. •So then I'm no longer the one doing these things
18 — it's sin dwelling within me that's to blame. •I know that the good doesn't dwell within me, that is, in my flesh, because although I want to do
19 what's right I'm unable to do it, •for instead of doing the good that I want
20 to do, I do the evil thing that I *don't* want to do. •Now if I do the very thing that I don't want to do, that means it's not me doing it, it's sin dwelling
21 within me that's doing it. •So it turns out to be a law that when I want to
22 do what's right, evil awaits me, •for although I agree with God's law in
23 my inmost self •I can see that there's another law in my bodily members which wars against the law of my reason and holds me captive to the law
24 of sin in my bodily members. •What a miserable state I'm in! Who can
25 save me from this body which is leading me to death? •Thanks be to God through our Lord Jesus Christ! So then, I myself serve God's law with my mind, but in the flesh I serve the law of sin.

[1] *Gal 5:17.*

7:7 Ex 20:17; Dt 5:21.
7:14 Here Paul uses "flesh," as he often does, to refer to our lives as lived "in sinful self-reliance," oriented away from God, as if He didn't matter.
7:15 "Choose." Traditionally translated "understand." As the context of this extended passage shows, what is at issue is not intellectual understanding — after all, I clearly understand that my actions are wrong and desire to follow the law — but the ability to carry out the choices I make. This meaning of the underlying Greek verb is apparent in other passages of the Bible as well.

Life in the Spirit, Life in Hope

8 •Thus there's no condemnation now for those who are in Christ Je- 1
sus. •For the law of the Spirit of life in Christ Jesus has freed you 2
from the law of sin and death. •What the Torah was unable to do be- 3
cause the flesh had weakened it, God has done — by sending His own
Son in the likeness of sinful flesh and as an offering for sin, He has condemned sin in the flesh. •He did this so that the just requirement of the 4
Torah would be fulfilled in us, who live according to the Spirit instead
of according to the flesh. •The thoughts of those who live according to 5
the flesh are in accordance with the flesh, while the thoughts of those
who live according to the Spirit are in accordance with the Spirit. •To 6
have a mind conformed to the flesh leads to death, but to have a mind
conformed to the Spirit leads to life and peace, •because the flesh's way 7
of thinking is hostile to God — it doesn't obey God's law, in fact it *can't*.
•And so those who are in the flesh are unable to please God. •But *you're* 8,9
not in the flesh — you're in the Spirit, since the Spirit of God dwells
within you. And if anyone doesn't have Christ's Spirit, he doesn't belong to Christ. •But if Christ is in you, even though your body is dead 10
because of sin, then your spirit is alive because of righteousness. •[m] And 11
if the Spirit of God Who raised Christ from the dead dwells within you,
then the One Who raised Christ from the dead will give life to your dead
bodies through His Spirit that dwells within you.

•So then, my brothers, we are under an obligation, but it's not to the 12
flesh and we're not obligated to live according to the flesh; •for if you 13
live according to the flesh you'll die, but if by the Spirit you put to death
the deeds of the body you'll live. •For all those who are led by the Spir- 14
it of God are sons of God. •[n] You didn't receive a spirit of slavery which 15
caused you to be afraid; you received a spirit of adoption, by which we
cry, "Abba, Father!" •The Spirit itself bears witness with our spirit that 16
we're God's children. •And if we're children, then we're also heirs — 17
heirs of God, co-heirs with Christ, if we suffer with him so as to be glorified with him as well.

•I consider that the sufferings of the present time simply don't com- 18
pare with the glory to come, which will be revealed to us. •Creation awaits 19
the revelation of the sons of God with eager anticipation, •for creation 20

[m] *1 Cor 3:16.*   [n] *Gal 4:5-7; Mk 14:36.*

8:1ff. The dilemma that the Torah places us in — that knowledge of the law doesn't free us from sin (7:7-25) — is resolved by Christ's redemptive death, which opens for us life in the Spirit, thus freeing us from sin and death.
8:3 "In the likeness of sinful flesh," i.e., a normal human being in appearance; thus, to all appearances he would be subject to sin.

St. Paul's Basilica in Rome.

was subjected to futility, not of its own will but because of the one who
21 made it subject, with the hope •that creation itself would be freed from
its slavery to corruption and be brought to the glorious freedom of the
22 children of God. •For we know that all creation has been groaning in la-
23 bor pains up till the present; •° moreover, we ourselves who have the Spirit as the first fruits are also groaning within ourselves as we await our adop-
24 tion as sons, the redemption of our bodies. •For it was through this hope
that we were saved, but a hope that can be seen isn't truly a hope — af-
25 ter all, who hopes for what they can already see? •But if we hope for
what we do not yet see, then we wait patiently.

26   •Likewise the Spirit also helps us in our weakness, for we don't know
how to pray as we should; instead, the Spirit himself pleads for us with
27 inexpressible groanings, •and the One Who is able to see what's in the
heart knows what the Spirit wishes, because the Spirit intercedes for the
28 saints in accordance with God's will. •Now we know that God works in
every way for the good with those who love God and are called in ac-

° *2 Cor 5:2-4.*

cordance with His plan. •Those God knew beforehand He also predes- 29
tined to be conformed to the image of His Son, so that he might become the firstborn of many brothers. •Now those He predestined, God 30
also called, and those He called He restored to His fellowship, and all
those whom He restored to fellowship He also glorified.

•What then shall we say in view of this? If God is for us, who can be 31
against us? •If God didn't spare His own Son but instead gave him up 32
for all of us, won't He also freely give us everything along with His Son?
•Who will accuse God's chosen ones? God Himself pardons them! •Who 33,34
will condemn them? Christ died and rose for us and is now at God's right
hand interceding for us! •Who will separate us from Christ's love? Af- 35
fliction, distress, persecution, famine, destitution, danger, or the sword?
•As it is written, 36

For your sake we're being put to death all day long,
we're regarded as sheep for the slaughter.

•But in all these things we are winning an overwhelming victory through 37
the One Who loved us. •I'm convinced that neither death nor life, nei- 38
ther angels nor principalities, neither things present nor to come nor
powers, •neither height nor depth nor any other created being will be 39
able to separate us from God's love in Christ Jesus our Lord.

The place of Jews and Gentiles in God's plan

9 •I'm speaking the truth now in Christ, I'm not lying: my conscience 1
bears me witness in the Holy Spirit •that I'm in great sorrow and the 2
pain in my heart is unceasing. •For I could wish that I myself were ac- 3
cursed and cut off from Christ for the sake of my brothers, my kinsmen
according to the flesh. •They are Israelites, and to them belonged the 4
adoption as sons, the glory of God's presence, the covenants, the giving of the Torah, the Temple worship, and the promises; •theirs were 5
the patriarchs, and from them came the Messiah according to the flesh
— may God Who is over all be blessed forever, amen!

8:36 Ps 44:22.
8:39 It is generally agreed that "height" and
"depth" are astrological terms, but here they probably refer to heavenly or angelic beings.
9:1 Paul now confronts a formidable objection to
his gospel: true, God's plan appears to be succeeding among the Gentiles, but isn't it failing
among the Jews, most of whom have not put their
faith in Jesus? Paul goes on to explain this seeming anomaly, but his anguish at Israel's lack of
faith is apparent.
9:4 "The glory of God's presence," esp. during
the Exodus. "The Temple worship" refers to the
splendor of Israel's liturgical services. "Of God's
presence" and "Temple" are not in the original.

6 •But it's not as if God's word has failed. For not everyone who comes
7 from the line of Israel truly belongs to Israel, •and the fact that they're
descended from Abraham doesn't mean they're all his children; rather,
8 **Through Isaac shall your descendants be named.** •That means
that it isn't Abraham's children in the physical sense who are God's children, it's the children of the promise who are considered to be Abra-
9 ham's descendants. •Now this is the wording of the promise: **I'll come
at about this same time next year and Sarah will have a son.**
10 •Moreover, Rebecca too conceived children from one man, our father
11 Isaac, •and though they still hadn't been born and hadn't done anything
for good or ill, nevertheless so that God's intended selection might con-
12 tinue •based on God's call rather than on any deeds, she was told, **The
13 older will serve the younger,** •as it is written,

> **Jacob I loved,
> but Esau I hated.**

14 •What shall we say, then? Shall we accuse God of being unjust? By no
15 means! •For God said to Moses,

> **I'll show mercy to whomever I show mercy,
> and I'll be compassionate to whomever
> I'm compassionate to.**

16 •So then, the deciding factor is not a man's desire or his exertions, but
17 God's mercy. •For Scripture says to Pharaoh, **For this very reason
have I raised you up: to demonstrate My power through you
18 and to proclaim My name in every land.** •So then, He shows mercy to whomever He wishes, and hardens whomever He wishes.
19 •You'll say to me, then, "Then why does God still blame anyone? Who
20 can resist His will?" •But on the contrary, who are you, a man, to talk
back to God? **The clay can't say to the potter,** "Why did you make
21 me like this?" •Doesn't **the potter who forms the clay** have the right
to make from the same lump of clay one vessel for special occasions and
22 another for everyday use? •Perhaps God, wishing to demonstrate His
wrath and make known His might, has been extremely patient with the

---

9:6-8 "Not everyone who comes from the line of
Israel..." Membership in Israel is contingent upon
the mystery of God's call and is not an entitlement
based on physical descent.
9:7 Gn 21:12.   9:9 Gn 18:10.   9:12 Gn 25:23.
9:13 Ml 1:2-3. Paul's point is that the true Israelite
is not determined by physical descent. Esau, the

elder twin brother, was not to be the father of
God's people despite his physical descent. It is
God's will, rather, that the true Israelite is such by
faith in Jesus, the Messiah.
9:15 Ex 33:19.   9:17 Ex 9:16.
9:20 Is 29:16; 45:9.   9:21 Jr 18:6; Ws 15:7.

vessels of wrath which are ripe for destruction, •and did this in order to 23
make known the wealth of His glory for the vessels of mercy which He
had previously prepared for glory. •It is precisely such vessels of His mer- 24
cy that we are, called from among not only Jews but also Gentiles, •as 25
He also says in Hosea,

> Those who were not My people I will call My people,
>   and she who was not beloved I will call beloved;
> •And in the very place where they were told, 26
>   'You're not My people.'
>   they will be called sons of the Living God.

•Isaiah cries out over Israel, **Even though the number of the sons** 27
of Israel may be like the sand of the sea, only a remnant will
be saved; •for the Lord will act swiftly to carry out His sentence 28
upon the earth. •And just as Isaiah foretold, 29

> If the Lord of Hosts hadn't left us descendants,
>   we would have become like Sodom,
>   we would have become like Gomorrah.

•What shall we say, then? That Gentiles who weren't seeking right- 30
eousness have attained righteousness, a righteousness based on faith,
•whereas Israel, which sought a righteousness based upon law, has not 31
been able to fulfill that law. •Why? Because Israel relied upon their own 32
efforts, rather than on faith. They stumbled over the stumbling stone,
•as it is written, 33

> Behold I am laying in Zion a stumbling stone,
>   a rock that will cause men to fall,
>   but whoever believes in him will not be
>   put to shame.

10 •Brothers, my heart's desire and my prayer for them to God is 1
for their salvation. •I'll bear them witness — they're zealous for 2
God, but their zeal is based on a misconception, •for by failing to un- 3
derstand God's saving righteousness and trying to establish their own
righteousness they haven't submitted themselves to God's saving righteousness. •For Christ brings the Torah to an end, so that everyone who 4
has faith may be righteous.

9:25 Ho 2:23.   9:26 Ho 1:10.   9:27-2 Is 10:22-23.   9:29 Is 1:9.   9:33 Is 28:16.
10:1ff Having explained how God's plan is being   continues to pray for Israel's salvation, even as
fulfilled despite Israel's lack of faith, Paul is nev-   he indicts them for their obstinacy (Chapter 10).
ertheless still in anguish over his "kinsmen." He

A potter: ancient Roman relief. (Rm 9:21)

5 •This is what Moses wrote about the righteousness that comes from
6 observance of the Torah: **Whoever observes it will live by it.** •But
the righteousness which comes from faith says: "**Don't say** in your
heart, **Who will ascend into Heaven** (that is, to bring Christ down)?
7 •or **Who will descend into the Abyss** (that is, to bring Christ up
8 from the dead)?" •What does it say?

> **The word is near you,**
> **in your mouth and in your heart,**

9 (that is, the word of faith we preach). •Because if you profess with your
mouth that Jesus is Lord and believe in your heart that God raised him
10 from the dead, you'll be saved. •For with your heart you believe and
are restored to fellowship with God, and your profession through your
11 mouth leads you to salvation. •Scripture says, **No one who believes**
12 **in him will be put to shame.** •The same Lord is Lord of all and he
13 bestows riches upon everyone who calls upon him, •for **whoever calls**
upon the Lord's name will be saved.

10:5 Lv 18:5.   10:6-8 Dt 30:12-14.
10:11-13 The quotations from Is 28:16 and Jl 2:32 clearly refer to God, but Paul quite matter of fact-
ly applies them to Jesus.

•But how can they appeal to him if they haven't put their faith in [14] him? And how can they put their faith in him if they haven't heard of him? How will they hear unless someone preaches? •Who will preach [15] if no one is sent out? As it's written, **How beautiful are the feet of those who bring good news!** •But not all have responded to [16] the good news, for as Isaiah says, **Lord, who has believed what they've heard from us?** •So faith comes from what's heard, and [17] what's heard comes through Christ's word. •But I ask, haven't they [18] heard? They certainly have!

> **Their voice has gone out to every land,**
> **their words to the ends of the inhabited world.**

•But I ask, didn't Israel understand? First Moses says, [19]

> **I'll make** you **jealous of those who aren't a nation,**
> **I'll make** you **angry with a foolish nation.**

•Then Isaiah makes bold to say, [20]

> **I was found by those who weren't seeking Me,**
> **I showed Myself to those who didn't ask for Me**.

•But regarding Israel He says, **All day long I held out My hands to** [21] **a disobedient and obstinate people.**

11 •[p] I ask, then, has God rejected His people? By no means! After [1] all, I too am an Israelite, a descendant of Abraham from the tribe of Benjamin. •**God has not rejected His people** whom He knew be- [2] forehand. Don't you know what Scripture says in the story of Elijah? How Elijah appeals to God against Israel: •**Lord, they've killed Your** [3] **prophets, torn down Your altars, and I alone am left, and now they're trying to kill me!** •But what is the Divine answer to him? **I've** [4] **kept seven thousand men for** Myself, **who haven't bent a knee to Baal.** •That's how it is at the present time as well — there's a rem- [5] nant chosen by grace. •But if they were chosen by grace then they [6] weren't chosen because of their works, since then grace would no longer be grace. •What does this mean, then? Israel failed to find what it was [7]

[p] Ph 3:5.

10:15 Is 52:7.   10:16 Is 53:1.   10:18 Ps 19:4.   10:19 Dt 32:21.   10:20-21 Is 65:1-2.
11:1ff Paul now outlines the reasons for hoping that Israel will be saved after all. First of all, the remnant of Israel (personified in Paul himself) has not been rejected. Second, Israel's lack of faith has already contributed to God's plan, for it has been instrumental in bringing salvation to the Gentiles. Finally, God has not withdrawn His call; His offer of salvation is still open.
11:3 1 K 19:10, 14.   11:4 1 K 19:18.
11:8 Dt 29:4; Is 29:10.

8 looking for. The chosen *did* find it, but the rest became hardened, •as it is written,

> **God gave them a numbness of spirit,**
> **eyes that are unable to see**
> **and ears that are unable to hear,**
> **to this very day.**

9 •And David says,

> **Let their table become a snare** and a trap,
> **a stumbling block and retribution to them;**
10 > **•May their eyes be darkened so as not to see,**
> **and their back forever bent.**

11 •So I ask, have they stumbled so as to be lost forever? By no means! Rather, their offense brought salvation to the Gentiles, which will cause 12 them to become jealous. •Now if their offense brought riches to the world and their failure riches to the Gentiles, imagine how much more their full number will bring!

13 •Now I'm speaking to you Gentiles. As long as I'm an apostle to the 14 Gentiles I'll go on praising my ministry •in the hope of somehow arous-15 ing the jealousy of my kinsmen and saving some of them. •For if their rejection brought reconciliation to the world, would their acceptance be 16 anything less than life from the dead? •If the first fruits are holy, so is the whole lump of dough, and if the root is holy then so are the branches.

17 •But if some of the branches have been broken off and you, a wild olive, have been grafted into their place to share in the rich root of the 18 olive tree, •don't despise the branches. If you boast, remember that 19 you're not supporting the root — it's the root that supports you. •Per-haps you'll reply, "The branches were broken off so *I* could be grafted 20 in." •That's quite true. They were broken off because they didn't believe, and you are in their place because of your faith. Rather than being proud 21 you should stand in awe, •for if God didn't spare the natural branches 22 He won't spare you either. •Here you can see God's kindness as well as His severity. With those who have fallen He's severe, but with you God is kind as long as you remain in His kindness; otherwise you'll be 23 cut off too. •But even those who fell will be grafted back in, unless they persist in their unbelief, for God has the power to graft them back in 24 again. •For if you were cut off from what is by nature a wild olive tree

11:8 Dt 29:4; Is 29:10.
11:9-10 The rabbis equated "table" with "altar," raising the possibility that Paul is applying Ps 69:22-23 to the Jewish Temple worship and ritual.

and, contrary to nature, were grafted into a cultivated olive tree, imagine how much more readily the branches which belong to the olive tree by nature will be grafted back into their own tree.

•I want you to understand this mystery, my brothers, so you won't 25 become smug and consider yourselves to be wise. Israel has been partially hardened until the full number of the Gentiles enters, •and in this 26 way all Israel will be saved, as it is written,

> **The Deliverer will come from Zion**
> **and he'll banish ungodliness from Jacob,**
> **•This will be My covenant with them,** 27
> **when I take away their sins.**

•With respect to the good news God regards them as enemies for your 28 sake, but with respect to the choice God made they are beloved for the sake of their forefathers, •for God's gift and His calling are irrevocable. 29 •Just as you were once disobedient to God but have now received mercy 30 because of *their* disobedience, •so too have they been disobedient because 31 of the mercy you received so that they may also receive mercy [now]. •For 32 God has consigned all to disobedience so that He may show mercy to all.

•O the depth and richness of God's wisdom and knowledge! How un- 33 fathomable are His judgments, how inscrutable His ways!

> **•For who has known the mind of the Lord?** 34
> **Who has been His counsellor?**
> **•Who has been the giver** 35
> **and God the One Who returned the gift?**

•q For all things are from Him, through Him, and in Him. To Him be 36 glory forever, amen.

F. PRACTICAL COUNSELS FOR THE LIFE IN CHRIST

12 •So I beg you by God's mercy, my brothers, to offer your whole lives 1 as a living sacrifice which will be holy and pleasing to God — this is your spiritual worship. •Don't pattern yourselves after the ways of this world; 2 transform yourselves by the renewal of your minds, so you'll be able to discern what God's will is, and what is good, pleasing, and perfect.

q *1 Cor 8:6.*

11:26-27 Is 59:20-21 (Septuagint); Is 27:9 (Septuagint).
11:34 Is 40:13 (Septuagint).   11:35 Jb 41:11.

St. Paul by A. Testa.

3 •By the grace that's been given to me I say to each one of you, don't think more highly of yourselves than you ought to. Instead, aim for a sober and accurate appraisal, based on the measure of faith that God 4 has provided to each of you. •ʳ For just as we have many members in 5 one body and all the members don't have the same functions, •in the same way we, many as we are, are one body in Christ, and each one 6 of us is a part of the other. •ˢ We all have different gifts and should use them in accordance with the grace that has been given to us — prophe- 7 cy should be exercised in proportion to the faith received, •if we have the gift of serving it should be used in service, the teacher should use 8 his gift to teach, •whoever is gifted in exhorting should encourage, who- ever makes contributions should be generous, whoever gives aid should do so eagerly, whoever shows kindness should do so cheerfully.

9 •Love should be genuine; hate what's evil, hold fast to what's good. 10 •Be devoted to one another in brotherly love, try to outdo one another 11 in showing respect. •Don't hang back when zeal is called for — serve the 12 Lord, aglow with the Spirit. •Rejoice in your hope, bear up when you're

ʳ *1 Cor 12:12.*   ˢ *1 Cor 12:4-11.*

afflicted, persevere in prayer. •Contribute to the needs of the saints, strive 13
to be hospitable. •ᵗ Bless those who persecute you — bless, and don't 14
curse them. •Rejoice with those who rejoice, weep with those who weep. 15
•Have an equal regard for one another; associate with the lowly and don't 16
be proud. Don't have an exaggerated opinion of your own wisdom. •ᵘ 17
Don't pay back evil with evil, **set your sights on what all consider
to be honorable.** •If possible live in peace with everyone to the extent 18
that you're able to. •Don't take revenge, my beloved — leave that to God's 19
wrath, for it is written, **Vengeance is Mine, *I* shall repay,** says the
Lord. •Instead, **if your enemy is hungry, feed him, if he's thirsty,** 20
**give him to drink, for by doing this you'll be heaping burning
coals on his head.** •Don't let evil defeat you; instead, overcome evil 21
with good.

13 •Every person should be subject to the governing authorities. For 1
all authority comes from God and the existing authorities have
been appointed by God. •Therefore, whoever resists authority resists 2
God's order, and those who resist will bring judgment upon themselves.
•For only wicked conduct need fear the rulers, not good conduct. Do 3
you want to be free from fear of whoever is in authority? Then do what's
good and you'll be praised by him, •because he's God's servant for your 4
good. But if you do what's evil you should fear, for not without reason
does the one in authority wield the sword. For he's God's servant, the
avenger who brings wrath to the evildoer. •Therefore it's necessary to 5
submit not only because of God's wrath but also for the sake of conscience. •ᵛ This is why you pay taxes, for the authorities are God's ser- 6
vants, busily engaged at this very thing. •Pay everyone what you owe 7
— taxes to the tax collectors, customs duties to the customs officials; respect those to whom it's due, honor those to whom honor is due.

•ʷ See that you owe nothing, except for your obligation to love one 8
another, for whoever loves his neighbor has fulfilled the Torah. •For **You** 9
**shall not commit adultery, you shall not murder, you shall not
steal, you shall not covet** and any other commandments can be
summed up in one sentence — **You shall love your neighbor as
yourself.** •Love does no harm to a neighbor, so love is the fullness of 10
the Torah.

•Do this, because you know what time it is, you know it's already time 11
for you to rise from your sleep, for now your salvation is nearer than when
you first believed. •The night is almost over, and the day is near. Be done 12

12:17 Pr 3:4.   12:19 Dt 32:35.   12:20 Pr 25:21-22 (Septuagint).   13:9 Ex 20:13-15; Dt 5:17-19.

with the deeds of darkness and clothe yourselves with the weapons of
13 light. •Let us conduct ourselves decently as we would during the day, not
in carousing and drunkenness, not in promiscuity and indecent behavior,
14 not in strife and envy. •Instead, clothe yourselves with the Lord Jesus
Christ and give no thought to doing what the flesh desires.

1 **14**•x Welcome the person whose faith is weak, and don't enter in-
2 to quarrels over your differing opinions. •One person may believe
it's permissible to eat everything, while another whose faith is weak will
3 eat only vegetables. •The person who eats everything shouldn't despise
the one who doesn't, and the person who doesn't eat everything should-
4 n't condemn the one who does, for God has accepted him. •Who are
you to judge someone else's servant? He stands or falls before his own
master, and he will stand, because the Lord is able to make him stand.
5 •One person considers a certain day to be more important than another, while another considers every day to be the same. Let everyone make
6 up their own minds. •The person who observes a certain day as special
is thinking of the Lord, and the person who eats everything eats with
the Lord in mind, because he gives thanks to God for this; and whoev-
7 er doesn't eat does so for the Lord and also gives thanks to God. •We
8 none of us live for ourselves and we none of us die for ourselves, •for
if we live we live for the Lord and if we die we die for the Lord. And so
9 whether we live or whether we die we belong to the Lord. •This is why
Christ died and came to life — so he'd be Lord of both the dead and
10 the living. •y Why do you condemn your brother? Why do you despise
11 your brother? After all, we'll all stand before God's judgment seat, •for
it is written,

**As I live, says the Lord, every knee shall bend to me,
and every tongue shall give praise to God.**

12 •So then each of us will render an account of ourselves to God.
13 •Therefore, let's not condemn each other any longer; instead, resolve
14 that you'll do nothing that would cause a brother to stumble or fall. •I
know and am certain in the Lord Jesus that nothing is in itself unclean,
15 but if someone thinks that it is unclean then it's unclean for him. •If your
brother is distressed by what you eat then your conduct is no longer based
on love. Don't allow what you eat to cause the downfall of someone for
16,17 whom Christ died. •So don't let our good be blasphemed. •After all, the
Kingdom of God doesn't consist of eating and drinking — it consists of

14:11 Is 42:53 (Septuagint).

righteousness, peace, and joy in the Holy Spirit. •Whoever serves God ₁₈ in this way will be acceptable to God and respected by men. •So then ₁₉ let's strive for what leads to peace and edification for one another; •don't ₂₀ destroy God's work for the sake of food. All foods are indeed clean, but it's evil if the person eating it considers it to be an offense. •It's good to ₂₁ avoid eating meat, drinking wine, or doing anything else that would cause your brother to stumble. •Keep what you believe in this matter between ₂₂ yourself and God. Blessed is he who can make his decision with a clear conscience. •But the person who is uncertain is condemned if he eats, ₂₃ because his decision isn't based on faith. Whatever doesn't come from faith is sin.

15 •We who are strong ought to bear with the failings of the weak ₁ and should not seek to please ourselves. •Each of us should try ₂ to please our neighbor for their own good and for their edification. •Christ didn't try to please himself; instead, as it is written, **The re-** ₃ **proaches of those who reproached You fell upon me.** •For what- ₄ ever was written in the past was written for our instruction, so that by our steadfastness and the encouragement of the Scriptures we might have hope. •May God, the source of steadfastness and encouragement, ₅ grant that you may live in harmony with one another in accordance with Christ Jesus, •so that with one mind and one mouth you may glorify ₆ the God and Father of our Lord Jesus Christ.

•Therefore, accept one another as Christ has accepted you, for the ₇ glory of God. •For I tell you that Christ became a servant for the cir- ₈ cumcised in order to show that God is truthful and to confirm the promises He made to the patriarchs, •and so that the Gentiles might glorify ₉ God for His mercy, as it is written,

> **Therefore I'll praise you among the Gentiles,**
> **Your name will I praise.**

•And again it says, ₁₀

> **Rejoice with His people, you Gentiles!**

•And again, ₁₁

> **Praise the Lord, all you Gentiles,**
> **let all the peoples praise Him.**

•And again Isaiah says, ₁₂

15:3 Ps 69:9.   15:9 2 S 22:50; Ps 18:99.   15:10 Dt 32:43.   15:11 Ps 117:1.

Plaque showing the beheading of St. Paul,
in the Tre Fontane church in Rome.

The root of Jesse shall come,
who will rise to rule the Gentiles,
and the Gentiles will hope in him.

13 •May God, the source of hope, fill you with all joy and peace through your belief in Him, so that you'll overflow with hope by the power of the Holy Spirit.

G. PAUL APPEALS FOR THE ROMANS' AID IN HIS PLANS FOR FUTURE EVANGELIZATION

14 •My brothers, I myself am fully satisfied that you yourselves are full of goodness, filled with every sort of knowledge, and able to instruct one 15 another. •Still, on some points I've written to you rather boldly as a re-16 minder, because God has given me the grace •to be a minister of Christ Jesus to the Gentiles and to perform a priestly service for God's good

15:12 Is 11:10.
15:16 Paul portrays himself as a priest, and the Gentiles as the offering being presented to God.

ROMANS

news, so that the offering of the Gentiles may be acceptable to God and sanctified by the Holy Spirit. •Therefore it is in Christ Jesus that I have 17 reason to boast of my work for God, •for I don't dare speak of anything 18 except what Christ has done through me to win the obedience of the Gentiles by word and deed, •by the power of signs and wonders, and 19 by the power of the Holy Spirit. As a result, all the way around from Jerusalem to Illyricum I've completed the proclamation of God's good news. •And so my ambition is to proclaim the good news where Christ's 20 name has never been heard so that I won't be building on someone else's foundations, •but as it is written, 21

**Those who were never told of Him shall see,
and those who haven't heard will understand.**

•This is why I've been prevented from coming to you so many times, 22 •but now since I no longer have any opportunities in these regions and 23 since for many years I've had a great desire to come to see you, •while 24 I'm on my way to Spain I hope to pass through and see you and be helped on my way by you, after I've enjoyed being with you for a while. •ᶻ Right now, however, I'm on my way to Jerusalem to help the saints, 25 •for Macedonia and Achaia have been pleased to make a contribution 26 to the poor among the saints in Jerusalem. •ᵃ They were pleased to do 27 it, and in fact they're indebted to the saints, for if the Gentiles have come to share in their spiritual blessings they have an obligation to help the saints with their material blessings. •So when I've finished this and 28 have safely turned this sum over to them, I'll go to Spain by way of you, •and I know that when I come to you I'll come in the fullness of 29 Christ's blessing.

•I beg you, my brothers, by our Lord Jesus Christ and the love of the 30 Spirit, to join me in my struggle by praying to God for me •that I may 31 be delivered from the unbelievers in Judea and that my service in Jerusalem may be acceptable to the saints •so that, God willing, I'll come 32 to you full of joy and will find rest with you. •May God Who gives peace 33 be with you all, amen.

ᶻ *1 Cor 16:1-4.* ᵃ *1 Cor 9:11.*

15:21 Is 52:15.

H. COMMENDATION OF PHOEBE
AND CLOSING GREETINGS

1,2 **16** •I commend to you our sister, Phoebe, who is a minister in the church at Cenchreae. •Receive her in the Lord in a manner worthy of the saints and help her with anything she may need from you, for she has been a benefactor to many people, including myself.

3,4 •Greet Prisca and Aquila, my co-workers in Christ Jesus. •They risked their own necks to save my life, and not only I but also the Gen-
5 tile churches thank them. •Also greet the church at their house. Greet
6 my beloved Epaenetus who is the first fruits of Asia for Christ. •Greet
7 Mary, who has worked so hard for you. •Greet Andronicus and Junias, my kinsmen and fellow prisoners; they are prominent among the
8 apostles and were in Christ before me. •Greet Ampliatus, my beloved
9 in the Lord. • Greet Urbanus, our co-worker in Christ, and my beloved
10 Stachys. •Greet Apelles, who is tried and true in the Lord. Greet those
11 who belong to Aristobulus' family. •Greet my kinsman Herodion. Greet
12 those in Narcissus' family who are in the Lord. •Greet Tryphaena and Tryphosa, laborers in the Lord. Greet the beloved Persis, who has
13 worked so hard in the Lord. •[b] Greet Rufus, chosen in the Lord, and
14 his mother, who is also my mother. •Greet Asyncritus, Phlegon, Her-
15 mes, Patrobas, Hermas, and the brothers who are with them. •Greet Philologus, Julia, Nereus, and his sister, as well as Olympas and all the
16 saints who are with them. •Greet one another with a holy kiss. All Christ's churches greet you.

17 •My brothers, I urge you to watch out for those who cause dissension and raise obstacles which are contrary to what you were taught. Shun
18 them, •for such persons are serving their own appetites instead of our Lord Christ, and by smooth speech and flattery they deceive the unsus-
19 pecting. •Word of your obedience has reached everyone and so I rejoice for you, but I want you to be wise regarding what's good and innocent
20 regarding what's evil. •Then God Who gives peace will quickly smash Satan beneath your feet. The grace of our Lord Jesus be with you.

21 •[c] My co-worker Timothy greets you, as do Lucius, Jason and Sosi-
22 pater, my kinsmen. •Tertius, the writer of this letter, greets you in the Lord.
23 •[d] My host Gaius greets you, along with the whole church at his house.
24 Erastus, the city treasurer, greets you, as does our brother Quartus. [•]

[b] Mk 15:21.   [c] Ac 16:1.   [d] Ac 19:29; 1 Cor 1:14; 2 Tm 4:20.

16:24 Some textual witnesses insert the following verse: "The grace of our Lord Jesus Christ be with you all. Amen."

ROMANS

I. PRAISE OF GOD'S GLORY

•To Him Who is able to strengthen you according to my gospel and 25
the proclamation of Jesus Christ, according to the revelation of the mystery which was kept secret for long ages •but is now revealed through 26
the writing of the Prophets and made known by order of the eternal God
to bring the obedience of faith to all nations — •to the God Who alone 27
is wise be glory forever through Jesus Christ, amen.

16:25-27 While the best manuscript tradition places this concluding doxology here, some manuscripts place it at the end of Ch. 14 or 15. A few manuscripts omit it entirely.

THE FIRST LETTER
TO THE

CORINTHIANS

Introduction to the
First Letter to the Corinthians

After leaving Thessalonica Paul travelled south through Greece, eventually winding up in Corinth. In that bustling commercial center and seaport he found fertile ground for the good news, and the church that he established there was as alive as the city itself. As reported in Acts (the portions relevant to the Corinthian correspondence are 18:1-18, 24-28), Paul followed his usual procedure of first preaching in the local synagogue and then turning to the Gentiles after encountering resistance among the Jews.

After leaving Corinth and returning to Antioch Paul set out once again. This time he spent about three years in the Ephesus area, and it was toward the end of his stay in Ephesus that he wrote the present letter, in 55 or 56 A.D. Apparently he wrote it partially in response to a letter the Corinthians had sent him requesting guidance and partially as a result of information he had received from members of "Chloe's household." This information had been very troubling, for it painted a picture of a church torn by internal divisions, at odds over basic principles governing behavior at the liturgy, and confused about everyday ethical questions.

The resulting correspondence is fascinating both for the detailed information it gives concerning the inner life of one of the earliest Christian communities as well as for what it tells about Paul himself. While lacking the sustained power of Romans, perhaps, 1 Corinthians covers a wide range of issues of continuing importance — liturgical, ethical, spiritual, and doctrinal.

A. GREETING

1 2 **1** •Paul, called by the will of God to be an apostle of Christ Jesus, and our brother Sosthenes, •to the church of God in Corinth, to those who have been sanctified in Christ Jesus, who are called to be saints, with all those people everywhere who call upon the name of our Lord 3 Jesus Christ — their Lord and ours — •may the grace and peace of God our Father and the Lord Jesus Christ be with you.

B. THANKSGIVING

4 •I constantly give thanks to God for you because of the grace God 5 has given you in Christ Jesus. •In him you have been enriched in every 6 way, in speech and in knowledge, •for our testimony about Christ has 7 become established in you to such an extent •that there's no grace you 8 lack, as you await the revelation of our Lord Jesus Christ •who will sustain you until the end, so that you'll be blameless on the day of our Lord 9 Jesus Christ. •God is faithful, and it was God Who called you to the fellowship of His Son, our Lord Jesus Christ.

C. PAUL ADDRESSES PROBLEMS WITHIN THE CORINTHIAN CHURCH

Divisions and factions

10 •I beg you, brothers, in the name of our Lord Jesus Christ, to all speak as one. Let there be no divisions among you — be united in thought 11 and purpose. •For some members of Chloe's household have informed 12 me, brothers, that there's quarreling among you. •[a] Here's what I mean:

---

[a] Ac 18:24-28.   [b] Ac 18:8; 19:29; Rm 16:23   [a] Ac 18:24-28.

1:12 "Kephas." This is the Aramaic for "Peter." It is known from tradition that Peter travelled widely and so it is entirely possible that he may have stayed for a time in Corinth. On the other hand, a faction among the Corinthians may have used Peter's name simply because of his prominence.

each of you says, "I follow Paul," "I follow Apollos," "I follow Kephas," or "I follow Christ." •Can Christ be divided? Was Paul crucified for you, 13 or were you baptized in Paul's name? •[b] I thank God that I baptized none 14 of you except Crispus and Gaius, •so no one can say they were bap- 15 tized in my name. •I baptized Stephanas' household, too; other than that 16 I know of no one else I baptized. •Christ didn't send me to baptize, he 17 sent me to proclaim the good news, but not with words of "wisdom," lest Christ's cross be deprived of its power.

•For the message of the cross is foolishness to those who are on their 18 way to destruction, but for those who are being saved — for us — it's the power of God. •For it's written, 19

**I'll destroy the wisdom of the wise,
and the insights of the intelligent I'll reject.**

•Where is the wise man? Where is the scribe? Where is the skilled 20 debater of this age? Hasn't God turned the wisdom of this world to fool- ishness? •For since, in God's wisdom, the world was unable to come to 21 knowledge of God with its own wisdom, God chose through the fool- ishness of our proclamation to save those who believe. •Jews ask for 22 signs and Greeks look for wisdom, •but we·proclaim Christ crucified — 23 a stumbling block for Jews and foolishness to Greeks, •but for those who 24 have been chosen, both Jew and Greek alike, Christ the power of God and the wisdom of God, •for God's foolishness is wiser than human wis- 25 dom, and God's weakness is stronger than human strength.

•For consider the fact that you were called. Not many of you were 26 wise according to the flesh, nor powerful or well-born, •but God chose 27 the foolish things of the world to shame those who are wise, the weak of the world to shame the strong; •God chose the base-born and con- 28 temptible of the world, things that are nothing, to shame what is, •so 29 that the flesh would have nothing to boast of before God. •Through God 30 you are in Christ Jesus, and through God Christ became our wisdom, righteousness, sanctification, and redemption, •so that as it is written, 31 **Whoever boasts, let him boast in the Lord.**

[b] Ac 18:8; 19:29; Rm 16:23.

1:17 The word "wisdom" had both positive and negative connotations in Judaism, but Paul is us- ing it here in its negative sense. As the letter pro- gresses it becomes clear that some of the Corinthians had developed an inordinate pride in their speaking and reasoning ability. Paul recalls them to that humility which is inseparable from the true spirit of Christ and is itself "wisdom." The Corinthians had forgotten that their call was based on God's freely given grace which flew in the face of human "wisdom" and their own un- worthiness. Paul constantly returns to this ironic contrast between the true wisdom which is re- garded as foolishness and the foolishness which is acclaimed as wisdom.
1:19 Is 29:14 (Septuagint).   1:31 Jr 9:24.

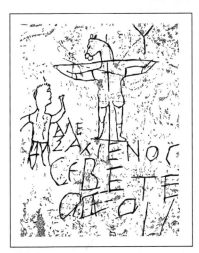

*Graffito discovered on the Palatine in Rome,
dating back to the 3rd century A.D. (1 Cor 1:23)*

2 ¹ •When I came to you, brothers, I didn't proclaim the mystery of God ² to you in high-sounding language or with a display of wisdom. •I had made up my mind to know nothing while I was among you except Je- ³ sus Christ, and the fact that he was crucified. •I came to you in weak- ⁴ ness, fear, and trembling, •and my message and proclamation were de- livered not with plausible words of "wisdom" but with a demonstration ⁵ of the Spirit and of power, •so that your faith would be based on the power of God rather than on human wisdom.

⁶ •Yet among the mature we do preach wisdom, but a wisdom which is not of this age nor of the rulers of this age, who are losing their pow- ⁷ er. •Instead we preach *God's* wisdom, a wisdom which is secret and hid- ⁸ den and which God ordained before the ages for our glory. •None of

2:1 The "mystery of God" which Paul proclaimed was God's saving righteousness, His plan for bringing salvation to both Jews and Gentiles.
2:6-3:3 Paul introduces a fundamental distinction. The Christian is called to live according to God's Spirit, which has been given to us so we can understand God's will for us. To live in the Spirit is to be oriented toward God. In their petty, prideful factionalism, however, the Corinthians have shown themselves to be still of the "flesh," understood not as matter but as a basic orienta- tion which relies upon human abilities ("wisdom")

and ignores God, which is to say, True Wisdom. Thus, those who are "of the flesh" are spiritually blind, unable to discern wisely.
2:8 The "rulers of this age" are almost certainly to be understood as angelic powers, here seen as hostile to God's saving plan. By leading their subjects, the human race, to crucify the Lord they unwittingly brought God's plan to fruition and showed their inability to fathom God's wisdom. In turn, God's plan will bring about their downfall and break their power over the human race. Cf. also below at 6:3.

the rulers of this age understood this, for if they *had* they never would have crucified the Lord of glory. •But as it is written, 9

What eye has not seen nor ear heard,
what human heart has not conceived,
What God has prepared for those who love Him,

•this God has revealed to us through His Spirit, for the Spirit is able 10 to search out everything, even the depths of God's intentions. •For 11 who can know what someone else intends? Surely only that person's own spirit knows! So, too, no one knows what God intends except the Spirit of God. •But the Spirit we have received is not the spirit of 12 this world but the Spirit that comes from God and enables us to know what it is that God has freely bestowed upon us. •And we proclaim 13 this in words taught by the Spirit rather than by human wisdom, words which explain spiritual matters to those who have the Spirit. •The un- 14 spiritual man is unable to accept what comes from the Spirit of God, since for him it's foolishness. He's unable to understand such matters because they can be evaluated only spiritually. •The spiritual man, on 15 the other hand, *is* able to evaluate all such matters and is subject to no one else's judgment.

•**For who knows the mind of God,** 16
    who can advise Him?

But we have the mind of Christ.

3 •I wasn't able to speak to you, brothers, as I would to the spiritual- 1 ly mature. Instead, I spoke to you as to children of this world, infants in Christ. •[c] I gave you milk to drink, because you were not yet able to 2 eat solid food. The fact is, you're *still* not able to eat solid food, •you 3 *still* belong to this world. For when there's jealousy and strife among you, don't you show that you belong to this world? Aren't you behaving in accordance with human standards? •When someone says, "I'm a 4 follower of Paul," while someone else says, "I follow Apollos," aren't you showing yourselves to be mere men? •After all, what is Apollos? 5 What is Paul? We're only the ministers through whom you came to believe — we each simply performed the task assigned to us by the Lord. •I planted, Apollos watered, but it was God Who caused the growth. 6 •Thus, neither the one who planted nor the one who watered amounts 7

[c] *Heb 5:12-13.*

2:9 Is 64:4; 52:15.   2:16 Is 40:13 (Septuagint).

8 to anything — only God Who caused the growth is of importance. •The one who plants and the one who waters are both equal, and each will 9 receive a reward corresponding to their labor. •We are God's co-workers. You are God's field, you are God's building.

10 •In accordance with the grace God has given me I laid the foundation the way a wise master builder would, while another is building upon those foundations. But each builder must take care how he proceeds. 11 •No one can lay any other foundation than the one which was laid, 12 which is Jesus Christ. •You can build on the foundation with gold, sil-13 ver, precious stones, wood, hay, or straw, •but the nature of each person's work will be made known, for it will be revealed on the day of the Lord. It will be revealed with fire, for the fire will show what sort 14 of work each has done. •If anyone's work lasts, he'll receive a reward; 15 •if anyone's work is burned up, he'll be punished — he himself will be 16 saved, but it will be through fire. •Don't you know that you're the Tem-17 ple of God, and that the Spirit of God dwells within you? •If anyone destroys God's Temple, God will destroy him, for God's Temple is holy, and you are that Temple!

18 •Don't deceive yourselves! If any of you think you're wise in this age, 19 become foolish, so you'll be *truly* wise. •The wisdom of this world is foolishness to God, for it is written,

He catches the wise in their cunning,

20 •and again,

The Lord knows the thoughts of the wise,
He knows that they're futile.

21 •So no one should put their pride in mere men — everything 22 is yours. •Paul, Apollos, Kephas, the world, life, death, the pres-23 ent, the future — it's all yours, •but you belong to Christ, and Christ belongs to God.

3:13-15 "The day of the Lord" will introduce the final judgment. "Fire" is seen not only as a means of punishment and destruction but also as having power to cleanse the sinner. Here too we see Paul's fundamental optimism — he almost always speaks of saving the sinner rather than of punishing the sinner in a vindictive spirit.

3:16 Paul normally uses the image of the Church as the Temple only when referring to his ministry. His preferred image for the Church is the Body of Christ.
3:19 Jb 5:13.
3:20 Ps 94:11.

A reminder of Paul's authority

4 •This is how you should regard us — as Christ's servants and stew- ₁ ards of God's mysteries. •Naturally, stewards must be examined and ₂ be shown to have been faithful. •For me it's of no importance if I'm ₃ judged by you or by some human tribunal — I don't even judge myself. •I'm not aware of anything against me, but that doesn't mean I'm ac- ₄ quitted, because the Lord is the one who will judge me. •So don't pass ₅ judgment before the proper time, before the Lord comes and brings to light what's hidden in darkness and reveals the motives of our hearts. Then God will commend each of us. •I've applied all this to myself and ₆ Apollos for your sake, brothers, so that through us you'll learn what "Don't go beyond what's written" means, and won't arrogantly despise one person in favor of another. •For who says you're so important? What ₇ do you have that you didn't receive? And if you received it, why do you boast as if it were your own? •Already you've become self-satisfied, al- ₈ ready you think you're rich! You've become kings and left us behind! I wish you *had* become kings, so we could reign with you! •For it seems ₉ to me that God has made us apostles the lowliest of all, as if we were condemned to death, because we've become a spectacle to the world, both to angels and to men. •We are fools for Christ, while you are wise ₁₀ in Christ; we are weak, but you are strong; you are honored, while we are despised. •Right up to the present moment we suffer hunger and ₁₁ thirst, we're poorly clothed and roughly treated, we wander about with- out a home. •ᵉ We labor and work with our own hands. When we're ₁₂ cursed we give blessings in return, when we're persecuted we endure it, •when we're reviled we respond cheerfully; we've become the world's ₁₃ garbage heap, the scum of the earth right up to the present.

•I'm not writing this to shame you, but to admonish you as my beloved ₁₄ children. •For though you may have innumerable guides in Christ, you ₁₅ don't have numerous fathers — *I* was the one who begot you in Christ Jesus through the good news. •So I urge you to become imitators of ₁₆ me. •That's why I sent Timothy to you — he's my beloved and faithful ₁₇ child in the Lord and will remind you of the way I walk in Christ, which is what I teach everywhere, in every church. •Some of you have become ₁₈ arrogant, as if I weren't coming to you, •but I'll come to you quickly if ₁₉ the Lord is willing and I'll find out what sort of power these arrogant people have, not just how well they speak. •For the Kingdom of God is ₂₀ not a matter of words but of power! •What do you want? Should I come ₂₁ to you with the rod, or in a spirit of love and gentleness?

ᵉ *Ac 18:3.*

Corinth. The rostrum of the orators, 1st century A.D.

Dealing with immorality in the community

1 5 •It's actually reported that there is fornication among you, fornication of a kind that's unheard of even among the Gentiles — a man
2 is living with his father's wife! •But you're puffed up with pride! Should-
n't you be grieving, instead? The perpetrator of this deed should be re-
3 moved from among you! •For though I'm absent in body I'm present in
spirit, and I've already passed judgment on the man who did this as if I
4 *were* present, •in the name of the Lord Jesus. When you've assembled
5 and my spirit is present with the power of our Lord Jesus, •you are to
hand that man over to Satan for the destruction of the flesh, so his spir-

[f] *Gal 5:9.*

5:1 Dt 22:30. In rabbinical theology "fornication" was often used in a technical sense to refer to unlawful marriages within forbidden degrees of consanguinity.
5:2 "Puffed up with pride." Perhaps the Corinthians felt they were exhibiting true Christian freedom.
5:6-8 Paul here presents in a very compact form his vision of the Christian life as a prolonged celebration of the Passover festival. Christ, the New Paschal Lamb, has been sacrificed; the Church, the new Israel, is embarked upon a New Exodus from slavery to sin and spiritual death to freedom and life; like the Old Israel, Christians must discard the old leavening of wickedness and celebrate the New Passover with the unleavened bread of moral renewal. This Passover/Exodus imagery will reappear twice again in the letter.

it may be saved on the day of the Lord. •ᶠ You have nothing to boast 6
about! Don't you know that "A little yeast leavens all the dough"? •Get 7
rid of the old yeast so you'll be a new batch of dough, as indeed you *are*
unleavened. Christ our Paschal Lamb has been sacrificed, •so let's cel- 8
ebrate the feast not with the old yeast, the yeast of wickedness and evil,
but with the unleavened bread of sincerity and truth.

•In the letter I wrote to you I warned you not to associate with the im- 9
moral, •not meaning, of course, the immoral of this world — the greedy, 10
thieves, idolaters — because then you'd have to leave this world! •What 11
I meant was that, if someone who bears the name "brother" is immoral,
greedy, idolatrous, abusive, a drunkard, or a robber, don't associate with
them, don't even *eat* with them. •What business is it of mine to judge 12
outsiders? Isn't it those within the church whom you're to judge? •God 13
will judge outsiders. **Remove the evil person from among you!**

6 •Do any of you dare bring your disputes with one another before the 1
unrighteous for a decision, instead of bringing the matter before the
saints? •Don't you know that the saints will judge the world? And if you're 2
the ones who will judge the world, are you incapable of judging minor
matters? •Don't you know that we'll be passing judgment on angels? And 3
here we're speaking of everyday affairs! •So then, if you have ordinary 4
lawsuits of this sort, why bring them before those who have no standing
in the church? •I say this to shame you. Isn't there even one person 5
among you wise enough to settle disputes between brothers? •But instead 6
brothers sue brothers, and before unbelievers! •Actually, having lawsuits 7
against one another is already a defeat for you; wouldn't it be better to
submit to the injustice? Wouldn't it be better to let yourselves be cheated? •Instead, you're the ones who wrong and cheat others, even broth- 8
ers! •Don't you know that the unjust will not inherit the Kingdom of God? 9
Make no mistake, neither fornicators, nor idolaters, nor adulterers, nor
perverts, nor sodomites, •nor thieves, nor the greedy, nor drunkards, nor 10
those who slander others, nor robbers will inherit the Kingdom of God.
•And that's what some of you were. But you were washed clean, you 11
were sanctified, you were admitted to fellowship with God in the name
of the Lord Jesus Christ and by the Spirit of our God.

5:13 Dt 17:7 (Septuagint).
6:2-3 In Jewish mythology of that time each nation was thought to have a ruling angel. Paul says
that Christians will judge those angels.
6:12-20 Paul returns here to the topic of sexual immorality. Apparently some in the community were
prepared to extend their freedom in dietary matters
to sexual ethics as well, as if it were simply a matter of satisfying a bodily appetite such as hunger.
Paul's reply rejects any division of man into distinct
spheres of body and spirit, and so too the corollary
that sins of the flesh don't affect the spirit.

12 •"Everything is permissible for me," but not everything is beneficial. "Everything is permissible for me," but I won't be enslaved by anything.
13 •"Food is for the stomach, and the stomach is for food," but God will do away with both. The body, on the other hand, is not for fornication
14 — it's for the Lord, and the Lord is for the body. •Now God raised the
15 Lord, and He'll raise us, too, through His power. •Don't you know that your bodies are parts of Christ's body? Shall I take parts of Christ's body,
16 then, and make them part of a prostitute's body? God forbid! •Don't you know that whoever joins himself with a prostitute becomes one body
17 with her? For Scripture says, **The two shall become one flesh.** •But
18 whoever joins himself to the Lord becomes one spirit with him. •Flee fornication! Every other sin you commit remains outside your body, but
19 whoever is guilty of fornication sins against his own body. •[g] Or don't you know that your bodies are Temples of the Holy Spirit within you, Who comes to you from God, and that you don't belong to yourselves?
20 •You were bought for a price, so glorify God in your bodies!

D. PAUL ANSWERS THE CORINTHIANS' QUESTIONS REGARDING MARRIAGE

1 7 •Regarding the things you wrote about — it's good for a man not
2   to touch a woman, •but to prevent immorality every man should have
3 his own wife, and every woman her own husband. •The man should ful-
4 fill his duties to his wife, and likewise the woman for her husband. •The woman has no authority over her body — her husband does. Likewise,
5 however, the man has no authority over his body — his wife does. •Don't deny one another, except perhaps for a short time by mutual agreement in order to devote yourselves to prayer, and then come together again
6 lest Satan use your lack of self-control to tempt you. •But I say this as
7 a concession; it's not a command. •I wish everyone were like myself, but all have their own gift from God, one of one sort, another of a dif-ferent kind.
8   •To those who are unmarried and to widows I say, it's good for them
9 to remain as I do. •But if they're unable to exercise self-control they

---

[f] Gal 5:9.   [h] Mt 5:32; 19:9; Mk 10:11-12; Lk 16:18.

6:16 Gn 2:24.
7:1ff At the same time that some members of the Corinthian church were indulging in gross im-morality and advocating libertinism, others were urging an exaggerated asceticism, especially in the

context of marriage. Paul opposes both extremes and exhibits his usual firm common sense.
7:9 "Than to burn." This phrase probably means "to burn with passion," but it may possibly mean to fall into sin and be condemned to Hell.

should marry, for it's better to marry than to burn. •[h] Those who are 10
married, I command you — not I, but the Lord — a wife shall not separate from her husband, •but if she does separate, she must either re- 11
main unmarried or be reconciled with her husband, nor should a husband leave his wife. •As for the rest, I say — not the Lord — if any broth- 12
er has a non-believing wife who agrees to live with him, he may not leave
her. •And if any wife has a non-believing husband who agrees to live 13
with her, *she* may not leave *him*. •For a non-believing husband is sanc- 14
tified by his wife, and a non-believing wife is sanctified by her husband.
Otherwise, your children would be unclean, but we know that they're
holy. •If a non-believer separates, however, let him go — a brother or 15
sister isn't bound in such cases, for God has called you to peace. •Does 16
a wife know for sure that she'll be able to save her husband? Does a
husband know that he'll be able to save his wife?

•The main point is the Lord assigned some role to each of you; each 17
of you should therefore continue to live as you were when God called
you — this is the instruction I give in all the churches. •Were you cir- 18
cumcised when you were called? Then don't try to remove the marks of
circumcision. Were you uncircumcised when you were called? Then don't
have yourself circumcised. •Neither circumcision nor uncircumcision is of 19
any importance; what's important is to obey God's commandments.
•Each of you should remain in the state you were in when you were called. 20
•Were you a slave when you were called? Don't worry about it, but if you 21
get the chance to become free, take advantage of it. •For any slave who 22
was called in the Lord is a freedman of the Lord. Likewise, whoever was
free when they were called is a slave of Christ. •You were bought for a 23
price, so don't become slaves of men. •Each of you, brothers, should re- 24
main before God in the same state in which you were called.

•Regarding girls who are betrothed — I have no command from the 25
Lord, but I'll give you my opinion as one who through the Lord's mercy is trustworthy. •In view of the present distress this is what I think — 26
it's best to remain as you are. •Do you have a wife? Then don't seek to 27
be free of your obligations. Are you without a wife? Then don't go looking for a wife. •But if you *do* marry, you've committed no sin. Never- 28
theless, people who marry will be afflicted with worldly concerns, and
I'd prefer to spare you that. •This is what I'm saying, brothers. Time is 29
short; from now on those who have wives should live as if they didn't,
•those who are weeping as if they weren't weeping, those who are re- 30
joicing as if they weren't rejoicing, those who are buying as if they had
nothing, •and those who make use of the world as if they weren't mak- 31
ing full use of it, for the world as we know it is passing away. •I want 32

you to be free from anxiety. The unmarried man concerns himself with
33 the Lord's affairs, with how to please the Lord, •while the married man
34 concerns himself with worldly affairs — how to please his wife — •and
is divided. Likewise, girls who are betrothed and unmarried women are
concerned with the Lord's affairs — how to be holy in body and spirit
— while a married woman is concerned with affairs of the world, such
35 as how to please her husband. •I'm saying this for your own good, not
simply to rein you in — I want you to preserve good order so you'll be
able to devote yourselves to the Lord without distractions.

36   •If anyone thinks he's behaving improperly toward his betrothed, if
his passions are strong and it must be so, he should do what he wishes
37 — he's committing no sin; they should get married. •But whoever has
his heart firmly set, who is under no compulsion but has control over
his desires and has decided in his heart to have her remain a virgin, he
38 does well. •And so the one who marries his betrothed does well, and
the one who doesn't marry does better.

39   •A woman is bound as long as her husband is alive, but if her husband dies she's free to marry whoever she wishes to, as long as he's in
40 the Lord. •But in my opinion she'll be happier if she remains as she is,
and I think that I too am in accord with God's Spirit.

A couple depicted on a Roman tomb (1st century A.D.). (1 Cor 7:2-3)

Regarding the eating of food that had been previously offered to idols

8 •Regarding meat that was offered to idols — we know that "we all ₁ have knowledge." Knowledge leads to arrogance, but love builds up. •Anyone who thinks he knows something still doesn't know as he ought ₂ to know, •but whoever loves God is known by God. •So concerning meat ₃,₄ that was offered to idols, we know that "there are no idols in the world" and that "there is no God but One." •For even if there are so called gods ₅ in heaven or on earth, as indeed there are many so-called "gods" and "lords," •there is still only one God for us, the Father from Whom every- ₆ thing comes and for Whom we live, and there's one Lord, Jesus Christ, through whom all things are and through whom we exist.

•But not everyone knows this. Some, because up till now they've been ₇ accustomed to idols, eat meat as if it really had been offered to idols, and since their conscience is weak they're defiled. •Now food will not com- ₈ mend us to God — if we don't eat we won't be any worse off, and if we do eat we won't be any better off. •But be careful that your freedom does- ₉ n't somehow cause those who are weak to fall. •For if someone sees you ₁₀ who have knowledge reclining at table in an idol's temple, and his con- science is weak, won't he be encouraged to eat meat that's been offered to idols? •And so your knowledge would lead to the weak person's down- ₁₁ fall — who is himself a brother for whom Christ died. •Therefore, who- ₁₂ ever sins against his brothers in this way and injures their weak con- sciences is sinning against Christ. •Thus, if food causes my brother to sin ₁₃ I'll never eat meat again, so I won't cause my brother to sin.

Paul's defense of his ministry as an apostle

9 •Am I not free? Am I not an apostle? Haven't I seen Jesus our Lord? ₁ Aren't you my work in the Lord? •If I'm not an apostle to others, I ₂ certainly am to you, for you're the seal of my apostleship in the Lord!

•This is my defense to those who sit in judgment over me. •Have we ₃,₄ no right to eat and drink? •Have we no right to travel with a Christian ₅

8:1ff Paul takes advantage of a specific issue (eating food that had previously been sacrificed to idols) to set out a fundamental principle of Christian morality — concern for the conscience of "weaker" persons.
9:1ff Paul now returns to a matter he first raised in Chapter 4. Apparently, in their "wisdom," some of the Corinthians felt able to pass judgment on Paul and other Christian missionaries. This is Paul's defense of his worth as an apostle, but even more than that, Paul sets out the principles that form the basis for his ministry.

wife, as do the other apostles, the brothers of the Lord, and Kephas?
6 •Are Barnabas and I the only ones who have no right to be free from
7 the necessity to work? •Who serves as a soldier at his own expense? Who
plants a vineyard but doesn't eat its fruit? Who shepherds a flock but does-
8 n't get any of the flock's milk? •Am I saying this on human authority, or
9 doesn't the Torah also say this? •For in the Law of Moses it's written,
You shall not muzzle the ox when it's threshing. Is it for oxen that
10 God is concerned? •Isn't He saying this for us all? For it was written for
us that the plowman should plow in hope and the thresher should thresh
11 in hope of gaining a share. •If we have sown spiritual seed for you, is it
12 so shocking that we should reap material benefits from you? •If others
share in this claim on you, don't we have even more of a right to do so?
   Nevertheless, we've made no use of this right; instead, we endure
everything rather than place an obstacle in the way of Christ's good
13 news. •Don't you know that those who perform the Temple services get
their food from the Temple, and those who serve at the altar share in
14 what's offered on the altar? •ⁱ So, too, the Lord commanded those who
15 proclaim the good news to gain their living from the good news. •And
yet I've made use of none of these things, nor am I writing this in order
to have it done for me — I'd rather die than let anyone deprive me of
16 my boast! •For proclaiming the good news is not my boast, since I do
so under compulsion — woe to me if I *don't* proclaim the good news!
17 •If I do it of my own free will, then I get a reward, but if not, I've sim-
18 ply been entrusted with a commission. •What then is my reward? My
reward is to proclaim the good news free of charge without asserting
my rights in the good news.
19   •For though I'm totally free I've made myself a slave to all in order to
20 win over as many as possible. •I became a Jew for the Jews in order to
win the Jews over; for those under the Torah I acted as if *I* were subject to the Torah — although I'm *not* subject to the Torah — in order
21 to win over those who *are* under the Torah; •for those outside the Torah
I became like one outside the Torah in order to win over those outside
the Torah, although rather than being outside God's law I'm subject to
22 Christ's law. •For those who were weak I became weak in order to win
over the weak. I've become all things to all men so that by all means I
23 might win some of them over. •I do all this for the sake of the good news
so that I'll be able to share in it.

ⁱ Mt 10:10; Lk 10:7.

9:9 Dt 18:1-3.

1 CORINTHIANS

•Don't you know that all the runners in the stadium race, but only one 24 gets the prize? Run to win! •Everyone who competes in an athletic con- 25 test trains rigorously, but while *they* do it to win a perishable crown *we're* competing for an imperishable crown. •So I don't run as if I didn't know 26 where the finish line is; when I box I don't just punch wildly. •On the 27 contrary, I discipline myself and bring my body under control, because I don't want to preach to others and then find *myself* disqualified.

A general moral exhortation

10 •I want you to bear in mind, brothers, that our ancestors were all 1 under the cloud and they all passed through the sea. •They were 2 all baptized into Moses in the cloud and in the sea; •they all ate the same 3 spiritual food •and they all drank the same spiritual drink. For they drank 4 of the spiritual rock that followed them, and that rock was Christ. •Nev- 5 ertheless, God was displeased with most of them, for He struck them down in the desert. •Now these events were warnings for us, not to long 6 for evil things like those evil people did. •Don't be idolaters, like some 7 of them were, as it's written, **The people sat down to eat and drink, and got up to dance.** •Don't turn to fornication like some of them 8 did — in one day twenty-three thousand fell in the desert. •Let's not test 9 Christ like some of them did, and were killed by the snakes. •Don't grum- 10 ble, like some of them did, and were killed by the Destroyer. •These 11 things happened to them as warnings, but they were written down for *our* instruction, for the end of the ages has come to us. •So anyone who 12 thinks they're standing should be careful not to fall. •The only tempta- 13 tions you've received are normal human ones. God is trustworthy and won't allow you to be tested beyond your strength — along with the temptation He'll also provide a way out, so you'll be able to endure it.

ⁱ *Mt 26:26-28; Mk 14:22-24; Lk 22:19-20.*

10:1ff Paul begins his moral exhortation with a renewed appeal to the image of the Church as the New Israel embarked upon a New Exodus from sin and death to life — the experience of the Passover and Exodus is the experience of the Christian life. The Corinthians must bear in mind that passing through the waters of baptism is no guarantee that they will reach the Promised Land. 10:4 At Ws 11:4 the water the Israelites received from the rock is identified with Wisdom. If Paul has this passage in mind he is identifying Jesus with the Wisdom of God, continuing a theme al-luded to at 1:24, 30. This is a further identifica-tion of Jesus as the New Torah, for the rabbis had come to equate the Torah with the revelation of the Divine and creative Wisdom. This is signifi-cant for Christology, for Wisdom was at the be-ginning with God. It is also significant for ethics and the spiritual life, Paul's chief concern in this passage, for it is the basis of Paul's vision of the Christian life as a living of Christ's life rather than as mere obedience to a written code. 10:7 Ex 32:6. 10:9 Some manuscripts read "the Lord" for "Christ."

*The Judean desert. Symbol of the temptations
and of the wanderings of the Chosen People. (1 Cor 10)*

14,15 •Therefore, beloved, flee idolatry. •I'm speaking as if to the wise —
16 judge for yourselves what I say. •ʲ The blessing cup we bless, isn't it a
sharing in Christ's blood? The bread we break, isn't it a sharing in Christ's
17 body? •Because there's one bread, we who are many are one body.
18 •Consider "Israel according to the flesh." Aren't those who eat the sac-
19 rifices sharers in the altar? •What am I saying? That food offered to an
20 idol is of any significance, or that an idol has any significance? •No, what
I'm saying is that the things the Gentiles sacrifice they sacrifice to demons
rather than to God, and I don't want you to become sharers with
21 demons. •You can't drink the Lord's cup *and* the cup of demons; you
22 can't share in the Lord's table *and* the table of demons. •Are we to pro-
voke the Lord to jealousy? Are we stronger than he is?

10:14-22 As he so often does, Paul stresses the communal/ covenant aspect of the Eucharist — his remarks are best understood in light of the Passover/Exodus experience. The events of the Passover and Exodus were constitutive for Israel as the people of God and are seen by Paul as types of the sacraments. Sharing in the sacramental life of the Church, especially in the Eucharist, is in this sense constitutive for the New Israel. Cf. also 5:7, 10:2-4; 11:20-34.
10:20 Dt 32:17 (Septuagint).

•"Everything is permitted," but not everything will benefit you. 23 "Everything is permitted," but not everything will build you up. •Everyone should look out for his neighbor's good rather than his 24 own. •Eat whatever's in the meat market without making inquiries 25 for the sake of your conscience, **•for the earth and everything** 26 **in it belongs to the Lord.** •If any of the unbelievers invite you 27 over and you wish to go, eat whatever's put before you without making inquiries for the sake of your conscience. •But if anyone tells you, 28 "This was offered in sacrifice," then don't eat it for the sake of the person who informed you and for conscience's sake — •I don't mean 29 your *own* conscience, I mean the other person's. For why should my freedom be limited by someone else's conscience? •If I share in the 30 food gratefully, why should I be criticized for something I give thanks for? •Whether you eat or drink or whether you don't, do everything 31 for the glory of God. •Give no offense to the Jews, the Greeks, or 32 to the church of God, •just as I try to please everyone in everything 33 I do. I look out for the good of the many, rather than my own good, so that they'll be saved.

11 •Be imitators of me, just as I imitate Christ. 1

E. PAUL ADDRESSES CERTAIN PROBLEMS WHICH HAVE ARISEN IN THE LITURGICAL GATHERINGS

Women's headdress

•I commend you because you always remember me and hold fast 2 to the traditions just as I handed them down to you. •But I want you 3 to understand that Christ is the head of every man, the husband is the head of his wife, and God is the head of Christ. •Any man who prays 4 or prophesies with his head covered disgraces his head, •while any 5 woman who prays or prophesies with her head uncovered disgraces her head — it's the same as if her head were shaved. •For if a woman 6 leaves her head uncovered, she may as well have her hair cut off, but since it's shameful for a woman to cut her hair off or be shaved, then she should cover her head. •A man, on the other hand, should *not* 7 cover his head, since he's the image and glory of God, while woman

10:26 Ps 24:1.

8 is the glory of man. •For woman was made from man, not man from
9 woman, •and woman was created for man, not man for woman.
10 •Therefore a woman should wear a sign of authority on her head for
11 the sake of the angels. •Nevertheless, in the Lord woman is not in-
12 dependent of man, nor is man independent of woman, •for just as
woman comes from man, so too man comes from woman, and every-
13 thing comes from God. •Judge for yourselves, is it proper for a woman
14 to pray to God with her head uncovered? •Doesn't nature itself teach
15 us that it's shameful for a man to wear his hair long, •while a woman's
16 long hair is her glory? For her hair is given to her as a covering. •But
if anyone is disposed to keep arguing — we have no such custom, nor
do the churches of God.

Their manner of celebrating the Lord's Supper

17 •But in giving these instructions I *don't* commend the fact that your
18 assemblies lead to harm rather than to good. •In the first place, when
you assemble as a church I hear that there are divisions among you,
19 and in part I believe it — •after all, it's necessary for there to be fac-
tions among you so that it will be apparent which of you are genuine.
20,21 •But when you assemble it's not to eat the Lord's supper, •for when
you eat each of you goes ahead with his own supper — one is hun-
22 gry, while another is drunk. •Don't you have homes to eat and drink
in? Do you despise God's church and shame those in need? What shall
I say to you? Shall I commend you? I certainly don't commend you
for this!
23 •For I received from the Lord what I handed down to you, that on
24 the night he was betrayed the Lord Jesus took bread, •and after blessing it he broke it and said, "This is my body which is for you. Do this
25 in remembrance of me!" •In the same way he took the cup after they
had eaten and said, "This cup is the new covenant in my blood. Do
26 this, whenever you drink it, in remembrance of me!" •For whenever
you eat this bread and drink this cup you proclaim the death of the
Lord, until he comes.
27 •Therefore, if anyone eats the bread or drinks from the cup of the
Lord unworthily, he'll be answerable for the body and blood of the Lord.
28 •Each of you should first examine yourself and then eat the bread and

11:10 Based on Qumran parallels, it is possible that the angels were thought to be present at litur-
gies and that therefore proper decorum should be maintained.

drink from the cup, •for whoever eats and drinks without recognizing 29
the body eats and drinks judgment to himself. •That's why so many of 30
you are weak and ill, and a considerable number have died, •but if we 31
examined ourselves we wouldn't be subject to judgment. •But when we're 32
punished by the Lord we receive guidance so that we won't be condemned with the world. •Therefore, my brothers, when you assemble 33
to eat, wait for each other. •If anyone is hungry, let him eat at home, 34
so your assembly won't lead to condemnation. I'll give you instructions
about the other matters when I come.

Regarding the purpose and relative importance of spiritual gifts

12 •Regarding spiritual gifts — brothers, I don't want you to lack un- 1
derstanding in this matter. •You know that when you were Gen- 2
tiles whenever you were seized by a spirit you used to be led off to dumb
idols. •This is why I want you to know that no one speaking under the 3
influence of God's Spirit can say, "Cursed be Jesus!" and no one can
say, "Jesus is Lord!" except under the influence of the Holy Spirit.

•[k] There are various gifts, but the same Spirit, •there are various min- 4,5
istries, but the same Lord, •and there are various ways to be active, but 6
the same God Who causes all these effects in everyone. •Some mani- 7
festation of the Spirit is given to each for the common good. •To one 8
it may be given to speak wisdom through the Spirit, to another it's giv-
en to speak deep knowledge according to the same Spirit. •To still an- 9
other faith may be given through the same Spirit, while to another the
one Spirit will give healing gifts. •To one may be given the ability to per- 10
form miracles, to another the gift of prophecy, to one the gift of distinguishing spirits, to another various tongues, to still another the interpretation of tongues. •One and the same Spirit causes all this, distrib- 11
uting individually to each as He wishes.

•[l] For just as the body is one but has many members, all the members 12
of the body — many though they are — are one body, and so it is with

[k] *Rm 12:6-8.* [l] *Rm 12:4-5.*

11:29 In the context, "recognizing the body" refers both to recognizing in the Eucharist the saving sacrifice of Jesus' body and blood as well as the Church's unity with Christ in the Eucharist. Every individual Christian shares the responsi-bility for maintaining that unity.

12:1-26 The idea animating this important pas-sage is that the Church as a Body is a unity, not a mere aggregate of individuals. Spiritual gifts must therefore be understood as being essen-tially at the service of the Church rather than be-ing the possessions of individual Christians.

13 Christ. •We've *all* been baptized in one Spirit into one body, whether
14 Jew or Greek, slave or free, and we've all drunk of one Spirit. •For the
15 body isn't one member — it's made up of many members. •If the foot
should say, "I'm not a hand, so I'm not part of the body," it would still
16 be part of the body for all that, •and if the ear should say, "I'm not the
eye, so I'm not part of the body," it would still be part of the body for all
17 that. •If the whole body were an eye, how could it hear? If the whole
18 body were an ear, how could it smell? •But as it is, God arranged the
members of the body — each one of them — as He wished them to be.
19,20 •If they were all just one member, what sort of body would that be? •As
21 it is, though, there are many members, but one body. •The eye can't tell
the hand, "I have no need of you," nor can the head tell the feet, "I have
22 no need of you." •On the contrary, the members of the body which seem
23 the weakest are much more necessary, •the members of the body which
seem less honorable are the ones we grant the most honor to, and our
24 private parts we treat with more modesty, •whereas there's no need to
treat our more presentable parts that way. But God has formed the body

Descent of the Holy Spirit. Bible of Borso d'Este (1433-1461).

in such a way as to give greater honor to the members which lack it, •so 25 that there will be no discord in the body and the members will feel the same concern for one another. •If one member suffers, all the members 26 suffer; if one member is honored, all the members rejoice.

•You are the body of Christ, and each individual is a member. •[m] God 27,28 has appointed some in the church to be, first, apostles, second, prophets, third, teachers, then miracle workers, those with the gift of healing, helpers, administrators, and those with various tongues. •Are all mem- 29 bers apostles? Are all prophets? Are all teachers? Do all work miracles? •Do all have the gift of healing? Can all speak in tongues? Can all in- 30 terpret tongues? •But strive for the greatest gifts. 31

And I'll show you an even better way.

13 •If I can speak both human and angelic tongues but don't have 1 love, I'm nothing but a gong sounding or a cymbal clashing. •[n] If 2 I have the gift of prophecy, understand every mystery, and possess all the deepest knowledge, if I have such complete faith that I can move mountains but I don't have love, I'm nothing. •And if I give all my pos- 3 sessions away and hand my body over to be burned but I don't have love, it does me no good at all.

•Love is patient, love is kind, it isn't jealous, doesn't boast, isn't ar- 4 rogant. •Love is not dishonorable, isn't selfish, isn't irritable, doesn't keep 5 a record of past wrongs. •Love doesn't rejoice at injustice but rejoices 6 in the truth. •Love endures all things, love has complete faith and stead- 7 fast hope, love bears with everything.

•Love never ends. Prophecy will pass away, speaking in tongues will 8 cease, knowledge will pass away. •Our knowledge is incomplete and 9 prophecy is incomplete, •but when what's perfect comes the imperfect 10 will pass away. •When I was a child I spoke like a child, thought like a 11 child, reasoned like a child. When I became a man, I put an end to child- ish ways. •Right now we see indistinctly, as in a mirror, but then we'll 12 see face to face. At present my knowledge is incomplete, but then I'll truly understand, as God understands me. •So these three — faith, hope, 13 and love — remain, but the greatest of them all is love.

---

[m] *Eph 4:11.*   [n] *Mt 17:20; 21:21; Mk 11:23.*

13:1ff This passage builds on what preceded it. Just as the gifts of the Spirit are for building up the life of the Church, so Paul reminds the Corinthians that the essence of that life of the Spirit "in Christ" is love. Individual achievements and gifts are to be measured against their success in strengthening the community's life of love "in Christ." This emphasis on the Church over the individual continues the Old Testament tradition that individuals were inspired by the Spirit for the good of Israel.

1,2 **14** •Strive for love and set your hearts on the gifts of the Spirit, but especially desire to receive the gift of prophecy. •The person who speaks in tongues speaks to God and not to men, since no one can un-
3 derstand him — he proclaims mysteries through the Holy Spirit. •But
4 whoever prophesies strengthens, encourages, and comforts others. •You strengthen yourself when you speak in tongues, but when you proph-
5 esy you strengthen the church. •I want you all to speak in tongues but I'm especially desirous that you should prophesy. It's far better to proph-esy than to speak in tongues, unless someone translates what you're say-ing so the whole church will be strengthened.

6 •Look at it this way, brothers. If I come to you speaking in tongues what good will it do you, unless I proclaim some revelation, deep knowl-
7 edge, prophecy or teaching? •Similarly, if inanimate objects that produce sounds, such as the flute or the lyre, don't produce distinct notes, how
8 will anyone know what's being played? •If I sound an uncertain trumpet
9 blast, who will prepare for battle? •So, too, when you speak in tongues — unless you can give an intelligible account of it, how will anyone know
10 what you're saying? You may as well be speaking to the air! •Or take an-other example — there are many different types of speech in the world,
11 and all are intelligible, •but if I don't know what the sounds mean I'll be like a foreigner to the person who's speaking, and he'll be a foreigner to
12 me. •So, since you're eager for gifts of the Spirit, strive to have an abun-
13 dance of those which build up the church. •Therefore, whoever speaks
14 in tongues should pray to be able to interpret them. •For when I'm pray-
15 ing in tongues my spirit is praying but my mind is idle. •What should I do? I'll pray with my spirit, but I'll also pray with my mind; I'll sing with
16 my spirit, but I'll also sing with my mind. •Otherwise, if you praise God in the Spirit, how will someone without special gifts be able to raise the "Amen!" to your thanksgiving, since he doesn't know what you're say-
17 ing? •You may be thanking God well enough, but no one else is being
18 strengthened. •I give thanks to God that I'm able to speak in tongues more
19 than any of you, •but in church I'd rather speak five words from my mind that provide instruction for others, than ten thousand words in tongues.
20 •Brothers, don't be childish in your thinking — be like children with
21 regard to evil, but be mature in your thinking. •In the Torah it's written,

> **Through foreigners**
> **and through the lips of foreigners**
> **I'll speak to this people,**
> **and even so they won't listen to me,**

14:21 Is 28:11-12.

says the Lord. •Therefore, speaking in tongues is a sign to non-believ- 22
ers rather than to believers, while prophecy is for believers rather than
non-believers. •So if the whole church were to gather together and be 23
speaking in tongues and uninstructed people or non-believers should
come in, they'd say you were out of your minds, wouldn't they? •But if 24
you were all prophesying when the non-believer or uninstructed person
came in he'd be convinced of his errors and be called to account by all
of you. •The secrets of his heart would be revealed — he'd fall on his 25
face and worship God, proclaiming, "God is truly with you!"

•What should you do, brothers? When you gather, each of you should 26
have a song, some teaching, a revelation, a message in tongues, or an
interpretation — everything should be done with a view toward strengthening the church. •If anyone wants to speak in tongues, let two or, at 27
most, three do so, but have them take turns and have one of them translate. •If there's no one there to translate, they should be silent in church 28
— let them speak to themselves or to God. •Let two or three prophets 29
speak while the others pass judgment, •but if someone sitting there re- 30
ceives a revelation, the first speaker should stop talking. •You can all 31
prophesy one at a time, so that you'll all learn and receive encouragement. •The prophetic spirit should be controlled by the prophets, •for 32,33
God is made manifest in peace, not in disorder.

As in all the churches of the saints, •women should remain silent in 34
church, for they're not permitted to speak. They should be subordinate,
as the Torah says, too. •If they want to learn about something they 35
should ask their husbands at home, because it's disgraceful for a woman
to speak in church. •Did the word of God come from you? Are you the 36
only ones it came to?

•If anyone thinks he's a prophet or that he's been favored with gifts 37
of the Spirit he'll realize that what I'm writing to you is a command of
the Lord. •Anyone who doesn't accept that should be ignored. •There- 38,39
fore, brothers, set your hearts on prophecy, but don't hinder speaking
in tongues. •Everything should be done in a proper and orderly fashion. 40

F. DOCTRINAL TEACHING:
THE RESURRECTION OF THE DEAD

15 •I want to remind you, brothers, of the good news I proclaimed 1
to you, the good news you received and in which you stand firm.
•You'll be saved through the good news if you hold fast to the message 2
I proclaimed to you, unless you believed in vain. •For I handed down to 3

Tomb of the Roman times with circular stone (1st century B.C.).

you as of primary importance what I, in turn, had received, namely that
4 Christ died for our sins in accordance with the Scriptures, •that he was buried, that he was raised on the third day in accordance with the Scrip-
5,6 tures, •and that he appeared to Kephas and then to the Twelve. •Then he appeared to more than five hundred brothers at once, the majority
7 of whom are still with us, although some have died. •Then he appeared
8 to James, then to all the apostles. •Last of all he appeared to me as
9 well, to one born at the wrong time, as it were, •for I'm the least of the apostles, not even worthy to be *called* an apostle, because I persecut-
10 ed God's church. •But through the grace of God I am what I am, and the grace He gave me has not been without result — I've worked hard-er than any of them, although it wasn't me working — it was the grace
11 of God working in me. •So whether it was me or them, this is what we proclaimed and this is what you believed.
12 •Now if Christ is proclaimed as raised from the dead, how can some
13 of you say that there's no resurrection of the dead? •If there's no resur-

15:1ff As a prolegomena to his discussion of resurrection from the dead, Paul reviews the content of the good news he had previously proclaimed to the Corinthians.

rection from the dead, then Christ wasn't raised either, •and if Christ was- 14
n't raised then everything we proclaimed is in vain, and so is your faith.
•Moreover we'll have been found to be false witnesses against God, for 15
we testified that God raised Christ, whom He couldn't have raised if the
dead in fact are not raised. •For if the dead are not raised, then Christ 16
wasn't raised either, •and if Christ wasn't raised your faith is worthless and 17
you're still in your sins, •and those who died in Christ have also perished. 18
•If our hope in Christ is for this life only, we're the most pitiable of men. 19

•As it is, Christ *was* raised from the dead, the first fruits of those who 20
have died. •For since death came through a man, resurrection from the 21
dead *also* came through a man, •for just as in Adam all men die, so too 22
in Christ they'll also come to life again. •Each will be raised in the prop- 23
er order — Christ the first fruits, then at his coming those who belong
to Christ will rise. •Then the end will come, when he'll deliver the King- 24
dom to his God and Father, when he'll do away with every ruler, authority, and power. •For Christ must reign until he's put all his enemies 25
under his feet. •The last enemy to be done away with will be death, •for 26,27
God has put everything under his feet. When it says that "everything" has been made subject to him it's clear that "everything" doesn't
include God. •When everything is made subject to him, then the Son 28
himself will be subjected to the One Who subjected everything to the
Son, so that God will be all in all.

•Otherwise, what's the point in people being baptized for the dead? 29
If the dead aren't actually raised, why are people baptized for them?
•Why do we run risks every hour of the day? •Every day I die. I do! I 30,31
swear it by the pride I have in you in Christ Jesus our Lord! •If in hu- 32
man terms I fought with wild beasts in Ephesus, what good did it do me?
If the dead aren't raised,

**Let's eat and drink,
for tomorrow we'll die!**

•Don't be led astray, 33

"Bad company ruins good morals!"

15:20 The "first fruits" was a harvest offering to God, but Paul is probably thinking once again of the Passover and Exodus. At Dt 26:1-11 the offering of the first fruits is explicitly described as a thank offering for the mighty works of the Lord in bringing Israel out of Egypt and into the Promised Land.
15:25 Ps 110:1.   15:27 Ps 8:6.

15:29 Apparently the Corinthians engaged in a form of baptism by proxy on behalf of dead relatives. Paul points out the inconsistency of engaging in such a practice while denying the resurrection of the dead.
15:32 Is 22:13.
15:33 This is a quotation from the Greek poet Menander.

34 •Come to your senses and stop sinning! Some of you don't know God — I say this to your shame.

35 •Perhaps someone will say, "How can the dead be raised? What kind
36 of bodies will they have?" •You fool! What you sow doesn't come to life
37 unless it dies! •What you sow isn't your body as it will be — it's a bare
38 kernel, like wheat or something of that sort. •God gives it the body He's
39 chosen for it, and each type of seed has its own body. •Not all flesh is the same; human flesh is of one sort, the flesh of domestic animals is of another; the flesh of birds is of one kind, while fish have another type.
40 •There are also heavenly bodies and earthly bodies, but the glory of heavenly bodies is one thing and the glory of earthly bodies is something else.
41 •The sun has one type of brightness, the moon another, and the stars yet another, for stars differ according to their brightness.

42 •So it is with the resurrection of the dead.

What is perishable when it's sown is imperishable
   when it's raised.
43 •What's sown in dishonor is raised in glory,
What's sown in weakness is raised in power;
44 •A physical body is sown, a spiritual body is raised.
45 Now if there's a physical body, there's also a spiritual body. •So it is written,

Adam, **the** first **man, became a living being;**
   the last Adam became a life-giving spirit.
46 •But the spiritual isn't first;
   first comes the physical, then comes the spiritual.
47 •The first man was made of dust,
   the second man came from Heaven.
48 •Those who are of the dust
   are like the man of dust,
And those who are of Heaven
   are like the man from Heaven,
49 •And just as we've borne the image of the man of dust,
   so too we'll bear the image of the man from Heaven.

50 •This is what I mean, brothers — it's impossible for flesh and blood to inherit the Kingdom of God, nor can what's perishable inherit what's imperishable.

15:45 Gn 2:7.

•° Behold, I'll tell you a mystery —   51
   not all of us will die,
But all of us will be transformed,
   •in a moment, in the twinkling of an eye,   52
At the sound of the last trumpet call,
   when the trumpet sounds,
The dead will be raised imperishable
   and we'll be transformed.
•For this corruptible body must be clothed   53
   in incorruptibility,
   and this mortal body must be clothed
   in immortality.
•And when this corruptible body is clothed   54
   in incorruptibility
   and this mortal body is clothed in immortality
The following passage of Scripture will come to pass,
•Death is swallowed up in victory.   55
Death, where is your victory?
Death, where is your sting?
•Sin is death's sting,   56
   and the Torah is sin's power,
•But thanks be to God, Who gives us victory   57
   through our Lord Jesus Christ.

•Therefore, my beloved brothers, be firm and steadfast. Constantly in- 58
crease your work for the Lord, in the knowledge that your labor in the
Lord is not in vain.

G. PAUL'S PLANS AND
OTHER PRACTICAL CONSIDERATIONS

16 •Regarding the collection for the saints — do just as I command- 1
ed the churches in Galatia to do. •On the first day of every week 2
each of you is to lay aside and save whatever you're able to, so that a
collection won't have to be made when I come. •When I arrive I'll send 3
whomever you approve to carry your gift to Jerusalem with letters of introduction. •If it seems proper for me to go too, they'll accompany me. 4

° 1 Th 4:15-17.
15:54-55 Is 25:8; Ho 13:14 (Septuagint).

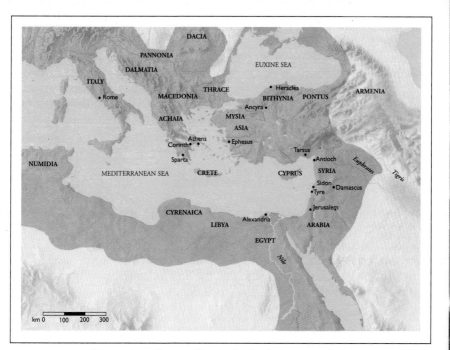

The eastern Roman Empire in the 1st century A.D.

5 •P I'll come to you when I go through Macedonia, for I'll be going
6 through Macedonia, •and I may stay with you awhile or even spend the
winter with you, so you'll be able to send me on to wherever I'm going.
7 •I don't want to see you now just in passing — I'm hoping to spend some
8 time with you if the Lord will permit it, •q but I'll stay in Ephesus until
9 Pentecost, •for a particularly effective door of opportunity has been
opened for me, though I have many adversaries.
10 •If Timothy comes, see that he's made welcome among you, for he's
11 doing the Lord's work just as I am, •so no one should look down on
him. Send him on in peace so he'll be able to come to me, for I'm waiting for him along with the brothers.
12 •Regarding our brother Apollos — I strongly urged him to go to you
with the brothers, but it was not at all God's will for him to go now —
he'll come to you when he has the chance.

P *Ac 19:21.* q *Ac 19:8-10.*

•Be watchful, stand firm in the faith, be manly, be strong! •Let all your 13,14 work be done in love.

•You know that those in Stephanas' household were the first converts 15 in Achaia and that they've devoted themselves to the service of the saints. I beg you, •obey them and all who labor and work as they do. •I rejoice 16,17 that Stephanas, Fortunatus, and Achaicus came, because they make up for your absence — •they've refreshed my spirit as well as yours. Give 18 such men recognition.

H. FAREWELL

•The churches of Asia greet you. Aquila and Prisca greet you fervently 19 in the Lord along with those in the church at their house. •All the broth- 20 ers greet you. Greet one another with a holy kiss. •This greeting is my 21 own writing — Paul's. •If anyone doesn't love the Lord, let him be 22 cursed! *Marana tha!* •The grace of the Lord Jesus be with you. •May 23,24 my love be with all of you in the Lord Jesus.

16:22 *Marana tha.* Aramaic for "Come, Lord!"

THE SECOND LETTER
TO THE

CORINTHIANS

Introduction to the
Second Letter to the Corinthians

2 Corinthians is undoubtedly one of Paul's most difficult letters. Unlike in Romans, theological complexity is not the main difficulty — in fact, specifically theological concerns occupy a relatively minor portion of the whole. Rather, its difficulty stems from its intensely personal character and its seeming lack of unity. This is not to deny the letter its share of theological insights (see Chapters 3-5 especially), but they must be viewed within the context of the letter as a whole, which is the crisis in Paul's relations with the Corinthians.

Paul had remained in Corinth for about two years, and his ministry there had been rewarded with great success. He had then, after a brief return trip to Palestine and Antioch, based himself in Ephesus, an important city on the western coast of Asia Minor, across the Aegean sea from Corinth. Problems had arisen in the Corinthian church, however, and Paul had been required to visit at least once, to send emissaries, and to write letters. Apparently Paul's visit had been a stormy one, involving a challenge to Paul's authority. After leaving Corinth, Paul had written a letter in which he demanded that his main antagonist be disciplined. This "painful letter" (as he himself termed it) had had the effect he had hoped for, and his emissary Titus had returned with the good news that the Corinthians were once more wholeheartedly behind Paul. Against this background, Paul wrote 2 Corinthians.

A. GREETING

1 **1** •Paul, an apostle of Christ Jesus by the will of God, and Timothy our brother to the church of God in Corinth, along with all the saints 2 in all of Achaia. •Grace and peace to you from God our Father and the Lord Jesus Christ.

B. STATEMENT OF THE LETTER'S THEME: PAUL'S RECORD IS OF SELFLESS SERVICE IN GOD'S GRACE

3 •Blessed be the God and Father of our Lord Jesus Christ, the com-
4 passionate Father and ever encouraging God! •He encourages us in all our afflictions so that we'll be able to encourage others who are in affliction by means of the encouragement we ourselves have received from
5 God. •For just as Christ's sufferings overflow and include us, so too
6 through Christ our encouragement is also unbounded. •If we suffer, it's for your encouragement and salvation; if we receive encouragement, it's so you'll be encouraged and enabled to endure the same sufferings we
7 suffer. •Our hope in you is firm, for we know that if you share the suffering, you also share the encouragement.
8 •For we want you to know, brothers, about our afflictions in Asia. We were so utterly weighted down, beyond our strength, that we doubted
9 whether we could go on living. •We were convinced that we had received the death sentence, but that was so that instead of trusting in ourselves
10 we would place our trust in God, Who raises the dead. •He delivered us from these terrible dangers of death, and He'll continue to deliver us. In
11 Him we have placed our hope and God will rescue us again. •You must help us by praying for us, so that many people will give thanks for the gift we received through the prayers of many people.

1:8-10 The Roman province of "Asia" had its capital at Ephesus, from which city much of Paul's Corinthian correspondence was written. What the afflictions he experienced there were we cannot be sure, but their serious nature is also alluded to at 1 Cor 15:32.

•For this is our boast — that our conscience can testify that we have 12 conducted ourselves in the world, and especially toward you, with the single hearted simplicity and sincerity of God, not by worldly wisdom but by the grace of God. •For we write to you only what you can read and 13 understand. I hope you'll fully understand, •as indeed you've partially un- 14 derstood us, that we are your boast just as you'll be our boast on the day of the Lord Jesus.

C. A REVIEW OF RECENT TROUBLED RELATIONS BETWEEN PAUL AND THE CORINTHIANS

•Because I was sure of all this I originally planned to come to you so 15 you'd have a double gift. •[a] I was going to visit you on my way to Mace- 16 donia and come to you again when I returned from Macedonia — and then be sent on my way to Judea by you. •In making this plan did I show 17 myself to be fickle? Do I make my plans according to the way of the world, saying "Yes, yes" and "No, no" in one breath? •As God is faithful, we 18 have not been saying both yes and no to you. •For Jesus Christ the Son 19 of God who was proclaimed among you by us — by Silas, Timothy, and myself — was not both "Yes" and "No"; instead, the "Yes" was in him. •For all God's promises find their "Yes" in him, which is why it's through 20 Jesus that we say "Amen" to the glory of God. •It's God Who establish- 21 es us in Christ with you and Who has anointed us, •Who has placed His 22 seal on us and given our hearts the Spirit as a down payment.

•I call on God as my witness, upon my life, that it was to spare you 23 that I decided not to go to Corinth. •Not that we lord it over your faith 24 — on the contrary, we're working *together* for your joy, for you stand firm in the faith.

2 •The fact is I made up my mind not to go to you again if that 1 would pain you, •for if I were to cause you pain who would there 2 be to cheer me up except those whom I had pained? •I wrote what 3 I did so that when I came I wouldn't receive pain from those who should have given me joy, for I was confident that as far as you were concerned my joy would be your joy. •I was in tears when I wrote to 4 you, and what I wrote came from my troubled and anguished heart. My intent was not to cause you pain but to let you know how great my love for you is.

1:22 The reference to being "sealed" is probably a reference to baptism.

Perga. View of the Hellenistic Gate (3rd century A.D.).
This town is among one of the first visited by Paul in his second missionary journey.

5 •But if anyone caused pain, it wasn't just me that he pained; not to
6 exaggerate, but to some degree the pain was caused to all of you. •This
7 punishment by the majority of you is sufficient for such a person, •so
you should forgive and encourage him now, lest he be swallowed up in
8 his overwhelming grief. •Therefore, I urge you to assure him of your
9 love, •because the reason I wrote was to test you and find out if you're
10 obedient in everything. •Anyone you forgive, I do too. Whatever I've
forgiven, if there *was* anything for me to forgive, has been forgiven for
11 your sake in the presence of Christ •to keep Satan from gaining an advantage over us — for we're well aware of his plans.
12 •When I came to Troas to proclaim the good news of Christ a door
13 of opportunity was opened for me in the Lord, •but I had no peace of
mind because I didn't find my brother Titus there, so I bade them farewell
and left for Macedonia.

2:5-11 While certainty is not possible, many believe the offense was a personal attack on Paul, probably a questioning of his authority.

D. THE NATURE OF APOSTLESHIP
THE SOURCE OF PAUL'S CONFIDENCE

•But thanks be to God Who continually leads us in triumph in Christ 14
and through us makes known the fragrance of the knowledge of God in
every place, •for we are the aroma Christ offers to God among those 15
being saved and among those who are perishing. •For some it is a dead- 16
ly fragrance which leads to death, for others it is a lifegiving fragrance
which leads to life. Who is worthy of these things? •For we're not like 17
so many other people who peddle the word of God for profit; we proclaim the word sincerely, having received it from God; we proclaim it in
the sight of God and in Christ.

3•Are we beginning to commend ourselves again? Or do we, like 1
some others, need letters of recommendation to you or from you?
•You are our letter, written on our hearts, for all to know and read. 2
•Yes, you're clearly a letter from Christ delivered by us, written not 3
with ink but with the Spirit of the living God, not on stone tablets but
on tablets of human hearts.

The superiority of the new covenant of the Spirit

•This confidence we have is in God through Christ. •Not that we can 4,5
take credit for anything ourselves, as if we had accomplished it on our own

2:14-16 A Roman "triumph" was a military victory parade which included, among other things,
the procession of captives and the burning of incense. As many scholars have pointed out, however, the "aroma" and "fragrance" alluded to in vv.
15-16 probably owe more to Old Testament sacrificial imagery, in which God is said to be pleased
by the odor of the sacrifice. Paul, of course, is
referring to his own sacrifices in his ministry, sacrifices he gladly makes for the spiritual welfare
of his converts.
3:1ff Here for the first time in the letter Paul
contrasts himself with other teachers. They appear to have come to Corinth bearing letters of
recommendation. At this point Paul's criticism is
restrained, although it seems apparent that
Paul's opponents must have placed greater emphasis on Jewishness and observance of at
least some of the Torah. Later, when it became
clear that these teachers were denigrating both
Paul's person and his ministry in pointedly per-

sonal terms, Paul reacted vigorously in defense
of his person, his ministry, and his authority
(Chapters 10-13).
3:4-18 The old covenant was a covenant of the
letter, the Torah, while the new covenant is a
covenant of the spirit. Therefore, since "the Lord
is the Spirit," the very person of Christ becomes
the focal point of the new covenant. Rather than
obeying commandments written in stone the
Christian becomes an imitator of Christ, the New
Torah. The Torah, according to rabbinic theology,
was the revelation of God, but, says Paul, it had
a glory which was destined to fade. Christ is a far
more perfect revelation of God and his glory will
never fade. As we gaze upon the revealed glory
of the Lord and become imitators of Christ we are
transformed into His image.
3:6 Paul, of course, is not denying the Torah's essential and glorious role in salvation history.
However, when opposed to the new covenant it
leads to death.

6 — our adequacy to the task comes from God. •He it is Who made us qual-
ified to become ministers of a new covenant, a covenant not based on a
written code but on the Spirit; for the letter kills, but the Spirit gives life.

7 •Now if the ministry of death which was carved in letters on stone
was so glorious that the Israelites were unable to gaze upon Moses' face
8 because his face was illuminated by this transitory brightness, •won't the
9 ministry of the Spirit be much more glorious? •For if the ministry that
brought condemnation was glorious, then the ministry that brings restora-
10 tion to fellowship with God will far exceed it in glory. •Indeed, in this
respect, what was once glorious is now without glory because its glory
11 has been surpassed, •for if the Torah which was transitory had glory,
then what's permanent will be far more glorious.

12,13 •Since we have this hope we act with great boldness, •unlike Moses
who placed a veil over his face so the Israelites wouldn't see the end of
14 what was fading away. •But their minds were hardened, for to this day
that same veil remains in place when they read the old covenant, be-
15 cause the veil is set aside only for those who are in Christ. •Instead, to
16 this day whenever Moses is read a veil lays over their hearts, •**but when-**
17 **ever you turn to the Lord the veil is taken away.** •Now the Lord
18 is the Spirit, and where the Spirit of the Lord is, there is freedom. •So
all of us who gaze with uncovered faces at the glory of the Lord are being transformed into his image, from one level of glory to the next, and
this comes from the Lord, who is the Spirit.

1 **4** •Therefore, since we received this ministry through God's mercy,
2 we do not lose heart. •We have renounced shameful deeds done
in secret, refusing to employ deceit or to water down the word of God.
Instead, by openly proclaiming the truth we commend ourselves to the
3 conscience of all men in the sight of God. •And even if our good news
4 is veiled, it is veiled only from those who are perishing. •The god of
this age has blinded the minds of the unbelievers so they won't see
the light of the good news of Christ's glory, who is the image of God.
5 •For we don't proclaim ourselves — we proclaim Jesus Christ as Lord
6 and ourselves as your servants for Jesus' sake. •For the God Who said,

---

3:7 This passage is a midrashic interpretation of
Ex 34:29-30. Paul is intent on showing the superiority of the new covenant to the old covenant
and how this superiority explains his ministry.
3:16 Ex 34:34.
4:1ff The surpassing glory of the new covenant
accounts for their boldness, knowing as they do

that they are God's appointed heralds. Thus their
confidence is in God, not in themselves.
4:3-6 The gospel is veiled only to those who
are spiritually blind because they follow the "god
of this age." Worship of what is not God in whatever form is idolatry and leads to spiritual blindness.

2 CORINTHIANS

"Out of the dark a light will shine," has caused His light to shine in our hearts to reveal the knowledge of God's glory in Christ's face.

Sharing in Jesus' death and life

•But we keep this treasure in clay vessels so that this extraordinary pow- 7 er will be seen to be from God and not from us. •We're afflicted in every 8 way, but we're not crushed, uncertain but not in despair; •although we're 9 persecuted we're not abandoned, knocked down but not dead — •we al- 10 ways bear the death of Jesus in our bodies so the life of Jesus may *also* be revealed in our bodies. •For in our lives we're constantly being deliv- 11 ered to death for Jesus' sake so that Jesus' life may also be revealed in our mortal flesh. •Therefore death is at work in us, but life is at work in 12 you. •But since we have the same spirit of faith which is in accordance 13 with these words of Scripture — **I believed, and therefore I spoke** — we too believe and therefore we also speak out, •because we know that 14 God Who raised the Lord Jesus will also raise us and bring us with you into His presence. •All this is for your sake so that as grace extends to 15 more and more people it may lead to an increase of thanksgiving to the glory of God.

•This is why we don't lose heart, for although our outer self is wast- 16 ing away our inner self is being renewed, day by day. •Our slight, mo- 17 mentary affliction is producing for us an eternal fullness of glory which is beyond all comparison, •and so we keep our eyes on what is unseen 18 rather than on what can be seen, for what can be seen is transitory but what is unseen is eternal.

5 •For we know that if the tent which is our earthly dwelling should 1 be destroyed we have a building from God, an eternal house not made by human hands. •Here we groan, because we long to put on 2 our heavenly dwelling, •and if we *are* clothed with it we won't be found 3 to be naked. •For while we live in this tent we groan in our troubled 4

4:7-5:10 Paul now returns to the theme of suf- fering. For the Christian, suffering has value and meaning because in it we share in Christ's re- demptive death so as to rise with him and share his life.
4:13 Ps 116:10 (Septuagint).
5:1-10 This passage is dense and complicated and is made more so by the way Paul shifts be- tween images of building and clothing. Our earth- ly bodies ("tents") are alive, but in comparison to the heavenly bodies we long for they are dead. It's not that we long for death — after all these bod- ies were made by God and are good — rather, we long to have our living deaths swallowed up and transformed in the heavenly life. Our courage is a result of faith, for through faith we know that even as our earthly lives are dying we are coming to life in Jesus, a life that will not end with bodily death.

Two peacocks, symbols of the resurrection. (2 Cor 4:14)
Church of the Transfiguration on Mount Tabor.

state of mind; we don't want to remove our clothing — we want to have clothing put over it so that what's mortal will be swallowed up by life. 5 •God is the One Who has prepared us for this, and He has given us the Spirit as a down payment.

6   •So we're always full of courage, even though we know that while we're 7 at home in the body we're away from the Lord, •for we walk through 8 faith, not by sight. •We're full of courage and we'd prefer to leave our 9 bodies and be at home with the Lord. •Therefore our ambition is to please 10 the Lord, whether we're at home or away. •[b] For all of us will have to appear before the judgment seat of Christ where each will receive either good or evil, depending on what we did while in the body.

Ambassadors of Christ's love

11   •Therefore, knowing as we do the fear of the Lord, we try to persuade others, but God knows us for what we are, and I hope that we're also

[b] *Rm 14:10.*

5:11-21 Paul appeals to the Corinthians to accept him as God's ambassador and to understand how this status affects all that he does, inspired as he is by the vision of Christ's love for all.

2 CORINTHIANS

well known to your consciences. •We're not commending ourselves to 12
you again — we're giving you an opportunity to boast about us, so you'll
have something to say to those who boast about appearances rather than
what's in the heart. •For if we've lost our minds, it's for God; if we're of 13
sound mind, it's for you. •The love of Christ urges us on, since we're 14
convinced that one man died for all and that as a result all have died. •He 15
died for all so that those who live might no longer live for themselves but
instead might live for the one who died and rose for them.

•Therefore, from now on we regard no one according to the flesh. If 16
at one time we looked upon Christ according to the flesh, we no longer
do. •Therefore, anyone who's in Christ is a new creation — the old has 17
passed away, behold the new has come! •All this is from God, Who rec- 18
onciled us to Himself through Christ and has given us this ministry of
reconciliation. •That is, in Christ God was reconciling the world to Him- 19
self, not counting their transgressions against them and entrusting us with
the message of reconciliation. •That makes us ambassadors for Christ, 20
just as if God Himself were making His appeal through us. We beg you
on behalf of Christ — be reconciled to God! •For our sake God had 21
Christ become sin, even though he was without sin, so that in Christ we
might become the righteousness of God.

6 •We are sharing in God's work and we urge you not to accept God's 1
grace in vain — •for He says, 2

At the acceptable time I heard you,
on the day of salvation I came to your aid.

Behold, now is the acceptable time; behold, now is the day of salvation!
•We give no one any cause to take offense, so that no fault may be found 3
with our ministry, •but as servants of God we commend ourselves in 4
every way possible with great steadfastness — in afflictions, in dire need,
in distress, •when beaten, in prison, subjected to mob violence, in hard 5
work, in sleepless nights, in fasting, •in purity, in knowledge, in patience, 6
in kindness, in the Holy Spirit, in sincere love, •in truthful words, in the 7
power of God, with weapons of righteousness for both attack and defense, •in honor and dishonor, in ill repute and good repute, whether 8

5:16 "According to the flesh"; i.e., Paul judged the
Messiah, Jesus, by the standards of, for example, Israel's national aspirations.
5:17 "A new creation." The Greek translates rabbinic terminology and thought, according to
which a person who was brought to true knowl-

edge of God was considered "a new creation."
6:1-7:4 Paul makes a final impassioned plea for
the Corinthians to accept his love and return it,
as well as to live lives worthy of God's promise.
6:2 Is 49:8.

9 regarded as impostors or truthful, •as unknown or well known, as dy-
10 ing and yet we're alive, as subjected to punishment but not killed, •as
sorrowful yet always rejoicing, as poor yet enriching many, as having
nothing yet possessing everything.
11 •We have spoken openly to you, Corinthians; our hearts are open
12 wide! •You're not constrained by *us*; you're constrained by your own af-
13 fections! •In return — I speak now as if I were speaking to my own children — open wide your hearts to us!

A warning against relationships with unbelievers

14 •Don't enter into relationships with unbelievers! After all, what partnership can there be between righteousness and wickedness? What do
15 light and darkness have to share? •What agreement can there be between
Christ and Belial? What is there in common between a believer and an
16 unbeliever? •What accommodation can there be between the Temple of
God and idols? *We* are the Temple of the Living God; as God has said,

> **"I will dwell and move about among them,**
> **I will be their God, and they shall be My people.**
17 > •Therefore, **come out of their midst**
> **and separate yourselves from them,"**
> **says the Lord;**
> **"Touch nothing that's unclean**
> **and I will take you in.**
18 > •**I will be** your **Father,**
> **and** you will be **My sons** and daughters,"
> **Says the Lord God Almighty.**

7 •Since we have these promises, beloved, let us cleanse ourselves from
every defilement of flesh and spirit and come to perfect holiness in
the fear of God.

A renewed plea for the Corinthians' love

2 •Make room for us in your hearts! We've wronged no one, we've cor-
3 rupted no one, we've taken advantage of no one! •I'm not saying this

6:16 Lv 26:12; Ezk 37:27; Jr 32:38.   6:17 Is 52:11.   6:18 2 S 7:14; 1 Ch 17:13.

to condemn you — as I've already said, you're in our hearts and we'll die together and live together. •I have great confidence in you, I have great pride in you. I'm wonderfully encouraged and despite all our afflictions I'm brimming over with joy. ₄

E. CONTINUATION OF PAUL'S ACCOUNT OF RECENT RELATIONS

•Even when we came to Macedonia our bodies had no rest. We were ₅ afflicted in every way — conflicts without, fear within. •But God, Who ₆ encourages the downhearted, encouraged us with the arrival of Titus. •It wasn't just his arrival that encouraged us, however, but the news ₇ of how you had encouraged Titus, for he told us of your longing for me and your sorrow, and of your zeal on my behalf. As a result, I rejoiced all the more! •For even if my letter caused you pain, I don't re- ₈ gret it now. Even if I regretted it at the time — for I can see the letter did hurt you, if only for a little while — •I rejoice in it now, not be- ₉ cause it caused you pain but because your sorrow led you to repent. For your sorrow was directed toward God, and so you lost nothing through us. •For grief which is directed toward God produces a re- ₁₀ pentance that leads to salvation and is not to be regretted, whereas sorrow in a purely human sense brings death. •Just look at how much ₁₁ earnestness was produced by this sorrow which was directed toward God — you were filled with a desire to defend yourselves, with indignation, fear, longing, zeal, and with eagerness to see just punishment administered. In every respect you've proved your innocence in this matter. •So even though I wrote to you, it wasn't because of the one ₁₂ who did wrong or because of the one who received the injury — it was so you'd be able to clearly see in the sight of God how eager you are in our behalf. •For this reason we're encouraged. ₁₃

And although we rejoiced because of our own encouragement, we rejoiced even more at Titus' joy, because his mind has been set to rest by you. •I may have been somewhat boastful about you to him, but I haven't ₁₄ been put to shame. Just as everything we told you was true, so too did our boasts to Titus prove true. •And his affection for you grows all the ₁₅ stronger when he recalls how you received him in fear and trembling. •I rejoice because I have every confidence in you. ₁₆

Cart with two wheels. Fragment of a Roman sepulchral stele (Turin).

F. THE COLLECTION FOR THE SAINTS IN JUDEA

1,2 **8** •We want you to know, brothers, about the grace God has given to the churches in Macedonia, •for although they've been sorely tried with afflictions their abundant joy and extreme poverty have overflowed 3 in a wealth of generosity. •I bear them witness — of their own accord they gave according to their means and even beyond their means, 4,5 •earnestly begging us to allow them a share in helping the saints. •It was beyond what we'd hoped for, but first they gave themselves to the Lord 6 and then to us by God's will. •As a result we've urged Titus to complete 7 among you this work of love, which he previously began. •Just as you excel in every other respect — in faith, speech, knowledge, earnestness, and in your love for us — so too may you excel in this work of love.

8 •I'm not issuing any orders; instead, by telling you how eager others 9 are to help I'm testing the genuineness of your love. •For you know the grace of our Lord Jesus Christ; although he was rich he became poor for 10 your sake so that you might become rich through his poverty. •I'll give

8:9 This is a reference to Christ's pre-existence. Cf. Ph 2:6-11.

you my opinion in this matter — this is in your own interest. A year ago you began to desire to do this, •and now you should complete what you 11 began, so that your ready desire to undertake this work may be matched by your completion of it from what you have. •For if you're willing to 12 give, your giving will be acceptable to God based on what you have, not based on what you don't have. •My intent is not that others should rest 13 while you are burdened, but that as a matter of equality •your current 14 surplus should make up for what they lack. Later, their surplus may make up for what you lack, so that everything will be equal. •As it is written, 15

> **The one who had much didn't have**
>   **an excessive amount,**
>   **and the one who had little was not in need.**

•Thanks be to God, Who put the same earnest concern for you into 16 Titus' heart. •Not only did he agree to the course of action we urged 17 upon him, but he's so very eager that he's going to you of his own accord. •We're sending with him the brother who is praised in all the 18 churches for his proclamation of the good news — •not only that, but 19 he's been chosen by the churches to be our travelling companion in this service of love we're performing for the glory of God and to show our willingness to help. •We're trying to avoid being blamed by anyone for 20 our handling of this generous gift, •for **our concern is to do what's** 21 **right**, not only **in God's sight** but **also** in the eyes **of men.** •With 22 them we're sending our brother whom we've tested many times and have found to be eager, but now he's even more eager because of the tremendous confidence he has in you. •As for Titus, he's my partner and co- 23 worker for you; as for our brothers, they're messengers from the churches, the glory of Christ. •So show the churches your love and the reason 24 we boast about you to them.

G. THE MATTER OF THE
COLLECTION ADDRESSED ONCE AGAIN

9 •It's superfluous for me to write to you about the help we're send- 1 ing to the saints. •I know how eager you are and I boast about you 2 to the Macedonians, saying that Achaia has been prepared since last year. As a result, your eagerness has stirred most of them up. •I'm send- 3

8:15 Ex 16:18.
8:20-21 Paul is quite aware of the precarious state of his relations with the Corinthians and is determined to leave no opening for misunderstanding.
8:21 Pr 3:4 (Septuagint).

ing the brothers so our boasting about you won't come to naught in this
4 matter, so you'll be ready just as I said you would. •Otherwise, if some
Macedonians come with me and find you unprepared we'll be humiliat-
5 ed for being so confident — not to mention you! •Therefore I thought
it was necessary to urge the brothers to go on ahead to you and arrange
for the generous gift you've promised, so it will be ready as a gift and
not as an exaction.
6   •Keep in mind that whoever sows sparingly will also reap sparingly,
7 and whoever sows bountifully will also reap bountifully. •Each should give
from the heart, not reluctantly or under compulsion, for **God** loves **a**
8 **cheerful giver.** •Moreover, God is able to provide you with every gift
so that you'll always have enough of everything and will have more than
9 enough for every good work, •as it is written,

> **He's generous, He gives to the needy,**
> **His righteousness lasts forever.**

10   •He Who supplies seed to the sower and bread for food will also provide your seed, cause it to multiply, and increase the yield of your right-
11 eousness. •You'll be enriched in every way for your generosity, which
12 will produce a thanksgiving to God through us. •For your contribution
to this service not only supplies what the saints lack, it's also producing
13 an outpouring of thanksgiving to God. •This test of your willingness to
help will lead people to glorify God for your obedience to your profession of the good news of Christ and for your generosity in sharing with
14 them and with everyone. •Then, as they pray for you, they'll long for
15 you because of the immeasurable grace God has given you. •Thanks be
to God for His inexpressible gift to you!

H. A DEFENSE OF PAUL'S MINISTRY AS AN APOSTLE

Paul's authority and power

1 **10**•I, Paul, myself appeal to you by the humility and gentleness of
Christ — I who am meek and mild with you when we're face to
2 face, but bold with you when I'm away. •I beg that when I come I won't
have to act boldly with the confidence I intend to display toward those
3 who think we behave in a worldly way. •For though we live in the world
4 we don't wage war in a worldly way. •The weapons we use in our cam-

9:7 Pr 22:8 (Septuagint).   9:9 Ps 112:9.

paign aren't worldly weapons, they're God's powerful weapons for destroying strongholds. We destroy sophistry •and every proud obstacle to 5 the knowledge of God and we capture every thought to bring it into obedience to Christ. •We stand ready to punish all acts of disobedience, once 6 your obedience is complete.

•Look the facts in the face. If anyone is confident that they belong to 7 Christ they should think again, because we belong to Christ as much as they do. •I may boast a little too much about our authority, which the 8 Lord gave us to build you up and not to destroy you, but I won't be put to shame. •I don't want it to look like I'm frightening you with letters. 9 •Then they'll say, "His letters are severe and powerful, but his person- 10 al presence is weak and his speaking ability isn't worth mentioning." •Those who think that way had better understand that our actions when 11 we come will be the same as what we say in our letters when we're away.

•Not that we dare put ourselves in the same class or compare our- 12 selves with those who think so highly of themselves, but when they measure themselves against one another and compare themselves to one another they show no understanding at all. •Our boasting won't exceed 13 the limits of our ministry; it will stay within the bounds of the commission God assigned to us, which includes you. •When we came to you 14 with the good news of Christ it wasn't as if our commission didn't include you and we were overreaching our authority, •so we're not going 15 beyond the limits of our ministry and boasting about the work of others. Our hope is that as your faith increases the scope of our activity will be greatly enlarged, •so that we'll be able to proclaim the good news to 16 lands beyond you and won't have to boast of work already done in someone else's area. •But **whoever boasts should boast in the Lord,** 17 •for the one whom the Lord commends is the one who's approved, not 18 the one who commends himself.

Paul's boasting

11 •I wish you'd bear with me in a little foolishness — please bear 1 with me! •For I'm jealous for you with the jealousy of God, be- 2 cause I betrothed you like a pure virgin to be presented to one husband — to Christ — •but I'm afraid that just as the serpent deceived Eve with 3 his cunning, your minds will somehow be led away from a sincere devotion to Christ. •For if someone comes and proclaims a different Je- 4

10:17 Jr 9:24.

sus than we proclaimed, or if you receive a different spirit than the one you received from us, or if you receive a different gospel than the one 5 you received from us, you bear with it quite readily! •I don't consider 6 myself to be in any way inferior to these "super apostles"! •Maybe I lack something in speaking ability, but not in knowledge! We made this clear to you repeatedly and in every possible way.

7 •Did I commit a sin by humbling myself so you could be exalted, be- 8 cause I proclaimed God's good news to you without any charge? •I robbed other churches by accepting money from them so I could serve 9 you, •and when I was among you and was in need I didn't burden any of you — the brothers who came from Macedonia took care of my needs. In every possible way I avoided being a burden to you, and I'll continue 10 to do so. •As Christ's truth is in me, this boast of mine will not be si- 11 lenced in the districts of Achaia! •Why? Because I don't love you? God knows I do!

12 •What I'm doing I'll continue to do, to eliminate any chance that those pretenders might find some pretext under which they might claim to be 13 regarded as our equals in the ministry they boast of. •Such men are false

Coin of King Aretas (9 B.C.-40 A.D.). (2 Cor 11:32-33)

apostles, dishonest workers who disguise themselves as apostles of Christ. •There's nothing remarkable in this; after all, even Satan disguises 14 himself as an angel of light, •so it should come as no surprise if Satan's 15 servants disguise themselves as servants of righteousness. Their end will be in accordance with their works!

•I repeat, no one should think I'm a fool, but if you do, accept me as a 16 fool just so I'll have a little something to boast about. •What I'm going to 17 say is not the way the Lord would have me speak; I'm speaking foolishly, in boastful confidence. •Since many others boast of their human merits, 18 I'll boast too! •[c] After all, you gladly put up with fools, since you're so wise, 19 •for if someone imposes upon you, preys upon you, takes advantage of 20 you, puts on airs, or slaps you in the face, you bear with it. •To my shame, 21 I have to admit that we were too weak to do that, but if anyone dares to boast — I'm speaking like a fool, now — I can be just as daring!

•Are they Hebrews? So am I! Are they Israelites? So am I! Are they 22 descended from Abraham? So am I! •Are they servants of Christ? Now 23 I'm speaking like a madman — I'm even more so! I've worked harder, spent more time in prison, been beaten more severely, and have often been in danger of death. •Five times I received forty lashes less one from 24 the Jews, •three times I was beaten with rods, once I was stoned, three 25 times I was shipwrecked — a day and a night I spent out on the deep! •In my many journeys I've been in danger from rivers, from robbers, 26 from my own race, from Gentiles; I've been in danger in the city and in the wild, on the sea and from false brothers. •I've toiled and been through 27 hardships, spent many sleepless nights, been hungry and thirsty; I've often gone without food, been cold and without sufficient clothing. •Apart 28 from these external things, I experience daily cares and anxiety for all the churches. •If anyone is weak, I too am weak! If anyone is led into 29 sin, I too am ablaze with indignation!

•If I must boast, I'll boast of my weakness. •The God and Father of 30,31 the Lord Jesus, Who is blessed forever, knows that I'm not lying. •[d] In 32 Damascus the ethnarch, King Aretas, kept watch over the city of the Damascenes in order to arrest me, •but I was lowered in a basket from 33 a window in the city wall and escaped his clutches.

12 •I must boast. It may serve no purpose, but I'll go on and talk about 1 visions and revelations from the Lord. •I know a man in Christ 2 who fourteen years ago was caught up to the Third Heaven — whether in the body or out of the body I don't know, God knows. •And I know 3

---

[c] *Ph 4:15-18.*   [d] *Ac 9:23-25.*

that this man — whether in the body or out of the body I don't know,
4 God knows — •I know that he was caught up to Paradise where he heard things too sacred to be put into words, things which no man may utter.
5 •I'll boast about this man, but as for myself I'll boast only of my weak-
6 nesses. •If I'm going to boast, I won't be a fool — I'll tell the truth! But I'll spare you, so no one will think more of me than what they can see
7 and hear of me. •But to keep me from getting puffed up as a result of these extraordinary revelations I was given a thorn in the flesh, an an-
8 gel of Satan, to beat me so I wouldn't get puffed up. •Three times I
9 begged the Lord to take it away from me, •but he told me, "My grace is enough for you, for my power is made perfect in your weakness." Therefore I'm all the more pleased to boast of my weaknesses, so that
10 Christ's power may dwell with me. •For this reason I delight in weakness, insults, hardships, persecution, and difficulties for Christ's sake, for when I'm weak, that's when I'm strong.

11 •I've been a fool, but you forced me to be one! I ought to be commended by *you* rather than by myself! I'm not one bit inferior to those
12 super apostles, even if I *am* nothing. •I patiently performed signs among you which proved that I'm an apostle — signs, wonders, and miracles.
13 •In what way were you treated worse than the other churches, except
14 that I wasn't a burden to you? Forgive me for this injustice! •This is the third time now that I've prepared to come to you. I don't want your possessions, I want you! After all, children shouldn't be saving up for their
15 parents, it's the parents who should be saving up for their children. •I'd gladly spend all my money and utterly exhaust myself for your souls. If
16 I love you so much, will you love me less? •Let it be agreed, then, that I wasn't a burden to you, but could it be that I was crafty and took ad-
17 vantage of you by deceit? •Well, I didn't take advantage of you through
18 anyone I sent to you, did I? •I urged Titus to visit you and sent a brother with him. Titus didn't take advantage of you, did he? Didn't we follow in the same spirit? Didn't we leave the same footprints?

19 •Have you been thinking all this time that we've been defending ourselves to you? We've been speaking in Christ in God's presence, and
20 it's all been for your edification, my beloved! •My fear is that I'll come and find that all is not as I would like it to be with you, and you'll find *me* to be other than you'd like me to be. I'm afraid that I'll find strife,
21 jealousy, anger, selfishness, slander, gossip, pride, and unholiness. •I'm afraid that I'll come again and God will humble me before you — I'll have to weep for many of those who sinned before and haven't repented of the impurity, immorality, and licentiousness they practiced.

Paul's plans to visit Corinth

13 •This is the third time I'm coming to you. **Any charge must** [1] **stand on the testimony of two or three witnesses.** •On [2] my second visit I warned those who sinned before and now I'm warning the rest of you again, that if I come again I won't spare you, •since [3] you want proof that Christ is speaking in me. He's not weak in dealing with you — he's powerful among you! •He was crucified in weak- [4] ness, but he lives by the power of God. We're weak in him, but in dealing with you we'll live with him by God's power.

•Test yourselves, see if you're living in faith, examine yourselves! Don't [5] you realize that Christ Jesus is in you? Or have you failed the test? •I hope [6] you'll find out that *we* haven't failed the test! •We pray to God that you [7] won't do anything wrong — not so we'll appear to be successes, but so you'll do what's right, even though we may seem to be failures. •After [8] all, we can't oppose the truth, we can only work *for* the truth. •We re- [9] joice when we're weak and you're strong; our prayer is for your perfection. •The reason I'm writing this while away from you is so that when I [10] come I won't have to be severe and use the authority the Lord has given me, that I'll be able to build you up, not tear you down.

I. CLOSING EXHORTATIONS AND FAREWELL

•Finally, brothers, rejoice! Mend your ways, encourage one another, [11] live in harmony and peace, and the God of love and peace will be with you. •Greet one another with a holy kiss. All the saints greet you. [12]
•The grace of the Lord Jesus Christ, the love of God, and the fel- [13] lowship of the Holy Spirit be with you all.

13:1 Dt.19:15.

THE LETTER TO THE

GALATIANS

Introduction to the Letter
to the Galatians

Galatians takes us to the heart of several issues which are central to an understanding of St. Paul and his gospel. The letter was written in response to a serious threat to the "truth of the gospel" among the churches of Galatia, a region located in what is now central Turkey. Apparently Paul had had to stop over among the Galatians as the result of a serious illness and had taken the occasion to proclaim the good news. At the time of writing, however, problems had arisen among the predominantly Gentile converts. Jewish Christian missionaries had appeared among them and had raised doubts among the Galatians regarding Paul and the gospel he had preached. These missionaries discounted Paul's claim to apostolic authority and asserted that he had taught the Galatians an abbreviated version of the good news. Paul had proclaimed the good news that Jesus is Messiah but, they maintained, he had failed to inform them about the need to be circumcised and to observe the Torah in order to be saved.

In the face of this fundamental challenge Paul responded with a passionate defense of both himself and of the gospel he preached. He adamantly maintained that his claim to be an apostle was based upon the personal call of Jesus himself, whom God had revealed to him. He also vigorously proclaimed the basic Christian truth that our relationship with God can never be restored by legal observance but only through accepting God's call to faith in Jesus. Included in this proclamation was the assurance that both Jews and Gentiles have equal access to salvation and a ringing call to the Christian life of freedom in the Spirit.

A. GREETING

1 2 3 4 5 **1** •Paul, an apostle not from men nor through a man but through Jesus Christ and God the Father, Who raised him from the dead, •and all those brothers with me, to the churches of Galatia. •Grace and peace be with you from God our Father and the Lord Jesus Christ, •who gave himself for our sins to deliver us from the present evil age in accordance with the will of our God and Father, •to Whom be glory forever and ever, Amen!

B. THE BASIS OF THE GOSPEL PAUL PROCLAIMED

6 7 8 9 •I'm amazed that you're so quick to desert the One Who called you by the grace of Christ and are turning to a different gospel. •There is no other good news, of course, but there are some who are disturbing you and trying to distort the good news of Christ. •But even if we or an angel from Heaven should proclaim a gospel contrary to the good news we proclaimed to you, let them be accursed! •As we said before and now repeat, if anyone proclaims a gospel contrary to what you received from us, let him be accursed!

10 •Who am I trying to gain favor with now, men or God? Am I seeking to please men? If I were still trying to please men, I wouldn't be a servant of Christ!

11 12 •I want you to know, brothers, that the good news I proclaimed is not a human gospel, •for I didn't receive it from a man nor was I taught it — I received it through a revelation of Jesus Christ.

1:1 "An apostle..." From the very beginning of the letter Paul signals that he will vigorously defend his authority and standing as an apostle against all challengers. The tone is quite uncharacteristic for Paul's greetings, normally so serene.
1:6 "I'm amazed..." marks an even more drastic departure from the usual epistolary format, for in place of the usual thanksgiving Paul gets right down to business, without any attempt to hide his concern.
1:10 Apparently Paul had been accused of trying to gain human favor by proclaiming a type of less rigorous, abbreviated gospel, in that he preached obedience to the Torah in the spirit, rather than according to the letter. Paul will vigorously assert that the new Christian freedom, far from being an abbreviation of the gospel, is of its very essence.

•[a] You've heard what my life was like in Judaism, that I went to ex- 13 traordinary lengths in persecuting the church of God and trying to destroy it, •[b] and that I advanced in Judaism beyond many contemporaries 14 of my race, so much more zealous was I for the traditions of my fathers. •[c] But when the One Who set me apart from my mother's womb and 15 called me through His grace was pleased •to reveal His Son to me so 16 that I might proclaim his good news to the Gentiles, I didn't immediately consult with flesh and blood, •nor did I go up to Jerusalem to see 17 those who were apostles before me. Instead, I went off to Arabia and later returned to Damascus.

•[d] Three years later I went up to Jerusalem to get to know Kephas, 18 and I stayed with him for fifteen days. •I saw no other apostles except 19 James, the Lord's brother. •Before God, what I'm writing to you is no 20 lie! •Then I went to the regions of Syria and Cilicia. •The Judean church- 21,2 es in Christ had no personal knowledge of me — •they only heard that 23 "the one who persecuted us is now proclaiming the faith he once tried to destroy," •and they glorified God because of me. 24

2 •[e] Fourteen years later I again went up to Jerusalem with Barnabas, 1 taking Titus along also. •I went because of a revelation; I met privately with those held in repute and set out for them the gospel I proclaim among the Gentiles, lest I should somehow be running or have run in vain. •But not even Titus who was with me and is a Greek was 3 required to be circumcised, •although it was urged by some false broth- 4 ers who slipped in to spy on the freedom we have in Christ Jesus and wanted to enslave us. •We didn't give in to them for a moment, so the 5 truth of the gospel would be preserved for you. •Those who were held 6 in repute — who they were makes no difference to me; God isn't influenced by such considerations — those who were held in repute added nothing. •On the contrary, when they saw that I had been entrusted 7 with the gospel for the uncircumcised just as Peter had been entrusted with the gospel for the circumcised — •for the One Who worked 8

[a] *Ac 8:3; 22:4-5; 26:13-18.*   [b] *Ac 22:3.*   [c] *Ac 9:3-6; 22:6-10; 26:13-18.*
[d] *Ac 9:26-30.*   [e] *Ac 11:30; 15:2.*

1:18 "Kephas." The Aramaic name for Peter, also derived from a word meaning "rock."
1:19 "James, the Lord's brother." In Semitic usage a relative was often referred to as a brother. In the Gospels it can be seen that James and Jesus had different mothers, cf. Mt 27:55; Mk 15:40-44; Lk 23:49; Jn 19:25.
2:4 Note the very strong language Paul uses:

Jewish Christians who advocate obedience to the Torah are termed "false brothers" who want "to enslave us," so that a return to observance of the Torah would be slavery.
2:5 While Paul constantly preaches respect for the consciences of others, he will not compromise on a matter of principle — to compromise "the truth of the gospel" is not true charity.

Saint Paul on his missionary travels, by Venzo (Italy).

through Peter for the apostleship of the circumcision also worked
9 through me for the Gentiles — •and when they realized the grace that
had been given to me, James and Kephas and John, who were considered the pillars, gave me and Barnabas the right hand of fellowship.
10 We were to go to the Gentiles, and they to the circumcision. •Their
one concern was that we should remember the poor, which was the
very thing we were eager to do.
11 •But when Kephas came to Antioch I opposed him to his face, be-
12 cause he was clearly wrong. •For before certain men came from James,
Kephas ate with the Gentiles, but when they came he drew back and
separated himself because he was afraid of those who favored circum-
13 cision. •The rest of the Jews also joined in the hypocrisy — even Barn-

2:9 The use of the term "pillars" may derive from
the image of the Church as the new Temple of
God, and these disciples as the principal support
for that Temple on earth.
2:10 "The poor." The Jerusalem church. Paul
was eager for his Gentile converts to contribute
to the Jerusalem church as a sign of the unity between Jew and Gentile which Christ had brought.
2:12 For a Jew to eat with Gentiles was to become ritually impure, since Gentiles were considered "unclean."

abas was carried away by their hypocrisy. •But when I saw that their ac- 14
tions were inconsistent with the truth of the gospel I told Kephas in front
of them all, "If you, a Jew, live like a Gentile and not like a Jew, how
can you force the Gentiles to live like Jews?"

•We're Jews by birth and aren't Gentile sinners, •[f] but we know that 15,16
we can be restored to fellowship with God only through faith in Jesus
Christ, not by observance of the Torah. We have believed in Jesus Christ
so that we'll be restored to fellowship with God through faith in Christ
and not by observance of the Torah, because no one **at all can be re-**
stored to fellowship with God by observance of the Torah. •But sup- 17
pose, as we seek to be restored to fellowship with God in Christ, we
ourselves are found to be sinners? Does Christ then serve the interests
of sin? Not at all! •But if I once again build up what I've torn down, I 18
show that I myself am a violator of God's law. •For through the Torah 19
I died to the Torah, so as to live for God. I've been crucified with Christ!
•It's no longer I who live, it's Christ who lives in me! And this life I live 20
now in the flesh, I live through faith in the Son of God, who loved me
and gave himself up for me. •I won't reject God's grace, for if right- 21
eousness came through the Torah then Christ died in vain.

C. THE MEANING OF FAITH AND TORAH
AND THEIR PLACE IN GOD'S PLAN

3 •You foolish Galatians! Who has cast a spell over you? Before your 1
eyes Jesus Christ was publicly portrayed as crucified! •All I want to 2
know from you is this — did you receive the Spirit as a result of observing the Torah or from listening and believing? •How can you be so 3
foolish? Having begun with the Spirit will you now finish with the flesh?
•Has your experience of all this been for nothing, if it truly was for noth- 4

---

[f] *Rm 3:20-22.*

2:16 Ps 143:2.
2:17-18 If in their new life in Christ, Jewish Christians are led to violate Torah rules of purity, can
it be said that Christ has led them into sin? On
the contrary, the purpose of the Torah was to prepare us to receive God's grace in Christ. To return to Torah observance is to reject that grace
and to be exposed as a true sinner.
2:19 The true purpose of the Torah was to lead
to the realization that reconciliation is necessary
and that this cannot be effected by legal observance. This realization leads to death with Christ

to the Torah, but also to resurrection with him to
life in the Spirit.
3:1-6 Paul begins his exposition with an appeal
to the Galatians' own experience: without having
been circumcised, they received the Spirit as witness of Christ's redemptive death and resurrection. Since this occurred through faith rather than
observance of the Torah this means that faith, not
legal observance, is the operative principle. To
now turn to legal observance would be a retreat
from the truth of the gospel. Abraham's experience foreshadows their own.

5 ing? •Does God give you the Spirit and work miracles among you be-
6 cause you observe the Torah or because you listen and believe? •[g] Thus, Abraham **believed God, and it was credited to him as righteousness.**
7   •[h] You can see, then, that those who believe are the sons of Abraham.
8 •Scripture foresaw that God would restore the Gentiles to fellowship with Him through faith and so it proclaimed the good news to Abraham be-
9 forehand, **Through you God will bless all the nations.** •Therefore,
10 those who believe are blessed with Abraham, who had faith. •For every-one who relies on observance of the Torah is under a curse, as it is writ-ten, **Whoever fails to observe everything in the book of the Torah**
11 **is cursed!** •Now, that no one is restored to fellowship with God by ob-servance of the Torah is evident, because **The righteous man shall**
12 **live by faith.** •But the Torah is not based on faith; instead, **Whoever**
13 **does these things will live by them.** •Christ set us free from the Torah's curse by becoming a curse for us, as it is written, **Whoever hangs**
14 **on a tree is cursed.** •So it is that in Christ Jesus the blessing of Abra-ham is able to come to the Gentiles, so that through faith we may re-ceive the promise of the Spirit.
15   •My brothers, let me give you an example. No one can set aside
16 someone's will or modify it once it's been ratified. •Now the promises were made to Abraham and his descendant. It doesn't say, "And his de-scendants," as if it were referring to many people; rather, it refers to
17 one person, **And your descendant,** which is to say, Christ. •This is what I'm getting at; the Torah, which came four hundred and thirty years after the covenant had already been ratified by God, cannot invalidate
18 the covenant so as to set aside the promise. •[i] For if the inheritance were dependent upon the Torah, it would no longer come from the promise,
19 whereas God *did* give it to Abraham by a promise. •What, then, was

---

[g] *Rm 4:3.*   [h] *Rm 4:16.*   [i] *Rm 4:14.*

3:6 Gn 15:6.
3:7-14 Paul next appeals to Scripture to under-score that only through faith and not through ob-servance of the Torah is it possible to be restored to fellowship with God.
3:8 Gn 12:3.
3:10 Dt 27:26 (Septuagint).
3:11 Hab 2:4.
3:12 Lv 18:5.
3:13 Dt 21:23.
3:15-18 Having shown in the preceding verses that the call of the Gentiles to faith had been promised through Abraham, Paul now appeals to

the example of a will to show that the promise takes precedence over the Torah.
3:16 Gn 12:7.
3:19-22 Paul maintains that the Torah was of a lower order than the promise because the Torah was promulgated by angels and only as a tem-porary measure. The belief that God used inter-mediaries in his dealings with humans was com-mon in Judaism. Verse 20 has been variously translated, but the general thrust is that the Torah is ancillary and subordinate to God's original promise to Abraham.

the purpose of the Torah? It was added so that transgressions would be seen for what they are, to be in effect until the descendant to whom the promise was made came, and was promulgated by angels through an intermediary. •Now there's no need for an intermediary when one par- 20 ty acts alone, and God is one.

•So then, is the Torah contrary to God's promises? Not at all! Only 21 if the Torah were able to give life would fellowship with God come from the Torah. •But Scripture confined everything under the power of sin 22 so that what was promised might be given to those who believe, based on faith in Jesus Christ.

•Before faith came we were imprisoned under the Torah, confined 23 until such time as this faith was to be revealed. •So the Torah had cus- 24 tody of us until Christ came to restore us to fellowship with God through faith. •Now that faith has come we're no longer in its custody. 25

•Through faith you're all sons of God in Christ Jesus, •for all of you 26,27 who were baptized into Christ have clothed yourselves with Christ. •There's neither Jew nor Greek, there's neither slave nor free, there's 28 neither male nor female — you're all one in Christ Jesus. •ʲ And if you 29 belong to Christ then you're Abraham's descendants, heirs in accordance with the promise.

4 •Here's what I mean; as long as the heir is a minor, he's no different 1 than a slave, even though he owns everything — •he's subject to 2 guardians and trustees until the day that was set by his father. •It's the same 3 with us — when we were minors we were subject to the elementary principles of the world. •But when the fullness of time had come, God sent 4 forth His Son, born of a woman, born under the Torah, •ᵏ to redeem those 5 who were under the Torah, so we could be adopted as God's sons. • And 6 proof that you're His sons can be seen from the fact that God has sent the Spirit of His Son into our hearts, to cry, "Abba, Father!" •Therefore you're 7 no longer a slave — you're a son, and if you're a son you're also an heir.

ʲ Rm 4:13.   ᵏ Rm 8:15-17.

3:23-4:7 Paul concludes this section with several more metaphors — of imprisonment, sonship, and tutelage — to drive home the point that Christians are heirs of the promise and have been freed by Christ from the Torah.

D. EXHORTATION TO HOLD FAST
TO FREEDOM IN FAITH

8 •Back then when you didn't know God you were slaves to things that
9 by nature are not gods. •Now that you know God — or, rather, are
known by God — how can you turn back once again to those poor,
10 weak, elementary principles? Do you want to be their slaves again? •You
11 observe days and months and seasons and years. •I'm afraid that all my
work for you may somehow have been in vain.

12 •My brothers, I beg you, become like me as I have become like you!
13 You did me no wrong — •you know that it was due to an illness of the
14 flesh that I first proclaimed the good news to you, •and although my
condition was a trial for you, you didn't despise or disdain me; instead,
15 you received me like an angel of God, like Jesus Christ. •What has become of your blessed joy? For I bear you witness, if it had been possi-
16 ble you would have torn your eyes out and given them to me! •Have I
17 become your enemy, then, by telling you the truth? •They court your
favor, but they don't mean you well — they want to have you for them-
18 selves so you'll court *their* favor. •Now it's always good to be made much
19 of for a good purpose, and not just when I'm present with you. •My chil-

*Hebron. The Sanctuary which holds the tombs of Abraham
and of the Patriarchs, models in faith. (Gal 4:21-31)*

dren, once again I'm suffering birth pains until Christ takes form in you. •I wish I were with you now and could change my tone, because now 20 I'm at a loss to understand you.

•Tell me, you who wish to be subject to the Torah, don't you under- 21 stand what the Torah says? •For it's written that Abraham had two sons, 22 one born of a slave woman and the other born of a free woman. •The 23 one who was born of the slave woman was born according to the flesh, but the one who was born of the free woman was born through a prom- ise. •This is an allegory — these women are two covenants. One covenant 24 is from Mount Sinai and bears children into slavery — this is Hagar. •Now 25 Hagar is Mount Sinai in Arabia and corresponds to the present Jerusalem, which is in slavery with her children. •The Jerusalem above, on the oth- 26 er hand, is free, and she is our mother, •for it is written, 27

> **Rejoice, barren woman, who have not given birth,**
> **break out and shout you who have not**
> **been in labor,**
> **Because the abandoned woman will have**
> **more children**
> **than the woman who has a husband.**

•Now brothers, you, like Isaac, are children of the promise. •But just 28,29 as at that time the son who was born according to the flesh persecuted the son born according to the Spirit, so it is even now. •But what does 30 Scripture say? **Send the slave woman and her son away, for the slave woman's son shall not share the inheritance with the son** of the free woman. •So then, my brothers, we're not children of the 31 slave woman but of the free woman.

5 •Christ freed us for freedom, so stand firm and don't submit once 1 again to the yoke of slavery.

•Listen now! I, Paul, tell you that if you have yourselves circumcised, 2 Christ will not be able to do you any good. •I bear witness once again 3 to every man who has himself circumcised that he must observe the whole Torah. •Those of you who seek to be restored to fellowship with 4 God through the Torah have separated yourselves from Christ, you've fallen away from grace. •For through the Spirit, by faith, we eagerly await 5 the hope of fellowship with God. •For in Christ Jesus neither circumci- 6 sion nor uncircumcision have any meaning — what matters is faith work- ing through love.

---

¹ *1 Cor 5:6.*   4:27 Is 54:1.   4:30 Gn 21:10.

7 •You were running well; who has deflected you from following the
8,9 truth? •Whoever persuaded you, it wasn't the One Who calls you! •ˡ A
10 little yeast can leaven the whole lump of dough. •I'm confident in the
Lord that you'll take the same view, and the person who's disturbing
11 you, whoever he is, will be punished. •My brothers, if I am still preaching circumcision, why am I still being persecuted? In that case, the scan-
12 dal of the cross has been abolished! •I wish those who are disturbing
you by preaching circumcision would go on and castrate themselves!

E. CHRISTIAN FREEDOM IN DAILY LIFE

13 •You've been called to freedom, brothers — just don't let your freedom become an opportunity for the flesh. Serve one another through
14 love. •For the whole Torah can be summed up in one command — **Love
15 your neighbor as yourself!** •But if you bite and devour one another, watch out that you don't destroy each other!
16 •But I tell you, walk according to the Spirit, and don't carry out the
17 desires of the flesh. •ᵐ For the flesh's desires are opposed to the Spirit,
and the Spirit is opposed to the flesh. They're opposed to each other so
18 you won't just do whatever you want. •If you're led by the Spirit, you're
19 not subject to the Torah. •Now it's evident what the works of the flesh
20 are — fornication, impurity, and indecent acts, •idolatry, sorcery, hatred,
21 strife, jealousy, anger, selfishness, dissension, factionalism, •drunkenness,
carousing, and similar things. I warn you now as I warned you before,
that those who do these things will not inherit the Kingdom of God.
22 •The Spirit's fruit is love, joy, peace, patience, kindness, goodness,
23 faith, •gentleness, self-control. There is no law against these things!
24 •Those who belong to Christ have crucified the flesh with its passions
25,26 and desires. •If we live in the Spirit, let us also follow the Spirit. •Let's
not be conceited, provocative, or envious toward one another.

ᵐ *Rm 7:15-23.*

5:12 Traditional translations often moderate the
coarseness of this passage with such eu-
phemisms as "make eunuchs of themselves" or
"mutilate themselves," but the Greek means quite
literally to "cut away." The words "by preaching
circumcision" are not in the original.
5:14 Lv 19:18.
5:20 The Greek word for "sorcery" is *pharmakeia*;
the first century sorcerer's stock in trade included a variety of drugs for different purposes. It is

believed that some of these concoctions purported to be abortifacient and contraceptive.
5:22ff Paul now summarizes the preceding verses. He has already noted (v. 14) that the Torah
can be summed up in the commandment to love.
Those who would live "in Christ" must live "by the
Spirit" (v. 16), and the life of the Spirit is expressed preeminently in love. Not only is the
Torah not opposed to this (v. 23), but this fulfills
the law of Christ, the New Torah.

6 •My brothers, if anyone is caught in some kind of transgression, those 1 of you who are spiritual should set him right in a spirit of gentleness. Watch out for yourself, so you won't be tempted too! •Bear one an- 2 other's burdens, and in this way you'll fulfill Christ's law. •For if anyone 3 thinks he's something even though he's nothing, he's only fooling himself. •Each of you should examine your own conduct and then you'll be 4 able to boast of yourself, without worrying about anyone else, •for you 5 will be bearing your own burden. •Whoever is taught the word should 6 share all that's good with the one who teaches. •Don't be deceived; God 7 cannot be outwitted. Whatever you sow, you'll also reap, •because who- 8 ever sows for his flesh will reap corruption from his flesh, whereas whoever sows for the Spirit will reap eternal life from the Spirit. •Let's not 9 grow tired of doing good, for in due time we'll also reap a harvest if we don't give up. •So then, let's continue to do good to everyone as long 10 as we have time, but especially to members of the household of the faith.

F. CONCLUDING EXHORTATION

•Look how large the letters are that I'm writing to you with my own 11 hand! •Those who want to put on a good show in the flesh are the ones 12 who are trying to force you to be circumcised, just so they won't be persecuted for the cross of Christ, •for these proponents of circumcision don't 13 observe the Torah themselves — they only want you to be circumcised so they'll be able to boast about your flesh! •Far be it from me to boast 14 of anything but the cross of Christ, through which the world is crucified to me and I to the world. •Neither circumcision nor uncircumcision is of 15 any significance — a new creation is all that matters. •May peace and 16 mercy be upon those who follow this rule, and upon God's Israel!

•In the future, let no one cause me trouble, for I bear the marks of 17 Jesus in my body!

•The grace of our Lord Jesus Christ be with your spirit, my brothers. 18 Amen!

6:15 In rabbinic thought a convert who was brought to a knowledge of God was said to be a "new creation."

THE LETTER TO THE

EPHESIANS

Introduction to the Letter to the Ephesians

Unlike so many of his other letters, Paul had no particular crisis in mind when he wrote Ephesians — no urgent moral concerns, no dangerous doctrinal deviations. Rather, the letter is an attempt to encourage the recipients to maintain unity in the truth of the gospel they have received. Paul's method of doing this is to review the plan of God which was revealed in Christ. By doing so Paul shows how great is God's power and glory and how great is the glory which we are called to share in, in Christ.

The review of God's plan for our salvation is contained in the first three chapters. Of note is Paul's deviation from his usual epistolary format, for a Blessing precedes the Thanksgiving section and in it Paul details the blessings we have received from God, our reasons for singing His praises. This not only sets the theme of the letter, it also sets the tone, for on several more occasions Paul will break out into prayer as he contemplates the sublimity of God's plan and the place in His plan which has been assigned to the human race.

The second half of the letter is a detailed discussion of various issues regarding life in Christ, including some of the most sublime words that have been written on marriage. Life in Christ is the fruit of faith, and is our response to our call. Of urgent importance to Paul is that the unity of the Christian in Christ should be manifested in unity of spirit in Christ's body, the Church.

A. GREETING

1 2 **1** •Paul, an apostle of Christ Jesus by the will of God, to the saints [in Ephesus] who are faithful in Christ Jesus — •grace and peace be with you from God our Father and the Lord Jesus Christ.

B. BLESSING

3 •Blessed be the God and Father of our Lord Jesus Christ Who has 4 blessed us in Christ with every spiritual blessing in the heavens. •He chose us in Christ before the foundation of the world to be holy and 5 blameless before Him. In His love •He destined us beforehand to be His adopted sons through Jesus Christ, according to the purpose and de- 6 sire of His will, •to the praise of the glorious grace He bestowed upon 7 us in His Beloved. •[a] Through Christ's blood we are redeemed and our 8 sins are forgiven — such is the wealth of His grace •which He poured 9 out upon us! With every manner of wisdom and understanding •He made known to us the mystery of His will, according to the purpose He dis- 10 played in Christ •as a plan for the fullness of time — to bring all things 11 together in Christ, things in the heavens and things on earth. •God ac- complishes all things in accordance with the purpose He has decided upon, and in Christ He chose and selected us in accordance with His 12 plan •by which we who were the first to hope in Christ might exist to

[a] *Col 1:14.*

1:3 "In the heavens." This introduces a prominent theme in Ephesians, in which Paul will refer frequently to "things in the heavens" (v. 10), "elemental spirits," and heavenly "powers." Both Jewish and pagan thought at the time held that human affairs — governmental, social, religious, etc. — were under the power or influence of spiritual beings, whether they were called angels, demons, or gods. Christ's mastery over this spiritual realm will thus be a source of "spiritual bless-

ing," as, in Christ, we extend the effects of his redemption to all aspects of our individual and corporate lives as human beings.
1:7 According to Judaic sacrificial theology "The life of the flesh is in the blood... it is the blood that makes an atonement for the soul" (Lv 17:11). Thus the reference to "blood" is properly understood within a sacrificial context, whereby the shedding of blood brings life. Cf. also 2:13.

praise His glory. •In Christ you who heard the word of truth — the good 13
news of your salvation — and believed it were sealed by the promised
Holy Spirit, •which is the pledge that we shall gain our inheritance when 14
God redeems what is His, to the praise of His glory!

C. THANKSGIVING

•And so, having heard of your faith in the Lord Jesus and your love 15
for all the saints, •I give unceasing thanks and mention you in my prayers 16
•that the God of our Lord Jesus Christ, the glorious Father, may give 17
you a spirit of wisdom and revelation by which you'll come to a knowledge of Him. •May the eyes of your hearts be enlightened so you'll come 18
to know what the hope is to which He calls you, how rich is His glorious heritage which will be shared among the saints, •and how extraor- 19
dinary is His great power for us who believe. The might of His power
can be seen in the work •He accomplished in Christ when He raised 20
him from the dead and had him sit at His right hand in the heavenly
realms, •far above every ruler, authority, power, and dominion, and 21
above any name that can be named, not only in this age but also in the
age to come. •[b] **He has put all things under his feet** and has giv- 22
en him as head over all things to the Church, •which is his body, the 23
fullness of the One Who fills all things in their totality.

D. IN CHRIST BOTH JEWS AND GENTILES
ARE RECONCILED AND ARE UNITED IN THE CHURCH

2 •[c] You used to be dead in the sins and transgressions •by which you 1,2
followed this world's way of life, following the ruler of the power of
the air, the spirit that is currently at work in those who are disobedient.
•We all once lived among them in the desires of the flesh; we did what 3
the flesh and our imagination wanted and were, by nature, children of
wrath, like the rest of them. •But God is rich in mercy and because of 4
the great love He had for us, •even when we were dead in our trans- 5

[b] *Col 1:18.*   [c] *Col 2:13.*

1:21 "Every ruler, authority, power, and domina-
tion." In this phrase Paul is referring to the "things
in the heavens" (v. 10), those spiritual beings or
influences which rule man in his corporate life.
1:22 Ps 8:6.

2:1-3 "The ruler of the power of the air" is believed to be a reference to Satan. "Children of
wrath" is a characterization of the entire human
race as liable to divine punishment because of
their sins.

EPHESIANS

gressions, He brought us to life together with Christ — you've been saved
6 by grace — •He raised us with him and had us sit together with Christ
7 in the heavenly realms •so that in the coming ages He could show the
extraordinary riches of His grace in His kindness toward us in Christ Je-
8 sus. •For by grace you have been saved through faith; and this was God's
9 gift, it didn't come from you, •not from your own efforts, so that no one
10 would be able to boast. •For we are His handiwork, created in Christ
Jesus for the purpose of carrying out those good works for which God
prepared us beforehand, so that we might lead our lives in the performance of good works.

Ephesus. Roman theatre with the Arcadian Road (1st-2nd century A.D.).

11 •Therefore, remember that formerly you who are Gentiles by birth,
you who are called the "uncircumcision" by what is called the "circumci-
12 sion" (made in the flesh by human hands), •remember that at that time
you were separated from Christ, alienated from the community of Israel
and strangers to the covenants made pursuant to the promise. You had
13 no hope and were without God in the world, •but now you who were
once far away have been drawn near through the blood of Christ.

•For he is our peace. He has made the two — Jews and Gentiles — 14 one, and in his flesh has torn down the dividing wall, the protective hedge, of enmity. •[d] He did this by setting aside the Torah with its com- 15 mandments and regulations, making peace by creating one new man in himself out of the two •[e] and reconciling them both to God in one body 16 by the cross, putting enmity to death by it. •He came and **proclaimed** 17 **the good news of peace** to you **who were far off, and peace to those who were near,** •for through him we both have access in the 18 one Spirit to the Father. •So then you're no longer strangers and aliens 19 but fellow citizens with the saints and members of God's household. •You 20 were built upon a foundation of apostles and prophets, and Christ Je- sus was its cornerstone. •In him the whole building is joined together 21 and grows into a holy Temple in the Lord, •and in him you are being 22 built together into God's dwelling place in the Spirit.

E. PAUL'S ROLE IN THE CHURCH AS APOSTLE TO THE GENTILES

3 •Because of this I, Paul, a prisoner for Christ [Jesus] on behalf of 1 you Gentiles — •for I'm sure you've heard of the stewardship of 2 God's grace that was given to me for you, •how the mystery was made 3 known to me in a revelation, as I've already written briefly. •[f] When 4 you read this you'll be able to understand my insight into the mystery of Christ, •which wasn't made known to other generations of the sons 5 of men as it has now been revealed to His holy apostles and prophets by the Spirit — •that the Gentiles are to be co-heirs, members of the 6 same body, sharers in the promise in Christ Jesus through the good news. •I became a minister of the good news by a free gift of God's 7 grace given me through the working of His power. •To me, the least 8 of all the saints, was given the grace of proclaiming to the Gentiles the unfathomable riches of Christ •and to reveal for all the plan of the mys- 9 tery that was hidden for ages in God, the creator of all things, •so that 10 the multi-faceted wisdom of God might now be made known through

---

[d] Col 2:14.   [e] Col 1:20.   [f] Col 1:26-27.

2:14-15 "The dividing wall..." The rabbis spoke of the Torah as a barrier which maintained Israel's separateness and purity by isolating them from the Gentiles.
2:17 Is 57:19.
3:10-11 By making God's plan of salvation known to "the rulers and powers in the heavens"

the way is opened to redeem human life in all its earthly aspects, to the extent possible through the action of individual human beings. This is the basis of Christian optimism from the social standpoint, but it is important to remember that Paul is not recommending a facile, utopian optimism.

11 the church to the rulers and powers in the heavens, •in accordance with
12 the eternal plan He carried out in Christ Jesus our Lord. •In Christ we
13 have free and confident access to God through our faith in him. •There-
fore I ask you not to lose heart because of the afflictions I'm suffering
on your behalf — this is your glory.

14,15   •Because of this I bend my knees to the Father. •From Him every
16 family in the heavens and on earth is named, •so that from the riches
of His glory He may grant you inner strength and power through His
17 Spirit. •May Christ dwell in your hearts through faith, firmly rooted and
18 established in love, •so that with all the saints you may be able to un-
19 derstand the breadth, the length, the height, and the depth, •and know
Christ's love which surpasses all knowledge so that you may be filled with
all God's fullness.

20   •Now to Him Who is able to do so much more than all we can ask
21 for or imagine, by the power at work in us, •to Him be glory in the
church in Christ Jesus for all generations, forever and ever. Amen.

F. EXHORTATION TO GROWTH IN THE LIFE IN CHRIST

1 **4** •So I urge you — I, a prisoner in the Lord — to conduct yourselves
2 in a manner worthy of the calling to which you've been called, •[g] with
3 humility, gentleness, and patience. Bear with one another in love, •make
4 every effort to maintain unity of spirit in the bond of peace. •There is
one body and one Spirit, just as you were called to the one hope of your
5,6 calling. •One Lord, one faith, one baptism, •one God and Father of us
all, Who is above all, through all, and in all.
7   •Grace has been given to each of us according to the extent of Christ's
8 gift. •Therefore Scripture says,

> **When he ascended on high he led
> prisoners into captivity,
> he gave gifts to men.**

[g] *Col 3:12-13.*

4:1ff Having painted a breathtaking picture of God's plan of salvation, Paul turns to the individual life of Christians. He reminds the Ephesians that no matter how awe inspiring the mystery of God may be, each individual Christian must work out their salvation in their daily life, no longer alone, however, but as a part of Christ's body, the Church.

4:7-11 Some have argued that the descent referred to was Christ's return on Pentecost to bestow the gifts of the Spirit. Among other factors we may note that Ps 68:18 (quoted) was used at the Jewish feast of Pentecost to commemorate the lawgiving at Sinai, the quintessential gift-giving of the Old Testament.

•(Now what can "he ascended" mean except that he also descended, 9 into the lower regions of the earth? •The one who descended is also the 10 one who ascended far above all the heavens in order to fill all things.) •To some the gift he gave was to be apostles, to others it was to be 11 prophets, to others it was to be evangelists, pastors, or teachers. •This 12 was to equip the saints for the work of ministry, the building up of the body of Christ, •until we all attain to unity of faith and knowledge of the 13 Son of God — to mature manhood, to the extent of Christ's full stature. •Thus we'll no longer be infants, tossed and carried here and there by 14 every wind of teaching coming from human cunning, from their crafti- ness in developing deceitful schemes. •Instead, by speaking the truth in 15 love we'll grow in every way into him — Christ — who is the head •[h] upon whom the whole body depends. Joined together and united by 16 all the supporting ligaments, when each part is working as it should the head causes the body to grow and build itself up in love.

•Therefore I say this and bear witness in the Lord — you must no 17 longer live as the Gentiles do, with their futile reasoning. •Their under- 18 standing is clouded and they're alienated from God's life because of their ignorance, which is caused by the hardening of their hearts. •They've 19 grown callous and have given themselves over to licentiousness, greed- ily pursuing every sort of impurity. •That's not how you learned Christ, 20 •not if you heard about him and were taught the truth as it is in Jesus. 21 •[i] Put off the old man, your former way of life which is corrupted by de- 22 ceitful desires! •Be renewed in your mind and spirit •[j] and put on the 23,24 new man created in accordance with God's design in true righteousness and holiness.

•Therefore, put away falsehood and **let everyone speak the truth** 25 **to his neighbor,** because we're parts of one another. •**Be angry, but** 26 **don't sin.** Don't let the sun set on your anger, •and don't give the Dev- 27 il an opening. •The thief must no longer steal; instead, he must labor 28 and do honest work with his own hands so he'll have enough to give to those in need. •Let no bad word come from your mouths; instead, say 29 only what is necessary and will serve to edify, so that those who hear may receive grace. •Don't grieve the Holy Spirit, with Whom you were 30 sealed for the day of redemption. •Let all bitterness, anger, wrath, an- 31 gry shouting, and slander be put away from you, along with all malice. •[k] Be kind to one another, compassionate, forgiving each other just as 32 God forgave you in Christ.

[h] Col 2:19.   [i] Col 3:9.   [j] Col 3:10.   [k] Col 3:13.

4:25 Zc 8:16.   4:26 Ps 4:4 (Septuagint).

1,2 5 •Be imitators of God as beloved children. •Walk in love, just as Christ loved us and gave himself up for us to God as an offering and sac-
3 rifice with a pleasing fragrance. •Don't even mention any sort of forni-
4 cation, impurity, or greed among you, as is fitting among saints, •nor indecent behavior, foolish talk, or coarse joking. These things are im-
5 proper; it's better to give thanks. •For you should know that no forni- cator, or impure or greedy person — that is, no idolater — will have any share in the Kingdom of Christ and God.

6 •Let no one deceive you with empty words — it's through these things I've mentioned that God's wrath comes upon the disobedient.
7,8 •Therefore, don't associate with them, •for once you were darkness,
9 but now you're light in the Lord. Walk like children of light — •for the fruit of light is to be found in every sort of goodness, righteousness,
10 and truth — •and examine everything to see what's pleasing to the
11 Lord. •Don't participate in the unfruitful deeds of darkness; instead,
12 show them up for what they are, •for it's disgraceful to even mention
13 the things they do in secret. •But everything brought into the open by

Ephesus. The Library of Celsus (110-135 A.D.).

the light is clearly revealed, •and everything thus revealed is light. There- 14
fore it says,

> "Sleeper awake, and rise from the dead,
> And Christ will be your light."

•Be sure to walk carefully, wisely rather than foolishly. •[l] Make good use 15,16
of your time, for the days are evil. •Therefore, don't be foolish — un- 17
derstand what God's will is. •Don't get drunk on wine, which is dissi- 18
pation; instead, be filled with the Spirit. •[m] Speak to each other in psalms, 19
hymns, and spiritual songs; sing praise to the Lord in your hearts, •giv- 20
ing thanks always and for everything to God the Father in the name of
our Lord Jesus Christ.

•Be subject to one another out of reverence for Christ. •[n] Wives should 21,22
be subject to their husbands as they are to the Lord, •for the husband 23
is his wife's head just as Christ is the head of the church, and is himself
the Savior of the body. •But just as the church is subject to Christ, so 24
too wives should be subject to their husbands in everything. •[o] Husbands, 25
love your wives, just as Christ loved the church and gave himself up for
her, •to sanctify her by cleansing her with the bath of water and the word. 26
•In this way he'll be able to present the church to himself in its glory, 27
having neither stain nor wrinkle nor anything of that sort, but instead
holy and unblemished. •In the same way husbands should love their wives 28
just as they love their own bodies. The man who·loves his wife loves
himself, •for no one ever hates his own flesh. On the contrary, he nour- 29
ishes and cares for it just as Christ does for the church, •because we're 30
parts of his body.

•For this reason a man shall leave his father 31
    and mother
      and be joined to his wife,
   And the two shall be one flesh.

•This is a tremendous mystery. I'm applying it to Christ and the 32
church, •but each one of you should in the same way love his wife as 33
he loves himself, and the wife should respect her husband.

---

[l] *Col 4:5.* [m] *Col 3:16-17.* [n] *Col 3:18; 1 P 3:1.* [o] *Col 3:19; 1 P 3:7.*

5:14 It is generally believed that this verse is a great emphasis on the mutuality of love and re-
fragment of an early Christian hymn, probably spect which should characterize the marriage
used during the baptismal liturgy. union.
5:21-33 Paul, in this beautiful passage, places 5:31 Gn 2:24.

6 [1] •[p] Children, obey your parents [in the Lord], because it's the right [2] thing to do. •**Honor your father and mother!** This is the first com- [3] mandment that comes with a promise — •**that all may be well with** [4] **you and you may have a long life on earth.** •[q] And fathers, don't cause your children to resent you; instead, raise them by instructing and admonishing them as the Lord would.

[5] •Slaves, obey your earthly masters with fear and trembling and with [6] single-hearted devotion, just as you obey Christ, •and don't just try to impress them and curry favor. Instead, as servants of Christ who do God's [7] will from the heart, •serve your masters enthusiastically as if you were [8] serving the Lord and not a man. •For you know that if anyone does something good he'll receive the same thing from the Lord, whether that [9] person is a slave or free. •And you masters, do the same for them. Stop threatening your slaves, because you know that the Lord in Heaven is both your Lord and their Lord, and he doesn't play favorites.

[10,11] •Finally, become strong through the Lord's power and might. •Put on God's armor so you'll be able to stand up against the schemes of the [12] Devil, •for we're not engaged in a struggle with mere flesh and blood — we're fighting against the rulers and powers, against the cosmic pow- ers of this dark world, against the spiritual forces of evil in the heavens. [13] •Therefore, take up God's armor so you'll be able to oppose them on the day of evil and, by doing everything in your power, to remain stand- [14] ing. •So stand firm! **Gird your loins with truth and put on the** [15] **breastplate of righteousness!** •**Put on your feet the boots of pre-** [16] **paredness for the good news of peace!** •And along with all this take up the shield of the faith, with which you'll be able to extinguish all [17] the flaming arrows of the Evil One. •Take **the helmet of salvation** [18] and **the sword of the Spirit,** which is **the word of God.** •Pray at all times in the Spirit with every manner of prayer and supplication. To this end stay alert and persevere in supplication on behalf of all the saints, [19] •and on my behalf, that when I open my mouth God will give me the [20] words to boldly make known the mystery of the good news, •for which I'm an ambassador in chains. Pray that I'll speak out boldly as I should.

[p] *Col 3:20.*   [q] *Col 3:21-4:1.*

6:2-3 Ex 20:12; Dt 15:16.
6:5-9 Without fanfare Paul introduces a new el- ement into the master/slave relationship, for he points out that slaves, too, have God-given rights and that masters will answer to God for their treat- ment of servants. This principle may also be ap-

plied in complete faithfulness to Paul's thought to all relationships involving subordination.
6:14 Is 11:5; 59:17.
6:15 Is 52:7.
6:17 Is 59:17.

G. CONCLUSION

•[r] Tychicus, my beloved brother and faithful servant in the Lord, will 21 tell you everything, so you'll know about my situation, what I'm doing. •[s] I've sent him to you for that very reason, so you'll know how we are 22 and so he'll be able to give your hearts encouragement.

•Peace and love be to the brothers, with faith from God the Father 23 and the Lord Jesus Christ. •Grace be with all who love our Lord Jesus 24 Christ with an undying love.

[r] Ac 20:4; 2 Tm 4:12.   [s] Col 4:7-8.

THE LETTER TO THE

PHILIPPIANS

Introduction to the Letter
to the Philippians

Paul's ministry at Philippi is recounted in Acts (16:11-40; 20:6) but we can be sure that Acts' narrative is far from being the whole story, for it is clear from this letter that Paul's relations with the Philippians were particularly close and cordial. In fact, the Philippians had eagerly supported Paul in his missionary activities after he moved on, demonstrating a zeal for which Paul was especially grateful.

The letter was written to thank the Philippians for the assistance they had sent as soon as they heard about Paul's imprisonment. The letter is to be carried by Epaphroditus, the Philippian who had brought the aid to Paul. Epaphroditus had had to remain with Paul for some time due to illness.

The letter itself finds Paul in a relatively exalted frame of mind, almost hoping that he will meet a martyr's end. Far from being in any way depressed, he repeatedly speaks of his own joy and urges the Philippians to rejoice as well. The intent of the letter is basically to encourage and exhort the Philippians to continue their already outstanding efforts to advance the gospel. With this purpose in mind, he emphasizes the need for them to conduct themselves in a manner worthy of the good news, to hold fast to the faith, and to maintain an unselfish unity in Christ. Throughout the letter Paul expresses himself with great personal warmth, leaving a beautiful testimony to the sincere Christian love he and the Philippians shared.

A. GREETING

1 **1** •Paul and Timothy, servants of Christ Jesus, to all the saints in Christ
2 Jesus at Philippi, along with the bishops and deacons — •the grace
and peace of God our Father and the Lord Jesus Christ be with you.

B. THANKSGIVING

3,4   •I give thanks to my God every time I think of you. •Whenever I pray
5 for you I offer my prayer joyfully, •because of your partnership in the
6 good news from the first day up to the present. •Of this I'm convinced,
that the One Who began the good work in you will bring it to comple-
7 tion on the Day of Jesus Christ. •It's right that I should feel this way
about you because I have you in my heart, and because you all share
my grace, both in my imprisonment and in the defense and confirma-
8 tion of the good news. •For God is my witness that I long for all of you
9 with the affection of Jesus Christ. •My prayer is that your love will in-
10 crease more and more with knowledge and every manner of insight •so
that you'll be able to discover what's best and may be pure and blame-
11 less for the Day of Christ, •filled with the fruit of the righteousness that
comes through Jesus Christ, to the glory and praise of God.

C. THE GOSPEL IS BEING ADVANCED
DESPITE PAUL'S IMPRISONMENT

12   •I want you to know, my brothers, that the things that have hap-
13 pened to me have actually had the effect of advancing the gospel. •As
a result it's become known throughout the praetorium and to every-

---

1:13 "Praetorium" could either mean the headquarters of the Praetorian Guard in Rome or the res-
idence of a provincial governor, such as in Caesarea.

one else that I'm in chains for Christ, •and my chains have given the 14
majority of the brothers in the Lord the confidence to proclaim the
word even more fearlessly.

•Some proclaim Christ out of jealousy and contentiousness, but oth- 15
ers proclaim him out of good will, •and these do it out of love, because 16
they know I'm here for having defended the gospel. •Those who pro- 17
claim Christ out of jealousy do so insincerely in the hope of causing me
trouble while I'm in prison. •What does it matter? The important thing 18
is that one way or another Christ is proclaimed, whether from false or
sincere motives, and for that I rejoice. And I *will* rejoice, •for I know 19
that it will lead to my deliverance, through your prayers and the support
of the Spirit of Jesus Christ. •It is my eager expectation and hope that 20
I won't be ashamed, but that now as always Christ will be boldly honored in my person whether I live or die. •For me, to live is Christ and 21
to die is gain. •If I continue to live in the flesh that means I'll have fruit- 22
ful labor, yet I don't know which to prefer. •I'm torn between the two 23
alternatives — I wish to depart and be with Christ, for that is far better,
•but for your sake it's more necessary to remain in the flesh. •Since I'm 24,25
convinced of this, I know I'll stay and remain with you all to further your
progress and joy in the faith, •so that when I'm once more with you 26
your pride in me may overflow in Christ Jesus.

•The main thing is to conduct yourselves in a manner worthy of 27
Christ's good news, so that whether I come and see you or whether I'm
away I'll hear that you're standing firm in one spirit, working together
with one mind for the faith of the gospel •and not frightened in any way 28
by your enemies. This will be a sign to them of their coming destruction, but of your salvation which will come from God. •For God has gra- 29
ciously allowed you not only to believe in Christ but also to suffer for
him. •You're engaged in the same struggle which you saw me engaged 30
in, and now hear that I'm still engaged in.

D. EXHORTATION TO UNITY IN CHRIST

2 •If life in Christ provides any encouragement, any comfort in love, 1
any sharing in the Spirit, any affection and compassion, •then com- 2
plete my joy by being of one mind, sharing the same love, being united in spirit, and thinking as one. •Do nothing out of selfishness or a de- 3

1:19 "It will lead to my deliverance." This probably refers to vindication before the heavenly court
rather than before a human court. Jb 13:16 (Septuagint).

Philippi. Ruins of the Basilica (5th century A.D.).

sire to boast; instead, in a spirit of humility toward one another, regard
4 others as better than yourselves. •Each of you should look out for the
5 rights of others, rather than looking after your own rights. •Have the
same outlook among you that Christ Jesus had,

6   •Who, though he was in the form of God,
          did not consider equality with God
             something to hold on to.
7   •Instead, he emptied himself and took on
          the form of a slave,
       born in human likeness,
          and to all appearances a man.

2:6-11 Whether this passage was written by
Paul or was a pre-Pauline hymn, as many scholars believe, it is agreed that this passage refers
to Christ as pre-existing and represents some of
the "highest" Christology in the New Testament.
There are numerous allusions to Isaiah's Suffering Servant, in which the importance of
Christ's obedience is stressed. This obedience
was congenial to the rabbinic concept of complete loyalty to the Torah.
2:6 Is 53:12.
2:7 "the form of a slave," i.e., Jesus appeared to
be a normal human being, a slave of sin.

•He humbled himself and became obedient, 8
   even unto death, death on a cross.
•For this reason God exalted him 9
   and gave him a name above every
      other name,
•So that at the name of Jesus **every knee shall bend,** 10
   in the heavens, on earth, and below the earth,
•**And every tongue will proclaim** to the glory 11
   of God the Father,
      that Jesus Christ is Lord.

•So then, my beloved, be obedient as you always have been; not just 12
as you were when I was present — in my absence now you must be
even more so. Set about accomplishing your salvation with fear and trembling, •for God is the One Who is leading you both to desire and to work 13
for His chosen plan. •Do everything without grumbling or arguing •so 14,15
that you'll be blameless and pure, unblemished children of God amidst
a twisted and perverted generation, among whom you'll shine like stars
in the world. •Hold fast to the word of life, so that on the Day of Christ 16
I'll be able to boast that I didn't work or toil in vain. •[a] But even if I'm 17
poured out like a libation upon the sacrificial offering of your faith, I'll
rejoice and be glad with all of you, •and likewise you too should rejoice 18
and be glad with me.

E. NEWS OF TIMOTHY AND EPAPHRODITUS

•I hope in the Lord Jesus that I'll soon be able to send Timothy to 19
you, so that I'll be cheered by finding out about you. •I have no one 20
else like him who is so sincerely concerned about you, •for they all look 21
out for their own interests, not those of Christ Jesus. •But you know 22
Timothy's worth, and that he served with me in advancing the gospel
like a child serves his father. •Therefore I hope to send him as soon as 23
I see how things stand with me, •and I trust in the Lord that I too will 24
soon be able to come.

[a] *2 Tm 4:6.*

2:9 Is 52:13.
2:10-11 Is 45:23 (Septuagint).
2:17 A "libation" was a sacrificial offering of a liq-
uid, performed by pouring it out or, as here, by
pouring it over another sacrificial offering.

2:8 Is 53:7-8, "Even to death on the cross."
Christ's obedience was truly extraordinary, for it
embraced a shameful death which bore the
Torah's curse: "Cursed be everyone who hangs
on a tree" (Dt 21:33).

25 •I've thought it necessary to send you Epaphroditus, my brother, co-worker, and fellow soldier, whom you sent to minister to me in my need,
26 •since he was longing for all of you and was distressed that you had
27 heard that he was ill. •He *was* ill, in fact, and was close to death, but God had mercy on him, and not only on him but on me as well, so that
28 I wouldn't have grief upon grief. •So I'm all the more eager to send him so that when you see him again you'll rejoice, and I'll be free from
29 anxiety. •Receive him in the Lord, then, with joy, and honor people
30 like him, •because for the sake of Christ's work he came close to death, risking his own life to perform those services you yourselves were unable to perform for me.

1 3•And so, my brothers, rejoice in the Lord. To write the same things to you is no trouble for me and makes you more secure.

F. A WARNING AGAINST CHRIST'S ENEMIES AND AN EXHORTATION TO STAND FIRM IN THE FAITH

2 •Beware of those dogs, beware of the evil-doers, beware of the mu-
3 tilation. •We are the *true* circumcision, who worship God in spirit and
4 put our trust in Christ Jesus rather than in the flesh, •although I have reason for confidence in the flesh, as well. If anyone else thinks they
5 have reason for confidence in the flesh, I have better reasons! •[b] I was circumcised on the eighth day, from the people of Israel, the tribe of Benjamin, a Hebrew from Hebrews, a Pharisee with regard to the Torah,
6 •[c] a zealous persecutor of the church, blameless as to righteousness un-
7 der the Torah. •But whatever I had gained from all this, I have come to
8 consider it loss for the sake of Christ. •In fact, I consider everything to be loss for the sake of the surpassing greatness of knowing Christ Jesus my Lord. For his sake I've cast everything aside and regard it as so
9 much rubbish so that I'll gain Christ •and be found in him, having no righteousness of my own based on observance of the Torah but only that righteousness which comes through faith in Christ, the righteousness that

[b] *Rm 11:1; Ac 23:6; 26:5.*   [c] *Ac 8:3; 22:4; 26:9-11.*

3:2-3 This passage refers to Jews or Jewish Christians who wished to impose observance of the Torah on Gentile converts. "Dogs" was a term commonly used by Jews to refer to Gentiles, and now Paul tosses it back at his bitter opponents; "evildoers" may refer ironically to the harm they do while claiming to rely upon deeds done in observance of the Torah; "mutilation" was, in Greek, a derisively punning reference to circumcision and may also refer to the ban on mutilated persons belonging to the Jewish priesthood (Lv 21:5, 20; Dt 23:1).

comes from God and which is based on faith. •My goal is to know him 10 and the power of his resurrection, to understand the fellowship of his sufferings and become conformed to his death •in the hope of some- 11 how attaining resurrection from the dead.

•Not that I've already achieved this or that I'm already perfect! But I 12 continue to strive in the hope of making it my own, because Christ [Jesus] has made *me* his own. •My brothers, I don't consider that I've won 13 yet, and for this reason I forget what's behind me and reach out for what's in front of me. •I strain toward the goal to win the prize — of God's heav- 14 enward call in Christ Jesus. •So let us who are mature adopt this attitude, 15 and if your attitude is otherwise, God will reveal this to you as well. •But 16 let's conduct ourselves in the light of what we've already attained.

•My brothers, be imitators of me. Watch those who behave in ac- 17 cordance with the example we've given you. •I've told you many times 18 and now I tell you with tears in my eyes, there are many who behave like enemies of Christ's cross. •They'll end up being destroyed; their god 19 is their own desires — they glory in their shame, their concern is for earthly things. •But we are citizens of Heaven, and we eagerly await a 20 savior from Heaven, the Lord Jesus Christ. •He'll transform our lowly 21 bodies so that they'll have the same form as his glorious body, by means of the power that enables him to subject everything to himself.

4 •Therefore, my beloved brothers whom I long for, my joy and my 1 crown, be steadfast in the Lord.

G. CONCLUDING ADMONITIONS

•I urge Euodia and Syntyche to think as one in the Lord. •And I ask 2,3 you, my true comrade, to help these women who joined me in the struggle for the gospel, along with Clement and the rest of my co-workers — their names are in the Book of Life. •Rejoice in the Lord, always; again 4 I say, rejoice! •Let all know how considerate you are. The Lord is near. 5 •Don't be anxious; instead, give thanks in all your prayers and petitions 6 and make your requests known to God. •And God's peace which is be- 7 yond all understanding will keep your hearts and minds in Christ Jesus.

3:10 Paul wishes to understand the process by which, through suffering, we come closer to Christ.
3:18 Most commentators are in agreement that the "enemies of Christ's cross" are heterodox Christians, rather than the Jews.

3:19 The reference to "their own desires (lit., "belly")" is probably meant to apply in a broad sense to a life spent focused on oneself.
4:2 Euodia and Syntyche are women's names.

8 •And so, my brothers, whatever is true, whatever is honorable, whatever is just, whatever is pure, whatever is pleasing, whatever is gracious, if there is any excellence or anything praiseworthy, think of these things.
9 •What you have received from me, what you have learned, what you have heard, what you have seen in me, do these things, and the God of peace will be with you.

Philippi. View of the ruins.

H. PAUL'S THANKS FOR THE PHILIPPIANS' GENEROSITY

10 •It's a great joy to me in the Lord that now at last your concern for me has been revived — you *were* concerned but you had no opportu-
11 nity to show it. •Not that I suffered any want — I've learned to be con-
12 tent with what I have. •I know how to live in straitened circumstances, and I know how to live amid plenty. I've learned this secret under every conceivable circumstance, whether full or hungry, well provided for or
13 suffering want. •I'm able to do everything through the One Who strength-
14 ens me. •Nevertheless, you did well to share in my affliction.

•[d] You Philippians also know that in the beginning of my proclamation of the good news, when I left Macedonia, not one church extended a partnership to share in giving and receiving, except for you alone. •Even in Thessalonica you once and then again sent me help. •Not that I'm interested in receiving gifts — rather, I want to see the credits to your account keep increasing. •I have everything I need; in fact, I have *more* than enough. I've received what Epaphroditus brought on your behalf, and I'm fully supplied. It was a fragrant aroma, an acceptable sacrifice that was pleasing to God. •My God will fill all your needs by means of His glorious riches in Christ Jesus. •Glory be to our God and Father for ever and ever, amen. [15] [16,17] [18] [19] [20]

I. FAREWELL

•Greet each saint in Christ Jesus. The brothers with me greet you. •All the saints greet you, especially those who belong to Caesar's household. •May the grace of the Lord Jesus Christ be with your spirit. [21] [22] [23]

[d] *2 Cor 11:9.*

THE LETTER TO THE

COLOSSIANS

Introduction to the Letter
to the Colossians

Colossians is a companion letter to the Letter to Philemon. Both were written to the city of Colossae in Asia Minor, but whereas Philemon was written to a specific person, Colossians was written to the congregation there at large. Both letters were to be delivered by Tychicus.

Colossae was a relatively small town in the region of Phrygia and Paul had never personally been there. Instead, the Colossians had received the good news from a fellow Colossian named Epaphras. The letter itself was in response to a report Epaphras had brought to Paul in prison to the effect that the congregation was being unsettled by certain persons who were advocating doctrines which were at variance with what Epaphras had taught them. Probably at Epaphras' request, Paul wrote this letter to put the Colossians on guard against the new teaching and to urge them to hold fast to the faith they had received through Epaphras. The result is a marvel of tact, considering that Paul could claim no particular authority with respect to the Colossians.

Paul's exhortation to the Colossians rests firmly upon the person of Jesus Christ and the truth of the gospel. Jesus is superior to everything, both in the heavens and on earth, and has subjected all the powers and authorities. In Christ we share in God's fullness, for Christ is the fullness of God, and so it makes no sense for the Colossians to follow the rules and regulations of these inferior powers rather than the gospel of Christ. Moreover, Christ is the source of true wisdom and spiritual strength, and no human "philosophizing" can compare with the wisdom and strength we receive through the gospel.

A. GREETING

1 •Paul, an apostle of Christ Jesus by God's will, and our brother Tim-
2 othy •to the holy and faithful brothers in Christ at Colossae — grace
and peace be with you from God our Father.

B. THANKSGIVING

3 •When we pray for you we always give thanks to God, the Father of
4 our Lord Jesus Christ, •because we've heard of your faith in Christ Je-
5 sus and your love for all the saints •which comes from the hope stored
up for you in Heaven. You first heard of this hope in the word of truth,
6 the good news •that has come to you. This good news has been increasing and producing fruit in the whole world, just as it has among
you from the day you heard and came to know the grace of God in truth.
7 •[a] You learned the good news from our beloved fellow servant Epaphras,
8 who is a faithful minister of Christ on our behalf, •and he informed us
of your love in the Spirit.
9 •Therefore, from the day we heard of you we haven't ceased praying for you. May God fill you with the knowledge of His will through
10 wisdom and all manner of spiritual understanding, •that you may conduct yourselves in a manner worthy of the Lord and fully pleasing to him
— fruitful in every type of good work and increasing in knowledge of
11 God. •We pray that you will be strengthened with all the power of His
glorious might so that your steadfastness and patience will be perfected
12 and you may joyfully •give thanks to the Father Who made you worthy

---

[a] *Phm 23.*

1:6 As always, Paul stresses that the good news
is a free gift ("grace") from God, unmerited by any
actions on the part of those who have received it.
1:11 "His glorious might" refers to the power by
which God raised Jesus. Cf. also Rm 6:4.

1:12 The Greek word translated "portion" was the
same word used in the Septuagint which referred
to the "portions" of Palestine which were allocat-
ed to the twelve tribes of Israel.

to share in the portion of the saints in light. •He has rescued us from 13
the power of darkness and has brought us into the Kingdom of His
beloved Son, •[b] by whom we are redeemed and our sins are forgiven. 14

C. CHRIST IN US, THE MYSTERY OF GOD

•He is the image of the unseen God, 15
    the firstborn of all creation,
•For in him all things in the heavens and on earth 16
     were created,
    both the seen and the unseen,
Whether thrones, dominions, rulers, or powers;
    all things were created through him and for him.
•He is before all things 17
    and in him all things hold together.
•[c] He is the head of the body, 18
    of the church,
He is the beginning, the firstborn from the dead,
    so that he might be above all else,
•For in him all the Fullness was pleased to dwell 19
    •[d] and through him reconciled all things to Himself, 20
Making peace by the blood of his cross,
    reconciling everything on earth or in the heavens.

•You were once alienated from God and were His enemies both in in- 21
tent and in your evil deeds, •but now God has reconciled you through 22
Christ's body of flesh — by means of his death — so God will be able to
bring you before Himself, holy, unblemished, and blameless, •as long as 23

---

[b] Eph 1:7.   [c] Eph 1:22-23.   [d] Eph 2:16.

1:13-14 The idea of a New Exodus is a favorite Pauline theme and a metaphor which he often applies to the Christian life.
1:15-20 The background for this hymn-like passage is to be found in the Old Testament Wisdom literature, in which Wisdom becomes a personified attribute of God. The rabbis identified Wisdom with the Torah, whereas Paul applies these passages to Christ.
1:15ff This passage is considered to be a reference to Pr 8:22, in which Wisdom is described as begotten by God at the beginning. As the image of God Jesus is thus also the image of the Wisdom of God and is the New Torah, for the rabbis had come to equate the Torah with the Divine and Creative Wisdom.
1:16 This verse can be seen as a rejection of those dualist systems which maintained that God did not create all things but that a principle of evil was responsible for some aspects of creation. The "unseen" things probably refer to the "elemental spirits" (2:8) which were believed to have power over man's "corporate life," as manifested in religion and politics, for example.

you remain firmly established in the faith and aren't shifted from the hope of the gospel you heard — the gospel which has been proclaimed to every creature under Heaven, and of which I, Paul, am a minister.

24   •I rejoice in what I'm suffering for you now; in my flesh I'm completing what is lacking in Christ's afflictions on behalf of his body, that is, the

25 church. •I am a minister of the church in accordance with the responsibility God gave me with regard to you — to fully proclaim the word of

26 God, •the mystery which was hidden for ages and generations. But now

27 it has been revealed to His saints, •to whom God chose to make known the richness of this glorious mystery among the Gentiles — this mystery

28 is Christ in you, the hope of glory. •It is Christ whom we proclaim, and we admonish and instruct everyone in all wisdom so that we'll be able

29 to present each of them as perfect in Christ. •To this end I toil and strive, and Christ's mighty energy is at work in me.

Roman bridge in Turkey.

2 •For I want you to know how great my labor is on your behalf, as 1
well as on behalf of those in Laodicea and all those who haven't seen
me in person. •My goal is to encourage their hearts as they are drawn 2
together in love so that they may have the full wealth of conviction that
comes from understanding and leads to knowledge of God's mystery —
of Christ — •in whom all the treasures of wisdom and knowledge are 3
hidden. •I say this so no one will deceive you with a plausible sounding 4
line of argumentation. •For although I may not be present, I am with 5
you in spirit, and I rejoice to see how you maintain good order and how
firm your faith in Christ is.

D. EXHORTATION TO BE FIRM IN THE FAITH
AND TO RESIST JUDAIZING TENDENCIES

•Therefore, since you've received Christ Jesus the Lord, live your lives 6
in him; •be rooted and built up in him and firmly established in the faith 7
just as it was taught to you; be filled with thanksgiving. •See that no one 8
leads you into captivity by means of "philosophy" or the empty decep-
tions of human traditions, which follow the elemental spirits of the world
rather than Christ. •For in Christ the fullness of divinity dwells in bodily 9
form •and in him you reach completion; he is the head of every ruler 10
and power. •In him you also received a circumcision, one which was not 11
performed by hand; with Christ's circumcision you put off the body of
flesh — •[e] you were buried with him in baptism and in baptism you also 12
rose with him through faith in the power of God, Who raised Christ from
the dead. •[f] Although you were dead because of your transgressions and 13
because your flesh was uncircumcised, God brought you to life with Christ
by forgiving all our transgressions •[g] and canceling our commitment to 14
obey the decrees of the Torah, which stood as an accusation against us.
He set it aside and nailed it to the cross; •He stripped the rulers and pow- 15
ers and, in Christ, held a public triumph over them.

•[h] So let no one judge you in matters concerning food and drink, or 16
regarding festivals, new moons, or the Sabbath. •These things are a fore- 17

[e] *Rm 6:4.*   [f] *Eph 2:1-5.*   [g] *Eph 2:15.*   [h] *Rm 14:1-6.*

2:1 Laodicea was the major city of the region in
which Colossae was located.
2:8-9 The "elemental spirits" were the angelic beings which were thought to influence human rulers.
2:14 The words "of the Torah" are not in the original.

2:16-23 Having addressed the true basis for our
salvation in the preceding verses, Paul now proceeds to warn the Colossians against the practices
which some in the community have adopted.
These practices appear to have combined asceticism and ritualism based on Jewish influences.

18 shadowing of what is to come, but the reality is Christ's. •You are not to be disqualified by those who insist on self-mortification and worship of angels, based upon things they've seen in visions. Such people have become puffed up without reason by relying on their own world-centered
19 minds •[i] rather than holding fast to the Head, from which the whole body, with its joints and ligaments, receives what it needs and is held to-
20 gether, deriving its growth from God. •If you have died with Christ to the elemental spirits of the world, why do you observe rules and regu-
21 lations as if you were still living in the world? •"Don't touch this! Don't
22 taste that! Don't handle this!" •Don't all these rules concern things which are destined to be destroyed through use, and aren't they simply human
23 precepts and teachings? •These rules *appear* to be wise from the standpoint of piety, humility, and discipline of the body, but they're of no use in controlling self-indulgence.

E. PRACTICAL COUNSELS TO THE TRUE LIFE IN CHRIST

1 3 •If you've been raised with Christ, seek the things that are above,
2 where Christ is seated at God's right hand; •think about the things
3 that are above, not about things on earth, •for you've died and your life
4 is hidden with Christ in God. •When Christ, your life, appears, then you too will appear with him in glory.

5 •Put to death those parts of you which are earthly — fornication,
6 impurity, passion, evil desires, and that greed which is idolatry. •It's because of these things that God's wrath is coming [upon the disobe-
7,8 dient]; •you too used to do these things when you lived for them. •But now you must cast them all aside — wrath, anger, malice, slander, ob-
9 scene language from your mouths. •[j] Don't lie to one another, now
10 that you've stripped off the old man with his deeds •[k] and put on the new one, which is being renewed according to the image of its Cre-
11 ator for the knowledge of God. •Here there is no Greek or Jew, circumcised or uncircumcised, barbarian or Scythian, slave or free, but Christ is all and in all.

[i] *Eph 4:16.*   [j] *Eph 4:22.*   [k] *Eph 4:24.*

2:18-20 Paul held to the common Jewish view that the Torah was given to Moses by angelic intermediaries rather than directly from God. Thus he may be indulging in sarcasm at the expense of those who were introducing practices from the Jewish law when he refers to "angel worship."

Paul has no problem with curbing sensuality, but he is troubled by the fascination with intermediaries, who are subordinate to Christ.
2:21-22 These verses refer to dietary and purification regulations, probably of Jewish origin.

•[l] So then, as God's chosen ones, holy and beloved, clothe your- 12
selves with true compassion, kindness, humility, gentleness, patience;
•[m] bear with one another and forgive each other if anyone has a griev- 13
ance against someone else. Just as the Lord forgave you, you too
should do the same. •But over all these things put on love, which per- 14
fects and binds the whole. •Let the peace of Christ rule in your hearts, 15
the peace to which you were called in one body, and be thankful.

•[n] Let the word of Christ dwell in you richly; teach and admonish each 16
other with all wisdom; sing psalms, hymns, and spiritual songs to God
with thanks in your hearts. •Whatever you do whether in word or deed, 17
do it all in the name of Jesus the Lord, and give thanks to God the
Father through him.

•[o] Wives, be subject to your husbands, as is fitting in the Lord. •[p] Hus- 18,19
bands, love your wives and don't be harsh with them.

•[q] Children, obey your parents in all things, for that is pleasing to the 20
Lord. •[r] Fathers, don't cause your children to be resentful, so they won't 21
become discouraged.

•[s] Slaves, obey your earthly masters in all things, not just to impress 22
them and curry favor but with single-hearted devotion, in fear of the
Lord. •Whatever you do, let it be from the heart, as if you were work- 23
ing for the Lord rather than for men, •in the knowledge that as your 24
reward you'll receive an inheritance from the Lord. Serve Christ the
Lord, •[t] for the wrong-doer will be repaid for the wrong he has done, 25
and God will not play favorites.

4 •[u] Masters, do what's just and fair for your slaves, for you know that 1
you too have a Lord in Heaven.

•Persevere in prayer, stay awake while you pray and be thankful. 2
•At the same time, pray for us, that God may open for us a door of 3
opportunity to proclaim the mystery of Christ, for the sake of whom
I'm in prison. •Pray that I'll be able to make this mystery clear, since 4
I must speak of it. •[v] Conduct yourselves wisely toward outsiders, make 5
good use of your opportunities. •Always be pleasant in your speech 6
but season it with salt, so you'll always be able to answer everyone.

[l] Eph 4:2.   [m] Eph 4:32.   [n] Eph 5:19-20.   [o] Eph 5:22.   [p] Eph 5:25.   [q] Eph 6:1.
[r] Eph 6:4.   [s] Eph 6:5-8.   [t] Eph 6:9.   [u] Eph 6:9.   [v] Eph 5:16.

3:18-19 As always when Paul discusses family relations he stresses mutuality of obligations: the
husband's duties are no less binding than those of the wife.

Paul. Engraved ivory from Syria.

F. PERSONAL NEWS AND CONCLUSION

7   •ᵂ Our beloved brother Tychicus will tell you everything concerning my situation — he's a faithful minister and fellow servant in the Lord. 8   •ˣ I'm sending him to you so you'll know how things stand with us and 9   to encourage your hearts, •ʸ along with our faithful and beloved brother Onesimus, who is one of you. They'll let you know about everything that's going on here.

10   •ᶻ My fellow prisoner Aristarchus greets you, as well as Barnabas' cousin Mark (concerning whom you've received instructions — if he

ᵂ *2 Tm 4:12.*   ˣ *Eph 6:21-22.*   ʸ *Phm 10-12.*   ᶻ *Ac 27:2; Phm 24.*

4:10 "Mark"; believed to be Mark the Evangelist.

comes to you, receive him), •and Jesus who is called Justus. Of those 11 who are Jewish these are the only ones who are co-workers for the King- dom of God, and they've been a comfort to me. •Epaphras, one of you 12 and a servant of Christ [Jesus], greets you — he continually strives on your behalf in his prayers, that you may be perfect and fully convinced of all God's will. •I bear him witness that he's worked hard for you and 13 for those in Laodicea and Hierapolis. •ᵃ Demas and my beloved Luke, 14 the physician, greet you. •Greet the brothers at Laodicea as well as 15 Nympha and the church at her house. •And when you've read this let- 16 ter, have it read to the Laodicean church as well, and you should also read the letter from Laodicea. •ᵇ Tell Archippus, "See that you fulfill the 17 ministry you received in the Lord."

•The greeting is in my own hand — Paul's. Remember my chains! 18 Grace be with you!

ᵃ *2 Tm 4:10-11; Phm 24.*   ᵇ *Phm 2.*

4:13 Hierapolis was a city near Colossae.
4:15 It is equally possible, based on manuscript evidence and linguistic probabilities, that this phrase should read, "Nymphas and the church at his house."

THE FIRST LETTER
TO THE

THESSALONIANS

Introduction to the First Letter
to the Thessalonians

Paul's first letter to the church in Thessalonica is also one of the earliest of his letters which has been preserved and, thus, one of the earliest Christian writings. It is usually dated around 50-51 A.D. Of all Paul's letters its background is the most thoroughly described in Acts, stretching from 16:6 to 18:5. Briefly, Paul had had great initial success in Thessalonica (the capital of Macedonia) but was forced to leave because of the determined hostility of a part of the Jewish community there. Paul proceeded on through Greece, eventually winding up in Athens where he waited for his companions Silas and Timothy, who had stayed behind in Thessalonica to continue instructing the young community. After he was joined by Timothy he became anxious for the spiritual welfare of the Thessalonian church and sent Timothy back to check on matters. Timothy's return with a positive report was the occasion for this letter.

In structure this letter follows the usual format, except that the thanksgiving section is quite extended and is interwoven with relatively detailed accounts of Paul's previous relations with the Thessalonians. In addition to being thankful, Paul is also anxious to distinguish his mission from that of other itinerant preachers, who were common in the Hellenistic world at that time. He then goes on to deliver a brief moral exhortation as well as additional instruction regarding the *parousia*, the return of the Lord.

A. GREETING

1 ¹ •Paul, Silvanus, and Timothy to the church of the Thessalonians in God the Father and the Lord Jesus Christ — grace and peace be with you!

B. THANKSGIVING

² •We always give thanks to God for all of you and mention you in ³ our prayers, constantly •calling to mind before our God and Father your active faith, your loving labors, and your steadfast hope in our ⁴ Lord Jesus Christ. •For we know, brothers beloved by God, that you ⁵ have indeed been chosen, •because our proclamation of the good news didn't come to you in words alone but also with power, with the Holy Spirit, and with complete certainty. You know what we were like ⁶ for your sake while we were among you, •[a] and you became imitators of us and of the Lord, for although your acceptance of the word caused you considerable affliction, you received it with joy inspired ⁷ by the Holy Spirit. •As a result, you became an example for all the ⁸ believers in Macedonia and Achaia. •For the word of the Lord has gone forth from you not only in Macedonia and Achaia — news of your faith in God has reached every place, so that we have no need ⁹ to say anything! •Those people themselves recount what sort of reception we had among you, and how you turned to God from idols ¹⁰ to serve the living and true God •and to await His Son from Heaven — Jesus, whom He raised from the dead and who delivers us from the coming wrath.

[a] *Ac 17:5-9.*

1:7 "Achaia," i.e., Greece proper.

2 •For you yourselves know, my brothers, that our reception by you [1] was not in vain. •[b] Although we had previously suffered and been [2] mistreated in Philippi, as you know, God gave us the courage to proclaim God's good news to you in spite of considerable opposition. •For [3] the appeal we make is not based upon deceit or impure motives or deception. •On the contrary, since God has judged us worthy to be entrusted with the good news, we proclaim it with that in mind — not in [4] order to please men but to please God, Who is able to discern what's in our hearts. •We never resorted to flattery, as you know, nor did our [5] words serve as a cover for greed — God is our witness! — •and we did- [6] n't seek human honors, whether from you or from others, •although as [7] apostles of Christ we could have made demands upon you. Instead we were gentle with you, like a nursing mother comforting her child. •Such [8] was our affection for you that we were prepared to share with you not only God's good news but even our very selves, so dear had you become to us. •For you remember, brothers, how we labored and toiled — we [9] worked night and day so we wouldn't be a burden to any of you while we proclaimed God's good news. •You and God are witnesses to how [10] devoutly, uprightly, and blamelessly we behaved toward you believers, •and you also know how, like a father with his own children, •we ex- [11,12] horted you, encouraged you, and urged you to conduct yourselves in a manner worthy of God, Who calls you to the glory of His Kingdom.

•A further reason that we constantly give thanks to God is that when [13] you received the word of God that you heard from us you didn't accept it as mere human words but for what it truly is, the word of God which is at work in you believers. •You became imitators, brothers, of the [14] churches of God in Christ Jesus which are in Judea — you suffered the same things at the hands of your fellow countrymen as they did from the Jews, •who killed both the Lord Jesus and the prophets and drove [15] us out. They displease God and show their hostility to all men •by try- [16] ing to prevent us from proclaiming to the Gentiles that they can be saved. In this they constantly complete the full measure of their sins. But God's wrath has come upon them until the end!

•So, brothers, when we were separated from you for a little while you [17] were absent from our sight but not from our hearts, and we became all the more eager to see your faces — our desire to see you was strong,

[b] *Ac 16:19-24.*

2:14 "Fellow countrymen." This phrase tends to indicate that it is Gentiles rather than Jews who are persecuting the Thessalonians, and leads to the conclusion that the majority of converts were also of Gentile, rather than Jewish, origin.

18 indeed! •We wanted to come to you — I, Paul, tried to do so more than
19 once — but Satan thwarted our desires. •For what is our hope, our joy,
our crowning boast before our Lord Jesus Christ when he comes, if not
20 you? •*You* are our glory and our joy!

3 1 •[c] Therefore, when we could no longer bear it, we decided to remain
2 alone in Athens •and sent Timothy, our brother and co-worker for
God in the good news of Christ, to strengthen and encourage you in
3 your faith •so that no one would be disturbed by these afflictions. You
4 yourselves know that we are destined for this, •for when we were with
you we warned you that we would have to suffer affliction precisely as
5 it has come to pass, as you know. •This is why when I could no longer
bear it I sent to find out the state of your faith, lest the Tempter had
somehow tempted you and all our work might be for naught.

[c] *Ac 17:15.*

Athens. View of the Acropolis.

•[d] But Timothy has just now come to us from you and has given us 6 the good news about your faith and love, and that you hold our memory dear, longing to see us just as we long to see you. •Therefore, brothers, 7 in all our distress and affliction your faith has encouraged us, •because 8 now we can live if you stand firm in the Lord. •For what thanksgiving 9 can we render to God for all the joy we feel before our God for your sake? •More than ever we pray night and day to see your faces 10 and complete what's lacking in your faith.

•May God our Father and our Lord Jesus make straight our road to 11 you! •May the Lord cause you to increase and overflow with love for 12 one another and for everyone, just as we do for you, •so as to strengthen 13 your hearts to be blameless in holiness before our God and Father when our Lord Jesus comes with all his saints.

C. MORAL COUNSELS

4 •And so, brothers, we beg you and exhort you in the Lord Jesus that, 1 just as you learned from us how you should live if you are to please God, as you are now living, you should do so more and more. •For you 2 know the instructions we gave you through the Lord Jesus. •Your sanc- 3 tification is what God wills for you — you should avoid fornication; •you 4 should learn to exercise control over your body in holiness and honor, •and not in lustful passion as the Gentiles do, who don't know God; •let 5,6 no man sin and take advantage of his brother in this matter, for the Lord will avenge all these things, just as we warned you before. •For God 7 called us to holiness, not to impurity. •[e] Therefore, whoever rejects this 8 instruction rejects not man but God, Who gives His Holy Spirit to you.

•There's no need for us to write to you about brotherly love, for you 9 yourselves have been taught by God to love one another •and you do 10 this with regard to all the brothers in Macedonia. But we exhort you, brothers, to do even more. •Aspire to live a quiet life; mind your own 11 affairs and work with your hands, as we instructed you, •so you'll have 12 the respect of outsiders and will lack for nothing.

---

[d] *Ac 18:5.*   [e] *Lk 10:16.*

4:3 The Greek word *porneia*, here translated "fornication," was sometimes used in a technical sense in rabbinic theology with the meaning of "marriage within forbidden degrees of consanguinity." That meaning is also possible in this context.

4:11 "Work with your hands." Some of the Thessalonians may already have been neglecting their work because of expectations of an imminent *parousia*, an issue which is dealt with explicitly and forcefully in 2 Thessalonians. Cf. also 5:14.

D. DOCTRINAL INSTRUCTION: RESURRECTION FROM THE DEAD AND THE COMING OF JESUS

13 •Brothers, we want you to understand how it is with those who have fallen asleep, so you won't grieve like others do, who have no hope.
14 •For if we believe that Jesus died and rose again, then through Jesus God will also bring with him those who have fallen asleep.
15 •[f] Indeed, we can tell you, based on the Lord's teaching, that we who are alive, who remain until the Lord's coming, will not precede those
16 who have fallen asleep. •The Lord himself will come down from Heaven and issue a command, with an archangel's voice and a blast from
17 God's trumpet. Those who died in Christ will rise first, •then we who are living, who remain, will be caught up into the clouds with them to
18 meet the Lord in the air, and so we'll always be with the Lord. •Encourage one another with these words.

5 1 •But as for the specific time or occasion, brothers, there's no need
2 for us to write to you, •[g] for you yourselves are well aware that the
3 day of the Lord will come like a thief in the night. •Just when people are saying, "We have peace and security!" sudden destruction will come upon them, the way labor pains come to a pregnant woman, and there
4 will be no way for them to escape. •But brothers, you aren't in the dark, so the day of the Lord can't take you by surprise like a thief,
5 •for you're all sons of the light and sons of the day. We don't belong
6 to the night or to darkness, •[h] so let's not sleep like others do — let's
7 stay awake and be sober! •For those who sleep sleep at night, and
8 those who get drunk get drunk at night, •whereas we who belong to the day should remain sober, **clothed in the breastplate** of faith and
9 love and the **helmet** of hope **in salvation.** •God has not destined us for His wrath — He has destined us to gain salvation through our Lord
10 Jesus Christ, •who died for us so that whether we are awake or sleep-
11 ing we will live with him. •So encourage and strengthen one another, as you are doing.

[f] 1 Cor 15:51-52.   [g] Mt 24:43; Lk 12:39-40; 2 P 3:10.   [h] Mk 13:35-37; Eph 6:13-17.

4:13-18 The expectation that the Lord would return soon to bring about the "end of the world" was widespread in the early Church. Since many converts had a poorly developed understanding of the afterlife this sometimes led to concern for the fate of those who died before the Lord's *parousia* or coming.
5:8 Is 59:17.

E. CONCLUDING COUNSELS
ON LEADING THE LIFE IN CHRIST

•We beg you, brothers, to respect those who labor among you and 12
direct and admonish you in the Lord. •[i] Have the utmost respect for them 13
and love them for the sake of their work. Be at peace with one another. •We urge you, brothers, to admonish those who are lazy, encourage 14
the fainthearted, help the weak, and be patient with everyone. •[j] See 15
that no one pays back evil for evil; instead, always seek to do good to
one another and to everyone.

•Rejoice always, •pray constantly, •give thanks no matter what hap- 16,17,18
pens, for this is God's will for you in Christ Jesus. •Don't stifle the Spir- 19
it •or despise prophecy — •test everything and keep what's good. •Avoid 20,21,22
every kind of evil.

•May the God of peace Himself sanctify you completely, and may your 23
spirit, soul, and body be kept sound and blameless for the coming of
our Lord Jesus Christ. •He Who calls you is faithful, and He will do it! 24

•Brothers, pray for us, too! 25

F. GREETINGS AND FAREWELL

•Greet all the brothers with a holy kiss. •I adjure you by the Lord to 26,27
read this letter to all the brothers.

•The grace of our Lord Jesus Christ be with you! 28

[i] Mk 9:50.   [j] Mt 5:39ff.

THE SECOND LETTER TO THE

THESSALONIANS

Introduction to the Second Letter to the Thessalonians

This letter is believed to have been written shortly after 1 Thessalonians, in about 50-51 A.D. Apparently the first letter had not had the desired effect and the community continued to be disturbed by apocalyptic speculations and other disorders. New Christians were beginning to neglect work and their everyday responsibilities (3:6-15) as a result of their belief that the day of the Lord had already come (2:2). There may even have been attempts to capitalize on Paul's authority by using letters purporting to have been from him or by misrepresenting his oral teaching (2:2).

Paul's reply, delivered in forceful terms, has been the Church's ever since: nobody knows when the day of the Lord will come. The process is a mystery under the ultimate control of God. As they wait for the end, Paul's instruction to Christians is: "Don't grow weary of doing good" (3:13). In other words, Christians are not to turn from the world in favor of millennial speculation but instead are to continue in the world, but transformed "in Christ," to use a phrase which will feature prominently in Paul's future letters. Paul's prescription for those who fail to follow this advice is simple and stern: "Anyone who refuses to work should not be allowed to eat" (3:10). Nevertheless, as always with Paul, the bitter medicine is not to be administered in a vindictive or malicious spirit but is intended to shame the perpetrator and lead him to mend his ways (3:14-15).

A. GREETING

¹ **1** •Paul, Silvanus, and Timothy to the church of the Thessalonians in
² God our Father and the Lord Jesus Christ. •Grace and peace be with
you from God the Father and the Lord Jesus Christ.

B. THANKSGIVING

³ •We're bound to give thanks to God for you always, brothers, as is
proper, because your faith is growing wonderfully and the love each of
⁴ you has for one another is increasing. •As a result we ourselves boast
in the churches of God of your steadfastness and faith in all the perse-
⁵ cutions and afflictions which you endure. •This is proof that God's judg-
ment is just and it will lead to your being considered worthy of God's
⁶ Kingdom, for which you're suffering. •It's right for God to pay back in
⁷ suffering those who are causing you to suffer •and to give rest to you
who are suffering as well as to us at the revelation of the Lord Jesus,
⁸ when he comes from Heaven with his mighty angels, **•with a blazing
fire, to wreak vengeance on those who don't know God** and don't
⁹ obey the good news of our Lord Jesus. •They'll undergo the punishment
of eternal destruction and be shut off **from the face of the Lord and
¹⁰ from his glorious might** •when he comes on that day to be glorified
with his saints and to be marvelled at by all the believers, because you
¹¹ believed our witness. •We pray always that this will come to pass for
you, that God will consider you worthy of His call, and that by His pow-
¹² er He will fulfill every desire for goodness and every work of faith, •so
that the name of our Lord Jesus will be glorified in you, and you in it,
in accordance with the grace of our God and the Lord Jesus Christ.

1:8 Ps 79:6; Is 66:15; Jr 10:25.
1:9 Is 2:10, 19, 21. Note that "destruction" does of existence — but is essentially synonymous
not indicate annihilation — a complete cessation with separation from Christ and God.

C. WARNING AGAINST FALSE
TEACHING ON THE COMING OF JESUS

2 •Now as for the coming of our Lord Jesus and our being gathered to 1
him, we beg you, brothers, •not to be too quickly shaken in mind or 2
disturbed, whether by a spirit-inspired utterance, by preaching, or by a letter purporting to be from us and claiming that the day of the Lord has
come. •Let no one deceive you in any way. Unless the apostasy comes 3
first and the man who embodies all wickedness is revealed, who is doomed
to perdition •and opposes **and exalts himself against every** so-called 4
god and object of worship so as **to seat himself in God's Temple** and
proclaim that he's God — •Don't you remember that I told you all this 5
while I was still with you? •And now you know what's restraining him, so 6
that he'll be revealed at his proper time. •For the mystery of evil is already 7
at work; only the Restrainer is holding it back for the present, until he's
removed. •Then the wicked one will be revealed and the Lord **will slay** 8
him with the breath of his mouth and destroy him when he appears
at his coming. •[a] The wicked one's coming will be Satan's work and will 9
be accompanied by power and false signs and wonders •and with all man- 10
ner of wicked deception against those who are to perish, because they refused to love the truth and save themselves. •That's why God is sending 11
the power of error to cause them to believe what's false, •so that all who 12
delighted in wickedness instead of believing the truth will be condemned.

•But we must always give thanks to God for you, brothers beloved of 13
the Lord, because God has chosen you as first fruits to be saved through
sanctification by the Spirit and belief in the truth. •It was for this that He 14
called you through our good news to possess the glory of our Lord Jesus Christ. •So then, brothers, stand firm and hold fast to the tradition 15
we taught you, whether by word of mouth or by a letter of ours. •May 16
our Lord Jesus Christ himself and God our Father, Who loved us and
through His grace gave us everlasting encouragement and good hope,
•encourage and strengthen your hearts for every good work and word. 17

---

[a] Mt 24:2.

2:1-12 As in 1 Thessalonians, Paul refuses to
speculate about dates or times for the day of the
Lord. He reminds the Thessalonians that "the
mystery of evil" is already at work, but the cul-
mination of this process is being held in check
for an indefinite length of time by a mysterious
person or force called the "Restrainer." We are
unfortunately unable to establish the identity of
this "Restrainer," although there has been no
lack of theories. The three leading candidates
are the Roman Empire (or the Emperor himself),
some supernatural force, or Satan. Ultimately,
however, God is in control of this process (2:10-
12), and it is God Who will determine the "proper time" (2:6).
2:4 Dn 11:36. 2:8 Jb 4:9; Is 11:4.
2:13 Some manuscripts read "from the beginning" instead of "as first fruits."

D. CONCLUDING EXHORTATIONS
TO PRAY AND TO AVOID IDLE LIVING

1 **3** •Finally, pray for us, brothers, that the word of the Lord may spread
2 quickly and be glorified as it was among you •and that we may be
3 delivered from perverse and evil men, for not all have the faith. •But the
4 Lord is faithful and will strengthen you and protect you from evil. •We
have every confidence in you in the Lord that you are doing and will do
5 what we have commanded. •May the Lord guide your hearts to the love
of God and the steadfastness of Christ.

6 •Brothers, we command you in the name of the Lord Jesus Christ to
avoid any brother who leads an idle life which is not in accord with the
7 tradition you received from us. •You know how you should imitate us
8 — we weren't lazy when we were among you, •nor did we eat anyone's
bread without paying for it. Instead, we worked night and day, laboring
9 and toiling so as not to burden any of you. •Not that we didn't have the
right to be supported, but because we wanted to give you ourselves as
10 an example to imitate. •And indeed when we were among you we commanded that "anyone who refuses to work should not be allowed to eat."
11 •We hear that some of you are leading idle lives and are behaving like
12 busybodies instead of working. •We command and exhort such people
13 in the Lord Jesus Christ to work quietly and eat their own bread. •And
14 you, brothers, don't grow weary of doing good. •If anyone doesn't obey
our instructions in this letter, take note of him and don't associate with
15 him, so as to put him to shame. •Yet don't regard him as an enemy; instead, admonish him as a brother.

E. GREETING AND FAREWELL

16 •May the Lord of peace himself grant you peace at all times and in
all ways. The Lord be with all of you.
17 •This greeting is written with my own hand — Paul's. This is my sign
18 in every letter, this is how I write. •The grace of our Lord Jesus Christ
be with all of you.

3:17 It appears to have been Paul's usual practice to dictate his letters to a secretary, actually
writing only the last few lines himself. It is possible that in some letters the scribe also had a hand
in composing the letter.

Here, Paul writes the last few words in his own
hand, and states that this is his handwriting, as
a means of authenticating the letter and guarding against forgers attempting to claim his authority for their own purposes.

THE FIRST LETTER TO

TIMOTHY

Introduction to the First Letter
to Timothy

1 Timothy is largely devoted to matters of church organization: the qualifications of bishops and deacons; the treatment of various groups within the church, notably widows and elders, and behavioral guidelines for women, the rich, and slaves; how to deal with doctrinal deviations among the faithful; and practical advice on how Timothy is to comport himself while he is in charge of the church at Ephesus in Paul's absence.

Those scholars (the overwhelming majority) who regard 1 Timothy as pseudonymous have more freedom in assigning a date and place to the letter. Scholars who support Pauline authorship usually place it late in Paul's life, precisely because so little is known about Paul's life after he reached Rome. Among those who support Pauline authorship, Robinson makes the interesting suggestion that the letter was written between the two Corinthian letters, while Paul was based in Ephesus but was travelling throughout the Aegean region. The strength of this suggestion is that it places the letter at a time when Timothy was still somewhat new to Paul's work. This would explain why Paul spells out in such detail exactly what Timothy is to do, an aspect of the letter which is difficult to explain if it is placed later in Paul's life.

A. GREETING

1 **1** •Paul, an apostle of Christ Jesus by command of God our Savior and
2 Christ Jesus our hope, •to Timothy, my true child in the faith: grace,
mercy, and peace from God the Father and Christ Jesus our Lord.

B. TIMOTHY IS INSTRUCTED
TO OPPOSE FALSE TEACHERS

3 •As I urged you when I was leaving for Macedonia, remain at Ephesus and instruct certain persons to refrain from teaching false doctrines
4 •and occupying themselves with myths and endless genealogies, which
give rise to speculation rather than the working out of God's plan which
5 is received through faith. •The purpose of this instruction is to foster
that love which flows from a pure heart, a clean conscience, and sin-
6 cere faith. •Certain persons have departed from these principles and
7 have become sidetracked in fruitless discussions •out of a desire to be
teachers of the Torah, but they don't understand the words they use or
the matters about which they make confident assertions.
8,9 •Now we know that the Torah is good if it's used as a law, •in the realization that it's not intended for the righteous but for the lawless and
disobedient, godless sinners, the unholy and profane, patricides and mat-
10 ricides, murderers, •fornicators, sodomites, kidnappers, liars, perjurers,
11 and whatever else is opposed to sound teaching •in accordance with the
glorious good news of the blessed God with which I've been entrusted.
12 •I give thanks to Jesus Christ our Lord who has strengthened me, because by appointing me to his ministry he considered me trustworthy
13 — •I who had previously been an insolent and blasphemous persecutor.
14 But he had mercy on me because I acted ignorantly out of unbelief, •and
the grace of our Lord Jesus was given to me in abundance, along with

1:7 Here we learn, from the reference to the Torah, that the false doctrines have arisen from a Ju-
daizing tendency.

the faith and love which are in Christ Jesus. •This teaching may be trust- 15
ed and is worthy of complete acceptance — Christ Jesus came into the
world to save sinners, of whom I am the first. •The reason Christ Jesus 16
had mercy on me, the first of all sinners, was to demonstrate all his patience, as an example for those who were to believe in him for everlasting life. •To the King of ages, to the one, immortal, invisible God, 17
be honor and glory for ever and ever, amen.

•I'm entrusting you with this instruction, Timothy my child, in accor- 18
dance with the prophecies made about you long ago. May those words
inspire you to fight the good fight •with faith and a good conscience. 19
By rejecting conscience certain persons have made a shipwreck of their
faith. •Among them are Hymenaeus and Alexander, whom I've handed 20
over to Satan in the hope that they'll learn not to blaspheme.

C. THE ROLES AND QUALITIES OF
VARIOUS CATEGORIES OF BELIEVERS

2 •First of all, I urge that supplications, prayers, intercessions, and 1
thanksgivings be made for all men — •for kings and for all those in 2
positions of authority — that we may lead a peaceful, quiet life, holy
and respectable in every way. •Such a life is good and acceptable in 3
the sight of God our Savior, •Whose wish is that all may be saved and 4
may come to knowledge of the truth. •For there is one God and one 5
mediator between God and men — the man Christ Jesus, •who gave 6
himself as a ransom for all; this testimony was given at the time God
had chosen. •[a] I was made a herald and apostle to give this testimony 7
— I'm speaking the truth, I'm not lying — a teacher of the Gentiles in
faith and truth.

[a] 2 Tm 1:11.

1:17 This is believed to have been taken from an early liturgy.
1:20 Hymenaeus is mentioned at 2 Tm 2:17 in conjunction with a certain Philetus. They are described as claiming that the resurrection has already taken place. This probably means that they regarded resurrection of the dead as taking place symbolically in baptism, but denied an afterlife.

2:1ff The attitude expressed here toward civil authorities would be rather anachronistic if 1 Timothy had been written after the Neronian persecution of the middle to late 60's. It is instructive to compare these sentiments with the unrelenting hostility expressed in the Revelation to John.
2:6 "This testimony..." This obscure phrase may refer either to Jesus' death or his words.

Samothrace in Greece. Ruins by the Cabiri river.

The behavior of men and, especially, of women

8 •Therefore my desire is that at every place the men should lift holy
9 hands in prayer without anger or arguing. •[b] Likewise, the women
should dress in a modest, respectable manner, decorating themselves
sensibly, not with elaborate braids and gold, or pearls or expensive gar-
10 ments. •Instead, they should adorn themselves with good deeds, as is
11 proper for women who claim to be religious. •A woman should learn
12 in silence, and complete submissiveness. •I don't permit a woman to
teach, nor to have authority over a man; instead, she should be silent.
13,14 •For Adam was formed first, and then Eve. •Moreover it wasn't Adam
who was deceived, it was the woman who was deceived and sinned.
15 •But women will be saved by childbearing, if they persevere in faith,
love, and holiness, with modesty.

---

[b] *1 P 3:3.*
2:8 "At every place," i.e., where there is a church.
2:12 "A man" probably refers to a woman's husband.

The qualities of a bishop

3 •This teaching is trustworthy — "if anyone aspires to be a bishop [1] he desires to undertake an honorable task." •[c] Therefore a bishop [2] must be above reproach, married only once, temperate, sensible, respectable, hospitable, skillful in teaching, •not a drunkard, not a bul- [3] ly; instead he should be gentle, peaceable, and not greedy. •He should [4] manage his own household well and raise his children to be obedient and honorable. •(If someone doesn't know how to manage his own [5] household, how will he be able to care for the church of God?) •He [6] must not be a recent convert, so he won't become self-important and incur the judgment that befell the Devil. •He must be well regarded by [7] outsiders; otherwise, he may fall into disgrace and be trapped in the Devil's snare.

The qualities of deacons

•Likewise deacons must be honorable, not two-faced, not over-indul- [8] gers in wine, not greedy for material gain, •adhering to the mystery of [9] the faith with a clear conscience. •Moreover they should first be tested [10] and then, if they're found to be without fault, they may serve as deacons. •Their wives, too, must be honorable, not given to slander, temperate, [11] and trustworthy in all things. •Deacons should be men who have had on- [12] ly one wife and who guide their children and their households correctly, •for those who serve well as deacons acquire for themselves a good stand- [13] ing as well as great confidence in their faith in Christ Jesus.

•I hope to come to you soon, but I'm writing these things to you •in [14,15] case I'm delayed, so you'll know how to behave in the household of God, which is the church of the living God, the pillar and foundation of the truth. •The mystery of our religion is undeniably great — [16]

---

[c] Tt 1:6-9.

3:8-13 While some authors maintain that verse 11 refers to women deacons (the one Greek word in question can mean either "women" or "wives") the total context makes this unlikely, at least if "deacon" is understood as an ecclesiastical office. Verses 8-10 clearly view deacons as men, and verse 12 specifies that deacons are to be males (translated "men") who have had only one wife. In addition, 2:9-15 should be consulted regarding the letter's general attitude toward women; it is hard to visualize the author of those lines ordaining (in a technical sense) women as deacons. On the other hand, this passage probably envisions the wives of deacons assisting them in their ministry. Women were often deacons in the more general sense of the Greek word, as helpers. In Romans we have also seen Paul's patroness Phoebe referred to as a deacon or minister and engaged in helping Paul by delivering an important letter and establishing contact with the Roman church.

He was manifested in the flesh,
    vindicated in the spirit, seen by angels,
Proclaimed among the Gentiles,
    believed in throughout the world,
       taken up in glory.

D. THE ERRORS OF THE FALSE TEACHERS AND INSTRUCTIONS ON HOW TO COUNTER THEM

1 4 •Now the Spirit expressly states that in the end times there will be some who leave the faith. They'll follow deceitful spirits and the 2 teaching of demons, •led by the hypocrisy of liars whose consciences 3 have been deadened. •They forbid marriage and require abstinence from foods that God created to be received with thanksgiving by believers who 4 know the truth. •But everything created by God is good and nothing is 5 to be rejected when it's received with thanksgiving, •for it's sanctified by the word of God and by prayer.

6   •If you point this out to the brothers you'll be a good minister of Christ Jesus, nourished by the words of faith and the good teaching you've fol- 7 lowed. •Have nothing to do with profane myths and old wives' tales. 8 Train yourself in godliness, •for while physical training has a limited val- ue godliness is valuable from every standpoint, since it holds promise 9 both for this life and for the life to come. •This teaching is trustworthy 10 and deserves full acceptance — •the reason we toil and strive is because we've placed our hope in the living God, Who is the Savior of all, es- pecially of those who believe.

11,12   •Command and teach these things. •Let no one look down on you because you're young; be an example for the faithful in word, conduct, 13 love, faith, and purity. •Until I come, attend to reading, encouraging, 14 and teaching. •Don't neglect the gift that was given to you when, guid- 15 ed by prophecy, the council of elders laid hands on you. •Cultivate these things, devote yourself to them, so your progress will be clear to all. 16 •Keep a close watch over yourself and your teaching; persevere, for by doing this you'll save yourself as well as your listeners.

4:2 "Whose consciences have been deadened." Perhaps most literally, "whose consciences have been rendered insensible by cauterization." How- ever, it is also possible that the Greek means that their consciences have been branded as a sign that they belong to the demons.

4:10 "Strive." Some manuscripts read "are reviled." 4:13 "Reading," i.e., of Scripture in a public set- ting to his congregation. 4:14 This passage seems to envision prophetic speeches as a part of the ordination ceremony for church elders.

E. PRACTICAL GUIDANCE ON HOW TO TREAT CERTAIN CLASSES OF THE FAITHFUL IN GENERAL

5 •Don't reprimand an older man — encourage him as you would your ₁ father. Treat younger men as brothers, •older women like mothers, ₂ and younger women like sisters, with the utmost purity.

Widows

•Treat as widows only those who are truly widows. •If a widow has ₃,₄ children or grandchildren they should first learn to perform their religious duty toward their own household and repay their parents, for this is pleasing in the eyes of God. •A woman who is truly a widow ₅ and has been left alone sets her hope on God and continues both night and day in supplication and prayer, •but a widow who lives a life of ₆ self-indulgence is dead even though she's alive. •Issue these instruc- ₇ tions as well, so that they'll be irreproachable. •But if anyone doesn't ₈ provide for their relatives, especially their own family, they've renounced their faith and are worse than an unbeliever. •A widow should ₉ be put on the roll only if she's over sixty years old and has been married once; •she should have a reputation for good deeds, such as hav- ₁₀ ing raised children, shown hospitality, washed the feet of the saints, aided those who were afflicted, or devoted herself to all sorts of good works. •Refuse to put younger women on the roll, for when their sen- ₁₁ sual urges are aroused they're drawn away from Christ and want to get married, •then they're condemned for having broken their first ₁₂ promise. •Besides, they learn to be lazy and go about from house to ₁₃ house, and they become not only lazy but gossips and busybodies, saying things that shouldn't be said. •So I want young widows to marry, ₁₄ have children, manage their household, and thus give the adversary no opportunity to slander us, •for some have already turned aside to ₁₅ follow Satan. •If any woman believer has relatives who are widows she ₁₆ must help them herself — the church should be free of such burdens, so it can help those who are truly widows.

5:9 "Put on the roll." This whole passage appears to presuppose that the local church will have an official list of widows — perhaps corresponding to a formal organizational grouping — by which the church will be enabled to decide how to allocate the community's resources.

Mother and daughter (1 Tm 5:4);
a Roman terra-cotta from Myrina (Turkey).

Elders

17 •Elders who rule well should be considered worthy of double com-
18 pensation, especially those who labor at preaching and teaching, •[d] for
Scripture says, **Don't muzzle an ox while it's threshing,** and "The
19 worker deserves his pay." •Don't consider any accusation against an eld-
20 er unless it's **supported by two or three witnesses.** •Those who do
sin should be rebuked in front of everyone, so the others will be afraid.
21 •I charge you before God, Jesus Christ, and the chosen angels to fol-
22 low these rules impartially — do nothing based on favoritism. •Don't be

[d] Mt 10:10; Lk 10:7.

5:17 While some scholars claim to see a difference in function between "bishops" (3:1)
and "elders," the distinction appears forced. It
is more probable that the terms were used in-
terchangeably, or as "functional equivalents."
5:18 Dt 25:4. 5:19 Dt 19:15.
5:22 "Lay your hands on," i.e., ordain as an
elder.

too quick to lay your hands on anyone, and don't take part in anyone else's sins — keep yourself pure. •Stop drinking only water — take a little wine to aid your digestion and because of your frequent illnesses. 23

•The sins of some men are so evident that they go before them to judgment, while the sins of others follow behind. •Likewise, good works are evident, or even if they're not they can't be hidden. 24 25

Slaves

6 •All who are under the yoke of slavery should regard their masters as worthy of respect, so the name of God and our teaching won't be reviled. •Those whose masters are believers should not be insolent to them just because they're brothers — on the contrary, they should be even better servants because those who benefit from their service are believers and are beloved. 1 2

Roman slave (1 Tm 6:1); a bronze statue from Herculaneum (Italy).

F. CONCLUDING EXHORTATIONS, WARNINGS, AND COUNSEL

3 Teach and urge these things. •Whoever teaches differently and doesn't agree with our Lord Jesus Christ's sound words and with teaching
4 which is in accord with true religion •is blinded by pride and doesn't understand anything. Instead he has a sick craving for controversy and verbal disputes. These produce envy, discord, slander, unfounded suspicion,
5 •and constant irritation among men who have become depraved in mind and have been deprived of the truth — they think religion is a means of
6 gain. •Religious sentiment is indeed a great gain when it is free of con-
7 cern for material goods, •for we brought nothing into the world and can
8 take nothing out of it. •If we have food and shelter we should be con-
9 tent with that. •Those who want to be rich fall into temptations and snares, into many foolish and harmful desires which plunge them into
10 destruction and ruin. •For love of money is the root of all evil; in their desire for money, some have strayed from the faith and have been pierced with many sorrows.

11 •But you, O man of God, flee these things! Strive for righteousness,
12 true religion, faith, love, steadfastness, and gentleness. •Fight the good fight of faith, seize the eternal life to which you were called when you
13 nobly professed your faith before many witnesses. •I command you before God Who gives life to all things and before Christ Jesus who made
14 his noble profession when he testified before Pontius Pilate — •keep the commandment irreproachably and without blemish until our Lord Jesus
15 Christ appears. •His appearance will be made manifest at the proper time by the blessed and only Sovereign, the King of kings and Lord of
16 lords, •Who alone is immortal and dwells in unapproachable light. No one has seen Him, nor can He be seen. To Him be honor and power forever, amen.

17 •Command those who are rich in the present age not to be arrogant and not to place their hope in uncertain riches. Instead, we should place our hope in God, Who grants us all things in rich supply for our enjoy-
18 ment. •The wealthy should do good and grow rich in good deeds, be
19 generous and share, •and lay up for themselves a good foundation for the future so they'll be able to grasp the true life.

G. FAREWELL

•Timothy, guard what has been entrusted to your care! Avoid irreligious chatter, oppose that so-called knowledge which is false; •some who
profess it have missed the mark as far as the faith is concerned. Grace
be with all of you.

THE SECOND LETTER TO

TIMOTHY

Introduction to the Second Letter
to Timothy

In contrast to 1 Timothy, 2 Timothy is the most Pauline of the Pastoral Letters. It purports to be a letter of encouragement to Timothy and generally conforms to what we would expect of Paul in this situation. If it is pseudonymous, it is certainly remarkable for its sensitivity in portraying Paul as aging and alone, in prison for Christ. Again in contrast to 1 Timothy there are many personal references to well-known companions of Paul, references which, if authentic, tend to group this letter with Colossians and Philemon.

The dominant theme is the need to be faithful and steadfast. Particularly noteworthy is the way in which Paul always has Christ in mind throughout the letter; never does the letter sink into self pity, for Paul has complete faith in Christ. Paul's concern is not for himself but for the young churches which Timothy must oversee, lest they be led astray by false teachers.

A. GREETING

1 ¹ •Paul, an apostle of Christ Jesus by the will of God in accordance ² with the promise of the life which is in Christ Jesus, •to Timothy my beloved child — grace, mercy, and peace from God the Father and Christ Jesus our Lord.

B. THANKSGIVING AND EXHORTATION TO TIMOTHY

3 •I give thanks to God — Whom I serve with a clear conscience, as did my forefathers — when I mention you in my prayers, which I do un-
4 ceasingly, night and day. •When I remember your tears I long to see you
5 and be filled with joy. •[a] I remember your sincere faith — it dwelt first in your grandmother Lois and your mother Eunice and I'm certain it dwells
6 in you as well. •For this reason I remind you to stir up the flame of God's
7 gift, which is yours through the laying on of my hands, •for God didn't give us a spirit of cowardice — He gave us a spirit of power, love, and
8 good judgment. •So don't be ashamed to bear witness to our Lord, nor to me, his prisoner; instead, join with me in suffering for the good news
9 through the strength that comes from God. •He saved us and called us to a holy way of life, not because of what we had done but in accordance with His plan and His grace which He granted us in Christ Jesus before
10 the beginning of the ages. •It has now been made manifest through the appearance of our Savior Christ Jesus, who destroyed death and brought
11 life and immortality to light through the good news, •[b] for which I have
12 been appointed a preacher, an apostle, and a teacher. •This is the reason I'm suffering these things, but I'm not ashamed, for I know whom I've believed and I'm confident that he's able to guard what was entrust-
13 ed to me until that day. •Hold fast to the example of sound teaching that you received from me, in the faith and love which are in Christ Jesus.
14 •Guard the precious trust, through the Holy Spirit that dwells in us.

[a] *Ac 16:1.*   [b] *1 Tm 2:7.*

Rome. Trajan's Market (107-113 A.D.).

C. CALL TO TIMOTHY
TO SUFFER WITH PAUL IN CHRIST

•As you know, all those in Asia have deserted me, including Phygelus 15 and Hermogenes. •May the Lord grant mercy to the household of One- 16 siphorus, because he has revived me many times and has not been ashamed of my chains. •On the contrary, when he was in Rome he ea- 17 gerly sought me out and found me — •may the Lord grant that he may 18 find mercy from the Lord on that day! He also rendered many services for me at Ephesus, as you well know.

2 •So, my child, be strong in the grace which is in Christ Jesus. •The 1,2 things you heard from me before many witnesses, entrust them to faithful men who will be capable of teaching others. •Share in my suf- 3 fering like a good soldier of Christ Jesus. •No one serving as a soldier 4 can get entangled in affairs of everyday life, because he wants to please the one who enlisted him. •And an athlete isn't awarded the crown 5

2:4 The idea behind the phrase "affairs of every-day life" is probably that the soldier should not moonlight in a second job. The lesson for the Christian is that of singleness of purpose.

6 unless he competes in accordance with the rules. •The farmer who
7 works hard should be the first to receive a share of the harvest. •Think over what I'm saying, for the Lord will give you understanding in all
8 things. •Remember Jesus Christ who was raised from the dead and was descended from David, in accordance with the good news I pro-
9 claimed. •It's for that that I'm suffering and in chains like a criminal,
10 but the word of God cannot be chained. •The reason I'm willing to endure it all for the sake of those who were chosen, is so they'll be
11 able to attain salvation in Christ Jesus, with eternal glory. •This teaching can be trusted,

> If we've died with him we'll also live with him;
12 > •[c] if we endure we'll also reign with him;
> if we deny him, then he'll deny us too;
13 > •if we're unfaithful, he remains faithful,
> for he can't deny himself.

D. BE FAITHFUL AND OPPOSE FALSE TEACHING

14 •Keep reminding people of these things, warn them before God not to engage in disputes over words — such disputes serve no purpose
15 but the ruin of those who listen to them. •Make every effort to present yourself as acceptable to God, a laborer who need not be ashamed
16 and correctly interprets the word of truth. •Avoid irreligious chatter, for
17 it leads people to further wickedness •and their talk spreads like a can-
18 cer. Among them are Hymenaeus and Philetus. •They've departed from the truth by saying that the resurrection has already taken place, and
19 they are upsetting the faith of some. •Nevertheless God's firm foundation stands and bears this seal: **The Lord knows those who are His,** and "Let everyone who calls on the name of the Lord keep away
20 from evil." •In a great house there aren't just gold and silver vessels — there are also wooden and clay ones, some of which are for more hon-
21 ored use and some for less honored use. •So if someone purifies himself from these things he'll be a vessel that's destined for honored use,
22 set apart and useful to the master, ready for every good work. •Flee youthful passions, strive for righteousness, faith, love, and peace, to-

[c] Mt 10:33; Lk 12:9.

2:18 Hymenaeus and Philetus appear to have regarded resurrection as taking place symboli- cally at baptism and to have denied an afterlife. 2:19 Nb 16:5

gether with those who call upon the Lord from pure hearts. •Avoid fool- 23
ish and stupid controversies, because you know that they lead to quarrels. •A servant of the Lord should not quarrel — he should be kind to 24
everyone, skilled at teaching, tolerant, •able to correct opponents gen- 25
tly, in case God should grant them repentance and lead them to recognize the truth, •return to their senses, and escape the Devil's snares, 26
by whom they had been held captive to do his will.

3 •Understand this — in the final days there will be difficult times. •For 1,2
men will be selfish, greedy, braggarts, arrogant, abusive, disobedient
to their parents, ungrateful, unholy, •inhuman, merciless, slanderous, 3
lacking in self-control, brutal, enemies of what's good, •treacherous, reck- 4
less, conceited, given over to pleasure rather than being lovers of God.
•They'll have the outward appearance of piety but will deny the power 5
of religion. Avoid them! •For included among them are those who worm 6
their way into homes and mislead poor weak women who are burdened
with sins and influenced by all kinds of passions. •These women are al- 7
ways trying to learn but are never able to arrive at a knowledge of the
truth. •Just as Jannes and Jambres opposed Moses, so too these men 8
oppose the truth. They're corrupt in mind and their faith is worthless,
•but they won't get very far, for their folly will be apparent to all, just as 9
was the folly of Jannes and Jambres.

  ˙ •But you have followed my teaching, my way of life, my purpose, 10
my faith, my patience, my love, my steadfastness, •[d] my persecutions, 11
my sufferings, everything that happened to me in Antioch, in Iconium,
and in Lystra, all the persecutions I endured — and the Lord delivered
me from them all. •And in fact everyone who desires to live a holy life 12
in Christ Jesus will be persecuted, •while evil men and impostors will 13
grow ever worse, deceiving and being deceived. •But remain faithful to 14
what you've learned and believed, remembering from whom you
learned it. •Remember that from childhood you have been familiar with 15
the holy Scriptures, which are able to instruct you and lead you to salvation through faith in Christ Jesus. •All Scripture is inspired by God 16
and is useful for teaching, reproving, correcting, and training in righteousness, •so that the man of God may be fully capable of carrying out 17
every good work.

[d] *Ac 13:14-14:20.*

3:8 In Jewish legend Jannes and Jambres were said to have been the names of Pharaoh's magicians
(cf. Ex 7:11; 8:18-19).

Man wearing a cloak (2 Tm 4:13); Roman bronze statue.

1 4 •I charge you before God and Christ Jesus, who is to judge the liv-
2 ing and the dead, and by his appearance and his Kingdom — •pro-
claim the word, insist upon it whether it's convenient or inconvenient,
show error for what it is, reprove and encourage, but always display pa-
3 tience in your teaching. •The time will come when people will not tolerate sound teaching; instead, because their ears are itching, they'll fol-
4 low their own desires and gather teachers for themselves. •They'll stop
5 listening to the truth and will turn to myths. •But keep your self-control
at all times, endure suffering patiently, do the work of an evangelist, perform your ministry fully and completely.
6   •[e] As for me, my life is already being poured out like a libation — the
7 time of my departure is imminent. •I've fought the good fight, I've fin-
8 ished the race, I've kept the faith. •From here on the crown of righteousness is being laid aside for me, which the Lord, the just judge, will
award me on that day, and not only me but all those who have longed
for his appearance.

[e] Ph 2:17.

E. PERSONAL NEWS AND GREETINGS

•Do your best to come to me quickly. •[f] Demas has abandoned me [9,10] out of love for this present world and has gone to Thessalonica, Crescens has gone to Galatia, and Titus to Dalmatia — •[g] only Luke is with me. [11] Get Mark and bring him with you, for he's useful to me in the ministry. •[h] Tychicus I sent to Ephesus. •When you come, bring the cloak I left [12,13] at Troas with Carpus as well as the scrolls, especially the parchments. •[i] Alexander the coppersmith has done me considerable harm — the [14] Lord will repay him in accordance with his deeds! •Be on your guard [15] against him, for he strenuously opposed our teaching.

•At my first hearing no one came to my aid — they all abandoned [16] me, may it not be held against them! •But the Lord came to my aid [17] and strengthened me so that through me the proclamation of the good news might be fully accomplished and all the Gentiles might hear it, and I was delivered from the lion's mouth. •The Lord will deliver me [18] from all evil and will save me for his heavenly Kingdom, to him be glory for ever and ever, amen.

•Greet Prisca and Aquila and the household of Onesiphorus. •[j] Eras- [19,20] tus remained at Corinth and I left Trophimus ill at Miletus. •Do every- [21] thing in your power to come before winter. Eubulus greets you, as well as Pudens, Linus, Claudia, and all the brothers. •The Lord be with your [22] spirit. Grace be with all of you.

[f] Col 4:14; Phm 24; 2 Cor 8:23; Gal 2:3; Tt 1:4.
[g] Col 4:10, 14; Phm 24.
[h] Ac 20:4; Eph 6:21-22; Col 4:7-8.
[i] 1 Tm 1:20.
[j] Ac 19:22; 20:4; 21:29; Rm 16:23.

4:19 Prisca and Aquila were well known associates of Paul, mentioned not only in Acts but in 1 Corinthians and Romans as well.

4:21 "Linus." Possibly the same Linus who became the second pope. If so, this would be an argument for a Roman setting for the letter.

THE LETTER TO

TITUS

Introduction to the Letter to Titus

Titus was Paul's companion and co-worker during some of Paul's most productive years, although he is known only from Paul's letters and is not mentioned in Acts. That Paul had great confidence in him can be seen from the fact that Paul used him for very sensitive missions, such as trips to the recalcitrant church in Corinth bearing letters from Paul (cf. 2 Corinthians). This letter itself, however, offers little of a personal nature; it is brisk and businesslike in tone and, like 1 Timothy, is concerned with church organization, the threat posed by false teachers, and the need for the faithful to lead orderly, respectable lives.

At the time of writing Titus is in Crete, and Paul is writing to give him instructions on how to organize the new churches there. Among those who support Pauline authorship (the minority view), the suggestion is sometimes made that the letter was written while Paul was en route back to Jerusalem for his last visit.

A. GREETING

1 •Paul, a servant of God and an apostle of Jesus Christ for the purpose of advancing the faith of God's chosen ones and their knowl- **2** edge of religious truth, •in hope of the eternal life which was promised **3** before time began by God, Who never lies, and Who, •at the proper time, revealed His word in the proclamation with which I have been en- **4** trusted by the command of God our Savior — •[a] to Titus, my true child in our common faith; grace and peace from God the Father and our Savior Christ Jesus.

B. INSTRUCTIONS ON TITUS' MINISTRY IN CRETE, ESPECIALLY WITH REGARD TO FALSE TEACHERS

5 •The reason I left you in Crete was to correct any shortcomings and to appoint elders in every city in accordance with the instructions I gave **6** you — •[b] if the man is blameless, married once, and has children who **7** are believers and are not accused of profligacy or rebelliousness. •For a bishop, as God's steward, must be above reproach, not arrogant, not **8** quick-tempered, not a drunkard, not a bully, and not greedy. •Instead, he should be hospitable, he should love what's good, be prudent, up- **9** right, holy, and self-disciplined. •He must adhere to the true word as it was taught so he'll be able both to offer encouragement with sound teaching and to refute opponents.

10 •For there are many who are rebellious, who are empty talkers and **11** deceivers, especially those who support circumcision. •You must silence them, because they're upsetting entire households by teaching what they

---

[a] *2 Cor 8:23; Gal 2:3; 2 Tm 4:10.*   [b] *1 Tm 3:2-7.*

1:5-7 Here we clearly see that "bishop" and "eld-er" are essentially equivalent terms in the Pastoral Letters.

1:10 "Those who support circumcision," i.e., Jewish Christians who favored requiring Gentile converts to be circumcised.

shouldn't for the sake of dishonest gain. •One of them, a prophet of 12 their own, said:

"Cretans have always been liars,
    evil beasts, and lazy gluttons."

•This testimony can be trusted. Therefore rebuke them sharply so 13 they'll be sound in the faith •and won't give themselves over to Jew- 14 ish myths and the commandments of men who reject the truth. •Everything is pure for those who are pure, but for those who are 15 corrupt and unbelieving nothing is pure — both their minds and consciences are corrupt. •They claim to know God, but deny Him by their 16 actions; they're detestable and disobedient and unfit for any good deed.

C. PROPER BEHAVIOR OF THE FAITHFUL

2 •You, however, must say what is in accord with sound teaching. 1 •Urge older men to be temperate, serious, sensible, sound in faith, 2 love, and steadfastness. •Likewise, urge older women to be reverent in 3 their behavior, not slanderous nor slaves to· wine; they should teach what's good •and encourage young women to love their husbands and 4 children, •to be sensible, chaste, devoted homemakers, generous and 5 submissive to their husbands so the word of God won't be blasphemed. •Likewise, encourage the·young men to be sensible. •Be a model of good 6,7 works in every respect; in your teaching demonstrate integrity, seriousness, •and sound speech which is beyond reproach so that whoever op- 8 poses us will be ashamed and will have nothing bad to say about us. •Slaves are to be submissive to their masters in everything, to give sat- 9 isfaction and not be contentious; •they are not to pilfer but are to show 10 complete good faith so that in every respect they will adorn the teaching of God our Savior.

•For the grace of God has appeared with salvation for all men, 11 •teaching us to reject impiety and worldly passions and to live sober, 12 upright, and godly lives in this present age •as we await our blessed 13 hope — the appearance in glory of our great God and of our Savior Christ Jesus. •He gave himself for us to redeem us from all wicked- 14 ness and to purify for himself a people eager for good works. •Say 15 these things, encourage and reprove with authority — let no one disregard you.

1 3 •Remind them to be submissive to rulers and authorities, to be obe-
2 dient and ready for any good work; •to slander no one, to be peace-
3 able and gentle, to show consideration for everyone. •For we too were
once foolish, disobedient, deceived, enslaved by various desires and passions, spending our lives in malice and envy — we were hateful, and we
hated one another.

4   •But when the goodness and loving kindness
        of God our Savior appeared —
5   •not because of righteous acts we had performed
        but through His mercy —
    He saved us through the bath of rebirth
        and renewal in the Holy Spirit,
6   •which He poured out upon us so richly
        through our Savior Jesus Christ
7   •so that we might be restored to fellowship with God
        by his grace
    and become heirs in hope of eternal life.

8   •This teaching can be trusted, and I want you to insist upon it so that
those who have come to believe in God will be intent upon busying themselves with good deeds — these are good and are beneficial to others.
9 •But avoid foolish controversies, genealogies, strife, and disputes about
10 the Torah — these things are useless and futile. •Warn a heretic once or
11 twice and then have nothing to do with him, •in the realization that such
people are perverted and sinful and stand self-condemned.

D. CLOSING INSTRUCTIONS AND GREETINGS

12   •[c] When I send Artemas or Tychicus to you do everything in your power to come to me at Nicopolis, for I intend to spend the winter there.
13 •[d] Do everything in your power to send Zenas the lawyer and Apollos
14 on their way, and see that they lack nothing. •Our people should learn
to be occupied with good deeds so as to provide for urgent needs and
so they won't be unfruitful.
15   •All those with me greet you. Greet those who love us in the faith.
Grace be with all of you.

[c] Ac 20:14; Eph 6:21-22; Col 4:7-8; 2 Tm 4:12.   [d] Ac 18:24; 1 Cor 16:12.

3:1 The attitude expressed here toward civil authorities would be rather anachronistic if Titus had
been written after the Neronian persecution of the middle to late 60's. The unremitting hostility ex-
hibited in the Revelation makes an interesting
contrast.

THE LETTER TO

PHILEMON

Introduction to the Letter to Philemon

Philemon is a letter of extraordinary humanity and charm. While in prison Paul had come in contact with and converted a runaway slave named Onesimus. Onesimus' master, Philemon, was a prominent Christian in Colossae and Paul decided to send Onesimus back. In the letter he pleads with great tact and eloquence that Onesimus should be allowed to return to Paul to help him in his work.

In Galatians Paul had said that "in Christ" "there's neither slave nor free." Brave words, but words which had no legal authority in the Roman Empire. Powerless before the administrative apparatus of the Empire, Paul used his most powerful weapon, the moral authority of the gospel, to challenge Philemon to express his Christian faith in action.

Paul knew he was unable to revolutionize the social reality of his world by his efforts alone, but by his words and example he articulated the principles by which Christians of every age are called to transform their hearts and their daily lives, and in this way the world around them, by living the life of Christ and bringing the good news of this Way to all their brothers and sisters.

1 •Paul, a prisoner for Christ Jesus, and our brother Timothy to our
2 beloved fellow worker Philemon, •[a] our sister Apphia, our fellow soldier
3 Archippus, and the church at your house — •grace and peace be with
you from God our Father and the Lord Jesus Christ!

4,5 •I always give thanks to God when I mention you in my prayers, •for
I hear of the faith and love you have for the Lord Jesus and all the saints,
6 •and I pray that your fellowship in the faith may serve to lead you to a
7 deeper understanding of all the good that we have in Christ. •Your love
has been a great joy and comfort to me because the hearts of the saints
have been refreshed through you, my brother.

8 •Therefore, while I'm bold enough in Christ to order you to do what
9 should be done, •I prefer to base my appeal on your love for me — I,
10 Paul, an ambassador and now also a prisoner for Christ Jesus. •[b] I appeal to you on behalf of my child, Onesimus, whom I have begotten
11 while in prison. •He was formerly useless to you, but now is useful both
12 to you and to me. •I'm sending him back to you, which is to say, I'm
13 sending my heart. •I wanted to keep him with me so that he might serve
14 me on your behalf while I'm imprisoned for the gospel, •but I preferred
not to do anything without your knowledge because I wanted your good
15 deed to be voluntary rather than compelled. •Perhaps the reason he
was taken from you for a time was so you could have him back forev-
16 er, •no longer as a slave but as more than a slave — as a beloved brother, especially beloved to me, but how much more to you as well, both
in the flesh and in the Lord!

---

[a] *Col 4:17.*   [b] *Col 4:9.*

2 "The church at your house." "Your" is in the singular and it is generally accepted that it refers to
Philemon, a natural supposition since he appears
to have been a man of some means.
9 "Ambassador." The Greek word (*presbutes*) literally means "old man" and is very closely related to the word for "ambassador" (*presbeutes*).
Most commentators believe "ambassador" is the
intended meaning.

11 "Useless... useful." This is a pun on the name
Onesimus, which means "useful." It was a common name for slaves.
16 "In the flesh." This phrase refers to Onesimus
under the aspect of his simple humanity, whereas "in the Lord" refers to his status as a Christian
"brother."

•So if you regard me as a partner you'll receive him as you would 17
me, •and if he has wronged you or owes you anything, charge it to my 18
account. •I, Paul, am writing this with my own hand — I'll pay you back 19
(not to mention that you owe me your very self)! •Yes, my brother, you 20
can be of use to me in the Lord — refresh my heart in Christ!

•I write to you with complete confidence in your obedience, for I know 21
you'll do even more than I ask. •At the same time, prepare a guest room 22
for me, for I hope to be granted to you through your prayers.

•[c] My fellow prisoner Epaphras greets you in Christ Jesus, •[d] as do 23,24
Mark, Aristarchus, Demas, and Luke, my fellow workers.

•The grace of the Lord Jesus Christ be with your spirit! 25

THE LETTER TO THE

HEBREWS

Introduction to the Letter to the Hebrews

The Letter to the Hebrews is an address forwarded to its audience because the author was unable to be present to deliver the address in person.

Most scholars are in agreement that the recipients were Jewish Christians who were in danger of losing their faith and returning to Judaism. It appears that the author of Hebrews was well known, certainly by reputation, to the recipients of the letter, and was asked by third parties to write the letter in order to head off the impending crisis of faith. The letter is thus an extended polemic asserting the superiority of the New Covenant, the Christian faith, to the Old Covenant.

Who was the author? Early tradition, especially in the Eastern Church, testifies that Paul wrote the letter. Modern scholars almost universally reject this ascription, and ancient writers were aware of the difficulties involved as well. That there is a Pauline connection seems likely. On the other hand, the style and thought is quite distinct from that of Paul. The early Church Father Origen gave it as his opinion that only God knew the truth of the matter, because the style was clearly not Paul's.

The letter is written in a fine Greek style, probably the overall best in the New Testament, and presents its thesis in a sustained argument from beginning to end, without digressions. The author was a man of powerful intellect who could deal with complex Christological issues with a sure hand, painting with broad bold brush strokes but equally comfortable with detailed argumentation. He also possessed great tact and sensitivity. He had received a difficult commission in a crisis situation, but he resists the temptation to simply condemn the recipients. Instead, he carefully balances warnings and reprimands by providing encouragement and reasons for confidence. Central to the whole letter is the majestic picture of Jesus — Son of God through whom the universe was created, great high priest who can intercede with us before God, but also our brother who can sympathize with our weakness.

A. THE SON OF GOD REVEALS THE GREATNESS OF GOD'S SALVATION AND ITS SUPERIORITY OVER PREVIOUS REVELATIONS

1 •Of old God spoke to our fathers through the prophets many times
2 and in various ways, •but in these last days He has spoken to us
through a Son, whom He designated heir of all things and through whom
3 He created the universe. •He is the radiance of God's glory, the full expression of God's being, and he sustains the universe with his powerful
word. When he had brought about purification from sins he took his seat
4 at the right hand of the Majesty on high, •having become as much su-
5 perior to the angels as the name he inherited is superior to theirs. •For
to which of the angels did God ever say,

> **You are My son,**
> **this day have I begotten you.**

Or again,

> **I will be a Father to him**
> **and he will be a son to Me.**

6 •And again when He brings His firstborn into the world He says,

> **Let all God's angels worship him.**

7 •Of the angels He says,

> **He makes His angels winds,**
> **and His servants flaming fire,**

8 •while of His Son He says,

> **Your throne, O God, is forever and ever,**

1:1-4 The letter opens with a brief review of the *kerygma* of the early Church, the original proclamation of the good news. This summary strongly emphasizes the Son's glory and high dignity and combines two early approaches to Christology, that of pre-existence (for it was through the Son that the universe was created) and that of exaltation, which stresses Jesus' completion of God's plan of salvation.

1:3 Ws 7:26.
1:5 Ps 2:7; 2 S 7:14.
1:6 Dt 32:43 (Septuagint).
1:7 Ps 104:4 (Septuagint).
1:8-12, Ps 45:6-7; Ps 102:25-27 (Septuagint). Note that references to God in Scripture are here explicitly applied to the Son.

the righteous scepter is the scepter of
Your Kingdom.
•You loved righteousness and hated wrongdoing,   9
Therefore God, your God, has anointed you
with the oil of gladness,
far above your companions,

•and,   10

It was You at the beginning, Lord, who established
the earth,
and the heavens are the work of Your hands;
•They will perish, but You will remain,   11
they'll all grow old like a cloak,
•Like a mantle You will roll them up,   12
like a cloak they'll be changed.
You are ever the same,
and Your years will never end.

•And to which of the angels has He ever said,   13

Sit at my right hand,
till I make your enemies a stool
for your feet.

•Aren't all the angels ministering spirits who are sent to serve, for the   14
sake of those who are going to receive salvation?

2 •Therefore we must pay more attention than ever to what we've   1
heard so that we won't drift off course. •For if the word spoken   2
through angels was reliably established, and every transgression and act
of disobedience received just retribution, •how will we escape if we dis-   3
regard so great a salvation? It was first proclaimed by the Lord, then was
confirmed for us by those who had listened. •At the same time God bore   4
witness through signs and wonders and all sorts of mighty deeds, and
by distributing the gifts of the Holy Spirit according to His will.

1:13 Ps 110:1.
2:1ff Chapter 2 is balanced at the beginning and
end: at the beginning by a warning concerning the
possibility of punishment (2:1-3) and at the end
by reassurance that we will receive help from Jesus, the merciful and faithful high priest (2:17-18).
2:2-4 The true purpose in establishing Jesus' su-

periority to the angels now becomes apparent,
for "the word spoken through angels" refers to
the Torah, which was believed by Jews of that
time to have been revealed through the inter-
mediation of angels. The salvation proclaimed by
Jesus is thus as superior to the Torah as Jesus
himself is to the angels.

5 •For it wasn't to angels that God subjected the world to come, about
6 which we are speaking. •Someone testified somewhere,

> **What is man, that You should think of him,**
> **the son of man, that You should be concerned**
> **for him?**
7 **•You made him less than the angels for a while,**
> **and crowned him with glory and honor,**
8 **•You placed all things beneath his feet.**

In making all things subject to man, God left nothing beyond his control. Right now we're not yet able to see all things subjected to man,
9 •but we do see Jesus, who **for a little while was made lower than
the angels** so that he could taste death for all, now **crowned with glory and honor** because of the death he suffered.

10 •It was fitting that God, for Whom and through Whom all things exist, should through suffering perfect the pioneer of their salvation so as
11 to lead many sons to glory. •For the one who sanctifies and those who
are sanctified have one and the same origin, for which reason Jesus is
12 not ashamed to call them brothers, •for instance, when he says,

> **I will proclaim Your name to my brothers,**
> **I will praise You before the assembly;**

13 •and again,

> **I will put my trust in Him;**

and again,

> **Here am I, with the children God has given me.**

14 •Now since the "children" are all made of flesh and blood, he too shared
in the same flesh and blood so that through his death he would destroy
15 the one who has power over death, that is, the Devil, •and in this way
would deliver those who all their lives were in bondage through fear of
16 death. •For it's surely not with the angels that he's concerned; no, **He**

2:5-18 The author now turns to the humanity of
Jesus, to establish Christ's solidarity with us in
preparation for discussing his role as high priest.
A priest must be one with those he represents.
Jesus must be a high priest, however, because
only the high priest could preside at the Day of
Atonement rituals, and the author sees Jesus as
fulfilling the Day of Atonement sacrifices.
2:6-8 Ps 8:4-6.

2:9 "Jesus... was made lower than the angels,"
i.e., by becoming a human being Jesus was subject to the angels, like all other humans.
2:10 "Pioneer." The Greek word most commonly refers to the founder of a city. In this context it
is applied to Jesus in the sense of one who goes
ahead and leads the way.
2:12 Ps 22:22. 2:13 Is 8:17-18 (Septuagint).
2:16 Is 41:8-9.

is concerned with the descendants of Abraham. •Therefore he 17
had to become like his brothers in every respect so he could become a
merciful and trusted high priest before God and expiate the sins of the
people. •For since he himself was tested through what he suffered, he's 18
able to help those who are tempted.

B. CHRIST THE TRUSTWORTHY
AND COMPASSIONATE HIGH PRIEST

3 •Therefore, holy brothers, who share in a heavenly calling, think 1
of Jesus, the apostle and high priest of the faith we profess, •for 2
he is trusted by God Who appointed him, just as **Moses was trusted in God's household.** •But Jesus is worthy of far more glory than 3
Moses, just as the founder of a household deserves more honor than
the house itself. •Every house is founded by someone, but God is the 4
founder of everything. •Now **Moses was trusted in all God's** 5
house as **a servant,** bearing witness to the things that were to be
spoken by God in the future, •but Christ is trusted as a son over God's 6
house — and *we* are His house if we maintain our confidence and
pride in our hope.

•Therefore, as the Holy Spirit says, 7

> **Today if you hear His voice,**
> •**Harden not your hearts as in the rebellion,** 8
> **on the day of temptation in the desert,**
> •**Where your ancestors put Me to the test** 9
> **and knew My works •for forty years.** 10
> **Therefore I became provoked with that generation**
> **and said, "Their hearts always stray,**
> **they don't know My ways."**
> •**As I swore in My wrath,** 11
> **"They shall never enter My rest!"**

•Take care, brothers, that none of *you* have evil, unbelieving hearts 12
in rebellion against the living God — •encourage one another every day, 13
as long as there is a day to be called "today," so that none of you will
become hardened by the deceitfulness of sin. •After all, we have become 14

3:1ff In Chapters 3 and 4 we find similar bal-
ancing sections: 3:7-4:13 is an extended warning of the consequences of loss of faith, 4:14-
16 provides reasons for being confident, to reassure the readers.
3:2,5 Nb 12:7. 3:7-11 Ps 95:7-11 (Septuagint).

God speaks to Moses from the burning bush.
(Raphael, 1483-1520)

partners with Christ, if only we maintain our original confidence firm to
15 the end, •as it is said,

> **Today if you hear His voice,**
> **Harden not your hearts as in the rebellion.**

16 •Who were those who heard God's voice yet rebelled? Wasn't it all those
17 who came out of Egypt under Moses? •And with whom was He **pro-
voked for forty years**? Wasn't it with those sinners whose **corpses**
18 **fell in the desert**? •Who was it that He **swore** wouldn't **enter into**
19 **His rest,** if not those who were disobedient? •And so we see that it
was because of their unbelief that they were unable to enter.

1 **4**•Therefore, as long as God's promise to allow us into His rest remains open, we should fear lest any of you be considered to have
2 fallen short. •For we, too, received the good news, just as those before

3:15 Ps 95:7-8 (Septuagint).
3:17 Nb 14:29.
3:18 Nb 14:22-23; Ps 95:11.

4:1ff Chapter 4 develops the idea of God's "rest,"
which was introduced in Chapter 3. This term signifies salvation, the fulfillment of God's plan.

us did, yet the word did them no good since it didn't meet with faith in those who heard it. •It is we who have believed who are entering into ₃ God's rest, as He said,

> **As I swore in My wrath,**
> **"They'll never enter into My rest!"**

And yet God's work was complete from the creation of the world, •for ₄ Scripture speaks somewhere about the seventh day in these words, **On the seventh day God rested from all His work.** •And again in the ₅ previous passage, **They'll never enter into My rest.** •It follows, there- ₆ fore, that some will enter God's rest, but since those who received the good news in former times were barred because of their unbelief, •God ₇ once again set a day, "Today," saying much later in David's Psalms the words which have already been quoted,

> **Today if you hear His voice,**
> **Harden not your hearts.**

•If Joshua had given them rest, God would not have later spoken about ₈ another day. •So then, there remains to God's people the Sabbath rest, ₉ •for whoever enters God's rest receives rest from his labors, just as God ₁₀ rested from *His* labors. •So let us zealously strive to enter that rest, for ₁₁ we don't want to fail by following this same example of unbelief.

•For the word of God is living and active, sharper than any two-edged ₁₂ sword. It pierces to the dividing line between soul and spirit, joints and marrow, and it can discern the innermost thoughts and intentions of the heart. •No creature can hide from Him — everything is naked and laid ₁₃ bare to the eyes of Him, to Whom we must render an account.

•Therefore, since we have a great high priest who has passed through ₁₄ the heavens — Jesus the Son of God — let us hold fast to the faith we profess. •For our high priest isn't one who is unable to sympathize with ₁₅ our weaknesses; he was tempted in every way we are, yet never sinned. •Therefore, let us confidently approach the throne of grace to receive ₁₆ mercy and find grace to help us in time of need.

5 •For every high priest is chosen from among men and appointed to ₁ represent them before God, to offer gifts and sacrifices for their sins. •Such a high priest is able to deal patiently with those who have gone ₂ astray through ignorance, since he himself is subject to human weakness; •and because he too is weak he must offer sacrifice for his own ₃

4:3 Ps 95:11.   4:4 Gn 2:2.   4:5 Ps 95:11.   4:7 Ps 95:7-8 (Septuagint).   5:3 Lv 9:7.

4 sins as well as for those of the people. •Moreover, no one can take the honor of the high priesthood for himself — he can only be chosen by God, as in the case of Aaron.

5 •And so it was with Christ: he did not assume the dignity of the high priesthood on his own but was chosen by the One Who said to him,

> **You are My son,**
> **this day have I begotten you,**

6 •or as He says in a different place,

> **You are a priest forever,**
> **in the line of Melchizedek.**

7 •[a] When Jesus was in the flesh he offered prayers and supplications to the One Who was able to save him from death, accompanied by loud cries and tears, and God heard him because of his devotion and rever-
8 ence. •Son though he was, he learned obedience from what he suffered,
9 •and when he was made perfect he became the source of eternal sal-
10 vation for all who obey him, •and God declared him high priest **in the line of Melchizedek.**

C. EXHORTATION TO GREATER MATURITY

11 •Concerning this we have much to say and it will be difficult to ex-
12 plain, since you've become hard of hearing. •[b] By this time you should be teachers, and yet once again you need someone to teach you the ABCs
13 of God's word — you need milk instead of solid food. •Anyone who lives on milk is still a child and is inexperienced in the word of righteousness,
14 •whereas solid food is for the mature, those who have practiced and trained themselves so that they can distinguish between good and evil.

1 **6** •Let us leave behind the elementary teaching of Christ, then, and move on to the mature teaching, instead of once again laying the foundation — repentance from dead works, reliance upon faith in God,
2 •instruction about baptisms, the laying on of hands, resurrection of the

---

[a] *Mt 26:36-46; Mk 14:32-42; Lk 22:39-46.*   [b] *1 Cor 3:2.*

5:5 Ps 2:7.   5:6 Ps 110:4.
6:2 "Instructions about baptisms." This phrase probably contrasts various Jewish ritual ablutions and purification ceremonies to the rite of Chris- tian initiation. The word "enlightenment" (6:4, 10:32) also is a probable reference to Baptism, based on early Christian terminology.

dead, and eternal judgment. •And this we shall do, if God will allow it. ₃
•For it's impossible to restore to repentance those who have once been ₄
enlightened, who have tasted the heavenly gift and became sharers in
the Holy Spirit, •who have tasted the goodness of God's word and the ₅
powers of the coming age, •and yet have fallen away and so are cru- ₆
cifying the Son of God of their own accord and are holding him up to
contempt. •For earth which drinks the rain that repeatedly falls upon ₇
it and brings forth vegetation which is useful to those for whom it was
cultivated receives a blessing from God, •but if **it produces thorns** ₈
and thistles it's worthless and is on the verge of being cursed — in
the end it will be burned.

•But even though we speak in this way, beloved, we feel sure that ₉
you are destined for better things — those that pertain to salvation. •For ₁₀
God is not so unjust as to overlook your deeds and the love you've shown
for His name by serving the saints, as you continue to do. •Our desire ₁₁
is for each of you to show the same zeal for bringing about the fulfillment of your hope right to the end. •Don't be lazy! Imitate those who ₁₂
through faith and patience are inheriting the promises.

•When God made His promise to Abraham He **swore by Himself,** ₁₃
since there was no one greater for Him to swear by, •saying, **Surely,** ₁₄
I will bless you and make your descendants numerous! •And ₁₅
so, after waiting patiently, Abraham obtained what God had promised.
•Men swear in the name of someone greater than themselves, and the ₁₆
oath serves as a guarantee to put an end to any dispute. •Likewise, ₁₇
when God wished to provide the heirs of the promise with an even more
convincing demonstration of how unchangeable His will was, He confirmed it with an oath. •He did this so that, as a result of two un- ₁₈
changeable things about which it's impossible that God should play false,
we who have fled to His protection would be provided a powerful encouragement to grasp the hope that lies before us. •This hope is our ₁₉
soul's anchor, firm and reliable; it leads behind the sanctuary curtain,
•where Jesus has gone as a forerunner on our behalf — he has become ₂₀
a high priest **forever in the line of Melchizedek.**

6:8 Gn 3:17-18. 6:14 Gn 22:16-17.
6:18 "Two unchangeable things." This phrase
refers to the preceding verse (6:17); the "two...
things" are the promise and the oath.
6:19-20 Lv 16:2; Ps 110:4. By entering the inner
sanctuary Jesus secures access to God for us.
This is possible because of the superiority of Jesus' priesthood, sacrifice, and covenant, the
themes of the next sections of the letter. In Judaism, only the high priest entered the sanctuary,
but now, in union with Jesus, our hope, we will be
led into the heavenly Holy of Holies, into God's
presence. The Temple liturgy is but a shadow of
the reality that Jesus' sacrifice has gained for us.

Jerusalem. The Dome of the Rock,
under which is kept the rock of the Sacrifice of Isaac.

D. CHRIST'S PRIESTHOOD SUPERIOR
TO THE AARONIC PRIESTHOOD

1 7 •This **Melchizedek, the king of Salem and a priest of the Most High God, met Abraham as Abraham was returning from** 2 **his defeat of the kings. Melchizedek blessed him** •and **Abraham** apportioned to Melchizedek **a tenth of everything** he had captured. The name Melchizedek first of all means **king of righteousness,** but 3 he was also **king of Salem,** that is, the king of peace. •He is without father, mother, or genealogy; there was no beginning or end to his life, and like the Son of God he remains a priest forever.

4   •You can see how great he is, because the patriarch Abraham gave 5 him a tenth of the spoils. •Those descendants of Levi who become priests have a commandment by which, in accordance with the Torah, they levy

7:1-2 Gn 14:17-20.
7:2 "Salem," later Jerusalem, is related to the Hebrew word for "peace."
7:3 Scripture contains no reference to either the birth or the death of Melchizedek, and so the author says his life has not ended; cf. 7:8.
7:5 Nb 18:21.

a tithe on the people, that is, they take a tenth from their brothers, even though they too are descended from Abraham. •Melchizedek could not 6 trace his descent to them, and yet he collected tithes from Abraham and blessed Abraham who had received the promises. •Now there can be no 7 dispute that the superior person is the one who blesses the inferior. •In 8 one case the tithes are collected by mortal men, while in the other by one whom Scripture affirms is alive. •And in a manner of speaking Levi 9 (who himself receives tithes) actually paid tithes through Abraham, •for 10 he was still in his father's loins when **Melchizedek met Abraham.**

•So then, if perfection had come through the Levitical priesthood — 11 for the people received the Torah from the priesthood — what need would there have been for another priest to arise, **in the line of Melchizedek** rather than in the line of Aaron? •But when there's a 12 change in the priesthood this must signify a change in the law, as well. •Now the one concerning whom these things were said belongs to a dif- 13 ferent tribe, and no one from that tribe has ever officiated at the altar. •For it's clear that our Lord arose from Judah, and Moses said nothing 14 about priests with regard to that tribe. •The matter becomes even more 15 obvious if another priest arises in the likeness of Melchizedek, •one who 16 has become a priest by the power of an indestructible life rather than in accordance with a law concerning physical descent, •for it is testified, 17

> **You are a priest forever,**
> **in the line of Melchizedek.**

•On the one hand an earlier law is set aside because it has proved weak 18 and ineffective — •for the Torah brought nothing to perfection — on 19 the other hand a better hope is introduced by means of which we can draw near to God.

•Moreover, to the extent that this took place with an oath — for the 20 others became priests without an oath being taken, •but in the case of 21 this priest an oath was taken when God said to him,

> **The Lord has sworn**
> **and shall not change His mind,**
> **"You are a priest forever"** —

•to that same degree Jesus has become the guarantee of a better 22 covenant. •There is an additional difference — those priests were nu- 23 merous because death cut their ministry short, •whereas Jesus' priest- 24

7:9-10 "Levi." The author refers not only to the individual but to the entire priestly tribe of his descendants. Their priesthood is thus seen to be in- ferior to that of Melchizedek.
7:17 Ps 110:4
7:21 Ps 110:4.

25 hood is permanent because he remains forever. •Thus he is able for all time to bring complete salvation to those who approach God through him, since he's always alive to intercede for them.

26 •And it fit in with our needs to have such a high priest — holy, innocent, undefiled, set apart from sinners, and exalted above the heav-
27 ens. •Unlike the high priests, he has no need to offer daily sacrifices first for his own sins and then for those of the people — he did that
28 once and for all when he offered himself up. •The Torah appoints as high priests men who have their share of weaknesses, whereas God's oath, which came after the Torah, appoints His Son, who has been made perfect forever.

E. SUPERIORITY OF CHRIST'S NEW COVENANT

1 8 •Now this is the main point in what we've been saying: that is just the type of high priest we have. He has taken his seat at the right
2 hand of the throne of Majesty in Heaven, •a minister in the sanctuary,
3 the true tent that was set up by the Lord, not by man. •Every high priest is appointed to offer gifts and sacrifices, which means that this priest,
4 too, must have something to offer. •Now if he were on earth he wouldn't be a priest at all, since there are already priests who offer gifts in ac-
5 cordance with the Torah. •Those priests serve in a copy and shadow of the heavenly sanctuary, as Moses was warned when he was about to erect the tent, **See that you make everything according to the pat-**
6 **tern you were shown on the mountain.** •But now Jesus has received a ministry which is far superior to theirs; it's as superior as the covenant he mediates is, and is based on better promises.

7 •For if the first covenant had been perfect there would have been no
8 need for a second, •but God finds fault with them, and says,

> **Behold the days will come, says the Lord,**
> **when I'll make a new covenant with the house**
> **of Israel,**
> **and with the house of Judah.**
9 > **•It won't be like the covenant I made with their**
> **ancestors**
> **on the day I took their hand and led them**
> **out of Egypt.**

7:27 Lv 9:7.
8:1 Ps 110:1.

8:5 Ex 25:40.
8:8-12 Jr 31:31-34 (Septuagint).

For they didn't abide by My covenant
and so I rejected them, says the Lord,
•This is the covenant I'll make with the house of Israel   10
after those days, says the Lord:
I will put My laws in their minds
and write them on their hearts;
I will be their God
and they shall be My people.
•They won't need to teach their fellow citizens   11
or their brothers, saying, "Know the Lord!"
Because they'll all know Me,
from the least of them to the greatest.
•For I'll have mercy on their unrighteousness   12
and will no longer remember their sins.

•By speaking of a "new" covenant, God has declared the first one to be 13 obsolete, and what has become old and obsolete will soon disappear.

9 •The first covenant had regulations governing worship and an earth- 1 ly sanctuary. •A tent was erected — the outer one, which is called 2 the Holy Place — and in it were the lampstand, the table, and the bread of offering. •Behind the second curtain was the tent called the Holy of 3 Holies, •which contained the gold incense altar and the ark of the 4 covenant which was completely covered with gold. In the ark was a gold jar containing manna, Aaron's staff which had sprouted, and the stone tablets of the covenant. •Above the ark were the cherubim of glory 5 which overshadowed the mercy seat — now is not the time to speak of these things in detail.

•Once everything has been prepared in this manner, the priests con- 6 tinually enter the outer tent, performing their liturgical duties, •but on- 7 ly the high priest enters the inner tent, and he goes in only once a year when he takes blood to be offered for the inadvertent sins committed by himself and by the people. •In this way the Holy Spirit indicates that 8 the way into the sanctuary has not yet been opened up as long as the outer tent still stands. •This is a symbol of the present time, during which 9

9:2-5 Ex 25-26 passim. "The mercy seat" (9:5) was made of gold and was where the blood of sacrificed animals was sprinkled by the high priest during the rituals performed on the Day of Atonement.
9:6 Nb 18:2-6.
9:7 Lv 16:2-34. "Once a year," i.e., on the Day of Atonement.
9:8 The restriction on entry into the sanctuary indicates that as long as the old covenant was in effect there was no open access to God. This will come with the sacrifice of Jesus, and is of key importance in Hebrews.

Jerusalem. Roof of the Holy Sepulchre,
inhabited by the Ethiopian monks.

gifts and sacrifices are offered that cannot perfect the worshipper's con-
10 science. •They only deal with food and drink and various purification
rites — regulations for the body which are in force up to the time the
new order is established.

11   •But when Christ came as the high priest of the good things that have
come, he passed through that greater and more perfect tent which is
not made by human hands — that is, it's not part of this creation —
12 •and entered once and for all into the sanctuary bearing his own blood
rather than the blood of rams and bullocks, and thus secured for us an
13 eternal redemption. •For if the sprinkling of blood from rams and bulls
and the ashes of heifers can sanctify those who are ritually unclean so
14 that their flesh is purified, •then the blood of Christ will have a far greater

9:11 Some manuscripts read "that will come" rather than "that have come."
9:13 Lv 16:15-16; Nb 19:9, 17-19.

effect! Through the eternal Spirit he presented himself as an unblemished offering to God and will purify our consciences from ineffective practices so that we'll be fit to worship the living God.

•Therefore, Jesus is the mediator of a new covenant. Those who 15 have been called may now receive the promised eternal inheritance because a death has occurred which redeems them from transgressions under the first covenant. •In the case of a will it's necessary to 16 establish that the person who made the will has died — •the will on- 17 ly takes effect after death; it has no power while the person who made it is still alive. •This is why the first covenant had to be inaugurated 18 with blood. •After Moses had proclaimed every commandment of the 19 Torah to the whole people he took the blood of the bullocks — with water, scarlet wool, and hyssop — and sprinkled both the book as well as all the people, •saying, **This is the blood of the covenant God** 20 **has commanded you to obey.** •Then he also sprinkled the tent 21 and all the liturgical vessels with blood in the same way. •In fact, un- 22 der the Torah almost everything is purified with blood, and forgiveness is possible only when blood is shed.

•Thus it was necessary to purify the copies of the heavenly realities 23 with these rites, but the heavenly realities themselves could only be purified with greater sacrifices than these. •For Christ didn't enter a sanc- 24 tuary made by human hands which only represented the true sanctuary — he entered Heaven itself to appear now before God on our behalf. •Nor did he do this intending to offer himself many times, the way the 25 high priest enters the sanctuary every year bearing blood which isn't his own. •If that had been so he would have had to suffer repeatedly, start- 26 ing from the creation of the world. Instead, he appeared once and for all near the end of the age to remove sin by his sacrifice. •And just as 27 it has been ordained that men should die once and then be judged, •so 28 too Christ was offered once to bear the sins of many and when he appears a second time it won't be to deal with sin — it will be to bring salvation to those who eagerly await him.

10 •Now since the Torah has but a shadow of the good things to 1 come rather than their exact likeness, the same sacrifices which are offered year after year can never perfect those who draw near to worship. •Otherwise, wouldn't they have ceased to be offered? If those 2 who were worshipping had been cleansed once for all, wouldn't they

9:19-20 Ex 24:6-8.   9:22 Lv 17:11.
9:21 Lv 8:15.   9:28 Is 53:12.

3 have lost all consciousness of sin? •As it is, these sacrifices are a year-
4 ly reminder of sin, •for the blood of bulls and rams is unable to take
away sins.

5   •Therefore, when Christ came into the world he said,

> **Sacrifice and offering You didn't desire,**
>   **but You've prepared a body for me;**
6 **•Burnt offerings and sin offerings**
>   **gave You no pleasure.**
7 **•Then I said, "Behold, I've come to do**
>   **Your will, O God,"**
>   **as it's written about me**
>   **in the scroll of the book.**

8 •First he says, **Sacrifices and oblations, burnt offerings and offerings for sin You didn't desire, nor did they please You** —
9 these are offered according to the Torah — •then he says, **Behold I
come to do Your will.** He does away with the first in order to es-
10 tablish the second. •That "will" has sanctified us through the offering
of Jesus Christ's body once and for all.

11   •Every priest daily stands at worship and time after time offers the
12 same sacrifices, which can never take away sins. •But when Jesus had
offered one sacrifice for sin for all time **he took his seat at God's
13 right hand,** •to wait **until his enemies are** finally **made a foot-
14 stool for his feet.** •For with one offering he has perfected forever
those who are being sanctified.

15   •The Holy Spirit also bears witness to us, for after saying,

16 > **•This is the covenant I'll make for them**
>   **after those days, says the Lord;**
> **I'll put My laws in their hearts**
>   **and I'll write them in their minds,**

17 •he adds,

> **Their sins and misdeeds**
>   **I'll remember no more.**

18 •And where these things have been forgiven, there's no longer a need
for sin offerings.

10:5-7 Ps 40:6-8 (Septuagint).
10:12-13 Ps 110:1.
10:16-17 Jr 31:33-34.

F. CULMINATING EXHORTATION TO FAITHFULNESS

A call to faith

•So, brothers, since through the blood of Jesus we have the confi- 19
dence to enter the sanctuary •by the new and living way he opened 20
for us through the curtain — that is, the way of his flesh — •and since 21
we have a great high priest who has charge over God's household,
•let us approach with true hearts and the full assurance of our faith, 22
with hearts sprinkled clean from a guilty conscience and bodies washed
with pure water. •Let us hold fast to the profession of our hope with- 23
out wavering, for the One Who made the promise to us is faithful. •Let 24
us also consider how we can rouse one another to love and good
works. •Don't neglect your assemblies, as some are in the habit of do- 25
ing; encourage one another, especially because you can see the day
of the Lord drawing nearer.

•For if, after receiving knowledge of the truth, we sin deliberately, 26
there no longer remains a sacrifice for sins. •What remains instead is 27
the fearful prospect of judgment and a blazing fire that will consume
God's adversaries. •Anyone who rejects the law of Moses **dies** with- 28
out mercy **at the testimony of two or three witnesses.** •Think 29
how much worse a punishment will be deserved by someone who tram-
ples on the Son of God, regards as unclean the blood of the covenant
by which he was sanctified, and insults the Spirit of grace! •We know 30
Who it was Who said,

Vengeance is Mine, I shall repay,

and,

The Lord will judge His people.

•It's a fearful thing to fall into the hands of the living God! 31
•Recall the early days of your faith! After you were enlightened you 32
stood firm through a hard struggle which involved suffering. •At times 33
you were publicly insulted and mistreated, while at other times you stood
by those who were so treated. •You shared the sufferings of prisoners 34
and accepted the seizure of your possessions with joy, because you knew

10:19 Entrance to the sanctuary should be understood as a metaphor for access to God.
10:26-31 The author is clearly concerned here with
the possibility of apostasy, comparing a fall from

faith in Jesus to a Jew turning from the Torah to
idolatry (v. 28 refers to the punishment for idolatry).
10:28 Dt 17:6.
10:30 Dt 32:35-36.

Yad Vashem, Jerusalem. A memorial of the Holocaust.

³⁵ you had a better and more permanent possession. •So don't lose your
³⁶ confidence, because it will lead to a great reward. •You need to be steadfast if you want to do the will of God and receive what He promised.

³⁷ •For in just **a little while**
    he who is coming will come — he won't delay!
³⁸ **•But My righteous one will live by faith,**
    and if he draws back My soul has no
      pleasure in him.

³⁹ •We aren't the kind of people who draw back and are destroyed — we
have faith and will preserve our lives.

10:37-38 Hab 2:3-4 (Septuagint).

Examples of faith from the Old Testament

11 •Faith is confidence in what's hoped for, conviction about things that ₁ can't be seen. •Through faith the ancients won God's approval. ₂
•Through faith we understand that the world was created by the word ₃ of God, so that what is seen came to be from what can't be seen.
•Through faith Abel offered God a better sacrifice than Cain's, and ₄ thus was approved as righteous. God approved of his gifts and through faith Abel, though dead, still speaks. •Through faith Enoch was taken ₅ up so that he wouldn't see death, and **he wasn't found because God had taken him up,** for it is affirmed that, before he was taken up, **he had pleased God.** •Now it's impossible to please God without faith, ₆ because to even approach God you have to believe that God exists and that He rewards those who seek Him. •Noah received divine warning ₇ of events which were as yet unseen; through faith he took heed and constructed an ark in which his household could be saved. His faith was a condemnation of the world, and through it he became an heir of the righteousness that comes from faith.
•Through faith Abraham obeyed when he was called to leave for a ₈ place that he would receive as an inheritance. He left without knowing where he was to go. •Through faith he sojourned in the promised land ₉ as a foreigner, living in tents with Isaac and Jacob — co-heirs of the same promise. •For he was looking forward to a city whose foundations were ₁₀ built and formed by God. •Through faith Abraham received the power ₁₁ to father children, even though Sarah herself was barren and he was beyond the usual age, because he trusted the One Who made the promise. •And so from one man — one who was as good as dead — was ₁₂ born a multitude of descendants, **as numerous as the stars in the sky, as innumerable as the sand on the seashore.**
•They all died in faith without having received what was promised, ₁₃ but they had seen it and greeted it far in advance and acknowledged that they were foreigners and exiles on earth. •Those who say such ₁₄ things make it clear that they're seeking a homeland. •If they'd been ₁₅ thinking about the land they left they would have had the opportunity to return, •but now they're striving for a better land, a heavenly one. ₁₆ Therefore God is not ashamed to be called their God, because He has prepared a city for them.
•Through faith Abraham offered up Isaac when God tested him — ₁₇ Abraham had received the promises, and yet he offered up his only son

11:5 Gn 5:21-24 (Septuagint).   11:12 Gn 22:17

18 •of whom it had been said, **Through Isaac your descendants shall**
19 **carry on your name.** •He reasoned that God could raise Isaac from the dead, and so in a sense Abraham did receive him back from the dead.
20 •Through faith in what was to come Isaac blessed Jacob and Esau.
21 •Through faith Jacob, when he was dying, blessed each of Joseph's sons
22 and **bowed in worship over the top of his staff.** •Through faith Joseph, as his life was coming to an end, spoke of the exodus of Israel and gave orders regarding the disposition of his bones.
23 •Through faith Moses, when he was born, was hidden for three months by his parents because they could see he was a beautiful child
24 and they didn't fear the king's edict. •Through faith Moses, when he had
25 grown up, refused to be called a son of Pharaoh's daughter, •choosing to suffer with God's people rather than enjoy the transitory pleasures of
26 sin. •From his standpoint, to endure insults for the sake of the Messiah was greater wealth than all the treasure of Egypt, because he kept his
27 eyes fixed on the reward. •Through faith he left Egypt and felt no fear of the king's anger — he was steadfast because it was as if he could see
28 the Invisible One. •Through faith he kept the Passover and sprinkled the
29 blood so that the Destroyer wouldn't touch their firstborn sons. •Through faith they passed through the Red Sea as if it were dry land, while the Egyptians were swallowed up when they attempted to do the same.
30 •Through faith the walls of Jericho fell down after the Israelites had
31 marched around them for seven days. •Through faith Rahab the prostitute survived when those who were disobedient perished, because she had received the Israelite spies in peace.
32 •Should I say more? I wouldn't have sufficient time to tell about Gideon, Barak, Samson, Jephthah, David and Samuel and the
33 prophets, •who through faith overcame kingdoms, did what was right,
34 obtained what had been promised, shut the mouths of lions, •put out raging fires, escaped the ravening sword, drew strength from weakness,
35 were mighty in battle, and put foreign armies to flight. •Women had their dead returned to them by resurrection; some were tortured but refused
36 to accept release, preferring to receive a better resurrection; •others were
37 mocked and scourged, put in chains and imprisoned. •They were stoned, they were sawed in half, they were murdered by the sword, they went about dressed in sheepskins and goatskins, in need and afflicted, tor-
38 mented, •wandering the deserts and mountains, living in caves and holes in the ground — yet the world wasn't worthy of them.

11:18 Gn 21:12.   11:21 Gn 47:31

•They all gained approval through their faith, but they didn't receive 39
the promise •because, with us in mind, God had something better in 40
store — only with us were they to be made perfect!

A call to perseverance

12 •Therefore, since we're surrounded by such a cloud of witnesses, 1
let us put aside every burden and sinful entanglement, let us persevere and run the race that lies before us, •let us keep our eyes fixed 2
on Jesus, the pioneer and perfecter of our faith. For the sake of the joy
that lay before him he endured the cross and thought nothing of the
shame of it, and is now seated at the right hand of God's throne. •Think 3
of Jesus, who endured so much hostility from sinners, and don't let your
souls grow weary or lose your courage.

•In your struggle against sin you haven't yet resisted to the point of 4
shedding blood. •You have forgotten the words of encouragement which 5
are spoken to you as sons,

> **My son, don't take lightly the Lord's discipline,**
> **nor become discouraged when He punishes you.**
> **•For the Lord disciplines everyone He loves,** 6
> **He chastises everyone He accepts as a son.**

•Endure your trials as a form of discipline; God is treating you like sons, 7
for what son is there who isn't disciplined by his father? •Everyone has 8
shared in this discipline, so if you don't receive it you must be illegiti-
mate and not real sons. •After all, we had earthly fathers who disciplined 9
us and we respected them; all the more reason, then, to be subject to
the Father of spirits so we can live! •For our earthly fathers disciplined 10
us for a short time according as it seemed right to them, whereas God
disciplines us for our own good so that we'll be able to share in His holiness. •For the present, all discipline seems to bring grief rather than 11
joy, but later it will yield the peaceful fruit of righteousness to those who
have been trained by it.

•Therefore, **lift your drooping arms and strengthen your weak-** 12
ened knees, •make straight paths for your feet so that the lame 13
foot will be strengthened rather than twisted.

12:2 "Pioneer." Cf. 2:10, where this somewhat   12:12 Is 35:3 (Septuagint).
unusual word is also applied to Jesus.   12:13 Pr 4:26 (Septuagint).
12:5-6 Jb 5:17; Pr 3:11-12 (Septuagint).

Jerusalem. Zion Gate.

14 •Strive to be at peace with everyone and seek that holiness without
15 which no one will see the Lord. •See that no one lacks the grace of God,
that no root of bitterness sprouts up to cause trouble, causing many to
16 be stained by it, •that no one among you is a fornicator or an irreligious
17 person like Esau, who sold his birthrights for a single meal. •For, as you
know, when he later wanted to inherit the blessing he was rejected because he was given no opportunity to change what he had done, even
though he tearfully sought to do so.
18 •For you have not come to a mountain that can be touched, to a
19 blazing fire, to darkness, gloom, or a storm; •nor have you come to
a trumpet blast or a voice whose words caused those who heard them

12:15 Dt 29:18 (Septuagint).

to beg that no further message should be spoken to them, •because 20
they couldn't bear the command, **If even a beast should touch the
mountain, it must be stoned!** •Indeed, so terrifying was the spec- 21
tacle that Moses said, "**I'm** trembling and **afraid!**" •Instead, you've 22
come to Mount Zion, the city of the living God, the heavenly Jerusalem
with its thousands of angels. •You have come to the festal gathering 23
and the assembly of the firstborn whose names are written in Heav-
en, to a judge who is God of all, to the spirits of the righteous who
have been made perfect. •You have come to Jesus, the mediator of 24
the new covenant, and to the sprinkled blood that proclaims a better
message than Abel's blood.

•See that you don't reject the One Who is speaking, for if those who 25
rejected the One Who warned them on earth could not escape, what
chance will we have to escape if we reject the One Who warns us from
Heaven? •At the first warning His voice shook the earth, but now He 26
has promised, "**Once more I will shake** not only **the earth** but **heav-
en** as well." •Now the words "once more" clearly indicate that the cre- 27
ated things which have been shaken will be removed, so that what is un-
shaken may remain. •Therefore, we who are to receive an unshakable 28
Kingdom should be grateful and should worship God in an acceptable
manner with reverence and awe, •for our **God is a consuming fire.** 29

G. PRACTICAL COUNSELS, CLOSING
EXHORTATIONS, AND PERSONAL MESSAGES

13 •Let brotherly love continue. •Don't forget your duty to be hos- 1,2
pitable, for some who were hospitable had angels as guests, without knowing it. •Remember those in prison as if you were imprisoned 3
with them, and those who are mistreated, for like them you are still in
the body. •Marriage should be held in honor by all of you, and the mar- 4
riage bed should remain undefiled, for fornicators and adulterers will be
judged by God. •Keep your life free from love for money, be satisfied 5
with what you have, for God has said, **I will never abandon you or
forsake you.** •Thus, we may confidently say, 6

12:20 Ex 19:12-13.
12:21 Dt 9:19.
12:26 Hg 2:6 (Septuagint).
12:29 Dt 4:24.

13:2 Gn 18:1-8; 19:1-3.
13:5 Dt 31:6, 8.
13:6 Ps 118:6 (Septuagint).

**The Lord is my helper,
I shall not be afraid;
What can mere man do to me?**

7 •Remember your leaders who proclaimed the word of God to you;
8 consider the outcome of their way of life and imitate their faith. •Jesus
9 Christ is the same yesterday and today and forever. •Don't be carried
away by all kinds of strange teachings, for it's good for the heart to be
strengthened by grace rather than by food which has been of no use to
10 those who partake of it. •We have an altar from which those who serve
11 the tent have no right to eat. •For the blood of animals is carried into
the sanctuary by the high priest as an offering for the forgiveness of sin,
12 while the bodies of the animals are burned outside the camp. •There-
fore Jesus too suffered outside the gate in order to sanctify the people
13 with his own blood. •So let us go out to him outside the camp and share
14 the abuse he bore, •for our city here is not a lasting one — we seek the
15 city which is to come! •Therefore, let us continually offer through him
a sacrifice of praise to God, the fruit of lips that acknowledge His name.
16 •Don't forget to do good and to share what you have, for these are the
sacrifices which are pleasing to God.
17 •Obey your leaders and submit to them, for they keep watch over your
souls and will have to give an accounting. Let them perform their duties joyfully rather than with groaning, for to cause them sorrow would
be of no advantage to you.
18 •Pray for us, for we are convinced that we have a clean conscience
19 and we wish to behave creditably in all things. •I especially urge you to
pray that I may be restored to you quickly.
20 •May the God of peace, Who brought our Lord Jesus — the great
shepherd of the sheep — up from the dead through the blood of the
21 eternal covenant, •supply you with every good thing to help you to do
His will, and may He accomplish in us what is pleasing in His sight
through Jesus Christ, to whom be glory forever and ever. Amen.
22 •I urge you, brothers, bear with my exhortation, for I have written
23 briefly to you. •Our brother Timothy has been released, and if he comes
quickly I'll see you with him.
24 •Greet all your leaders and all the saints. Those from Italy send their
25 greetings to you. •Grace be with all of you!

13:10 "The altar" is used metaphorically to refer to the victim on it, here, Jesus.
13:11 Lv 16:27.

THE
CATHOLIC
LETTERS

THE LETTER OF

JAMES

Introduction to the Letter of James

This letter is traditionally ascribed to James "the brother of the Lord," who, along with Peter and John, was considered one of the "pillars" of the early Church. (In Jewish usage of the time, the word "brother" often referred to cousins or other close relatives.) Following the Resurrection he became prominent in the Jerusalem church and, when the apostles were scattered abroad by the Herodian persecution (in about 42 A.D.), he became the leader of that church. He had a reputation for great holiness and is said to have been respected even by many of the Pharisees. He was martyred in 62 A.D. by the Sadducees, who took advantage of the delayed arrival of a new Roman governor to charge James with having violated the Torah, as reported by Josephus in his *Jewish Antiquities*.

Unlike other New Testament letters but in keeping with this literary genre, James is not organized around a unifying theme which is developed as the letter progresses. Instead, it is composed of short sermon-like exhortations on specific topics without any real linkage between the sections. The first chapter, however, appears to serve as a thematic introduction to the rest of the letter, in that it contains short statements of most of the themes which are developed at greater length in the rest of the letter. It may be best to view this letter as a type of encyclical, to be circulated among the fledgling Christian communities for the purpose of providing encouragement in dealing with the difficulties they faced as they waited for the Lord.

A. THEMATIC INTRODUCTION

1 **1** •[a] James, a servant of God and of the Lord Jesus Christ, to the twelve
2 tribes in the Diaspora — greetings! •[b] My brothers, consider it a cause
3 for joy whenever you encounter various trials, •for you know that test-
4 ing of your faith produces steadfastness, •and the goal of your stead-
5 fastness should be to be perfect and complete, lacking nothing. •If anyone of you lacks wisdom he should ask God, Who gives generously and
6 without reproach to all, and God will give him wisdom. •[c] But he must
ask in faith and without doubting, for whoever doubts is like a wave on
7 the sea which is driven and tossed about by the wind. •Such a person,
8 who wavers and is undecided in everything he does, •should not expect
to receive anything from the Lord!

9,10 •Let the poor brother boast of his high position, •and let the wealthy
brother boast of his lowliness, for he will pass away like a flower of the
11 field. •For the sun rises with its scorching heat and dries up the grass,
and its flower falls and its beauty perishes — so too will the rich man
wither away in the midst of his pursuits.

12 •Happy the man who is steadfast in temptation! When he has been
proved worthy he will receive the crown of life that God promised to
13 those who love Him. •Let no one who is being tempted say, "I'm being tempted by God," for God cannot be tempted by evil, and He Him-
14 self tempts no one. •Each person is tempted when he is lured away and
15 enticed by his own desires. •Then desire conceives and gives birth to
sin, and when sin becomes full grown it brings forth death.

16,17 •Don't be deceived, beloved brothers of mine! •Every good gift and
every perfect present is from above and comes down from the Father
of lights, in Whom there is no variation or darkness due to change.

---

[a] Ac 15:13; Gal 1:19; 1 P 1:1.   [b] 1 P 1:6.   [c] Mt 21:21.

1:1 "The twelve tribes in the Diaspora." Probably a metaphorical reference to the Christian
communities scattered throughout Palestine,
Phoenicia, and Syria.

1:10-11 Is 40:6-7.
1:17 "The Father of lights" refers to God as the
creator of the various heavenly bodies.

•Of His own will He brought us forth by the word of truth to be the ¹⁸ first fruits, as it were, of His creatures.

•Remember this, my beloved brothers! Everyone should be quick to ¹⁹ listen, but slow to speak and slow to anger. •For a man's anger does ²⁰ not achieve the righteousness God demands. •Lay aside, therefore, all ²¹ filth and evil excess and humbly accept the word that has been planted in you and is able to save your souls.

•[d] Be doers of the word and not just hearers, who deceive themselves. ²² •For anyone who is a hearer of the word and not a doer is like a man ²³ observing his own face in a mirror, •for he looks at himself, then turns ²⁴ away and at once forgets what he looked like. •But the person who looks ²⁵ into the perfect law — the law of freedom — and sticks with it, who is not a forgetful hearer but a doer, he shall be blessed in his actions.

•If anyone considers himself to be religiously observant but doesn't ²⁶ restrain his tongue and deceives himself, his religion is worthless. •This ²⁷ is pure and undefiled religion in God's eyes — to care for widows and orphans in their distress, to keep yourself unstained by the world.

B. AGAINST FAVORING THE RICH OVER THE POOR

2 •My brothers, your faith in our Lord Jesus Christ of glory must not ¹ allow of favoritism. •Suppose a man should enter your assembly with ² a gold ring on his finger and dressed in splendid clothing and a poor man also comes in, dressed in shabby clothes; •if you show more re- ³ spect to the man wearing the fine clothing and say, "Please sit right here," but tell the poor man, "You can stand," or "Sit there by my foot-stool," •haven't you set up distinctions among yourselves, and haven't ⁴ you become judges with bad intentions?

•Listen, my beloved brothers! Didn't God choose the poor of the earth ⁵ to be rich in faith and heirs of the Kingdom He promised to those who love Him? •But you have humiliated the poor man! Isn't it the rich who ⁶

---

[d] Mt 7:21, 26.

1:18 In Jewish theology the harvest was likened to a new creation, and the first fruits of the harvest were offered to God. James sees our redemption as a new creation, and the first Christians as the first fruits of the harvest.
1:25 "The perfect law — the law of freedom," i.e., the Christian good news.
2:1 "Of glory." This phrase may refer to the He-brew concept of God's *Shekinah* or presence (translated into Greek as "glory"). Jesus would then be seen as the abiding presence of God, the glory of God made man.
2:2 "Assembly." Lit., "synagogue." This is the on-ly instance in the New Testament where a Christian assembly is referred to in this manner.

J A M E S

Qumran. Archaeological remains of the community buildings.

7 oppress you and drag you into court? •Aren't they the ones who blas-
8 pheme the honorable name that was invoked over you? •If you really
fulfill the royal law in accordance with the passage from Scripture, **Love**
9 **your neighbor as yourself,** you're doing well. •But if you show favoritism, then you're committing a sin and stand convicted as violators
10 of the Torah. •For whoever keeps the whole Torah but stumbles with
11 regard to one commandment has become guilty of all of it. •For the One
Who said, **You shall not commit adultery,** also said, **You shall not
murder.** If you don't commit adultery but do commit murder, you vio-
12 late the Torah. •Speak and act in a way befitting those who will be judged
13 by the law of freedom. •For judgment is without mercy to the one who
has shown no mercy, but mercy triumphs over judgment.

2:7 "The honorable name," i.e., of Jesus. The
name of the Lord was, of course, "invoked over"
Christians at baptism.

2:8 Lv 19:18.
2:11 Ex 20:13-14; Dt 5:17-18.

C. AGAINST FAITH WITHOUT WORKS

•What good is it, my brothers, if someone claims to have faith, but 14 doesn't show it in his actions? Faith can't save him, can it? •[e] If a broth- 15 er or sister is in need of clothes and lacks food for the day •and one of 16 you says to them, "Go in peace; stay warm and eat well!" what good is it? •And so faith by itself is dead, unless it is manifested in works. 17

•But perhaps someone will say, "You have faith and I have works." 18 Prove to me that you have faith without considering your works, and I'll prove to you from my works that I have faith! •You believe that God is 19 one. You do well — the demons also believe, and they tremble with fear! •You foolish man, do you want to know that faith without works is use- 20 less? •Wasn't our father Abraham shown to be righteous by his works 21 when he offered his son Isaac on the altar? •You can see that faith went 22 along with his works, and by works his faith was made perfect, •and the 23 Scripture was fulfilled which said, **Abraham believed God, and it was credited to him as righteousness,** and he was called a friend of God. •You can see that a man is shown to be righteous by his works, and not 24 by faith alone. •Likewise, wasn't Rahab the prostitute also shown to be 25 righteous by her works when she took the messengers in and sent them out by a different way? •For just as the body is dead without spirit, so 26 too faith without works is dead.

D. ON CONTROLLING THE TONGUE

3 •Not many of you should be teachers, my brothers, for you know 1 that those of us who are will be judged more strictly. •We all stum- 2 ble frequently — if there's anyone who doesn't stumble in his speech then he's a perfect man, able to maintain control over his whole body. •Now we put bits into horses' mouths so that they'll obey us, and then 3 we can guide their whole bodies. •Look at ships, too; although they're 4 so big and are driven by strong winds, they're guided to where the helms- man's will wishes them to go by a very small rudder. •In the same way, 5 although the tongue is a small part of the body its pretensions are great.

Look how a tiny fire can set a huge forest ablaze, •and the tongue 6 is a fire! The tongue is a world of unrighteousness within us, staining

[e] Mt 25:42-43.

2:21 Gn 22:1-14.   2:23 Gn 15:6.   2:25 Jos 2:1-21.

the whole body and setting the cycle of our existence afire, and set on
7 fire itself by Gehenna. •For every type of animal, bird, reptile, or sea
8 creature can be tamed and has been tamed by the human race, •but
no one can tame the tongue — restlessly evil, full of deadly poison.
9 •With it we bless the Lord and Father, and with it we curse men, who
10 were made in the image of God — •from the same mouth come bless-
11 ings and curses! My brothers, this should not be so. •Can a spring pour
12 forth both sweet and bitter water from the same source? •[f] Can a fig
tree produce olives, my brothers, or a grapevine figs? Nor can salt water produce fresh water.

E. AGAINST ENVY AND SLANDER

13   •Who among you is wise and intelligent? Let him show it by his good
14 life, with a humility born of that wisdom. •But if you harbor bitter jealousy or selfish ambition in your heart, don't boast and lie against the
15 truth. •This is not the wisdom that comes down from above — this is
16 earthly, worldly, and demonic! •For where there is jealousy and selfish
17 ambition there is also disorder and every kind of bad deed. •The wisdom from above is first of all pure, then peaceable, kind, reasonable,
18 and full of good fruits, impartial and sincere. •The harvest of righteousness is sown in peace by those who are peacemakers.

1   **4** •Where do wars and fighting among you come from? Don't they
2   come from your passions warring within you? •You desire, and you
don't possess, so you murder; you are filled with jealousy, yet you cannot get what you want, so you quarrel and fight. You don't possess be-
3 cause you don't ask. •You ask but don't receive because you ask wrong-
4 ly, wishing to squander it on your passions. •You adulterous wretches!
Don't you know that love of the world is enmity with God? So whoever wants to be a friend of the world makes himself an enemy of God.
5 •Or do you suppose that Scripture is nothing but empty words when it
6 says, "The spirit dwelling within us is given to jealous desires"? •[g] But
the grace He gives is greater, and so Scripture also says

---

[f] *Mt 7:16.*   [g] *1 P 5:5-9.*

4:4 In the Old Testament the covenant between
God and Israel was frequently portrayed
metaphorically as a marriage (the classic expression of this metaphor is in the first three
chapters of Hosea). By extending the metaphor,
those who break the covenant are committing
adultery.
4:5 The origin of this quotation is not known. It
may come from an apocryphal Jewish writing.
4:6 Pr 3:34 (Septuagint).

God opposes the arrogant
but gives grace to the humble.

•Therefore be subject to God. Resist the Devil and the Devil will flee 7 from you. •Draw near to God and He will draw near to you. Cleanse 8 your hands, you sinners, and purify your hearts, you waverers. •Be 9 wretched, lament and weep; let your laughter turn to mourning and your joy to dejection. •Humble yourselves before the Lord and He will 10 exalt you.

•Don't slander one another, brothers. Whoever speaks ill of a broth- 11 er or passes judgment on his brother speaks against the Torah and judges the Torah. If you judge the Torah, you're not a doer of the Torah but a judge. •There's only one lawgiver and judge, He Who is able to save or 12 destroy, so who are you to pass judgment on your neighbor?

F. AGAINST THE RICH,
THEIR ARROGANCE AND INJUSTICE

•Come now, you who say, "Today or tomorrow we'll go to this or 13 that city and spend a year doing business there and making money." •You don't know what your life will be like tomorrow! You're like a mist 14 that appears for a little while and then disappears! •What you should 15 say is, "If the Lord wills it we'll live and we'll do this or that," •but in 16 your arrogance you boast. All such boasting is evil. •For whoever knows 17 what he should do and doesn't do it is committing a sin.

5 •Come now, you rich, weep and wail at your coming misery! 1 •[h] Your riches have rotted and your clothing has become moth-eat- 2 en, •your gold and silver have corroded, their rust will be a witness 3 against you and will devour your flesh like fire. You have stored up treasure for the last days! •Behold, the wages you withheld from the 4 laborers who reaped your fields are crying out, and the cries of the harvesters have reached the ears of the Lord of Hosts. •You've lived 5 off the land in luxury and self-indulgence, you've fattened your hearts on the day of slaughter. •You have condemned, you have killed the 6 just man. He doesn't resist you.

[h] Mt 6:19.

4:14 Pr 27:1.   5:4 Dt 24:14-15.

Job, model of patience and of confidence. (Jm 5:11)

G. ON PATIENTLY AWAITING
THE COMING OF THE LORD

7 •Therefore be patient, brothers, until the coming of the Lord. Behold, the farmer waits for the valuable yield of the earth, patiently waiting un-
8 til it receives **the early and late rains.** •You be patient, too; strength-
9 en your hearts, for the coming of the Lord is at hand. •Don't grumble against each other, brothers, lest you be judged, for the judge is stand-
10 ing at the door. •Take the prophets who spoke in the name of the Lord
11 as an example of suffering and patience, brothers. •Behold, those who

ᶠ *Gal 3:20.*

5:7 Dt 11:14; Jr 5:24; Jl 2:23. "The early and late rains" is explicable only in a Palestinian or Syrian setting, where the farmers relied upon the spring and fall rains. In Scripture the spring and fall rains were a common image for God's power to order His creation and for His love in providing for His people.
5:11 Ps 103:8; 111:4.

were steadfast are the ones we call blessed. You've heard of the steadfastness of Job and you have seen the Lord's purpose, that **the Lord is compassionate and merciful.**

H. CONCLUDING COUNSELS

•[i] Above all, my brothers, don't swear, whether by Heaven, earth, or 12 some other oath; let your "yes" be "yes" and your "no," "no," lest you come under condemnation. •Is anyone among you suffering under adversity? He should pray! Is anyone cheerful? He should sing songs of praise! •[j] Is anyone among you sick? He should call the elders of the 14 church, and have them pray over him and anoint him with oil in the name of the Lord — •prayer rooted in faith will save whoever is ill and 15 the Lord will raise him up, and even if he has sinned the Lord will forgive him. •So confess your sins to one another and pray for each other 16 so that you may be healed — the prayer of a good man can accomplish great things. •Elijah was a man like us in every way and when he 17 earnestly prayed that it wouldn't rain it didn't rain on earth for three years and six months, •and when he prayed again the sky sent rain and the 18 earth brought forth its fruit. •My brothers, if anyone among you strays 19 from the truth and someone brings them back, •remember that a person who brings back a sinner from the error of his ways will save his 20 own soul from death and will make up for a multitude of sins.

[i] *Mt 5:34-37.*   [j] *Mk 6:13.*

5:14 This passage is the scriptural basis for the   5:17-18 1 K 17-18.
Sacrament of the Anointing of the Sick.

THE FIRST LETTER OF

PETER

Introduction to the First Letter of Peter

According to an ancient tradition of the Church, the First Letter of Peter was written by the apostle Peter. The letter is addressed to Christian communities which are located in a large stretch of territory in the northern half of Asia Minor, modern Turkey. All indications from the letter are that its recipients were of predominantly Gentile origin and were relatively recent converts.

The purpose of the letter is to encourage its recipients to continued growth in the faith, especially in light of the persecution they have lately been suffering from the pagans among whom they live. Several themes are employed for this purpose. Prominent among them is the reminder of Christ's death and resurrection on their behalf; the example of Christ's suffering is presented as a model for both the community in its relations with the outside world as well as for their personal lives.

Another prominent theme is that of baptism. Through the image of rebirth and washing the recipients of the letter are regularly reminded of their baptisms and what that means for them. Indeed, so pointed is this theme in certain parts of the letter that some scholars have speculated that portions of it may have been adapted from a baptismal liturgy. While this theory probably goes too far, the letter is instructive in the way it treats baptism.

A third theme is that of their calling. The readers are reminded that they were chosen and called by God Himself. This calling has constituted them as "a people set apart," and the recollection of God's choice of them should inspire them to focus on the hope they have received through Christ.

A. GREETING

1 **1** •Peter, an apostle of Jesus Christ, to those who are sojourners in the diaspora of Pontus, Galatia, Cappadocia, Asia, and Bithynia, 2 •who were chosen according to the foreknowledge of God the Father through sanctification by the Spirit for obedience to Jesus Christ and to be sprinkled with his blood: may grace and peace be yours in abundance.

B. REJOICE IN THE FAITH AND LIVE THE FAITH

3 •Blessed be the God and Father of our Lord Jesus Christ! In His great mercy we have been reborn to a living hope through the resurrection 4 of Jesus Christ from the dead •and to an imperishable, undefiled, and 5 unfading inheritance, which is reserved in Heaven for you •who by God's power are guarded through faith for the salvation which is ready to be 6 revealed in the last days. •You rejoice in this, although for a short time 7 now you may have to suffer various trials •so that your faith, more precious even than perishable gold which is tested with fire, may be tested and shown worthy of praise, glory, and honor at the revelation of Je- 8 sus Christ. •Although you haven't seen him you love him, and although you don't see him now you believe in him and rejoice with an inex- 9 pressible and glorious joy •because you are attaining the salvation of your souls, the goal of your faith.

10 •The prophets who prophesied about the grace that was to be yours 11 carefully searched and inquired about this salvation. •They inquired as to what person or circumstance was being revealed when the Spirit of Christ within them foretold Christ's sufferings and the glory that would 12 come after his sufferings. •It was revealed to them that they were serv- ing not themselves but you when they announced the things which

---

1:1 "Sojourners in the diaspora." Drawn from Jewish imagery, this phrase describes those who are temporarily living outside their homeland, scattered among foreigners. For Jews, of course, this was literally true, but as here applied to Gentile converts it is intended to be understood in a spiritual sense.

have now been proclaimed to you in the good news through the Holy Spirit which was sent from Heaven — *angels* long to get a glimpse of these things!

•Therefore, gird up the loins of your understanding! Be sober, and 13 have your hope totally focused on the grace that will come to you at the revelation of Jesus Christ. •Live as obedient children, and not accord- 14 ing to the desires of your former ignorance — •He Who called you is 15 holy, and so you too should be holy in all your conduct, •since it is writ- 16 ten, **You shall be holy because I am holy.**

•And if you invoke as "Father" the One Who judges each of us im- 17 partially according to our deeds, then you should live your lives in fear throughout the time of your sojourn, •for you know that you weren't 18 redeemed from the futile ways of your fathers with perishable things like silver and gold — •you were redeemed with the precious blood of 19 Christ, as if by the blood of an unblemished and spotless lamb. •He 20 was selected before the beginning of the world but was revealed at the end of time for your sake. •Through him you believe in God Who 21 raised him from the dead and glorified him, so that your faith and hope are in God.

•Since you've purified your souls through obedience to the truth for 22 sincere brotherly love, you should love one another earnestly from the heart. •You've been born anew, not from perishable seed but from im- 23 perishable seed, through the living, abiding word of God, •for 24

> **All flesh is like grass,**
> **and all its glory like a flower of the field**
> **The grass withers**
> **and the flower falls to the ground,**
> **•But the word of the Lord lasts forever.** 25

This word is what was proclaimed to you in the good news.

2 •So lay aside all malice and deceit, all hypocrisy, envy, and slander. 1 •Long like newborn babes for pure, spiritual milk, so that through 2 it you may grow up to salvation, •for **you have tasted that the Lord 3 is kind and merciful.** •Approach him, a living stone who was rejected 4 by men but is chosen and precious in God's sight, •and like living stones 5 let yourselves be built up into a spiritual house, a holy priesthood to offer spiritual sacrifices which are acceptable to God through Jesus Christ.

1:16 Lv 11:44-45; 19:2.   2:3 Ps 34:8.
1:24-25 Is 40:6-8 (Septuagint).

6 •For Scripture says,

> **Behold, I will lay a stone in Zion,**
> **a cornerstone, chosen and precious;**
> **Whoever believes in it shall not be put to shame.**

7 •For you who believe it has great value, but for those who don't believe

> **The stone the builders rejected**
> **has become the cornerstone;**

8 •and

> **A stone they'll trip over,**
> **a rock they'll stumble on.**

They stumble because they disobey the word — for this they were born.

9 •But you are **a chosen race, a royal priesthood, a holy nation, a people set apart by God to proclaim His saving deeds,** Who called you out of darkness into His marvelous light.

10 •Once you **were not a people,**
> but now **you're God's people,**
> **You had not received mercy,**
> but now **you have received mercy.**

C. HOW THE CHRISTIAN SHOULD FACE HOSTILITY

11 •Beloved, I beg you as strangers and sojourners to abstain from all
12 desires of the flesh that war against the soul. •Your conduct among the Gentiles must be good, so that if people speak against you as evildoers they'll see your good deeds and glorify God on the day of His visitation.
13 •For the Lord's sake be subject to every human institution, whether
14 to the Emperor as the supreme authority •or to governors sent by the Emperor to punish wrongdoers and praise those who do what's right,
15 •for it's God's will that by doing good you'll silence the ignorance of fool-

2:6 Is 28:16 (Septuagint).
2:7 Ps 118:22.
2:8 Is 8:14-15.
2:9-10 Is 43:20-21; Ex 19:5-6; Ho 2:23. As the New Israel, chosen by God (1:2), the Gentile converts are described in terms drawn from the Old Testament, where they were applied to the Old Israel.

2:11 Here the theme from 1:1 is recalled, but while the spiritual sense of being "strangers" in the world (not belonging, like resident aliens in a foreign land) remains, the concerns of this section are very pertinent to the here and now problems facing the converts.

ish people. •Live as free men, but without using your freedom as an ex- 16
cuse for evil; instead, conduct yourselves as servants of God. •Respect 17
everyone, love the brotherhood, fear God, and honor the Emperor.

•Household servants should be subject to their masters with all respect, 18
not only to kind and good masters but also to those who are unjust. •For 19
if anyone endures the pain of unjust suffering out of awareness of God,
that is a grace. •What credit do you deserve if you accept a beating af- 20
ter having done wrong? But if you suffer for doing what's right yet bear
with it, that's a grace in the eyes of God. •This is what you were called 21
to and this is why Christ suffered for you — to leave you an example
for you to follow in his footsteps.

•He did no wrong, 22
and no deceit was found on his lips.

•When he was reviled he didn't reply in kind, when he suffered he made 23
no threats; instead, he entrusted himself to the One Who judges justly.
•It was he who bore our sins in his body on the cross so that we 24
could die to sin and live in righteousness; **by his wounds you've been
healed.** •For you were **like sheep who had gone astray,** but now 25
you've returned to the Shepherd and Guardian of your souls.

3 •[a] Likewise, you wives should be subject to your husbands so that 1
even if they don't respond to the word they may be won over without a word by the behavior of their wives — •when they see your rev- 2
erent and chaste behavior. •[b] Don't try to be beautiful by braiding your 3
hair, wearing gold jewelry, and putting on fine clothing. •Instead, let your 4
beauty be that of the person hidden in your heart, the imperishable beauty of a gentle and quiet spirit, which is precious in the sight of God. •For 5
this is how the holy women of former times who hoped in God made
themselves beautiful, by being subject to their husbands — •just as Sarah 6
obeyed Abraham and called him "lord." You've become her children if
you do what's right and let nothing cause you to fear.

•[c] Likewise you husbands, treat your wives considerately since the fe- 7
male is the weaker sex, and show them respect since they're co-heirs
of the grace of life; do this so that your prayers may be answered.

---

[a] *Eph 5:22; Col 3:18.*   [b] *1 Tm 2:9.*   [c] *Eph 5:25; Col 3:19.*

2:22-25 Is 53:9 (22); Is 53:7 (23); Is 53:5-6 (Septuagint) (24-25). The quotations and surrounding
verses strongly recall Isaiah's "Suffering Servant."
The use of this imagery is considered character-
istic of "primitive" Christianity.

3:6 Gn 18:12.
3:7 "Co-heirs." This passage is strongly reminiscent of Paul's writings in its expression of the new
relationship between men and women "in Christ."

A man carrying a stone. (1 P 2:7) Roman engraved stone.

8 •Finally, you should all be of one mind; be sympathetic, love one an-
9 other, be compassionate and humble. •Don't pay back evil for evil or curse for curse; on the contrary, respond with blessings, for this is your calling and in this way you'll obtain a blessing.

10 •For whoever **would love life**
   and see good days
   Must keep his tongue from evil
   and his lips from speaking falsehood.
11 **•He must turn away from evil and do good,**
   seek peace and strive for it.
12 **•Because the Lord's eyes are upon the righteous,**
   and His ears hear their prayers,
   But the face of the Lord is against those who do evil.

3:10-12 Ps 34:12-16.

•Who will harm you if you're zealous for what's right? •[d] But even if you **13,14** do suffer for what's right, you're blessed! Have no **fear of them and don't be frightened,** •but in your hearts **revere** Christ as **the Lord.** **15** Always be ready with a reply for anyone who demands an explanation for the hope you have within you, •but do it humbly and respectfully **16** and have a clean conscience, so that when people malign your good behavior in Christ they'll be put to shame. •It's better to suffer for doing **17** what's right, if that's God's will, than for doing wrong! •For Christ died **18** for our sins once and for all, a righteous man for the unrighteous, so that he could lead us to God. He was put to death in the flesh but was brought to life in the spirit, •and it was in the spirit that he went and **19** proclaimed the good news to the spirits in prison, •who in former times **20** had refused obedience while God waited patiently for the ark to be built in the days of Noah. A few people, eight souls to be exact, were saved through water. •The water of baptism, which corresponds to the flood, **21** now saves you, not by removing dirt from the body but as an appeal to God for a clean conscience through the resurrection of Jesus Christ. •He **22** has gone to Heaven and is at the right hand of God, where angels, authorities, and powers are subject to him.

4 •So since Christ suffered in the flesh you too should arm yourselves **1** with the same attitude (for whoever suffers in the flesh is finished with sin) •so as to live what time remains in the flesh no longer according **2** to human passions but according to the will of God. •For in the past **3** you had sufficient time to do what the Gentiles like to do — living in debauchery, desire, drunkenness, revelry, carousing, and disgusting idolatry. •Now, they're surprised that you don't join them in the same reck- **4** less dissipation, and so they revile you, •but they'll have to give an ac- **5** count to the One Who's ready to judge the living and the dead. •For **6** this is why the good news was also proclaimed to those who are dead — so that although they were judged in the flesh like men, they may live in the spirit like God.

[d] *Mt 5:10.*

3:14-15 Is 8:12-13.
3:18-20 This passage with its reference to "the spirits in prison" has long puzzled commentators. An early view was that it referred to the spirits of humans from the time of Noah. Many modern authors favor the view that the spirits were the disobedient angels of Gn 6, probably to be identified with the powers and authorities who figure prominently in several of Paul's letters and were regarded as having power over humans. Thus, when Christ "proclaimed the good news" (3:19), it was probably not with a view toward their conversion but to announce their final subjugation (3:22). In v. 18 many manuscripts read "suffered" for "died."

7 •The end of all things is at hand, so be serious and sober for your
8 prayers. •Above all be constant in your love for one another, because
9 love covers a multitude of sins. •Be hospitable to each other without com-
10 plaining. •To the extent that each of you has received a gift, use it to
11 serve one another as good stewards of God's varied grace. •If anyone
speaks, let it be the words of God, if anyone serves, let it be with the
strength God supplies, so that in all things God may be glorified through
Jesus Christ, to whom be glory and might forever and ever, amen.

D. HOW CHRISTIANS SHOULD
FACE ACTIVE PERSECUTION

12 •Beloved, don't be surprised at the fiery ordeal which has come among
13 you to test you, as if something strange were happening; •instead, rejoice
in so far as you're sharing in Christ's sufferings, so that when his glory is
14 revealed you may rejoice and exult. •If people heap abuse on you because
of Christ's name, blessed are you! because the Spirit of glory and of God
15 is resting upon you. •Let none of you suffer for being a murderer, a thief,
16 a criminal, or a troublemaker, •but if you suffer for being a Christian, don't
17 be ashamed! Rather, glorify God in that name. •For it's time now for the
judgment, starting with God's own household, and if it begins with us, what
will be the fate of those who refuse to believe God's good news?

18 •And if **the righteous will be saved only with
difficulty,
where will the godless and sinners wind up?**

19 •Therefore, let those who suffer in accordance with God's will entrust
their souls to a faithful creator and do good.

1 5 •Therefore I exhort those of you who are elders — as a fellow elder and a witness of Christ's sufferings and a partaker in the glory
2 that will be revealed — •tend God's flock which has been placed in your
care. Oversee them, not because you must, but willingly as God would
have it, not out of a desire for material gain but because it's your eager
3 desire. •Don't lord it over those in your care; instead, serve as models
4 for your flock, •and when the head shepherd is revealed you'll receive

---

4:18 Pr 11:31 (Septuagint).
5:1-4 "Elder" was the usual early Christian term for

a bishop. The Greek word for bishop that replaced
"elder" appears in 5:2, and means "overseer."

an unfading crown of glory. •Likewise, you young men, be subject to 5 the elders. All of you should clothe yourselves with humility toward one another because

> ## God opposes the arrogant
> ## but gives grace to the humble.

•[e] So humble yourselves beneath God's mighty hand so that He'll ex- 6 alt you at the proper time; •cast all your cares on Him, because He cares 7 for you.

•Be sober and watchful. Your adversary the Devil goes about like a 8 roaring lion seeking someone to devour. •Resist him and be firm in your 9 faith, since you know that the same sufferings are being visited upon your brotherhood throughout the world. •The God of all grace Who 10 called you to eternal glory in Christ will Himself restore, strengthen, and establish you, after you've suffered for a little while. •To Him be power 11 forever, amen!

E. CONCLUSION

•[f] I've written to you briefly through my faithful brother Silvanus (so 12 I regard him) to exhort you and bear witness that this is the true grace of God. Be steadfast in it. •[g] Your chosen sister in Babylon greets you, 13 as does my son Mark. •Greet one another with the kiss of love. Peace 14 to all of you who are in Christ.

---

[e] *Mt 23:12; Lk 14:11; 18:14.* [f] *Ac 15:22, 40.* [g] *Col 4:10; Phm 24.*

5:5 Pr 3:34 (Septuagint).
5:12 "Silvanus." Probably to be identified with Paul's companion Silas (cf. Acts 15-17, passim).
5:13 "Your chosen sister in Babylon." Lit., "She in Babylon who is chosen," i.e., the church in Rome. "Babylon," with its Old Testament associations of wickedness and persecution of God's people, was the early Church's designation for Rome. Its use at the end of the letter, along with the use of the phrase "fiery ordeal" (4:12), has led some scholars to suggest that the latter part of this letter may have been written after the outbreak of the Neronian persecution. Thus, the guardedly positive attitude toward the state (2:13-17) is replaced by a hostility that necessitates the use of a code-word.

THE SECOND LETTER OF

PETER

Introduction to the Second Letter of Peter

The relatively small amount of literature devoted to the study of the closely related letters, 2 Peter and Jude, revolves largely around such issues as authorship, date of composition, the relation of 2 Peter to 1 Peter, and the identity of the heretics who are denounced in both Jude and 2 Peter.

Regarding Jude, little can be definitively said. The author of the letter himself states that he is "a servant of Jesus Christ and brother of James," which is traditionally taken to mean that he is, with the author of James, one of the "brothers" of the Lord (Mt 13:55; Mk 6:3). Jude was most probably a Jewish Christian, based not only on his general outlook but also upon his knowledge of the Jewish apocryphal works *1 Enoch* and *The Assumption of Moses.*

Of the two letters, 2 Peter is the more polished production. Its purpose was to urge the readers to progress in the life of virtue, as a necessary adjunct to their faith. The need for such encouragement is occasioned by the presence of false teachers who misinterpret Scripture and lead dissolute lives. After denouncing these false teachers at length, their presence is related to the end time, with the warning that when the day of the Lord will actually come is not known to us: "for the Lord one day is like a thousand years, and a thousand years is like one day."

A. GREETING

1 **1** •Symeon Peter, a servant and apostle of Jesus Christ, to those who have received a faith of equal worth with ours through the saving will 2 of our God and Savior Jesus Christ: •may grace and peace abound to you through knowledge of God and Jesus our Lord.

B. CHRISTIANS CALLED TO THE LIFE OF VIRTUE

3 •His divine power has bestowed on us everything that pertains to life and godliness through our knowledge of the One Who called us 4 by His own glory and power. •Through His glory and power He has bestowed on us the great and precious promises, so that through them you may escape from the corruption that passion brought into the 5 world and may come to share in the divine nature. •For this very reason you should make every effort to supplement your faith with virtue, 6 your virtue with knowledge, •your knowledge with self-control, your 7 self-control with steadfastness, your steadfastness with godliness, •your godliness with mutual affection, and your mutual affection with love. 8 •If you make these things your own and cause them to grow, they'll keep you from being idle or unfruitful in the knowledge of our Lord 9 Jesus Christ. •Whoever lacks these things is blind and shortsighted, 10 forgetting that he was cleansed from his past sins. •Therefore, brothers, you must spare no effort to give your call and election a firm foun- 11 dation, for if you do this you'll never stumble. •In this way your entry into the everlasting Kingdom of our Lord and Savior Jesus Christ will be richly provided for.

12 •Therefore I intend to constantly remind you of these things, even though you are aware of them and are firmly established in the truth

---

1:1 "Symeon Peter." In only one other passage in the New Testament (Acts 15:14) is Peter referred to as Symeon, and that by James, Jude's brother.

1:3 Some early manuscripts read only "through glory and power."

you have. •I think it proper to keep reminding you of these things as 13 long as I have life, •since I know that I'll soon be putting off this bodily 14 dwelling of mine, as our Lord Jesus Christ has made clear to me. •And 15 so I'll make every effort to ensure that you'll always remember these things after my departure.

C. FALSE TEACHERS CONDEMNED

•When we made known to you the power of our Lord Jesus Christ's 16 coming we didn't depend on cleverly contrived myths, for we were eye-witnesses of his majesty. •[a] When he received honor and glory from God 17 the Father and these words came to him from the Magnificent Glory, "This is My beloved Son in whom I am well pleased!" — •[b] we ourselves 18 heard that voice from Heaven because we were with him on the holy mountain. •Moreover we have the prophetic word which is even more 19 certain. You will do well to pay close attention to it, like a light shining in some dark place until the day dawns and the morning star rises in your hearts. •Above all you must understand that no scriptural prophe- 20 cy is a matter of your own individual interpretation, •for no prophecy 21 ever came because a man wished for it — men prophesied from God only because they were moved by the Holy Spirit.

2 •But there were also false prophets among the people, just as there 1 will be false teachers among you who will secretly bring in destruc-tive heresies and will even deny the Master who redeemed them — there-by bringing swift destruction upon themselves. •Many people will follow 2 their licentiousness and through them the Way of truth will be blas-phemed. •In their greed they'll exploit you with false words, but sentence 3 was passed upon them long ago, and their utter ruin is assured.

•For if God didn't spare the angels when they sinned but instead held 4 them captive in dark pits and handed them over to be kept for judgment; •if He didn't spare the ancient world but protected Noah, a herald of 5 righteousness, with seven others when He brought a flood upon this god-less world; •if He condemned the cities of Sodom and Gomorrah to de- 6

---

[a] *Mt 17:1-5; Mk 9:2-7; Lk 9:28-35.*   [b] *Jude 4-16.*

1:13 "As long as I have life." Lit., "as long as I'm in this tent," "tent" being a metaphor for life in the body.
1:15 "Departure." In Greek, "exodus," a metaphorical way of referring to death.

2:1 "The people." I.e., Israel.
2:4 Cf. Jude 6. This is probably a reference to the story of the rebellious angels in Gn 6, as ex-panded by the Jewish apocryphal work *1 Enoch.*

struction and reduced them to ashes, thus making them an example to
7 godless people of what is to come; •if He rescued the just man Lot, who
was tormented by the licentious way of life of those unprincipled peo-
8 ple — •for the soul of that just man was tormented day after day by the
9 lawless deeds he saw and heard while he lived among them — •then
the Lord is able to rescue religious people from their trials and keep the
10 wicked under punishment for the day of judgment, •especially those who
follow the way of the flesh and corrupting passion and scorn authority.

Bold and self-willed, they're not afraid to blaspheme heavenly beings,
11 •whereas angels who are much greater in power and might don't de-
12 nounce them in such insulting terms before the Lord. •But these false
teachers are like brute animals — born subject to instinct, born to be
caught and slaughtered — and they blaspheme what they're ignorant
13 of. They'll be destroyed just like the animals •and they'll suffer in payment for the suffering they've caused. They consider daytime revelry to
be a pleasure and are stains and blots, reveling in their deceitful ways as
14 they feast with you. •They have eyes only for adultery and their appetite
for sin is insatiable. They ensnare weak souls and have hearts well trained

*Capharnaum. The city of Peter was later extended up
to the red-domed Orthodox church.*

in greed, accursed wretches! •They've left the straight way and gone 15
astray, following the way of Balaam son of Bosor, who loved gain from
wrongdoing •but was rebuked for his offense — a dumb ass spoke with 16
a human voice and turned the prophet aside from his madness.

•They're waterless wells and mists driven by a storm; gloomy dark- 17
ness has been reserved for them, •for they hold forth with empty boasts 18
and by arousing sensual passions of the flesh they seduce people who
are only just beginning to escape from those who live in error. •They 19
promise them freedom, but they themselves are slaves of depravity, for
anyone who is overcome by something becomes that thing's slave. • For 20
if after fleeing the corruption of the world through the knowledge of our
Lord and Savior Jesus Christ they once again become entangled with
these things and are overpowered, their last state is worse than their first.
•It would have been better for them if they had never come to know the 21
Way of righteousness, rather than to come to know the Way and then
turn away from the holy commandment that was handed down to them.
•Their actions illustrate the truth of the proverbs, 22

> "The dog returns to its own vomit,"

and,

> "A washed sow goes back to its mud wallow."

D. THE DAY OF THE LORD DELAYED

3 •Beloved, this is now the second letter I've written to you. By means 1
of these reminders I've tried to stir up within you a sincere disposition •[c] to remember the words previously spoken by the holy prophets 2
as well as the commandment of our Lord and Savior which you received
from your apostles. •First of all you must realize that in the last days 3
there will be people who will follow their own desires and will scoff •and 4
say, "What about his promise to come? Since the day the fathers fell
asleep everything has remained the same as it was at the beginning of
creation." •They willfully ignore the fact that through the word of God 5
the heavens existed long ago, and earth was formed from water and
through water. •Through them the world that then existed was flood- 6

[c] Jude 17-18.

2:15-16 Nb 22:4-35. Balaam's name had, by
New Testament times, become practically synonymous with rebellion against God. Many
manuscripts have "Beor" rather than "Bosor".
2:22 Pr 26:11.

7 ed and destroyed by water. •By the same word the present heavens and earth have been saved for fire, kept for the day of judgment when the impious will be destroyed.

8 •But beloved, there's one thing you shouldn't lose sight of — for the Lord one day is like a thousand years, and a thousand years is like one
9 day. •The Lord's promise is not delayed as some would reckon "delay." On the contrary, he's being patient with you because he doesn't want anyone to be destroyed — he wants everyone to come to repentance.
10 •[d] But the day of the Lord will come like a thief. On that day the heavens will disappear with a roar; the elements will be consumed with fire
11 and the earth and everything done on it will be found out. •Since all these things are to be destroyed in this way, what must you be like as regards
12 leading holy and godly lives? •You should await and hasten the coming of the day of God, as a result of which the heavens will be destroyed by
13 fire and the elements will melt away in the heat. •[e] But in accordance with his promise we are awaiting **a new heavens and a new earth,** in which righteousness will dwell.

14 •Therefore, beloved, since we're expecting these things, make every
15 effort to be found by him spotless, unblemished, and at peace. •Consider our Lord's patience to be an opportunity for furthering your salvation, just as our beloved brother Paul wrote to you with the wisdom he has
16 been given. •This is what he says about these matters in all his other letters as well. There are some things in his letters which are difficult to understand — ignorant and unstable people distort them, just as they dis-
17 tort the other scriptures, to their own destruction! •So you, beloved, who know this beforehand, be on guard against being carried away by the errors of unprincipled people and losing your own stability.

E. CLOSING DOXOLOGY

18 •Grow in the grace and knowledge of our Lord and Savior Jesus Christ. To him be glory, both now and to the day of eternity. Amen.

---

[d] *Mt 24:43; Lk 12:39; 1 Th 5:2; Rv 16:15.*   [e] *Rv 21:1.*

3:8 Ps 90:4.
3:10 Other manuscript traditions replace "will be found out" with "will vanish" or "will be burned up."
3:13 Is 65:17; 66:22.
3:16 "Other scriptures." Opinion is divided as to whether this phrase refers to Paul's letters as al-
ready being accorded the authority of Scripture. No definitive judgment is possible based on this verse alone, although it is clear that Paul's writings carried great weight in the Church from a very early date.

General Introduction to the Johannine Letters

The three letters of John provide a glimpse of a community, or more exactly, a group of communities, beset with internal conflict. The unnamed Christian communities involved are traditionally believed to have been located in Asia Minor and to have been founded by the apostle John. The conflict was doctrinal in nature and centered around the nature and significance of Jesus. As nearly as we can tell from the letters, which of course give only a partial picture, the heretics who were troubling the communities appear to have questioned the humanity of Christ and to have stressed the need for Christians to have a direct relationship with the Father. For the heretics, Jesus' role in salvation was to lead us to knowledge of the Father, not to die as an expiation for sins. Moral deviations may also have arisen, fueled by the conviction that those who were in fellowship with the Father could do no wrong.

Against these views, the letters of John maintain the full humanity of Jesus, his sacrificial death for our sins, and the need to remain in solidarity with the apostolic teaching that was received "in the beginning."

THE FIRST LETTER OF

JOHN

A. PROLOGUE

1 **1** •ᵃ What was from the beginning, what we have heard, what we have seen with our eyes, what we have looked at and touched with our 2 hands, concerning the word of life — •ᵇ the life was made visible and we saw it, and we testify and proclaim to you the everlasting life which 3 was with the Father and was made visible to us — •what we have seen and heard we also proclaim to you so you too may be in fellowship with us. Our fellowship is with the Father and with His Son, Jesus Christ, 4 •ᶜ and we're writing these things so that our joy may be complete.

B. GOD IS LIGHT

5 •This is the message we heard from him and which we announce to 6 you — God is light and there is no darkness in Him. •ᵈ If we say we're in fellowship with Him yet walk in darkness we're lying and don't fol- 7 low the truth, •but if we walk in the light as He is in the light we're in fellowship with one another and the blood of His Son Jesus cleanses us 8 from all sin. •If we say we're without sin we deceive ourselves, and there's 9 no truth in us. •If we confess our sins He is faithful and just and will for- 10 give us our sins and cleanse us from all unrighteousness. •If we say we haven't sinned we make Him a liar and His word isn't in us.

ᵃ *Jn 1:1.* ᵇ *Jn 1:14.* ᶜ *Jn 15:11.* ᵈ *Jn 12:35.*

1:1-4 While there are similarities between the prologues to 1 John and the Gospel of John, there are important differences. The primary emphasis in 1 John is on the reality of the experience of Jesus in his humanity, which appears to have been denied by the heretics.
1:3 The theme of the letter is apparent in this verse. Its purpose is to maintain fellowship between the writer(s) (we) and the readers (you). The author specifies that "we" are in fellowship with both the Father and the Son, as opposed to the heretics, who deny the Son.

1:5-10 This paragraph and the following two (2:1-6, 7-11) introduce and develop several important themes. The first is the metaphorical contrast of light and dark, which prepares us for a continual series of antithetical pairs — truth and falsehood, love and hate, sight and blindness, obedience and disobedience, etc. The typically Semitic metaphor of "walking" (meaning the conduct of our lives) also features prominently.
1:8-10 The insistence that we have all sinned should be seen as a reply to the heretics, who apparently claimed to be incapable of sinning (no

2 •[e] My children, I'm writing these things to you so you won't sin, but ¹ if anyone *does* sin we have an Intercessor with the Father, Jesus Christ the Just. •He is the expiation for our sins, and not only for *ours* but for ² the sins of the whole world. •[f] This is how we can be sure that we know ³ [God] — if we keep His commandments. •Whoever says, "I know [God]," ⁴ but doesn't keep His commandments is a liar, and there is no truth in him, •[g] but whoever *does* keep His word, the love of God is truly per- ⁵ fected in him. This is how we know that we're in him — •whoever claims ⁶ to be in fellowship with [God] should walk in the same way Jesus walked.

•[h] Beloved, I'm not writing a new commandment to you — it's an old ⁷ commandment which you had from the beginning. This old commandment is the word you heard. •Yet I *am* writing you a new commandment, ⁸ which is true in [Jesus] and in you, because the darkness is passing away and the true light is already shining. •Whoever claims to be in the light ⁹ but hates his brother is still in the darkness. •Whoever loves his brother ¹⁰ remains in the light and causes no scandal to others. •But whoever hates ¹¹ his brother is in darkness and walks in darkness, and he doesn't know where he's going because the darkness has blinded his eyes.

•I'm writing to you, my children, ¹²
    because your sins have been forgiven by his name.
•I'm writing to you, fathers, ¹³
    because you know the one who is from the
      beginning.
I'm writing to you, young men,
    because you have conquered the Evil One.
•I write to you, children, ¹⁴
    because you know the Father.
I write to you, fathers,
because you know the one who is from
    the beginning.

---

[e] *Jn 14:16.*   [f] *Jn 14:15.*   [g] *Jn 14:23.*   [h] *Jn 13:34.*

matter what their actual behavior) as a result of their claimed fellowship with the Father. While insisting that all Christians do sin, however, John goes on in the following paragraphs to make two important points: first, we are obligated to adhere to a certain standard of conduct, and that standard is Jesus (2:6); second, if we fall, Jesus will intercede for us, because he is the expiation for the sins of the whole world (2:1-2).

2:3 This is the first of the so-called "test" verses — verses which contain the phrase "this is how you can know" or similar language — which provide a standard which can be used to measure the fidelity of the various teachers the community may be exposed to. Cf. also 2:5; 3:16, 19, 24; 4:2, 6, 13; 5:2. 2:7 "From the beginning" is another phrase which implicitly indicates the standard to be used in judging doctrine — apostolicity.

*Sign directing customers to a brothel, engraved
in a foot-path in Ephesus. (1 Jn 2:16)*

I write to you, young men,
    because you're strong;
The word of God remains in you
    and you've conquered the Evil One.

15 •Don't love the world or what's in the world. If anyone loves the world
16 the love of the Father isn't in him, •because everything *in* the world —
sensual lust, covetousness, and overbearing self-confidence — is *of* the
17 world and is not from the Father. •The world too is passing away as well
as its desires, but whoever does God's will lasts forever.

2:15 "The world" is used metaphorically of life
lived on a purely "natural" level, disregarding God.
2:16 "Sensual lust." Lit., "desires of the flesh."
"Covetousness." Lit., "desire of the eyes."
"Overbearing self-confidence." Lit., "pride of life."

C. STEADFASTNESS IN THE FAITH

•My children, it's the last hour. You've heard that Antichrist is com- 18
ing and now many Antichrists have come, which is how we know that
it's the last hour. •They came *from* us but they weren't *of* us, for if they'd 19
been of us they would have remained with us. This was all to show that
none of them were with us. •[i] But you, too, were anointed by the Holy 20
One and all of you have knowledge. •I write to you not because you don't 21
know the truth but because you *do* know the truth, and you know that
no lie is from the truth. •Who *is* the liar, if not whoever denies that Je- 22
sus is the Messiah? This is the Antichrist — whoever denies the Father
and the Son. •No one who denies the Son has the Father, but whoev- 23
er acknowledges the Son has the Father as well. •So then, you should 24
let what you heard from the beginning remain in you. If what you heard
from the beginning does remain in you, you'll also remain in fellowship
with the Son and with the Father. •[j] And this is the promise he gave to 25
you — life everlasting.

•I write these things to you about those who would deceive you, •but 26,27
the anointing you received from him remains with you and you have
no need for anyone to teach you — as his anointing teaches you about
everything, and it's true and is not a lie — just as it taught you, remain in him.

•And now, my children, remain in Jesus so that when he appears 28
we may be confident and not be put to shame by him at his coming.
•If you know that [God] is just, you also know that everyone who does 29
what's right was born of Him.

3 •[k] You see what love the Father has given us so we might be called 1
children of God — and so we are! This is why the world doesn't know
us — because it didn't know him. •Beloved, we're now God's children, 2
but it's not yet clear what we *will* be. We know that when [Jesus] appears we'll be like him, because we'll see him as he is. •Everyone who 3
has this hope in him purifies himself, just as he is pure.

---

[i] *Jn 14:26.*   [j] *Jn 5:24.*   [k] *Jn 1:12.*

2:18-25 The appearance of persons who deny
that Jesus is the Messiah (lit., "Antichrists") is for
the author a sign of the end times. While "Antichrist" has often been considered to refer to a
specific individual, this passage most probably
uses the term generally of Christ's opponents. As
throughout the letter, the inseparability of Father
and Son is strongly stressed.
2:20 The reference to "anointing" most probably
has to do with the gift of the Holy Spirit. While
there is some question, "Holy One" probably
refers to the Son rather than to the Father.

A mortally wounded warrior. Marble statue (3rd century BC.). (1 Jn 3:15)

4,5 •Whoever sins violates the law, for sin is lawlessness. •¹ You know that
6 [Jesus] appeared to take away sins, and there is no sin in him. •No one
7 who remains in him sins; no one who sins has seen or known him. •My
children, let no one deceive you. Whoever does what's right is righteous,
8 just as *he* is righteous; •ᵐ whoever sins is from the Devil, because the
Devil was a sinner from the beginning. This is why the Son of God ap-
9 peared — to destroy the works of the Devil. •No one who was born of
God is a sinner, because His seed remains in him, and he's unable to
10 sin because he's born of God. •This is how the children of God and the
children of the Devil can be known — whoever doesn't do what's right
is not from God, nor is he who doesn't love his brother.
11 •ⁿ For this is the message you heard from the beginning, that we should
12 love one another, •not like Cain who was from the Evil One and slew his
brother. And why did he slay him? Because his own works were evil while
13 his brother's works were good. •Don't be surprised, brothers, if the world
14 hates you. •We know that we've passed over from death to life because
15 we love the brethren — whoever doesn't love remains in death. •Every-

¹ Jn 1:29.   ᵐ Jn 8:40-47.   ⁿ Jn 5:24.

one who hates his brother is a murderer, and you know that no murderer has eternal life within him. •This is how we came to know love — he 16
laid down his life for us; we too should lay down our lives for our brothers. •Whoever has worldly goods and sees a brother in need but closes 17
his heart to him — how can love for God remain in him? •My children, 18
let's not love in word or speech alone but in actions and truth.
•This is how we'll know that we're of the truth and will reassure our 19
hearts before him •when our hearts condemn us, because God is greater 20
than our hearts and He knows everything. •Beloved, if our hearts don't 21
condemn us we can be confident before God, •and whatever we ask for 22
we'll receive from Him because we obey His commandments and do
what's pleasing in His sight. •[o] And this is His commandment, that we 23
believe in the name of His Son Jesus Christ and love one another, just
as he commanded us to. •Whoever obeys His commandments remains 24
in [God], and [God] remains in him. And this is how we know that He
remains in us — from the Spirit He gave us.

4 •Beloved, don't believe every spirit — test the spirits to see if they're 1
from God, because many false prophets have gone out into the
world. •This is how you'll know the Spirit of God: every spirit that ac- 2
knowledges that Jesus Christ came in the flesh is from God, •and every 3
spirit that doesn't acknowledge Jesus is not from God. This is the spirit of Antichrist; you've heard that it's coming and now it's already in the
world. •My children, you're from God and have conquered them, for 4
He Who is within you is greater than the one who's in the world.
•[p] They're from the world and so what they say is from the world and 5
the world listens to them. •[q] We are from God; whoever knows God lis- 6
tens to us, while whoever is not from God doesn't listen to us. From this
we can recognize the spirit of truth and the spirit of error.

D. GOD IS LOVE

•Beloved, we should love one another, because love is from God and 7
everyone who loves is born of God and knows God. •Whoever doesn't 8
love doesn't know God, because God is love. •[r] This is how God's love 9

[o] *Jn 13:34; 15:12.* [p] *Jn 15:19.* [q] *Jn 8:47.* [r] *Jn 3:16.*

4:1-3 This is an indication of the heretics' claim to be spirit-inspired. This section closes with a renewed appeal for continued solidarity and a strongly worded reminder of "our" teaching authority.

was made clear to us. God sent His only begotten Son into the world
10 so that we might have life through him. •This is what love is: not that
we loved God but that He loved us and sent His Son as the expiation
11 for our sins. •Beloved, if God so loved us we, too, should love one an-
12 other. •ˢ No one has ever seen God, but if we love one another God remains in us and His love is made perfect in us.

13   •This is how we know that we remain in Him and He remains in us
14 — from the Spirit He has given us. •We have seen and bear witness
15 that the Father sent His Son as the Savior of the world. •Whoever acknowledges that Jesus is the Son of God, God remains in him and he
16 remains in God. •We know and believe in the love God has for us.

God is love, and whoever abides in love abides in God, and God abides
17 in him. •This is how love is made perfect among us so that we may be
confident on the day of judgment, because just as He is, so are we too
18 in this world. •Fear has no place in love. Perfect love casts all fear aside
because fear has to do with punishment, and a person who is afraid is
19,20 not perfected in love. •We love because He first loved us. •If anyone
says,"I love God," but hates his brother he's a liar, for whoever doesn't
love his brother whom he *can* see is unable to love God, Whom he *does-*
21 *n't* see. •We have this commandment from [Jesus] — whoever loves God
must also love his brother.

1 **5** •Everyone who believes that Jesus is the Messiah is born from God,
and everyone who loves the parent also loves the parent's offspring.
2 •This is how we know that we love God's children, when we love God
3 and follow His commandments. •ᵗ For this is love for God, that we keep
4 His commandments, and His commandments are not burdensome. •For
every child who is born from God conquers the world, and the victory
5 that conquers the world is our faith. •Who is it that conquers the world
6 but the one who believes that Jesus is the Son of God? •This is the one
who came through blood and water, Jesus Christ — not just by water
alone but by water and blood — and the Spirit is the witness because
7,8 the Spirit is the truth. •For there are three witnesses, •the Spirit, water,
9 and blood, and the three are as one. •We accept the testimony of men,
and God's testimony is greater. This is God's testimony, that He bore
10 witness to His Son. •Whoever believes in the Son of God has God's testimony within himself; whoever *doesn't* believe God makes Him a liar,
because he doesn't believe the testimony God gave about His Son.

ˢ *Jn 1:18.*   ᵗ *Jn 14-15.*

•[u] And this is the testimony, that God gave us eternal life, and this life is in His Son. •Whoever has the Son has life; whoever doesn't have the Son of God doesn't have life. 11 12

E. CLOSING ASSURANCES

•I write these things to you, who believe in the name of the Son of God, so that you'll know that you have eternal life. •This is the confidence we have in [God], that if we ask for something which is in accordance with His will He hears us. •And if we know that He hears whatever we ask for, we know that we have what we requested of Him. 13 14 15

•If anyone sees his brother committing a sin which is not a mortal sin, he will ask and [God] will give life to those whose sin is not mortal. There is also mortal sin; I do not say that you should plead with [God] concerning that. •All wrongdoing is sinful, but there are some sins which are not mortal. 16 17

•We know that no one born from God sins — [God] protects him and the Evil One cannot touch him. •We know we're from God, and that the whole world is in the power of the Evil One. •We know that the Son of God has come and has given us understanding so that we can know the One Who is true, and we are in the true One, in His Son Jesus Christ. He is the true God and everlasting life. •My children, be on your guard against idols. 18 19 20 21

[u] Jn 3:36.

THE SECOND LETTER OF

JOHN

•The Elder to the chosen lady and her children, whom I love in truth ₁ — and not only I but also all those who know the truth, •because of the ₂ truth which dwells in us and will be with us forever. •Grace, mercy, and ₃ peace will be with us from God the Father and from Jesus Christ, the Son of the Father in truth and love.

•I was delighted to find some of your children walking in truth, just ₄ as we were commanded by the Father. •ᵃ Now I beg you, lady, not as ₅ if I were writing you a new commandment but the one we've had from the beginning — let us love one another! •And this is love, that we walk ₆ according to His commandments; this is the commandment just as you heard from the beginning — that you should walk in love. •For many ₇ deceivers have gone out into the world who deny that Jesus came in the flesh — such a person is a deceiver and an Antichrist. •See that you ₈ don't lose what we worked for but will receive your full reward. •Every- ₉ one who goes too far and doesn't remain true to Christ's teaching does- n't have God; whoever remains true to Christ's teaching, he has both the Father and the Son. •If anyone comes to you but doesn't bring this ₁₀ teaching, don't receive him into your house and don't greet him, •for ₁₁ whoever greets him shares in his evil works.

•Although I have much to write to you, I don't want to use paper and ₁₂ ink — I hope to come to you and speak face to face, so that our joy may be complete. •Your chosen sister's children greet you! ₁₃

ᵃ *Jn 13:34; 15:12, 17.*

1 "The Elder." That the author could identify him- self in this absolute manner argues both that he was well known to the community to which the let- ter was sent and that he was a man of more than ordinary stature."The chosen lady," i.e., a sister church, cf. also 13.

4 "Walking" is a typically Jewish metaphor for the conduct of a person's life.

6 "From the beginning." As in 1 John, this phrase provides a standard of apostolicity against which the teaching the community is exposed to may be compared.

7 As in 1 John, "Antichrist" appears to refer to op- ponents of Jesus the Messiah (Christ) in gener- al, rather than to a specific individual.

THE THIRD LETTER OF

JOHN

•The Elder to his beloved Gaius, whom I love in the truth. 1

•Beloved, I pray that you will prosper in all things and will enjoy good 2 health, just as your soul is prospering. •I was delighted when some broth- 3 ers came and bore witness to your truth — to how you walk in the truth. •I can have no greater joy than to hear that my children are walking in 4 the truth.

•Beloved, you show yourself to be faithful when you do anything for 5 the brothers, especially when they are strangers. •Those brothers bore 6 witness to your love before the church; you will do well to send them on their way in a manner worthy of God, •for they set out on behalf of 7 the Name and have accepted nothing from the Gentiles. •Therefore, it 8 is our duty to support such men so that we may be fellow workers in the truth.

•I wrote something to the church, but Diotrephes, who likes to assert 9 his authority, doesn't acknowledge us. •Therefore, if I come I'll bring up 10 what he's doing — making unjustified accusations against us! And not content with that, he refuses to welcome the brethren and stops those who wish to welcome them and expels them from the church.

•Beloved, imitate good, not evil. Whoever does what's good is from 11 God, while whoever does what's evil has not seen God. •Demetrius is 12 well spoken of by everyone, as well as by the truth itself. We too bear witness to him, and you know our witness is true.

•I had many things to write to you, but I don't want to write to you 13 with pen and ink. •I hope to see you very soon, and then we'll talk face 14 to face. •Peace be with you! The friends greet you. Greet each of the 15 friends by name.

---

7 "The name," i.e., of Jesus. While some would argue that the reference to "Gentiles" betrays a contempt for non-Jews on the part of a predominantly Jewish Christian community, it is more likely that the Elder is simply appealing for financial assistance for missionaries who are going to the Gentiles. Like Paul, they wished to be self-sufficient rather than appear to be sponging off their converts.

9 "Likes to assert his authority." Lit., "likes to be first."

12 It is not clear, but is certainly possible, that the Demetrius who is here commended was the bearer of this letter.

THE LETTER OF

JUDE

•ᵃ Jude, a servant of Jesus Christ and brother of James, to those who ₁ are called — beloved in God the Father and protected for Jesus Christ — •may you have mercy, peace, and love in abundance. ₂

•Beloved, I was diligently occupied in writing to you about our com- ₃ mon salvation when I decided that it was necessary to write this letter to you and urge you to fight for the faith that was handed down once and for all to the saints. •ᵇ For certain persons who were long ago marked ₄ down for condemnation have snuck in under false pretenses. These impious men distort and change the love of our God into licentiousness and deny our only Lord and master, Jesus Christ.

•I want to remind you, although you're already fully aware of all this, ₅ that the Lord Who delivered the people out of the land of Egypt later destroyed those who didn't believe. •And the angels who didn't keep to ₆ their proper place but instead left their dwelling, they've been kept by Him in darkness in eternal chains until the great day of judgment. •Like- ₇ wise Sodom and Gomorrah, as well as the nearby cities that indulged in the same type of immorality and followed unnatural desires, serve as an example by undergoing the punishment of eternal fire.

⌐ •It's the same with these men. As a result of their dreaming they de- ₈ file their bodies, reject authority, and blaspheme the heavenly beings. •ᶜ Michael the Archangel, on the other hand, when he was disputing with ₉ the Devil over the body of Moses, didn't take it upon himself to pro-

ᵃ Mt 13:55; Mk 6:3.   ᵇ Rv 12:7.   ᶜ 2 P 2:1-18.

5 Nb 14:29-30.
6 Gn 6:1-4 alludes briefly to the angels who deserted Heaven to take human wives. This episode was greatly elaborated upon in *1 Enoch*, a popular and influential Jewish apocryphal work which is explicitly cited at v. 14.
7 "Followed unnatural desires." Lit., "went after different flesh." Just as the angels sinned by lusting after humans (v. 6), the Sodomites sinned in lusting after Lot's angelic visitors. Jude appears to be focusing more on the idea of rebellion, re-

fusal to accept one's proper place, than on sexual misconduct as such.
8 "Dreamings" most likely refers to visions, used by the heretics to bolster their claims. "Authority." Lit., "lordship." This is an unusual word and may be best understood as referring to the sovereignty of God rather than to authority in general. Unfortunately, this does not add significantly to our knowledge of the heresy.
9 This is a reference to *The Assumption of Moses*, a Jewish apocryphal book.

nounce judgment on the Devil because of his blasphemies. Instead he
10 said, "May the Lord rebuke you!" •But these men blaspheme what they
don't understand, and what they *do* understand — by instinct, like brute
11 animals — leads to their destruction. •[d] Woe to them! They've followed
the way of Cain and for the sake of gain abandoned themselves to Balaam's error; they have joined in the rebellion of Korah and have been
12 destroyed. •They're a blot on your love feasts, shamelessly carousing and
looking after themselves. They're waterless clouds carried along by the
13 wind, autumn trees without fruit — twice dead and uprooted — •wild
waves of the sea foaming with their shameful deeds, wandering stars for
whom the gloom of darkness has been reserved forever.
14 •It was about them that Enoch prophesied in the seventh generation
after Adam when he said, "Behold, the Lord came with His myriads of
15 angels •to execute judgment upon all, to rebuke all the impious for all
the ungodly acts they committed and for all the harsh words that unholy
16 sinners have spoken against Him." •They're grumblers and complain-
ers who follow their own desires, their mouths spout boasts as they flat-
ter others for the sake of gain.
17 •[e] But you, beloved, should remember the words of warning spoken
18 by the apostles of our Lord Jesus Christ, •for they said to you, "In the
last days there will be people who scoff at you and follow their own god-
19 less desires." •These are the ones who create divisions, who are sensu-
20 al and devoid of the Spirit. •But you, my beloved, should build yourselves
21 up in your most holy faith; pray in the Holy Spirit; •keep yourselves in
the love of God and wait for the mercy of our Lord Jesus Christ which
22,23 leads to eternal life. •Be merciful with those who waver, •save others by
snatching them from the fire, and on still others have mercy with fear,
hating even the garment stained by the flesh.
24 •To Him who is able to preserve you from stumbling and can bring
25 you blameless and rejoicing into the presence of His glory, •to our only God and Savior through our Lord Jesus Christ, be glory, majesty, power, and authority, before all ages, now, and for all ages to come, Amen!

[d] *Rv 2:14.*   [e] *2 P 3:2-3.*

11 Nb 22:1-35; 16:1-35.   14 Gn 5:18, 21-24.

THE REVELATION TO

JOHN

Introduction to the Revelation to John

While a knowledge of the events which led John to write the Revelation is essential to an understanding of this book, it would be a mistake to think that it is of relevance only to the historian. The Revelation was written in response to events during a particular stage of history and must be understood first within that context. Nevertheless it deals with the timeless problems common to every age and associated with all human existence within history —the tension of good and evil, the pressure to conform to the spirit of the age, the need to look beyond the present life in determining what stand we will take. The Revelation thus is a statement about the present rather than a forecast of future events in a rigidly historical sense.

In spite of its often blood-curdling imagery, which may strike some readers as downright un-Christian, the Revelation's response to these problems is unquestionably steeped in the teaching of Christ. The sensational imagery serves a serious purpose, in that it highlights the enormity and deforming power of sin. Furthermore, it should be noted that the sufferings described are symbolic of the misfortunes caused by human sinfulness, which involves a violation of our relationship with God as well as with our fellow man. As symbolic, they should not be taken literally as divinely inflicted. God acts in history, but we are not privy to the mystery of His actions. As part of the mystery of free will and evil, God permits us to taste the consequences of our own actions, but in the hope that it will lead us to repentance. True, the wicked will receive their deserts, but the only victory John holds out for the saints on earth is the victory of Christ's cross.

A. PROLOGUE AND GREETING TO THE CHURCHES

1 •The revelation of Jesus Christ, which God gave him to show his servants what must soon take place, and which he made known by sending his angel to his servant John, •who bore witness to the word of God and to the testimony of Jesus Christ —to everything he saw. •Blessed be whoever reads this revelation and those who listen to the words of this prophecy, and blessed be those who heed what's written in it, for the appointed time is near.

•John to the seven churches in Asia: grace be to you and peace from the One Who is, Who was, and Who is to come, from the seven spirits before His throne •and from Jesus Christ the faithful witness —the firstborn of the dead and the ruler of the kings of the earth.

To the one who loves us and freed us from our sins by his blood — •who made us a Kingdom, priests to his God and Father —to him be glory and power forever, amen!

•[a] **Behold, he's coming on the clouds!**
Every eye **will see** him,
including those who **pierced** him;
All the tribes of the earth will mourn him.

Yes! Amen!

•"I am the Alpha and the Omega," says the Lord God, Who is, Who was, and Who is to come —the Almighty.

---

[a] *Mt 24:30; Mk 13;26; Lk 21:27; 1 Th 4;17; Jn 19:34, 37.*

1:3 The Greek indicates that John expects that the Revelation will be read aloud, probably in church.

1:4 Seven is the number which symbolizes fullness and completion, and figures prominently throughout the Revelation. Here the number seven serves to indicate that the Revelation is addressed, at least in intent, to the whole Church, although formally it is addressed only to the seven churches listed.

1:7 Dn 7:13; Zc 12:10.

1:8 Alpha and Omega are the first and last letters of the Greek alphabet. "The Almighty" translates the Greek "Pantokrator," lit. "ruler of all." In the Septuagint "Pantokrator" was used to translate the Hebrew "Lord of hosts."

B. JOHN IS COMMISSIONED BY JESUS

•I, John, your brother and partner in the suffering, the Kingdom, and 9 the steadfast endurance which we have in Jesus, found myself on the island called Patmos for proclaiming the word of God and for witnessing to Jesus. •I was in the spirit on the Lord's day when I heard a loud 10 voice like a trumpet behind me •saying, "Write what you see in a scroll 11 and send it to the seven churches: to Ephesus, Smyrna, Pergamum, Thyatira, Sardis, Philadelphia, and to Laodicea."

•I turned to see whose voice was speaking to me and when I turned 12 I saw seven gold lampstands, •and among the lampstands I saw **one like** 13 **a son of man, dressed in a long robe with a gold** girdle around his breast. •**The hair of his head was as white as snow** white **wool** 14 **and his eyes were like** flames **of fire.** •**His feet were like polished** 15 **brass** that's been refined in a furnace **and his voice was like the roar of rushing waters.** •In his right hand he had seven stars and from 16 his mouth came a sharp, double-edged sword, and his face shone like the sun at its brightest.

•When I saw him I fell at his feet as if I were dead, but he put his right 17 hand upon me and said, "Don't be afraid! I am the first and the last, •I am he who lives. I was dead, but now I live forever and ever, and I 18 hold the keys of Death and Death's realm. •So write down what you 19 have seen —what is, and what will take place hereafter. •This is the se- 20 cret meaning of the seven stars you saw in my right hand, and of the seven gold lampstands: the seven stars are the angels of the seven churches and the seven lampstands are the seven churches."

C. THE SEVEN LETTERS TO THE CHURCHES OF ASIA

2 •"To the angel of the church in Ephesus, write: 'So says the one 1 who holds the stars in his right hand, who walks among the sev-

---

1:9 "In the spirit," i.e., in a trance. Patmos is an island off the coast of Asia Minor to which John was banished by a Roman provincial governor.
1:12-13 As we learn at 1:20, the seven lampstands represent the seven churches, the seven stars their angels. The lampstands are probably the menorahs which stood in the Temple in Jerusalem. Thus, the setting is the heavenly Temple, where Jesus moves among the seven lamps, symbolically demonstrating his continu-ing presence with and concern for the churches. As for the angels, these are analogous to the angels who were thought to be responsible for nations — the "powers" which frequently mentioned in the Pauline letters. Jesus' garb may mirror that of the high priest.
1:13 Dn 10:5.
1:14 Dn 7:9.
1:14-15 Dn 10:6.
1:15 Ezk 1:24; 43:2.

Ephesus. Ruins of the temple of Artemis.

2 en gold lampstands: •I know what your works are, how you've toiled and persevered, and I know you can't abide evil men. You've tested those who call themselves apostles but aren't, and you've found them to be 3 false. •You're steadfast — you've suffered for the sake of my name and 4 haven't grown weary. •But I have this against you — you've lost your 5 first love. •So think of where you've fallen from; repent and do the works you did before. If you don't, I'll come to you and move your lampstand 6 from its place. •But you have this in your favor — you hate the works 7 of the Nicolaitans, which I hate too. •Whoever has ears, let them hear what the Spirit says to the churches! Whoever is victorious, I'll allow him to eat from the tree of life in God's Paradise.'"

8 •"To the angel of the church in Smyrna, write, 'So says the one who 9 is first and last, who was dead and came to life. •I know of your suffering and your poverty, but you're rich! I also know how you're slandered by those who claim to be Jews but aren't, who instead belong to Satan's 10 synagogue. •Don't fear what you're about to suffer. Behold, the Devil is going to throw some of you into prison in order to test you, and you'll suffer for ten days. Be faithful unto death, and I'll give you the crown of

2:6 Little is known about the Nicolaitans. They figure more prominently in the letters to Pergamum and Thyatira.

2:10 The period of "ten days" signifies that the sufferings Christians will undergo will be of limited duration.

life. •Whoever has ears, let them hear what the Spirit says to the church- 11
es! Whoever is victorious will not be harmed by the second death.'"

•"And to the angel of the church in Pergamum, write, 'So says the 12
one who has the sharp, double-edged sword, •I know where you dwell 13
— where Satan's throne is! — yet you hold fast to my name and didn't
renounce your faith in me even in the days of Antipas, my faithful witness who was killed there, where Satan dwells. •But I have a few things 14
against you — you have some there who hold to the teaching of Balaam,
who taught Balak to entice the sons of Israel to sin, to eat meat that had
been offered to idols and to commit fornication. •Likewise you also have 15
among you some who follow the teaching of the Nicolaitans. •So repent! 16
If you don't I'll come quickly to you and make war against them with the
sword of my mouth. •[b] Whoever has ears, let them hear what the Spir- 17
it says to the churches! To whoever is victorious I'll give some of the hidden manna, and I'll also give them a white stone with a new name written on it, which no one will know except the one who receives it.'"

•"And to the angel of the church in Thyatira, write, 'So says the Son 18
of God, whose eyes are like flames of fire and whose feet are like polished brass. •I know what your works are, and I know about your love, 19
your faith, your service and your steadfastness, and your recent works
are better than what you did earlier. •But I have this against you — you 20
tolerate that woman Jezebel, who claims to be a prophetess. She teaches and misleads my servants, so that they commit fornication and eat
meat that has been sacrificed to idols. •I gave her time to repent, but 21
she won't repent of her fornication. •Behold, I'll throw her onto a 22
sickbed, and if they don't repent of her works those who commit adultery with her will suffer terribly. •I'll kill her children with plague and let 23
the churches know that I am the one who can see into minds and hearts,
and I'll deal with each of you according to your works. •But to the rest 24

[b] Jn 6:48-50.

2:11 "The second death;" i.e., spiritual death.
2:13 "Where Satan's throne is!" Pergamum was the first city to have a temple dedicated to the Emperor.
2:14 Nb 22-24. The word "fornication" is used here in its common metaphorical sense of being unfaithful to God. John is condemning a lax atti-tude toward the pagan society which surrounded the early Christians, a problem Paul also had to address in his Corinthian correspondence.
2:17 Is 62:2. In the ancient world "a white stone" was commonly used as an admission to-ken to banquets. The reference to "manna" in-dicates that those who refuse to attend pagan ritual banquets will gain admission to the heav-enly banquet. The new name, of course, is that of Jesus.
2:20 1 K 16:31; 2 K 9:22, 30. The teaching of the prophetess appears to have been the same as that of the Nicolaitans at Pergamum: she pro-moted what John regarded as a compromising at-titude toward the surrounding paganism.
2:24 "The deep secrets of Satan." It is unclear whether John is speaking ironically or sarcasti-cally or whether this was truly a phrase used by the followers of the prophetess.

of you in Thyatira I say, those of you who don't accept that teaching —
who haven't learned what they call "the deep secrets of Satan" — I won't
25 put any other burden on you. •Hold firmly to what you have until I come,
26 •and whoever is victorious and follows my ways till the end,

To him I'll give authority over **the nations,**
27 •And **he'll rule them with an iron rod,**
    shattering them like clay pots,

28 •just as I've received such authority from my Father, and I'll give him
29 the morning star. •Whoever has ears, let them hear what the Spirit says
to the churches!'"

1 3 •"And to the angel of the church in Sardis, write, 'So says the one
who has the seven spirits of God and the seven stars, I know what
your works are and I know that you're considered to be alive, but you're
2 dead. •Wake up! and strengthen what remains to you but is on the verge
of dying, for I haven't found your works brought to completion in God's
3 eyes. •[c] So remember what it was that you heard and received; hold fast
to it and repent. If you don't wake up I'll come like a thief, and you won't
4 know at what hour I'll come upon you. •But there are a few of you in
Sardis who haven't soiled your garments; they will walk with me all
5 dressed in white because they're worthy. •[d] Whoever is victorious will
be clothed like that in white robes and their names will not be blotted
out of the Book of Life. I'll vouch for them before my Father and be-
6 fore His angels. •Whoever has ears, let them hear what the Spirit says
to the churches!'"

7 •"And to the angel of the church in Philadelphia write, 'So says the
one who is holy and true,

Who holds **the key of David,**
Who opens and no one can close,
    and closes and no one can open,

8 •I know what your works are. Behold, I've set before you an open door
which no one can close. I know that your power isn't great, yet you've
9 kept my word and haven't denied my name. •Behold I'll make those from
the synagogue of Satan — who call themselves Jews but aren't, who are
lying — behold I'll make them come and kneel at your feet, and they'll

[c] Mt 24:43-44; Lk 12:39-40.   [d] Mt 10:32; Lk 12:8.

2:26-27 Ps 2:8-9 (Septuagint).   3:8 "An open door" was a metaphor for an op-
3:7 Is 22:22.   portunity to proclaim the good news.

know that I love you. •Because you heeded my call to be steadfast, I'll 10 protect you in the time of trial which is going to come upon the whole world to test those who dwell upon the earth. •I'm coming soon! Hold 11 on to what you have so that no one will take your crown. •Whoever is 12 victorious, I'll make him a pillar in the Temple of my God and he'll never leave the sanctuary. On him I'll write the name of my God and the name of the city of my God —the new Jerusalem which will descend out of Heaven from my God — as well as my new name. •Whoever has ears, 13 let them hear what the Spirit says to the churches.'"

•"And to the angel of the church in Laodicea, write, 'So says the 14 Amen, the witness faithful and true, the source of God's creation, •I know 15 what your works are and I know that you're neither hot nor cold. Would that you *were* either hot or cold! •And so, because you're lukewarm and 16 are neither hot nor cold, I'll vomit you out of my mouth! •For you say, 17 "I'm rich, and have become wealthy; I need nothing," not realizing that you're wretched —miserable and poor, blind and naked. •I advise you 18 to buy from me gold that's been refined in fire so you'll be rich, and white robes, so you can dress and not reveal the shame of your nakedness. Buy eye salve to rub into your eyes so you'll be able to see. •Whoever 19 I love I rebuke and discipline, so be zealous and repent. •Behold, I'm 20 standing at the door and knocking. If anyone hears my voice and opens the door I'll come in to him and eat with him, and he with me. •Who- 21 ever is victorious I'll allow to sit with me on my throne, just as I was victorious and sat down with my Father on His throne. •Whoever has ears, 22 let them hear what the Spirit says to the churches!'"

D. THE SEVEN SEALS

The vision of God and the Lamb in Heaven

4 •After this I looked, and behold there was an open door in Heaven, 1 and the first voice that I'd heard speaking to me like a trumpet said, "Come up here and I'll show you what must happen after this." •At once 2 I found myself in the spirit, and behold there was a throne there in Heaven and there was Someone seated on the throne. •The One seated on 3 the throne appeared like jasper or carnelian, and all around the throne

3:20 Once more we encounter the image of the messianic banquet as a symbol of Heaven.
4:1-11 All the following details are intended to express the majesty of God.

4:2-3 Ezk 1:26-28. The rainbow is a sign of God's mercy and His promise to Noah that He would never again destroy the human race.

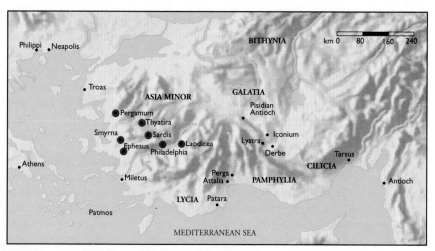

The Seven Churches of the Apocalypse. (Rv 2:1-3:22)

4 was a rainbow that was like emerald in appearance. •Surrounding the throne were twenty-four thrones, and on them sat elders who were
5 dressed in white robes with gold crowns on their heads. •From the throne came thunder, lightning, and voices. Before the throne burned seven
6 torches of fire, which are the seven spirits of God, •and before the throne was like a sea of glass, like crystal.

In the middle, around the throne, were four living creatures which were
7 covered with eyes, front and back. •**The first** living creature was like **a lion, the second** living creature was like **a young bull, the third** living creature had **a human face,** and **the fourth** living creature was
8 like **an eagle** in flight. •**Each one** of the four living creatures had **six wings apiece,** and they were covered with eyes inside and out. Night and day they never ceased to say,

> **"Holy, holy, holy,**
> **is the Lord God, the Almighty,**
> Who was, Who is, and Who is to come."

9 •And when the living creatures give glory, honor, and thanks to the One seated on the throne — the One Who lives forever and ever —

4:4 While it is not possible to be certain of the identity of the twenty-four elders, they serve to highlight the glory of God as He sits in state in His heavenly court.

4:6-7 Ezk 1:5-10. The sea is a symbol of cosmic chaos and evil, as will become apparent later.
4:8 Ezk 1:8; Is 6:2-3.

•the twenty-four elders fall down before the One seated on the throne 10 and worship the One Who lives forever and ever, and they throw their crowns before the throne, saying,

> •"Worthy are You, our Lord and God, 11
> to receive glory, honor, and power,
> Because You created all things,
> and through Your will they exist and were
> created!"

5 •In the right hand of the One seated on the throne I saw a scroll that 1 was covered with writing both inside and out and was sealed with seven seals. •Then I saw a mighty angel proclaim in a loud voice, "Who 2 is worthy to open the scroll and break its seals?" •And there was no one 3 in the heavens, on the earth, or below the earth who was able to open the scroll or look at it. •I wept and cried because no one was found wor- 4 thy to open the scroll or look at it. •Then one of the elders said to me, 5 "Don't weep! Behold, the Lion of the tribe of Judah, the Root of David, has been victorious — he can open the scroll and its seven seals."

•Then I saw a Lamb amid the throne, the four living creatures, and 6 the elders. It was standing as if it had been slain and had seven horns and seven eyes, which are the seven spirits of God sent to the whole earth. •The Lamb came and took the scroll from the right hand of the 7 One seated on the throne, •and when he took the scroll the four living 8 creatures and the twenty-four elders fell down before the Lamb, each holding a harp and a gold bowl full of incense, which are the prayers of the saints. •They sang a new song and said, 9

> "Worthy are you to take the scroll
> and to open its seals,
> Because you were slain and by your blood
> redeemed for God
> a multitude from every tribe and tongue,
> every people and nation,
> •You have made them a Kingdom, priests for our God, 10
> and they shall rule over the earth."

•Then I looked, and I heard the voice of many angels around the 11 throne, the living creatures, and the elders — the angels numbered in

5:1 Scholars generally agree that the scroll con- tains the details of God's redemptive plan, the des- tiny of the world.

5:6 Paradoxically, the Lion, symbol of strength, is shown to be the Lamb who was slain. Horns and eyes were traditional symbols of power and wisdom.

12 the thousands and tens of thousands, •and cried out in a loud voice,

> "Worthy is the Lamb who was slain to receive
> power, wealth, wisdom, and might,
> honor, glory, and blessing!"

13 •And I heard every creature in the heavens, on the earth, below the earth, and on the sea, saying,

> "To the One seated on the throne and to the Lamb
> Be blessing, honor, glory, and power,
> For ever and ever!"

14 •Then the four living creatures said, "Amen!" and the elders fell down and worshipped.

The first six seals are opened

1 6 •Then I watched while the Lamb opened the first of the seven seals, and I heard the first of the four living creatures say in a voice like 2 thunder, "Come!" •I looked, and behold a white horse, and the rider seated upon it had a bow. A crown had been given to him and he went out, a conqueror going forth to win victory.

3 •When he opened the second seal I heard the second living creature 4 say, "Come!" •Out came another horse, as red as fire, and the rider seated upon it had the power to take peace from the earth so that people would slay one another, and he had been given a great sword.

5 •When he opened the third seal I heard the third living creature say, "Come!" I looked, and behold a black horse, and the rider seated upon 6 it had a scale in his hand. •Then I heard something like a voice among the four living creatures saying, "A quart of wheat or three quarts of barley for a day's wages, but don't harm the olive oil and wine!"

7 •When he opened the fourth seal I heard the voice of the fourth liv- 8 ing creature say, "Come!" •I looked, and behold a pale horse, and the rider seated upon it, his name was Death, and Death's realm went with him. They were given power over one fourth of the earth, to kill with

---

6:1-8 The first four riders symbolize evils which God will permit to come upon the earth for the purpose of bringing the human race to repentance.

6:2 The rider armed with a bow is patterned after the Parthians, who were a powerful threat to the Romans in their eastern territories during the first century, a threat that was welcomed by some of the disaffected local populations.

6:5 The black horse symbolizes famine, portrayed by the exorbitant prices for basic foodstuffs.

6:8 "A pale horse." Lit., "pale green," the color of decay and death.

sword and famine, with disease and the wild beasts of the earth.

•When he opened the fifth seal I saw under the altar the souls of those 9 who had been slain for the word of God and because of the witness they had given. •They cried out in a loud voice and said, "How long, 10 O Lord, holy and true, before You judge the inhabitants of the earth and avenge our blood?" •Then they were each given a long white robe 11 and were told to rest a little longer, until the number of their fellow servants and brothers was fulfilled — those who were to be killed just as they had been.

•e When he opened the sixth seal I looked and there was a powerful 12 earthquake. The sun turned as black as coarse sackcloth and the whole moon became like blood, •the stars of the sky fell to the earth the way 13 a fig tree drops its fruit in summer when it's shaken by the wind •and the 14 sky disappeared like a scroll being rolled up. Every mountain and island was moved from its place. •Then the kings of the earth, the nobles, the 15 tribunes, the wealthy, the powerful, and every slave and free man hid themselves in caves and among the rocks on the mountains. •f **And they** 16 **said to the mountains and the rocks, "Fall on us** and **hide us** from the face of the One seated on the throne, and from the wrath of the Lamb, •because the great day of their wrath has come and who can re- 17 sist it?"

Interlude: those who came through the persecution are sealed

7 •After this I saw four angels standing at the four corners of the earth, 1 restraining the four winds so that no wind blew on either land or sea or against any tree. •Then I saw another angel coming up from the ris- 2 ing of the sun, holding the seal of the living God. He cried out in a loud voice to the four angels who had been given power to harm the earth and the sea •and said, "Don't harm the earth, the sea, or the trees un- 3 til we seal the servants of our God on their foreheads!" •Then I heard 4 the number of those who had been sealed — one hundred and forty-four thousand sealed from the tribes of the sons of Israel.

---

e Mt 24:29; Mk 13:24-25; Lk 21:25.   f Lk 23:30.

6:11 White robes were a common symbol in Jewish apocalyptic writings, signifying victory and purity.
6:12-17 In this passage the wrath of God and (paradoxically) of the Lamb, epitomized by the cosmic earthquake, is seen striking terror into all levels of society.

6:16 Ho 10:8.
7:4ff The 144,000 from the twelve tribes of Israel are to be taken as symbolic of the fullness of the human race, and not of Jews alone. Cf. 7:9, 13-14 and 14:1.

5 •From the tribe of Judah, twelve thousand sealed,
from the tribe of Reuben twelve thousand,
from the tribe of Gad twelve thousand,
6 •from the tribe of Asher twelve thousand,
from the tribe of Naphtali twelve thousand,
from the tribe of Manasseh twelve thousand,
7 •from the tribe of Simeon twelve thousand,
from the tribe of Levi twelve thousand,
from the tribe of Issachar twelve thousand,
8 •from the tribe of Zebulon twelve thousand,
from the tribe of Joseph twelve thousand,
from the tribe of Benjamin twelve thousand sealed.

The sheep are led to pasture. (Rv 7:17) Roman lamp (1st century A.D.).

•After this I looked, and behold a vast crowd which no one could ₉
ever count from every nation, tribe, people, and tongue, standing before the throne and the Lamb and dressed in long white robes with
palm branches in their hands. •They were crying out in a loud voice ₁₀
and saying,

> "Victory to our God Who is seated
>   upon the throne,
> and to the Lamb!"

•Then all the angels stood around the throne, the elders, and the living ₁₁
creatures. They fell on their faces before the throne and worshipped God,
•saying, ₁₂

> "Amen! Blessing, glory, wisdom, thanks, honor,
>   power, and might
> be to our God forever and ever, amen!"

•Then one of the elders spoke and said to me, "Who are the people ₁₃
dressed in long white robes, and where have they come from?" •I said ₁₄
to him, "My lord, you're the one who knows!" Then he said to me,
"These are the ones who came through the terrible persecution. They
washed their robes and made them white in the blood of the Lamb.

> •Therefore they stand before God's throne ₁₅
>   serving Him day and night in His sanctuary,
>   and the One seated on the throne will
>   shelter them.
> •**No longer will they hunger or thirst,** ₁₆
>   **nor will the sun strike them**
>   **nor the scorching heat,**
> •For the Lamb in the center of the throne will ₁₇
>   **shepherd them**
> **and guide them to springs of living water,**
> **and God will wipe every tear** from their eyes."

7:13-14 Those in the long white robes are car-   7:16 Is 49:10.
rying palm branches, symbolic of victory and re-   7:17 Ps 23:1-2; Is 25:8.
joicing, and have washed their robes, rendering
them pure. Cf. 6:11.

E. THE SEVEN TRUMPETS

The seventh seal opens the way for the trumpets

1 8•When the Lamb opened the seventh seal there was silence in Heav-
2 en for about a half an hour. •Then I saw the seven angels who stand
before God, and seven trumpets had been given to them.

3 •Another angel came and stood at the altar holding a gold censer, and
he was given a large amount of incense so he could add it to the prayers
4 of all the saints at the gold altar before the throne. •And the smoke of
the incense went up with the prayers of the saints from the hand of the
5 angel who stood before God. •Then the angel took the censer, filled it
from the fire at the altar, and threw it onto the earth, and there was thunder and lightning, voices crying out, and an earthquake.

6 •Then the seven angels who held the seven trumpets prepared to
sound them.

The first six trumpets

7 •The first angel blew his trumpet, and hail and fire mixed with blood
fell upon the earth and consumed a third of the earth, a third of the trees,
and all the green grass.

8 •Then the second angel blew his trumpet, and something like a huge
mountain blazing with fire was thrown into the sea. A third of the sea
9 was turned to blood, •a third of the creatures living in the sea died, and
a third of the ships were destroyed.

10 •The third angel blew his trumpet, and a huge star fell from the sky,
blazing like a torch, and it fell on a third of the rivers and springs of wa-
11 ter. •The name of the star was Wormwood, and a third of the water was
turned to wormwood. Many people died from the water, because it had
been made bitter.

12 •Then the fourth angel blew his trumpet. A third of the sun was strick-
en, a third of the moon, and a third of the stars, so that they lost a third
of their light. A third of the day was darkened, and likewise a third of
the night.

8:6-12 Like the plagues that fell upon Egypt at the time of the Exodus (which they resemble), these misfortunes are limited in extent and are intended to lead men to repentance. This imagery is part of the symbolism by which John portrays the Church as the New Israel and our redemption as the New Exodus (a favorite theme of Paul, as well).

•Then I looked, and I heard an eagle cry out with a loud voice as it 13 flew in midair, "Woe, woe, woe, to the inhabitants of the earth from the rest of the trumpet blasts the three angels are about to blow!"

9 •Then the fifth angel blew his trumpet, and I saw a star that had fall- 1 en from Heaven to earth, and he was given the key to the pit of the abyss. •Then he opened the pit of the abyss and smoke came up from 2 the pit as if it were coming from a huge furnace, and the sun and air were darkened by the smoke from the pit. •Then from the smoke lo- 3 custs went out over the earth and they were given the type of authori- ty that scorpions have on earth. •They were told not to harm the grass, 4 the trees, or any green plant —only the people who didn't have the seal of God on their foreheads. •They weren't given authority to kill them, 5 but they were allowed to torment them for five months, and their tor- ment was like that of a scorpion when it stings someone. •In those days 6 men will seek death but won't find it, they'll long to die but death will flee from them.•In appearance the locusts resembled horses made ready 7 for battle, and on their heads were things like gold crowns. Their faces were like men's faces, •their hair was like women's hair, and their teeth 8 were like lions' teeth. •They had chests like iron breastplates, and the 9 sound of their wings was like the sound of many horse-drawn chariots rushing into battle. •They had tails with stings, like scorpions, and it was 10 with their tails that they had power to harm people for five months. •The 11 king they have ruling over them is the angel from the abyss who in He- brew is named Abaddon, and in Greek Apollyon ("the Destroyer").

•The first woe is over; behold, there are still two woes to come after 12 this one.

•Then the sixth angel blew his trumpet, and from the four horns of 13 the gold altar standing before God I heard a voice •telling the sixth an- 14 gel, who was holding the trumpet, "Release the four angels who are bound at the great river Euphrates!" •The four angels were released, hav- 15 ing been prepared for this hour, day, month, and year, to kill a third of mankind. •The number of the horsemen was double ten thousand times 16

9:1 "A star," i.e., an angel. "The abyss" repre- sents those elements of creation which oppose God's will, humans included. Note that the locusts which issue from the abyss have human features and attack only humans, not grass, trees, or plants.
9:13 The horns are on the four corners of the al- tar (cf. Ex 27:2).

9:13-19 The demonic horde of horsemen from beyond the Euphrates are modeled after the Parthians, whose cavalry had twice inflicted crushing defeats on Roman armies prior to the time the Revelation was written. As with the ear- lier plagues, their powers are limited (9:18), nor did their depredations lead people to repent.

Horse and rider; Roman bronze statue. (Rv 9:17)

17 ten thousand, and I heard their number. •This is how the horses and their riders looked to me in my vision —they had breastplates that were fiery red, deep hyacinth blue, and sulfur yellow. The horses' heads were
18 like lions' heads and from their mouths came fire, smoke, and sulfur. •A third of mankind was killed by these three plagues, by the fire, smoke,
19 and sulfur coming from their mouths. •The power of the horses is in their mouths and in their tails, for their tails are like snakes with heads, and with them they inflict harm.
20 •The rest of the people who hadn't been killed by these plagues didn't turn away from what they'd made with their own hands, they didn't stop worshipping demons and **idols of gold, silver, bronze, stone, and wood, which** can **neither see, nor hear, nor walk.**
21 •Nor did the people repent of their murders, their sorcery, their fornication, or their thievery.

9:20 Ps 135:15-17.
9:21 The Greek word for "sorcery" is *pharmakeia*. The first century sorcerer's stock in trade included a variety of drugs for different purposes. It is believed that some of these concoctions purported to be abortifacient and contraceptive.

Interlude:
The little scroll and the two witnesses

10 •Then I saw another mighty angel coming down from Heaven, wrapped in a cloud with the rainbow over his head. His face was like the sun and his legs were like pillars of fire, •and in his hand a little scroll was opened. He set his right foot on the sea and his left foot on the land •and shouted in a loud voice like a lion roaring, and when he shouted the seven thunders spoke with their voices. •When the seven thunders had spoken I was going to write it all down, but I heard a voice from Heaven say, "Seal up what the seven thunders said, and don't write it down!" •Then the angel I saw standing on the land and the sea

> **Raised his right hand to Heaven**
>   **•and swore by the One Who lives forever** and
>   ever —

by the One Who created the heavens and what's in it, the earth and what's in it, and the sea and what's in it — "there shall be no more delay! •On the day the seventh angel blows the trumpet blast he is to sound, the mystery of God which He proclaimed to His servants the prophets will be fulfilled."

•Then the voice I heard coming from Heaven spoke to me again and said, "Go take the scroll that lies open in the hand of the angel standing on the sea and the land." •So I went up to the angel and told him to give me the little scroll, and he said to me, "Take it and eat it. It will turn your stomach sour, but in your mouth it will be as sweet as honey." •So I took the little scroll from the angel's hand and ate it. In my mouth it was as sweet as honey, but when I'd eaten it it turned my stomach sour. •Then they said to me, "You must once again prophesy about many peoples, nations, tongues, and kings!"

10:1 "Another mighty angel." The first mighty angel appeared at 5:2. This angel is clearly a delegate of God, for his appearance has characteristics of divine manifestations: the cloud, the rainbow, the pillars of fire. These are also reminiscent of the Exodus.
10:5-11 Dn 12:7. There has been delay: the seven seals have been opened, six trumpets have sounded, but mankind has not repented. But now there is to be no more delay; the mystery of God announced through the prophets will be fulfilled. This fulfillment is to be announced through prophecy; the message will be sweet, but at the same time will be bitter for the prophets (cf. 11:7-10).

11 ¹ •I was given a stick like a measuring rod and told, "Get up and measure the Temple of God and the altar, and count the peo-
² ple who are worshipping in the Temple. •ᵍ Leave out the outer court of the Temple, don't measure it, for it's been given to the Gentiles.
³ They'll trample the holy city for forty-two months. •I'll give my two witnesses authority and they'll prophesy for one thousand two hun-
⁴ dred and sixty days, dressed in sackcloth." •The two witnesses are the two olive trees and the two lamps standing before the Lord of the earth.
⁵ •If anyone tries to harm them fire will come from their mouths to de-vour their enemies —if anyone tries to harm them this is how they'll
⁶ be killed. •They have authority to shut up the sky so that no rain will fall during the time they prophesy, and they have authority to turn the water on earth into blood and to strike the earth with every kind of
⁷ plague as often as they want. •When their witness comes to an end the beast that comes up from the abyss will make war against them,
⁸ conquer them, and kill them. •Their corpses will lie in the street of the great city which is symbolically called Sodom and Egypt, where their
⁹ Lord was also crucified. •For three and a half days the peoples and tribes and languages and nations will look at their corpses and won't
¹⁰ allow them to be laid in a tomb. •The inhabitants of the earth will re-joice over them, they'll cheer and exchange gifts, because the two
¹¹ prophets had tormented the inhabitants of the earth. •But after three and a half days the breath of life entered them from God and the prophets rose to their feet, and those who had been watching them
¹² were overcome with fear. •Then they heard a loud voice from Heav-en telling them, "Come up here!" So they went up to Heaven in a
¹³ cloud while their enemies watched them. •At that very hour there was a powerful earthquake and a tenth of the city fell. Seven thousand peo-ple were killed in the earthquake and the rest became frightened and gave glory to the God of Heaven.
¹⁴ •The second woe has passed. Behold, the third woe will come soon.

ᵍ Lk 21:24.

11:1-2 Ezk 40:3; Zc 2:1-2. Many scholars believe that the Temple stands for the faithful within the Church, but opinion is divided regarding the significance of the outer court and the rest of the holy city. Some would argue that the outer court represents Christians who have been unfaithful, while others believe that it is a symbol for pagans who persecuted Christians.
11:4 Zc 4:3, 11-14. The "two witnesses" who "are the two olive branches and the two lamps" are to be identified with Christian prophets and witnesses in general; a portion of the Church as a whole rather than with any particular historical figures.
11:13 Hope seems at times to be out of place in the Revelation, but this is a misconception. Here, nine-tenths of the people repent. Following this overwhelming repentance the Lord is enthroned in Heaven (11:15).

The seventh trumpet

•Then the seventh angel blew his trumpet, and loud voices in Heav- 15
en could be heard saying,

> "The kingdom of the world has passed to
>   our Lord, and to His Messiah;
> He shall reign for ever and ever."

•Then the twenty-four elders who sit on their thrones before God fell 16
on their faces and worshipped God, •saying   17

> "We thank you Lord, God Almighty,
>   Who is and Who was,
> Because You have assumed Your great power
>   and begun Your reign,
> •The nations raged,   18
>   but Your wrath has come,
>   the time for the dead to be judged,
> The time for Your servants the prophets to be
>   rewarded,
>   the saints and those who fear Your name,
>   the great and the small,
> The time to destroy those who destroy the earth!"

•Then God's Temple in Heaven was opened and the ark of His covenant 19
was seen in His Temple. Lightning bolts flashed, thunder sounded, and
there was an earthquake and heavy hail.

F. SEVEN VISIONS

12 •Then a great sign was seen in the sky —a woman clothed with 1
the sun, with the moon beneath her feet and a crown of twelve
stars on her head. •She was pregnant and was crying out in the pangs 2
of childbirth. •And another sign was seen in the sky — a huge red drag- 3
on with seven heads and ten horns, and on its heads were seven diadems.
•Its tail swept a third of the stars from the sky and threw them down to 4
the earth. The dragon positioned itself before the woman so that it could

---

12:1ff The child is Jesus, the woman represents
the People of God, the messianic community. As
Giblin notes, the identification of the woman as
Mary, while not the literal meaning of the text, is
a legitimate "application" of it.

Jerusalem in a mosaic at Madaba, Jordan (6th century A.D.). (Rv 11:2)

5 devour her child as soon as she gave birth. •She gave birth to a son, a male child who will **rule** all **the nations with an iron rod,** but the 6 child was snatched up to God and His throne. •Then the woman fled into the desert where God had prepared a place for her where she could be cared for for one thousand two hundred and sixty days.

7 •[h] Then war broke out in Heaven. Michael and his angels fought against 8 the dragon. The dragon and his angels fought back •but they were de-9 feated and no longer had a place in Heaven. •[i] Then the huge dragon — the ancient serpent who is called the Devil and Satan, who deceived the whole world — was thrown down to earth and his angels were thrown 10 down with him, •and I heard a loud voice in Heaven saying,

> "Now salvation and power have come,
>   the Kingdom of our God
>   and the authority of His Messiah,

[h] *Jude 9.*   [i] *Lk 10:18.*

12:5 Ps 2:9.
12:7-12 Victory in Heaven is paralleled by victory on earth through the blood of the Lamb, the triumph of the cross.

For the accuser of our brothers has been thrown down,
who accused them night and day before our God.
•They conquered him through the blood of the Lamb   11
and through the word of their testimony,
Love of life did not cause them to shrink from death.
•So rejoice, you heavens,   12
and you who dwell in them!
But woe to the earth and the sea,
because the Devil has come to you,
greatly enraged
because he knows his time is short."

•When the dragon saw that he'd been thrown down to earth he 13 began to pursue the woman who had given birth to the male child, •but the woman was given the two wings of a huge eagle so she could 14 fly into the desert to the place where she was to be hidden from the serpent and cared for there for three and a half years. •Then the ser- 15 pent spewed water from his mouth like a river in order to sweep her away in a flood, •but the earth helped the woman —it opened its 16 mouth and drank in the river the dragon had spewed from its mouth. •The dragon was enraged with the woman and went off to wage war 17 against the rest of her offspring —those who keep God's command-ments and accept the testimony of Jesus. •And he stood on the sands 18 of the sea.

13 •Then I saw a beast rising out of the sea, with ten horns and sev- 1 en heads. On its horns were ten diadems and on its heads were blasphemous names. •The beast I saw was like a leopard, but its feet 2 were like a bear's and its mouth was like a lion's mouth. The dragon gave the beast his own power, his throne, and his great authority. •One 3 of the beast's heads looked like it had a fatal wound, but its fatal wound had healed. The whole world was amazed by the beast and followed it. •They worshipped the dragon because it had given the beast its own au- 4 thority, and they worshipped the beast, saying, "Who can compare with the beast, and who can fight with it?"

12:13-17 Satan's defeat has not extinguished his hatred. Following Jesus' triumph Satan pursues the Church.
13:1-7 Dn 7:3-8, 21. Most scholars identify the beast from the sea with the Roman Empire and the seven heads bearing blasphemous names with the Roman Emperors, who claimed divinity. The wounded head is generally believed to rep-resent Nero. Perhaps because the people were in awe of his sheer evil, it was widely believed that Nero would be reincarnated.

5 •Then the beast was allowed to utter boasts and blasphemies and was
6 given authority for forty-two months. •It opened its mouth to blaspheme
God, blaspheming His name and His dwelling as well as those who dwell
7 in Heaven. •And the beast was allowed to make war on the saints and
conquer them, and to have authority over every tribe, people, tongue,
8 and nation. •All the inhabitants of the earth will worship the beast —
that is, all those whose names weren't written before the creation of the
world in the Book of Life of the Lamb who was slain.

9 •Whoever has ears, let them hear!
10 •**If anyone is to be taken into captivity,**
into captivity he shall go.
If anyone is to be slain by the sword,
by the sword he shall be slain.

In this is the steadfastness and faith of the saints.
11 •Then I saw another beast rising up from the earth with two horns
12 like a lamb, but it spoke like a dragon. •It wielded all the authority of
the first beast in its presence, it made the earth and all its inhabitants
13 worship the first beast, whose fatal wound had healed. •And the second beast performed impressive signs, even making fire come down
14 from the heavens to earth in front of everyone. •With the signs it was
allowed to perform in the presence of the beast it deceived the inhabitants of the earth, and told the earth's inhabitants to make an im-
15 age of the beast who was wounded by the sword yet survived. •The
second beast was allowed to give life to the beast's image, so that the
beast's image could speak and have all those who wouldn't worship
16 the beast's image slain. •And he had everyone —rich and poor, slave
17 and free —marked on either their hands or their foreheads •and
wouldn't allow anyone to buy or sell unless they had the mark, either
18 the name of the beast or the number of its name. •Here wisdom is
needed —let whoever has a discerning intellect figure out the beast's
number, for it's the number of a man, and its number is six hundred
and sixty-six.

13:10 Jr 43:11.
13:11 The second beast which derived power
from the first is the governing body in the province
of Asia which was in charge of the imperial cult.
13:18 In Greek and Hebrew the letters of the al-
phabet had numerical values. While any pro-
posed solution to the number 666 is open to objections, the most widely accepted is that it represents the Greek words *Neron Kaisar* (Nero
Caesar) transliterated into Hebrew, which yields
the number 666.

14 •Then I looked, and behold I saw the Lamb standing on Mount 1 Zion, and with him was a crowd one hundred and forty-four thousand strong, each of whom had the Lamb's name and the name of the Lamb's Father written on their foreheads. •And I heard a voice from 2 Heaven like the sound of rushing waters or the sound of loud thunder, and the voice I heard was like harpers playing on their harps. •The 3 crowd was singing a new song before the throne, before the four living creatures and the elders. The only ones who were able to learn the song were the hundred and forty-four thousand who had been redeemed from the earth. •They were all virgins —men who hadn't defiled them- 4 selves with women. They follow the Lamb wherever he goes. They had been redeemed from among men as the first fruits which had been set aside for God and the Lamb, •and no lie could be found on their lips 5 —they were unblemished.

•Then I saw another angel flying in midair, preparing to proclaim the 6 good news for all time to those who live on earth, to every nation, tribe, tongue, and people, •and he cried out in a loud voice, "Fear God and give 7 glory to Him, because the hour of His judgment has come! Worship the One Who made the heavens and earth, the sea and springs of water!"

•A second angel followed, saying, "Babylon has fallen, Babylon the 8 Great! Who made all the nations drink the wine of her impure passion!"

•A third angel followed them and cried out in a loud voice, "Anyone 9 who worships the beast and its image, and accepts the beast's mark on their forehead or hand, •will also drink the wine of God's anger. It will be 10 poured full strength into the cup of His wrath, and they'll be tortured with fire and sulfur before the holy angels and the Lamb. •The smoke from 11 their torments will rise for ever and ever, there will be no relief, either by night or by day, for those who worship the beast and its image or for anyone who accepts the mark of its name." •In this is the steadfastness 12 of the saints, who keep God's commandments and faith in Jesus.

•Then I heard a voice from Heaven saying, "Write this: 'Blessed are 13 the dead who from here on die in the Lord!'" "Yes, indeed!" says the Spirit, "they'll have relief from their toil, for their works will go with them."

14:1-5 This passage builds on the theme of Israelite holy war: the chaste men were soldiers of the Lamb who maintain the ritual purity required of holy warriors. As first fruits, their lives have been offered to God as a symbol of all who are to be redeemed. Zp 3:13.

14:6 Note the universality of the proclamation of the good news.

14:8 Is 21:9. The name Babylon, with its associations with wickedness and persecution of God's people, stands for Rome, but also for all arrogant power at war with God.

14:12 In the face of all the horror and suffering in the world, the saints do not lose faith in the redemption God offers through Jesus.

The vintage. Mosaic from Israel. (Rv 14:18)

14 •Then I looked, and behold I saw a white cloud and seated on the cloud was one like a son of man. On his head he had a gold crown
15 and in his hand was a sharp sickle. •Then another angel came out of the Temple, calling in a loud voice to the one seated on the cloud, "Take your sickle and bring in the harvest, because the hour for the
16 harvest has come, and the earth's harvest is ripe." •Then the one seated on the cloud swung his sickle on the earth, and the earth was harvested.
17 •Then another angel came out of the Temple in Heaven, with a
18 sharp sickle in its hand. •And another angel came from the altar — he was in charge of the fire —and he called in a loud voice to the angel with the sharp sickle, "Take your sickle and gather the grapes from
19 the earth's vineyard, because its grapes are ripe." •So the angel swung its sickle on the earth and gathered the earth's vintage and threw it
20 into the great vat of God's anger. •The vat was trampled outside the city, and blood ran out of the vat to the height of a horse's bridle for two hundred miles.

14:14-20 Dn 7:13. The harvest was a traditional symbol for God's judgment.

G. THE SEVEN PLAGUES AND SEVEN BOWLS

15 •Then I saw another great, awe-inspiring sign in the sky: seven ₁ angels with the seven last plagues through which God's anger achieves its ultimate expression.

•Then I saw something like a sea of glass mixed with fire, and I al- ₂ so saw those who had conquered the beast. They had defeated the one whose name is a number and were standing by the glass sea, holding God's harps, •singing the song of God's servant Moses and the song ₃ of the Lamb,

> "Great and awe-inspiring are Your works,
>   Lord God Almighty!
> Just and true are Your ways,
>   King of nations!
> •Is there anyone who doesn't fear You, Lord,   ₄
>   or glorify Your name?
> Because You alone are holy;
>   all the nations will come
>   and worship before You,
> For Your righteous deeds have been revealed!"

•After this I looked, and the sanctuary of the heavenly Tent of Tes- ₅ timony was opened. •The seven angels with the seven plagues came ₆ out of the sanctuary, dressed in pure, bright linen and with a gold belt around their breasts. •Then one of the four living creatures gave the ₇ seven angels seven gold bowls full of the anger of God, who lives for- ever and ever. •The sanctuary was filled with smoke from God's glory, ₈ and no one could enter the sanctuary until the seven plagues of the sev- en angels were finished.

16 •Then I heard a loud voice from the sanctuary say to the seven ₁ angels, "Go pour the seven bowls of God's anger onto the earth!"

•The first angel went off and poured his bowl onto the earth, and ug- ₂ ly painful sores developed on those who bore the mark of the beast and had worshipped its image.

15:5ff. The Tent of Testimony was the travelling Israelite Temple, whose arrangement and cultus are described in Exodus chs. 25-31, 35-40. The imagery of this passage is drawn especially from Ex 27:3 and 38:21.

16:1ff The plagues enumerated here are clearly patterned after the plagues of Egypt described in Exodus. Rome is thus the persecutor of the New Israel, just as Egypt under Pharaoh persecuted the Israelites.

3 •The second angel poured its bowl into the sea. The sea's water turned to blood, as if it came from a corpse, and everything in the sea that had life died.

4 •The third angel poured its bowl into the rivers and springs of water,
5 and they turned to blood. •Then I heard the angel of the waters say,

> "Just are You, O holy One, Who are and Who were,
>   for having rendered this judgment —
6 •They shed the blood of the saints and prophets
>   and You've given them blood to drink.
> They deserve it!"

7 •Then I heard the altar say,

> "Yes, Lord God Almighty!
>   Your judgments are just and true."

8 •The fourth angel poured his bowl onto the sun, and it was allowed
9 to scorch men with fire. •They were scorched by the searing fire; and they blasphemed the name of God Who has power over these plagues, but they didn't repent and give Him glory.

10 •The fifth angel poured its bowl onto the beast's throne. The beast's kingdom was darkened and the people bit their tongues in their pain.
11 •They blasphemed the God of Heaven because of their pain and their sores, but they didn't repent of their deeds.

12 •The sixth angel poured its bowl into the great river Euphrates. Its water was dried up, to prepare the way for the kings from the east.
13 •Then I saw three unclean spirits like frogs come out of the mouths of
14 the dragon, the beast, and the false prophet. •They were the spirits of demons who performed signs, and they went to all the kings of the world
15 to gather them for battle with God Almighty on His great day. •[j] "Behold, I'm coming like a thief! Blessed are they who stay awake and keep their clothes at hand, so they won't have to walk around naked and let
16 others see their shame." •Then the spirits gathered them at the place called, in Hebrew, Armageddon.

17 •Then the seventh angel poured its bowl into the air, and a loud voice
18 came from the throne in the sanctuary, saying, "It is done!" •Then there were lightning bolts and thunder claps, and there was a powerful earth-

[j] Mt 24:43-44; Lk 12:39-40.

16:16 2 K 23:29. "Armageddon" means Mount Megiddo, the site of several famous battles in Israelite history. This is a symbolic location, not to be taken literally, for the crisis John sees coming involves Rome and all comparable earthly powers.

quake that was stronger than any earthquake since the time there were first men on earth. •The great city was split into three parts and the 19 cities of the Gentiles fell. And God remembered Babylon the Great, giving it the cup filled with the wine of His anger and wrath. •Then every 20 island fled and no mountains could be found. •Huge hailstones weigh- 21 ing a hundred pounds came down from the heavens on the people, and they blasphemed God for the plague of hail, because the plague was so terrible.

H. THE PUNISHMENT OF BABYLON

17 •Then one of the angels with the seven bowls came and said to 1 me, "Come, and I'll show you the punishment of the great whore who lives near many waters, •with whom the kings of the earth com- 2 mitted fornication and who made the inhabitants of the earth drunk with the wine of her fornication." •So he took me to the desert in the spir- 3 it. There I saw a woman seated on a scarlet beast, which was covered with blasphemous names and had seven heads and ten horns.•The 4 woman was dressed in purple and scarlet and was adorned with gold and precious stones and pearls. She had a gold cup in her hand full of disgusting, unclean things from her fornication. •On her forehead was 5 written a name which is a mystery, "Babylon the Great, the mother of whores and all the abominations of the earth." •Then I saw that the 6 woman was drunk with the blood of the saints and the blood of those who had borne witness to Jesus.

As I looked at her I was filled with amazement, •so the angel said to 7 me, "Why are you so surprised? I'll explain the mystery of the woman and the beast who carries her, with its seven heads and ten horns. •The 8 beast you saw was, but now is not. It's about to come up from the abyss and will go forth to its destruction. The inhabitants of the earth whose names were not written in the Book of Life from the creation of the world will be amazed when they see the beast, because it was but now is not, yet will appear. •This calls for a penetrating mind, one with wisdom. The 9 seven heads are seven hills, on which the woman is seated. There are

17:2 "Fornication" is used here in its metaphorical sense of idolatry: worship of what is not God.
17:4 Jr 51:7. Purple and scarlet were the colors of royalty.
17:9 The "seven hills" clearly set the location as Rome.
17:9-13 These references to the various kings most plausibly refer to the turmoil of the years 67-70 A.D. Many scholars argue that the Revelation is not necessarily tied to specific events and that the numbers cited are largely symbolic. John's message is that of the inevitable downfall of every power which wars against the Father and the Lamb.

10 seven kings as well — •five have fallen, one is now, the other has not
11 yet come, but when he comes he'll remain for only a little while. •The
beast that was and now is not is itself the eighth, yet is one of the sev-
12 en and will go to its destruction. •The ten horns you saw are ten kings
who have not yet reigned, but after the beast they'll receive authority as
13 kings for one hour. •The ten kings are of one mind and will give their
14 power and authority to the beast. •They'll do battle with the Lamb but
the Lamb will defeat them, because the Lord of lords is also the King of
kings and those with Him are called, chosen, and faithful."

15   •Then the angel said to me, "The waters you saw, where the whore
16 lives, are peoples and crowds and nations and tongues. •The ten horns
you saw, and the beast, they'll hate the whore and will make her naked
17 and desolate — they'll eat her flesh and burn her with fire. •For God
has led them to do His will, to be of one mind and give their kingdom
18 to the beast until God's words are fulfilled. •And the woman you saw is
the great city that rules the kings of the earth."

Bacchus; Roman bronze sculpture. (Rv 17:2)

18

•After this I saw another angel coming down from Heaven. 1
He had great authority and the earth was illuminated by his glory, •and he called out in a mighty voice, saying, 2

"Babylon has fallen, Babylon the Great!
and has become a dwelling place for demons.
It has become a haunt for unclean spirits,
for all the unclean and despicable birds,
•For from the wine of her immoral passions 3
have all the nations drunk.
The kings of the earth whored after her
and the merchants of the earth grew rich
off her unbridled luxury."

•Then I heard another voice from Heaven say, 4

"Leave her, my people, so you won't take part
in her sins
nor receive a share of her punishment
•For her sins reach as high as Heaven, 5
and God has not forgotten her iniquities.
•Repay her in kind, pay her back double for her deeds, 6
mix her a double dose in the cup she mixed.
•To the degree that she praised herself 7
and lived in luxury,
give her that much torment and grief.
For she says to herself, 'Here I sit, a queen;
I'm no widow; mourning shall never be mine!'
•Because of this her plagues will all come in a day — 8
death, sorrow, and famine —
She'll be consumed by fire,
for God Who judges her is a mighty Lord."

•The kings of the earth who shared in her luxury and fornication will 9
weep and wail over her when they see the smoke from the fire. •They'll 10
stand at a distance for fear of her torments, and say,

18:1-24 This passage reveals the true nature of
Rome's idolatry. It was not so much the worship
of dumb idols as the worship of material wealth
and comfort, arrogant self-confidence, and callous
indifference: in a word, self-worship, rather than
worship of God. John's vivid evocation of the glory that was Rome is a reminder that it is our attitude toward material goods, not the goods themselves, that is the source of sin. John focuses not
on the actual destruction of the city, which is left
to our imagination, but on the reactions of the onlookers, which reflect their spiritual state.

"Woe, woe, for the great city,
　for the mighty city of Babylon —
Your judgment came in just one hour!"

11　•The merchants of the earth will weep and mourn over her, since there
12 is no one to buy their goods — •gold, silver, precious stones, pearls, fine
linen, purple cloth, silk and scarlet cloth; all sorts of rare woods, objects
13 wrought from ivory, expensive wood, bronze, iron, and marble, •cin-
namon, spice, incense, myrrh and frankincense, wine and oil, fine flour
and wheat, cattle and sheep, horses and carriages, slaves and human
lives.

14　　•"The fruit that was the desire of your soul
　　　has left you,
　　All the fine and splendorous things
　　　have been lost to you,
　　　never to be seen again!"

15 •The merchants who sold these goods and grew rich off her will stand
at a distance for fear of her suffering, and they'll weep and mourn
16 •and say,

　　"Woe, woe, for the great city!
　　　who was clothed in fine linen,
　　　　purple and scarlet,
　　　and was adorned with gold jewelry,
　　　　with precious stones and pearls.
17　　•In one hour all this wealth was laid waste!"

　　Every ship's captain and everyone sailing to that place, all the sailors
18 and others who work on the sea, stood at a distance •and cried out when
they saw the smoke from the fire and said, "What could compare with
19 the great city?" •Then they threw dust on their heads, weeping and wailing and crying out,

　　"Woe, woe, for the great city
　　　where all those with ships at sea
　　　grew rich from her wealth —
　　In one hour she was laid waste!
20　　•Rejoice over her, O Heaven,
　　　you saints, apostles, and prophets,
　　For God has executed judgment against her on
　　　your behalf!"

•Then a mighty angel picked up a stone like a huge millstone and 21
threw it into the sea, saying,

> "With like violence shall the great city of Babylon be
>   cast down
>   and be seen no more!
> •The sound of harpists and musicians, flute and   22
>   trumpet players,
>   shall be heard in you no more!
> Craftsmen at their trades
>   shall be found in you no more,
> And the sound of a millstone
>   shall be heard in you no more!
> •The light of a lamp   23
>   shall shine in you no more,
> The voice of a bride and groom
>   shall be heard in you no more!
> For your merchants were the most powerful on earth,
>   and all the nations were led astray by your sorcery.
> •In her was found the blood of prophets and saints,   24
>   the blood of all those who were slain on the earth."

19 •After this I heard what seemed like the sound of a large crowd 1
in Heaven, crying,

> "Alleluia!
> Salvation, glory, and power belong to our God,
>   •for His judgments are just and true,   2
> He judged the great whore
>   who corrupted the earth with her fornication,
> And He avenged the blood of His servants,
>   which had been shed by her."

•Once again they cried,   3

> "Alleluia!
> The smoke will rise from her, forever and ever!"

•Then the twenty-four elders, and the four living creatures all fell down 4
and worshipped God as He sat on His throne, saying,

> "Amen, Alleluia!"

5   •Then a voice came from the throne,

> "Praise our God,
> all you His servants,
> And you who fear Him,
> both great and small!"

6   •Then I heard what seemed like the sound of a large crowd, or the sound
of rushing water or the sound of mighty thunderclaps, saying,

> "Alleluia!
> The Lord has established His Kingdom,
> God the Almighty!

7   •Let us rejoice and be glad,
> let us give glory to Him!
> For the wedding of the Lamb has come
> and his bride has made herself ready.

8   •She has been allowed to dress
> in fine linen, pure and bright"

the fine linen is the good deeds of the saints.

Roman seamen; engraved sepulchral stone (2nd century A.D.). (Rv 18:17)

•[k] Then the angel said to me, "Write this down! Blessed are those who 9
are called to the Lamb's wedding feast!" Then he said to me, "These
are God's words, and are true." •At this I fell at his feet and worshipped 10
him, but he said to me, "Don't do that! I'm a fellow servant with you
and your brothers who bear witness to Jesus. Worship God! The testimony of Jesus is the spirit of prophecy."

I. SEVEN VISIONS

The first six visions

•Then I saw Heaven opened up, and behold a white horse, and its 11
rider is called Faithful and True, and he judges and makes war right-
eously. •His eyes were flaming fire and on his head were many di- 12
adems. He had a name written which no one knew but himself, •and 13
he was wearing a robe which had been dipped in blood. His name is
The Word of God. •The armies in Heaven followed him on white hors- 14
es, dressed in pure white linen. •From his mouth came a sharp sword 15
with which to slaughter the nations, and he **will rule them with an
iron rod.** He will trample out the wine vat of God Almighty's furious
wrath. •On his robe and on his thigh a name is written — King of kings 16
and Lord of lords.

•Then I saw an angel standing on the sun and shouting in a loud 17
voice to all the birds flying in midair, "Come gather for God's great
supper! •You'll eat the flesh of kings, of tribunes, of mighty men, the 18
flesh of horses and their riders — the flesh of all men, slave and free,
great and small." •Then I saw the beast and the kings of the earth 19
gathered with their armies to wage war against the rider of the horse
and his army. •The beast was seized along with the false prophet 20
who'd been performing signs in the beast's presence, by means of
which he'd led astray those who bore the sign of the beast and had
worshipped the beast's image. The two of them were thrown alive
into the burning lake of sulfur. •The rest were killed with the sword 21
that comes from the mouth of the horse's rider, and all the birds ate
their fill of their flesh.

[k] *Mt 22:2-3.*

19:7 The Lamb's bride is, of course, the Church.
19:11-16 The rider on the white horse is the Son of Man, first seen at 1:12-18.
19:15 ·Ps 2:9.

20 •Then I saw an angel coming down from Heaven with the key
to the abyss and a heavy chain in his hand. •He seized the dragon, that ancient serpent — which is the Devil or Satan — and bound
him for a thousand years, •then he threw him into the abyss, locked
it, and sealed it so he'd no longer be able to deceive the nations until
the thousand years were up. After that he'll have to be set loose for a
little while.

•Then I saw thrones, and those seated on them had been given the
power to judge. I also saw the souls of those who had been beheaded
for bearing witness to Jesus and the word of God, and who had not worshipped the beast or its image and hadn't received its sign on their foreheads or hands. They came back to life and reigned with Christ for a
thousand years. •The rest of the dead didn't come back to life until the
thousand years were up. This is the first resurrection. •Blessed and holy
are those who share in the first resurrection —the second death will have
no power over them. Instead, they'll be priests of God and of Christ,
and they'll reign with him for a thousand years.

•When the thousand years were up, Satan was released from prison
•and he went forth to deceive the nations in the four corners of the
earth —that is, Gog and Magog —and gather them for war. Their number was like that of the sands of the sea. •They went up over the breadth
of the earth and surrounded the camp of the saints and the beloved
city, but fire came down from Heaven and consumed them. •The Devil who had deceived them was thrown into the burning lake of sulfur
along with the beast and the false prophet, where they'll suffer night
and day, forever and ever.

•Then I saw a great white throne and the One seated upon it, from
Whose face the heavens and earth fled, but no place was found for
them. •Then I saw the dead, both great and small, standing before the
throne. Books were opened, and another book was opened —the Book
of Life. The dead were judged from what was written in the books, according to their deeds. •The sea gave up the dead who were in it, and
Death and Hades gave up the dead who were in them. Each of them
was judged according to their deeds. •Both Death and Hades were
thrown into the flaming lake. This is the second death —the flaming
lake. •Anyone who couldn't be found written in the Book of Life was
thrown into the lake.

20:4 The resurrection of those who had been witnesses to Christ is, of course, not an earthly resurrection, nor is their reign an earthly reign.

20:7-10 This passage is a reminder that in the
Revelation John did not see an end to history, but
saw the divine activity in history.

21 •[j] Then I saw a **new heavens and a new earth** — the first heav- ₁
ens and the first earth had passed away and the sea was no more.
•And I saw the holy city, new Jerusalem, coming down out of Heaven from ₂
God, prepared as a bride is adorned for her husband. •Then I heard a loud ₃
voice from the throne say, "Behold, God's dwelling is now with men. **He
shall dwell with them and they shall be His people, and** God Himself will be with them. •**He'll wipe every tear** from their eyes and death ₄
shall be no more — no more grief or crying or pain, for what came before
has passed away."

•Then the One seated on the throne said, "Behold, I'll make all things ₅
new!" He also said, "Write this down, for these words are trustworthy
and true." •Then He said to me, "It is finished! I am the Alpha and the ₆
Omega, the beginning and the end. Those who thirst I'll allow to drink
freely from the spring of living water. •Whoever is victorious shall in- ₇
herit all these things, and **I shall be his God and he shall be My
son.** •But as for the cowardly, the unfaithful, perverts, murderers, for- ₈
nicators, sorcerers, idolaters, and all liars —their portion lies in the flaming lake of fire and sulfur, that is, the second death."

The New Jerusalem

•Then one of the seven angels who had the seven bowls full of the ₉
seven last plagues came and said to me, "Come, I'll show you the Lamb's
bride!" •So he took me in the spirit to a great high mountain and showed ₁₀
me the holy city Jerusalem coming down out of Heaven from God •with ₁₁
God's glory. Its splendor was like the radiance of a precious stone, like
jasper but as clear as crystal. •It had a great high wall with twelve **gates** ₁₂
and on the gates were twelve angels. Inscribed on the gates were the
names of the twelve **tribes of the sons of Israel. •There were three** ₁₃
gates on the east, three gates on the north, three gates on the

---

[j] *2 P 3:13.*

21:1-8 Is 65:17. "The sea", symbol of chaos and
the source of evil, "was no more." This marks the
transition to the true future, but this future inter-
penetrates the present: "God's dwelling is now
with men," and the present is transformed by
God's glory. Those who thirst, all who wish to be
made anew, can drink freely. All who reject this
condemn themselves, while those who accept
God's transforming grace will be His children.

21:3 Ezk 37:27; Lv 26:11-12.
21:4 Is 25:8.
21:7 2 S 7:14; Ps 89:26-27.
21:9ff The Lamb's bride, who is a city, the New
Jerusalem, is presented in a vision of resplendent
beauty and perfection, in contrast to the whore,
Babylon the Great. This is the contrast between
the Church and the arrogance of earthly power.
21:12-13 Ezk 48:30-35.

Tree of Life. Marble from Israel (6th century A.D.). (Rv 22:2,14,19)

14 **south and three gates on the west.** •And the city's wall had twelve foundations, on which were the names of the Lamb's twelve apostles.

15 •The angel who was speaking with me had a gold measuring rod with
16 which to measure the city, its gates, and its walls. •The city was laid out in a square, its length equal to its breadth. The angel measured the city with the rod and it was fifteen hundred miles —its length, breadth, and
17 height were all equal. •Then he measured the wall and it was two hundred and sixteen feet high according to human measurement, that is, an
18 angel's. •The material used in making the wall was jasper, while the city
19 was made of pure gold, as clear as glass. •The twelve foundations of the city's walls were adorned with every sort of precious stone —the first with jasper, the second with sapphire, the third with chalcedony, the fourth
20 with emerald, •the fifth with onyx, the sixth with carnelian, the seventh with chrysolite, the eighth with beryl, the ninth with topaz, the tenth with chrysoprase, the eleventh with turquoise, and the twelfth with amethyst.
21 •The twelve gates were twelve pearls, each gate made from a single pearl. The city's street was made of pure gold, as clear as glass.

22 •I saw no Temple in the city, for the Lord God Almighty and the Lamb
23 are the city's Temple. •The city had no need for the sun or the moon

21:22ff Note the explicit replacement of the Temple with the presence of God and the Lamb.

to shine on it, for God's glory illuminated the city, and the Lamb was its lamp. •The nations will walk by its light, and the kings of the earth 24 will bring their glory into it. •Its gates will never be shut, for there shall 25 be no night there. •They'll bring into it the glory and wealth of the na- 26 tions, •but nothing impure will enter it, nor will anyone who does any- 27 thing abominable or false —only those who are written in the Lamb's Book of Life.

22 •Then the angel showed me the river of the water of life. It sparkled 1 like crystal and came from the throne of God and the Lamb. •It 2 flowed **down the middle** of the city's street, and **on either side of the river was the tree of life,** bearing fruit twelve times a year, once a month. The tree's **leaves** are **for healing** the nations. •There shall 3 no longer be anything in the city that's accursed. The throne of God and the Lamb shall be in it. His servants will worship Him •and will see His 4 face, and His name will be on their foreheads. •There will no longer be 5 night, and they'll have no need for a lamp's light or for the light of the sun, for the Lord God will shine upon them and they'll reign forever and ever.

J. EPILOGUE:
ATTESTATION TO THE BOOK

•Then the angel said to me, "These words are trustworthy and true, 6 and the Lord, the God who inspired the prophets, has sent His angel to show His servants what must soon take place. •Behold, I'm coming 7 soon! Blessed are they who keep the prophetic words of this book!"

•I, John, am the one who heard and saw these things. And when I heard 8 and saw them I fell down in worship at the feet of the angel who showed me these things. •But he said to me, "Don't do that! I'm a fellow servant 9 both of you and of the prophets and those who keep the words of this book. Worship God!" •Then he said to me, "Don't seal up the prophet- 10 ic words of this book, for the time of their fulfillment is near. •Let evildo- 11 ers continue to do evil, let the filthy go on soiling themselves, let the right-eous continue to do what's right, and let whoever is holy still be holy."

•"Behold, I'm coming soon, and I'll bring my rewards with me, to re- 12 pay everyone according to their deeds. •I am the Alpha and the Omega, 13 the first and the last, the beginning and the end."

22:2 Ezk 47:12
22:12 Christ is now the speaker.

14 •Blessed are those who wash their robes and so will have the right to
15 eat from the tree of life, and to go through the gates into the city. •Outside will be the dogs —sorcerers, fornicators, murderers, idolaters, and all those who love and do what's false.

16 •"I, Jesus, have sent my angel to you to bear witness to all this in the churches. I am of the root and race of David, the bright morning star."

17 •The Spirit and the Bride say, "Come!"
And let whoever hears say, "Come!"
Come, whoever is thirsty,
whoever wants to receive the gift of living water!

18 •I will bear witness to everyone who hears the prophetic words of this book. If anyone adds to them God will inflict on them the plagues de-
19 scribed in this book, •and if anyone removes any words from this prophetic book, God will take from him his share in the tree of life and the holy city, which were described in this book.

20 •The one who bears witness to these things says, "Yes, I'm coming soon!" Amen, come, Lord Jesus!

21 •The grace of the Lord Jesus be with you all.

GLOSSARY

Aaron The brother of Moses. Aaron and his descendants were chosen by God to be High Priests of Israel. He belonged to the Israelite tribe of Levi.

Abel The second son of Adam and Eve (the first human beings created by God). Abel was murdered out of jealousy by his older brother Cain, because God had been pleased by Abel's sacrifice but not by Cain's.

Abiathar One of the two High Priests appointed by King David.

Abraham The ancestor of all Israelites who was called by God to leave his home in Mesopotamia and become the father of a nation God would make.

Abyss The place in the depths of the earth where the evil spirits were held captive by God until the day of judgment.

Adam The first man created by God. His name means "man."

Agrippa See, Herod Agrippa and Herod Agrippa II.

Akeldama A cemetery near Jerusalem.

Alexandria One of the largest and most important cities of the Mediterranean world. Located in Egypt, Alexandria was both a major commercial center as well as one of the most notable centers of Hellenistic learning. It was also home to a large and thriving Jewish community.

Alpha and Omega The first and last letters of the Greek alphabet. Used in a metaphorical sense to mean the beginning and the end.

Amen A Hebrew word signifying agreement with a statement that has been made: "let it be" or "may it be so." As used by Jesus, however, it is a solemn affirmation of the truth of his own statement that will follow.

Ancient of Days As used in the Book of Daniel, this expression refers to God in His majesty and wisdom.

Angel This Greek word means "a messenger." In late Old Testament and New Testament times angels took on increased importance in Jewish thought as members of the heavenly host and were believed to exercise great influence over human affairs.

Antioch Next to Rome itself and Alexandria, Antioch in Syria was the greatest city in the Roman Empire. It was a major center for trade with the East and early on became one of the most important centers for Christianity. There was a town of the same name in Pisidia, a district in modern Turkey.

Antipas See, Herod Antipas.

Apollos A learned Jew who collaborated in Paul's mission in the area around the Aegean Sea. He hailed from Alexandria, one of the major centers of Jewish learning in the ancient world.

Apostle A Greek word meaning "one who is sent out." In the New Testament it refers to Jesus' inner circle called The Twelve. They became the first bishops.

Aquila and Priscilla Man and wife. Jewish converts to Christianity who were among Paul's closest collaborators.

Archelaus Son of Herod the Great who ruled Samaria, Judea, and Idumaea following his father's death in 4 B.C. He was deposed by the Romans in 6 A.D.

Areopagus A hill in central Athens where the city council used to meet. The name was also used to refer to the council itself.

Aretas King of Nabatea, a Semitic desert kingdom to the south and east of Palestine. Nabatea controlled a number of important caravan routes.

Ark of the Covenant A box used by the Israelites to hold the tablets of the Torah and, perhaps, other sacred objects. After the first Temple was built the Ark was kept in the inner sanctuary, the Holy of Holies. The lid of the Ark was covered with gold and was known as the Mercy Seat. On the Day of Atonement the High Priest entered with the blood of the sacrifice and, among other rites, sprinkled blood on the Mercy Seat.

Artemis Also known as Diana. The Greek and Latin mother goddess, who had an important shrine at Ephesus in Asia Minor.

Athens The major center of Greek civilization.

Atonement, Day of The holiest day of the Jewish year. On this day the High Priest offered sacrifice for all the sins of the whole people of Israel. In Hebrew it is called Yom Kippur.

Augustus Originally a title (meaning "Imperial majesty") applied to the first Roman Emperor, Gaius Octavius (63 B.C. - 14 A.D.).

Baal The principal god of the ancient Canaanites, the Semitic inhabitants of Palestine before the arrival of the Israelites.

Babylon The ancient capital of the Mesopotamian empires of Babylonia and Chaldea. It became a symbol of corrupt power and wickedness.

Balaam A pagan seer who was summoned by Balak, the king of Moab, to curse the Israelites as they were preparing to enter the land of Canaan.

Balak The pagan king of the ancient Semitic kingdom of Moab, located on the eastern side of the Dead Sea. He was king at the time of the entry of Israel into Canaan following the Exodus from Egypt.

Beelzebul A name perhaps derived from a derisive Hebrew pun on the pagan god Baal. In the New Testament it refers to the Devil as the chief of all evil spirits.

Boaz In Old Testament times a rich landowner from Bethlehem whose story is told in the Book of Ruth. He married Ruth, the Moabite widow, and figures in Matthew's genealogy of Jesus.

Burnt offering A sacrificial offering of an animal in which, after being slaughtered, the entire animal was consumed by fire. In other sacrifices parts of the animal would be retained for consumption.

Caesar Derived from Julius Caesar, it became a title for all Roman Emperors.

Cherubim Representations of winged creatures with human faces. They were placed on or near the Ark of the Covenant in the Holy of Holies (inner sanctuary of the Temple) to prevent any unauthorized person from approaching the Seat of God. There is some indication that the cherubim were believed to support or carry God.

Christ A Greek word translating the Hebrew "Messiah" or "The Anointed One." The name was applied by the Jews to the Savior of Israel foretold by the prophets.

Claudius Roman Emperor from 41 to 54 A.D.

Clean/Unclean Also Pure/Impure. Refers to the suitability or unsuitability of a person to approach God in prayer or worship (thus, ritual purity: suitability for participating in the sacred rites). The Jews had elaborate rules for maintaining ritual purity. Entire classes of people were considered unclean, or at least suspect, by the strictest sects.

Corinth An important commercial center and seaport in ancient Greece.

Damascus A major city of Syria located on the edge of the Syrian Desert. It was a major center for caravans and is one of the oldest continuously occupied cities in the world.

David, **City of** Bethlehem, the ancestral home of David, located south of Jerusalem in the Judean hill country. The term is also used to refer to the oldest part of Jerusalem, which was captured by David.

David The greatest king of ancient Israel and the founder of the royal dynasty. Traditionally, authorship of the Psalms is ascribed to David, and it was from David's line that the Messiah was to come.

Deacon A Greek word meaning "servant." In the early Church it was originally applied to seven assistants to the apostles, and later to a category of assistants to the early elders or bishops.

Dead Sea A body of water located on the eastern border of Palestine in a deep valley, over 1,200 ft. below sea level. The Jordan River empties into the Dead Sea, the waters of which are so salty that it can support no life.

Decapolis A Greek word meaning "ten cities." A league of ten Hellenized cities in Palestine.

Dedication, **Feast of** Also known as Hanukkah. This feast celebrates the purification and reconsecration of the Temple after it had been desecrated by the aggressively Hellenistic Syrian regime of the Seleucid Empire in the period after the return from the Babylonian Exile.

Diaspora A Greek word meaning "scattered." It refers to those Jews of the ancient world who for centuries before New Testament times had both emigrated and been exiled from Palestine and settled throughout the Mediterranean basin as well as in Mesopotamia. The Jews of the Diaspora were actually more numerous than Palestinian Jews and in fact comprised a significant portion of the total population of the Roman Empire. They were especially numerous in major urban centers such as Alexandria, Antioch, and Rome itself, but were found in almost every other city and province as well.

Drusilla The wife of Felix, the Roman governor of Judea, and the sister of Herod Agrippa II, a vassal king of the Roman Empire.

Elders In the New Testament the term "elder" or, in Greek, "presbyter," was interchangeable with "bishop." Among the Jews the term was applied to the leading authorities in the synagogues and in civic life.

Elijah The wonderworking prophet of the Old Testament who led the resistance against accommodation of the Israelite religion with the pagan Canaanite religion. He was so popular in later times that he came to be considered representative of all the prophets, and appears as such at the Transfiguration of Jesus. The prophet Malachi prophesied that Elijah would return before the Messiah.

Epicureans Followers of the Greek philosopher Epicurus, one of the largest philosophical schools in the early New Testament period in the Hellenistic cities. Epicurus taught that happiness was the greatest good in life.

Essenes A Jewish sect whose life was characterized by great concern for ritual purity. The sect is believed to have arisen in the Maccabean period about 150 B.C. based upon the belief that the High Priesthood had been usurped. They are believed to be the authors of the Dead Sea Scrolls, a collection of writings discovered in caves in the desert near the Dead Sea where the Essenes maintained a center at Qumran.

Eunuch A male who has been castrated. Eunuchs were often used as high officials by ancient kings.

Exile, The After the death of Solomon, David's son, the kingdom of Israel was divided into northern and southern kingdoms, known respectively as Israel and Judah. In 721 B.C. Israel was conquered by the Assyrian Empire and many of its inhabitants were exiled to Mesopotamia. In the sixth century B.C. Judah was conquered by the Chaldean Empire and many of its inhabitants were again exiled to Mesopotamia in the 580s and 570s B.C. Beginning in 538 B.C. Cyrus of Persia, conqueror of the Chaldean Empire, allowed the Jews to return to Judah.

Exodus The departure of the Israelites from slavery in Egypt, led by Moses. After forty years of wandering in the desert the Israelites entered Canaan, the land promised by God to Abraham. The Exodus was accompanied by many signs of God's concern as well as the giving of the Ten Commandments to Moses on Mount Sinai. It became the formative event in Jewish religious consciousness.

Fasting Abstaining from food as a form of penance and expression of contrition of sin. In the Old Testament a strict fast was observed from dawn to dusk on the Day of Atonement. By the time of the New Testament fasting had become more common and was considered an exemplary form of piety, along with prayer and almsgiving. The early Church followed the Pharisaic custom of fasting twice a week.

Felix Roman governor of Judea, 52-60 A.D. His tenure was characterized by cruelty toward the Jews.

Festus Roman governor of Judea, 60-62 A.D.

Gabriel Traditionally, an archangel, one of the most important of God's angels along with Michael and Raphael. Gabriel figures as God's messenger to Zechariah and Mary in Luke's Gospel.

Gallio Roman governor of Achaia (Greece), 51-52 A.D.

Gamaliel The most renowned Pharisee at the time of Christ and famous in later times as well. He was known for his tolerance and humanity.

Gennesaret, Sea of The Sea of Galilee.

Gentile A non-Jew.

Gerezim, Mount The mountain in Samaria on which the Samaritans worshipped.

Gethsemane, Garden of A garden located outside the city wall on the east side of Jerusalem, in the Kidron Valley at the foot of the Mount of Olives.

Glory This Greek word was often used to translate the Hebrew "Shekinah," which referred to the Divine Presence.

Gog and Magog In the New Testament they refer to the forces of evil in rebellion against God.

Gomorrah With Sodom this was one of the wicked Cities of the Plain which was destroyed by God in the time of Abraham and Lot.

Hades The Greek name for the underworld: Hell.

Herod the Great Herod was an ethnic Idumaean, a Semitic people of southern Palestine who had been largely, though somewhat superficially, Judaized. Through a combination of cunning and ruthlessness he ingratiated himself to a series of Roman rulers and eventually, in 40 B.C., was declared by the Roman Senate to be king of Judea, succeeding to the Hasmonean dynasty which had been founded by the Maccabee family. The years of his reign, which lasted until 4 B.C., were marked by the rebuilding of the second Temple on a magnificent scale and by a series of murders which included many of his closest family members, including his wife and several sons.

Herod Agrippa A grandson of Herod the Great, he ruled all of Palestine from 41 A.D. to 44 A.D.

Herod Agrippa II Son of Herod Agrippa. He ruled only small portions of northern Palestine.

Herod Antipas Son of Herod the Great who ruled Galilee and Perea (a portion of present day Jordan) until 39 A.D.

Herodians That group of political opportunists in Palestine who supported the rule of the Herodian family.

High Priest The head of the Jewish priestly hierarchy. On the Day of Atonement the High Priest offered sacrifice for his sins and those of the whole people, a theme taken up in the Letter to the Hebrews.

Hosannah A Hebrew acclamation believed to signify "royal power."

Isaiah One of the five "major" prophets in the Old Testament, he advocated, in vain, a policy of neutrality for Judah in the great power politics of his day. In the New Testament era he was notable for the use made of his "Suffering Servant" prophecies, which the early Church applied to Jesus as the Messiah.

Israel Also known as Jacob, one of the Patriarchs, the son of Isaac and Rebecca and the grandson of Abraham. Later the name was applied to the whole Chosen People as well as to the northern kingdom.

Jeremiah A "major" prophet of the Old Testament, his prophetic career spanned the last years of the kingdom of Judah and the early years of the Exile. Jeremiah spoke out especially against the faithlessness of the Israelites.

Jericho An ancient city located near the point in the Jordan Valley where the Jordan River enters the Dead Sea. It was also near Jericho that the Israelites entered the Promised Land.

Jerusalem The Holy City of Israel; former ruling seat of the Davidic dynasty, the political center of Roman Palestine and site of the Temple, the religious focus for Jews throughout the ancient world.

Jonah Old Testament protagonist of the Book of Jonah who was forced by God to successfully preach repentance to the pagan power of Assyria. Jonah fled this prophetic calling by seeking to cross the sea in the opposite direction, but through God's will he was shipwrecked, swallowed by a whale, and safely deposited on land to carry out God's will.

Judah One of the twelve tribes of the nation of Israel. Its territory included the area stretching south of Jerusalem to the Negev Desert. From Judah came the royal line of David, as well as the Messiah. Following the breakup of the Davidic kingdom the name was applied to the southern Israelite kingdom.

Judea The territory of the tribe of Judah, a Roman province in New Testament times.

Law The word — in Greek, "nomos" — used to translate the Hebrew "Torah."

Levites Members of the tribe of Levi, one of the twelve tribes of Israel. This tribe supplied the men who performed various auxiliary functions in the Temple worship.

Lord This word translates the Greek "Kyrios," and was used in a variety of senses. It could be used as a polite form of address to an acknowledged superior, master, or leader. On the other hand, it was used in Greek translations of the Hebrew Bible to refer to God Himself: The Lord. This convention was followed to avoid direct use of God's holy name, Yahweh in Hebrew.

Lot The nephew of Abraham. He was a righteous man who lived in the proverbially wicked city of Sodom. When God destroyed Sodom and Gomorrah, Lot and his family were the only ones who were saved.

Manna A substance resembling bread that God provided for the sustenance of the Israelites during their Exodus through the desert.

Melchizedek In the time of Abraham Melchizedek was the king of Salem (later known as Jerusalem) and priest of God Most High. He blessed Abraham after Abraham had waged a successful campaign against enemies.

Messiah A Hebrew word meaning "anointed" and translated "Christ" in

Greek. Though originally used at times to designate a variety of persons who were considered to be appointed by God, the term came to be applied to the Savior of Israel who was to come to deliver Israel from oppression and usher in the age in which all the prophecies would be fulfilled.

Michael One of the most important of the angels, believed to have fought with and defeated Satan.

Moloch A god of the pagan peoples of Palestine in pre-Christian times. The cult of Moloch involved human sacrifices, including that of infants.

Moses A member of the tribe of Levi, Moses led Israel's Exodus from Egypt to the Promised Land of Canaan and received from God on Mount Sinai the tablets containing the Ten Commandments. He was considered in many ways the founder of Israel as an organized nation with an identity of its own, its lawgiver and greatest prophet.

Nazirites Individuals who were under a vow. The vow could last for a short or long time. John the Baptist, for example, was a lifetime Nazirite.

Nicolaitans An early heretical sect in Asia Minor who were accused of condoning immorality and the eating of flesh that had been offered to idols.

Niniveh The great capital of the Assyrian Empire, a symbol of arrogant power in rebellion against God. It was destroyed in 612 B.C.

Noah The only righteous man left on earth at the time of the Flood (or Deluge) that washed away all the evil inhabitants of the earth. He and his family, along with two of each species of living creature, were saved when God instructed Noah to construct an ark.

Olives, Mount of A mountain directly to the east of Jerusalem, separated from the city itself by the Kidron Valley. The Garden of Gethsemane is near the foot of the Mount of Olives.

Parable A Greek word meaning "a comparison." A parable could take a variety of forms, from a brief simile or metaphor to a longer illustrative or allegorical story.

Paradise A Persian word in origin, it referred to an enclosure such as the blissful garden where Adam and Eve, the first humans, lived before they sinned. It later came to mean the heavenly dwelling place of the righteous dead.

Passover This great feast of the Jews commemorates the deliverance of Israel from slavery in Egypt. Specifically, it commemorates the night before their departure when a lamb was slaughtered and its blood smeared on the door posts of their houses. Then God sent the Angel of Death to kill the first born sons of all those (the Egyptians) whose houses were not marked in this manner, while "passing over" the houses of the Israelites. Thus the feast is celebrated with a meal at which God's concern for His Chosen People and His saving power are remembered.

Patriarchs, Fathers Strictly speaking, this term refers to the very early ancestors of Israel such as Abraham, Isaac, and Jacob, but it was also used to refer to certain other significant figures in Israel's past.

Pentecost From the Greek word for "fifty." A Jewish harvest festival occurring fifty days after Passover.

Pharaoh The ancient Egyptian monarch.

Pharisees A Jewish sect noted for its strict adherence to the Torah, especially the rules of ritual purity, perhaps as a way of extending the purity which characterized the Temple cult to daily life. This movement was led by scribes, experts in the Torah and its interpretation, and was centered in the synagogues (lit., "gathering places"). Following the Roman destruction of the second Temple, the Pharisaic movement gave rise to Rabbinic Judaism.

Philip Son of Herod the Great. Following his father's death, Philip ruled Galilee and parts of present day Syria and Jordan.

Phoenicia Coastal district along the Mediterranean directly north of Palestine, now in modern Lebanon. Its ancient inhabitants were renowned as a maritime trading nation throughout the Mediterranean world.

Phylacteries Small leather boxes containing excerpts from the Scriptures. Devout Jews bound phylacteries around their brows while praying.

Pontius Pilate Roman governor of Judea from 26 A.D to 36 A.D.

Preparation, Day of Friday, the day before the Jewish Sabbath (Saturday), during which preparations were made for the Sabbath observances.

Priests A category of men, originally drawn from descendants of Aaron from the tribe of Levi, who were dedicated to the service of the Temple cult, in particular the offering of the required sacrifices.

Prophet An individual chosen by God to communicate a message or the will of God.

Proselyte A Gentile convert to Judaism. There were some variations in Jewish practice. Generally, a proselyte was required to undergo baptism and circumcision, and to offer a sacrifice before he was considered a true Jew, but some Jewish circles taught that circumcision was not necessary for a Gentile to be admitted to worship. Gentiles, such as the centurion Cornelius in Acts 10, who were unwilling to take all three steps but attended the synagogue and in most other respects lived as Jews, were known as God-fearers.

Rabbi A Hebrew term of respect meaning "Teacher."

Rite/Ritual Set procedure associated with sacred functions, usually having to do with the offering of sacrifice. Under Jewish law there were various requirements for maintaining a state of purity in order to be eligible to participate in the sacred rites.

Ruth In the Old Testament Book of Ruth, a Moabite widow who married Boaz, an Israelite. Ruth and Boaz are both listed in Matthew's genealogy of Jesus.

Sabbath One of the seven days of the week, it was to be dedicated to the service of God. The Jewish Sabbath was Saturday, the last day of the week. The Christian Sabbath was changed to Sunday, the first day of the week, the day of Jesus' resurrection.

Sadducees The aristocratic priestly caste which traced its descent to Zadok, one of two High Priests appointed by King David.

Samaritans Inhabitants of the the central section of Palestine known as Samaria, after its capital city of the same name. The Samaritans were descended from the Israelites of the northern kingdom of Israel and Gentile settlers from the time of the Exile. They were despised by the Jews as half-breeds and especially because they set up a rival sanctuary to Jerusalem.

Sanctuary A building dedicated to the worship of God, and especially the inner portion where sacrifice is performed. This innermost part of the Jewish Temple was known as the Holy of Holies.

Sanhedrin The supreme council or court of the Jews. It was headed by the High Priest and members were drawn from the priestly class as well as from among other respected elders and scribes.

Satan While in some Jewish circles Satan may have been conceived as a tester sent by God, in the New Testament he is a fallen angel who seeks to draw men into rebellion against God.

Scribes The class of non-priests who were dedicated to the study and interpretation of Scripture and the sacred traditions.

Scripture A translation of a Greek word meaning "writings." In New Testament times the term referred to the sacred books of the Old Testament.

Septuagint The Greek translation of the Hebrew Old Testament, written for the benefit of Jews of the Diaspora whose first language was Greek. The Septuagint was translated in Alexandria, traditionally by seventy scholars. Its abbreviation in critical studies is LXX, the Roman numeral for 70.

Sinai, Mount Mountain on the Sinai peninsula between Israel and Egypt proper where Moses received the tablets of the Ten Commandments from God during the Exodus.

Sodom With Gomorrah, one of the two wicked Cities of the Plain that were destroyed by God. Lot and his family were the only inhabitants to be saved. The traditional location for these two cities is under the southern part of the Dead Sea.

Son of Man An Aramaic term. Originally it simply meant "a man." In the New Testament, drawing on the Book of Daniel, it appears in some instances to have been a title that Jesus applied to himself. There is still considerable dispute as to its exact significance.

Stoics An ancient school of philosophers who taught detachment as the key to happiness. They were known for adherence to duty and their high moral standards.

Tabernacles, Feast of The feast of the autumn harvest, in October. It was also known as the Feast of Booths, because during the festival shelters were erected as a reminder of the way Israel had lived in the desert during the Exodus.

Temple Originally the Israelites worshipped in many places, especially on "high places," prominent hilltops. David's son Solomon erected the first Temple as a central sanctuary in Jerusalem. The first Temple was destroyed by the Chaldeans in 587 B.C. A second Temple was rebuilt following the return from the Exile and then greatly expanded by Herod the Great. The second Temple was destroyed by the

Romans in 70 A.D. during their conquest of Jerusalem in the Jewish Revolt.

Tiberias, Sea of The Sea of Galilee.

Tiberius Roman Emperor from 14 to 37 A.D.

Torah The Jewish "law," quintessentially the Ten Commandments. The word, however, had taken on the far broader meaning of the totality of God's revelation which could serve as a guide for one's life. In this sense it included the first five books of the Bible, the Pentateuch, but was also extended far beyond that at times.

Unleavened Bread, Feast of the The seven day Israelite festival commemorating the Exodus, during which Passover was celebrated. During the seven day festival only unleavened bread was eaten, in commemoration of God's command to the ancient Israelites at the first Passover.

Vow Solemn promise to God, usually to perform some act in return for a favor granted. Other vows could bind a person to a particular type of life, as with some Nazirite vows.

Zealots The extreme nationalist Jewish party that advocated armed rebellion against the Romans.

Zion The mountain on which Jerusalem was built. Also refers to the city itself.

Pictorial credits:
Edizioni San Paolo Archive

Printed in Italy
Society of St. Paul - Rome.